A Letter to the Reader

Read this book carefully and think about what is said. Compare everything in it to the holy Scriptures. A copy of the New Testament is in the back of the book. The only creed a Christian should have is the Word of God, the Bible.

You must not think of the first part of this book as being divine or as part of the Scriptures. It is only a guide to help you understand the teachings that our Creator has given us through the inspired writers of the Old and New Testaments of His Scriptures. You must never allow any writings of man to replace the divine writings of the Scriptures, but we hope that the messages in the first part of the book will help you to study the Scriptures and to follow them so you can receive the abundant life God offers. Compare the first part of the book with the New Testament Scriptures to make sure we have told you the truth.

The most important decision on earth is to become right with God and His Son, Jesus Christ. Salvation, as presented by the Bible, means being forgiven of sins, entering into fellowship with Almighty God, and receiving eternal life. The saved are blessed with abundant living now and a reward in heaven later. The highest goal of every person on earth should be to receive and live in God's salvation. The Bible says, "For what will a man be profited, if he gains the whole world, and forfeits his soul? Or what will a man give in exchange for his soul?" (Matthew 16:26). Our families, food, clothing, shelter, and education are of great value; but the salvation of the soul is the most valuable blessing that we can ever receive.

Once again, we urge you to read this book carefully. Study the "Guide to Eternal Life" found on the pages following the New Testament. When you understand how to become a Christian, make arrangements to become one immediately. After you have obeyed the gospel, live the Christian life that is outlined in this book and is clearly taught in the New Testament.

Remember to think of others. After you have read this book, share it with someone else so that he or she can read it and be taught how to become a Christian. We want as many people as possible to become Christians and go to heaven. This book can teach the way of salvation to as many people as read it. Take as your mission not only to be a Christian, but also to see that other people read this book as they study the Bible so that they may learn how to become God's children and serve Him.

We at Truth for Today World Mission School wish you a happy Christian life and pray that we will one day meet in heaven.

INTO THE ABUNDANT LIFE

INTO THE ABUNDANT LIFE

INCLUDES A COMPLETE NEW TESTAMENT

Truth for Today World Mission School
P.O. Box 2044
Searcy, AR 72145-2044

© 2007 Truth for Today World Mission School, Inc.,
P.O. Box 2044, Searcy, AR 72145-2044

Originally published as *Becoming a Faithful Christian.*

1st printing, 1999	6th printing, 2005
2nd printing, 2000	7th printing, 2006
3rd printing, 2000	8th printing, 2006
4th printing, 2001	9th printing (third edition), 2006
5th printing (revised), 2003	10th printing, 2007

ISBN-13: 978-0-9795390-1-5
ISBN-10: 0-9795390-1-3

Authors include Eddie Cloer, Nick Hamilton, Mike Knappier, Owen Olbricht, Neale Pryor, David Roper, and Ian Terry.

Illustrations by Isaac Alexander.

Dedication

To All Those Noble Souls
who want to serve
the true and living God
by obeying the teachings
of the New Testament

*"'And you will know the truth, and
the truth will make you free'" (John 8:32).*

*"Now these were more noble-minded
than those in Thessalonica, for they
received the word with great eagerness,
examining the Scriptures daily to see
whether these things were so" (Acts 17:11).*

Contents

Contents

1

The Question of God

A building is no stronger than its foundation. All the different parts of a building will be affected by the foundation upon which the building sits.

What a foundation is to a building, the question "Does God exist?" is to life. Our belief or disbelief in God forms a foundation for our thinking which colors or interprets all of our thoughts about life.

Therefore, the most profound question anyone can ask is the question "Does God exist?" The reason this question is so significant is that the answer given to it will affect all the answers to all our other questions about life.

For example, let us say that a man answers this question by saying, "No, God does not exist." Then, as this man answers the question "How shall I live in this world?" he will conclude, "I may live any way I choose. After all, I am not a created being, and I am not accountable to any higher power. The only obligation I have is to support the happiness and productivity of fellow human beings in a reasonable way.

Beyond this, what I do with my life is up to me. Since I will not live again beyond death, I must squeeze from life all the living I can."

Now, let us say that a man answers the question "Does God exist?" by saying, "Yes, He does exist." He will have an altogether different answer to the question "How shall I live in this world?" In response to this question, he may say, "I have been created by an Almighty Being. He clearly had a purpose for my existence, and I must discover that purpose. Only by finding His will and living by it can I find the peace and purpose that my Creator intended for my life. I know that someday He will call me into account for the way I have lived in His world."

Let us consider the question "Does God exist?" very carefully. Are there compelling reasons for believing that God exists? The Bible does not begin with an argument about the existence of God. It actually begins with an affirmation about God: "In the beginning God created the heavens and the earth" (Genesis 1:1). Scattered throughout the Bible, however, are rational evidences for the existence of God. Some are given directly, and some are given indirectly; some are expressly stated, and others are implied. Let us summarize several of them by considering two. If you will think deeply about these two reasons, they will lead you to believe confidently that God really does exist.

THE EVIDENCE OF THE WORLD

The first evidence that compels us to believe that God really does exist is that given by the world around us and above us. The earth and the universe eloquently proclaim the existence of God.

We live on a planet which we call Earth. It is part of a solar system which revolves around the sun. This solar system has unquestioned order and design. All the planets stay in their orbits and never run into each other. They encircle the sun at the right speed and at the right distance. The earth's relation to the sun creates day, night, and seasons. It is always at a proper distance from the sun. If we were any further away from the sun, we would freeze; if we were any closer, we would fry.

Scientists tell us that numerous other solar systems beyond ours exist in space. We do not even know for sure the dimensions of the universe. Our telescopes cannot take us to its edge; our minds cannot comprehend its width. Although there is much we do not know about the universe, one thing about it we know for certain—it is a universe characterized by order and design. It is not haphazard and chaotic; it is unified and organized.

The existence of the universe demands that we draw one of two conclusions about it: Either it was created or it just happened. If one argues that the universe just happened, he must either conclude that the universe just happened from nothing or that it resulted from some kind of cosmic explosion from already existing matter. Of the two major conclusions, the only reasonable one is that the universe was created. How could we believe with integrity that the universe came from nothing? How could we believe with rationality that the universe resulted from a cosmic explosion and that matter is the only thing that has always been?

Suppose a man came to me with a book in his hand. He gave the book to me and asked me to look at it. I began to examine it. I noticed the book had on the front cover "Cruden's Complete Concordance." I also noticed that it had "Zondervan" printed in the place for the publisher. As I thumbed through the pages, I observed that it contained all the different names, places, and phrases of the King James Version of the Bible listed in alphabetical order, with the different references of their appearance in the Bible listed underneath them. On the cover of the book, it was stated that over 200,000 references were listed in the book. I might say to the man, "I believe I will contact the publishing company and see if I can acquire a copy of this book."

The man then said, "You cannot buy a copy of this book. This book was neither published by Zondervan nor compiled by Alexander Cruden. The book just happened. We found it in its completed state. It came into existence from nothing." I would say to him, "Are you telling me that all these listings of the names, places, and phrases of the King James Version of the Bible were not compiled by someone? Are you telling me that these over 200,000 references came into existence from nothing? Are you saying that this book was not composed, printed, and bound?"

If the man should reply, "Yes, that is what I am saying," I then would say, "I know that you are mistaken. I respect you as a human being, but my ability to reason will not allow me to accept your conclusion concerning the origin of this book. I can say without any fear of being disproven that this book did not just happen." I can be confident about my answer to this man because my ability to reason will not allow me to draw any other conclusion concerning the origin of the book.

Suppose another man came to me and handed me an electric razor. The man said to me, "I want you to look at this razor. An electrical cord may be plugged into the bottom of it, and through the use of electrical energy you can turn on this razor and shave your face. It will remove the whiskers from your face without cutting your skin. Inside the bottom part of the razor is a battery. While the razor is plugged into an electrical outlet, electric energy is stored in this battery for future use. Then, when you are away from an electrical outlet, you may turn on the razor, and it will run without being plugged into an electrical outlet. It can be used at home and also while you are traveling." I might say to the man, "This would be a most helpful appliance. I do travel often, and an appliance like this would be very useful to me. I believe I will see if I can purchase a razor similar to this one."

Imagine that the man said to me, "Oh, no. This razor cannot be bought. It was not created. It just happened. Not too far from here was a factory which contained all types of materials—plastics, metals, wood, etc. An explosion occurred in that building. These materials were thrown up into the air. While in the air, parts of these materials somehow came together, and after a while they developed into this appliance. Amidst the rubble and debris of the devastated building, we found this razor. It was not designed or manufactured; it resulted from this explosion." I would say to this man, "Are you asking me to believe that this razor was not designed, engineered, and carefully put together? Are you affirming that this razor resulted from chaotic chance, not intelligence?" If the man still insisted that the razor resulted from an explosion, I would say to him, "You must be mistaken regarding the razor. I cannot conceive of a razor coming into existence in this way." I would be absolutely positive about my response to this man. My ability to reason will not permit me to draw any other conclusion.

The conclusion which we have drawn with confidence regarding the book and the electric razor is a conclusion which we must draw with even more confidence about the universe. No amount of scientific rhetoric and terminology can make us believe that the universe came from nothing or resulted from an explosion. The universe is far more highly engineered and designed than a book or an electric razor. If we cannot believe that a book just happened or that an electric razor resulted from an explosion, how can we believe that the universe came from nothing or resulted from an explosion of mindless matter? All who have studied the universe in any detail have come away from such a study with the realization that the universe is a marvel of complex design and precision.

What we have concluded by reason, the Bible affirms. Psalm 19:1 says, "The heavens are telling of the glory of God; and their expanse is declaring the work of His hands." In other words, if we should sit down upon the ground on a clear night and look up into the starry sky, we will find ourselves in a wonderful worship service. The preacher will be the darkened sky with its myriad of stars. We will be the congregation. The auditorium will be the grass upon which we are sitting. The preacher will declare silently but eloquently that the stars did not just happen but were created. The starry sky will proclaim the glory of God. As we leave this worship service, we will say, "The message I heard by this preacher has to be right. My reason will not allow me to accept any other message."

Paul, one of the writers of the New Testament, wrote, "For since the creation of the world His invisible attributes, His eternal power and divine nature, have been clearly seen, being understood through what has been made, so that they are without excuse" (Romans 1:20). The visible, tangible things of the universe prove the existence of the unseen, invisible hand of God. They tell of His Almighty power and His supernatural character. We learn of the existence of God through general revelation—the world around us and the world above us. Paul also said, "And yet He did not leave Himself without witness, in that He did good and gave you rains from heaven and fruitful seasons, satisfying your hearts with food and gladness" (Acts 14:17). The world of our planet and the world of the universe witness to the existence of God.

In a popular children's story, Robinson Crusoe was shipwrecked on a deserted island. When he washed ashore from the shipwreck, he immediately looked around for other survivors. None were to be found. He alone had survived the wreck. He searched throughout the island for other human beings but found none. He concluded that he was all alone on the island. He made for himself a type of house out of branches and logs. He lived on the wild fruit which grew on the island. He trapped and killed wild animals for meat and clothing. One day as he walked across the seashore, he saw in the soft sand the footprints of another human being. He immediately knew that one of three conclusions would be true: Maybe someone had made those footprints and left. Perhaps the one who had made those footprints had died, and Crusoe would find him dead on the island. Maybe the one who had made those footprints was still alive on the island. The truth that someone other than himself had been on that island made his heart skip with joy. The footprints proved it. He could be absolutely certain about it. He searched throughout the island, and eventually, on one Friday, he found the native that had made the footprints. He named him Friday after the day on which he found him.

We are much like the storybook character Robinson Crusoe. We have before us the footprints of the earth, the stars, the sun, and the moon. These prints were made by an Almighty Being. Crusoe would have been foolish to have looked at those footprints and concluded that they had come from nothing. Even so, we would be unwise to ignore reason and to conclude that the earth and the universe have just happened, that they have come from nothing.

The world around us and the world above us point to only one conclusion: An Almighty God is behind this physical earth and the physical universe which is beyond it. We can be confident about this, just as confident as we are that a book cannot just happen from nothing and an electric razor cannot result from an explosion.

THE EVIDENCE OF MAN

Second, we can believe with confidence that God really does exist because of the evidence which comes to us through the existence of man. The existence of man proclaims the existence of God.

Man is a far greater marvel than the physical universe. Think of his intellectual powers. He can reason, believe, love, dream, plan, and design. There are people who speak three and four languages fluently. Scientists tell us that one cell in a person's brain is more complex than the finest computer we can now build.

Think of man's spiritual nature. Man has always been a worshiping being. The most primitive of tribes of people look up in worship to some higher power. Man has within him a sense of "ought." He has a moral consciousness within him. Sometimes this consciousness is not very refined, but it is always present.

Think of man's physical body. You can spend a lifetime studying any part of the human body and never exhaust the research which could be done.

Think of life itself. We cannot create it, and we cannot revive it when it dies. We cannot fully explain it, and we cannot totally control it. The marvel of man declares the existence of his Maker.

Suppose we are in a classroom listening to a distinguished professor lecture about the origin of life. Skipping over the scientific terminology and explanations he uses, he says, in essence, "In the beginning a little cell of some kind existed, and it had some kind of life form in it. It multiplied, grew, and developed. A type of sea creature emerged. It multiplied, grew, and developed. A type of land creature emerged. It multiplied, grew, and developed. Finally, with the passing of millions of years, the creatures known as human beings evolved."

As we listen to the professor, we are confronted

with three problems which his theory does not solve. He skips over these problems as if they are insignificant and unworthy of mentioning, but his treatment of these problems makes it impossible and unreasonable to accept his theory. The first problem is explaining the origin of life. His theory assumes that life came from nothing. Any person would find it impossible to believe that a book came from nothing and that an electric razor resulted from an explosion, and life is far more complex than a book or a razor. Man can create a book and a razor, but he cannot create life. Yet the professor would ask us to believe that life came from nothing.

The second problem is explaining the existence of natural law. The professor's theory assumes that natural law came from nothing. Our world is governed by natural laws. If you do not eat or take food into your body in some way, you will die. You cannot ignore or evade this law. No one is excused from it. If you do not sleep, your body will collapse in exhaustion. You cannot break this natural law. Neither can you overcome the natural law of death. The death rate of human beings is 100 per cent. There are no exceptions. The professor implies by his theory that natural law just happened.

The third problem is the explanation for the existence of the family. The human race is made up of families. We cannot find a time in recorded human history when the family did not exist. The professor would have us believe that man evolved into maturity at the very time that woman evolved into maturity. They just happened to find companionship enjoyable and so man and woman have continued to build family relationships throughout recorded history. Man is different from woman, and woman is different from man; yet they are alike in compatibility and companionship. The professor says they emerged into maturity at the same time and this resulted in the family. In other words, he argues that the family came from nothing—that it is only an accidental happening.

Our minds will not allow us to conceive that life came from nothing, that natural law came from nothing, and that the human family came from nothing. The only rational way that the existence of man can be explained is with the understanding that an Almighty Being created him and placed him upon this earth for a special reason.

What we have concluded by reason, the Bible clearly declares. In the first chapter of the Bible, we are told, "Then God said, 'Let Us make man in Our image, according to Our likeness...'" (Genesis 1:26). Human life came from divine life, according to the Bible. We are further told, "God created man in His own image, in the image of God He created him; male and female He created them. God blessed them; and God said to them, 'Be fruitful and multiply, and fill the earth, and subdue it; and rule over the fish of the sea and over the birds of the sky and over every living thing that moves on the earth'" (Genesis 1:27, 28). God gave human beings a spiritual nature, a likeness to Himself. He created the family, making humans male and female. God created the natural laws that would govern all earth life.

Reason demands that we admit that human life was created by an Almighty hand and for a divine reason. Without hesitation, we can say, "For You formed my inward parts; You wove me in my mother's womb. I will give thanks to You, for I am fearfully and wonderfully made; wonderful are Your works, and my soul knows it very well" (Psalm 139:13, 14).

A missionary once said, "I have been in several countries of the world, and I have had a similar experience in every country. For example, when children are taught that two plus two equals four, they always respond in the same way. They think about it and then conclude that this is right. Something in their minds reaches out to that concept and accepts it as truth. Likewise, when people in all these different countries are taught that God created the earth, the universe, and man, they think about it and then conclude that this concept has to be right. Something in their minds reaches out to that teaching and accepts it as truth. I have received this response in every nation and country where I have gone."

If you will think about the existence of man—his life, his intelligence, his spiritual nature, his moral consciousness, and his physical body—you will surely conclude that he could not have just happened, but was created by an Almighty Being. You can be confident that God really does exist. The existence of man proves it.

CONCLUSION

Think deeply about these two evidences we have considered—the evidence of the world and the evidence of man. The conclusion which they demand is so certain and undeniable that the Bible says, "The fool has said in his heart, 'There is no God'" (Psalm 14:1).

It is also reasonable to believe that the God who

made us will call us one day into judgment and will require an accounting of how we have lived. This is the very reason God sent Jesus into the world and has given us the Bible. He wanted us to know why we are here and what is expected of us. Jesus said, "He who rejects Me and does not receive My sayings, has one who judges him; the word I spoke is what will judge him at the last day" (John 12:48).

The most amazing truth which Jesus and the Bible reveal to us is that God wants to adopt us as His children. The One who made the sun, the moon, the stars, the earth, and the entire universe seeks my fellowship in His eternal family! He has invited me into His family through the gospel of His Son. As I obey this gospel by faith in Jesus, repentance of sin, confession of Jesus, and baptism into Christ's body, I am adopted into His spiritual family (Ephesians 1:5; Galatians 4:6). According to the Scriptures, you can know not only that God really does exist but also that you are really His child!

STUDY QUESTIONS
(answers on page 259)

1. What is the most profound question anyone can ask?
2. Why is the question "Does God exist?" so profound?
3. What does the Bible begin with?
4. What is the first evidence that compels us to believe in God?
5. What three problems confront anyone who leaves God out of his explanation for the existence of man?

CREATOR OR CHANCE?

Dr. A. Cressy Morrison, former president of the New York State Academy of Science, said:

The evidence is strongly suggestive of this directive purpose back of everything. . . . We have found that the world is in the right place, that the crust is adjusted to within ten feet, and that if the ocean were a few feet deeper we would have no oxygen or vegetation. We have found that the earth rotates in twenty-four hours and that were this revolution delayed, life would be impossible. If the speed of the earth around the sun were increased or decreased materially, this history of life, if any, would be entirely different. We find that the sun is the one among thousands which could make our sort of life possible on earth, its size, density, temperature and the character of its rays all must be right, and are right. We find that the gases of the atmosphere are adjusted to each other and that a very slight change would be fatal. . . .

Considering the bulk of the earth, its place in space and the nicety of the adjustments, the chances of some of these adjustments occurring is in the order of one to a million, and the chances of all of them occurring cannot be calculated. . . . The existence of these facts cannot, therefore, be reconciled with any of the laws of chance. . . . A review of the wonders of nature demonstrates beyond question that there are design and purpose in it all. A program is being carried out in all its infinite detail by the Supreme Being we call God.

A. Cressy Morrison, *Man Does Not Stand Alone* (New York: Fleming H. Revell Co., 1944), 94, 95; quoted in Batsell Barrett Baxter, *I Believe Because* . . . (Grand Rapids, Mich.: Baker Book House, 1971), 66.

2

Is the Bible God's Word?

The Bible claims to be inspired by God (2 Timothy 3:16, 17). The Greek phrase translated "inspired by God" literally means "God-breathed." Great secular writers, such as Leo Tolstoy, have been "inspired" by a variety of stimuli—including principles and events—but the Bible asserts that *God Himself* is its source of inspiration. Peter, an apostle and author of several New Testament books, wrote that biblical prophecies were not the result of "an act of human will, but men moved by the Holy Spirit spoke from God" (2 Peter 1:21).

The purpose of this lesson is to introduce you to this inspired Book. A few proofs of the Bible's divine origin will be included, but the primary aim of this chapter is to create an interest in this amazing volume—to encourage you to read it for yourself. As you read the Bible and follow its precepts (James 1:21–25), you will begin to understand why this remarkable Book has had such an impact on people through the ages.

15

This chapter features what one writer called "Seven Wonders of the Wonderful Word": the wonders of its antiquity, modernity, diversity, unity, theme, influence, and comfort. Other marvels of the Bible could be mentioned, such as its historical and geographical accuracy and its impartiality, but these seven are sufficient to cause us to exclaim with one of the writers of the Book of Psalms, "Your testimonies are wonderful"! (Psalm 119:129a).

ITS ANTIQUITY

The Bible is one of the oldest books in all the world! Books generally do not have the opportunity to become very old. They are so fragile. Fire consumes them, and water dissolves them. Insects eat them, and careless fingers tear them.

The Bible, in its completed form, is almost two thousand years old. Parts of it are fully twice that old. No other book in the world can be compared with this! The age of the Bible reveals its endurance and indestructibility.

The most ancient writings are in the Old Testament: Genesis, Exodus, Leviticus, Numbers, and Deuteronomy. They were written by Moses and contain the account of the beginning of man and the beginning days of recorded time. It can be safely said that these writings have come from the *oldest complete manuscripts in the possession of man today*!

The Bible has reached this ancient age in spite of man's frequent and continued efforts to destroy it! Again and again, the most powerful governments that the earth has known have sought to eradicate this Book. Men have died on the gallows for reading it and have been burned at the stake for owning it.

Tortures too fiendish to describe have been visited upon people for studying its pages—yet there are more Bibles on the earth today than there are copies of any other book ever written!

At the end of the third century, the Roman Emperor Diocletian decreed death for any person who owned a copy of the Bible. He also condemned to death the members of a prisoner's household—for not reporting his disobedience. In this way, the mighty Roman ruthlessly set out to remove the writings which condemned his own vicious life and tyranny. After two years, Diocletian boasted, "I have completely exterminated the Christian writings from the face of the earth."

A century later, another Roman emperor, Constantine, was impressed by Christianity and desired to have copies of the New Testament made for all of the churches of his empire. He offered a substantial reward to anyone who could discover and deliver to his officers a copy of God's Word. Within twenty-four hours, fifty copies of the Scriptures were offered to the emperor—in spite of the fact that Diocletian thought he had destroyed them all!

Though written upon perishable materials in ink that is quick to fade—defying the ravages of time, the forces of nature, and the destructive conspiracies of man—the Bible has survived to our present century. Only God's providence can account for its long and fabulous history.

ITS MODERNITY

As ancient as it is, the Bible is also a modern book in many respects. We do not expect old books to be up-to-date in their teachings. A ten-year-old science textbook is obsolete. One a century old is a curiosity. The medical information given in *Salmon's Embryology*, printed in the year 1700, would send a modern doctor into hysterical laughter. The *Pharmacopia Londensis* of 1600 seems even more ridiculous; if a physician were to practice medicine in accordance with that famous text, those who regulate medical practices would put him in jail!

To illustrate how even a few years can make a difference, here is a statement from a textbook on botany that is about 150 years old:

> In Italy there groweth an herb . . . which hath a blossom of pure white possessing a rare fragrance, yet withal hath this strange property: the blossoms, placed under damp stones and suffered there to remain, in ten days transform themselves into venomous scorpions, the bite of which is death.

You may say, "Be fair. After all, we have learned a great deal in the last century and a half. You cannot expect old books to be up-to-date." That is the point! Moses, for instance, wrote 3,500 years ago, yet you will not find his writings contradicting modern science and knowledge. Entire books have been written on "the scientific foreknowledge of the Bible," stressing that modern facts of astronomy and cosmology and other scientific fields can be found in the pages of the Bible. Facts such as these are included:

The earth is round (Isaiah 40:22; Proverbs 8:27).
The earth is suspended in space (Job 26:7).
Space is too large to be measured or the stars counted (Genesis 15:5; Jeremiah 33:22).

The oceans have natural lanes in them (which are used for shipping to this day) (Psalm 8:8).

These volumes do not assert that the Bible is a scientific treatise. Rather, they stress that, when Bible writers touched on themes relating to science, unlike other writers of their day, they did not contradict scientific fact.

The most fascinating illustrations of the timeless quality of the Bible are in the area of medicine. Written in a world that knew nothing of modern hygiene or health practices, the law given to Moses as recorded in the Old Testament is filled with instructions about cleanliness, sanitation, quarantine, and other methods for preventing and controlling disease.

For example, it is standard procedure for a surgeon to wear a mask as he operates. Also, when one goes into the room of someone who is especially susceptible to disease, he wears a mask. Why? Because he does not want to spread germs. More than three thousand years before germs were discovered by scientists, God had Moses give these instructions: "And the leper in whom the plague is . . . he shall put a covering upon his upper lip, and shall cry, Unclean, unclean" (Leviticus 13:45; KJV).

Another medical advancement is the blood transfusion. Years ago, it was considered sound medical practice to "bleed" people; many literally were bled to death. Today, however, it is understood that the blood is the lifestream of the body. Turn now to Moses' statement in Genesis 9:4: "Only you shall not eat flesh with its life, that is, its *blood*." (Emphasis mine.) In other words, Moses said: The *life* of the flesh is in the *blood* (see also Leviticus 17:11–14).

Books have been dedicated to the medical accuracy of the Bible. These cover a wide range of medical practices. Here is a sample:

> Both men and women contain the "seed" of life
> (Genesis 3:15; 22:18).
> It is wise to decontaminate yourself and your clothing after coming in contact with possibly diseased men or animals (Numbers 19:5–22).
> Eating an animal that died naturally is dangerous
> (Leviticus 17:15).

Isn't that amazing? The oldest volume in our possession is as modern as twenty-first-century medical concepts!

The modernity of the Bible can be illustrated with all of its varied subjects. Can anyone claim that the world has matured beyond the ethical standards of this Book? Have we found any superior knowledge that leaves its precepts behind? No! Modern man has not begun to pass the wisdom of the Bible; if the world continues to exist for another thousand years, God's Word will be just as up-to-date in the thirty-first century as it is in the twenty-first!

ITS DIVERSITY

All that we have said to this point would be sufficiently amazing if the Bible were just one book, dealing with one subject. However, that is not the case.

The Bible is one of the most diverse books in the world. First, it is in reality two volumes—the Old Testament and the New Testament—separated from each other by some four or five centuries. Second, each one of these volumes is further divided into a number of books—thirty-nine in the Old Testament and twenty-seven in the New Testament, making a total of sixty-six. Third, these sixty-six books were written by more than forty different writers. Fourth, these forty-plus men lived over a span of almost two thousand years! Finally, these authors wrote on every subject known to literature—plus one. The "plus one" is a subject no other book contains: true *prophecy*. This is God's realm alone! Hundreds of prophetic statements in the Bible have come to pass perfectly and accurately. Space will permit only a few examples:

> *Prophecies of Nations:* Numerous prophecies were given regarding the rise, decline, and fall of nations. For instance, Israel's history is vividly portrayed in Deuteronomy 28:47–68. Prophecies were also given concerning many other nations, including Assyria (see Isaiah 10:12, 24, 25; 2 Kings 17:24; 18:13) and Babylon (see Isaiah 13; Daniel 5:28).

> *Prophecies of People:* The work of King Josiah was foretold more than three hundred years before he was born (1 Kings 13:2; 2 Kings 23:15, 16), as was the reign of Cyrus of Persia (see Isaiah 44:28; 45:1). The amazing story of Sennacherib's inability to capture Jerusalem is also worth mentioning (see 2 Kings 19:32–35).

> *Prophecies of Christ:* Of the approximately eight hundred prophecies in the Old Testament, over three hundred are centered in the person of Jesus Christ. Chapter 4 of this book lists many of these prophecies and their fulfillment.

The diversity of the Bible proves that it is from God. This is especially true because in that diversity we find unity. No part of human life and spirituality is overlooked in this Book of all books. It touches all the phases of human existence in principle and in divine guidance.

ITS UNITY

If the Bible were one book, written by a single author, we would naturally expect all of its parts to harmonize. Even if it were one book written by forty-plus men on one subject, the chances of complete agreement would be very slight. Therefore, to claim that forty-plus men wrote sixty-six books on so many different subjects, and that their words are in perfect agreement, leaves the mind stunned. One might say, "They must have worked together very closely and carefully to achieve so remarkable a work!" History proves that they could not have. Most of these men never saw each other. They were separated by centuries and had no opportunity to plan or revise their writings. The harmony must be explained in some other way.

The fact cannot be denied: Complete unity exists between all of the parts and writers of the Scriptures. Men have tried but failed to find even a single disagreement in the writings. The Bible is one book, a unified whole.

Consider, for instance, its two main parts: the Old Testament and the New Testament. Though they represent two separate covenants (or agreements) for two separate groups of people, they are tied together beautifully. Someone has said, "The Old Testament is the New Testament concealed, and the New

Testament is the Old Testament revealed." The Old Testament is the *root*, and the New Testament is the *fruit*.

Let us note a few contrasts between the *first* book of the Bible and the *last* book of the Bible:

(1) Genesis begins with the creation of the heavens and the earth; Revelation ends with the creation of the new heavens and the new earth.

(2) Genesis relates the coming of light and the creation of the sun and moon; Revelation tells of the end of their service to man—for in the New City (heaven), God and the Lamb (Jesus) are the light.

(3) In Genesis, man meets Satan and suffers defeat. In Revelation, another battle is fought; this time, Satan loses and, through Jesus, man is the victor.

(4) In Genesis, man is cast out of the Garden of Eden, where the first man and woman lived; in Revelation, he is reinstated with God.

(5) Finally, Genesis tells how man loses the privilege of eating of the Tree of Life—lest sin be made immortal. In Revelation, with sin destroyed, man is invited to eat of the Tree of Life so that he may live forever!

Yes, the unity of the book is marvelous. When we look at that unity, we stand amazed and conclude that God is the Author of it.

ITS THEME

The unity of the Bible is possible only if *one Mind* supervised the compilation of its contents. Since no human author could have lived over the fifteen-plus centuries which elapsed during this period of literary activity, only God can properly be called the Author of the Book. This was what Peter had in mind when he said, "Men moved by the Holy Spirit spoke from God" (2 Peter 1:21b).

Again, to have unity, not only was one author necessary, but also *one theme* was needed—in order that the whole might be drawn together. What is the theme of this Book? It is not "The Story of Mankind," although mankind provides the reason for the theme. It is not "The Story of the Jews," although they figure prominently in the working out of the theme. The theme of the book is "The Story of a Man," *one Man—Jesus Christ.*

It has been well said that the Bible revolves around the Coming One. The message of the Old Testament is "He is *coming*." The message of the Gospel Accounts is "He is *here*." The message of the rest of the New Testament is "He is *coming again*."

An interesting study can be made of each book of the Bible from the standpoint of how it reveals Jesus. Books could be written on "Jesus in Genesis," "Jesus in Exodus," "Jesus in Leviticus," and so forth. For instance:

Jesus is in Genesis 1, for "All things came into being through Him" (John 1:3a).

Jesus is in Genesis 3, for it is He who would later be "her [the woman's] seed" and would bruise the head of Satan (Genesis 3:15; Galatians 3:16).

Jesus is in Genesis 4, as He is foreshadowed in the sacrifice of Abel's lamb. (See Hebrews 12:24.)

Jesus is also in Genesis 6, for the salvation in the ark is a type [symbol] of the salvation to be found in and through Him. On and on we could go.

This, then, is the theme that gives the Word its wonderful unity: *Jesus Christ.* Jesus—the Redeemer who was to come, the Savior who did come, and the King who will come again—binds the words of the sixty-six books into one unified document.

ITS INFLUENCE

Of all the writings in the earth's libraries, the Bible has exerted the most potent influence on mankind. It has changed the flow of history, erected empires, cast down conquerors and kings. It has brought blessings and success to those who have obeyed its precepts, and it has brought death and destruction to those who have fought against it. The powers of the Bible are many and varied, but let us notice especially its power to change lives and to uplift men.

A man by the name of John G. Paton wanted to go to the New Hebrides Islands as a missionary. At first the British government refused to let him go. They said the tribesmen were savage cannibals who ate friends as well as enemies. But Paton persisted, and finally they gave in. In 1858, a British ship landed John and his wife on the island. An armed guard stood by while the crew built the missionaries a house in which to dwell. Then they sailed away, convinced they would never see the couple again.

The people with whom the Patons worked were brutal and cruel. Within a few years, Mrs. Paton died of a tropical disease. John had to lie upon her grave for ten days and nights, mustket in hand, to keep the natives from digging up her body and eating it. But he stayed on the island for thirty years and taught them the Word. At the end of the time, the British government published an official document saying that the former cannibals of the New Hebrides had become the most advanced and cultured of all the native tribes that lived under the British flag!

Wherever the Bible has gone, mankind has been made better. The Bible itself abounds with stories of changed lives. A dishonest tax collector became honest and generous (Luke 19:1–9). A murdering blasphemer developed into a great apostle (Acts 7:58; 8:1, 3; 22:4–21). Many other examples are given.

What God has done through the power of the Bible for others, He can do in your life. If you will read and live His Word, He will change you into the image of His Son, Jesus Christ.

ITS COMFORT

In granting comfort, as in every other field of service to man, the Bible is unique, unprecedented, and unparalleled! There has never been and never will be any other trustworthy light that can enable man to see beyond the grave. The Scriptures offer the reader hope and assurance for his own eternity, and they bring comfort to his heart when a loved one is taken away by death.

Death is an enemy. All the poetry and philosophy of man's devising can never change that grim and somber fact. Of course, to the Christian, it is an enemy whose defeat has been predetermined. By the power of Christ, death is forced to serve as an usher to introduce the redeemed into the presence of the Lord. Nevertheless, it remains *an enemy*! This enemy enters palaces and huts alike. It separates a husband from his wife. It tears the little baby from its mother's arms. It turns sweet happiness into dark despair.

When a loved one dies, people will request, "Say some words that will comfort us." Where shall those words come from? From literature? From a poet? From a philosopher? Search all your great books, and you will not find a line penned by mortal man that can bring lasting comfort and hope when death strikes your home. Only one source offers words of strength and comfort: the Bible. You can read words like these from God's book:

> Even though I walk through the valley of the shadow of death, I fear no evil, for You are with me; Your rod and Your staff, they comfort me (Psalm 23:4).

> But now Christ has been raised from the dead, the first fruits of those who are asleep.
> . . . But when this perishable will have put on the imperishable, and this mortal will have put on immortality, then will come about the saying that is written, "Death is swallowed up in victory" (1 Corinthians 15:20–54).

> Then we who are alive and remain will be caught up together with them in the clouds to meet the Lord in the air, and so we shall always be with the Lord. Therefore comfort one another with these words (1 Thessalonians 4:17, 18).

> And He will wipe away every tear from their eyes; and there will no longer be any death; there will no longer be any mourning, or crying, or pain; the first things have passed away (Revelation 21:4).

Through the ages, these words—and others like them in the Bible—have dried tears, given hope, and brought comfort to literally millions. Indeed, it is a wonderful book!

CONCLUSION

We have considered seven wonders of the Bible: It is old, but ever new! It is diverse, but with a perfect unity—a unity centered in Jesus! It is powerful in its influence, but tender in its comfort! The Bible is the inspired Word of God; there is no other adequate explanation.

STUDY QUESTIONS
(answers on page 259)

1. What does "inspired by God" mean as used in 2 Timothy 3:16?
2. The Roman emperor Diocletian tried to eliminate the Bible and its message. Did he succeed?
3. How does Leviticus 13:45 show the Bible's relevance?
4. How do the differences within the Bible prove that it is from God?
5. What is the theme of the Bible?
6. Of all the writings in the earth's libraries, which book has exerted the most influence?
7. What comfort does the Bible offer its reader?
8. List seven wonders of the Bible that prove that it is the inspired Word of God.

WORD HELPS

Scriptures—the Bible, both Old and New Testaments. The Old Testament was God's law for Jews and led the way for the New Testament (Galatians 3:24), which is for all people to follow today. It contains a summary of God's creation of the world, the laws given to His chosen people Israel, inspired poetry, and the teachings of God through His prophets.

3

Who Is God the Father?

God. No person or thing is superior to Him. He alone has full authority. He is over all.

The word "God" belongs rightfully to one being only, although man has made the mistake of trying to worship man-made ideas and images of stone, wood, and clay. Only one being is God; He alone is the object of all true worship. Any worship given to another so-called being, whether imagined or living, is false worship.

If we wanted to explain in just a few words the honor due God, we could find no greater and no simpler expression than 1 Timothy 1:17: ". . . to the King eternal, immortal, invisible, the only God, be honor and glory forever and ever. Amen." The truth about God is summed up in a statement recited repeatedly by ancient Israel: ". . . The Lord is our God, the Lord is one! You shall love the Lord your God with all your heart and with all your soul and with all your might" (Deuteronomy 6:4, 5). In light of who God is, Jesus declared the resolve that should be implanted in every heart: "You shall worship the Lord your God, and serve Him only" (Matthew 4:10b).

The true God is described in the Scriptures as "three" in nature. That is, He is one, yet He is three—God the Father; God the Son; and God the Spirit. The three persons of the Godhead are equal with each other, and each is eternal. Each possesses a distinct personality, reflecting supernatural intelligence, emotion, and will; however, these three are but one in essence, nature, and purpose.

This concept of God as one yet three is called the Godhead, the Divine Family, or the Trinity (Acts 17:29; Romans 1:20; Colossians 2:9).[1] This great truth is far beyond our human understanding—but not beyond our believing, for it is plainly taught in the Word of God. We accept it by faith—not because we have imagined it, not because we have reasoned that it could be true, and not because we have learned such a truth by studying the world around us. We accept this truth and believe it because it has been given to us in the inspired writings of the Scriptures.

The idea that God is the Father, the Son, and the Holy Spirit is not explained directly in the Scriptures, but it is implied. Writings in the Old Testament which suggest the idea of the Godhead include the divine name itself, which is the Hebrew word "Elohim," a word that is plural in form. Other writings in the Old Testament employ plural pronouns with reference to

---

[1]The three Greek words which can be translated "Godhead" appear only one time each in the Scriptures (Acts 17:29; Romans 1:20; Colossians 2:9; KJV). The terms "Divine Family" and "Trinity" are not found in the Scriptures, and we use them in this lesson only as explanations.

God—such as Genesis 1:26, which says, "Let Us make man in Our image. . . ."[2]

In the New Testament we read about the three members of the Godhead. At the baptism of Jesus, the Holy Spirit descended upon Him in the shape of a dove, while the voice of the Father declared, "This is My beloved Son . . ." (Matthew 3:17). When our Lord promised His disciples that He would send the Holy Spirit, He made a reference to the Spirit, God, and Himself: "When the *Helper* comes, whom I will send to you from the *Father*, that is the Spirit of truth, who proceeds from the Father, He will testify about *Me*" (John 15:26; emphasis mine).

The work of man's redemption involves all three members of the Godhead. Peter wrote, "According to the foreknowledge of *God the Father*, by the sanctifying work of *the Spirit*, to obey *Jesus Christ* and be sprinkled with His blood . . ." (1 Peter 1:2; emphasis mine). The Godhead is also seen in our approach to God in prayer, for Paul said that through *Jesus* all have "access in one *Spirit* to the *Father*" (Ephesians 2:18; emphasis mine).

The Great Commission pictures baptism as being administered in the name of the Trinity: "Go therefore and make disciples of all the nations, baptizing them in the name of the Father and the Son and the Holy Spirit, teaching them to observe all that I commanded you; and lo, I am with you always, even to the end of the age" (Matthew 28:19, 20).

Throughout the Bible, God the Father is always referred to with a personal pronoun in the male gender ("He"). He is the Father, the Creator, Jehovah,

---

[2]Three other examples are found in Genesis 3:22; 11:7; Isaiah 6:8.

the Almighty, and the Lord God. He always stands first among the three members of the Godhead. The Bible shows Him to be above all in wisdom, power, love, mercy, and justice. As the One who planned, designed, and created the universe, He is the supreme authority and sovereign ruler over all powers and authorities. He is the Father of those who worship and obey Him. In Him all creatures, including human beings, live and move and exist (Acts 17:28).

God is to be worshiped by all people, all nations, and all tribes as the only true God. He can be approached only through Jesus Christ. We cannot come to Him through angels, saints, or other people—living or dead, regardless of how good they may be or may have been. The only real mediator between God and man is His Son, Jesus (1 Timothy 2:5). The only way available for man to come to the Father is Jesus. Jesus said, "I am the way, and the truth, and the life; no one comes to the Father but through Me" (John 14:6).

The second member of the Godhead is the Lord Jesus Christ. Through Him God the Father created the earth and man (Colossians 1:16). In His relation to man, Jesus is called the "Son of Man"; in His relation to God, He is called the "Son of God." He is the only member of the Godhead who has taken on a human body and lived physically here on earth. He is the Savior and Redeemer of mankind. He is to be worshiped and adored by all people. He has provided the means by which the whole earth can come to the Father in worship.

For this reason also, God highly exalted Him, and bestowed on Him the name which is above every name, so that at the name of Jesus every knee will bow, of those who are in heaven and on earth and under the earth, and that every tongue will confess that Jesus Christ is Lord, to the glory of God the Father (Philippians 2:9–11).

The third member of the Godhead is the Holy Spirit. He has the same nature and make-up as God and Christ. Like them, He is referred to with personal pronouns, and references to Him are always in the male gender ("He"). He is always mentioned third when spoken of in the Bible in connection with the other two members of the Godhead. He is spoken of in the New Testament as the means by which man is guided and instructed. He is our Helper through the Scriptures. He inspired the writing of the Old and New Testaments; therefore, the Scriptures are referred to as the "sword of the Spirit" (Ephesians 6:17), the tool that He uses to do His work. He indwells (lives in) those who have become children of God (1 Corinthians 6:19, 20).

God the Father, Jesus the Son, and the Holy Spirit exist together eternally and make up the Godhead. While there is much that we do not know about them, we can be certain that each one exists and that the three of them make up the all-glorious Trinity. They are united and exist as one. They are eternal, distinct and different from all created things, and they are one in will and purpose.

Beyond the nature of God as three persons, what else do we know about God the Father? Basically, the Bible teaches one great, overall truth about Him: *He is the only true and living God, and He should be worshiped as such by every person.* No one can read any part of the Bible, the Old Testament or the New Testament, without seeing this truth forcefully taught.

Let us look further into the question "Who is God the Father?"

OUR CREATOR

God created everything. He made all things, and He owns all things. Nothing exists that He has not made or allowed to be made, and everything that exists belongs to Him.

The earth and mankind did not develop accidentally; they were created by the gracious hand of God. This is the reason why we should not worry about scientifically dating the age of the earth. The world has a miraculous beginning, and this causes it to look older than it really is. God created, to some extent, a mature earth. He did not try to fool man, but He had to make a full-grown earth to provide for man's existence.

He made Adam and Eve, the first couple, as adults, not as babies. Had you and I been present on the day that He created them, they might have appeared to us as a couple in their twenties; but they had just been given life. Even so, the earth was formed by God's miracle of creation at the beginning with full-grown vegetation, water, air, and life-sustaining dirt.

Flowing from the truth that God has created all things are other truths about God that we need to understand. What are they?

He is the being behind all realities.

All that exists can be divided into two categories: that which is God and that which is not God. God is the first and most basic reality. Everything else was created by Him or was allowed to be made by His authority, and therefore is not God.

He is eternal.

> Before the mountains were born or You gave birth to the earth and the world, even from everlasting to everlasting, You are God (Psalm 90:2).

> But You are the same, and Your years will not come to an end (Psalm 102:27).

God is without beginning and will be without end. He was before time, having created time at a juncture in eternity. He is the eternally existent One to whom the past, present, and future are like a moment in time. He lives in the eternal now. He sees the past and the future as clearly as He sees the present. He has forever been, and He will forever be.

He is almighty.

> "'Ah Lord God! Behold, You have made the heavens and the earth by Your great power and by Your outstretched arm! Nothing is too difficult for You'" (Jeremiah 32:17).

> "Behold, I am the Lord, the God of all flesh; is anything too difficult for Me?" (Jeremiah 32:27).

He can do anything in keeping with His nature. Of course, He cannot look upon wickedness with favor, and He cannot be tempted by evil, because He is righteous (Habakkuk 1:13). He cannot deny His own nature because of His truthfulness (2 Timothy 2:13), for He cannot lie (Titus 1:2). In line with His nature, however, He can do anything. Nothing is too hard for Him.

He is all-knowing.

"Am I a God who is near," declares the Lord, "and not a God far off? Can a man hide himself in hiding places so I do not see him?" declares the Lord. "Do I not fill the heavens and the earth?" declares the Lord (Jeremiah 23:23, 24).

The eyes of the Lord are in every place, watching the evil and the good (Proverbs 15:3).

He knows everything immediately, accurately, and completely. He does not have to learn anything. He needs no counselor or teacher.

He is present everywhere.

Where can I go from Your Spirit? Or where can I flee from Your presence? If I ascend to heaven, You are there; if I make my bed in Sheol, behold, You are there. If I take the wings of the dawn, if I dwell in the remotest part of the sea, even there Your hand will lead me, and Your right hand will lay hold of me. If I say, "Surely the darkness will overwhelm me, and the light around me will be night," even the darkness is not dark to You, and the night is as bright as the day . . . (Psalm 139:7–12).

". . . He is not far from each one of us; for in Him we live and move and exist . . ." (Acts 17:27, 28).

Anywhere we go, God is there. We cannot hide from Him or conceal anything from His all-seeing eyes. Neither distance nor darkness can remove us from His presence.

He is the only true and living God.

He is living (Matthew 16:16), and He is true

(1 Thessalonians 1:9). As a son may look like his father, human beings are in some ways like God, our Creator. Like man, God sees, hears, speaks, feels, wills, and acts. However, God cannot be seen; He is a spirit who can be present everywhere at the same time (John 4:24).

Who, then, is God the Father? He is the eternal Being and Creator of everything, three in nature, all-wise, almighty, and present everywhere.

Since God created all things, everything belongs to Him, and He deserves our worship. All material things are His possessions, all the creatures of the earth are His, and all the peoples of the earth are His. It is right that we worship and serve Him. If we give special honor and worship to another god of any kind, we are worshiping and serving a lie.

OUR PROVIDER

God not only created this universe, but He also takes care of it today. He keeps it from falling apart, breaking down, or failing to function as He intended (Colossians 1:16, 17).

This fact is proven by reason as well as by revelation. Logical thinking tells us that God created this earth and continues to manage it. Nothing about this earth maintains itself. It is obvious that some almighty hand holds it together. Man cannot even care for himself. He cannot make the air he breathes, the water he drinks, or the sunshine he needs. He is totally dependent upon the earth to run as it should.

The testimony of the revelation of God's Word is that God holds the world together. At the creation of the heavens and the earth, He set in motion natural laws to make His world continue.

Then God said, "Let there be lights in the expanse of the heavens to separate the day from the night, and let them be for signs and for seasons and for days and years" (Genesis 1:14).

Then God said, "Behold, I have given you every plant yielding seed that is on the surface of all the earth, and every tree which has fruit yielding seed; it shall be food for you; and to every beast of the earth and to every bird of the sky and to every thing that moves on the earth which has life, I have given every green plant for food"; and it was so (Genesis 1:29, 30).

In addition to maintaining natural laws, He upholds the universe and all the forces connected with it with His divine care.

"You alone are the Lord. You have made the heavens, the heaven of heavens with all their host, the earth and all that is on it, the seas and all that is in them. You give life to all of them and the heavenly host bows down before You" (Nehemiah 9:6).

Specifically, He preserves man and beast: "... O Lord, You preserve man and beast" (Psalm 36:6). He feeds all the living things of the earth: "He gives to the beast its food, and to the young ravens which cry" (Psalm 147:9). He watches over the birds of the air: "Look at the birds of the air, that they do not sow, nor reap nor gather into barns, and yet your heavenly Father feeds them. Are you not worth much more than they?" (Matthew 6:26); "Are not two sparrows sold for a cent? And yet not one of them will fall to the ground apart from your Father" (Matthew

10:29). He rules over the nations of the people of the world: "He makes the nations great, then destroys them; He enlarges the nations, then leads them away" (Job 12:23). He protects and blesses the righteous: "But transgressors will be altogether destroyed; the posterity of the wicked will be cut off. But the salvation of the righteous is from the Lord; He is their strength in time of trouble" (Psalm 37:38, 39); "But the very hairs of your head are all numbered" (Matthew 10:30). He provides eternal life for those who come to Him and obey Him: "My sheep hear My voice, and I know them, and they follow Me; and I give eternal life to them, and they will never perish; and no one will snatch them out of My hand" (John 10:27, 28).

Most of the cities in the world have some kind of transportation system for the people. The vehicles that make up these systems obviously must be cared for. If they are not kept in running order by changing the oil, fixing the broken parts, and replacing any worn-out parts, they will soon be left on the side of the street. All machines need care. We do not know of a machine on earth that does not need maintenance. The earth is like a giant machine. It must be cared for and provided for, and the Bible says that it is held in place by the God of heaven (Hebrews 1:3).

How grateful we should be to God for watching over us and providing for us! No one should doubt that God's providence is for the good of man (Acts 14:17), for He causes the sun to rise on the evil and the good (Matthew 5:45). It is the proven story of all who have served Him that He will not withhold any good thing from those who walk faithfully (Psalm 84:11; Romans 8:28).

OUR REDEEMER

God is our Redeemer, our Savior. He loves us and wants to save us from sin. The only hope we have for eternity is in Him.

His love for us is difficult to explain. It is greater than any human love we can ever know. Even though all people have sinned and separated themselves from Him by choice, He seeks to save them. He has offered salvation to us through Christ by sending Him into the world to make the ultimate sacrifice for our salvation.

God, being completely righteous, cannot excuse sin. We could not pay the penalty for our sin without experiencing eternal death. God sent Jesus to the cross to bear the punishment for our sin. Anyone who comes to Him by receiving and obeying His message of salvation will receive the benefits of Jesus' death. For this reason, the Bible describes God as our Savior (Titus 1:3), just as it describes Jesus as our Savior (Titus 2:13). God planned our redemption before the foundation of the world (1 Peter 1:20). Now He lovingly waits for all people to hear His message, repent (change their minds and their lives), and receive His salvation (2 Peter 3:9).

Picture a boy who has an abusive father. His father speaks to him only to rebuke him. Whenever the boy makes a mistake, his dad gives him a beating. After living for years in this type of relationship with his dad, he has come to regard his dad as a stern judge, not as a loving father. He fears his dad, but he does not love him. He does not even enjoy being with him. Whenever he hears the word "father," he thinks of being slapped or beaten. This unfortunate boy will find it hard to see in the word "father" the beautiful meaning which the word was meant to convey.

Some people have a similar feeling about the word "God." They have been taught all of their lives to see God as only a judge who waits for them to make a mistake so He can punish them by casting them into hell. Jesus taught us to see God as our Father. He said that we are to address Him as "Father" when we pray (Matthew 6:9). He said that God loves us with a sacrificial love (John 3:16). No greater love can be imagined than the love He has for us. He desires our fellowship and will abide in us when we obey Him (John 14:23). If we go astray from Him, He will receive us back in loving forgiveness when we return to Him by repenting (Luke 15:19–32).

God has done more for each of us than any human being is able to do for us. How should we respond to His great love? We should love Him back, expressing our love by obeying His Word and by worshiping Him as the one and only God. We must walk in reverence and respect before Him.

OUR JUDGE

While He is a loving, gracious Father, God will also judge us. He is the One to whom we must give an account at the end of time.

It is only reasonable to believe that each of us must give an account to the One who made us—and what reason dictates, the Bible declares to be true (Revelation 20:12). How will God judge us? His judgment will be personal, with each person giving an account to Him (Romans 14:12). His judgment will be specific, with each one held responsible for what he or she has said (Matthew 12:36, 37) and done (2 Corinthians 5:10). His judgment will be universal, with all nations gathered before Him (Matthew 25:32).

God will judge us through Jesus Christ. With righteousness as His standard (Acts 17:30, 31), His judgment will be final and eternal (Matthew 25:46). No appeals will be made after His verdict is given.

The story is told of a young man who was knocked unconscious when two vehicles crashed. An eyewitness of the accident pulled the boy to safety just before the vehicles exploded into flames. The boy could have been burned to death.

After being rescued, the young man opened his eyes and looked up into the face of the man who had saved his life. He would never forget that face. The boy recovered from the accident, and years passed. When he was older, he got into serious trouble. He broke the law and was arrested for his crime. When he was brought before the judge for trial, he was amazed; for he recognized this judge as the very man who had saved him years before. Without hesitating, he blurted out, "Your Honor, do you remember me? You pulled me from a crashed vehicle years ago and saved my life." The judge thoughtfully said, "Yes, I remember. I wanted the best for the person I saved. I was happy that I was able to rescue you so that you could continue your life. However, you must see this fact: Years ago, when I pulled you from the vehicle, I was your 'savior'; but today I am your 'judge.'"

God is pictured in the Bible as both our Savior and our Judge. He sent His Son to deliver us from sin. He has given the highest sacrifice to save us. What will happen if we do not listen, if we reject His salvation? Then, He will have to condemn us, for He is our eternal Judge.

We have one major duty in life. Seeing who God is, we must bow before Him in obedience to His will. We must worship Him as the true and living God. Such a response involves opening His Word and studying it carefully. He wants to be our loving Savior, not just our eternal Judge.

CONCLUSION

In light of these facts about God, we cannot be without an opinion about Him. A decision about Him must be made. The only reasonable response is to acknowledge Him as the true and living God and serve Him in faith and obedience.

A school teacher once told her class, "Two chemists, Karl Scheele of Sweden and Joseph Priestley of England, discovered oxygen around 1775." Immediately a little girl raised her hand and asked, "What did we breathe before they discovered oxygen?" Of course, the teacher had to explain that oxygen has always been in our atmosphere, but we just did not know about it or have a name for it until these chemists discovered it.

Our world is made of two types of realities: the realities that we can see with the eye and touch with our physical hands, and the truths that we cannot see or touch. The realities in the first group are quite evident to us, for we are continually working with and holding real objects. Realities of the second type are not as clear to us. We are less aware of them. We know they are there, but they are sometimes in the background of our thoughts. In our minds, we may know that one-fifth of our air is made of oxygen and that we cannot live without breathing it, but we do not think about it—we just breathe it. We are more aware of a pencil—a seen reality which we can pick up and write with—than we are of air, one of the unseen realities.

The point is this: The fact that we cannot see some realities does not mean that they are not real. They are just as real as the objects we see, even though we cannot see them or touch them.

The greatest reality that we cannot see is God. We cannot touch Him with our physical hands, put Him in a test tube and analyze Him, or see Him with our physical eyes; yet He is the supreme reality. He is the basis of every reality, whether the reality is seen or unseen.

A missionary was telling some people about the true God. He described God's mighty power, His love, and His wisdom. An elderly man listened to him with eager interest. After a few minutes, the aged gentleman stood up and exclaimed, "I knew that this God existed, but I just did not know His name until now!"

God is our Creator, Provider, Redeemer, and Judge. Anyone who denies that God exists, or fails to obey Him and serve Him, has made the greatest mistake that can be made. That person has rejected his or her Maker, denying the great truth behind the existence of man and the existence of the universe. Do not make this mistake! Worship God as the true and living God; bow before Him in humble obedience.

God loves you and invites you to come into His family. He wants you to walk with Him in daily fellowship in this life. He wants you to live with Him in eternity, in that eternal city called heaven.

STUDY QUESTIONS
(answers on page 260)

1. The word "God" belongs rightfully to one Being only. Why?
2. List the Old Testament passages that suggest the idea of the Godhead.
3. How do the baptism of Jesus, the work of man's redemption, prayer, and Great Commission baptism all support the idea of God's being one yet three (the Godhead)?
4. What is the only way available for man to come to God?
5. What Scriptures teach that God cannot be approached through angels, saints, or other people, living or dead?
6. How can the Lord Jesus be both the "Son of Man" and the "Son of God"?
7. While there is much we do not know about the members of the Godhead, there is much we can know. What are some of the facts taught in the Bible?
8. What truths flow from the truth that God created all things?
9. What evidence do we have that God continues to work in His world?
10. How will God judge us?

WORD HELPS

apostles—the twelve men chosen by Jesus to be His special messengers (Matthew 10:2–4). After the death of Judas, Matthias was named an apostle (Acts 1:23, 26). Later, Paul was added to their number (Acts 9:15, 16; 1 Timothy 2:7). Jesus taught that the inspired teaching and preaching of His apostles was to be obeyed (Matthew 16:19).

baptism—from a Greek word meaning "to immerse in water." God authorized baptism for the forgiveness of sins. (See Matthew 28:19, 20; Romans 6:1–4; Acts 2:38; 8:36.)

Christian—one who has obeyed the gospel of Christ.

confession—a statement of one's belief in Jesus Christ as the Son of God and one's acceptance of Him as Lord and Savior. (See Acts 8:37; Romans 10:10; 1 Timothy 6:12.)

disciple—learner or follower. In Acts 11:26 the disciples of Jesus were first called Christians.

Gospel Accounts—the first four books of the New Testament (Matthew, Mark, Luke, and John), which tell of Jesus' life, death, and resurrection.

Great Commission—Jesus' command to His disciples to go and preach the gospel to every person (Matthew 28:18–20; Mark 16:15, 16).

mediator—one who "goes between" to solve a problem. Jesus, the Son of God, is the mediator between God and man. He solves the problem of sin.

providence—God's care of and providing for man. (While the word "providence" is not used this way in the New Testament, this is a biblical teaching, as in Romans 8:28.)

redeemer—one who "buys back." By His death, Jesus bought back, or paid a ransom for, people's lost souls.

redemption—being "bought back" after living away from God. Christians are often referred to as "the redeemed."

repentance—the act of changing one's way of thinking and therefore one's way of living.

saint—New Testament Christian.

salvation—deliverance from sin; salvation can be provided only through Jesus.

savior—one who saves another from danger or death. Jesus, our Savior, saves us from sin and eternal death.

4

Is Jesus The Son of God?

At the heart of Christianity lies the truth that Jesus the Christ is the Son of God. Christ is the center of our religion. He is the foundation of our faith (1 Corinthians 3:11), the subject of our preaching (Acts 8:35; 1 Corinthians 1:23), the object of our confession (Matthew 10:32), and the basis of our hope (1 Timothy 1:1). Therefore, a strong faith in Him is essential (John 8:24). We have plenty of good reasons for believing in the deity of Christ. God has not asked us to believe anything which He did not give us abundant evidence for believing (John 20:31). The evidence is strong, and it has caused thousands through the centuries to believe. This lesson presents some reasons for believing that Jesus is God's Son. Examine them carefully. If you already have strong faith, silently pray as did the disciples, "Lord, increase my faith." If you are burdened by doubts, pray as did the father of the demon-possessed child in Mark 9:24a, "I do believe; help my unbelief."

BECAUSE HE FULFILLS
OLD TESTAMENT PROPHECY

Consider some of the prophecies made hundreds of years prior to the birth of Jesus. His birth was prophesied. His genealogy involved Abraham, Judah, and David (Genesis 12:3 / Matthew 1:2; Genesis 49:10 / Matthew 1:2, 6). Abraham had many descendants, yet even the family was specified in prophecy (Jeremiah 23:5; Isaiah 11:1 / Matthew 1:6). His virgin birth was predicted in Isaiah 7:14 and fulfilled in Matthew 1:18–25. Bethlehem was chosen as the place of His birth (Micah 5:2). It was also prophesied that His birth would be accompanied by the killing of many children (Jeremiah 31:15 / Matthew 2:16–18).

The prophets foretold His flight into Egypt (Hosea 11:1 / Matthew 2:13–15), His life in Galilee (Isaiah 9:1, 2 / Matthew 4:12–16), and His victorious entry into Jerusalem (Zechariah 9:9 / Matthew 21:1–11). His work was also predicted. The prophets said that a forerunner would go before Him (Malachi 3:1; Isaiah 40:3 / Matthew 3:1–3). They spoke of His ministry of healing (Isaiah 53:4 / Matthew 8:16, 17), His teaching by parables (Isaiah 6:9, 10 / Matthew 13:10–17), His mission among the Gentiles (Isaiah 42:1–4 / Matthew 12:15–21), and His rejection by the rulers (Psalm 118:22 / John 1:11).

Jesus' death was pictured in prophecy in great detail. The Old Testament portrayed His betrayal by a friend (Psalm 41:9 / Matthew 26:47–50) for thirty pieces of silver (Zechariah 11:12 / Matthew 26:14–16). Ancient Scriptures foretold how He would behave before His enemies (Isaiah 53:7 / Matthew 27:12, 14), how He would die (Psalm 22:16 / Matthew 27:35a), and how His clothing would be divided by the casting of lots (Psalm 22:18 / Matthew 27:35b, c). Also predicted were His dying words (Psalm 22:1 / Matthew 27:46), His bones not being broken (Psalm 34:20 / John 19:33), His side being pierced (Zechariah 12:10 / John 19:37), His burial (Isaiah 53:9 / Matthew 27:57–60), His resurrection (Psalm 16:10 / Luke 24:1–9; Acts 2:25–32), and His ascension (Psalm 68:18 / Luke 24:50–53).

It was comparatively simple for the prophets to say that a Savior would come. However, when they added over three hundred specific details, they built up a framework of certainty which cannot be denied.

Think of what the fulfillment of these prophecies means. Human foresight and wisdom cannot peer even twenty-four hours into the future to predict future events with absolute certainty. Political pollsters, by the use of agents scattered throughout the country, can predict an election's outcome—sometimes! These prophecies about Jesus would be like someone predicting who will be the president four hundred years from now, his place of birth, his lineage, his schooling, the length of his tenure, and the place and manner of his death.

True prophecy can be tested, for it reveals future events. It contains details that cannot be fulfilled accidentally. A prophecy is seen as accurate only after its historical fulfillment. No evidence, either written or oral, can set aside the strength of this argument from the fulfillment of prophecy. It proves on the one hand that Jesus was divine and on the other hand that the men who penned the prophecies were inspired.

BECAUSE HIS CLAIMS OF DEITY
ARE IN HARMONY WITH HIS WORKS

Jesus made bold, fantastic claims for Himself.

He said that He existed before Abraham (John 8:58), that He was with God before the world was (John 17:5, 24), that He came down from heaven (John 6:38, 62), that He had all authority in heaven and on earth (Matthew 28:18). Many who deny His deity speak of Him simply as a "good" man. However, if He was not what He claimed to be, He was a liar and a fraud—definitely not a "good" man!

His works showed that His claims were true. Jesus performed many miracles. Biblical historians testified to His miraculous works (Matthew 11:4, 5; John 20:30, 31). Even secular historians testified that He worked miracles.

His works were one with His words. He said, "I am the Light of the world" (John 8:12a); then He made the blind to see light (John 9:6, 7). He said, "I am the bread of life" (John 6:35a), and He fed five thousand men with a few loaves and two fish. He said, "I am the resurrection and the life" (John 11:25a); then He raised Lazarus from the dead (John 11:43, 44).

BECAUSE HE LIVED A SINLESS LIFE

Those who knew Jesus claimed that He lived a sinless life. These men were inspired by God!

> For we do not have a high priest who cannot sympathize with our weaknesses, but One who has been tempted in all things as we are, yet without sin (Hebrews 4:15).

> Who committed no sin, nor was any deceit found in His mouth (1 Peter 2:22).

Those who studied His life considered Him *good* (Luke 18:18). Even His enemies, who constantly sought to find fault with Him, knew of His goodness. He did a most unusual thing—He challenged them to examine Him and see if they could find anything wrong with Him (John 8:46a).

His goodness was acknowledged at His death. Consider the comments of Pilate's wife (Matthew 27:19), Pilate (Matthew 27:23), Herod (Luke 23:14), the thief on the cross (Luke 23:41), the centurion (Matthew 27:54), and even Judas (Matthew 27:4).

BECAUSE OF THE CONTINUING EFFECT HIS LIFE HAS ON THE WORLD

Many memorials honor His life: the Lord's Day (Revelation 1:10), the Lord's Supper (1 Corinthians 11:20–29; Matthew 26:26–28), baptism (Romans 6:3–5), and even the dating of our calendars (B.C. and A.D.). He is, without question, the world's greatest man—and without a single mark of greatness as man counts greatness. He had no great heritage, no formal education (John 7:15), no wealth, no political or military power, and no athletic prowess; yet no one would question the influence He has had on mankind for the last twenty centuries. If He were a mere man, could not the world produce a greater one today? The world has two thousand years of advancements to draw from. In the midst of our advanced learning, the world is hungry for real leadership. Everyone can look to Jesus Christ; He is the Way. He has been and is all things to all men. "His name will be called Wonderful Counselor, Mighty God, Eternal Father, Prince of Peace" (Isaiah 9:6b).

CONCLUSION

Surely, Jesus is the Son of God. Further examine

these reasons for believing that He is God's Son. Believe that He is, and give your life to God through Him.

STUDY QUESTIONS
(answers on page 261)
1. What truth lies at the heart of Christianity?
2. Jesus' birth, life, and death were prophesied in great detail. Give a few examples.
3. What do the fulfilled prophecies about Jesus prove?
4. Jesus made bold, fantastic claims for Himself. What are some of them?
5. How did Jesus' works harmonize with His words?
6. Give some examples of how Jesus' goodness was acknowledged.
7. How does Jesus' life continue to affect our world?

WORD HELPS
ascension—going up, being lifted up. The Ascension was the event when Christ, after being resurrected from death, was taken back into heaven to be with God.

deity—God; the nature of God; being God.

genealogy—a listing of ancestors. Jesus' genealogy (Matthew 1:1–16) showed that He was the fulfillment of prophecies about the Promised One of God.

Lord's Day—the first day of the week (Sunday) was set aside for worship by the New Testament church (Acts 20:7).

Lord's Supper—a memorial instituted by Jesus which consists of eating unleavened bread and drinking the fruit of the vine (grape juice). (See 1 Corinthians 11:20, 23–26.) The New Testament church observes this supper every first day of the week.

resurrection—the raising of a dead person back to life. The Resurrection (of Jesus) is the proof that Jesus has power over death and that those who follow Him will be able to live forever with Him in heaven after their life on earth.

5

Who Is
The Holy Spirit?

The question is not *"What* is the Holy Spirit?"
Rather, the question is *"Who* is the Holy Spirit?" This
is the question because the Holy Spirit is a being, an
individual with personality, the third member of the
Godhead. He is more than a force or a power; He is
a living heavenly person.

HE IS LIKE A PERSON
All information available in the Bible points to
the fact that the Holy Spirit is a divine person. He
has the same personal traits as do the Father and the
Son.

He Has the Attributes of a Person
The attributes of the Holy Spirit indicate that He
is a living person, an individual, instead of just a
force:

1. *He has judgment*: "For it seemed good to the
Holy Spirit" (Acts 15:28a).

2. *He has a mind*: "And He who searches the

hearts knows what the mind of the Spirit is" (Romans 8:27a).

3. *He wills*: "But one and the same Spirit works all these things, distributing to each one individually just as He wills" (1 Corinthians 12:11).

4. *He has knowledge*: "Even so the thoughts of God no one knows except the Spirit of God" (1 Corinthians 2:11b).

5. *He has emotions* (love, grief, joy): "Now I urge you, brethren, by our Lord Jesus Christ and by the love of the Spirit, to strive together with me in your prayers to God for me" (Romans 15:30); "Do not grieve the Holy Spirit of God, by whom you were sealed for the day of redemption" (Ephesians 4:30); "You also became imitators of us and of the Lord, having received the word in much tribulation with the joy of the Holy Spirit" (1 Thessalonians 1:6).

The fact that the Holy Spirit possesses these traits reveals that He is a person.

He Performs the Activities of a Person

The Holy Spirit acts as a person and not merely a force. He can do the following:

1. *He can teach and remind*: "But the Helper, the Holy Spirit, whom the Father will send in My name, He will teach you all things, and bring to your remembrance all that I said to you" (John 14:26).

2. *He bears witness*: "When the Helper comes, whom I will send to you from the Father, that is the Spirit of truth who proceeds from the Father, He will testify about Me" (John 15:26).

3. *He guides into truth*: "But when He, the Spirit of truth, comes, He will guide you into all the truth" (John 16:13a).

4. *He speaks*: "For He will not speak on His own initiative" (John 16:13b; see also Acts 8:29; 11:12; 1 Timothy 4:1).

5. *He hears*: "But whatever He hears, He will speak" (John 16:13c).

6. *He discloses*: "And He will disclose to you what is to come" (John 16:13d).

7. *He forbids*: "They passed through the Phrygian and Galatian region, having been forbidden by the Holy Spirit to speak the word in Asia" (Acts 16:6).

8. *He gives life*: "He who raised Christ Jesus from the dead will also give life to your mortal bodies through His Spirit who dwells in you" (Romans 8:11b).

9. *He reveals*: "For to us God revealed them through the Spirit" (1 Corinthians 2:10a; see also Ephesians 3:3–5).

10. *He searches*: "For the Spirit searches all things, even the depths of God" (1 Corinthians 2:10b).

11. *He promises*: "In order that in Christ Jesus the blessing of Abraham might come to the Gentiles, so that we would receive the promise of the Spirit through faith" (Galatians 3:14; see Acts 2:33).

12. *He fellowships*: "The grace of the Lord Jesus Christ, and the love of God, and the fellowship of the Holy Spirit, be with you all" (2 Corinthians 13:14; see also Philippians 2:1).

13. *He intercedes*: ". . . but the Spirit Himself intercedes for us with groanings too deep for words. . . . He intercedes for the saints according to the will of God" (Romans 8:26, 27).

14. *He indicates and predicts*: ". . . the Spirit of Christ within them was indicating as He predicted

the sufferings of Christ and the glories to follow"
(1 Peter 1:11).

15. *He invites*: "The Spirit and the bride say,
'Come'" (Revelation 22:17a).

16. *He leads*: "Jesus, full of the Holy Spirit, returned from the Jordan and was led around by the
Spirit in the wilderness" (Luke 4:1); "For all who are
being led by the Spirit of God, these are sons of God"
(Romans 8:14).

A person can engage in each of these activities,
while a mere force cannot. Therefore, the Holy
Spirit should be seen as a person.

He Can Be Mistreated

The words used to describe the slights and injuries
done to the Holy Spirit are usually terms associated
with the mistreatment of a person. They are not generally used to indicate wrongs committed against a
non-living power or force. The Holy Spirit can be
mistreated in these ways:

1. *He can be blasphemed*: ". . . but blasphemy
against the Spirit shall not be forgiven. . . . whoever
speaks against the Holy Spirit, it shall not be forgiven him, either in this age or in the age to come"
(Matthew 12:31, 32).

2. *He can be lied to*: "But Peter said, 'Ananias,
why has Satan filled your heart to lie to the Holy
Spirit...?'" (Acts 5:3a).

3. *He can be resisted*: "You men who are stiff-
necked and uncircumcised in heart and ears are always resisting the Holy Spirit" (Acts 7:51a).

4. *He can be grieved*: "Do not grieve the Holy
Spirit of God, by whom you were sealed for the day
of redemption" (Ephesians 4:30).

5. *He can be insulted or despised*: ". . . and has insulted the Spirit of grace?" (Hebrews 10:29).

6. *He can be quenched*: "Do not quench the Spirit" (1 Thessalonians 5:19).

The statements made concerning how the Holy Spirit can be mistreated indicate that He is a person. Ill treatment of powers or forces are usually not described in the above manner, except in a poetic or figurative context. The contexts of these verses do not indicate that the language is figurative.

He Has a Separate Existence

Another indication that the Holy Spirit is a person is that He is not only mentioned along with the Father and the Son as having their nature and character, but He also has His own distinct and separate existence.

He is mentioned as descending on Jesus when He was baptized (John 1:33). When the Son came out of the water of baptism, the Spirit descended on Him and the Father spoke from heaven (Matthew 3:16, 17; Luke 3:21, 22). The Father remained in heaven, the Son remained on earth, and the Spirit came to dwell with Jesus.

A person can speak evil against Jesus and be forgiven—but if he speaks against the Holy Spirit, he cannot be forgiven (Matthew 12:32). How can one speak against Jesus and not against the Holy Spirit if they are the same person? In giving this teaching, Jesus must have realized their separateness.

Luke 4:1 says that Jesus was full of the Holy Spirit, just as others were said to be full of the Holy Spirit (Acts 6:3, 5; 7:55; 11:24). Surely, all will agree that the people who were full of the Holy Spirit in these cases in Acts were not the same person as the Holy Spirit. Jesus and the Holy Spirit also must be recognized as distinctly separate beings.

John wrote that the Holy Spirit was not yet given (John 7:39), for Jesus was not glorified. This was stated while Jesus was already on earth with the apostles. The Holy Spirit must be someone other than Jesus if the Holy Spirit had not yet been given.

In John 14:26 Jesus stated that He would send the apostles "another Helper," which (according to John 14:16) was to be the Holy Spirit. How could Jesus send them "another" Helper if He was the Helper? Likewise, how could the Holy Spirit be "another" Helper if He and Jesus are the same?

Jesus said He would not send the Spirit until He had gone away (John 16:7). He also said that the Spirit would not speak on His own initiative, but would speak what He heard from Jesus (John 16:13). The information given in the New Testament about Jesus and the Holy Spirit indicates that they are two independent, separate heavenly persons.

HE IS DIVINE

The Holy Spirit is mentioned along with the Father and the Son, as their equal, having the same status. People are to be baptized in the name of the Father, the Son, and the Holy Spirit (Matthew 28:19). Paul mentioned the three together, as having the same status, in 2 Corinthians 13:14: "The grace of the Lord Jesus Christ, and the love of God, and the fellowship of the Holy Spirit, be with you all." The Spirit, God ("the Father"; 1 Corinthians 8:6), and the Lord ("Jesus"; 1 Corinthians 8:6) are the Ones who administer the spiritual gifts (1 Corinthians 12:4–6) which are said to be given according to the will of the Spirit (1 Corinthians 12:11).[1]

The evidence in the New Testament clearly and powerfully shows that the Father, the Son, and the Holy Spirit are distinct, individual heavenly beings of like nature. They are joined together as one in their relationship with each other and in their service to mankind.

Qualities possessed only by God are ascribed to the Holy Spirit. Note five attributes which He shares with the Father and the Son:

1. *He is eternal*: The following are Bible statements concerning the eternal nature of (1) the Holy Spirit—"How much more will the blood of Christ,

---

[1]Miraculous gifts have ceased to exist. We can be confident of this because of the clear statement of 1 Corinthians 13:8–13. In three chapters of 1 Corinthians we find Paul's discussion of miraculous gifts (12—14). In the middle of this discussion, he declared that love is more important than any miraculous gift (13:1–3). Then he described love (13:4–7). In the final section of the chapter (13:8–13), he showed that love, as a greater gift, would outlast the spiritual gifts. Paul was saying, "Prophecies will fail, tongues will cease, and the [miraculous] knowledge will be done away." These gifts caused Paul to say that "we know in part and we prophesy in part; but when the perfect comes, the partial will be done away" (vv. 9, 10). These miraculous gifts were to cease when "the perfect comes."

Since "perfect" means "complete," it stands in contrast with that which is "in part." The "partial" is miraculous knowledge and prophecy, which revealed the Word of God orally. It is most natural, then, to realize that the complete or "perfect" is the full revelation given to man in the written record of the New Testament. This complete revelation of God's will, "the faith which was once for all handed down to the saints" (Jude 3), came into general possession around the end of the first century. When the "complete" came, the "partial" was done away. Since the New Testament records the complete will of God (2 Timothy 3:16, 17; 2 Peter 1:3), miraculous gifts are no longer needed to provide further revelation. (Phil Sanders, "Does Anyone Have Miraculous Gifts Today?" *Truth for Today* [April 1995]: 49.)

who through the eternal Spirit offered Himself without blemish to God, cleanse your conscience from dead works to serve the living God?" (Hebrews 9:14); (2) the Father—"Your throne is established from of old; You are from everlasting" (Psalm 93:2); and (3) Jesus—"Jesus Christ is the same yesterday and today and forever" (Hebrews 13:8); "For in this way the entrance into the eternal kingdom of our Lord and Savior Jesus Christ will be abundantly supplied to you" (2 Peter 1:11).

2. *He is all-knowing*: This knowledge is spoken of in Bible passages concerning (1) the Holy Spirit— "For to us God revealed them through the Spirit; for the Spirit searches all things, even the depths of God" (1 Corinthians 2:10); (2) the Father—"And there is no creature hidden from His sight, but all things are open and laid bare to the eyes of Him with whom we have to do" (Hebrews 4:13); and (3) Jesus—"But Jesus, on His part, was not entrusting Himself to them, for He knew all men, and because He did not need anyone to testify concerning man, for He Himself knew what was in man" (John 2:24, 25).

3. *He is all-powerful*: Several Bible passages mention this power over everything in relation to (1) the Holy Spirit—"The Holy Spirit will come upon you, and the power of the Most High will overshadow you" (Luke 1:35b); "And Jesus returned to Galilee in the power of the Spirit" (Luke 4:14a); "But you will receive power when the Holy Spirit has come upon you" (Acts 1:8a); (2) God—"For nothing will be impossible with God" (Luke 1:37); and (3) Jesus—". . . 'All authority has been given to Me in heaven and on earth'" (Matthew 28:18).

4. *He is present everywhere*: The ability to be ev-

erywhere belongs to (1) the Holy Spirit—"Where can I go from Your Spirit?" (Psalm 139:7a); (2) the Father—"But will God indeed dwell on the earth? Behold, heaven and the highest heaven cannot contain You" (1 Kings 8:27a); "'Can a man hide himself in hiding places, so I do not see him?' declares the Lord. 'Do I not fill the heavens and the earth?'..." (Jeremiah 23:24); and (3) Jesus—"I am with you always, even to the end of the age" (Matthew 28:20b).

5. *He has creative power*: These Bible passages portray each member of the Godhead as Creator: (1) The Holy Spirit—"... the Spirit of God was moving over the surface of the waters" (Genesis 1:2); (2) the Father—"It is He who made the earth by His power, who established the world by His wisdom, and by His understanding He stretched out the heavens" (Jeremiah 51:15); and (3) the Son—"For by Him all things were created, both in the heavens and on earth, visible and invisible, whether thrones or dominions or rulers or authorities—all things have been created through Him and for Him" (Colossians 1:16).

CONCLUSION

The Holy Spirit is described in terms that can apply only to God. From these terms we can draw the conclusion that the Holy Spirit shares the divine nature with the Father and the Son and is one with the Father and the Son, but that He is a distinct personality. He is an important, central person of the Bible.

STUDY QUESTIONS
(answers on page 262)

1. Explain why the question should be "*Who* is the Holy Spirit?" rather than "*What* is the Holy Spirit?"
2. What five attributes indicate that the Holy Spirit is a living "person"?
3. How does the fact that the Holy Spirit can be mistreated indicate that He is a person?
4. What qualities does the Holy Spirit share with the Father and the Son?

WORD HELPS

attributes—features or characteristics. Romans 1:20 says, "For since the creation of the world His invisible attributes, His eternal power and divine nature, have been clearly seen, being understood through what has been made, so that they are without excuse."

miraculous gifts—special God-given abilities—such as tongue-speaking, healings, and prophecy—given to the early church before the writing of the New Testament was completed. These gifts are no longer needed or available. (See Ephesians 4:5; Matthew 28:18–20.)

THE WORK OF THE HOLY SPIRIT IN CHRISTIANS TODAY

1. He sets us free from the law of sin and death (Romans 8:2–8).
2. He will bring about our resurrection (Romans 8:11).
3. He helps in our prayers (Romans 8:26; Ephesians 6:18).
4. He intercedes in our behalf (Romans 8:26, 27).
5. He leads us (Romans 8:14).
6. He seals us as a pledge for the day of redemption (2 Corinthians 1:22; Ephesians 1:13, 14; 4:30).
7. He has fellowship with us (2 Corinthians 13:14).
8. He gives us access to the Father (Ephesians 2:18).
9. He strengthens the inner person (Ephesians 3:16).
10. He brings unity (Ephesians 4:3).
11. He sanctifies us (2 Thessalonians 2:13).

6

Did God Become Man?

The first four books of the New Testament (Matthew, Mark, Luke, and John) tell the most amazing story ever told. They reveal to us how God became man. They say that Jesus Christ, God's Son, entered this world as a man, died for our sins, and brought—for those who would receive it—salvation, or forgiveness of our sins, and eternal life.

The New Testament is not so much a history book as it is a study of salvation, the heart of which is how the divine Son of God became one of us in order to save us. Therefore, Matthew, Mark, Luke, and John are not just studies of the Lord's life. They are more like missionary messages. They give us "selective history," telling us the key events that relate to the bringing of salvation to man. John 21:25 says, "And there are also many other things which Jesus did, which if they were written in detail, I suppose that even the world itself would not contain the books that would be written."

What are some of these major events that we are

told about in the New Testament regarding Jesus' providing salvation for us? What is the truth concerning Jesus Christ?

JESUS WAS/IS GOD

The first truth that we must accept about Jesus is that He was and is God.

Was His birth His beginning? No. Our Lord's birth in Bethlehem was not the beginning of His existence. His birth was only His taking a physical body and becoming man.

"God" is somewhat like a family name. Your family name is what identifies you with the other members of your family. It is the link that joins individual family members into a single family unit. In a similar way, "God" is a family name. In the Scriptures we see God the Father, God the Son, and God the Spirit. The second member of this Godhead, Jesus, became man for us.

One passage that clearly declares that Jesus is God eternal is John 1:1–5.[1] John said that Jesus is God and has always been God.

In the beginning was the Word,[2] and the Word

---

[1] John begins his Gospel before history. He begins with God in eternity.

[2] "Philo of Alexandria has much to say about the *Logos*, which in his system was an intermediary principle between God and man, but he denied the possibility of the *Logos* becoming flesh. When John says that the *Logos* did become flesh he is clearly presenting a different kind of *Logos* from Philo. For all his great [learning], Philo could not present a *Logos* capable of dwelling among men, who could move men into action and give power to men to become sons of God. This was a new element in the contemporary Greek world" (Donald Guthrie, *A Shorter Life of Christ* [Grand Rapids, Mich.: Zondervan, 1970], 73).

was with God, and the Word was God. He was in the beginning with God. All things came into being through Him, and apart from Him nothing came into being that has come into being. In Him was life, and the life was the Light of men. The Light shines in the darkness, and the darkness did not comprehend it.

We need to think about four great truths that come out of this passage:

(1) We see that Jesus was not a creation. How could Jesus become a man without a previous existence? In regard to no other person can we see the difference between birth and beginning or say that his life did not begin when he was conceived, but we can say it concerning Jesus. He did not become God's Son at His birth or when He arose from the dead. He is God, supreme and without beginning. He has always been and will always be.

He spoke of the glory that He had with the Father before the world existed (John 17:5). He said, ". . . I came forth from the Father. I came forth from the Father and have come into the world . . ." (John 16:27, 28). He also said, "For You loved Me before the foundation of the world" (John 17:24b). Every other person has entered life through physical birth, but Jesus knew neither beginning of days nor end of life (Hebrews 7:3). He is fully eternal and fully God.

Unlike us, He chose to be born and to enter the experience of life. During His earthly life, He did not set aside His deity, but He laid aside only the voluntary use of His characteristics as God. At any time, He could have drawn upon any of His divine powers or exercised the divine choices that He had (Philippians 2:6).

(2) We see that God created the world through Jesus. He is the true Lord of the universe. First Corinthians 8:6 says it: "Yet for us there is but one God, the Father, from whom are all things and we exist for Him; and one Lord, Jesus Christ, by whom are all things, and we exist through Him." Colossians 1:16 says it also: "For by Him all things were created, both in the heavens and on earth, visible and invisible, whether thrones or dominions or rulers or authorities—all things have been created through Him and for Him."

(3) We see that Jesus gives life to the living, and He can revive the dead (see John 11:25). He is the author of life.

(4) We must conclude that He is the Lord of life and death. He made all things and takes care of all things, giving life and ruling over death.

Can we understand everything about our Lord's earthly life? Obviously, we cannot. How can man fully understand God? One does not have to understand a truth to believe it. I do not understand how God created the earth, but I believe that He did. I do not understand how Jesus arose from the dead, but I believe that He did. Likewise, I do not understand how God, Jesus Christ, could become man, but I believe that He did.

JESUS, GOD'S SON, BECAME MAN

The next truth about Jesus that we need to think about is that He became man fully. Let us allow this truth to enter into our minds: Jesus, God's Son, was clothed with flesh! Jesus was, is, and always will be the Son of God; but at His birth He became the Son of Man.

Paul described how Jesus gave up heaven to come to earth (Philippians 2:5–8). Notice how Jesus came down from heaven to become one of us.

First, He left heaven. He left the rich love of His Father's presence. He walked away from a place where no hatred existed—a place that was free from envy, jealousy, and suspicion. He left the beautiful harmony of heaven—a place without discord, conflicts, or arguments, a place without misunderstandings or confusion. He left the abundant resources of heaven. He chose to leave a place where there could be no lack of funds, where no one was poverty-stricken, and where no one was ever hungry or thirsty.

Second, He became man. His birth did not mark His origin, but only His appearance as a man on the stage of time. Jesus was the meeting place of eternity and time, the perfect blending of deity and humanity, the junction of heaven and earth. He consented not only to be born, but to be fully human so that He could die. As God, He became man. He was the Son of God, but He became the Son of Man.[3]

This is the great truth of Christianity. If you can believe this truth, then you can believe every other truth within Christianity. Yes, the staggering truth of Christianity is that Jesus of Nazareth was God made into man—that He took on humanity without loss of deity, so that He was as truly and fully God

---

[3]"Not God indwelling a man. Of such there have been many. Not a man Deified. Of such there have been none save in the myths of pagan systems of thought; but God and man, combining in one Personality the two natures, a perpetual enigma and mystery, baffling the possibility of explanation" (G. Campbell Morgan, *The Crises of the Christ* [Old Tappan, N.J.: Fleming H. Revell Co., 1936], 79).

as He was human. One who can believe this part of Christianity will have no trouble believing the rest of it.

John wrote that "the Word became flesh, and dwelt among us" (John 1:14a). In other words, God became man; the divine Son became a Jew; the Almighty appeared on earth as a helpless human baby, unable to do any more than lie in His bed, stare, wriggle, and make noises. He needed to be fed, to have His clothes changed, and to be taught to talk like any other child. This was not an illusion or a deception; the babyhood of the Son of God was a reality. The more you think about it, the more amazing it becomes. It is because of their misbelief—or at least inadequate belief— about the incarnation that people have difficulties with other truths in the gospel story. Once the incarnation is grasped as a reality, the other difficulties pass away.[4]

Third, He became a servant of men. He did not live as a king in a palace, but as a servant in poverty. He came not to be served, but to serve. He came to show us what God is like and what true manhood is like (Mark 10:45).

Fourth, He submitted to death. Without submitting to death, He could not have been fully human. He identified completely with man. He submitted to the worst kind of death, even death on a cross. I want to die in my sleep. How about you? In this sense, we are not like Jesus. He submitted to a torturous, painful death—willingly, voluntarily, and without coercion.

---

[4] J. I. Packer, *Knowing God* (Downers Grove, Ill.: InterVarsity Press, 1973), 46.

HE LIVED AMONG US
AS THE GOD-MAN

Another truth concerning Jesus that we need to think about is that He lived among us as the God-Man.

We would expect the earthly life of the God-Man to be very unusual. The God-Man would be different from all other people. We should not be surprised to find that Matthew, Mark, Luke, and John present His earthly life as being superior to any other human who has ever lived.

If God became man, a special birth would be necessary. He had such a birth: The Gospels of Matthew and Luke tell of His being born of a virgin named Mary. He had an earthly mother, but no earthly father, for He was conceived by the Holy Spirit (Matthew 1:20).

We would also expect His life to be perfect, marked by divine teachings that could not have come from mortal man. No wonder we read that no one had ever spoken the way He spoke (John 7:46). The people who met Him and heard Him teach were amazed at His life and His messages.

If He was God in the flesh, why should we be surprised that He manifested power beyond human ability by working miracles and wonders? We are told that He worked obvious miracles which even His enemies regarded as being above and beyond the laws of nature. He raised the dead (John 11:43, 44), healed the blind (Mark 8), and multiplied bread and fish (John 6). The fact that He had such power should not seem strange to us. After all, He created all things and sustains all things.

Would we not expect His death to be one of a kind

in the history of the world? For God to die on a cross would have to be the most astonishing event of all time. The Gospels show that this was the case. At Jesus' death, the sky turned black, the earth quaked, the veil of the temple was torn, and tombs opened. Many godly people rose from their graves and appeared alive in Jerusalem after Jesus' resurrection (Matthew 27:50–53). When the God-Man died, a special event took place—an event which had been planned from the foundation of the world.

Would we not also expect the God-Man to have power over death? Indeed, He arose from the dead. This truth is one of the clearest truths told us about His life. All four Gospel writers described His resurrection in great detail. He gave Himself for our sins, but He arose from the dead so that we might know that He was truly divine.

CONCLUSION

Here, then, are three truths about Jesus that we must never forget: He was and is God, He became man, and He lived among us as the God-Man.

These three truths about Jesus can encourage us in two ways. First, they remind us that our Savior is not a helpless man, but God—the almighty, eternal, creating, and sustaining God.

Second, we see in the preexistence of Jesus the truth of His love for all mankind. His coming to earth and His dying for our sins provided our only hope for salvation. Jesus was willing to come and give us that hope. He gave Himself for our salvation, but would the people of the earth receive that message and be saved? Would Jesus be giving up everything for only a small response? Jesus was willing to take that risk for us. He became our Savior. No one else could save us. If He had not come, we would have no hope.

Can you imagine becoming an ant? You would have to lay aside many of your assets as a human being, such as your human body, your strength, and your talents. You would have to live under the limitations of an ant. Jesus did not become an ant, but His descending from His lofty state in heaven to being a man in Palestine was a far greater act of humility than that of a man becoming an ant. Yes, Jesus became Man so that we might become children of God.[5]

Let us rejoice in what Jesus did for us and resolve right now that we will obey Him and follow Him.

STUDY QUESTIONS
(answers on page 262)

1. What do the first four books of the New Testament reveal?
2. Was Jesus' birth His beginning?
3. List four great truths that come out of John 1:1–5.
4. What were the four descending steps Jesus took as He became one of us?
5. What truth is so central to Christianity that if you believe it you can believe every other truth?
6. How was Jesus' birth a special birth?
7. What three truths about Jesus must never be forgotten?
8. How was Jesus' becoming a man a far greater step down than a man's becoming an ant?

---

[5]"The Eternal Being who knows everything and who created the whole universe became not only a man but (before that) a baby, and before that a [fetus] inside a Woman's body. If you want to get the hang of it, think how you would like to become a slug or a crab" (C. S. Lewis, *Mere Christianity*, rev. ed. [New York: Macmillan Publishing Co., 1952], 155).

WORD HELPS

incarnation—the appearance of the Son of God in a human body; Jesus' coming to earth to live as a human man.

indwell—to live within, as the Holy Spirit dwells, or lives, within Christians (1 Corinthians 6:19, 20).

preexistence—having been alive before the world was created. This nature belongs only to the Godhead (God the Father, God the Son, and God the Spirit). Jesus existed before becoming man. He is an eternal being who always has been, is, and always will be. (See John 1:1–11.)

7

How Shall We
View Jesus?

University students are often assigned research projects. They do not always enjoy doing research. Perhaps there are two reasons for their attitude toward research. First, research is often hard work. Someone has said, "I do not enjoy reading, but I enjoy having read." Many students do not enjoy doing research, but they enjoy having done research. Second, much research is open-ended. Research sorts through what we know and what we do not know—and sometimes what we do not know is much more evident than what we do know. A student could well conclude some research project by saying, "Before I started this research project, I did not know anything about this subject. Now that I have completed this project, I know that no one knows anything about this subject!" Such a conclusion can be very discouraging.

All of us want to know the truth about certain key subjects. We are not satisfied with open-ended, inconclusive discussions about them. This is especially true of the subject of Jesus Christ. We do not want to hear someone's opinion about Him or a discussion of vague theories about Him; we desire to know the *truth* about Him. Our deepest questions about Him are specific and to the point: Who is Jesus? Is He really God's Son? What does He say about life and salvation?

The Bible is the only truly accurate book in this world. God gave it to us so that we can be sure about His teachings (2 Peter 1:3). God does not want us to go through life being inconclusive about Jesus. He wants us to know who Jesus is and what He came to do. He wants us to have the absolute truth about Him so that we can build lives of confidence and assurance upon that truth.

The Bible gives us the only authentic picture we have of Jesus. It tells us who He is in two ways: First, we see who He is by noticing what He is *called* in the Scriptures. Second, we see who He is by observing the *characteristics* which are attributed to Him.

Let us consider carefully what He is called in the Bible. If a man is introduced to us as a preacher and teacher by someone we trust, we know who that man is and basically what kind of person he is. The terms "preacher" and "teacher" give us a distinct picture of him.

The Scriptures do not leave us in doubt about Jesus' identity. He is specifically referred to in terms that cannot be misunderstood. As we study carefully what Jesus is called in the Scriptures, we learn who He is.

HE IS OUR SAVIOR
First, the Scriptures call Jesus "Savior." The word

"savior" refers to someone who rescues others from extreme danger.

The birth narrative recorded in Matthew mentions that an angel appeared in a dream to Joseph, who was to be the earthly father of Jesus. The angel said,

> . . . "Joseph, son of David, do not be afraid to take Mary as your wife; for the Child who has been conceived in her is of the Holy Spirit. She will bear a Son; and you shall call His name Jesus, for He will save His people from their sins" (Matthew 1:20, 21).

As you can see, Jesus was not to be just any kind of savior; He was to be a unique Savior. If a man saves a child from a burning building, we call him a savior. If a man delivers food to starving people, he is called the savior of the people. Jesus, according to the Scriptures, saves us from our sins. He is our spiritual Savior.

Every responsible person must confront as his number-one difficulty the guilt of sin. Someone has said that if we were to tie tape recorders around our necks and record every word that came from our mouths in a forty-eight hour period, we could easily see that we are sinners. If we were to sit down and listen to each word, think of the motivation behind each statement, and ponder the tone in which we spoke, we would surely conclude that we did not always say what we should have said. Likewise, we could use a video camera to capture forty-eight hours of our lives on film. When we reviewed our every action and deed, we could easily see that we are sinners. We would be smitten with the truth that we often do what we should not and often do not do what we should. We do not even need the Bible to tell us that we are sinners. When we look closely at our words and deeds, we know that we are sinners. The Bible, however, declares this truth about us in unequivocal language. Paul reminded Christians, "... 'There is none righteous, not even one'" (Romans 3:10).

What can be done about our sin? We cannot forgive ourselves. Our sin is not only against others, but it is also against God. Who can help us with our most urgent need? Psychology cannot forgive us. Positive thinking cannot. Pretending we are not sinners will not save us. What can be done? God's answer to our desperate condition is Jesus. Joseph was told that Jesus' name (which means "Jehovah is salvation") was determined in heaven because of the function He would fulfill on earth. (See Matthew 1:21). At His birth, the angel announced to the shepherds on a hill in Palestine, "For today in the city of David there has been born for you a Savior, who is Christ the Lord" (Luke 2:11). The principal purpose in Jesus' coming to this earth was to save us from our sins (1 Corinthians 15:3).

A touching story is told of a soldier in Napoleon's army. He had been a brave, loyal soldier. In between battles, he was in his tent reviewing his obligations and family concerns. He had listed on a sheet of paper the debts he had and the money he needed for the care of his family. A wave of discouragement swept over him as he realized that he did not have the money needed for his debts and family expenses. Deeply depressed, he wrote across the bottom of the page on which he had listed his financial obligations, "Who is there who could pay all these debts?" Feeling defeated, he laid his head on his arm and went to sleep. Unknown to the soldier, Napoleon was making his way through the camp of his soldiers, checking their conditions and evaluating their strength. As he passed the young soldier's tent, he called for inspection, but no answer came from inside the tent. He walked over and looked inside. He saw the sleeping soldier and the pathetic question written across the bottom of the page. Napoleon reached down, picked up his pen, and wrote underneath the question, "I will," and then signed it, "Napoleon."

When we look at our debt of sin and our critical need for salvation, we also cry, "Who is there who can pay all these debts?" Someone far greater than Napoleon has answered, "I will." Jesus, the Savior of the world, through His death upon the cross, has brought to us the offer of complete salvation.

The Bible is clear that Jesus is our one and only Savior. Peter said, "And there is salvation in no one else; for there is no other name under heaven that has been given among men by which we must be saved" (Acts 4:12). If you want to be saved from your sins that you might stand before God in an acceptable state, you must come to Christ (John 14:6; Mark 16:16). According to the Bible, He is our Savior.

AS THE CHRIST

Second, Jesus is called "the Christ," which means "anointed one." "Christ" in the Greek language is the same as "Messiah" in the Hebrew language. The New Testament identifies Jesus as the Promised One, the Chosen One of God.

The prophets had foretold that a special servant of God was coming:

For a child will be born to us, a son will be given to us; and the government will rest on His shoulders; and His name will be called Wonderful Counselor, Mighty God, Eternal Father, Prince of Peace. There will be no end to the increase of His government or of peace, on the throne of David and over his kingdom, to establish it and to uphold it with justice and righteousness from then on and forevermore. The zeal of the Lord of hosts will accomplish this (Isaiah 9:6, 7).

Micah had prophesied, "But as for you, Bethlehem Ephrathah, too little to be among the clans of Judah, from you One will go forth for Me to be ruler in Israel. His goings forth are from long ago, from the days of eternity" (Micah 5:2). The New Testament proves that Jesus is that One whom the prophets had predicted was coming.

Toward the end of His earthly ministry, Jesus was walking with His disciples toward Caesarea Philippi. As they walked along, Jesus asked His disciples, "Who do people say that the Son of Man is?" His disciples said, "Some say John the Baptist; and others, Elijah; but still others, Jeremiah, or one of the prophets" (Matthew 16:13, 14). After their response, Jesus then asked, "But who do you say that I am?" Peter answered Him. He said, "You are the Christ, the Son of the living God" (Matthew 16:15, 16). Jesus complimented Peter for his answer. He said, "Blessed are you, Simon Barjona, because flesh and blood did not reveal this to you, but My Father who is in heaven" (Matthew 16:17). In other words, Jesus was saying, "Peter, you did not arrive at this conclusion upon the basis of what man has said. You have received this answer from God in heaven."

This was a divine revelation, not a human deduction.

Think about how the New Testament refers to Jesus. As it calls Him "the Christ," it is identifying Him as the One, the special Chosen One of God. He is not the forerunner of the One; He is the One. He did not predict the coming of the Chosen One; He was the fulfillment of all the prophecies concerning the Chosen One. He was not just associated with the Chosen One, but He was that very One.

AS THE SON OF GOD

Third, Jesus is identified in the New Testament as the Son of God, the second member of the Godhead.

John the Baptist was chosen by God to prepare the way for the earthly ministry of Jesus. He did this work by preaching repentance and administering the baptism of repentance for the forgiveness of sins (Mark 1:4). John pointed the people who responded to his preaching toward the Messiah who was to come. In their repentance and baptism, the people were pledging to receive the Messiah when He came (Acts 19:4). As John fulfilled the mission which God had given to him, all Judea and all the districts around the Jordan went out to him and were baptized by him (Matthew 3:5). One day when John was baptizing people in the river, Jesus appeared on the banks of the Jordan. John, at this point in time, did not know for sure that Jesus was the Messiah (John 1:29–31)— but he did know that Jesus was a better man than he. That being the case, he responded to Jesus' request by saying, in effect, "I need to be baptized by You, but you want me to baptize You?" Jesus said, "Permit it at this time; for in this way it is fitting for us to fulfill all righteousness" (Matthew 3:15). John was doing God's work. He was a God-sent man. Jesus desired to be completely submissive to God's will while on this earth. For this reason, He was obediently baptized by John—not because He had sins that needed forgiveness, because He needed repentance, or because He needed to receive the Messiah when He came. He was the Messiah, but He submitted to John's baptism to fulfill the will of God, to fulfill all righteousness.

As John brought Jesus out of the water following the immersion, the Spirit of God descended upon Him in the form of a dove. When John saw this miraculous occurrence, he knew that Jesus was the Messiah (John 1:32–34). Then, a voice from heaven—the very voice of God—spoke, saying, "This is My beloved Son, in whom I am well-pleased" (Matthew 3:17). Incorporated in these verses of the New Testament is God's testimony that Jesus is His Son.

The apostle John said that we have been given three testimonies that Jesus is the Son of God. He said, "For there are three that testify: the Spirit and the water and the blood; and the three are in agreement" (1 John 5:7, 8). The Holy Spirit testified that Jesus is God's Son by descending upon Him in the form of a dove after Jesus' baptism. The Holy Spirit also gave this testimony at other times in the Gospels. The "water" must refer to the baptism of Jesus, when the Father declared from heaven that Jesus is His Son. The "blood" to which John referred must represent Jesus' death. The miraculous events which surrounded the Crucifixion testified to Jesus' deity. John said, "If we receive the testimony of men, the testimony of God is greater; for the testimony of God is this, that He has testified concerning His Son" (1 John 5:9). If three honest men were united in testifying concerning a certain truth, we would accept their testimony—and so would any court of law in the land. How much more should we accept the testimony of God! He has given testimony concerning His Son—a testimony of the Spirit (in the form of a dove at His baptism), of the water (when the Father's voice was heard at His baptism), and of the blood (when the miracles occurred at His death).

Who is Jesus? The Scriptures leave no doubt about the answer. The New Testament clearly teaches that Jesus is God's Son. Jesus cannot be ignored. To ignore Him is to ignore God.

AS LORD

Fourth, the New Testament calls Jesus "Lord." He is our Supreme Ruler, with all authority from God.

After Jesus' resurrection from the dead, He appeared to His disciples, demonstrating that He had really arisen from the dead. Jesus told His disciples,

> All authority has been given to Me in heaven and on earth. Go therefore and make disciples of all the nations, baptizing them in the name of the Father and the Son and the Holy Spirit, teaching them to observe all that I commanded you; and lo, I am with you always, even to the end of the age (Matthew 28:18–20).

Ten days after Jesus' ascension to the Father, the Holy Spirit was poured out upon the apostles. On that day, the Day of Pentecost, Peter spoke to a large crowd which had gathered. He gave evidence which proves that Jesus is the Christ. As he reached the climax of his sermon, he asked his hearers to conclude that God had made Jesus both "Lord and Christ" (Acts 2:36). Paul, after describing the way Jesus humbled Himself to become man and obeyed even to the point of death, wrote,

> For this reason also, God highly exalted Him, and bestowed on Him the name which is above every name, so that at the name of Jesus every knee will bow, of those who are in heaven and on earth and under the earth, and that every tongue will confess that Jesus Christ is Lord, to the glory of God the Father (Philippians 2:9–11).

Paul also wrote of Jesus, "And He [God] put all things in subjection under His feet, and gave Him as head over all things to the church, which is His body, the fullness of Him who fills all in all" (Ephesians 1:22, 23).

What does the Lordship of Jesus mean to us, according to the New Testament? In practical terms, it means that we are to submit to Him. Jesus said, "Why do you call Me, 'Lord, Lord,' and do not do what I say?" (Luke 6:46). He further said, "Not everyone who says to Me, 'Lord, Lord,' will enter the kingdom of heaven, but he who does the will of My Father who is in heaven will enter" (Matthew 7:21). Are you willing to submit to the teachings of Christ? Second, it means that we must give Christ priority in our lives. We must give Him our loyalty and our love. He is the only Lord honored by heaven, and He must be the only Lord enthroned in our hearts.

Someone has said, "In each heart, there is a cross and a throne. If I place myself on the throne, I must put Christ on the cross. If I put Christ on the throne, I must put myself on the cross." No one can have two Lords. If you say "yes" to the Lordship of Christ, you must say "no" to your own will and wishes. No one can have two masters; you will love one and hate the other (Matthew 6:24).

The New Testament says that Jesus is Lord. God has placed everything under His feet. He is King of kings and Lord of lords.

CONCLUSION

Who, then, is Jesus? The only completely accurate book in the world says that He is our Savior, the Christ, the Chosen One of God, the Son of God, and our Lord. This is the truth about Him. You do not have to wait for other research to be done before you can know for sure who He is. The Bible tells us the absolute truth about Him.

Jesus' coming into the world divided the calendar into B.C. and A.D. Matthew 25:31–46 says that He will divide the human race, the saved from the lost. Pilate thought that Jesus was standing before him for judgment, but in reality Pilate was standing before Jesus. On the final day of the world, the saved will stand on the right of Jesus' throne, while the lost will stand on the left of His throne. Your response to Jesus will make the difference as to whether you stand on the right or on the left. You can only stand on the right through His salvation. He said, "I am the way, and the truth, and the life; no one comes to the Father but through Me" (John 14:6). You will either come to God through Jesus, or you will experience eternal doom. He came that we might have life (John 10:10); without Him we abide in eternal death.

Jesus invites us to come to Him for salvation. Other religious leaders invite you to come to their systems or their teachings. Only Jesus, the Son of God, can invite you to come to *Him*. He said, "Come to Me, all who are weary and heavy-laden, and I will give you rest" (Matthew 11:28).

STUDY QUESTIONS
(answers on page 263)

1. To what does the word "savior" refer?
2. How is Jesus a unique Savior?
3. What does "the Christ" mean?
4. How do we know that Jesus is the Son of God?
5. To what do the Spirit, the water, and the blood refer in 1 John 5:7, 8?
6. What did Peter ask his hearers to conclude about Jesus in Acts 2?
7. What does the Lordship of Jesus mean to us in practical terms?

WORD HELPS

city of David—Bethlehem.

crucifixion—death by hanging on a cross; a Roman form of execution. Jesus, though guiltless, was crucified for our sins.

King of kings and Lord of lords—a reference to Jesus and His greatness. He is above all others.

Pentecost (Day of Pentecost)—the Jewish feast of weeks, also known as Feast of Harvest; the day the church began (Acts 2).

submission—obedience to God and His Word.

8

Why Did Jesus Come to Earth?

What would you say if a news reporter came up to you as you were walking along the side of the road in your city and asked you, "What do you believe is the greatest single event that has occurred since the beginning of the world?" How would you answer him? What incident is bigger than all other events in human history? My answer would have to do with the Lord Jesus' coming into the world to be our Savior.

The most far-reaching occurrence in the history of the world has to be the life—the incarnation, the becoming flesh—of Jesus, God's Son. Paul wrote that even though Jesus existed in the form of God, He did not regard this equality with God as something to be clung to at all costs. He "emptied Himself, taking the form of a bond-servant," and was "made in the likeness of men" (Philippians 2:7). According to John, "the Word became flesh, and dwelt among us, and we beheld His glory, glory as of the only begotten from the Father, full of grace and truth" (John 1:14).

We could say that *Christ was just as much human as if He were not divine at all, and He was just as much divine as if He were not human at all*. So completely did Jesus identify with the human race in His becoming man that He was born as all humans are born (Luke 2:6), grew as all humans grow (Luke 2:40), was subject to all the sufferings to which all humans are heirs (Hebrews 5:8, 9), and lived in a body that could be affected by disease, decay, and death—a body that humans could even kill on a cross (Philippians 2:8, 9). He was thoroughly a man and was called the Son of Man, yet He was entirely divine and must be acknowledged as the Son of God (Hebrews 2:14, 17, 18). He was the perfect joining of humanity and deity into one personality. He became man without sacrificing His deity; He remained divine even though He became like us.

The nature of Jesus' coming to earth raises serious questions: Why did Jesus come to earth the way He did? What was the purpose of His entering the human race, living among us, and dying upon a cross? Why did the divine Son of God lower Himself to the extent of becoming wholly man? The answers to these questions can be summarized in a single sentence: *"He came to call out—by His ministry, death, and resurrection—a people for His name whom He would call His church"* (Mark 10:45; Luke 19:10).

In other words, the result of His visit to this earth is the church. Jesus did not write a book, found a college, or establish a physical family. The only reality that His earthly ministry produced was the church. The only body Jesus ever said He would build was a spiritual body which He termed "My church" (Matthew 16:18). The only foundation Jesus laid during

His ministry was the foundation for the church. Hence, the church can be said to be *the singular creation* of the earthly advent of Christ.

AFFIRMED BY THE GOSPELS

This truth is forcefully affirmed by the Gospel Accounts. Each of the Gospels points to and leads up to the church, the kingdom of heaven, that Jesus would establish on the first Pentecost following His death and resurrection.

As one studies the life of Christ in the Gospels, he is struck by three topics that spring up about His ministry: (1) the mission He set out to accomplish, (2) the way His work prepared for something more, and (3) the way His work was to continue.

First, the Gospels indicate that Jesus did not set out to evangelize the world during His personal ministry. After choosing His apostles, He did not give them a special worldwide commission for their preaching; rather, He calmed their zeal by saying, "Do not go in the way of the Gentiles, and do not enter any city of the Samaritans; but rather go to the lost sheep of the house of Israel" (Matthew 10:5b, 6). To our amazement, during His ministry Jesus limited Himself to Palestine. He never went to the countries outside of the Roman world. His mission was accomplished by His preaching and teaching in a very small area of the world. Had Jesus set out to evangelize the world during His personal ministry, He would have gone about His work in an entirely different way, employing different wide-scale strategies and methods.

Second, the Gospels indicate that Jesus' life, works, and death were preparing for something to come. Jesus preached, "Repent, for the kingdom of heaven is at hand" (Matthew 4:17b). He taught His disciples to pray, "Your kingdom come" (Matthew 6:10a). Jesus was careful to prevent the crowds from being overwhelmed by His miracles and, in reaction, rallying behind the idea of making Him their earthly king. He did not allow the multitudes of people to dictate His schedule. When He worked a miracle, Jesus sometimes asked the recipient of the miracle to "tell no one" (Matthew 8:4).[1] He chose twelve apostles and personally trained them, but it is apparent that He was training them for the work that they would do after His departure (John 14:19).

Third, the Gospels picture Jesus' ministry as having a sense of incompleteness about it. Jesus did what the Father had sent Him to do; but at the end of His life on earth, He prepared His apostles to expect other events and revelations following His ascension. Jesus said to the apostles, "But the Helper, the Holy Spirit, whom the Father will send in My name, He will teach you all things, and bring to your remembrance all that I said to you" (John 14:26). He also told them, "But when He, the Spirit of truth, comes, He will guide you into all the truth; for He will not speak on His own initiative, but whatever He hears, He will

---

[1]See also Matthew 9:30; 12:16; 17:9; Mark 1:44; 3:12; 5:43; 7:36; 8:30; 9:9; Luke 4:41; 8:56; 9:21. J. W. McGarvey wrote concerning the strange command "tell no one": "It is accounted for by the necessity of guarding against such undue excitement among the people as might have provoked an interference from the military authorities, and such as would have rendered the people incapable of calm thought in reference to the teachings of Jesus. (See also Mark 1:45.) Sometimes, as occasion required, he reversed his course, and commanded men to go tell what he had done for them" (J. W. McGarvey, *The New Testament Commentary: Matthew and Mark* [N.p., 1875; reprint, Delight, Ark.: Gospel Light Publishing Co., n.d.], 75).

speak; and He will disclose to you what is to come" (John 16:13). After the Resurrection and just before the Ascension, Jesus commanded His apostles to wait in Jerusalem until they received power from on high. Following the reception of power, they were to preach repentance and remission of sins to all nations, starting in Jerusalem (Luke 24:46–49).

These characteristics of our Lord's ministry before and after His death clearly show that His ministry on earth was that of bringing together the essential elements for the building of His kingdom, the church. In Matthew 16:18 Jesus announced to His disciples the burden of His earthly work: "I also say to you that you are Peter, and upon this rock I will build My church; and the gates of Hades will not overpower it." *Jesus did not come to preach the gospel; He came so that there might be a gospel to preach.*

The famous sculptor Gutzon Borglum, who chiselled out the remarkable Mount Rushmore in South Dakota, also sculptured a head of Abraham Lincoln for the Capitol in Washington, D.C. He carved it from a block of marble in his studio. It is said that when the woman who came in each morning to clean his studio saw the lifelike sculpture for the first time, she stood in astonishment for a moment and then asked, "How did he know that Lincoln was locked in that block of stone?" The answer to her question is that Borglum could see what others could not. He had the eye of an artist, the perception of a sculptor. He could see the face in the block before his skilled hands and visionary mind brought it out.

With the aid of the Gospels, we can see what Jesus saw during His earthly ministry. Locked up in His ministry was the vision of and preparation for the coming kingdom. He preached about it, prepared for it, and purchased it with His blood.

CONFIRMED BY ACTS

The New Testament book of Acts confirms that Jesus' ministry, death, and resurrection had behind them the controlling purpose of creating the church, of bringing in the kingdom. The Gospels candidly announce the truth, and Acts confirms the announcement by living-color illustrations.

Ten days after our Lord's ascension, the Holy Spirit was miraculously given to the apostles on Pentecost (Acts 2:1–4); the gospel of the death, burial, and resurrection of Jesus was preached for the first time; people were invited to respond to this gospel by faith, repentance, and baptism for the forgiveness of their sins (Acts 2:38; Luke 24:46, 47); and three thousand accepted that invitation by receiving the Word which was preached and by being baptized (Acts 2:41). Therefore, following Jesus' ministry as night follows day, the church of our Lord was born.

The remaining story of Acts is the story of the church's moving, as a flame of sacred love, from Jerusalem to Judea and Samaria and beyond, to other parts of the Roman Empire. Whenever inspired preaching occurred in Acts, hearers responded, coming into the church by obeying the Word preached. Whenever a mission trip took place in Acts, churches were left in its wake in new areas of the world. The three missionary trips of Paul in Acts planted churches throughout the world, from Jerusalem to Illyricum (Romans 15:19). No one can read Acts without observing anew the overwhelming conclusion that the church is the outcome of Christ's earthly advent.

A preacher once said, "We must employ the same methods that Jesus employed in our task of evangelizing the world. Let us gather around us twelve men and train them for future work. Jesus shows us how to evangelize the world in the method He used." Certainly, Jesus was perfect in everything He did. A thorough study of His ministry, however, reveals that His mission during His ministry was not that of evangelizing the world. It was that of laying the foundation for the church; it was that of putting the pieces of the blueprint together for the evangelization of the world. In His approach to His work, He employed ways and means suitable for the fulfillment of His unique mission, a mission which was different from the worldwide evangelistic mission He has given to His followers.

We do not see in Acts that the apostles and other inspired men used the same approaches that our Lord used. They did not try to imitate His way of teaching, gathering around them twelve other men to train. Instead, through their preaching and teaching, the apostles and other inspired men brought people into the church. These new Christians were then nurtured, trained, encouraged, and taught for service and evangelism *by the church as a part of the church.* Acts shows us the life of the church as the outcome of the earthly ministry of Jesus. The life of Christ makes up 48 percent of the New Testament; the other 52 percent is composed of what the life, death, and resurrection of Christ produced—the church.

REAFFIRMED BY THE EPISTLES

The New Testament epistles stress the application of the truth that the church is the natural fruition of

Christ's earthly life and death. The Gospels assert this truth, Acts amplifies it, and the Epistles apply it. The Epistles show us how to respond to the life of Christ by being His spiritual body.

The Epistles were written to people who had chosen to come to Christ through faith and obedience. They lived at a time when the effect of Christ's life, death, and resurrection was in fresh focus. The import of the messages of the inspired men was that Christ is honored as Lord and His human life among us is properly received by our becoming and being His church.

In every epistle the followers of Christ are urged to live and serve as Christ's spiritual body. The Epistles, when brought together, actually provide a "guidance manual" on how to be and live as the church of Christ in all kinds of circumstances and in different places. They teach us how to apply Christ's earthly ministry to our lives.

We submit to Jesus as Lord by entering His body through obedient faith. Paul likened the final act of this faith response to putting on, or being clothed with, Christ (Galatians 3:27). According to the Epistles, no one has submitted to Jesus until he has entered His body through a baptism for salvation that has been preceded by faith, repentance, and confession of Jesus as God's Son.

We honor the life, death, and resurrection of Jesus by living and worshiping together as God's family in His spiritual body, the church. Paul said,

> There is neither Jew nor Greek, there is neither slave nor free man, there is neither male nor female; for you are all one in Christ Jesus (Galatians 3:28).

> For just as we have many members in one body and
> all the members do not have the same function, so
> we, who are many, are one body in Christ, and in-
> dividually members one of another (Romans 12:4,
> 5).

> . . . there may be no division in the body, but that
> the members may have the same care for one an-
> other. And if one member suffers, all the members
> suffer with it; if one member is honored, all the
> members rejoice with it.
> Now you are Christ's body, and individually
> members of it (1 Corinthians 12:25–27).

> On the first day of the week, when we were
> gathered together to break bread, Paul began talking
> to them . . . (Acts 20:7).

When we fail to live and worship as God's family,
as Christ's church, we take away from what Christ
came to accomplish and damage what He died to
establish.

Jesus has called us to be His body, His church. The
Epistles never describe His people as being any church
or body other than the church of Christ. According
to the Epistles, Jesus created only one way for us to
follow Him, only one way to serve Him, only one
way to receive His blood and the salvation He provides. That way is to live faithfully in this world as
His spiritual body.

A little girl found a Bible in the corner of the house.
She held it up and asked her mother, "What book is
this, Mother?" Her mother said, "That is God's book,
the Bible." The little girl, with piercing insight, advised, "Why don't we send it back to Him, since we
never use it?"

The truth is that we can read it and *still not really use it*. We can quote the Bible in every conversation, read it every day, and yet *fail to apply it*. Real application of the Bible requires us to follow it in the practical way of being Christ's church. When we become what the Bible teaches us to become, only then are we making the right and proper use of it.

CONCLUSION

The entire New Testament, therefore, joins together to teach that the church, the spiritual body of Christ, is the creation of Christ's mission in becoming man. The Gospels affirm it by promising it, Acts confirms it by picturing it, and the Epistles reaffirm it by practically applying it to life.

Since the New Testament says that the only way for us to respond to the One who lived, died, and arose from the dead for our salvation is by entering His church and living as faithful members of it, the question that follows is this: "Are you in His body?" What a mistake it would be to come to the end of life and discover that you had completely missed the true purpose of life! Perhaps there is something even sadder—missing the purpose for which the Son of God came to this earth. As surely as the New Testament gives us God's divine message of salvation, as surely as Christ came to this earth in human form, anyone who does not enter His body will learn at the end of life's journey that he has missed the reason why Christ came to this earth. *This conclusion is the basic teaching of the entire New Testament!*

When Christ came to the end of His brief life here, He could say, "Father, I have done what You asked Me to do. I have fulfilled Your mission for Me." Better it is to live a few years on this earth within the circle of God's will, fulfilling His purposes, than to live a long life in a palace, reigning over the kingdom of selfish pursuits. At the end of life, scores of people are only able to say, "God, I have lived out the years that You gave me on this earth, and I have done only what I have wished to do. I have pursued the mission I chose for myself."

May it be that when we come to the close of life, we can say, "Lord, I have discovered from the Scriptures what You wanted me to be and do, and I have dedicated myself to that mission. I have sincerely tried to glorify You on the earth, and I have sought to live the plan that You gave to me. I have lived as the church of Christ."

STUDY QUESTIONS
(answers on page 264)

1. What is the greatest event that has ever occurred in the history of the world? Give a reason for your answer.
2. Was Jesus completely man or just partially man?
3. Was Jesus completely divine or just partially divine?
4. Why did Jesus come to earth? What one purpose did He come to fulfill?
5. Show how Jesus' ministry was preparation for something to come.
6. What is the function of the Epistles in the New Testament?
7. Can we respond properly to the life of Jesus without being His church?
8. Can we fulfill Jesus' mission for us in this world without living as His church?

WORD HELPS

added to the church—made part of God's obedient people. All who obey the terms laid down by Jesus in the Great Commission are added by God to the body of the saved (Acts 2:41, 47).

church of Christ—not a building, but the group of those who have obeyed the gospel and have been added to the church (as in Acts 2:36–47).

epistle—a letter. Many New Testament books (Romans through Revelation) were written as letters to Christians.

evangelism—the practice of sharing the gospel. Timothy, for example, was told to do the work of an evangelist in 2 Timothy 4:5.

Gentile—a non-Jewish person.

Jewish—of the race of Jews, or Israelites; being a descendant of Abraham through Jacob.

kingdom of God—the reign and rule of Jesus in the hearts and lives of men.

righteousness—the nature of being without guilt or sin. Since this is impossible for man himself, being "righteous" means receiving the forgiveness of God and becoming justified, cleansed of all sin, before God. The Christian exhibits this right relationship with God through living daily according to His Word.

9

*The Cross
And the Church*

Those familiar with the New Testament concept that Christ paid for our sins would agree that "the Christ without the cross would be as powerless to save sinners as the cross without the Christ." However, the good news of the gospel is that Christ, the Anointed One of God, gave His physical life on the cross for our sins (1 Corinthians 15:3).

The heart of the story of the Bible is the sacrifice made by the Son of God on the cross for man. The pages of the Old Testament, with its prophecies, and the pages of the New Testament, with its historic reality, drip with the blood of Christ. Henry C. Thiessen calculated that the story of the last three days of Jesus' life take up about one-fifth of the Gospels. If the three and one-half years of Jesus' public ministry had been treated in as great detail as His death, the Gospels would comprise a book 8,400 pages long.[1]

---

[1]Henry C. Thiessen, *Lectures in Systematic Theology* (Grand Rapids, Mich.: Wm. B. Eerdmans Publishing Co., 1949), 313.

R. A. Torrey estimated that 1 out of every 53 verses in the New Testament makes a specific reference to Christ's death.[2] Christianity is the only religion in the world that has as its center the offering of a divine sacrifice for sin and the resurrection of that sacrifice from the dead.

In a world of sin and sinners, of guilt and godlessness, of separation and suffering, the cross is *God's power for salvation*; it is the divine solution for the world's ultimate problem. He is the propitiation for our sins—that is, the One who pays for the wrong we have done and makes things right for us. It is written: "For the word of the cross is foolishness to those who are perishing, but to us who are being saved it is the power of God" (1 Corinthians 1:18); "And He Himself is the propitiation for our sins; and not for ours only, but also for those of the whole world" (1 John 2:2).

Among our spiritual discord, separation from God, and disunity with God, the cross is *God's instrument of peace and reconciliation*. Paul wrote, "And through Him to reconcile all things to Himself, having made peace through the blood of His cross . . ." (Colossians 1:20). Ephesians 2:14–16 says, "For He Himself is our peace, who made both groups into one and broke down the barrier of the dividing wall . . . and might reconcile them both in one body to God through the cross, by it having put to death the enmity."

Where spiritual hunger and poverty abound, *God provides full redemption*. The riches of righteousness

---

[2]R. A. Torrey, *What the Bible Teaches* (New York: Fleming H. Revell Co., 1898), 144.

are freely given at the foot of the cross. Paul said, "But we preach Christ crucified . . ." (1 Corinthians 1:23). He further said that the crucified Christ "became to us wisdom from God, and righteousness and sanctification, and redemption" (1 Corinthians 1:30).

Without question, the Holy Spirit shines a light on the cross of Christ as the centerpiece, the central message of the Bible.

Because the cross is mixed together with all other truths regarding redemption, one would expect the church to flow from the cross as a stream from a spring, as healing rays from the sun. A careful reading of the New Testament confirms that this is the case. There cannot be a Christianity without Christ and His church; logical thinking tells us that there cannot be a living body without a head. The striking feature of the New Testament is its message that the cross and the church are intimately joined together, combined into one plan, as God's gift of grace to lost humanity. Out of all the nations of the earth, God calls forth by the cross a new family—one body in Christ—to be His chosen people.

Let us pursue this thought further: How is the church connected to the cross? What relationship do the cross and the church have to each other? What does the cross do for the church?

CREATED BY IT

First, the cross creates the church. The church emerges through the redemption of sinners. If there were no cross, there could be no church.

When a person responds in obedient faith to Christ as his Savior and the Son of God, he is washed from his sins in Christ's blood (Acts 22:16). Through that washing, he is added to the community of the redeemed, a society of the saved that the New Testament calls "the church." For this reason, Paul could speak of Jesus' purchasing the church with His blood. "Be on guard for yourselves and for all the flock, among which the Holy Spirit has made you overseers, to shepherd the church of God which He purchased with His own blood" (Acts 20:28). Clearly, Jesus died on the cross for the church. Paul said, "Christ also loved the church and gave Himself up for her" (Ephesians 5:25b). The purpose of the death of Jesus was to provide a "called-out" people who would live in the world in fellowship with Christ and give themselves to His spiritual work. Paul told Titus that Jesus "gave Himself for us to redeem us from every lawless deed, and to purify for Himself a people for His own possession, zealous for good deeds" (Titus 2:14).

After a gospel meeting in southern Arkansas, a lady came to the preacher with an unusual, touching story. She told of something which had occurred when she was four years old, living in Dallas, Texas. At that time her family lived near a busy highway, and their yard provided little space for children to play outside. One evening, she and several of the neighborhood children were playing ball in the yard. The ball bounced away from her and rolled into the highway. Without thinking, she ran after it. As she reached down to pick it up, she froze in horror at the sight of a big truck coming down the highway. Her brother, who was nine years old at the time, had seen her run into the highway. He had also seen the truck. Like a flash, he ran out behind her, hoping to bring her back to safety. He ran in front of the truck and shoved her out of the way, saving her from certain death at the risk of his own young life. That brief moment was enough time for the boy to save his little sister, but not enough time for him to save himself. The truck smashed into him, killing him instantly.

The lady said she does not remember much about the details of the tragedy, but she does recall how her brother's lifeless body was lifted from the street and placed on the porch of their house until an ambulance could come and carry it away. She said with deep meaning and an appreciation too special for words, "My brother died for me." She is a faithful Christian, but the opportunity for her life and service in the church today was created by the sacrifice of her brother many years ago.

In a similar but far deeper way, the church receives life from the sacrifice of Jesus. His death is not only an opportunity for us to enter life, but the source of continued life; His death is our atoning sacrifice, our means of forgiveness for past sins. Jesus came into this world, walked among us as the God-Man, and by His death purchased for Himself "a people for God's own possession" (1 Peter 2:9). The church is not made of brick and mortar; it is a people bought by blood.

We respond to Christ's sacrifice in three ways: First, we embrace the cross by *appreciating* what Christ did. Gratefully, the redeemed rejoice over Christ's gift of grace! Christ was rich with heavenly glory; yet for our sakes He became poor by leaving heaven and becoming man, that we through His poverty might be made spiritually rich (2 Corinthians 8:9).

Second, we must react by *accepting* the benefits of His death. True appreciation leads to proper acceptance. By faith and obedience to Christ, we take the benefits of His death into our lives (Romans 6:1–4). He died for all (Hebrews 2:9), but only those who obey Him receive the benefits of His death (Hebrews 5:8, 9). Third, we should respond to His sacrifice with *abounding service* (1 Corinthians 15:58). We belong to Christ from head to foot—body, soul, and spirit (1 Corinthians 6:19, 20). Accordingly, our business in this world now is that of rendering the service He designs, directs, and delights in.

CLEANSED BY IT

Second, the cross continually cleanses the church. Its purifying power daily flows to and through God's people. As surely as the blood of our physical bodies circulates through us, sustaining and purging us, the precious blood of Jesus courses through His people with life-sustaining strength.

We not only need *to be saved*, but we also need *to be kept saved*. The church is increased each time a sinner, through his obedience to the gospel of Christ, is washed in His blood and, by divine grace, placed in Christ. The Christian is cleansed continually with the blood as he daily walks in the light. John wrote, "But if we walk in the Light as He Himself is in the Light, we have fellowship with one another, and the blood of Jesus His Son cleanses us from all sin" (1 John 1:7). John put "cleanses" in the present active tense in the Greek language, indicating a constant, continual, present-fact washing.

A Christian is not a perfect person, though he seeks to sin less and to grow in Christ each day. *He is not faultless, but he should be blameless.* The presence of sin in the sinner's life necessitates salvation through the blood of Christ, and sin in the saint's life necessitates that he or she be kept saved by the blood of Christ. We will never outgrow our need for forgiveness in this world.

It is interesting to watch a child learn to ride his bicycle. He faces two primary problems in acquiring this new skill: getting the bicycle up and keeping it up. Salvation may be viewed as involving two steps even as learning to ride a bicycle does: The sinner must first *get right* with God, and then he must *stay right* with God. Getting right is necessary, but it is only the beginning. The same problem which made him a sinner in the first place—the stain of sin in his life—is the problem which could condemn him after he becomes a Christian if he is not continually cleansed (Acts 8:22). If he needed saving from his sins before becoming a Christian, will he not need saving from any sins he commits after he becomes a Christian?

The Christian remains saved as long as he "walks in the light." According to John the apostle, walking in the light involves two spiritual character traits. It begins with *trusting Jesus for salvation*: "And He Himself is the propitiation for our sins; and not for ours only, but also for those of the whole world" (1 John 2:2). Obviously, we cannot earn salvation (Ephesians 2:8, 9). Jesus said that if we will respond to Him in faith and obedience, He will save us. We must trust Him to do what He has said He will do. We walk by faith, not by sight (2 Corinthians 5:7).

Walking in the light also requires *honestly doing His will*. John wrote, "For this is the love of God, that we keep His commandments . . ." (1 John 5:3); "The one who says, 'I have come to know Him,' and does not keep His commandments, is a liar, and the truth is not in him; but whoever keeps His word, in him the love of God has truly been perfected" (1 John 2:4, 5a). Walking in the light means admitting our sinfulness (1 John 1:8, 10), acknowledging our sins to God (1 John 1:9), and correcting our sins in harmony with our ability (1 John 2:29). It means walking as He walked (1 John 2:6) and sincerely following the inspired revelation from God, the Scriptures (2 Timothy 3:16).

COMPELLED BY IT

Third, the cross compels and activates the church. It implants the spiritual motivation into the heart of the church to be the persons Christ wants us to be and to do the work He wants us to do.

Christians need continual cleansing as well as personal power. Christianity provides many noble motivations; the grace of God is the highest and most permanent. The cross controls the lives of Christians. Jesus said, "And I, if I am lifted up from the earth, will draw all men to Myself" (John 12:32). Paul wrote, "For the love of Christ controls us, having concluded this, that one died for all, therefore all died; and He died for all, so that they who live might no longer live for themselves, but for Him who died and rose again on their behalf" (2 Corinthians 5:14, 15).

The cross *fills* Christians with greater love for God and for each other. John wrote, "We love, because He first loved us" (1 John 4:19). As Christians meditate daily upon His love for His people, they are drawn to love Him more deeply. John further said, "We know love by this, that He laid down His life for us; and we ought to lay down our lives for the brethren" (1 John 3:16). Any review of Jesus' life produces new and stirring pictures of the depth and steadfastness of His love. Thinking about these images gives Christians a similar love for Jesus and for each other: "But we all, with unveiled face, beholding as in a mirror the glory of the Lord, are being transformed into the same image from glory to glory, just as from the Lord, the Spirit" (2 Corinthians 3:18).

The cross *fixes* in Christians a hatred and disdain for sin. Two powerful testimonials to the evil and devastation of sin are the cross of Calvary and the bottomless pit of eternal destruction. No one who understands the reason for the cross and the necessity of hell can argue that sinning has any merits. The child of God cannot forget that his redemption was bought by the painful death of God's Son on a cross outside of Jerusalem. God Almighty could provide atonement (payment) for sin only by the sacrifice of His Son. This costly event should compel every sensible person to abhor sin and shun it.

The cross *forces* Christians to give themselves completely to Christ's mission. It provides both the reason and the strength for Christians to serve God and help other people. Paul wrote, "I am under obligation both to Greeks and to barbarians, both to the wise and to the foolish" (Romans 1:14). He also said, "But by the grace of God I am what I am, and His grace toward me did not prove vain; but I labored even more than all of them, yet not I, but the grace of God with me" (1 Corinthians 15:10). No Christian is more fully motivated to do Christ's work than the one who understands and appreciates what God did for him at the cross.

The church of Christ carefully keeps the commandments of her Lord. She does His wishes and fulfils His plans, but she does not find the obedient life burdensome because of the constraining force of love and the inward inspiration of His grace. "For this is the love of God, that we keep His commandments; and His commandments are not burdensome" (1 John 5:3).

Keep in mind what Christ has done for you, remembering daily the sacrifice He made for you. This careful thinking about His gift of salvation can change you day by day into His image, driving you to do labors of love in His kingdom of grace.

CONCLUSION

By God's design, the church and the cross are tied together. The church is created, cleansed, and compelled by the cross.

As Jesus suffered upon the cross, two of the mocking questions hurled at Him from the lawless crowd below were "Why doesn't He save Himself?" and "Why doesn't God save Him?" (See Matthew 27:39–43.) Little did the crowd realize that they were striking at the very foundation of God's mission. If Jesus had saved Himself, or if God had delivered Him from His death on the cross, it would have been impossible for the church to live; for the church is composed of people who are forgiven of their past sins by the cross and are daily cleansed and purified by the cross. Furthermore, without the cross, the church would be without inner drive in her ongoing life, since the church is compelled by the cross to be God's people and to do God's work in God's way.

If you are outside of the church of Christ, hasten

to enter it, because in entering the church, you receive all the benefits of the cross. The church is nothing more than the body of people who have been redeemed by Christ's blood and are living as God's children.

Each person is surrounded in this world by God's generous gifts. He provides air for us to breathe, water for us to drink, land for us to live on, family relationships for us to enjoy, and countless other benefits. One would be at a loss to name all the kindnesses of God. Without a doubt, the supreme expression of His grace is the salvation He gives us through Christ. It involves the greatest cost to God, and it pays the highest dividends for those sinners who receive it.

Many have seen the gracious hand of God in the physical blessings He has given to them, but they have not received His salvation. Is this true of you? Through belief in Christ (Romans 10:10), repentance of sin (Acts 11:18), confession of Christ as God's Son (Romans 10:10), and baptism into Christ (Galatians 3:27), you may enter Christ's body (1 Corinthians 12:13), the place of grace, and receive His eternal life. Paul said, "Or do you not know that all of us who have been baptized into Christ Jesus have been baptized into His death?" (Romans 6:3); "In Him we have redemption through His blood, the forgiveness of our trespasses [sins], according to the riches of His grace which He lavished [gave generously] on us" (Ephesians 1:7, 8a).

Jesus, through His cross, invites you to the forgiveness and life that creates His body, the church. Will you accept His invitation?

STUDY QUESTIONS
(answers on page 264)

1. What is the heart of the story of the Bible?
2. What does Christianity have at its center that no other religion has?
3. Explain why there cannot be a churchless Christianity.
4. What three things does the cross do for the church?
5. Many have seen the gracious hand of God in physical blessings but have not received His gift of salvation. How can you enter the body of Christ?
6. Jesus, through His cross, invites you to have what two blessings?
7. The body of Jesus is created when those who come to Him receive forgiveness and life. What is this body called?

WORD HELPS

head of the church—Jesus Christ (Ephesians 1:22, 23).

reconciliation—bringing back together; mending a broken relationship. We are reconciled to God through Jesus Christ.

sanctification—being "set apart" for God's special purpose.

10
What Is "The Church"?

A man from another country and culture wanted to travel to the USA for a long visit. Having worked hard to learn English, he believed that he was ready for his trip. He made his long-awaited trip to America, and soon after his arrival, his knowledge of English was put to the test. He went into a small grocery store to buy several items. At the counter, he was told how much he owed. He reached into his pocket, took out his money, counted the right amount, and handed it to the clerk. He put his groceries in a sack and started to leave. As he was going out the door, the clerk kindly said, "Come back!" The visitor stopped, turned around, and came back to the counter. The clerk said, "May I help you?" Somewhat confused, the man said, "You told me to come back!"

The man had taken an expression which meant "Thank you for your business; let us help you again soon" and had interpreted it literally. His mistake in understanding the clerk's intended meaning resulted in a failure in communication.

All of us have had his kind of experience. We knew the words which were spoken to us, but we did not understand how those words were being used by the one speaking. We understood the words but completely missed the meaning that was being conveyed.

Any way you look at it, communication is difficult. Much is required of the speaker and of the hearer for communication to take place.

Consider the process of communication with regard to studying the Bible. For profitable communication between the Bible and us to take place, we must not only listen to the words that were used, but we must also seek the meaning which the inspired writer had in mind as he chose these words. This means that we must make an effort to understand the context in which a word or sentence appears. Honesty with God demands that we carefully search for the meaning which God intended for His message.

The word "church" is familiar to most of us. God talks to us at length about this word in the Scriptures. For communication to occur between God and us regarding this word, we must be willing to go into the biblical world and see the word meanings, illustrations, and thought forms which were used by Jesus, the apostles, and the other inspired men who wrote the Bible through God's Spirit.

What is "the church"? As the New Testament uses this word 114 times[1] in various contexts, in seventeen of its twenty-seven books,[2] what is being communi-

---

[1]Ethelbert W. Bullinger, *A Critical Lexicon and Concordance to the English and Greek New Testament* (Grand Rapids, Mich.: Zondervan, 1975), 153.

[2]Ibid. The word "church" is not used in Mark, Luke, John, 2 Timothy, Titus, 1 and 2 Peter, 1 and 2 John, or Jude.

cated to us? When Jesus established the church, what did He build?

A SPIRITUAL BODY

We must first recognize that the church is a spiritual body, the very spiritual body of Christ.

A picture which usually comes to our minds with the word "church" is a physical building in which worship takes place. The word is never used in the New Testament, though, to convey this meaning.

In the Scriptures, the word "church" denotes the body of those who have yielded to the gospel of Christ and have been redeemed by the blood of Christ in their assembled, local, and universal senses.

First, the body of the redeemed as they assemble or gather to worship God is called "the church." As Paul rebuked the church at Corinth for their lack of unity when they gathered, he used the word "church" for the assembly of Christians. He said, ". . . when you come together as a church, I hear that divisions exist among you . . ." (1 Corinthians 11:18).

Next, "church" is used for the body of the redeemed in a definite locale. The body of redeemed ones at Corinth is called "the church of God which is at Corinth" (1 Corinthians 1:2a).

Still further, "church" is used for the whole number of the redeemed ones throughout the world. Paul referred to the church in a universal sense when he said, "For the husband is the head of the wife, as Christ also is the head of the church, He Himself being the Savior of the body" (Ephesians 5:23).

Let us apply these New Testament uses of the word "church" to a specific event in Acts. The many residents and visitors in Jerusalem on the Day of

Pentecost (Acts 2:1–4) heard the external signs of the outpouring of the Holy Spirit and gathered around the apostles to see what was taking place. As Peter preached to the multitude, he convinced them that Jesus was both Lord and Christ (Acts 2:36). In pain of soul, many cried out, "What shall we do?" (Acts 2:37b). Since faith prompted their crying out, Peter did not need to tell them to believe, but he did need to tell them to do what they had not done—to repent and be baptized for the forgiveness of their sins (Acts 2:38). Three thousand gladly received the way of salvation, repented, and were baptized for the forgiveness of sins (Acts 2:38, 41).

Notice how Luke described what took place on that day. He first described the converts in terms of what they *had become* (Acts 2:41). Those who were obedient to the Word of the Lord were made into the Lord's church. They became part of a fellowship, a group. Second, Luke described them in terms of their *new behavior*. They had a new life in their behavior *toward God* (Acts 2:42). This body of redeemed people worshiped God and received divine instruction from the apostles. They had a new life in their behavior *toward each other* (Acts 2:44, 45). They looked out after each other, by bearing, sharing, and caring—bearing each other's burdens, sharing with those in need, and caring for each other. This body of believers is referred to later in Acts as the "church" (Acts 5:11).

When these redeemed ones in Jerusalem came together to worship God, they were "the church" (in the assembled sense). All the redeemed in Jerusalem could be referred to as "the church in Jerusalem" (in the local sense). As that church grew and spread, all the redeemed people in the world at that time could be referred to by saying, "When Jesus comes again, He is going to receive His church (in the universal sense) and take it to heaven."

A LIVING ORGANISM

Second, we need to see the church as an organism—a living thing.

Some think of the group of saved people called "the church" as an organization, as some kind of human club. They view it as something one joins or pledges himself to, and nothing more.

As a body of redeemed people, the church is a living organism, not a human organization. The church which Christ established is living and vibrant with God's life and blessings; it is not a man-made group which is energized completely by man's wisdom, designs, and activities.

Paul described the church at Corinth as the temple, the sanctuary, or the dwelling place of God. "Do you not know that you are a temple of God and that the Spirit of God dwells in you?" he said in 1 Corinthians 3:16.[3] Later, in 1 Corinthians 6:19, 20, Paul pictured the individual Christian as the temple of God as he condemned fornication as a sin against a person's body. First Corinthians 3:16 is a reference to the church, not the individual Christian.[4] Paul was affirming that God dwells among His people. He

------

[3]The Greek language has two words for "temple": *naos* and *hieron*. The word for "temple" used by Paul in this passage is *naos*, not *hieron*. *Naos* refers to the temple proper, the sanctuary—not the temple complex, as does the word *hieron*. Paul was affirming that the body of Christ is the dwelling place of God.

[4]In this sentence, the "you" is second person plural in the Greek text, indicating that a group of people are under consideration, not just an individual as in 1 Corinthians 6:19, 20.

dwells in His people individually (1 Corinthians 6:19, 20) and collectively (1 Corinthians 3:16). In Old Testament times, God's dwelling place was the tabernacle in the wilderness and later the temple in Jerusalem; but in the Christian Age, according to Paul, God dwells in His church, His people.

The church can be likened to a living building. As Paul was illustrating what the Ephesian Christians had become, he said that they comprised a building which was made up of Christians and was in a constant stage of growth. Paul said, "In whom the whole building, being fitted together, is growing into a holy temple in the Lord, in whom you also are being built together into a dwelling of God in the Spirit" (Ephesians 2:21, 22). The building he described rests upon the foundation of the apostles and prophets, with Christ being the chief cornerstone. The building itself is made up of Christians. It has no top or roof; it continually ascends upward as people obey the gospel and are added to it.

The church, then, is not an organization—it is a living organism inhabited by the Spirit of God. It is a body of Christians who are alive with the life of God and who form a dwelling place for God's Spirit. You could say that the church is God's earthly residence.

AN INTIMATE RELATIONSHIP

Third, the church should be thought of as an intimate relationship with Christ.

From the earthly viewpoint, it would be easy to think of membership in the church in terms of entering a special relationship with a group of people, with the people who make up the church. This view of the church, however, misses an important truth.

The church involves a vital, intimate, ongoing relationship; and that relationship centers on an intimate
relationship with *Jesus.*

The continuing relationship which the church has
with Jesus is so close that it is described as a body/
head relationship. Christians are the body, and Jesus
is the head. God has made the church the spiritual
body of Christ, the visible part of the invisible Christ
on earth today. As surely as the Lord needed a
physical body in which to accomplish His work of
redemption while on the earth, He now needs a
spiritual body in which the fruit of His redemptive
work can be made available to everyone, everywhere.
On the Day of Pentecost, therefore, fifty days after
Jesus' resurrection from the dead, the Holy Spirit
descended to form the church, that spiritual body of
Christ. From that day until this, every redeemed
person, at the time of His redemption, is placed by
the wondrous grace of God in that body.

In keeping with this relationship, the church in
the New Testament is commonly called by the inspired writers the "body" of Christ (Ephesians
1:21–23; 5:23). Those who obey the gospel of Christ
become, and literally function as, Christ's spiritual
body on earth, led by the head, Christ Himself. So
true is this that when one is baptized, the New Testament specifically says that he is baptized "into
Christ" (Romans 6:3; Galatians 3:27), or "into one
body" (1 Corinthians 12:13).

The church has the closest relationship to Jesus
into which a person can enter upon this earth. The
church is the fullness of Christ, for His body is the
fullness of Him who fills all in all (Ephesians 1:23).
Christ is the fullness of the church, for His people

are complete in Him (Colossians 2:10). The church, His body, is incomplete without Christ, the head (Ephesians 1:22). In the same way, Christ, the head, is incomplete without His body, the church (Colossians 1:18). All that the head of the church is and has belongs to the church, and all that the church is and has should belong to Christ, its head. As His church, therefore, Christians experience a daily, continual partnership with Jesus. Those in Christ are not just professors of Christianity; they are possessors of Christ. To those in His body, the fountain of the fullness of Christ is opened.

As Paul discussed the church in Ephesians 5, he compared its relationship to Christ by using the figure of the husband/wife relationship, with the husband illustrating Christ and the wife illustrating the church. He referred to this relationship first *in principle*. Christ is the head of the church even as the husband is the head of the wife (Ephesians 5:23). He spoke of this relationship second *in practice or function*. As the wife is to be subject to her husband in everything, even so the church is to be subject to Christ. It is to look to Jesus as its head, leader, and guide (Ephesians 5:24). Finally, Paul discussed this relationship *in purpose*. As a husband loves his wife, Christ loves the church and is preparing this body of believers in Him to live with Him in eternity (Ephesians 5:25–27).

The church of the New Testament, at its heart, is a relationship with Christ. It is not initially a relationship with people, but it immediately results in a relationship with other Christians, the other members of the church, even as the children of the same father are related to each other. Members of Christ's body are members of each other, but, first and foremost, the church is Christ's body. To be members of Christ's church we must enter a relationship with Christ, a relationship so intimate and special that we are part of Him even as a body belongs to the head.

CONCLUSION

Many are confused on the proper meaning of the word "church." Such confusion need not exist, for the Bible is clear on its meaning.

What is "the church"? It is a spiritual body made up of those who have obeyed the gospel of Christ, have become His people, and are worshiping and working as His people in a given community. They wear His name and are His spiritual body on earth. They honor Christ in all things. This spiritual body is a living organism in which dwells the Spirit of the living God. Being part of the church does not mean just participating in a human organization or having membership in a group. It means having an intimate, ongoing relationship with Christ.

The church, the body of Christ, is entered by faith. This faith response involves repentance (Acts 17:30, 31), confession of Jesus as God's Son (Romans 10:10), and baptism into Christ (Romans 6:3; Galatians 3:27). At the point of baptism, one's sins are washed away and, with his new birth completed, he becomes a part of the body of Christ (Acts 2:38, 41, 47; 22:16; 1 Corinthians 12:13).

The church of the New Testament is not a denomination. Denominations are man-made; the church in the New Testament is designed, created, indwelt, and sustained by the Lord. Denominations come from the earth, from man; the New Testament church comes from heaven, from God. The church belongs to Christ—it wears His name, meets together for His worship, does His work in the world, and is indwelt by His Spirit. (See the chart entitled "The New Testament Church" on page 170.)

The invitation is extended by Christ to all people to enter His church upon His terms of salvation (Revelation 22:17) and live in the world as His church.

STUDY QUESTIONS
(answers on page 265)

1. How necessary is it to understand how the Holy Spirit is using a word, such as the word "church," in the Scriptures?
2. Discuss the different ways the word "church" is used in the New Testament.
3. The church is the temple of God. What does this mean in the Christian's life today? Does this name for the church suggest how its members are to live, work, and worship?
4. In what sense is the church a "living" building?
5. In what ways can the husband/wife relationship illustrate the church's relationship with Jesus?
6. Describe clearly how one enters Christ's church.
7. In what sense does the church uniquely belong to Christ?

WORD HELPS

denomination—a group of religious congregations which are not found in the Bible, united under a specific set of beliefs, and governed by some kind of council. *Since no denominations are found in the New Testament, this is not a Bible word.*

fellowship—sharing interests, ideals, or experiences; that love which fills Christians' hearts for one another.

fornication—sexual sin; having a sexual relationship without being married.

11

The Next To the Greatest Story Ever Told

In 1965 a motion picture company released a cinema on the life of Christ which was called *The Greatest Story Ever Told*. Beginning with Christ's birth, the cinema depicts His earthly ministry, rejection, crucifixion, burial, and resurrection. Although the production of the cinema was not faithful to the divine record of the Bible in its portrayal of Jesus, its title is a reminder that the actual life of Christ is the greatest story ever told.

If the birth, life, death, and resurrection of Jesus is the greatest story ever told, what would be the next to the greatest story ever told? The answer is obvious as one reads the Book of Acts in the New Testament: The second greatest story ever told is the establishment of our Lord's church.

The story of the bringing in of the kingdom of God, the church, as one would expect, is filled with high adventure and gripping excitement. One chapter in Acts—chapter 2—relates the drama.

Let us review this chapter in Acts as if this one

119

chapter were an entire book or a complete story. This will allow us to divide the story into its compelling and inspiring parts. Each chapter in the book *The Next to the Greatest Story Ever Told* will present an exciting phase of the story of the establishment of the church.

CHAPTER ONE:
"THE DIVINE OUTPOURING"

As we begin the book, we open to the first chapter, which is entitled "The Divine Outpouring."

Luke, the writer of Acts, said, "When the day of Pentecost had come, they were all together in one place" (2:1). The setting of the story, therefore, is the historic city of Jerusalem on the Day of Pentecost. Isaiah (Isaiah 2:2–4) and Micah (Micah 4:1–3) had prophetically marked Jerusalem as the place where the law of the Lord would go forth in the beginning of the age called "the last days." Pentecost was an Old Testament feast day which celebrated the harvest of grain (Exodus 23:16). From all over the Roman Empire, Jewish men with their families had come to Jerusalem to keep this important Old Testament festival.

As the Day of Pentecost was getting fully under way, something unusual happened:

> And suddenly there came from heaven a noise like a violent rushing wind, and it filled the whole house where they were sitting. And there appeared to them tongues as of fire distributing themselves, and they rested on each one of them. And they were all filled with the Holy Spirit and began to speak with other tongues, as the Spirit was giving them utterance (Acts 2:2–4).

The apostles were the only ones to receive the outpouring of the Holy Spirit. Acts 2 and the context leading up to Acts 2 make that clear. First, "they" in Acts 2:1 means "the eleven apostles" mentioned in Acts 1:26. The apostles are the center of attention as the story unfolds. Second, the account of the coming of the Holy Spirit (Acts 2:1–21) nowhere indicates that anyone other than the apostles received the baptism of the Holy Spirit. The multitude that witnessed the apostles' speaking in different languages through the Spirit recognized and acknowledged only the apostles as the ones doing the speaking (Acts 2:7).

For three years prior to this outpouring of the Holy Spirit, promises in different circumstances had been made to the apostles about how Christ would one day baptize them with the Holy Spirit. At the beginning of Christ's ministry, John the Baptist had said, "As for me, I baptize you with water for repentance, but He who is coming after me is mightier than I, and I am not fit to remove His sandals; He will baptize you with the Holy Spirit and fire" (Matthew 3:11). Shortly before His ascension, Christ had said to them, "For John baptized with water, but you will be baptized with the Holy Spirit not many days from now" (Acts 1:5). The parting words of Christ to His apostles at His ascension instructed them to abide in Jerusalem until they had received the promise of the Father and were clothed with power from on high (Luke 24:46–49; Acts 1:4). Now, in this divine outpouring of the Holy Spirit which came on the morning of the Day of Pentecost, all of our Lord's promises concerning the coming of the Spirit upon the apostles were being fulfilled.

As the Holy Spirit was poured out from heaven, something was heard: "... there came from heaven a noise like a violent rushing wind ..." (Acts 2:2). Something was also seen: "And there appeared to them tongues as of fire distributing themselves, and they rested on each one of them" (Acts 2:3). Something was also experienced: The way people saw the coming of the Spirit was the apostles' speaking in tongues, or languages, as the Spirit empowered them. There can be no doubt that the apostles were speaking in the human languages of the people who had heard the sound resembling wind and had gathered to see what was happening. As the people spoke of what they were hearing from the apostles, they used the Greek words *dialektos* (translated "language"; Acts 2:6, 8) and *glossais* (translated "tongues"; Acts 2:11).

The apostles were baptized with the Holy Spirit for three divine purposes. First, they were baptized for the purpose of inspiration. The Holy Spirit would inspire them so they could give God's revelation to the world. Christ had promised the apostles, "But the Helper, the Holy Spirit, whom the Father will send in My name, He will teach you all things, and bring to your remembrance all that I said to you" (John 14:26). Now, through the coming of the Spirit, this promise of inspiration that Christ had made to His apostles would be realized.

Second, they were baptized with the Holy Spirit for the purpose of confirming that the message they preached was from God. They were empowered by the Holy Spirit to work miracles, signs, and wonders to confirm, or prove, the messages they would preach. Christ had promised, "These signs will accompany those who have believed: in My name they will cast out demons, they will speak with new tongues; they will pick up serpents, and if they drink any deadly poison, it will not hurt them; they will lay hands on the sick, and they will recover" (Mark 16:17, 18). This promise would be fulfilled through the Spirit as the apostles worked miracles to confirm that they were men sent from God. An illustration of its fulfillment is seen in Acts 14:3: "Therefore they spent a long time there speaking boldly with reliance upon the Lord, who was testifying to the word of His grace, granting that signs and wonders be done by their hands."

Third, the apostles were baptized with the Holy Spirit so that they would have the power to lay hands on other Christians and give them miraculous gifts. An example of this giving of power is recorded in Acts 8:14–24: Peter and John, two apostles, were sent out from Jerusalem to Samaria to pray for the new converts who had come to Christ through Philip's preaching, lay hands on them, and give to them the miraculous gifts of the Holy Spirit.

What does this beginning of the "next to the greatest story ever told" mean to you and me? It means that the revelation found in the New Testament was given to us through inspired men. We can trust the New Testament message to be accurate and infallible. God empowered His apostles through the baptism of the Holy Spirit; and the apostles, in turn, by the laying on of their hands, gave miraculous gifts of the Holy Spirit to other Christians. Since all the New Testament writers were inspired, Spirit-guided men, we can believe confidently that the New Testament is God's revelation to man.

CHAPTER TWO:
"THE POWERFUL SERMON"

Chapter two of *The Next to the Greatest Story Ever Told* is entitled "The Powerful Sermon." The day on which the church was established was a day of preaching. At first, apparently all the apostles spoke to the different national groups in their languages or dialects, declaring "the mighty deeds of God" (Acts 2:11). Then Peter stood up with the eleven and delivered a detailed sermon, speaking perhaps in Greek, the universal language of that day, proclaiming that Jesus was both Lord and Christ (Acts 2:14).

The people who had been drawn together by the sound of the rushing mighty wind were Jews, providing an audience of unusual potential for this first preaching of the gospel. They had an intellectual potential. They were believers in God and knew well the Old Testament Scriptures. They had a mental readiness for the reception of the gospel message. They also had the opportunity to take Christ to many nations. They had come from all parts of the Roman Empire. The opportunity was present for an immediate spread of Christianity by these people who would receive the gospel and would later return to their homelands with it.

Through inspiration, Luke provided us with a summary of the sermon Peter preached (Acts 2:14–36). This vital overview he gave of Peter's sermon can be outlined in two or three different ways; but let us outline it according to the formal elements of a typical speech, looking at its introduction, body, and conclusion.

Peter began the sermon by starting where his audience was. Some of the people had mockingly said,

"They are full of sweet wine" (Acts 2:13). Preachers of the gospel can get along without just about anything except a good reputation. Any preacher who does not have trustworthy character and a reliable reputation is doomed to failure before he opens his mouth to speak. He will not be believed or respected regardless of how powerful his presentation of the gospel may be.

It is no surprise, then, that Peter began this sermon with an answer to the accusation that had been made against the apostles. He responded to their misunderstanding of the facts with two truths: First, he stated what it was not. He appealed to their common sense. He said, "For these men are not drunk, as you suppose, for it is only the third hour of the day" (Acts 2:15). Peter was saying, "The explanation cannot be drunkenness, for no normal Jew would be drunk so early in the morning on such an important day as Pentecost. Common sense will tell you that we are not drunk." Second, Peter explained what it was. He appealed to Scripture as he said, "But this is what was spoken of through the prophet Joel" (Acts 2:16). He then proceeded to quote Joel 2:28–32 (Acts 2:17–21). There can be no doubt, then, that the outpouring of the Spirit on Pentecost is, at least in part, the fulfillment of Joel's prophecy regarding the beginning of the age called "the last days." We have Peter's word on it. His words, "This is what was spoken of through the prophet Joel," must be regarded as a complete and final answer to this question.

This outpouring of the Spirit began the age of "the last days." As the apostles were empowered by the baptism of the Holy Spirit, the miraculous age of the beginning of the church commenced. Later in Acts, the apostles laid their hands on other Christians, and sons and daughters prophesied, young men saw visions, old men dreamed dreams, and men and women bondservants prophesied (Acts 6:6; 8:4–8, 14–24; 21:8, 9). This outpouring upon the apostles was the spring which produced the miraculous stream of the early days of Christianity. God would use the miraculous gifts of the Spirit imparted by the laying on of apostolic hands for the guidance of the infant church until the written form of the New Testament appeared. With the completion of the written form of the New Testament, the deaths of the apostles, and the deaths of those on whom the apostles had laid their hands, the miraculous beginning of the church ended and the age of the Spirit guiding the church through the written Word commenced.

Peter's introduction, then, pointed out to the multitude what the event was not and what the event was. He appealed to their common sense, and he appealed to Scripture. He took his audience from where they were to where they would be ready to consider the evidence for Jesus' being the Messiah.

The body of Peter's sermon consists of a presentation of different lines of evidence for believing that Jesus is the Christ. If you were asked to stand before an assembly of thousands of people and list the evidence for believing that Jesus is the Christ, what evidence would you list? Let us see what evidence he gave and check our list against his.

When the repetition is eliminated, Peter listed and explained five lines of evidence. First, he pointed to *the evidence of the miracles of Christ*. He said, ". . . Jesus the Nazarene, a man attested to you by God with miracles and wonders and signs which God performed through Him in your midst, just as you yourselves know" (Acts 2:22). It was the testimony of the miracles that had convinced Nicodemus that Christ had come from God. During his night interview with Christ, Nicodemus said, "Rabbi, we know that You have come from God as a teacher; for no one can do these signs that You do unless God is with him" (John 3:2). If a completely credible source of information, an undeniably reliable document, declared to us that Jesus worked true miracles, we would be forced by that testimony to respond to the miracles of Christ the same way that Nicodemus did—we would be compelled to believe that He came from God. The Word of God, the Bible, the most reliable source of information on earth, testifies that Christ worked actual miracles. This evidence can point to only one conclusion—He was "approved" of God, confirmed by the miracles He worked as being God's Son. Peter reminded his audience of the miracles of Christ and called for an acceptance of the logical conclusion which that evidence demands.

Second, Peter placed before his audience *the evidence of the Resurrection*. He said,

> This Man, delivered over by the predetermined plan and foreknowledge of God, you nailed to a cross by the hands of godless men and put Him to death. But God raised Him up again, putting an end to the agony of death, since it was impossible for Him to be held in its power (Acts 2:23, 24).

The Resurrection was a significant part of all the apostles' preaching. It was an argument that the Jews could not answer. The resurrection of Christ made cowards out of bold men and made bold men out of cowards. The Jews, who had boldly cried before

Pilate, "Crucify Him!" (Matthew 27:22), were drawing back in fear before the truth of the empty tomb. Peter, who had fearfully said at Christ's trial, "I do not know the man" (Matthew 26:72), was boldly preaching His resurrection before a vast assembly only a short distance from the empty tomb.

The Resurrection provides conclusive proof that Jesus Christ is God's Son. The only way anyone can deny the deity of Christ is to deny His resurrection from the dead. The Resurrection places Christianity in a category all by itself. Christianity is the only religion in the world of religions whose founder arose from the dead. It confirms His claims, authenticates His promises, and validates His religion.

Third, Peter argued from *the evidence of prophecy*. He quoted Psalm 16:8–11, a prophecy which predicted the resurrection of Christ:

> I saw the Lord always in my presence; for He is at my right hand, so that I will not be shaken. Therefore my heart was glad and my tongue exulted; moreover my flesh also will live in hope; because You will not abandon my soul to Hades, nor allow Your Holy One to undergo decay. You have made known to me the ways of life; You will make me full of gladness with Your presence (Acts 2:25b–28).

In his prophecy, David spoke in the first person. On the surface, it might appear that he was speaking of himself. Peter showed that David could not have been speaking of himself by pointing to two facts. First, he referred to David's death. David, the one who made the prophecy, died and was buried and was still in his tomb. As his evidence, he pointed to David's tomb, which was located in Jerusalem for all to see

(Acts 2:29). Second, he reminded them of God's promise to David (Acts 2:30). God had promised David that one of his descendants would eventually occupy his throne (2 Samuel 7:12). This promise, Peter said, has been fulfilled in Christ, for God has raised Him from the dead (Acts 2:31), placing Him at His right hand on a spiritual throne. Jesus came into the world through the lineage of David and now sits on a spiritual throne at God's right hand in heaven, reigning as King over His earthly kingdom, the church.

Peter made a similar argument from a prophecy in Psalm 110:1 at the end of his sermon (Acts 2:34, 35). His references to prophecy (Psalms 16:8–11; 110:1) proved that the One sent from God would be resurrected from the dead and exalted to God's right hand. Jesus, in His resurrection and exaltation, had clearly fulfilled both of these Old Testament prophecies.

Fourth, Peter used *the evidence of witnesses*. He said, "This Jesus God raised up again, to which we are all witnesses" (Acts 2:32). The Jews would have to acknowledge that the prophecy to which Peter had referred predicted a resurrection. Peter was seeking to confirm that Christ had arisen from the dead and had fulfilled that part of the prophecy. He forced his audience to face the testimony of eyewitnesses that Jesus had arisen from the dead. A witness is high-quality evidence. Any authentic court of law will accept the evidence of a witness as long as no contradictions are evident in his testimony. God not only affirmed the resurrection of His Son in His Word, but He placed in His Word the testimony of witnesses who, after His resurrection from the dead, saw Him, touched Him, ate with Him, and studied Him. Who could refuse such testimony?

Fifth, Peter pointed to *the evidence of the descent of the Holy Spirit*. He said, "Therefore having been exalted to the right hand of God, and having received from the Father the promise of the Holy Spirit, He has poured forth this which you both see and hear" (Acts 2:33). Just before Christ's departure to heaven, He promised to send the promise of the Father to the apostles (Luke 24:46–49). The multitude had seen and heard the results of the outpouring of the Spirit. These events gave them miraculous confirmation that Jesus had ascended to the Father's right hand, had received from the Father the promise of the Spirit, and had sent the Spirit forth upon the apostles.

These five lines of evidence establish an undeniable conclusion. Peter focused their attention on this conclusion with the word "therefore." Someone has said, "Whenever you see the word 'therefore' in the New Testament, you should stop and see what it is *there for*, for it is always *there for* a reason." Peter said, "Therefore let all the house of Israel know for certain that God has made Him both Lord and Christ—this Jesus whom you crucified" (Acts 2:36). His miracles, His resurrection from the dead, His fulfillment of prophecy, the testimony of witnesses, and the descent of the Spirit prove that Jesus is the Promised One of God, the Christ, and that He is Lord.

What does this chapter of *The Next to the Greatest Story Ever Told* mean to us? Does it not convince us that Christ is the center of Christianity? When one proves that Jesus is the Christ, he proves the credibility of Christianity. If Peter could not have proven that Christ was God's Son who died for our sins and arose from the dead, Christianity would have died on the day of its birth!

CHAPTER THREE:
"THE DEEP-FELT CRY"

The third chapter in *The Next to the Greatest Story Ever Told* is entitled "The Deep-Felt Cry." Many in Peter's audience were deeply moved by his sermon. Smitten in conscience, they cried out to Peter and to the rest of the apostles.

Luke wrote, "Now when they heard this, they were pierced to the heart, and said to Peter and the rest of the apostles, 'Brethren, what shall we do?'" (Acts 2:37). The King James Version of the Bible says that they were "pricked in their heart." This "pricking" of the heart is not the pricking similar to the pricking of one's finger with a needle or the pricking of one's hand by a thorn. It is an expression which means something like the breaking of the heart or like an arrow being shot through the heart. This same phrase is used in a different context in Acts 7:54: "Now when they heard this, they were cut to the quick, and they began gnashing their teeth at him." In this incident the Jews reacted to Stephen's sermon with anger. Their hearts were engulfed with anger; they were pierced through with hatred. The Jews who responded to Peter's sermon, however, were overwhelmed with conviction; they were distraught with guilt.

Perhaps the people who cried out actually interrupted Peter's sermon. Interruptions are not always desirable, but this was a blessed interruption indeed. A preacher was once preaching when a man interrupted his sermon with the question "Can I be baptized now?" The preacher stopped, looked directly at the man, and said, "My sermon can wait. If you want to be baptized, we will stop this sermon and baptize you into Christ. Then we will come back, and

I will finish the sermon." An interruption of this kind would not be an intrusion but an inspiration.

Their question was filled with excitement. They did not ask nonchalantly, "What shall we do?" Their question was more like, "What in the world can we do? We are in trouble. Do we have any hope?" Their question was asked in all seriousness.

Look carefully at their question: "Brethren, what shall we do?" They were addressing fellow Jews, hence, their use of the word "brethren." It has a nationality connotation, not a religious one. They had come to realize that before God they were in a terrible condition. They had participated in the crucifixion of the Messiah, the Savior whom God had sent into the world. Peter's sermon placed his listeners' sin before them as if in huge letters (Acts 2:23).

You have had to ask and answer many important questions in your life, but have you asked and answered according to the New Testament the question "What must I do to be saved?" Others present on the Day of Pentecost must have heard Peter's sermon and witnessed the miracles of Pentecost but turned and walked away without facing their guilt and asking this question. Sin in a person's life is a tragedy, a tragedy so great that Christ had to come into this world and die upon a cross to provide atonement (payment) for it. There is an even greater tragedy. When one refuses to face his guilt before God and seek God's solution to that guilt, he experiences the greatest tragedy of all.

CHAPTER FOUR:
"THE INSPIRED ANSWER"
The fourth chapter in the book *The Next to the*

Greatest Story Ever Told is a chapter entitled "The Inspired Answer." Guided by the Holy Spirit, Peter gave a plain answer to the convicted crowd's question: "Repent, and each of you be baptized in the name of Jesus Christ for the forgiveness of your sins; and you will receive the gift of the Holy Spirit" (Acts 2:38).

Shortly before His ascension, our Lord gave what is often called the Great Commission. Three full accounts of this commission are given in the New Testament: Matthew 28:18–20; Mark 16:15, 16; and Luke 24:46, 47. Each account has a different emphasis. Mark 16:15, 16 stresses the condition of faith. Luke 24:46, 47 emphasizes repentance and remission of sins. Matthew 28:18–20 highlights baptism. These three accounts indicate that salvation or remission of sins through God's grace was to be offered upon the three conditions of faith, repentance, and baptism. The wording of these accounts of the Great Commission leaves no doubt as to this understanding.

All three of the conditions expressed in the Great Commission are seen in Peter's answer to their question. Faith in Christ had been engendered in their hearts by Peter's sermon, and this faith prompted their crying out for instruction. Peter's answer to the Jews' question, therefore, mentions specifically repentance and baptism, the other two conditions mentioned in the Great Commission. He said, "Repent, and each of you be baptized in the name of Jesus Christ for the forgiveness of your sins . . ." (Acts 2:38). Notice where Peter placed the remission, or forgiveness, of sins in his answer. He did not promise salvation or forgiveness of sins before baptism, but after it. Peter was guided by the Holy Spirit, and the answer he gave was the Holy Spirit's answer, not his.

The answer given those who cried out is too clear to be misunderstood. In order to dodge the force and impact of this answer, some religious leaders have said that "for" in Acts 2:38 is translated from a Greek word which does not mean "in order to" but means "because of." That the Greek word *eis* is translated reliably by "for" or "in order to" is seen by comparing the numerous translations of the Bible. Pile them on top of each other—they all render the Greek word *eis* "for," "in order to," or an equivalent phrase. None render this word "because of." Peter's answer clearly places forgiveness of sins after baptism. Let God's answer to this question stand, and do not allow anyone to explain it away.

Someone has said that every verse in the New Testament has a twin. This is not always true, but it does have some truth to it. Some New Testament verses have twins, and when we look at the twin we see another way of saying the same truth. What is the twin of Acts 2:38? It is Acts 22:16. Saul had come to Damascus seeking the answer to his question "What shall I do, Lord?" (Acts 22:10a). He was a believer, for he had seen, spoken to, and been convicted by the Lord. His repentance was indicated by the question which he asked the Lord. He had even acknowledged the Lord, as is also evident in his question; but he was told to go to Damascus that he might be told what to do. He waited in Damascus in prayer and repentance for three days for the answer to his question. Ananias was sent to him with the answer. What did Ananias tell him? The answer Ananias gave him, you might say, is the twin of Acts 2:38. He said, "Now why do you delay? Get up and be baptized, and wash away your sins, calling on His name." If any doubt exists that baptism is for the forgiveness of sins, surely Acts 22:16 forever lays this question to rest.

A young man who was attending a private religious college once said that his Bible professor did not believe in baptism for the forgiveness of sins and was teaching this doctrine in his class. Someone asked him, "What have you done about it?" He said, "I asked my mother what to do about it, and she said that I should go to him after class and ask him to explain Acts 2:38. I did. I opened my Bible to Acts 2:38, went to him after class, and respectfully asked him to explain it. He said that Acts 2:38 really means 'because of' the remission of sins and not 'for' the remission of sins. I went home and mentioned what he had told me to my mother, and she said that I should go back and ask him to explain Acts 22:16. So I did. I went to him after class with my Bible open to Acts 22:16 and respectfully asked him to explain this verse. Do you know what the professor said? He said that he did not try to explain that verse but would just jump over it and go on to the next verse." Acts 22:16 cannot be explained away. It must be accepted or rejected.

Peter indicated that the answer he gave to this question was God's answer for the Christian Age, the final age of human history. He said, "For the promise is for you and your children and for all who are far off, as many as the Lord our God will call to Himself" (Acts 2:39). "You and your children" is an expression that refers to the Jews who would respond to the gospel, and "for all who are far off" is an expression that must refer to or include the Gentiles who would in time hear, accept, and obey the gospel. "As many as the Lord our God will call to Himself" is a phrase which includes all Jews and Gentiles who would ac-

cept the gospel in the future and come to Christ. If
the Gentiles are not included in the phrase "for all
who are far off," they are most assuredly included in
Peter's "as many as" phrase. Peter announced God's
plan not only for the Day of Pentecost but for all future
days of the Christian Age. He gave God's answer to
the question "What must I do to be saved?"

CHAPTER FIVE:
"THE WONDERFUL RESPONSE"

The fifth chapter in the book *The Next to the Greatest Story Ever Told* is entitled "The Wonderful Response." Luke told of the amazing acceptance of the
first preaching of the gospel message of salvation.
He said, "So then, those who had received his word
were baptized; and that day there were added about
three thousand souls" (Acts 2:41).

We are not told how long Peter and the other
apostles preached on that morning. Luke wrote, "And
with many other words he solemnly testified and
kept on exhorting them, saying, 'Be saved from this
perverse generation!'" (Acts 2:40). Peter not only
convinced them with evidence and argument; he also
compelled them with testimony and exhortation.

The listening audience accepted Peter's message
and acted upon it. Luke recounted, "So then, those
who had received his word were baptized; and that
day there were added about three thousand souls"
(Acts 2:41). These people were not just hearers of the
word; they became doers of it (James 1:25). They did
not just listen to it; they decided to live it. How
tragic it is that all most people ever do with sermons
is listen to them. Some, at least, in the great multitude
that heard Peter preach were not only convicted by

his message but, by yielding their minds and lives to that message, were converted to Christ. Three thousand gladly received the Word and were baptized. Before conversion can take place, one must gladly receive the Word of salvation. One of the major reasons that more people are not converted to Christ is that people do not gladly receive the Word into their hearts. The Word will always do its work if it is gladly received.

CHAPTER SIX:
"THE PROMISED BODY"

The sixth chapter in this book is entitled "The Promised Body." The three thousand who were baptized into Christ are pictured by Luke as the church. The prophets had foretold that a unique kingdom of God was coming (Daniel 2:44). John the Baptist, as he prepared the way for the coming of the Messiah, declared that the kingdom of heaven was near (Matthew 3:1, 2). During His ministry Christ Himself, the Messiah sent from God, called for repentance because the kingdom of heaven was at hand (Matthew 4:17). After His resurrection from the dead, during the forty days before His ascension, Christ spoke with the apostles and the disciples about the coming kingdom (Acts 1:3). In His final words to His apostles, Christ told them to wait for what the Father had promised (Acts 1:4). Ten days after His ascension, on a Sunday morning, the long-awaited time came. With the outpouring of the Holy Spirit (Acts 2:1–4), the first preaching of the gospel after the resurrection of Christ (Acts 2:14–36), and the response of three thousand to the gospel, the church was born. Those who were washed in the blood of Christ as they obeyed the gospel were made into Christ's church. From that day until this, every time someone hears the gospel and gladly obeys it by being baptized into Christ upon his faith, repentance, and confession of Jesus as God's Son, he is added to them (Acts 2:47)—these first ones, these three thousand who came to Christ at the very beginning on Pentecost.

From Pentecost forward in Acts, the church is spoken of as a present and living reality and no longer as a promise or prophecy. Luke said at the close of Acts 2, ". . . And the Lord was adding to their number day by day those who were being saved" (Acts 2:47). At the end of Peter's second sermon recorded in Acts, Luke wrote, "But many of those who had heard the message believed; and the number of the men came to be about five thousand" (Acts 4:4). Following the deaths of Ananias and Sapphira (Acts 5:1–10), Luke wrote, "And great fear came over the whole church, and over all who heard of these things" (Acts 5:11). When a persecution grew out of the stoning of Stephen (Acts 6:8—7:60), Luke said, ". . . And on that day a great persecution began against the church in Jerusalem, and they were all scattered throughout the regions of Judea and Samaria, except the apostles" (Acts 8:1). According to Luke, then, the church, the unique kingdom of God, had come.

It is said that one day someone came to Marshall Keeble, a great gospel preacher, and, pointing to his heart, said, "Brother Keeble, I like to feel it. I like to feel it right here." Brother Keeble had the marvelous ability to respond in an unforgettable way when he was placed on the spot. Pointing to his Bible, he answered this person, "Well, I like to read it. I like to read it right here." Feelings, of course, are important, but we must not let them lead us. Only the Bible, God's Word, should lead us. When our feelings are based upon our sincere reception and obedience of His Word, we will have the genuine joy spoken of in the New Testament.

CONCLUSION

We close the book *The Next to the Greatest Story Ever Told* and begin to think about what we have read. It dawns upon us that we have thought about something that is far more significant than anything that appears in our newspapers or on the local or national news on television. We have literally been able to pull back the curtains which conceal the past and, through the inspired Book of Acts, see the most historic and far-reaching event, next to the life, death, and resurrection of Jesus, in the history of the world. We have witnessed the actual beginning of the church, the unique, long-awaited kingdom of God. With its beginning, we have watched the ushering in of the final age of human history, the Christian Age or "the last days" age.

Another book follows in importance this book that we have read. We could call it *The Third Part of the Greatest Story Ever Told*. It would be the story of your conversion to Christ, the story of your becoming a part of the church which Jesus built. The story, of course, would be different for each of us. For many of us the story could easily be written, but for others of us the story could not be written at all simply because it has not taken place. How is it with you? Has the story taken place? Have you become a New Testament Christian?

If you are not a New Testament Christian, you

know now how to become one. By your gladly receiving the Word of the gospel and by your obedience to it, you can be born into the kingdom of God, the very kingdom of heaven we have seen in Acts 2.

STUDY QUESTIONS
(answers on page 265)

1. In what sense can we say that the establishment of the church is the next to the greatest story ever told?
2. What evidence can you give that only the apostles were baptized with the Holy Spirit on the Day of Pentecost?
3. Discuss the divine reasons that the apostles were baptized with the Holy Spirit.
4. What does the baptism of the apostles in the Holy Spirit mean to us today?
5. Discuss the evidence for the deity of Christ which Peter presented in his sermon.
6. How vital is the resurrection of Christ to God's scheme of redemption? Could we think of Christ in any sense as being God's divine Son if He had not arisen from the dead?
7. Can you think of a greater tragedy than being in sin?
8. Explain the different emphases that the three accounts of the Great Commission (Matthew 28:18–20; Mark 16:15, 16; Luke 24:46, 47) have on the conditions of salvation.
9. Discuss how Acts 22:16 supports Acts 2:38.

WORD HELPS

conversion—the act of changing one's heart and becoming a Christian.

miraculous age—the time period when the apostles and others they laid their hands on could work miracles. This was during the infancy of the church. While God still answers prayer, the miraculous age ended with the death of the last apostle (Ephesians 4:11–13; 1 Corinthians 13:8–10).

Nicodemus—a teacher who came to Jesus by night. Jesus taught him how to enter the kingdom of God (John 3).

revelation—truths revealed or made known by the Holy Spirit. God's revelation to man is the Bible.

12
The Church of The New Testament

Of necessity, living in this world requires making decisions. Most of our decisions are small, momentary, and somewhat insignificant. Other decisions are so critically important that they affect the way we will live before God in this life and will determine our eternal destiny. These decisions which influence life and eternity require serious thinking and prayerful research before being made. No more far-reaching decision can be considered than the decision to enter the New Testament church. The decision we make regarding this question will influence our daily living for God, our spiritual identity, our worship, and our spiritual service. This question, then, must be thoughtfully considered until it is answered according to the clear teachings of the Scriptures and our best unprejudiced reasoning.

Our world is filled with different religious groups which plead for our commitment and allegiance. A decision must be made. Which is the New Testament church? How shall we decide?

Commonsense guidelines obviously must be followed to help us think carefully about the evidence and make the right choice, the choice which will please God. If we follow these guidelines with integrity, we can identify the New Testament church in the world today.

What are these guidelines?

HOW WAS THE CHURCH IDENTIFIED IN THE FIRST CENTURY?

The first view of the church given in the New Testament is found in the latter part of Acts 2. The Gospels have created in us an expectation, an anticipation, for a picture of the church through their record of prophecies about it given by Jesus and His apostles (Matthew 16:18; Mark 9:1; Acts 1:4–8). Then, in Acts 2, as the church is established, a living picture of the church is set before us by the Holy Spirit.

This picture of the church helps us to see the main characteristics of it. No longer are we left to wonder what the church which Jesus established looks like in real life.

Survey carefully the chief traits of the church in the picture of it given by Luke in Acts 2:

> They were continually devoting themselves to the apostles' teaching and to fellowship, to the breaking of bread and to prayer.
>
> Everyone kept feeling a sense of awe; and many wonders and signs were taking place through the apostles. And all those who had believed were together and had all things in common; and they began selling their property and possessions and were sharing them with all, as anyone might have need.

Day by day continuing with one mind in the temple,
and breaking bread from house to house, they were
taking their meals together with gladness and sincerity of heart, praising God and having favor with
all the people. And the Lord was adding to their
number day by day those who were being saved
(Acts 2:42–47).

What characteristics of the church do we see in this
picture?

Strong in Commitment

The first trait is a steadfast commitment to the
apostles' doctrine or teaching. Luke said, "They were
continually devoting themselves to the apostles'
teaching and to fellowship, to the breaking of bread
and to prayer" (Acts 2:42).

This commitment of the church to the apostles'
teaching manifested itself in a faithful following of
their teaching; in their fellowship together in worship, service, and giving; in their observance of the
Lord's Supper or the "breaking of bread";[1] and in
prayer. Christ was their head, and they were recognizing His leadership of His church by honoring His
Word which had been given to them through the
apostles.

We must not allow the divisions of the Christian
world to confuse the simplicity of following Christ as
His church. The church is not a man-made body. It
is a group of people who have yielded to the message

---

[1]The frequency of the observance of the Lord's Supper is not discussed in this passage by Luke, but he does intimate in Acts 20:7 that
the supper was partaken by the church every first day of the week,
the day on which Jesus arose.

of the Holy Spirit and, therefore, by their obedience to the gospel, have been bonded together by the Holy Spirit into Christ's church. They belong only to Christ. They look to no human leadership but are guided by the head of the body, Christ, through His revealed Word. They view faithfulness to Christ in terms of abiding in His inspired Word. The Bible guides Christians' worship, their work as Christ's hands in the world, and their daily living for Christ.

As we look at the Holy Spirit's picture of the church, we see the trait of strong commitment.

Unselfish in Compassion

Another characteristic that we cannot miss in this divine picture of the church is the church's unselfish compassion for each other. Their sincere obedience to the truth produced in them a compassionate love for each other. Luke said, "And they began selling their property and possessions and were sharing them with all, as anyone might have need" (Acts 2:45).

Jews had come from all over the Roman Empire to keep the Day of Pentecost. They thought that this Pentecost would be a normal one; but, to their complete surprise, it was not. It was the historic day toward which the prophets had looked. After hearing Peter's message, many of the Jews decided to become Christians (Acts 2:41). Their obedience to Christ meant a radical change for them. For one thing, they needed to stay in Jerusalem and be taught further by the apostles about the church of which they had become a part. The sudden decision to stay in Jerusalem would be difficult for some of them because they had made no advance plans for such a stay. They would need housing and food, no doubt. How did other

Christians who did not face such a crisis respond to these brothers and sisters in distress from distant places? Their response is a picture of compassion and love that is seldom equalled. Some sold houses and land in order to care for these brethren. Their actions illustrate the trait of compassion which Christ intended always to be a part of His church.

A truth which makes their sharing beautiful beyond description is that the gifts were completely voluntary. Their giving was not forced or demanded by the apostles (Acts 5:4). It sprang from hearts of tender compassion and Christlike love. Christ had produced in them a new nature, one of unselfish sympathy.

Their giving was not just giving or sharing so that all might be equal or have the same amount of goods. It was not communal living; it was caring love. They gave to those in need. They satisfied *needs*, not *greeds*. They knew that *every emergency demands urgency*. As people developed needs, others acted in love to meet those needs—even if it called for sacrificial giving!

Luke later said of the church, "For there was not a needy person among them, for all who were owners of land or houses would sell them and bring the proceeds of the sales and lay them at the apostles' feet, and they would be distributed to each as any had need" (Acts 4:34, 35). He also said, "And not one of them claimed that anything belonging to him was his own, but all things were common property to them" (Acts 4:32b).

Compassion is a basic attribute of Christ's church. His church cannot exist where faithful obedience to His Word is not present; neither can His church exist unless compassion abounds as an expression of the very heart of Christ. True Christians have an active brotherly love which is created by God's love dwelling in their hearts. John wrote, "But whoever has the world's goods, and sees his brother in need and closes his heart against him, how does the love of God abide in him?" (1 John 3:17).

In the Spirit's first picture of the church, unselfish compassion is plainly a significant trait.

United in Christ

A third characteristic of Christ's church seen in this picture is its unity. The Holy Spirit, through the obedience of these people to the gospel and to the apostles' teaching, had given the members of Christ's church a oneness of mind. Luke said, "And all those who had believed were together and had all things in common" (Acts 2:44). He further said, "Day by day continuing with one mind in the temple, and breaking bread from house to house, they were taking their meals together with gladness and sincerity of heart" (Acts 2:46).

As we behold this beautiful unity which existed in the church that Jesus built, let us remind ourselves of the importance of this first picture of the church. This picture gives us the result of Christ's earthly life and death. What kind of church did Christ come to establish or create? Is it a big organization with many bodies which wear different names, live by different creeds, and have no fellowship with each other? Or did He create a united body over which He reigns as head? In Acts 2 we see the clearest image in perhaps all of the New Testament of what Christ wants His church to be and of how He wants it to live in the world. This picture unmistakably reveals that unity of mind and life characterized that church. This has to be what Christ desires for His church today. The division which prevails throughout the religious world is a sure sign that man, in his worldly wisdom, has left Christ's church and has manufactured churches of his own.

The unity of the Lord's church can be illustrated in marriage. A man and a woman who are different in background experiences and family life become one in marriage (Ephesians 5:31). After their wedding ceremony, they emerge as a new family. They belong to each other now, and they take on a new nature. Selfish ambitions and personal goals die; new ambitions and goals for the good of this new family come to life. They dwell together in unity, being of one heart and soul, working together for the maintenance, love, and future of their home. How were they given this unity? It was given by their common consent to enter marriage and their fulfillment of the marriage law. How do they maintain this unity? They maintain it by loving each other, caring for each other, forgiving one another, honoring their marriage vows, and honoring the blessed state of marriage.

Is this not true of the church? How do we enter the unity of the church? By personal consent, we decide to yield our lives to the gospel of Christ and enter His body, the church. As we enter that body, we are united by the Holy Spirit to Christ and to every member of it. With one heart and soul, we begin to love, serve, and live as His body. How do we maintain this unity? We keep it intact by loving and forgiving each other and by honoring the Word of Christ in worship, service, and daily living.

An undeniable characteristic of Christ's church

is unity. Christ's true church cannot exist where division remains. We are given this unity by the Holy Spirit when we enter Christ's body; and, as we live as His body, we will either maintain it or harm it. Division in the body of Christ should be unthinkable to every Christian. According to the Holy Spirit's picture, the one place where unity is to be found in this world is in the body of Christ.

HOW CAN THE CHURCH BE IDENTIFIED TODAY?

Consider Its Beginning

One of the identifying marks of the New Testament church is the time of its beginning. Any church which began at a different time from the New Testament church is obviously not the New Testament church.

Three-fourths of the way through His personal ministry, Jesus promised, "I will build My church" (Matthew 16:18). He fulfilled His promise on the first Pentecost Day following His resurrection (Acts 2:41–47). From this Pentecost Day forward, the church is spoken of as being in existence throughout the rest of the New Testament (Acts 5:11; 7:38; 8:1, 3).

Suppose someone said, "My church started in the Old Testament." His church is too early. The Old Testament predicts the coming of the kingdom, but it does not record its establishment. Suppose someone said, "My church started during the third century A.D." His church is too late. This cannot be the New Testament church. The New Testament does not end looking for the establishment of the church some day in the future. Rather, it ends with the Roman Empire quaking under the mighty spread of the church throughout the world.

In general, the Protestant churches sprang into existence during the sixteenth century, during or after the Reformation. No denomination of any kind is found in the New Testament. The New Testament church was established, and then centuries later, as apostasies from the New Testament order began to occur, denominations were formed. The picture in the New Testament is that of people becoming Christians, living, and worshiping as the body of Christ long before any denominations came into existence.

As you consider a specific church, ask, "When was its actual beginning?" If it goes back to any time other than the time of the first Pentecost after our Lord's resurrection, it cannot be the New Testament church.

Consider Its Aim

Another identifying characteristic of the New Testament church is its purpose or aim. The New Testament church has no other goal in this world but to be the New Testament church. It does not seek to be similar to it, akin to it, or nearly it. It intends to be it!

When considering the question "Which is the New Testament church?" you may ask of a specific church, "What is its aim or purpose in this world?" The New Testament church was the body of Christ in the world. Paul said, "So we, who are many, are one body in Christ, and individually members one of another" (Romans 12:5). Any church that is not seeking to be the body of Christ in its community is simply not the New Testament church.

Christ did not ask His disciples to be a sect. He asked them to be His living body in the world. This body is to wear His name, worship together in His name, and do His work in the world for His glory.

Consider Its Practices

Still another identifying mark of the New Testament church is its practices. It is one thing to say that a church is the New Testament church, but it is quite another for that church to demonstrate its identity by its practices. Anyone can claim to be the New Testament church, but the proof of the claim is always in the practice.

The practices of the New Testament church are easily seen in the New Testament. The New Testament church met for worship every first day of the week and broke bread in remembrance of the Lord's death (Acts 20:7; 1 Corinthians 11:20; Hebrews 10:25). Christians would sing together, making melody in their hearts and edifying one another. The New Testament gives no indication that they used instrumental music in their worship, nor does it give any command to do so (Ephesians 5:19; Colossians 3:16). They gave of their material prosperity on the first day of each week for the carrying on of God's work and the helping of the poor (1 Corinthians 16:1, 2). They prayed together and considered God's will which was being revealed by inspired men (Acts 2:42). (See pages 250 through 254.) Practices such as venerating icons and using candles or incense in worship are not authorized and are not a part of the practice of a New Testament church. Each congregation of the New Testament church governed itself through overseers or elders (1 Timothy 3:1–7), looking to Jesus as the only head of the church. Deacons (1 Timothy 3:8–11) and evangelists (2 Timothy 4:1, 2) served the church under the oversight of the elders.

To identify the New Testament church, we must list the characteristic practices of the New Testament church and then compare this list with the churches we see around us. When we find a true match, when we find a church which follows the New Testament pattern, we have found the New Testament church, the Lord's church.

Consider Its Designations

Another identifying mark of the New Testament church is its designations. The descriptive phrases which are used for the New Testament church in the Bible set it apart from denominations.

The New Testament church is referred to in the New Testament as "the body of Christ" (Ephesians 4:12), "the church of God" (1 Corinthians 1:2), "the churches of Christ" (Romans 16:16), the "church of the firstborn" (Hebrews 12:23), "the kingdom of heaven" (Matthew 16:19), and simply "the church" (Ephesians 1:22). These phrases describe the nature and identity of the church. They are descriptions more than they are names.

What if you are considering a church which is known by a phrase or name which is not found in the New Testament? Surely we must admit that this is unacceptable. First, if this church is the New Testament church, why does it use a name for itself which is foreign to the New Testament? Second, if this church is the New Testament church, why does it not use a New Testament phrase for the church to indicate to all that it is the New Testament church? Third, it is possible for a New Testament church to be using a phrase foreign to the New Testament as a name without really thinking about it. Surely, when this is called to their attention, they will gladly change to the New Testament names so that no one will mistake them for something other than the New Testament church.

If a church wants to be the New Testament church, develops the characteristics of the New Testament church, and wants everyone to know that it is the New Testament church, it should apply to itself the names given in the New Testament for the New Testament church and only those.

CONCLUSION

The Holy Spirit's picture of the New Testament church reveals three striking attributes which set Christ's church apart from all other religious bodies for all time. First, His church is a group of people who have been obedient to His Word and who steadfastly abide in His inspired Word. Second, His church is characterized by compassion for each member, a loving concern which considers a needy member of the church of greater significance than even material concerns and treasures. Third, each person who enters Christ's church through the gospel is made one with Christ and with all the other members by the Holy Spirit and maintains that unity by his love and daily adherence to Christ's Word. The church is pictured as one family with one heart and life!

How, then, can we be Christ's church today? Two words suggest the method: "duplicate" and "dedicate." Let us duplicate the way of becoming a follower of Christ that is found in this lesson. These people heard Christ's Word as it was preached by Peter and cried, "What shall we do?" Peter told them, "Repent, and each of you be baptized in the name of Jesus Christ for the forgiveness of your sins ..." (Acts 2:38). Through the faith planted in them by the Word, they repented and were baptized for the forgiveness of their sins, and the Lord added them to His church. This is Christ's way of making people His own. When someone today follows this way, Christ will do for him what He did for them. He loves each of us even as He loved them; He died for us even as He died for them.

Let us obey Christ's Word and dedicate ourselves to living as His church. According to the picture in Acts 2, this should be done by holding to Christ's Word, living with the heart of Christ, and keeping the unity which the Holy Spirit has given to His church in Christ.

Now that we know what Christ's church looks like, let us make the decision to become Christ's church.

STUDY QUESTIONS
(answers on page 266)

1. Discuss the meaning of the phrase "continually devoting themselves to the apostles' teaching" (Acts 2:42). What does this phrase mean for us today?
2. Describe the type of unity which the Jerusalem church had.
3. How is the church of Christ supposed to look today?
4. Why is deciding which is the New Testament church a far-reaching decision?
5. List verses of Scripture which show that the New Testament church began on the Day of Pentecost in Acts 2.
6. When did denominations spring up?

7. Who composes the body of Christ—individual Christians or denominational churches? (See 1 Corinthians 12:24.)
8. Why should a church designate itself the same way the church in the New Testament is designated?
9. Should the practices of the New Testament church be followed today?

WORD HELPS

abide in Him—to love, study, and obey Jesus' teachings (John 8:30–32).

breaking bread—the taking of the Lord's Supper. (See Acts 2:42; 20:7.)

deacons—qualified men (1 Timothy 3:8–13) who are selected to serve the congregation. They serve under the elders (Philippians 1:1; Acts 20:28).

elders—mature Christian men who are selected to oversee local congregations (1 Timothy 3:1–7).

instrumental music—songs played on man-made devices such as string, wind, and brass instruments, keyboards, or drums. Such music is not mentioned in the New Testament in relation to the worship of the church. God wants singing to be part of our public worship (Hebrews 2:12b; Ephesians 5:19; Colossians 3:16). Singing in private devotions is encouraged in James 5:13.

Protestant—the name given to man-made religious groups whose faith and practice are based on the principles of the Protestant Reformation. The leaders of this movement "protested" against some Catholic practices (such as recognizing the authority of popes and priests). While this movement did reject some errors, the New Testament church must be based on God's Word—not on any reaction to what others may be practicing.

13

Special Words
For God's People

Have you ever tried to picture heaven based on the Bible's description? It will probably be very different from what we expect. Our heavenly home will surely be greater than what we imagine and more glorious than the earthly symbols of gold, glass, and pearl which are used to describe it.

The same was true for those who tried to picture what God's messengers were describing as a "kingdom" and a "church." These terms are used so often in the Scriptures that we probably cannot hope to understand God's plan of salvation without understanding these two words.

THE WORD "KINGDOM"

The kingdom of God is both foretold and revealed as a kingdom in the two testaments of the Bible. It was prophesied (foretold) in the Old Testament and in the early part of the New Testament, and it is presented as a reality on earth in Acts 2 and throughout the rest of the New Testament. Since the kingdom was sometimes portrayed in figures and symbols in prophecy, the reality of it is greater and more glorious than the picture of it given by the prophets. The prophetic picture was accurate, but it was veiled in mystery because of the figurative language which was used.

The word "kingdom" is significant in the New Testament as well as in the Old, but we are especially interested in its use in the New Testament. God's kingdom is presented in the New Testament as the fulfillment of Old Testament prophecies. One is at a loss to understand Christ's church without a thorough grasp of the use of this word in the Bible. (See Appendix 4 on page 281.)

Let us examine this word from three angles, each of which relates to its use in connection with the church which Christ established.

Its Political Use

The word "kingdom" is first used in the Bible in a political sense, in reference to the realm of one who is the supreme head, the sovereign, the powerful ruler of that realm.

The political use of the word "kingdom" is also illustrated by Jehovah's relationship with the nation of Israel. At first in Israel's history, God was their king. He was the Sovereign head of their government as well as the head of their religion. Israel's government at this time was a *theocracy*, a nation ruled by God. Moses and the sons of Israel, when they saw that God had destroyed the Egyptians in the Red Sea, sang, "The Lord shall reign forever and ever" (Exodus 15:18). As Israel encamped in front of Mount Sinai, the nation was told by the Lord, "Now then, if you will indeed obey My voice and keep My covenant, then you shall be My own possession among all the peoples, for all the earth is Mine; and you shall be to Me a kingdom of priests and a holy nation" (Exodus 19:5, 6a). Jehovah gave Israel the laws by which they were to live, and all justice and religious activities were administered in His name. He led Israel in her battles and received credit for her victories (Numbers 21:34). He was the King of Israel, and Israel, as a nation under His rule, was His domain.

During the days of Samuel, Israel, motivated by the desire to be like the nations around her, asked that God give her an earthly king. God granted the people's request and gave them Saul as their first king. The king of Israel was not to be a monarch in the strictest use of the term. He was responsible to Jehovah as an assistant ruler and a servant. His authority was to be limited by the law of Moses. He was to be the servant of Jehovah and was to serve as His earthly representative. He was to defend Israel against enemies, lead Israel in righteousness, and bind the nation together in unity.

A kingdom in the political sense, then, involved a king who was sovereign, a domain of some kind, subjects to rule, and laws made by the king to carry out his rule. Kingdoms could be large or small; they could involve a domain of physical land or a nomadic nation. The main idea in the word "kingdom" is the rule of a king and the obedience of the citizens to that king.

Its Prophetic Use
The word "kingdom" also has a prophetic use in

the Scriptures. This political term was used by the Holy Spirit to foretell the work which God purposed to do in the world in the last age of the world, the Christian Age.

A major Old Testament "kingdom" prophecy is found in Daniel 2. Daniel was guided by the Holy Spirit to write, "In the days of those kings the God of heaven will set up a kingdom which will never be destroyed, and that kingdom will not be left for another people; it will crush and put an end to all these kingdoms, but it will itself endure forever" (Daniel 2:44). Daniel's revelation taught important truths regarding the prophesied kingdom. First, it would be a special kingdom, or a kingly rule, set up by the God of heaven. Second, it would be a kingdom which would be eternal or unending. Third, it would be above all the other kingdoms of the world in power and endurance.

Moreover, prophecy concerning the coming of this kingdom of God had a place of central importance in the preaching of John the Baptist (Matthew 3:1, 2) and in the preaching and teaching of Jesus (Matthew 4:17). The gospel was spoken of by Christ as the gospel of the kingdom (Matthew 9:35). The twelve apostles and the Seventy (Luke 10:1–20) were sent out by Jesus to announce that the kingdom of heaven was at hand (Matthew 10:7; Luke 10:9). More than one-third of Jesus' parables unfold truths about the kingdom. Jesus taught His disciples to pray for the kingdom to come (Matthew 6:10).

Based upon how often John and Christ taught about the kingdom, several facts may be learned: First, the coming of the kingdom was of great significance in God's plan. Second, the coming of the kingdom was near, "breaking in," or "at hand." Third, the kingdom which was coming was clearly the fulfillment of Daniel's prophecy. Fourth, the arrival of the kingdom was God's work, not man's. Fifth, when it arrived, the kingdom could only be entered by people when God's conditions of entrance were met (John 3:5).

From Acts 2 forward, the kingdom is always spoken of as a reality, as being present. Jesus had said to Nicodemus, "Truly, truly, I say to you, unless one is born of water and the Spirit he cannot enter into the kingdom of God" (John 3:5). But of Philip's preaching Christ in Samaria, Luke wrote, "But when they believed Philip preaching the good news about the kingdom of God and the name of Jesus Christ, they were being baptized, men and women alike" (Acts 8:12). Philip could not have preached this message had the kingdom not been present.

The prophetic use of the word "kingdom," then, refers to the spiritual reign of God over those who have submitted to His will for the world. It refers to a reign and a realm—the reign being the spiritual reign of God over a life, and the realm being the spiritual sphere where that reign of God is evident. This kingly rule of Christ is included in the word "church": As one submits to the will of Christ by receiving the gospel, he is brought into the body of Christ, the church; and as he lives in submission to the head of the church, Christ Jesus, he lives in and as part of God's earthly kingdom. The kingly rule of Christ over people's hearts creates the church. "The kingdom of God" and "the church of Christ," then, are expressions which can have the same meaning, as Jesus revealed in Matthew 16:18, 19.

Its Present-Day Use

The political background, the prophetic use, and the New Testament reality of the word "kingdom" require a present-day, practical use of the word.

First, it should be used in the sense of *prophetic fulfillment*. The kingdom of which Daniel spoke has come. God's special work in the world in a form of kingly rule, a reign which involves a spiritual realm, is now present. Those who have bowed to the will of God have come under that kingly rule. The prophecies about God's coming kingdom have been fulfilled.

Second, we should use the word "kingdom" in the sense of *a present-day reality*. The kingdom of God is no longer something which is to come. Christ reigns now over those who have come into His church through obedient faith. In a sense, our prayer should no longer be "Your kingdom come," but "May I fully submit to Your will that You may reign over my life and that I might live in Your kingdom."

Third, we should use this word in reference to *an earthly part of God's heavenly rule*. God's specially chosen people, the church, are the earthly part of His kingdom. Jesus and the New Testament writers have shown that the church is the kingdom of God or the kingdom of Christ which has come. Submission to a king creates a citizenship, a kingdom. Jesus called this community of obedient believers His church (Matthew 16:18, 19).

Fourth, we should see this word in the context of *a spiritual rule*. Faithful Christians are under the spiritual rule of Christ today and expect to enter into a fuller and closer relationship with God, Christ, and the Holy Spirit in eternity to come. The church is the kingdom now, but its members look forward to the eternal kingdom which is to come. The word "kingdom" has a future meaning to it. Christ said, "Not everyone who says to Me, 'Lord, Lord,' will enter the kingdom of heaven . . ." (Matthew 7:21). Paul wrote, "The Lord will rescue me from every evil deed, and will bring me safely to His heavenly kingdom; to Him be the glory forever and ever. Amen" (2 Timothy 4:18). Paul was in the kingdom of God, but he looked forward to entering into the heavenly kingdom. He saw the kingdom as a fulfillment of prophecies in the Old and New Testaments, both as a present-day reality shown in the church which Christ built and a promise for eternity.

As one moves through the New Testament, he notices a decreasing use of the word "kingdom," whether it is "the kingdom of heaven," "the kingdom of God," or another phrase referring to the kingdom. References to the kingdom occur forty-nine times in Matthew, fifteen times in Mark, thirty-nine times in Luke, five times in John, eight times in Acts, fourteen times in Paul's Epistles, two times in the General Epistles, two times in Hebrews, and three times in Revelation. Hence, the word "kingdom" has a continued but decreasing use in the New Testament. (See Appendix 4 on page 281.)

Matthew is the only New Testament writer who uses "kingdom of heaven." Mark, Luke, and John only use "kingdom of God." While the use of the word "kingdom" decreases when one gets to Acts, the use of the term "church" increases. It is as if the term "kingdom" is replaced by the Holy Spirit with the word "church."

THE WORD "CHURCH"

A very special significance attaches to the word "church" because of its key relation to the entire New Testament message. "Church" is an English translation of a word which appears 114 times in the Greek New Testament. It is probably accurate to say that one cannot hope to understand Christ's way of salvation for the world today without understanding the use of this word in the New Testament.

Its Secular Use

The word was first of all a common, everyday word without any particular religious meaning.

A sample of this use surfaces in Acts 19 in connection with the riot which occurred in Ephesus. A disturbance regarding Christianity developed. The people rushed into a nearby theater, and confusion prevailed. The writer, Luke, said of their gathering, "So then, some were shouting one thing and some another, for the *assembly* was in confusion and the majority did not know for what reason they had come together" (Acts 19:32; emphasis mine).

The word used by Luke for the assembly in this verse is *ekklesia,* the word translated into English with our word "church." Finally, the town clerk spoke, saying,

> But if you want anything beyond this, it shall be settled in the lawful *assembly*. For indeed we are in danger of being accused of a riot in connection with today's events, since there is no real cause for it, and in this connection we will be unable to account for this disorderly gathering (Acts 19:39, 40; emphasis mine).

Luke then added, "After saying this he dismissed the *assembly*" (Acts 19:41; emphasis mine).

Three times in this account of a town meeting, Luke used the Greek word *ekklesia* (Acts 19:32, 39, 41). He used it to mean just a gathering, for the assembly he called an *ekklesia* in verses 32 and 41 is pictured as a mob in verse 30. The assembly or *ekklesia* in the theater was not called together; it just happened in all the confusion and flow of events. Luke also called a lawful assembly where legal matters are settled an *ekklesia* in verse 39.

In light of Luke's usage of *ekklesia*, it is best to think of the word, in its secular use, as referring to an assembly of any kind. Sometimes an assembly is convened or summoned together, and sometimes an assembly just happens. Luke called each of these types of assembly an *ekklesia*.

Some language experts today believe that the secular use of *ekklesia* in New Testament days had more the meaning of "just an assembly" than the meaning of "a called-out assembly." The use of this word by Luke in Acts 19 would seem to confirm their conclusions.

Luke's use of *ekklesia* gives us an insight into how this word was used in the secular world before our Lord used it in a religious sense. This background of the word will be a basis on which we can build a better understanding of our Lord's use of *ekklesia*.

Its Religious Use

The word *ekklesia* had also a religious use in the New Testament.

It is clear from the Old Testament that in the Jewish background to Christianity the concept of an

assembly of God's people is present. In the Septuagint, the Greek translation of the Old Testament
Scriptures, the "congregation" of Israel, which is
qahal in Hebrew, was translated into Greek with the
word *ekklesia*, especially when the "congregation"
consisted of Israel gathered before the Lord for religious purposes (Deuteronomy 18:16; 31:30; 1 Kings
8:65; Acts 7:38).

The word "synagogue" was also used originally
to refer to an assembly of people gathered together
for a specific purpose. Later, the word was applied
to an assembly of Christians who had gathered for
worship. James used both Greek words, *sunagoge* and
ekklesia, apparently because he had Jewish Christians
in mind as the readers of his book. He used *sunagoge*
for a congregation of Christians who had gathered
for worship (James 2:2), and he used *ekklesia* for the
body of believers in a given locality (James 5:14).

As our Lord selected a word that would designate
those who would be God's unique people through
His salvation, He chose the word "church" (Matthew
16:18), which probably meant an "assembly" in its
secular use, but an "assembly of God's people" in its
Old Testament use. Our Lord took a secular word
and gave it a special religious meaning. In His selec-
tion of this word, He drew from its secular and religious backgrounds and added new meanings of His
own. The word, in the use Jesus gave it, refers to the
universal people of God who have been redeemed
by Christ's blood, whether they are assembled or not
(Acts 8:3; Ephesians 1:22).

Another idea which is brought out in the New
Testament in connection with the word *ekklesia* is the
concept of one's being "called out" or "set apart."

While this thought was probably not in the common use of the word, it is an important part of the meaning in Christ's special use of it. This idea is projected into the word by the nature of the people designated.

Peter told the multitude on the Day of Pentecost, "For the promise is for you and your children and for all who are far off, as many as the Lord our God will call to Himself" (Acts 2:39). Paul told the Thessalonians to "walk in a manner worthy of the God who calls you into His own kingdom and glory" (1 Thessalonians 2:12). It was through the gospel that God had called them. Paul said, "It was for this He called you through our gospel, that you may gain the glory of our Lord Jesus Christ" (2 Thessalonians 2:14). Those people who were called to God through the gospel were called "the church" (1 Corinthians 1:1–3).

Furthermore, Paul told the church at Colossae, "For He rescued us from the domain of darkness, and transferred us to the kingdom of His beloved Son, in whom we have redemption, the forgiveness of sins" (Colossians 1:13, 14). Peter said to "proclaim the excellencies of Him who has called you out of darkness into His marvelous light" (1 Peter 2:9b). Peter also wrote, "But like the Holy One who called you, be holy yourselves also in all your behavior" (1 Peter 1:15).

Jesus used the word "church" to refer to all of God's people in the Christian Age without respect to locality or particular time. Although no Christian today is a member of the congregation which was established on Pentecost, all true Christians of all times and of all places are members of the same church of the Lord which was established on that day. The church was established once for all time in Jerusalem on the first Pentecost Day after Jesus' resurrection. It had but one birthday; it is not born again and again each century or after periods of apostasy.

Its Practical Use

We would expect the meaning given to the word "church" by Jesus and the Holy Spirit to be brought out in a practical way in the New Testament, and this we indeed find to be the case.

In practical use, inspired writers used the word "church" in four ways. First, they used it to refer to a congregation of God's people in a given locality. Paul wrote unto "the church of God" at Corinth, to those who had been sanctified in Christ Jesus (1 Corinthians 1:2). The church in Philippi was referred to as "the saints in Christ Jesus who are in Philippi" (Philippians 1:1). The saints in Thessalonica were referred to as "the church of the Thessalonians in God the Father and the Lord Jesus Christ" (1 Thessalonians 1:1). All the Christians in a given locality were called "the church" of that place. An expression of the universal church is the local congregation of Christians. When one becomes a member of Christ's church, he will be a part of the body of Christians where he lives.

Second, the inspired writers used "church" in talking about the local congregations of a region. Luke wrote, "So the church throughout all Judea and Galilee and Samaria enjoyed peace, being built up; and going on in the fear of the Lord and in the comfort of the Holy Spirit, it continued to increase" (Acts 9:31). Sometimes the church in a region was designated in the plural as "churches." Paul was writing to "the churches of Galatia" as he wrote the letter to the Galatians (Galatians 1:2). It would be a scriptural use of the word "church" to speak of the church in Europe or the churches in Europe.

Third, the New Testament writers used the word "church" to show how the church is made up. They used it regarding the type of people in the churches. Paul referred to "the Gentile churches" in Romans 16: "Greet Prisca and Aquila, my fellow workers in Christ Jesus, who for my life risked their own necks, to whom not only do I give thanks, but also all the churches of the Gentiles; also greet the church that is in their house . . ." (Romans 16:3–5).

Fourth, these inspired writers used the word "church" in reference to a congregation gathered for worship. The church exists when it is not assembled for worship, but the word "church" is used in a special way for the assembly of the church in a given locality. Paul referred to the Corinthians as a church when they assembled themselves together (1 Corinthians 11:18). He told women to keep silent in the churches: "The women are to keep silent in the churches; for they are not permitted to speak, but are to subject themselves, just as the Law also says" (1 Corinthians 14:34). He is obviously referring to the worship assembly of the church in this passage.

In whatever way one refers to the church, he is speaking of those who have been brought into the body of Christ by submission to the gospel of Christ. A Christian has been called out of the world and darkness and placed by God's grace into that body which Christ and the inspired writers of the New Testament called "the church."

CONCLUSION

Surely this brief study of the words God chose to refer to His people challenge us to enter His kingdom, His church. God took these secular words and, giving additional meaning to them, applied them to the people who are called into salvation through the gospel of His grace. These words refer to all who have submitted to the rule of God and have been redeemed by the blood of Christ. Through the long years of the Patriarchal and the Mosaical ages, God planned for His special people. He has fulfilled all that He inspired His messengers to foretell. Now it is up to you to enter His kingdom and be added to His church.

STUDY QUESTIONS
(answers on page 267)

1. Discuss God's relationship to Israel in terms of a king and a kingdom.
2. What responsibilities did Saul, the first king of Israel, have as the king over God's kingdom, Israel?
3. What lessons can be learned from Daniel's prophecy concerning the coming kingdom? (See Daniel 2:44.)
4. Notice the decreasing use of the word "kingdom" in the New Testament. What does this mean?
5. Explain how one can be in the kingdom of God today and yet look forward to the eternal kingdom. (See 2 Timothy 4:18.)
6. How often does the word "church" appear in the New Testament, and what significance does this suggest about the word?
7. Give the simple secular use of the word "church" as reflected in the New Testament. Name a verse where it is so used.
8. Does the word "church" in its secular sense always refer to a religious assembly? Does it always refer to a "called-

out" assembly, one that is called together for a special purpose?

WORD HELPS

bride of Christ—the church. The church's relationship to Christ is compared to a man's relationship with his wife. (See Ephesians 5:22–29.)

parables—Jesus often used stories from everyday life to illustrate spiritual truths (Matthew 13:34).

Patriarchal Age—one of three distinct periods in Bible history. The first was the Patriarchal Age, when God spoke directly to the heads of the families. The next was the Mosaical Age, when the children of Israel followed the Law given to Moses (including the Ten Commandments). This lasted until the death of Jesus on the cross. The final age is the Christian Age. In this age, all the saved are added to the church, and the New Testament is the only divine standard for doctrine and worship. This age will last until the second coming of Jesus.

prophecy—the inspired words of a prophet, viewed as a revelation of God's will; sometimes a prediction of the future made by divine inspiration.

Samuel—a great Old Testament prophet, priest, and judge.

sovereign—a king or other ruler, one who has the greatest of power. In 1 Timothy 6:14, 15, the Lord Jesus Christ is said to be "the blessed and only Sovereign, the King of kings and Lord of lords."

THE NEW TESTAMENT CHURCH

FOUNDER: CHRIST Matthew 16:18	WHERE: JERUSALEM Isaiah 2:3; Acts 2:5, 47	WHEN: A.D. 33 Acts 2	HEAD: CHRIST Ephesians 1:22
ORGANIZATION Philippians 1:1	**ELDERS:** Tit. 1:5; 1 Pet. 5:1–3; Acts 20:28; 1 Tim. 3:1–7; **DEACONS:** Acts 6:1–6; 1 Tim. 3:8–13; **MEMBERS:** Acts 2:41–47; Col. 1:13; 1 Cor. 1:2		
DESIGNATIONS FOR THE CHURCH Ephesians 3:15	**THE CHURCH:** Col. 1:18, 24; **THE BODY OF CHRIST:** Eph. 1:22, 23; **THE KINGDOM:** Acts 8:12; **THE CHURCHES OF CHRIST:** Rom. 16:16; **THE CHURCH OF GOD:** 1 Cor. 1:2; Acts 20:28; **THE FAMILY OF GOD:** Eph. 2:19; 1 Tim. 3:15; **DISCIPLES OF THE LORD:** Acts 9:1; **THE TEMPLE OF GOD:** 1 Cor. 3:16; **THE CHURCH OF THE FIRSTBORN:** Heb. 12:23		
DESIGNATIONS FOR CHRISTIANS Ephesians 3:15	**DISCIPLES:** Acts 11:26; **SAINTS:** 1 Cor. 1:2; Phil. 1:1; **CHILDREN OF GOD:** Gal. 3:26; 1 Jn. 2:1; **BRETHREN:** Lk. 8:21; Gal. 6:1; **CHRISTIANS:** Acts 11:26; 26:28; 1 Pet. 4:16		
CREED	**JESUS CHRIST:** Mt. 16:16–18; Acts 8:37		
RULE OF FAITH AND PRACTICE: WORD OF GOD	**ALL POWER:** Mt. 28:18–20; Rom. 1:16; Heb. 4:12; **CHURCH GOVERNMENT:** 2 Tim. 3:16, 17; 2 Pet. 1:3; **SEED OF THE KINGDOM:** Mt. 13:3; Lk. 8:11; **SWORD OF THE SPIRIT:** Eph. 6:17		
WORSHIP	**SINGING:** Col. 3:16; **PRAYER:** 1 Thess. 5:17; **TEACHING:** Acts 20:7; **COMMUNION:** Acts 20:7; 1 Cor. 11:23; **CONTRIBUTION:** 1 Cor. 16:1, 2		
MISSION	**SAVE SOULS:** Mt. 28:18–20; Jn. 6:45; Eph. 3:10; 1 Tim. 4:16		
WARNING	**ABIDE IN THE TRUTH:** Gal. 1:6–8; Mt. 15:9, 13; 2 Cor. 11:3; Rev. 22:18, 19; 2 Jn. 9		

14

The Divine Designations Of the Church

A careful reading of the New Testament reveals that the church was created to be a special organism. It is, therefore, referred to in special ways by the inspired writers. These references can be divided into three groups. They are used with specific meaning, to express function, ownership, and relationship. They were given by divine direction and fulfill a divine purpose.

The phrases used by the Holy Spirit to refer to the church should not be thought of as mere illustrations.[1] The New Testament calls the faithful followers of Christ His "church," His "body," and His "kingdom." These divine designations[2] identify, character-

---

[1] The church is often illustrated in the New Testament, for example, as a sheepfold (John 10:1), a vineyard (Matthew 20:1), or a precious pearl (Matthew 13:45, 46). Such images help us to understand the church better; but they are only illustrations, not ways to identify the church.

[2] "Designations," as used here, means the biblical ways of referring to the church.

ize, and describe the church which the Lord established. Consider them carefully.

DESIGNATIONS OF FUNCTION

Some designations given to the church in the New Testament relate to the function of the church as a body, a living thing. These designations highlight what the Lord's church is in purpose, design, and action.

What Christ established is referred to simply as "the church" (Colossians 1:18, 24). This phrase means "an assembly of people who have become followers of the Lord." These people are referred to in an assembled sense (1 Corinthians 11:18), a local sense (1 Corinthians 1:2), a regional sense (1 Corinthians 16:1), and a universal sense (Ephesians 5:23). This designation declares the basic meaning of what Christ established—a group of people redeemed by His blood who live for Him, worship Him, and do His work.

Individual members of the church are called "Christians," since they are trying to be like Christ. (The word "Christian" means "Christ-like.") The name Christian was first given to the disciples at Antioch (Acts 11:26). The circumstances of the giving of this name are unclear, but we can be certain that God chose it for His people. As a name, it is found three times in the New Testament (Acts 11:26; 26:28; 1 Peter 4:16).

The Bible also refers to members of the church as "saints," those who have been sanctified. These are people who have been set apart as God's chosen ones. Paul addressed the Ephesians by saying, "Paul, an apostle of Christ Jesus by the will of God, to *the saints* who are at Ephesus and who are faithful in Christ Jesus" (Ephesians 1:1; emphasis mine). The King James Version of the Bible has "peculiar people" in Titus 2:14. The New Testament in the back of this book says "a people for His own possession." The basic meaning of "holy" or "saint" is "set apart for God." God's church is "a people for God's own possession," a holy people, a people set apart for God. Christians have been called with a holy calling (2 Timothy 1:9); they are to live in holy conduct and godliness (2 Peter 3:11); they seek to appear before Him on the last day "holy and blameless and beyond reproach" (Colossians 1:22b).

Some translations of the Bible have "Saint" in the titles of the Gospels of Matthew, Mark, Luke, and John, and have entitled Revelation "The Revelation of St. John the Divine." These titles to these New Testament books came from man, not God. The New Testament labels everyone in Christ as a "saint." The church is even referred to as "the churches of the saints" (1 Corinthians 14:33). People are set apart for God when they become Christians.

In addition, the church is referred to as the "body" of Christ (Ephesians 1:22, 23). This term is sometimes used as an illustration of what the church is like in function (1 Corinthians 12:12–27) and sometimes to indicate what the church actually is, as a term of identification. When used as a designation, the phrase "body of Christ" stresses the function as well as the relationship of the church: The church is the spiritual body of Christ on earth, and it is related to Christ as a body is to its head. In this spiritual body of Christ, individual Christians are said to function as "members" of the body, each Christian being a member of it and working as part of the body. Paul wrote of the church at Corinth, "Now you are Christ's body, and individually members of it" (1 Corinthians 12:27). The church is also referred to as "the kingdom" (Acts 8:12). Sometimes the expression used is "the kingdom of heaven" (Matthew 16:18, 19), and sometimes it is "the kingdom of God" (John 3:3). Both phrases reflect the spiritual nature of the dominion and rule of the church/kingdom (John 18:36). The church is a group of followers of Christ who have submitted to the rule of God upon earth. Christ is King and is now reigning over His kingdom, the church (1 Corinthians 15:24, 25). Consequently, the church has a divine head, or king, and it is governed by divine authority. Members of the church have bowed to the authority of King Jesus and are living as "citizens" of His spiritual kingdom (Philippians 3:20), though they dwell on earth.

Those who are part of the kingdom of God are likewise described as "citizens" of the kingdom of heaven (Matthew 16:18, 19). Paul said, "For our citizenship is in heaven, from which also we eagerly wait for a Savior, the Lord Jesus Christ" (Philippians 3:20). He also wrote, "So then you are no longer strangers and aliens, but you are fellow citizens with the saints, and are of God's household, having been built on the foundation of the apostles and prophets, Christ Jesus Himself being the corner stone" (Ephesians 2:19, 20). Christ is our King (1 Corinthians 15:24, 25), and only those who live under Christ's rule are in His kingdom (Matthew 7:21).

Christians are citizens in the eternal kingdom of which Daniel spoke in the Old Testament (Daniel 2:44). The writer of Hebrews described it as an "unshakable" kingdom: "Therefore, since we receive a kingdom which cannot be shaken, let us show gratitude . . ." (Hebrews 12:28). The next time you ask yourself where you will be one thousand years from today, if you are a Christian, you can tell yourself, "I will be in the eternal kingdom!" God's kingdom is not here today and gone tomorrow—it is eternal.

DESIGNATIONS OF OWNERSHIP

Three ways of referring to the church in the New Testament emphasize the possession-type of relationship that the church has to God and Christ. These phrases suggest ownership and leadership.

First, the church is referred to as "the church of Christ." In Paul's conclusion to his letter to the Romans, he sent greetings from the churches of Achaia: "All the churches of Christ greet you" (Romans 16:16b). This designation emphasizes the ownership and the identity of the church. The church is the church of Christ because Christ founded it, purchased it, owns it, and serves as its head. When one is converted to Christ, he belongs to Christ (1 Corinthians 6:20). He becomes so completely identified with Christ that he is called a Christian, a follower of Christ (Acts 11:26; 26:28; 1 Peter 4:16). The special assembly of followers of Christ, then, is called the church of Christ to show who the church is, who owns it, and who is part of it.

Second, the church is referred to as "the church of God" (1 Corinthians 1:2). If the church is referred to in the New Testament as the church of Christ, we would also expect it to be referred to as the church of God, for Jesus said that He and His Father are one (John 10:30). God planned the church before the foundation of the world (Ephesians 3:10, 11). He sent Christ into the world to prepare for the church (Matthew 16:18) and to purchase it with His blood (Acts 20:28). Just as God was in Christ at the cross reconciling the world to Himself (2 Corinthians 5:19), even so God was with Christ in the founding and purchasing of the church.

Third, members of the church are described as "slaves" or "servants." Those who submit to Christ and obey Him are servants. When the New Testament was written, the slave/master relationship was part of the society of the Roman Empire. A slave was totally under the control of his master. He had no rights and no real possessions. He did not even own himself. No wonder this term and relationship is used to illustrate our surrender to Christ and our life under His Word. Paul wrote, "If I were still trying to please men, I would not be a bond-servant of Christ" (Galatians 1:10b; see Philippians 1:1). He further said, "We are destroying speculations and every lofty thing raised up against the knowledge of God, and we are taking every thought captive to the obedience of Christ" (2 Corinthians 10:5).

Christians—those who claim Christ as their Master—can no longer be masters over their own lives. They must "crucify" their own wills. That is, they must destroy their own sinful human desires and put God's commands first in their lives. Paul said, "But may it never be that I would boast, except in the cross of our Lord Jesus Christ, through which the world has been crucified to me, and I to the world" (Galatians 6:14). He further said, "From now on let no one cause trouble for me, for I bear on my body the brand-marks of Jesus" (Galatians 6:17).

DESIGNATIONS OF RELATIONSHIP

Several ways in which the New Testament refers to the church stress the idea of relationship. This is to be expected, since being a member of the Lord's church involves various relationships.

In addition to the slave/master relationship and the body/head relationship which have already been mentioned, the word "Christian" itself expresses the beautiful relationship which church members have to their Lord. They are His followers; they live for Him and wear His name. The apostle Paul described his religious life after becoming a Christian in the now famous words "For to me, to live is Christ and to die is gain" (Philippians 1:21). Christ was not just first in Paul's life—Christ *was* his life! The sum and substance of Paul's life was Christ. He was truly a Christian.

The New Testament also describes the church as "the family of God." Paul said that Christians are "of God's household" (Ephesians 2:19). He told Timothy that he was writing to him so that he might know how to conduct himself in "the household of God, which is the church of the living God" (1 Timothy 3:15). At the time of one's conversion to Christ, God adopts him as His child, giving him family privileges and making him an heir of eternal life along with Christ (Romans 8:15–17; Ephesians 1:5). Christians have a heavenly Father to pray to and a loving Savior—an elder brother, Jesus—to pray through. As brothers and sisters, they love, help, and encourage each other (Acts 2:44).

Members of the church are referred to as "the children of God." They have a special relationship with God; He is their Father, and they are His children. When believers are baptized into Christ, they are adopted as God's "sons" (Ephesians 1:5). As His children, Christians have an eternal inheritance (Ephesians 1:11) and the strength and support of God's earthly family (1 Timothy 3:15; Ephesians 2:19–22). In this spiritual, heavenly family, God is the Father (Matthew 6:9), Jesus is the elder brother (Romans 8:17), and all Christians are brothers and sisters (2 Peter 3:15; 1 John 2:8–11).

God has a special love for His children (1 John 3:1). He protects them from Satan and provides for their daily needs. Jesus taught that if an earthly father gives good gifts to his children, then the children of Almighty God—the perfect Father in heaven—can expect Him to give them even more beautiful gifts when they ask Him! (See Matthew 7:11.)

Members of the early church considered each other not only brethren, but also friends (2 Peter 3:15; 3 John 15) who stand together in a beautiful comradeship. Christians are the highest type of friends.

John concluded his third epistle by writing, "Peace be to you. The friends greet you. Greet the friends by name" (3 John 15). He called the Christians around him "friends," and he called the Christians who would be receiving the letter "friends." Jesus called His disciples friends, and John is no doubt using this term after Jesus' example. Jesus had said to His disciples,

> Greater love has no one than this, that one lay down his life for his friends. You are My friends if you do what I command you. No longer do I call you slaves, for the slave does not know what his master is doing; but I have called you friends, for all things that

I have heard from My Father I have made known
to you (John 15:13–15).

Someone has said, "A friend is someone who stays
with you when everyone else leaves." Jesus is this
type of friend. When no one else could help us, He
laid down His life for us. Christians are to be this
type of friend to each other (1 John 3:16). Christians
are "friends."

The first-century church was often referred to as
"the disciples of the Lord" (Acts 9:1), or simply "disciples" (Acts 9:26; 11:26). The word "disciple" means
learner or follower; it suggests the continual relationship which exists between the Christian and his Lord.
A disciple is one who has committed himself to
someone greater than he, one who has learned from
the greater one, and one who continuously seeks to
learn more from the greater one through instruction
and imitation. He is not just a listener; he is a learner, an understudy. His Lord is his Master, his Teacher (John 13:13).

The word "disciple" is especially used in the
Gospels, appearing 238 times in them. It is found
twenty-eight times in Acts, and it does not appear in
the Epistles or Revelation. Perhaps the reason for the
obvious change in terminology as we go from the
Gospels to Acts to the Epistles is that during Christ's
life on earth, His followers were called "disciples"
in reference to Him. Afterwards, in Acts, the Epistles,
and Revelation, they were called "saints" in reference
to their holy calling or "brethren" in relation to one
another.

In the Great Commission given to His apostles
before His ascension, Christ commanded, "Go there-

fore and make disciples of all the nations, baptizing them in the name of the Father and the Son and the Holy Spirit, teaching them to observe all that I commanded you; and lo, I am with you always, even to the end of the age" (Matthew 28:19, 20). In this way, He gave a continuing use to the word "disciple," even though it is not often seen in the latter part of the New Testament.

A disciple is a doer of the Word. James said, "But prove yourselves doers of the word, and not merely hearers . . ." (James 1:22). A disciple is more than a student; he is an imitator of Christ, a follower of Christ.

From another viewpoint, the New Testament church is called "the temple of God." Paul said to the Christians at Corinth, "Do you not know that you are a temple of God and that the Spirit of God dwells in you?" (1 Corinthians 3:16). The church as an assembly of Christians forms a dwelling place for God. God's sanctuary today is a living body, the church. Individual Christians are called "saints" because they are set apart by the gospel to do sacred work and to provide a dwelling place for God (1 Corinthians 1:2).

In one passage, the New Testament refers to the church as the "church of the firstborn" (Hebrews 12:23). The church sustains a unique relationship with the future because each member of the church is "enrolled in heaven." The future for the Christian does not hold fear and dread because of the eternal hope Christ gives him. These relationship-type designations give insight into what the church is and how the church should live. They tell Christians how to live on earth and tell how the saved will be with God in the future.

CONCLUSION

God changed Abram's name to Abraham because the name Abram no longer fit him. Abram was told that he would be the father of a multitude (Genesis 17:5). The name Abram means "exalted father." Abram was a meaningful name, but it did not represent the future Abram would have. The name Abraham means "father of a multitude," the right name for a man who would father a nation of people. The designation God gave to Abraham meant something to God and to Abraham. Even so, the designations God gave to the church mean something to God, and they should mean much to us.

There are proper ways to refer to the New Testament church, and they should be used. We confuse the identity of the church by using nonbiblical designations for it. If a group of people seek to be the New Testament church and want to be known as the New Testament church, they should use the designations given in the New Testament for the church. A church can call itself the New Testament church and not be the New Testament church; but if it truly is the New Testament church, it should refer to itself with the proper New Testament language.

The commitment to being God's church today must be shown even in the way members designate and describe themselves. Using the designations that God used for His church is at least a beginning place for Christians who are trying to practice in their lives what God wants His church to be and to do. When Christians call themselves what God called the church, they are setting themselves on the right path, going toward what God wants them to be and become. (See Appendix 3 on page 279.)

STUDY QUESTIONS
(answers on page 268)

1. How is the word "kingdom" used in the New Testament in connection with the church?
2. Why does Paul refer to the church as "the church of Christ"? What other designation for the church suggests ownership?
3. Why should we use the designations for the church that are given in the New Testament?
4. What is accomplished when we refer to the church the way the Bible does?
5. Why is the church called "the family of God"?
6. What is the basic meaning of the word "Christian"? How does one live when he lives as a Christian?
7. How did Paul describe his life as a Christian in Philippians 1:21?
8. What does it mean to be a "child of God"? Give characteristics of this relationship with God.
9. How often does the word "disciple" appear in the New Testament?
10. Give the characteristics of a disciple.
11. Give the basic meaning of the word "saint." When does a person become a "saint"? What are the characteristics of a saint?

15

Christ, the Head Of the Church

An old story tells of a group of boys who came running into a store. They bought a few things and rushed out. Within minutes they topped the hill just beyond the store and went out of sight. A few minutes later, another boy came running into the store, out of breath. He excitedly asked the store clerk, "Have you seen a group of boys come by?" The store clerk said, "Yes. They were here not more than fifteen minutes ago. They were in a big hurry and didn't stay long." The boy said, "Which way did they go? I'm their leader!"

This boy, the group's leader, is an example of the kind of leadership all of us have seen too often—a leadership which is not out front leading but is behind wondering which way the followers went! The trouble with human leadership is its frailty and faults. Human leadership, at some time or other, brings disappointment. People are always going to be people.

Does the church also have poor leadership at

times? Does the ship bound for heaven have a captain who is subject to human weakness and failures? As the church journeys from earth to the eternal shore of the great forever, must its members depend upon a broken compass?

Such fears are relieved by the words of inspiration which assert that the head of the church is none other than Jesus Christ. Paul wrote, "Christ also is the head of the church, He Himself being the Savior of the body" (Ephesians 5:23–25). He is the head of the church because He loved it and died for it. Jesus has a right to lead the church because of His great sacrifice. Let the phrase "Christ also is the head of the church" enter deeply into your thinking. Seeing Christ as the head of the church gives assurance to those who are members of Christ's church, for it reminds them of the unerring guidance they receive. It should also be a reason for non-Christians to enter the church—so that they might come under the infallible leadership of Christ.

Let us contemplate the reassuring theme of "Christ, the Head of the Church," by considering the ways in which He is the head of the church.

HE IS THE HEAD IN AUTHORITY

First, Christ is the head of the church in authority. He is the Lord, and He leads by His law.

After His resurrection from the dead and His ascension to heaven, Christ was seated at God's right hand in the heavenly places, "far above all rule and authority and power and dominion, and every name that is named, not only in this age but also in the one to come" (Ephesians 1:21). God "put all things in subjection under His feet, and gave Him as head over

all things to the church, which is His body . . ."
(Ephesians 1:22, 23). Paul emphasized this same truth
in Colossians, when he said, "He is also head of the
body, the church; and He is the beginning, the firstborn from the dead, so that He Himself will come to
have first place in everything. For it was the Father's
good pleasure for all the fullness to dwell in Him"
(Colossians 1:18, 19). According to the writer of Hebrews, God will speak to us through His Son during
the last days, or the Christian dispensation (Hebrews
1:1, 2). He has highly exalted Jesus and has bestowed
on Him the name which is above every name, "so
that at the name of Jesus every knee will bow, of those
who are in heaven and on earth and under the earth,
and that every tongue will confess that Jesus Christ
is Lord . . ." (Philippians 2:10, 11). The Scriptures
assure us that Christ will reign as head of the church
or king of the kingdom until the end of time, and
then, when all rule, authority, and power are abolished, He will deliver the kingdom to God the Father
(1 Corinthians 15:23, 24).

Jesus' church lives under His authority and leadership. Even in a "me"-focused age, people in Christ's
church cannot demand their own way. They cannot
say "Me first" and acknowledge Jesus as Lord at the
same time. Every decision a Christian makes is a
spiritual decision, guided by obedience to His Lordship.

HE IS THE HEAD IN EXAMPLE
Second, Christ is the head of the church in ex-
ample. He is a perfect pattern in obedience to God.
He leads by His sinless life.

Peter said that Christ committed no sin, and no

deceit was found in His mouth. When He was reviled, He did not revile in return. When suffering, He uttered no threats (1 Peter 2:21–23).

Christ never needed to apologize for a mistake He had made. No need ever arose for Him to retract a misspoken word. His heart never knew a sinful thought. His enemies scrutinized His life but were unable to find a single sin.

The head of the church is perfect in character even as He is perfect in authority. His church is to heed His commands and imitate His life. John wrote, "The one who says he abides in Him ought himself to walk in the same manner as He walked" (1 John 2:6). Because of the unique leadership Jesus gives to the church, Paul could charge others, "Be imitators of me, just as I also am of Christ" (1 Corinthians 11:1).

From one viewpoint, Christ *became* our perfect Savior. By living a perfect life before God, He became perfectly qualified to be our Savior and could offer to God a sinless life for the atonement (payment) for sin. The writer of Hebrews argued, "Although He was a Son, He learned obedience from the things which He suffered. And having been made perfect, He became to all those who obey Him the source of eternal salvation" (Hebrews 5:8, 9).

Nathaniel Hawthorne wrote the story "The Great Stone Face" which reminds us that we become what we behold; we imitate what we admire. A gracious face, chiselled in the side of a mountain, overlooked a valley where a village of oppressed people lived. The community believed that someone with a face similar to the great stone face would one day come as their deliverer. A boy of the village continually thought about the stone face with aspiration and desire. In time, through his beholding and admiring the stone face, the youth grew into the likeness of the face, and the community soon recognized him as their deliverer.

The truth that we become what we behold is especially true of the church. Paul said, "But we all, with unveiled face, beholding as in a mirror the glory of the Lord, are being transformed into the same image from glory to glory, just as from the Lord, the Spirit" (2 Corinthians 3:18).

The church of Christ looks to His life as a model of how to live. He is our head in example. Not only do its members look at Him, but they also look unto Him (Hebrews 12:2) as He ever leads the church with His perfect life.

HE IS THE HEAD IN LOVE

Third, Christ is the head of the church in love. He leads and commands His people with His wonderful love.

The evening before His death, Jesus told His disciples, "A new commandment I give to you, that you love one another, *even as I have loved you*, that you also love one another. By this all men will know that you are My disciples, if you have love for one another" (John 13:34, 35; emphasis mine). He further told them, "This is My commandment, that you love one another, *just as I have loved you*" (John 15:12; emphasis mine).

This love which Christ shows for people leads His followers in three ways. First, it causes them *to love Him*. John said, "We love, because He first loved us" (1 John 4:19). Second, His love causes Christians *to love each other*. John wrote, "We know love by this, that He laid down His life for us; and we ought to lay down our lives for the brethren" (1 John 3:16). Third, His love causes His followers *to do His will.* Christ said, "If you love Me, you will keep My commandments" (John 14:15).

As the angels watched the earthly ministry of Christ, they must have been in awe. The day before His death on the cross, He took a basin and a towel, and in love and humility washed His disciples' feet! The King of kings knelt before His disciples in loving service. Christ not only became a man, but He became a servant of men. He took the form of a man and lived the life of a bondservant (Philippians 2:7).

John introduced this important scene with these words: "Jesus, knowing that the Father had given all things into His hands, and that He had come forth from God and was going back to God" (John 13:3). At a time when Christ was especially conscious of His authority, position, and future, He condescended (lowered Himself) to do the work of a servant in harmony with the life of a servant which He had lived. He did not flaunt His supremacy and strength, His power and position. In love, He used it to teach His disciples the lesson of humility.

As the head of the church, He lovingly serves with His power and authority! He did not relinquish His position as Lord when He washed the disciples' feet; He used His position as Lord to serve them and to build in them the spirit of service. He said to them, "You call Me Teacher and Lord; and you are right, for so I am. If I then, the Lord and the Teacher, washed your feet, you also ought to wash one another's feet. For I gave you an example that you also should do as I did to you" (John 13:13–15).

Jesus has portrayed in the highest possible way what love is and how true love is manifested. He leads His church with His love. As Christians live in the atmosphere of His love, breathe that atmosphere, and respond to it, they are remade into His image. No wonder John said, "Beloved, let us love one another, for love is from God; and everyone who loves is born of God and knows God. The one who does not love does not know God, for God is love" (1 John 4:7, 8).

CONCLUSION

Assuredly, Christ is the head of the church in authority, in example, and in love and service. He leads His church through His Lordship, through His perfect life, and through His compelling love.

The head of any organization or body should give the credibility, authenticity, and strength he possesses to the organization or body he leads. This is certainly true of Christ and the church. The Christ, the divine Son of God, gives His spotless perfection, infinite wisdom, matchless integrity, and almighty strength to the church with His headship and leadership.

The church of Christ was founded by Christ, is led by Christ, and wears Christ's name. Whatever Christ possesses, He imparts to His church; whatever future Christ has, the church has. He promises to sustain His church today and to sanctify her for her future, "that He might present to Himself the church in all her glory, having no spot or wrinkle or any such thing; but that she would be holy and blameless" (Ephesians 5:27).

If Christ has created the church, imparted to the

church His love and salvation, and has crowned the church with His promise of eternal glory, who would not want to be in His church?

Are you part of the church led by Christ?

STUDY QUESTIONS
(answers on page 268)

1. Give examples of leadership that does not really lead.
2. How is Jesus the head of the church in authority? Give passages of Scripture which teach that Jesus has all authority.
3. How long is Christ to reign as head of the church? (See 1 Corinthians 15:23–25.)
4. How did Jesus become our perfect Savior? (See Hebrews 5:8, 9.)
5. Conversion to Christ is an event in time, but transformation into His image is a process over time. Discuss this process of transformation. (See 2 Corinthians 3:18.)
6. What does Christ's washing of the disciples' feet teach us about daily living for Christ?
7. How do Christians "wash each other's feet" today?

WORD HELPS

purchased—bought. When we say that Christians have been "purchased by the blood of Christ," this refers to the death of Jesus on the cross for our sins.

transformed—changed. The Christian is to change in order to take on a new character in the image of Jesus. Romans 12:2 says, "And do not be conformed to this world, but be transformed by the renewing of your mind, so that you may prove what the will of God is, that which is good and acceptable and perfect."

16
How Do You Enter the Church?

Some things are expensive but are not really valuable—like fine clothing; some things are inexpensive but valuable—like sunshine or rain; some things are very expensive and very valuable—the church of Christ falls into this category.

The New Testament leaves little doubt about the priceless worth of the church. Its value is brought out in at least three ways: First, we see its worth in *its divine origin.* It was planned and purposed in the eternal counsel of heaven (Ephesians 3:10, 11), and it was prepared for through the earthly ministry of Jesus (Matthew 4:17). It was a divine forethought, not a mistaken afterthought. Second, we see its worth in *its precious cost.* We are told by Paul that it was purchased by the blood of Christ (Acts 20:28). The ultimate purpose of the death of Christ was to bring the church into existence. If purchase price indicates value, then the church, having been purchased by Christ's blood, is certainly the most valuable of all earthly bodies. Third, we see its worth in *the great value* that is placed upon it. Christ urged us to seek the kingdom of heaven above all other pursuits. He said, "Again, the kingdom of heaven is like a merchant seeking fine pearls, and upon finding one pearl of great value, he went and sold all that he had and bought it" (Matthew 13:45, 46). He not only likened the church to a precious pearl, but He likened it to the most precious of all pearls!

This supreme value of the church suggests that ignoring the New Testament church would be the greatest of all mistakes. A millionaire is like an orphan if he does not find and enter the Lord's church. The greatest man outside of the church becomes the least of men.

In light of the unmistakable worth of the church, reason dictates that we sincerely ask, "How is the church entered?" Perhaps no greater question can be considered. Let us devote ourselves to finding the New Testament answer to this question.

THE ANSWER ANNOUNCED

Christ was definite about what He wanted His disciples to do after He returned to heaven from His earthly ministry. Three rather full accounts of His commission are recorded in the New Testament (Matthew 28:18–20; Mark 16:15, 16; Luke 24:46, 47). The significance of these accounts can hardly be overestimated. They give Christ's guidance for His disciples for the entire Christian Age.

Christ first gave a worldwide charge to His disciples, by saying, "Go into all the world and preach the gospel to all creation" (Mark 16:15). Second, He specified the conditions upon which salvation is to be offered as the gospel is preached. He told His disciples what to do—"Go," and He told them what to say—"Preach the gospel." With the words "go" and "gospel," He summarized their future work.

One time, according to Mark, Christ gave the commission and emphasized the condition of belief. He said, "Go into all the world and preach the gospel to all creation. He who has believed and has been baptized shall be saved; but he who has disbelieved shall be condemned" (Mark 16:15, 16). Baptism is clearly mentioned as a condition in this record of the commission, but the emphasis seems to be upon belief.

According to Luke, Christ gave the commission at another time and stressed repentance. He said, "Thus it is written, that the Christ would suffer and rise again from the dead the third day, and that repentance for[1] forgiveness of sins would be proclaimed in His name to all the nations, beginning from Jerusalem" (Luke 24:46, 47). Repentance, a turning from sin to God, was to be a main idea in the gospel preaching of the Christian Age.

Matthew pictured Christ as giving the commission on a mountain in Galilee, where He emphasized baptism. He said, "All authority has been given to Me in heaven and on earth. Go therefore and make disciples of all the nations, baptizing them in the name of the Father and the Son and the Holy Spirit, teaching them to observe all that I commanded you; and lo, I am with you always, even to the end of the age" (Matthew 28:18–20).

Obviously, then, the three conditions upon which salvation is to be extended are belief, repentance,

---

[1]Some manuscripts read "and" here instead of "for."

and baptism, each of which was singled out by our Savior and stressed in the three accounts of the Great Commission.

These three conditions are evident and are easily perceived. No one can take seriously Jesus' commission without acknowledging these conditions and recognizing their significance in the Lord's plan. They constitute the terms or conditions of entrance into the Lord's kingdom or church. They are to govern the entire Christian Age.

THE ANSWER AMPLIFIED

The conditions of salvation are not only unmistakably given in the New Testament, but they are also clearly illustrated in the Acts of the Apostles.

For example, the book begins with the thrilling story of the establishment of the church. In Acts 2 a multitude of people who were convicted by Peter's sermon cried out, "What shall we do?" Belief in Jesus had prompted their crying out. Peter commanded them to repent and be baptized for the forgiveness of sins (Acts 2:38). Three thousand were baptized that day (Acts 2:41). Accordingly, Acts 2:47b says, "And the Lord was adding to their number day by day those who were being saved." The group to which they were added is later referred to as the church (Acts 5:11). Our Lord, in His final commission, had specified belief (faith), repentance, and baptism as the conditions upon which salvation was to be proclaimed. The people who entered the church on Pentecost complied with these three conditions.

Another example is found in Acts 8. In the latter part of Acts 8, Philip was told by an angel to go south for further preaching (Acts 8:26). At a certain intersection, Philip saw an Ethiopian eunuch traveling down the road in a chariot (Acts 8:27, 28). This man was a very religious man, but he was not yet a Christian. Philip was instructed by the Holy Spirit to go near and join the Ethiopian (Acts 8:29). Running to him, he discovered that the Ethiopian was reading in the Book of Isaiah but did not understand what he was reading (Acts 8:31). Philip started with the passage which the Ethiopian had been reading and unfolded to him the story of Christ (Acts 8:35), telling him, no doubt, all about Christ's coming into this world and dying for our sins.

As they traveled along, talking about Christ, they came to some water. The Ethiopian asked, "Can I be baptized?" Since the Ethiopian believed, it was appropriate for him to be baptized.[2] They stopped the chariot and waded down into the water, and Philip immersed the Ethiopian (Acts 8:38). Following his baptism, the Ethiopian went on his way rejoicing.

Once again, the terms our Lord laid down for salvation in His final commission were followed. Belief in Christ became a reality as a result of the preaching done by Philip (Acts 8:35, 36). The Ethio-

---

[2]Verse 37 of Acts 8 does not appear in many reliable manuscripts of Acts. This has led to the conclusion that this verse may not be part of the original text of the New Testament. It must be granted, however, that the leading statement posed in this verse by Philip is the most natural thought to raise in this circumstance. The Ethiopian eunuch did not know of Christ or about whom the prophet was writing. Then, after only one conversation about Christ, the eunuch wanted to be baptized. Hence, the statement "If you believe with all your heart, you may" is most appropriate and can never be out of place in the preparations made for baptism. The confession of Christ as God's Son is an affirmation of faith and grows out of the condition of the Great Commission to believe.

pian was a religious man who was sincerely trying to do the will of God. Repentance, therefore, is evident from his acceptance of the message about Christ which Philip brought him. Baptism is portrayed in this account more clearly than in any other in the Book of Acts. Both Philip and the Ethiopian waded down into the water, and Philip immersed him. (See the chart entitled "Examples of Conversion in Acts" on page 200.)

Imagine that you live in a kingdom and know the king as a personal friend. One day, while in a conversation with the king, you are told that if you will return later to see him, he will forgive your taxes. You receive this news with joy and resolve to return to see him in one month. Eventually, you return to see the king, anticipating the forgiveness of your taxes. Upon your arrival at the palace, you are told that the king has gone on a trip to another country. You tell the royal gatekeeper that the king told you that your taxes would be forgiven if you returned to see him. The gatekeeper says, "The king has made special arrangements for you." He ushers you into a room which is occupied by twelve administrators. You tell them your story. In response, they say, "When the king was here, he had the power to forgive taxes through just a word, but the king is now gone. He left behind specified terms upon which taxes are to be forgiven. You will now have to abide by these terms. You must first return to your home; second, write a letter to us stating your story; third, list all the members of your family; and fourth, sign the letter in the presence of three witnesses. When these terms are met, your taxes will be forgiven."

Compare this story with what Christ has actually

done. When He was here, He would often forgive sins with just a word. For example, He forgave the thief on the cross (Luke 23:43). However, when Christ got ready to leave this earth and return to heaven, He gave us the terms upon which salvation would be imparted to people during the Christian Age. In addition, He indicated that His commission was to be in effect until the end of the world (Matthew 28:20). Now that the King is gone, His terms of forgiveness are in effect.

THE ANSWER APPLIED

These terms of entrance into the church should be applied to each of us. The final commission of Christ has not changed. It is the same today as it was when it was given. The terms of salvation are precisely the same for us as they were for those who heard the first sermon preached by Peter. Christ sets the terms of entrance into the church and does the actual adding to it. Men's arguments and instructions do not alter His last will and testament. The King is gone, and the terms He set down for the Christian Age must be followed.

Where do you stand in respect to His terms of entrance into His church? Do you believe? The source of faith is the Word of God (Romans 10:17). Man's wisdom, learning, or accomplishments cannot produce faith. Do you believe in God? Do you believe that Christ is His Son and the Savior of mankind?

Have you repented of your sins (Acts 17:30, 31)? Have you turned from sin to the living God? Have you committed your heart to the will of God regardless of what it means and regardless of where it leads?

Have you stated publicly that you believe in Jesus as God's Son (Romans 10:10)? Have you confessed with your lips that Jesus is Savior and Lord?

Have you been baptized? The baptism of the Great Commission is by immersion (Romans 6:4), into Christ (Romans 6:3; Galatians 3:27), for the forgiveness of sins (Acts 2:38; 22:16), and in the name of the Father, the Son, and the Holy Spirit (Matthew 28:19, 20). Have you been baptized according to the New Testament pattern?

When one today adheres to the terms which Christ laid down in His final commission, is it not reasonable to believe that our faithful Lord and Savior adds him to His church or kingdom? No one can explain away the Lord's terms. We must not permit any substitution for them or any corruption of them. True commitment to Christ will allow nothing but obedience.

CONCLUSION

Have you entered the New Testament church? Would you like to enter it today?

It is surely the greatest and grandest news for us that the church found in the New Testament can be entered by anyone who will sincerely comply with the Lord's terms of entrance. All nations, all races, and all peoples can enter into His kingdom and be one in Christ (Ephesians 2:14).

Wisdom demands that we start at the beginning, making sure the foundation is true. If you have not obeyed the Lord's terms of salvation, fulfill those terms completely and immediately. Enter His kingdom, and from now on live as a citizen of His kingdom and of His kingdom alone.

The church of Christ is not really valuable to you unless you enter it.

STUDY QUESTIONS
(answers on page 269)

1. Describe the incomparable worth of the Lord's church.
2. Are the conditions of the Great Commission binding upon Christians today?
3. Why can we not be saved today as the thief on the cross was saved?
4. How can one become a member of the church today?
5. Do men add the saved to the church?
6. Is there any reason to believe that, if one does what was done in the Book of Acts to become a Christian, God will not do for him what He did for those who obeyed His will in the Book of Acts?
7. How can one be sure that he is in Christ's church?
8. When the Lord's conditions of salvation are corrupted, has great damage been done?

WORD HELPS

Jesus' last will and testament—the New Testament (Hebrews 9:15–17).

peculiar—different; set apart. First Peter 2:9 says of Christians, "But ye are a chosen generation, a royal priesthood, an holy nation, a peculiar people; that ye should show forth the praises of him who hath called you out of darkness into his marvellous light" (KJV).

EXAMPLES OF CONVERSION IN ACTS

HEARD	BELIEVED	REPENTED	CONFESSED	BAPTIZED	SAVED
Jews Acts 2	"they were pierced to the heart" (v. 37)	"Repent" (v. 38)		"be baptized" (v. 38); "were baptized" (v. 41)	"for the forgiveness of your sins" (v. 38)
Samaritans Acts 8	"when they believed" (v. 12)			"they were being baptized" (v. 12)	
Ethiopian Acts 8	["if you believe"] (v. 37)		["I believe that Jesus Christ is the Son of God" (v. 37)]	"baptized" (v. 36); "he baptized him" (v. 38)	"went on his way rejoicing" (v. 39)
Saul Acts 9; 22; 26		fasting and praying (9:9, 11)	"Lord" (9:5)	"was baptized" (9:18); "be baptized" (22:16)	"wash away your sins" (22:16)
Cornelius Acts 10; 11	"believes in Him" (10:43)	"repentance that leads to life" (11:18)		"baptized" (10:47); "ordered . . . to be baptized" (10:48)	"forgiveness of sins" (10:43)
Lydia Acts 16				"baptized" (v. 15)	
Jailer Acts 16	"believe in the Lord Jesus" (v. 31); "having believed" (v. 34)	"washed their wounds" (v. 33)		"was baptized" (v. 33)	"you shall be saved" (v. 31); "rejoiced greatly" (v. 34)
Corinthians Acts 18	"were believing" (v. 8)			"were . . . being baptized" (v. 8)	

17

The Unity Of the Church

T. B. Larimore, a gospel preacher whose Christlike spirit was recognized by all who knew him, explained the family unity of Christ's church with Psalm 133:1: "Behold, how good and how pleasant it is for brothers to dwell together in unity!" Some things are good but not pleasant. An operation to remove a cancerous growth is lifesaving, which is good, but it is not pleasant for the patient. Some things are pleasant but not good. Play is pleasant and enjoyable on special occasions, but continual play would be bad. Brother Larimore observed that we find few things in this world that are both good and pleasant, actually beneficial to us and at the same time enjoyable to experience. He showed that both of these qualities are found in unity in Christ, in brothers dwelling together in one accord.[1] Who would disagree with him?

---

[1]T. B. Larimore, "Unity," in *Biographies and Sermons*, ed. F. D. Srygley (n.p., n.d.; reprint, Nashville: Gospel Advocate, 1961), 35–36.

According to the New Testament, unity in Christ is not only good and pleasant to us; but, even more important, it is good and pleasing to God. Just before Jesus was betrayed into the hands of lawless men on the darkest night of the world, He prayed for the unity of those who would believe on Him in the future. He prayed to His Father, "I do not ask on behalf of these alone, but for those also who believe in Me through their word; that they may all be one; even as You, Father, are in Me and I in You, that they also may be in Us, so that the world may believe that You sent Me" (John 17:20, 21).

If you were scheduled to be executed tomorrow, and you knelt to pray tonight, for what would you pray? Would you pray for small, unimportant plans? Would you not pray for the hopes that are the dearest and most important in the world to you? Do we not see how Christ valued unity as we read His prayer for unity the night before He was crucified? The unity of the believers had to be the dearest and most important longing in the heart of Jesus, or He would not have prayed for it on the night before His death.

When Paul wrote to the terribly divided church at Corinth, a church beset by many problems and weaknesses, he first gave them a forceful call to unity: "Now I exhort you, brethren, by the name of our Lord Jesus Christ, that you all agree and that there be no divisions among you, but that you be made complete in the same mind and in the same judgment" (1 Corinthians 1:10). At the time that Paul wrote to the Corinthians, A.D. 54 to 56, denominations did not exist. The only church that existed was the Lord's church, and Paul, by the inspiration of the

Holy Spirit, told God's church at Corinth to dwell together in unity. He not only pleaded for this unity, but he pleaded for it in the very name of Jesus Christ.

Let us look at the unity of the church in greater detail. The two passages already quoted make it obvious that Christ's church is to have a beautiful unity, but what kind of unity is it to have? What is the nature of that unity? Understanding the unity Christ prayed for should help us understand more about the church itself.

UNITY IN BECOMING PART OF A BODY

First, let us try to understand the God-given unity of the body of Christ as one people. The New Testament speaks of a unity that is natural and basic to being in Christ. This unity occurs by the grace of God when one enters Christ's body. Anyone who has genuinely become a member of the body of Christ has received this unity.

The New Testament world was divided into two main communities: Jewish and Gentile. The division between these two groups was as wide as any division which might exist between two races today. Yet Paul affirmed that Jew and Gentile had become *one* in Christ:

> For He Himself is our peace, who made both groups into one . . . (Ephesians 2:14).

> . . . that in Himself He might make the two into one new man, thus establishing peace, and might reconcile them both in one body to God through the cross . . . (Ephesians 2:15, 16).

> There is neither Jew nor Greek, there is neither
> slave nor free man, there is neither male nor fe-
> male; for you are all one in Christ Jesus (Galatians
> 3:28).

Christ, through His death on the cross, has made into one all people who come into Christ, regardless of background or race. Jews and Gentiles, two distinct races, were recreated into a new race and were called Christians. Christ did not make Jews into Gentiles or Gentiles into Jews. He did not raise the Gentile up to the position of privilege occupied by the Jew; neither did He bring the Jew down to the position of the Gentile. He raised both Jew and Gentile to a heavenly position in Christ which was far greater than any privilege or position ever promised to or possessed by either. The Jew was to forget that he was a Jew, and the Gentile was to forget that he was a Gentile.

The same is true in the church today. Each person is to think only of what he is in Christ. Christ is Savior and Lord to all Christians. In this divine oneness, all national, racial, social, and family differences are removed.

Through Christ, people are reconciled to—or brought together with—God (Colossians 1:20). Then, through that reconciliation, Christians are brought together with one another and "are being built together into a dwelling of God in the Spirit" (Ephesians 2:22). Before two can be united with each other, they must be united with God.

History contains examples of peoples, like the Normans and the Saxons in England, who were continually at war with each other. Hostility and hatred perpetually characterized them. Through the centuries, however, the peoples mixed and married, until eventually these two communities of people had merged into one. The separate nations, as unique communities, ceased to exist. The wars ended, of course, because the division between them no longer existed. The intermingling of the two communities produced one new community of people who loved and respected each other.[2]

In a similar way, all human divisions and barriers are broken down in Christ; one new body of people is created by God's marvelous grace. In His body, people do not see Jew or Greek, slave or freeman, rich man or poor man, male or female, white or black. Christians only see that they "are all one in Christ Jesus" (Galatians 3:28b).

To understand the unity in Christ, then, we must first know about the unity which Christians are given when they enter His body. It is appropriate, and even necessary, to tell new Christians when they enter the body of Christ that they are now one with all other members of His body. The church must think and act in agreement with this truth. No ranks, no barriers, no divisions, and no tribes matter in Christ's body. All the members have become one with Christ and one with each other.

UNITY IN TEACHING

Second, unity in teaching is found in Christ. Unity is given by the Spirit when people enter the body of Christ, but this unity is kept by each member's

---

[2]R. C. Bell, *Studies in Ephesians* (Austin, Tex.: Firm Foundation Publishing House, 1971), 17.

obedience to the teachings of the Scriptures.

Christians are bound together by a unity of teaching and belief. Christ's body is not a collection of people guided by unproven beliefs about God and guesses about life. Members of His body are united by God's divine revelation of truth.

As Paul discussed the unity of the church of Christ, he urged Christians to keep the unity of the Spirit in the bond of peace. He named seven "one's" which form the basic teaching for keeping unity in Christ's body. He said, "There is one body and one Spirit, just as also you were called in one hope of your calling; one Lord, one faith, one baptism, one God and Father of all who is over all and through all and in all" (Ephesians 4:4–6). The body of which Paul wrote is the spiritual body of Christ, the church (Ephesians 1:22, 23). The Spirit is the third member of the Godhead who gave us the revelation of the Scriptures. The one hope is the eternal hope put in the heart of every Christian through the gospel (Colossians 1:23). The one Lord is the Christ, the Son of the living God, the One who died for our sins and was raised for our justification. The one faith is the belief in Christ and His Word which comes from the testimony of the Scriptures (Romans 10:17). The one baptism is the baptism which Christ commanded in the Great Commission and which will be in effect until the end of the Christian Age (Matthew 28:19, 20). The one God is the eternal God who created and provides for the earth, the only true and living God. Concerning the seven "one's," R. C. Bell said, "These unalterable, final facts demand either acceptance or repudiation. No other reaction is possible; a man who rejects even one of them is not to consider himself a Christian at all."[3]

Union is one thing, but unity is another. Union can be achieved by force, but unity can only be found in devotion. Union can be created by tying two people together with ropes, but unity can only come when hearts are tied together with faith and love. People of divided minds and wills can experience a type of union, but people can only dwell together in one accord through speaking the same truths and being one in mind and judgment.

Paul not only pleaded for unity in 1 Corinthians 1:10, but he told exactly the kind of unity for which he was pleading—a unity of agreement, without divisions, complete in mind and judgment. This kind of unity is brought about by submission to Christ's will. In Acts 2, on the day the church was established, each person submitted to the message of the Spirit delivered by inspired men. This submission resulted in unity based on a shared belief in God's teaching: "They were continually devoting themselves to the apostles' teaching. . . . And all those who had believed were together and had all things in common" (Acts 2:42–44). Paul wrote to the brethren in Philippi, ". . . let us keep living by that same standard to which we have attained" (Philippians 3:16).

UNITY IN DAILY LIVING

Third, unity is to be seen in the day-to-day living of the body of Christ. The unity which is given by the Holy Spirit when people enter Christ is kept not only by each member's obedience to the plain teachings of the Scriptures, but also by each member's

---

[3]Ibid., 24.

following a practical, commonsense approach to living together in one accord in Christ.

Paul encouraged the Philippian brethren to live together in love and harmony. He said, "Make my joy complete by being of the same mind, maintaining the same love, united in spirit, intent on one purpose" (Philippians 2:2). He further said, "I urge Euodia and I urge Syntyche to live in harmony in the Lord" (Philippians 4:2). These verses necessarily demand that each member of Christ's body live by the teachings of the Bible. In order to keep unity, Christians sometimes have to keep their opinions and wishes to themselves.

The church is never to demand that a brother do anything that would go against his own conscience. Paul said,

> Therefore let us not judge one another anymore, but rather determine this—not to put an obstacle or a stumbling block in a brother's way (Romans 14:13).

> Now we who are strong ought to bear the weaknesses of those without strength and not just please ourselves. Each of us is to please his neighbor for his good, to his edification. For even Christ did not please Himself; but as it is written, "The reproaches of those who reproached You fell on Me" (Romans 15:1–3).

Practical unity often requires give-and-take. The selfish man will never know unity with others. He will always live in a little kingdom which is bounded on all four sides by his selfish demands. He cannot come out of that kingdom for genuine fellowship with others, and no one else can enter it for genuine fellowship with him.

This practical unity in Christ grows out of a careful attempt on the part of each member of Christ's body to think of his brother or sister with love and grace. The Christian is to be less demanding about his own opinions and wishes. He is to do nothing from selfishness or empty conceit, but with humility of mind, he is to regard others as more important than himself (Philippians 2:3). He is not to look out for his own interests; he is to look out for the interests of others (Philippians 2:4). As he so lives, he is uniquely exhibiting the mind of Christ (Philippians 2:5–8).

CONCLUSION

Christ's body, therefore, is to be known for its unity. This unity has a threefold nature. Christians are united as one body, as believers of one teaching, and as people who treat each other thoughtfully in daily living. Unity comes by God's grace when new Christians enter into His body. It is kept and experienced through the body's complete commitment to the teachings of the Scriptures. Unity is enjoyed by the church because each member is concerned about the spiritual life of fellow Christians.

God seeks to bring all the clanging discord in His world into harmony in Christ: "For it was the Father's good pleasure for all the fullness to dwell in Him, and through Him to reconcile all things to Himself, having made peace through the blood of His cross; through Him, I say, whether things on earth or things in heaven" (Colossians 1:19, 20). Christ, through His gospel, calls us to this unity in His body. God planned

it (Ephesians 3:6), Christ prayed for unity and provided the possibility for it (John 17:21; Ephesians
2:16), Paul pleaded for unity (1 Corinthians 1:10), and
the Spirit produces it (Ephesians 4:1–6).

Should we not accept this unity by receiving it
and living in it?

STUDY QUESTIONS
(answers on page 270)

1. In what way is unity in Christ both pleasant and good?
2. What was Christ's special prayer for His church on the
    night before His crucifixion? (See John 17:21–24.)
3. Discuss the plea for unity given by Paul in 1 Corinthians
    1:10.
4. Explain the unity which Christ's church has as a body.
5. When is the unity of the church given to one who is enter-
    ing the church?
6. Define the unity of the church in teaching. What is the
    difference between having unity as a body and having
    unity in teaching?
7. How are unity and submission to the will of Christ relat-
    ed?
8. What is the difference between having unity in teaching
    and having unity in daily living?
9. What are some steps Christians must sometimes take in
    order to keep practical unity in the church?

WORD HELPS

conscience—the internal moral witness found in humans;
    sometimes thought of as an inner voice which tells us right
    from wrong. The conscience needs to be educated by the
    Word of God.

Euodia and Syntyche—two Christian women who were disput-
    ing with each other (Philippians 4:2). Paul urged them to
    live in peace with each other.

18

Eternal Reward And Punishment

One of the most difficult concepts for our minds to grasp is "eternity," a never-ending existence. Everything in our physical universe, what we can see and touch, had a beginning and will have an end; therefore, grappling with the concept of eternity can be overwhelming. Since eternity is outside our experience, understanding it is almost impossible for our minds.

We may readily concur with God's giving us heaven with its wonders, even though we realize that what we did in this short life could not possibly earn us the right to be there throughout eternity. At the same time, we may object to the horrors of hell, thinking that what we did in this short life could not have been bad enough to deserve unending punishment. We may think that the righteous deserve God's mercy and grace more than the unrighteous deserve His vengeance.

Some make the mistake of thinking that eternal punishment cannot be harmonized with God's love, mercy, and grace. Therefore, they seek to interpret the Bible so that it will be consistent with a God who is only loving, kind, and forbearing (1 Timothy 1:2; 1 John 4:8). They overlook the other side of God: He is also a God of wrath and vengeance.[1] He hates lawlessness (Hebrews 1:9), shows "severity" (Romans 11:22), and is a "consuming fire" (Hebrews 12:29). We read, "Behold then the kindness and severity of God; to those who fell, severity, but to you, God's kindness, if you continue in His kindness; otherwise you also will be cut off" (Romans 11:22). Hebrews 10:31 says, "It is a terrifying thing to fall into the hands of the living God."

The kindness of God is portrayed in the New Testament in His dealings with Peter (Luke 22:31, 32), Paul (1 Timothy 1:15, 16), and others. His wrath is seen in the deaths of Ananias and Sapphira (Acts 5:1–10) and of Herod (Acts 12:20–23). God struck these people dead for their wrongdoing.

God's dealings with the disobedient show that He is capable of severe punishment. Those who see God as only a God of love overlook His hot displeasure with sin and His punishment of those who do not submit to His will.

A PREVIEW OF PUNISHMENT

While we wish that the pleasantries in life would never end, we want pain to terminate immediately. What is pleasant and enjoyable is not punishment. Retribution for wrongdoing can be administered only by making us endure those things that are disagree-

---

[1]Read Romans 1:18; 2:8; 3:5; 12:19; Ephesians 5:6; Colossians 3:6; 2 Thessalonians 1:8.

able to us. If what God says He will do seems hurtful, such should be expected. How else could God punish sinful man?

What Will Punishment Be Like?

As we have already concluded, the Bible teaches that the punishment of the wicked at the end of time will be forever. We cannot imagine what "eternal punishment" will be like (Matthew 25:46).

Annihilation? Some teach that no one will be punished forever. They believe that "eternal punishment" means that the disobedient will be annihilated. They believe that passing out of existence is everlasting punishment. They base this doctrine on verses which declare that the wicked will be destroyed or will receive eternal destruction (Matthew 10:28).

The Greek word *apollumi*, which is translated "destroy" in Matthew 10:28, is also translated "perishing" (Matthew 8:25) and "lost" (Luke 15:4, 6). The wine skins which Jesus alluded to in Matthew 9:17 would be ruined, but not annihilated; and the sheep, the coin, and the son that were lost (*apollumi*) were found (Luke 15:6, 9, 24). Jesus came "to seek and to save that which was lost" (Luke 19:10), and He promised that "he who has lost his life for My sake will find it" (Matthew 10:39). That which has been annihilated cannot be found or saved. In every conclusive context, the word *apollumi* means "to be lost," "to ruin," "to perish," or "to destroy," but cannot mean "to be annihilated."

The wicked will continue to be punished without end, throughout eternity: "And the smoke of their torment goes up forever and ever; they have no rest day and night" (Revelation 14:11). The same description is given in Revelation 20:10 concerning the punishment of the devil, the beast, and the false prophet, who were thrown into the lake of fire earlier, in Revelation 19:20. If the lake of fire annihilates those who are thrown into it, the beast and the false prophet who earlier had been thrown into the lake of fire should have burned up by the time the devil was thrown into it more than a thousand years later (Revelation 20:2, 3). They were still in the lake of fire and would continue to be tormented there "day and night forever and ever" (Revelation 20:10).

Those who reject God's grace under the new covenant will be considered deserving of worse punishment than was administered to those in Israel who violated the law of Moses (Hebrews 10:29). Since death was the worst punishment given to those who violated Moses' law, there must be a punishment that is to be dreaded even more than death. That punishment is hell.

Actual Punishment? Hell (Gk.: *gehenna*[2]) is a real place that is mentioned exclusively by Jesus,[3] except for one other reference, James 3:6. A clear difference should be noted between Hades, the intermediate place for the dead, and hell, the place where the wicked will be punished.

The word *gehenna* was first applied to a ravine located on the south side of Jerusalem, belonging to

---

[2]*Gehenna* is a transliteration into Greek of a Hebrew word that is the combination of two Hebrew words, *ge*, meaning "valley," and *Hinnom*, the owner of the valley.

[3]See Matthew 5:22, 29, 30; 10:28; 18:9; 23:15, 33; Mark 9:43, 45, 47; Luke 12:5; James 3:6.

the sons of Hinnom. The place had become abominable and loathsome to God and man, because idolatrous worshipers had burned their children there.[4] By Jesus' day, it had become a disposal place for Jerusalem's garbage. It stank, was infested with worms, and smoked from continual fires. The word *gehenna* was used by Jesus as a fitting description of the place of punishment for the wicked.

Jesus alluded to the fire of Gehenna as a furnace of fire (Matthew 13:42, 50). This fire is eternal and cannot be quenched (Matthew 3:12; 18:8; 25:41; Mark 9:48[5]). He also said that the "worm" will not die. If the fire and the worms consumed the carcasses, then the fire would cease and the worms would die out for want of anything to consume. Even though Jesus may not have intended for the fire and the worms to be thought of as literal, He did use terms that would indicate the unending nature of the punishment.

If the fire is not literal, why did Jesus repeatedly use the word "fire"? On the other hand, how could He describe to us in an understandable way the punishment of souls except in physical terms? Perhaps in the same way heaven is described in physical terms to convey its beauty. Jesus used physical terms to help us understand the awfulness of hell.

What type of punishment will be experienced in hell? What can the disobedient expect?

(1) Those who are being sent to hell will be told to "depart" (Matthew 7:23; see 25:41; Luke 13:27). They will be separated from God.

---

[4]See 2 Kings 23:10; see 2 Chronicles 28:3; 33:6; Jeremiah 7:31, 32; 19:6.

[5]See Mark 9:43; Luke 3:17.

(2) Those in hell will be punished away from God's presence (2 Thessalonians 1:9). This may indicate that God will not see, hear, or help them.

(3) The devil and his angels, as well as every wicked person who has ever lived, will be in hell (Matthew 25:41).

(4) Hell is a place of torment with fire and brimstone (Revelation 14:10; see 20:10; 21:8).

(5) Those in hell will continue to be destroyed (2 Thessalonians 1:9).

(6) They will not be allowed to enter God's eternal kingdom (1 Corinthians 6:9; Galatians 5:21).

(7) They will be suffering the wrath of God (Matthew 3:7; see Romans 2:5; 5:9; Ephesians 5:6; Colossians 3:6). It will be poured out without mixture (Revelation 14:10).

(8) They will be in outer, utter darkness (Matthew 8:12; see 22:13; 25:30; 2 Peter 2:17; Jude 13).

(9) They will receive damnation (Mark 16:16; John 5:29; 2 Thessalonians 2:12; 2 Peter 2:3; KJV).

(10) They will be in a state of corruption (Galatians 6:8).

(11) They will suffer God's vengeance (Romans 12:19).

The reaction of those being punished is indescribable: They will be suffering tribulation and distress (Romans 2:9). Jesus said they will be weeping and gnashing their teeth, which is descriptive of intense pain (Matthew 8:12; 13:42, 50; 22:13; 24:51; 25:30; Luke 13:28).

All that is said about hell is dreadfully bad; nothing good is said. Those who go there will have to associate forever with every evil person who has lived, as well as with the devil and his angels (Matthew 25:41)! They will never be with God or with the righteous. They will live in darkness forever. God, who is light, will be absent. The sun, galaxies, stars, and every light of our universe will not exist. Without God and these lights, there is only darkness.

Who Will Go to Hell?

We are told who will be punished. Paul described them as those who are stubborn and have unrepentant hearts, those who are "selfishly ambitious and do not obey the truth, but obey unrighteousness," and those who do evil (Romans 2:5, 8, 9). Also, he wrote that they include those "who do not know God and . . . do not obey the gospel of our Lord Jesus" (2 Thessalonians 1:8). Paul gave lists of people who will not go to heaven, which means that they will go to hell (1 Corinthians 6:9; see Galatians 5:21; Ephesians 5:5). Because of the lives they have lived, hell will be their eternal abode.

No wonder the New Testament speaks of fear. Paul wrote, "Therefore, knowing the fear of the Lord, we persuade men" (2 Corinthians 5:11). In the same vein, Peter wrote, "If you address as Father the One who impartially judges according to each one's work, conduct yourselves in fear during the time of your stay on earth" (1 Peter 1:17). Jesus said, "Do not fear those who kill the body but are unable to kill the soul; but rather fear Him who is able to destroy both soul and body in hell" (Matthew 10:28). Paul also wrote, "So then, my beloved, just as you have always obeyed, not as in my presence only, but now much more in my absence, work out your salvation with fear and trembling" (Philippians 2:12).

"Perfect[6] love casts out fear" (1 John 4:18), and perfect love will keep us obedient (John 14:15, 21; 1 John 5:3). We should develop both a love and a fear of God. Our love for God should draw us near Him to serve Him, and our fear of God should move us to respect Him enough to do His will (1 Peter 1:17).

All that has been stated should be enough to convince us that we do not want to go to hell. Hell was not designed for us, but for the devil and his angels. Because of the trouble he has caused throughout the history of the world, the devil deserves forever and ever the hottest hell God can design. If we say this, however, we should realize that those who do not obey God but follow the devil deserve more than a slight reproof for their sins.

Our greatest goal should be to reach heaven and escape the punishment of hell. The most lowly place in heaven, if heaven has lowly places, is to be preferred throughout eternity over the best place in hell, if hell has a best place. We can avoid the horrors of hell by living as God wants us to live and by helping others to prepare to go to heaven.

A PREVIEW OF HEAVEN

One exciting promise that Jesus made is "Your reward in heaven is great" (Matthew 5:12; Luke 6:23). We who are Christians have hope (Ephesians 4:4) of a life in heaven that far exceeds this one in glory, which is one blessing that makes being Christians worthwhile. No other people have so many songs about heaven or sing so frequently about a future

---

[6]The Greek word translated "perfect" is *telios,* meaning "mature."

home. Our expectation of heaven carries us with joy through the many trials and burdens that drive others to sorrow and despair (1 Thessalonians 4:13). Jesus said, "I came that they might have life, and might have it abundantly" (John 10:10). An abundant life is not without problems. Paul wrote, "And indeed, all who desire to live godly in Christ Jesus will be persecuted" (2 Timothy 3:12). The persecution Paul endured led him to say, "If we have hoped in Christ in this life only, we are of all men most to be pitied" (1 Corinthians 15:19). He wrote about his hardships for Christ, "If from human motives I fought with wild beasts at Ephesus, what does it profit me? If the dead are not raised, let us eat and drink, for tomorrow we die" (1 Corinthians 15:32; see Isaiah 22:13).

The New Testament gives us much to look forward to. Heaven, in the sense of the eternal home of the saved, is not mentioned in the Scriptures frequently or described in detail, but the blessings of heaven are alluded to many times.

The Christian's hope of a home in heaven is one that brings us joy (Romans 12:12). This is a better promise than was made to those under the old covenant (Hebrews 8:6; 10:34). They were promised the land of Canaan, with long life and prosperity if they kept the covenant God made with them (Deuteronomy 4:13; 5:33). If all we are promised is a place on an earth restored to its pristine state, then God's promises to us under the new covenant, the basis of our hope, are not that much better than the land promises God gave to Israel (Deuteronomy 28:1–14). Our hope, however, is a place forever in heaven (1 Peter 1:3, 4) instead of a plot of land with prosperity and long life on earth.

What Is Heaven Like?

In order to understand heaven as described in the Bible, we must realize that "heaven" is used of three different realms (2 Corinthians 12:2–4): (1) the sky where the clouds are (Deuteronomy 11:11) and where the birds fly (Psalm 79:2), (2) the universe filled with stars and constellations (Genesis 1:14–18; Deuteronomy 1:10), and (3) God's dwelling place, where the redeemed of the earth will live forever (1 Peter 1:3, 4). This last reference is the concern of this lesson.

The expression "kingdom of heaven" is used to refer to (1) God's eternal kingdom (Matthew 13:43), (2) the kingdom prepared for the saved (Matthew 25:34), and (3) the kingdom of Christ which He preached was at hand and about which He sent others to preach. This kingdom was referred to as the "kingdom of heaven" (Matthew 4:17); the "kingdom of God" (Mark 1:15), "My kingdom" (Luke 22:30), and the "kingdom of His beloved Son" (Colossians 1:13). A unifying thread which runs through these terms correlates them in meaning, for each of them refers to heaven's reign. Christ's special reign, which He preached was at hand (Matthew 4:17), began with His ascension (Ephesians 1:19–23) and will end when He returns (1 Corinthians 15:24). This lesson will stress the kingdom the saved will enter as their eternal reward (Matthew 25:34). Only the context can determine which of these uses of the term is meant in each passage.

Since heaven is not a physical dimension, we must realize that the physical terms used to describe it can only hint at the realities of that spiritual realm. Paul wrote concerning this realm, "We look not at the things which are seen, but at the things which are not seen; for the things which are seen are temporal, but the things which are not seen are eternal" (2 Corinthians 4:18). Although God describes heaven in earthly terms, it must not be thought of as physical. The earth is not to be renovated or changed into a spiritual habitation. If it were, then we could not take seriously Him who sits on the throne, who said, "Behold, I am making all things new" (Revelation 21:5). Nor could we take literally the statement "Then I saw a new heaven and a new earth; for the first heaven and the first earth passed away . . ." (Revelation 21:1).

The new Jerusalem, the city for the saved, is described as being made of the most costly materials known on earth (Revelation 21:11–21). Such a description is awesome, almost beyond human imagination. It is the picture God wanted us mortals to have. We will all be awestricken when we are glorified in His kingdom (1 Thessalonians 2:12; Hebrews 2:10), behold its splendor and glory (Romans 8:18), and become partakers of that glory (1 Peter 5:1). He will be "glorified in His saints" (2 Thessalonians 1:10). We will also be impressed that this is not a passing realm, but will provide for us as citizens of heaven an "eternal weight of glory far beyond all comparison" (2 Corinthians 4:17). Compared with the earth, it is "a better possession and a lasting one" (Hebrews 10:34), "a better country, that is, a heavenly one" (Hebrews 11:16).

The most wonderful aspect of heaven will be our association throughout eternity with God, Jesus, the Holy Spirit (Revelation 21:3), and all the wonderful saved people who have lived. No fellowship on earth can compare with the eternal fellowship we will have in heaven.

If we could gaze but for a moment on the glory of heaven and see the fellowship we will experience, we would be so excited about going there that we would spend every waking moment dreaming about it, working toward it, and planning for it. Paul wrote, "For I consider that the sufferings of this present time are not worthy to be compared with the glory that is to be revealed to us" (Romans 8:18).

What Will Be in Heaven?

Symbols are used to help us understand heaven. Heaven will not have items we need here on earth, like the sun, the moon, or a lamp; nor will there be any night there, for the Lamb (Jesus Christ) will be the light (Revelation 21:23, 25; 22:5). Our having ready access to God will mean that a temple will not be needed, for God and the Lamb will be the temple (Revelation 21:22).

We will not need physical food, for life will be sustained by the water of the river of life and by the fruit of the tree of life (Revelation 22:1, 2). No longer will we be away from God, for "He will dwell among them, and they shall be His people, and God Himself will be among them" (Revelation 21:3). The throne of God and of the Lamb will be there, and because of this, no curse can be there (Revelation 22:3). Only righteousness will be in our new dwelling place (2 Peter 3:13).

What Will We Be Like?

Our physical bodies will be changed into spiritual bodies (1 Corinthians 15:44, 51–54). Physical bodies would be unsuitable for the spiritual dimension we will enter, for "flesh and blood cannot inherit the kingdom of God" (1 Corinthians 15:50). God's spirit realm is natural for Him, since He is a spirit (John 4:24), and for the angels, since they also are spirits (Hebrews 1:14). We cannot understand what the body in that dimension will be like, but we have the assurance "that when He appears, we will be like Him, because we will see Him just as He is" (1 John 3:2). In order for us to see God, we must enter His dimension, for physical beings cannot see God (1 Timothy 6:16). Jesus "will change our lowly body to be like his glorious body, by the power which enables him even to subject all things to himself" (Philippians 3:20, 21; RSV). When this happens, we "will see His face" (Revelation 22:4), a face that none of us in our physical bodies can behold and live (Exodus 33:20).

When we are changed, we will have the glory of heavenly beings. We will be "glorified with" Christ (Romans 8:17), having entered into glory, honor, and peace (Romans 2:7, 10). In our new state we "will shine forth as the sun in the kingdom" of our Father (Matthew 13:43). "Just as we have borne the image of the earthy, we will also bear the image of the heavenly" (1 Corinthians 15:49).

We will be eternal beings with "eternal life," no longer able to die (Luke 20:36; Revelation 21:4). "Eternal life" means quality of life as well as length of life, which can refer to a present possession[7] or to the life we will receive as a reward for believing in Jesus and serving Him.[8]

---

[7]See John 3:36; 5:24; 6:47, 54; 1 John 5:11, 13.
[8]Matthew 19:29; Mark 10:30; Luke 18:30; John 10:28; Romans 2:7; 6:22; 1 Timothy 6:12.

What Will We Be Doing?

God has not given us a full description of what we will be doing in heaven, and perhaps for good reason. We might not consider what spiritual beings do to be very exciting, since we are physical. Since our happiness is usually based on physical things, we might have difficulty getting excited about the spiritual activities of heaven.

In heaven we will know only happiness, for God "will wipe away every tear from their eyes; and there will no longer be any death; there will no longer be any mourning, or crying, or pain; the first things have passed away" (Revelation 21:4). Those physical aspects of this life that have caused us sorrow or have been a curse to us will no longer exist (Revelation 22:3). The saved will enter into the "joy" of our Master (Matthew 25:21, 23). We will get to rest from the toils of this life (Revelation 14:13; Hebrews 4:8–11).

Throughout eternity we will rejoice, because we will be with the Father (Revelation 21:3), with Jesus (John 12:26[9]), with the angels (Luke 9:26), and with those who are saved (Matthew 13:43). We will joyfully serve Jesus (Revelation 22:3) and reign with Him forever (2 Timothy 2:12; Revelation 22:5). He will be glorified in the saints (2 Thessalonians 1:10), which must mean that Jesus will be highly honored and revered (Philippians 2:10, 11) by those He has saved. Heaven will be a wonderful place of love, fellowship, and rejoicing.

---

[9]See John 14:3; 17:24; 2 Corinthians 5:6–8; Philippians 1:23; Colossians 3:4; 1 Thessalonians 4:17.

Who Will Go to Heaven?

The glories of heaven are not given on the basis of merit, but on the basis of grace (2 Thessalonians 2:16). We will not be able to brag that we have earned heaven by our good works (Ephesians 2:8, 9; Titus 3:5). We will simply say, "We have done only that which we ought to have done" (Luke 17:10). Heaven will be given to us as an inheritance.[10] An inheritance is not earned; it is a gift. Those who are heirs are the children of God (Romans 8:16, 17; Galatians 3:6, 7, 29). By being born again of water and Spirit (John 3:5), we are born of God (John 1:12, 13). In this way we become children of God and heirs of heaven through faith and baptism (Galatians 3:26, 27).

Those who will not enter heaven are those who rebel against God and live immoral lives (1 Corinthians 6:9, 10; Galatians 5:19–21). Because they have not been cleansed by the blood of Jesus, they will remain defiled and cannot enter heaven (Revelation 21:27; 2 Peter 3:13). Those who will enter heaven are those who have been cleansed by Jesus' blood (Ephesians 5:25–27; Colossians 1:19–22).

CONCLUSION

The thought that God will punish forever and ever those who have not obeyed Him is horrifying, but the teaching is in His Word. The punishment of the unrighteous will be as eternal as the blessings of the righteous. This certainty should motivate us to seek to please God in everything we do. If we gain

---

[10]See Acts 20:32; see 26:18; Ephesians 1:11, 14, 18; 5:5; Colossians 1:12; 3:24; Hebrews 9:15; 1 Peter 1:4.

eternity with Him in heaven and avoid the everlasting fire with the devil and his angels, every effort, every hardship, every minute of service will be worthwhile.

STUDY QUESTIONS
(answers on page 270)

1. Some conclude that eternal punishment cannot be harmonized with God's love, mercy, and grace. Why is this conclusion wrong?
2. Why is the view that the disobedient will be annihilated a false doctrine?
3. What kind of punishment can be expected in hell?
4. How does Paul describe those who will be punished?
5. What should be our greatest goal?
6. How is the Christian's hope of heaven a better promise than was made to those under the old law?
7. In what three ways is "heaven" used?
8. Why will heaven not have the items we need here on earth?
9. Who will go to heaven?

WORD HELPS

divisions of Christendom—denominational differences. In contradiction to the prayer of Jesus (John 17:21) and plain New Testament teaching (1 Corinthians 1:10–13), some men have introduced man-made churches and doctrines that divide believers.

19

Repentance

We sometimes allow the circumstances we are in to determine our spiritual values. An unforgettable scene in Luke 16, which tells of the rich man and Lazarus, illustrates how this is true. The rich man had no thought of others in this life and apparently no thought of his spiritual needs. His concerns were limited to the little world of his own selfish desires and ambitions. At death, he went into eternity to face the results of what he had done. He went from luxury into torment in the spirit world called "Hades" (Luke 16:23).

After death, his priorities completely changed. All other considerations paled. He became occupied with two significant thoughts: First, he became (perhaps for the first time) concerned for his soul. He pleaded for mercy, for grace. Jesus said, "And he cried out and said, 'Father Abraham, have mercy on me, and send Lazarus so that he may dip the tip of his finger in water and cool off my tongue, for I am in agony in this flame'" (Luke 16:24).

Second, he voiced concern for the spiritual condition of his brothers. This may have been the first time in his life that he had verbalized any spiritual love for his brothers. A few moments of torment had given him the heart of a missionary. He pleaded,

> Then I beg you, father, that you send him to my father's house for I have five brothers in order that he may warn them, so that they will not also come to this place of torment (Luke 16:27, 28).

When he was told that his brothers should read the law and the Prophets like everyone else, he pleaded, "No, father Abraham, but if someone goes to them from the dead, they will repent" (Luke 16:30). Was this the first time the word "repent" had ever been spoken by him? Death had changed his thinking and his interests! He knew what his brothers needed—transforming repentance!

Time and eternity will convict us all that the big issue of life is repentance! May we not wait until death for this realization to hit us with force. Jesus said, "I tell you, no, but unless you repent, you will all likewise perish" (Luke 13:3, 5). Paul pushed away all exceptions to the command of repentance with his declaration to the Athenians: "Therefore having overlooked the times of ignorance, God is now declaring to men that all people everywhere should repent" (Acts 17:30). Mankind travels one of two roads before God: the way of repentance or the way of rebellion. God delays the coming of Jesus for one reason—to allow more time to bring men to repentance: "The Lord is not slow about His promise, as some count slowness, but is patient toward you, not wishing for any to perish but for all to come to repentance" (2 Peter 3:9). The final destiny of each man hangs upon whether or not he repents: "But for the cowardly and unbelieving and abominable and murderers and immoral persons and sorcerers and idolaters and all liars, their part will be in the lake that burns with fire and brimstone, which is the second death" (Revelation 21:8).

The church is made up of the people who have answered the call to New Testament repentance. Christians are those who have named the name of the Lord and departed from wickedness (2 Timothy 2:19). Through conversion to Christ, they have been delivered from the domain of darkness, and have been transferred into the kingdom of God's Son (Colossians 1:13). They have committed themselves to living as obedient children of God, refusing to return to the former lusts in which they lived in ignorance and disobedience (1 Peter 1:14). Their desire is to be like the One who called them. They are striving to imitate Him in all their behavior, acknowledging in their conduct their Lord's desire: "You shall be holy, for I am holy" (1 Peter 1:16).

Repentance, therefore, is a cornerstone word and a chief attitude for anyone seeking to be a Christian, a member of the Lord's church. The nature of the church is reflected in the basic meaning and implications of this word. Repentance stands as a designation for the kind of people God calls His church: the church is made up of the penitent ones. When Peter explained the baptisms of Gentiles at Cornelius' house to Jewish Christians in Jerusalem, these Jewish brethren responded by saying, "Well then, God has granted to the Gentiles also the repentance that leads to life."

(See Acts 11:18.) It was clear to them, and it should be clear to us, that the door of true life is only opened by true repentance.

What is repentance? Let us define this word more graphically so that there is no mistaking what it is and what it means. We will use the backdrop of Saul's conversion to illustrate it.

TURNING FROM SIN

First, repentance is turning from sin, making a change in direction regarding wickedness.

Repentance is more than personal improvement, more than a way to have better control of one's life. It is a deep-seated resolve, a decision to abandon all that is foreign to God. This resolve contributes to a total change that Jesus called a new birth (John 3:3).

Repentance is not just regretting that one has sinned. One can be sorry that he has sinned because of the embarrassment that sin has brought upon him or because of a penalty that he has had to pay for his sin. Judas regretted that he betrayed Jesus, but he did not repent (Matthew 27:3). Peter, who denied Christ (Matthew 26:34, 69–75), repented; Judas only regretted. One can be deeply distraught that he sinned, yet never repent.

Repentance is not just conviction of sin. On the Day of Pentecost, Peter pointed out the sins of the Jews who were listening to him. His words brought conviction to their hearts, and they cried out, "What shall we do?" (Acts 2:37). However, Peter did not regard their conviction as repentance; for in his response to their query, he said, "Repent, and each of you be baptized in the name of Jesus Christ for the forgiveness of your sins; and you will receive the gift of the Holy Spirit" (Acts 2:38).

Repentance is not just godly sorrow. Godly sorrow for sins precedes and produces repentance, according to Paul:

> For the sorrow that is according to the will of God produces a repentance without regret, leading to salvation, but the sorrow of the world produces death (2 Corinthians 7:10).

Godly sorrow is part of the process of repentance, but it is not repentance itself.

Repentance would not even be defined as a reformation of life. Rather, it produces a reformation of life. If repentance does not effect a changed life, then it is not genuine repentance; but the reformed life is not in itself repentance. John the Baptist urged the people coming to him, "Therefore bear fruit in keeping with repentance" (Matthew 3:8). Actual repentance precedes the fruits of repentance, a changed life.

Repentance has to do with a resolute change of one's will regarding sin. It involves intellect, emotions, and conscience. This change of mind about sin is so comprehensive in the human personality that it enables a person to give up a way of life. At baptism, one can be immersed into his own spiritual death to sin, crucifying the old self, so that the body of sin might be destroyed (Romans 6:6).

This meaning of repentance can be seen in Saul's conversion. Saul of Tarsus was a Pharisee, a Hebrew of Hebrews (Philippians 3:5). Regarding the law of Moses, he said he was found blameless (Philippians 3:6). In other words, no legitimate accusation could be brought against him regarding his failure to keep the Law. As a Pharisee—as a Jew of high standing in Judaism—Saul believed that Jesus was an impostor and that He intended to destroy Judaism. Saul thought that he must oppose this Jesus with the fury of a devastating persecution. Without a doubt, he considered anyone who followed Jesus his enemy. With relentless energy and intense determination, he sought to put an end to Christ's church.

As he branched out in his persecution of the church, Saul asked for the backing of the high priest (Acts 9:1, 2). When he received the authority he desired, he left for Damascus to carry out his plan. As he journeyed to Damascus, the Lord Jesus appeared to him in a brilliance that exceeded the sun at high noon. Blinded by the light of the Lord's presence, Saul crumpled to the ground. When Saul realized with earthshaking conviction the truth that the One speaking to him was Jesus the Christ, the Son of God, he asked in deep penitence and contrition, "What shall I do, Lord?" (Acts 22:10). He was instructed to go to Damascus, where he would be told what to do (Acts 9:6). When he arrived, he waited for three days in fasting and prayer until the answer was brought to him by Ananias.

Saul repented. He made a resolute change of will regarding his way of life. His life had been dedicated to Judaism and the persecution of Christ's church; when he repented on that Damascus road, his life took an entirely new direction. He turned from his old life with a revolutionary change of will which affected his entire personality—intellect, emotions, and conscience. Later, he said, "Whatever things were gain to me, those things I have counted as loss for the sake of Christ" (Philippians 3:7).

Christians are people who, like Saul, have turned from sin in repentance. The lifestyle of God's people is that of abstaining from every form of evil (1 Thessalonians 5:22), refusing to be conformed to this world (Romans 12:2), overcoming evil with good (Romans 12:21), and putting to silence any false charge against them by excellent behavior (1 Peter 2:12).

TURNING FROM SIN TO CHRIST

Second, repentance is turning to Christ. It is not just a negative reaction to evil; it is also a positive response to Christ.

Paul commended the Thessalonians because in their repentance they had "turned to God from idols to serve a living and true God" (1 Thessalonians 1:9). If one turned from sin but did not turn to God, he would not have repented in the complete sense of this term in the New Testament.

New Testament preaching in its main thrust exalted Christ. Luke's description of Philip's preaching in Samaria is an example of the type of preaching all inspired men did: "Philip went down to the city of Samaria and began proclaiming Christ to them" (Acts 8:5). As people responded to this type of preaching, they renounced sin and received Christ by yielding to the gospel message. After the preaching of Paul at Ephesus, both sides of repentance were evident. Luke said,

> And fear fell upon them all and the name of the Lord Jesus was being magnified. Many also of those who had believed kept coming, confessing and disclosing

their practices. And many of those who practiced magic brought their books together and began burning them in the sight of everyone (Acts 19:17b–19a).

The repentant Ephesians acknowledged Christ and abandoned their sinful practices.

Saul's repentance was both a turning from sin and a turning to Christ. He was on his way to persecute Christians as he journeyed to Damascus. Living under the Law of Moses, he had been free from moral and ceremonial crimes. He had not been a wicked prodigal in any sense. His repentance, therefore, did not affect his core desire to please God; he had been driven by this desire from his youth and had manifested such in his faithful keeping of the Law of Moses. His persecution of Christians, however, was a terrible sin. Consequently, his repentance before God resulted in the rejection of his former belief that serving God required persecuting Christians and denouncing Christ. It also required a turning to Christ, an acknowledgment of Him as Lord, and a humble bowing in submission to His will.

Paul himself described his repentance in Philippians 3:8–11:

> ... I count all things to be loss in view of the surpassing value of knowing Christ Jesus my Lord, for whom I have suffered the loss of all things, and count them but rubbish so that I may gain Christ, and may be found in Him, not having a righteousness of my own derived from the Law, but that which is through faith in Christ, the righteousness which comes from God on the basis of faith, that I may know Him and the power of His resurrection and the fellowship of

His sufferings, being conformed to His death; in
order that I may attain to the resurrection from the
dead.

Therefore, Saul turned from sin to Christ. Repentance
to him was both negative and positive, a turning
from his former way of life and a turning to a new
and better way of life in Christ.

The church, Christ's body of penitent people, lives
in submission to Christ. The members of it have become one with Christ. Through repentance, the
Christian has entered a life of holiness and righteousness. He has been crucified with Christ, and in his
new life which has resulted from his repentance, he
lives by faith in the Son of God (Galatians 2:20). As
God's penitent people, Christians wear Christ's name,
live in union with Christ, exalt Christ in worship,
and are constrained to be righteous by their anticipation of going to be more fully with Him at His coming or at death.

TURNING FROM SIN TO CHRIST
FOR LIFE

Third, repentance is a turning from sin to Christ
for life. Jesus did not invite anyone to take a religious
vacation, a brief respite from wickedness. He asked
for total commitment, which He referred to as a birth
of water and the Spirit, a birth from above (John 3:5).
So radical and lasting is this transformation that Paul
compared it to a spiritual circumcision, a complete
removal of the body of flesh through the working of
God:

And in Him you were also circumcised with a cir-

cumcision made without hands, in the removal of
the body of the flesh by the circumcision of Christ
(Colossians 2:11).

Paul said that conversion means discarding the
old self and putting on the new self, as one would
remove shabby, dirty, worn-out clothes and lay them
aside with the intent of never returning to them
(Ephesians 4:24; Colossians 3:10). God lifts us up
from sin and death and gives us life in Christ when
we are redeemed by the blood of Christ (Colossians
2:13).

Repentance involves an ongoing commitment. In
our response to God, we are to put to death the deeds
of the body. Henceforth, one task we have as Christians is to keep these deeds from resurfacing. Paul
said, "Therefore consider the members of your
earthly body as dead to immorality, impurity, passion, evil desire, and greed, which amounts to
idolatry" (Colossians 3:5). He also said,

> But now you also, put them all aside: anger, wrath,
> malice, slander, and abusive speech from your
> mouth. Do not lie to one another, since you laid aside
> the old self with its evil practices (Colossians 3:8,
> 9).

Paul wrote of a putting away at one point in time, a
point of death, and of a continual putting aside, an
ongoing repentance.

Where could we turn for a more vivid illustration
of this meaning of repentance than to the conversion
of Saul? Someone has said, "We have not yet seen
what God can do with one man who is totally con-

verted to Him." If we have not, we come very close to it in the life of Saul. The impact in the world as a result of the conversion of Saul has been felt for two thousand years. His decision to follow Christ was final and irrevocable. He laid his life at the foot of the cross for the service and good that Christ could do with it.

As Alexander the Great brought his army ashore for a great battle, it is said that he commanded that the ships be set afire once they were vacated. Alexander would not consider the possibility of a retreat. There would be no turning back for him or for his men. Any future they had was straight ahead, not behind. So it was with Saul. He left no room in his heart for any kind of reservation or any possibility of retreat.

God's people, the church, have made a commitment—one so strong that it may be labeled a transformation, a passing from death to life (1 John 3:14). They have put on the new man in Christ for life. This happened at one point in time, as their conversion to Christ took place, but heart cleansing is a continual obligation for them (Romans 6:2b). The old man has been put to death, but he will try to come back to life if any opportunity is given for his resurrection (Romans 6:12, 13). The Christian must be careful to walk in wisdom, not in foolishness (Ephesians 5:17). He does not participate in the unfruitful deeds of darkness, but rather exposes them (Ephesians 5:11). He has died, and his life is hidden with Christ in God (Colossians 3:3). The Christian has presented himself to God as one who is alive from the dead and as one whose body is dedicated to righteousness (Romans 6:13).

CONCLUSION

Everyone accountable before God has the obligation to repent and to live the life that repentance requires. Repentance is a profound changing of the will, a turning from sin to Christ for life. It is brought about by conviction of sin, godly sorrow, and the goodness of God. It results in a transformation which brings to life a new person who is hidden with Christ in God.

The church is a community of new persons. They are not perfect, but they are in pursuit of purity, godliness, and righteousness. Their lifetime commitment is to be vessels of honor in the Lord's service.

Three incentives for repentance can easily be identified in the Scriptures. First, Paul said that the goodness of God leads to repentance: "Or do you think lightly of the riches of His kindness and tolerance and patience, not knowing that the kindness of God leads you to repentance?" (Romans 2:4). Second, Peter mentioned the promise of reward: "Therefore repent and return, so that your sins may be wiped away, in order that times of refreshing may come from the presence of the Lord" (Acts 3:19). Third, John referred to the fear of punishment:

> Now in those days John the Baptist came, preaching in the wilderness of Judea, saying, "Repent, for the kingdom of heaven is at hand. ... The axe is already laid at the root of the trees; therefore every tree that does not bear good fruit is cut down and thrown into the fire" (Matthew 3:1–10).

Repentance in and of itself is not enough to please God, but repentance does create within us the spirit of submission. Such a spirit compels us to obey all of God's commands which He has made requisite to coming into Christ. It opens up one's life to God's will.

It has been said that the last word of our Savior was not the Great Commission but His call for five of the seven churches of Asia to repent (Revelation 1—3). If you have not repented and come into the body of Christ to live as God's penitent people, you have no greater need. If you are a Christian, living as a new person in Christ, your supreme obligation is to live the commitment you have made.

STUDY QUESTIONS
(answers on page 271)

1. How did death change the thinking of the rich man?
2. Why is "repentance" a cornerstone word and a chief attitude for anyone seeking to be a Christian?
3. Why is repentance more than regret that one has sinned?
4. Explain why repentance is not just godly sorrow.
5. How can repentance be seen in Saul's conversion?
6. Why did Paul commend the Thessalonians?
7. How is repentance more than confession of sins?
8. What are the three scriptural incentives for repentance?

A GUIDE FOR FURTHER BIBLE STUDY

Who should repent?—2 Peter 3:9; Acts 17:30, 31; Luke 13:3.

New Testament examples of repentance—The Prodigal Son (Luke 15:11–24); Zaccheus (Luke 19:2–8).

The cost of repentance—Matthew 10:34–39; Luke 12:51–53.

Examples of conversions—Acts 2:36–47; 8:5, 6, 12, 18–22, 26–39; 9:1–18; 10:1–48; 16:13–15, 25–34; 18:8; 19:1–5.

Christian influence—Matthew 5:13–16; 1 Corinthians 15:33.

Jesus shed His blood for all people—Salvation is provided for the obedient (Hebrews 9:11–14); the blood of bulls and goats is insufficient to take away sins (Hebrews 10:4); His blood has redeemed us (1 Peter 1:18, 19); Jesus tasted death for everyone (Hebrews 2:9).

When we look at the cross we learn—that we need a Savior (Romans 3:23; 5:12); how much God loves us (John 3:16); that Christ loves people even though they are sinners (Romans 5:8, 9); that salvation is a gift from God (Ephesians 2:8–10).

Jesus' death on the cross saves us when we contact His blood through baptism—We are buried with Him in baptism (Romans 6:3, 4); baptism saves (1 Peter 3:21).

How can you live as a Christian after obeying the gospel?
1. *Have a great commitment to spiritual growth.* Make every effort to grow (2 Peter 1:1–10). Plan to grow (Philippians 3:7–15).
2. *Study the Bible.* Accurately handle the Word (2 Timothy 2:15). Grow in knowledge (2 Peter 3:18). Study the Scriptures daily (Acts 17:11). Receive the Word with humility, and obey it (James 1:21–25).
3. *Add the Christian graces to your life.* Add faith, moral excellence, knowledge, self-control, perseverance, godliness, brotherly kindness, and love (2 Peter 1:5–7).
4. *Pray regularly.* Pray for wisdom (James 1:5, 6). Pray without ceasing (1 Thessalonians 5:17).
5. *Worship regularly (with other Christians, if possible).* Do not forsake the assembly (Hebrews 10:25). If there is no church in your area, you can start one in your home (see page 275). Worship in spirit and truth (John 4:24).
6. *Tell others about Jesus.* Teach everyone you can (Matthew 28:18–20; Mark 16:15, 16). Share this book with friends, and help them to become Christians.
7. *Do good works.* Those saved by Jesus are created to do good works (Ephesians 2:10).

20
What Will You Do With Jesus?

Even as large and as complex as this world is, according to the divine Scriptures, it is only a place of preparation for the life we will live in eternity. Therefore, life here is only a brief beginning. Every human being is a living soul, destined to live beyond this world in heaven or hell. The New Testament describes for us everlasting life and everlasting destruction (Matthew 25:46). There is no place in-between eternal life and eternal death for us to abide in the hereafter. At death or when Jesus returns, our destiny is sealed forever. There will be no second opportunities to change our relationship with God after entering the world of eternity. What a sobering thought! What we do about Jesus has eternal implications. We plead with you to decide that you will become a Christian and live your life for Christ so that you may have the abundant life now (John 10:10) and eternal life in the world to come (1 John 2:25).

You have come to the end of this study of becoming a faithful member of "the church," as that theme is presented in the Scriptures. You have been briefly introduced to Jesus Christ—the Son of God—who came into the world and demonstrated by His life, teachings, and love what God is like and what God's will is. He died for our sins on the cross, making it possible for everyone who obeys His message of salvation to become and live as a child of God. Further, you have studied carefully the nature of the church which resulted and continues to result from His life and death. You have seen how one enters that church and lives in this world as that church. You have now come to the big question, the most serious question you have ever thought about: "What shall I do about Jesus?"

It is the sincere prayer and earnest hope of all Christians that you will resolve in your heart to become a Christian and be a faithful follower of Christ for the rest of your life. In the course of your study, maybe you have already said to yourself, "I want to be a Christian." Maybe you have thought, "I have some questions about becoming a Christian and when I get those questions answered, I will become one."

If you are asking questions, carefully read the remaining part of this book. It will provide some answers. Also, it lists and explains some steps that you need to take in order to fulfill your desire to become and live as a Christian.

STEP ONE: SALVATION

The first step to take, of course, is to become a Christian. Anyone, anywhere in the world, can become a Christian if he believes in Christ (John 8:24), repents (or turns from his sins; Acts 17:30), confesses Jesus as the Christ (Romans 10:10), and is baptized into Christ for the remission of sins (Acts 2:38).

Let us answer some questions you may ask:

"What About Children?"

The New Testament never mentions the baptism of infants or small children. They do not need to be baptized, for they are safe in their innocence before the Lord. Since they do not know right from wrong, they are not accountable in God's sight. When they become conscious of what is required of them by the Lord, then they should become Christians (as should all people) by obeying the Lord's way of salvation. In their innocence, however, they are safe before God, for they have not sinned. As they are, with their minds seeking to understand, putting their faith completely in those who lead them, their confiding trust and teachableness is an example for adults to imitate (Matthew 18:3). Jesus said of children, "For the kingdom of heaven belongs to such as these" (Matthew 19:14b).

As a young person or adult who understands the way of salvation, who knows that you have sinned before God, and who knows that you must become a Christian to be saved, you now need to obey the Lord's plan of salvation.

"What Must I Do?"

In our studies, you have seen how to become a Christian. You can become a Christian by accepting the evidence and testimony of the Scriptures about Jesus' being the Son of God. The only truly accurate book in the world, the Bible, has told you who Jesus is and what He came into the world to do. Do you accept this message? If you do, then you have come to believe that Jesus Christ is the Son of God who came into the world to die on the cross to save you from your sins and make it possible for you to be a child of God.

You must also ask yourself, "Have I turned from my sins?" You will never be perfect in this world, but by repenting you resolve to put away sin from your life and sincerely follow the Word of the Lord from now on. Following your genuine repentance, Jesus will be your Lord, and the Scriptures will be the guidebook by which you will live.

You must next find someone to baptize you into Christ for the remission of your sins. There may be a church of Christ in your community. If so, find a member of that church and ask him to introduce you to a Christian man who will baptize you into Christ. When you are introduced to that Christian man, tell him that you want to confess Jesus as the Christ before others and that you wish for him to baptize you into the spiritual body of Christ for the forgiveness of your sins. He will be happy to assist you.

"How Can I Find the Church of Christ?"

In this day of religious confusion, you will want to make sure that you have contacted a group of people who have entered the Lord's church and are continuing to be the Lord's church. One way you can tell is to notice how they refer to themselves. They will not wear any man-made names. They will call themselves a church of Christ and will refer to themselves by the other designations for the church that are found in the Scriptures. If you see that they have given themselves a name which is not a biblical way of referring to the church, that is a sign that they are part of a denomination and are something separate and different from the Lord's church.

Another way you can tell if a group is a church of Christ is by checking to see if they are following the Word of God. Here are some questions that you can ask them to determine their goals and purposes:

Are you simply trying to be the church of the New Testament?

When you gather on Sunday for worship, what is your worship service like?

Do you partake of the Lord's Supper every Sunday as in Acts 20:7?

Do you sing without instrumental accompaniment according to the New Testament example?

Do you pray in Jesus' name?

Do you study the Word of God as your only creed and guide?

Do you give each Sunday as you have been prospered (1 Corinthians 16:1, 2)?

How are you organized as a church? Do you have more organization than preachers, teachers, elders, and deacons?[1]

Do you have earthly headquarters, or do you just look to Christ as your head?[2]

What is your mission in this world: Are you seeking to fulfill our Lord's Great Commission (Matthew 28:19, 20)?

---

[1]The organization of the churches of the New Testament was simple and basic. First, there were ministers and teachers who preached and taught the Word. Second, each congregation that had become mature enough had a plurality of elders (sometimes called "overseers," "shepherds," and "pastors") who would guide and watch over the congregation. Third, each congregation had deacons who served the church under the oversight of the elders.

[2]The New Testament names only one head of the church: Christ. His church has no earthly headquarters; each congregation of the church follows only the leadership of Christ.

You would be wise to ask these questions, for you are seeking to understand who they are. You want to become a member of the Lord's church, not a member of a denomination. (See page 275.)

If you cannot find a church of Christ, then you should establish one. Find a sincere man who is interested in serving the true God. Ask him to read this book as he studies his Bible. Then ask him if he will join you in becoming a Christian and in being the Lord's church in your community. If he wants to follow Christ, you can baptize each other. Locate a church baptistery or make arrangements for the use of a swimming pool. If necessary, you can go to a nearby stream, lake, or pond (where you would have enough water to immerse someone).

When you baptize him, make sure that you fulfill three commands of the Scriptures. First, ask him this question: "Do you believe that Jesus Christ is the Son of God?" We see this command in Romans 10:10. He should affirm that he believes in Jesus as God's Son.

Second, you need to make sure that you are baptizing the man into the body of Christ—the church—for the forgiveness of sins. Before you baptize him, describe out loud what is taking place, both for the benefit of those present and as a reminder to him of what is happening. Here is one example of how you could state it (based on Matthew 28:19, 20; Romans 6:3; Acts 2:38; and Mark 16:16):

> I am baptizing you in the name of the Father, the Son, and the Holy Spirit, into the spiritual body of Christ, the church of the New Testament, for the forgiveness of your sins through the blood of Jesus Christ, in obedience to Christ's command.

Third, as you baptize him, make sure that you immerse him completely. Remember, baptism in the New Testament is a burial in water (Romans 6:4). Here is an illustration of how baptism can be done:

In the deep water of a baptistery or swimming pool, the one being baptized may be leaned backward until he is fully immersed.

Once you have baptized him, have him baptize you in the same way. He needs to ask you the same question, and he should state clearly why he is baptizing you, just as you did when you baptized him.

After your baptism, you are a Christian, a member of the Lord's church. Even if the Lord's church has not existed in your community in the past, it does now—for you are the church of Christ! You have established the church where you live by becoming a Christian.

STEP TWO: LIVING AS A CHRISTIAN

Of course, the second step that you need to take is a continuous, never-ending step—namely, that of living the Christian life. You now are a Christian, and you will want to live as one. (See the chart entitled "What Elders Are To Be, All Christians Are To Be" on page 278.)

How does a Christian live? A good way to summarize the life of a Christian is to say that he is what his name implies: a follower of Christ. He is a CHRIST-ian, one who lives the way Christ lived (Philippians 1:21). Life to the Christian is Christ.

Searching the Scriptures

Anyone who follows Christ will be characterized by one important trait: submission to the Father's will. Jesus was perfect in every way, but one charac-teristic of His life that you and I can set out to imitate is faithful obedience to the Father. Christian living, then, means searching the Scriptures for God's will and then humbly, reverently, and lovingly obeying that will. A Christian stays close to the Word of God. He reads it daily and tries to put into practice what he learns from it.

Trying to Imitate Jesus' Lifestyle

Three other principles that should guide us in our living for Jesus include the "golden rule," compas-sion, and prayer. A good way to imitate Jesus is always to ask ourselves, "How would I like to be treated?" The "golden rule" (Matthew 7:12) is followed when we decide how we would like to be treated and then proceed to treat others that way. This rule was Christ's way of living, and it is the best way to live in this world.

Jesus was a man of compassion. The word "com-passion" means "feeling with" others. Jesus loved the poor, the needy, and the lonely. His heart went out to them. He ministered to them. Likewise, a Christian should be a person who is concerned about others and continually manifests that love by helping them if he can (Matthew 9:36).

Even though Jesus was the Son of God, He prayed

to the Father often—privately, publicly, and in small groups. A Christian also prays to God continually.

Since you are now a Christian, God is your Father. He has claimed you as His own. Pray to Him regularly with a believing heart. Ask for His will to be done in your life, praying to Him in the name of Jesus. Here is a sample of how you can pray to God:

Address God: Dear Father,
Praise Him: Hallowed be Your name.
Thank Him: How grateful we are for the blessings You have given. . . . (Name some of them.)
Petition Him: Here is what we need, as far as we can tell. Grant these requests if they are in harmony with Your will.
Petition Him: Forgive our sins as we forgive others. Deliver us from evil.
Praise Him: To You be all the glory.
Close: In Jesus' name we pray to You. Amen.

You probably recognized this pattern as taken in part from our Lord's model which He taught His disciples in Matthew 6:9–13. Part of His prayer would not apply to us (for example, the part about the request for the kingdom to come, since His kingdom came at Pentecost), but much of it does apply to us. Remember, the pattern given is just a sample and is intended to be only a suggested order to follow when one is expressing his own thoughts to God.

Let us stress this truth: You will not be perfect. Human beings cannot be perfect, but we can dedicate our hearts to the doing of His will. When we fail, we can get up, dust ourselves off, and set out again to do His will. The important thing is that we are striving to do His will. We will be saved by God's grace—

through faith, not by perfection (Ephesians 2:8). Having faith means honestly seeking to do His will.

When we fail in such a way that we hurt others, let us apologize to them and assure them that we are sorry and that we will seek to do better in the future (James 5:16). If we sin and our sin has hurt the church as a whole, we can come before the church, ask for forgiveness, and request that our brothers and sisters in Christ pray for us (James 5:16). God will forgive us, and the church will forgive us.

One section of the Scriptures that you may want to read first as you enter your life as a Christian is the beginning of the New Testament—Matthew, Mark, Luke, and John—the life of Christ. This reading and study will give you an understanding of how Jesus lived on this earth. Everything you learn about Him will help you to follow Him more closely.

STEP THREE: WORSHIPING GOD

The third step you need to take as you seek to be a Christian is to begin worshiping God regularly. If a church of Christ exists in your neighborhood, you will want to meet with them on Sunday and any other times that they meet for corporate worship. On each Sunday, they will meet to sing, pray, study God's Word, keep the Lord's Supper, and give of their means as God has blessed them. You should participate with them in each of these expressions of worship. (See page 150.)

If no congregation of the Lord's church meets in your community, you can begin regular, faithful worship of God in your home. It does not matter to God where the church meets, as long as we meet to worship Him. There is no command in the New Testament to worship in a special building. Scriptural worship can take place anywhere two or three are gathered in the name of Jesus (Matthew 18:20).

Meeting as the Church
In the New Testament we notice that the early Christians met on the first day of the week, or Sunday. This was the day when the Lord arose from the dead. When those first Christians came together for worship on Sunday, they partook of the supper that Jesus instituted to be observed in memory of His death and resurrection. It is clear that they partook of this supper each Sunday. It was the "Lord's Supper" (1 Corinthians 11:20), taken on each Lord's Day. Study carefully Hebrews 10:25; 1 Corinthians 11:22; 16:1, 2; and Acts 20:7.

Observing the Lord's Supper
When Christ created the Lord's Supper, He used two elements: fruit of the vine and unleavened bread. Our Lord was eating the Passover with His disciples when He told them to keep this supper. The Passover supper included only unleavened bread and a beverage, which was a mixture of the fruit of the vine (juice from some kind of grape) and water. Jesus told His disciples to eat of the bread and remember His body that was given for them. He told them to drink some of the cup, or fruit of the vine, and remember His blood that was shed for them.

You will want to follow our Lord's instructions and the example of the Christians in the Book of Acts. Each Sunday, those of you who have been obedient to Christ should gather for worship. You should sing, pray, and study God's Word. At some point in the worship service, partake of this supper that Jesus gave you. Have available some unleavened bread in a plate. Ask God to receive your thanks for the bread that represents Christ's body and for His great sacrifice. Then, pass the bread to each Christian who wishes to partake of it and remember Jesus' body.

Second, take the cup or cups which contain the fruit of the vine. Pray to God, giving thanks for the cup and the precious blood that Jesus shed for our forgiveness. After the prayer, pass the cups to the Christians present, so that each may partake of the cup and remember that Jesus' blood was shed for us.

Putting Aside, or Giving

Each Christian is to "put aside and save" in order to give to the Lord's work. At an appropriate point while the church is gathered for worship, every Christian should be given an opportunity to give out of his or her prosperity, as the New Testament teaches (1 Corinthians 16:1, 2). Some type of basket or other container may be passed around to allow for this giving, or a place may be provided for Christians to leave the money which they have set aside for God. Remember that this is an expression of worship and should be done reverently and joyfully. The donations should be used to do the work of the church. For example, the money may be used to preach the gospel to others, to help the poor, to purchase Bibles for study, and any other purpose that might be in harmony with the work of the church. Decisions on how to use what is collected should be made by the church and not by only one individual.

Here is an example of how a worship service may be planned:

Prayer
Song or songs
A discussion of a chapter from the Scriptures or a sermon if a capable teacher or preacher is available
Song
A Scripture reading concerning the Lord's Supper
Observance of the Lord's Supper
Song
Giving as each has prospered
Song
Prayer

However the service is arranged, each of these elements of worship is to be included.

Singing

Following the institution of the Lord's Supper, Jesus and His disciples sang a hymn (Matthew 26:30). Paul's instruction to the Christians in Corinth reveals that the early church employed singing in their worship assemblies (1 Corinthians 14:15; see v. 26).

One fact we know about the first-century Christians is that they were committed to doing things God's way (Acts 2:42; 4:19, 20; 5:29). While God accepted the use of musical instruments in the worship of the Old Testament, the early Christians did not use them in their assemblies. They must have done what they did because of apostolic teaching, which came from God (Matthew 16:17b; 1 Corinthians 2:9–11). The New Testament was written by those same Spirit-inspired men who instructed the earliest Christians.

The apostles knew the real purpose of worship, and their instruction equipped the early church for worship that would please God. We may safely conclude that if God had wanted the church to use instruments in worship, He would have given that instruction to the apostles—but He did not. Once we understand what worship really is and what God wants worship to accomplish, we understand that instruments of music do not contribute to the process.

Conducting Congregational Meetings

In order for the local congregation to conduct its work "properly and in an orderly manner" (1 Corinthians 14:40), the men of the congregation will need to meet from time to time. This is especially true if there are no elders. These meetings will not be for the purpose of making laws for God, but to ensure that the worship and work of the local body is done in a Christlike way. Meetings will provide the appropriate time and place for making decisions on worship times, making assignments for helping with the worship service, planning for good works, and discussing other spiritual matters. It is essential that each one who participates in the meeting conduct himself in a Christlike fashion (Ephesians 4:1–3). Someone once said, "Everyone has a right to his say, but no one has a right to expect his way." This is a good motto.

As congregational matters are discussed, these questions should be asked about each decision:

- Is it scriptural?
- Will it glorify God?
- Will it edify?
- Will it work?

The men will need to agree upon the frequency and time for these meetings. They should choose a time when the greatest number of men will be able to attend. One of the mature Christian brothers should be selected to lead the meetings. It is wise to vary who takes this responsibility. This is not a position of authority, but an expedient way to proceed. Decisions made should represent a consensus of the men. Someone ought to keep a record of the decisions. A meeting might follow this order:

Prayer
Old business—discussion left from past meetings; reports on progress and assigned responsibilities
New business—consideration of needs, future plans, assignments, and spiritual concerns
Prayer

Worshiping God Daily

You will want to worship God daily in your heart and with your physical family. At each meal, pray to God, giving thanks for the food He has given before you eat. Pray regularly with your family, bringing before God the needs that you have and giving Him thanks and praise for all that He has done for you.

Of course, you will want to worship God at times other than on Sunday. You will always meet on Sunday, including in that worship service the observance of the Lord's Supper and the contribution. Beyond that, you may want to meet with fellow Christians at other times during the week for Bible study, prayer, and singing. It is important for Christians to meet together often, worship together, and encourage one another in the Lord.

As a servant of the Lord, you should let Him talk to you daily by reading and studying His Word. You can also talk to Him daily by praying to Him.

STEP FOUR: DOING GOOD WORKS

The fourth step that you need to take is that of serving the Lord. You are now a Christian, a follower of Christ, so live the way He lived. We are told that He went about doing good (Acts 10:38).

Sharing the Gospel

Christians are to evangelize, to share the gospel. Jesus told us just before He went back to heaven to "go into all the world and preach the gospel . . ." (Mark 16:15). Christ died to create the gospel; now we must work to see that it is preached to every person. One way that you can evangelize is to ask others to read this book. Encourage them to become Christians. Let us do all we can to lead others to Christ.

Edifying Others

Another task of the Christian is to edify others. The word "edify" means to build up. When you have an established congregation of fifteen or more, please write to Truth for Today World Mission School (use the address on page 303), and we will send you some materials to assist you in studying the Bible. Let us continue to grow in our knowledge of Christ and His way, and let us encourage others to grow with us.

Helping Others

You will also want to engage in works of benevolence. Ask yourself, "What can I do to help the poor?"

You cannot be like Christ if you do not care for the needy (Matthew 25:31–46).

Here is a list of some good works Christians do:

> Teach others the gospel
> Minister to the sick
> Assist children in learning about God
> Feed the hungry
> Help widows and orphans
> Visit those in prison
> Practice hospitality
> Distribute Christian literature
> Invite others to worship services
> Pray for others
> Read the Bible to those who cannot read

Jesus came into this world to serve. He came not to be ministered unto, but to minister unto others and to give His life as a ransom for many (Mark 10:45). We cannot die for others the way Jesus did; but we can live for others by teaching them the gospel, helping them to grow in Christ, and showing compassion for them when they are hurting.

CONCLUSION

Have you read the story of the Ethiopian nobleman in Acts 8? If not, pause in your reading of this book and read that story. Philip was sent to him to teach him the gospel. Gladly, the Ethiopian received the gospel and became a Christian.

Philip was an inspired man. This book that you are reading is not inspired (except for the last section, the New Testament). However, in these pages, you have read what the New Testament teaches about the salvation Christ brought and the church He established. These pages have pointed you to the inspired book, the Bible. Compare what you have read here to the Scriptures, and you will see that we have tried to teach you what the New Testament teaches.

God gave the Ethiopian an opportunity to be saved. It was not a long, drawn-out study; but it was sufficient to teach him how to become a Christian and live as a Christian. We have tried to provide the same teaching for you. The opportunity is now yours. May you take full and complete advantage of this opportunity. We bid you a sincere farewell. May God's rich blessings fall upon you as you obey the gospel that He has given through His Son. We will be looking forward to meeting you in heaven, if not before.

STUDY QUESTIONS
(answers on page 272)

1. Why does the question "What will you do with Jesus?" have eternal implications?
2. Do infants and small children need to be baptized? Why or why not?
3. What is the purpose of baptism?
4. What are some questions that will help you to find the church of Christ?
5. What Scripture teaches that baptism is a burial in water?
6. What is a good way to summarize the life of a Christian?
7. Why will a Christian stay close to the Word of God?
8. Each Sunday the church will meet to worship God. What expressions of worship should be used?
9. What two elements did Jesus use when He created the Lord's Supper?
10. What are the four steps you need to take in order to become a Christian and live as a Christian?

Appendix 1

Answers To Study Questions

THE QUESTION OF GOD
(questions for Chapter 1 are found on page 13)

1. The most profound question anyone can ask is "Does God exist?"
2. The question "Does God exist?" is profound because how we answer this question will affect all the answers to all our other questions about life.
3. The Bible begins with an affirmation about God.
4. The first evidence that compels us to believe in God is the evidence of the world. The earth and the universe eloquently proclaim the existence of God.
5. If the existence of man is not attributed to God, we cannot explain (1) the origin of life, (2) the existence of natural law, and (3) the existence of the family.

IS THE BIBLE GOD'S WORD?
(questions for Chapter 2 are found on page 28)

1. The Greek phrase translated "inspired by God" literally means "God-breathed." Secular writers are said to be "inspired" by a variety of stimuli, but the Bible asserts that God Himself is its source of inspiration.
2. Diocletian was unsuccessful in his attempt to destroy the Bible. In fact, one hundred years later, when another Roman emperor announced that he wanted to reproduce the

New Testament, fifty copies were presented to him within twenty-four hours.
3. Written in a world that knew nothing about hygiene or health practices, Moses' books demonstrate modern concepts. Though written three thousand years before scientists discovered germs, Leviticus 13:45 gives instructions to aid in preventing the spread of disease.
4. While the Bible includes every subject known to literature and was written by forty-plus authors over more than two thousand years, it demonstrates complete unity.
5. The theme of the Bible is the story of a Man—Jesus Christ.
6. The Bible has exerted more influence on mankind than any other book. It has changed the flow of history, erected empires, and brought blessings and success to those who have obeyed its precepts.
7. The Bible offers the reader hope and assurance for his own eternity, and it brings him comfort when a loved one is taken away.
8. Wonders of God's Word include its antiquity, its modernity, its diversity, its unity, its theme, its influence, and its comfort.

WHO IS GOD THE FATHER?
(questions for Chapter 3 are found on page 45)

1. Only one Being is the true and living God. He created the world and is the only being who is eternal, all-powerful, all-knowing, and ever-present.
2. The Old Testament concept of the Godhead is seen in Genesis 1:26, Genesis 3:22, Genesis 11:7, and Isaiah 6:8.
3. The baptism of Jesus, the work of man's redemption, prayer, and Great Commission baptism show instances of the Father, the Son, and the Holy Spirit working in co-operation.
4. The only way for man to come to God is through Jesus Christ. He is the only authentic mediator between God and man.
5. John 14:6 and 1 Timothy 2:5 teach that God cannot be approached through angels, saints, or other people (living or

dead). Jesus Christ is the only way to the Father.

6. Jesus is called the "Son of Man" to reflect His relationship to mankind; and in His relationship to God, He is called the "Son of God."

7. Some of the facts taught in the Bible about God are these: (1) The Father, the Son, and the Holy Spirit exist. (2) The Three make up one glorious Godhead. (3) They are united and exist as one. (4) They are eternal, distinct and different from all created things. (5) They are one in will and purpose.

8. These truths rest on the fact that God created all things: (1) He is the One behind all realities. (2) He is eternal. (3) He is almighty. (4) He is all-knowing. (5) He is present everywhere. (6) He is the only true and living God.

9. We are told in Colossians 1:16, 17 that God continues to work in the world, holding all things together. Logic and observation also tell us that an almighty hand maintains the earth with its natural laws. He continues to provide air, water, and sunshine for the earth and its people.

10. God's righteous judgment through Jesus Christ will be personal, specific, and universal.

IS JESUS THE SON OF GOD?
(questions for Chapter 4 are found on page 52)

1. At the heart of Christianity lies the truth that Jesus Christ is the Son of God.

2. Jesus' birth was prophesied, including some specifics of His genealogy. The place and nature of His birth were predicted. Prophets foretold His flight into Egypt and the massacre at the time of His birth. Prophecies told of His life in Galilee, His victorious entry into Jerusalem, His forerunner, and His work. His ministry, His teaching in parables, His mission among the Gentiles, and His rejection by the Jewish rulers were all predicted. Jesus' betrayal and death were pictured in prophecy in great detail. His dying words were recorded in advance, along with information about His burial, resurrection, and ascension. (See pages 48 and 49.)

3. The fulfillment of prophecies concerning Jesus' life shows

that Jesus was divine and that the men who wrote the
Bible were inspired.

4. Jesus claimed to exist before Abraham and said that He
   was with God before the beginning of the world. He taught
   that He came from heaven and had all authority on
   earth.

5. Jesus said that He was the light of the world; then He made
   the blind to see. He called Himself the bread of life, and
   He fed five thousand. He claimed to be the resurrection
   and the life, and He raised Lazarus from the dead.

6. Jesus' goodness was acknowledged by Pilate's wife, by
   Herod, by the thief on the cross, and even by Judas.

7. The Lord's Day, the Lord's Supper, baptism, and the dating
   of our calendars are evidences of Jesus' impact on our
   world today.

WHO IS THE HOLY SPIRIT?
(questions for Chapter 5 are found on page 62)

1. The question is *"Who?"* rather than *"What?"* because the
   Holy Spirit is a being, a divine individual with personality.

2. The fact that the Holy Spirit demonstrates judgment, mind,
   will, knowledge, and emotions shows that He is a living
   person, not just a force.

3. Ill treatment of powers or forces is not usually described
   with words like "grieved," "insulted," or "quenched,"
   except in a poetic or figurative context. The context of these
   verses does not indicate that the language is poetic or
   figurative. If one can "grieve" or "insult" the Holy Spirit,
   then He must be a person.

4. The Holy Spirit shares with the Father and the Son the
   qualities of being eternal, all-knowing, all-powerful, and
   present everywhere. Like the Father and the Son, the
   Spirit has creative power.

DID GOD BECOME MAN?
(questions for Chapter 6 are found on page 71)

1. The first four books of the New Testament—the Gospels—
   reveal how God became man.

2. Birth was not the beginning for Jesus. He shared the Father's glory before the world existed.

3. John 1:1–5 teaches these four great truths: (1) Jesus was not a creation. (2) God created the world through Jesus. (3) Jesus gives life to the living. (4) Jesus is Lord of life and death.

4. Jesus descended by (1) leaving heaven, (2) becoming man, (3) serving men, and (4) submitting to death.

5. The fact that God became man is the central truth of Christianity.

6. Jesus' birth was unique because He was born of a virgin.

7. We must never forget that Jesus (1) was and is God, (2) became a man, and (3) lived on the earth as the God-Man.

8. Jesus was God: For Him to become man was a greater step down than a man's becoming an ant.

HOW SHALL WE VIEW JESUS?
(questions for Chapter 7 are found on page 84)

1. The word "savior" refers to someone who rescues others from extreme danger.

2. Jesus is a unique Savior in that He saves us from our sins. He is a spiritual Savior.

3. "The Christ" means "the anointed or chosen one of God."

4. We know that Jesus is the Son of God because God announced Him as His Son at Jesus' baptism. John the apostle said that we have been given three witnesses: the Spirit, the water, and the blood.

5. In speaking of the Holy Spirit, the water, and the blood, the apostle was referring to the events in the life of Jesus. The Spirit descended upon Him when He was baptized in water, and the blood refers to the events surrounding His death.

6. Peter challenged his hearers to accept Jesus as Lord and Christ (Acts 2:36).

7. If Jesus is Lord (and He *is*), then we must submit to His teaching and give Him first place in our lives.

WHY DID JESUS COME TO EARTH?
(questions for Chapter 8 are found on page 95)

1. The Lord's coming to earth was the greatest event in human history. Our salvation depended on His coming to die on the cross.
2. Jesus was completely man and completely divine.
3. Jesus was completely divine and completely human.
4. Our Lord came to call out—by His ministry, death, and resurrection—a people whom He would call His church.
5. Jesus chose twelve apostles and personally trained them, but it is apparent that He was training them for the work they would do after His departure (John 14:19).
6. The Epistles show us how to respond to the life of Christ by being His spiritual body.
7. No, we cannot respond properly to the life of Jesus without being His church.
8. We cannot fulfill Jesus' mission for us in this world without living as His church.

THE CROSS AND THE CHURCH
(questions for Chapter 9 are found on page 108)

1. The heart of the story of the Bible is the sacrifice of His life made by the Son of God on the cross for men.
2. At the center of Christianity alone is the offering of a divine sacrifice for sin and the resurrection of that sacrifice from the dead.
3. A churchless Christianity cannot exist; because a head cannot function without a body, nor can a body function without a head.
4. The cross (1) creates the church, (2) cleanses the church, and (3) compels, or activates, the church.
5. One enters Christ's body through belief in Him (Romans 10:10), repentance of sin (Acts 11:18), confession of Christ as God's Son (Romans 10:10), and baptism into Christ (Galatians 3:27).
6. Jesus invites us to have forgiveness and life.
7. The body of Jesus is the church.

WHAT IS "THE CHURCH"?

(questions for Chapter 10 are found on page 118)

1. Understanding the use of words by the Holy Spirit is crucial. We must be willing to study the biblical world to see the word meanings, illustrations, and thought forms used by Jesus and the apostles. (See pages 110 through 116 and Appendix 3 on page 279.)

2. The word "church" refers to the body of those who have obeyed the gospel of Christ and have been redeemed by the blood of Christ. This body is "the church" as a local assembly of Christians in one place. Also, it can refer to all of the redeemed ones throughout the world.

3. The fact that the church is the temple of God means that God dwells among His people. For this reason, we are to live, work, and worship as people indwelt by God.

4. Christians make up a "living" building, the church. Each Christian should be in a constant state of growth.

5. Christ is the head of the church even as the husband is the head of the wife. Christ loves the church as a husband loves his wife.

6. One enters Christ's church through faith, repentance, confession, and baptism. God adds each saved person to His church; man does not.

7. The church wears the name of Christ, meets together for His worship, and does His work in the world. The Holy Spirit of Christ lives in Christians.

THE NEXT TO THE GREATEST STORY EVER TOLD

(questions for Chapter 11 are found on page 140)

1. The church is the fulfillment of the Great Commission (Matthew 28:20) and is the body of Christ on the earth.

2. The pronoun "they" in Acts 2:1 refers to "the eleven apostles" in Acts 1:26. Nowhere does the Bible indicate that anyone other than the apostles received the baptism of the Holy Spirit on the Day of Pentecost.

3. The apostles were baptized with the Holy Spirit to enable them to reveal God's message, to confirm that the message

was from God, and to pass on miraculous gifts to other Christians.

4. The baptism of the apostles in the Holy Spirit confirms that the New Testament was given to us by inspired men.

5. As evidence of Christ's deity, Peter spoke of His miracles, His resurrection, the fulfillment of prophecy, the evidence of witnesses, and the descent of the Spirit.

6. Christ's resurrection is vital to God's scheme of redemption. Christ could not be thought of as God's divine Son if He had not arisen from the dead.

7. No tragedy is greater than that of being lost in sin.

8. Concerning the conditions of salvation, Mark 16:15, 16 emphasizes faith; Luke 24:46, 47, repentance and forgiveness of sins; and Matthew 28:18–20, baptism.

9. Acts 22:16, in conjunction with Acts 2:38, proves that baptism is in order to receive the remission of sins.

THE CHURCH OF
THE NEW TESTAMENT

(questions for Chapter 12 are found on page 153)

1. "Continually devoting themselves to the apostles' teaching" means faithfully following what the inspired apostles had taught. Christians must have this same firm commitment to the Word of God.

2. The church in Jerusalem shared a oneness of mind, heart, and doctrine (teaching).

3. Today's church should be known for its compassion and obedience to the Word of God. Each person who has obeyed the gospel is made one with Christ and with all other members of the church. Christians are a family with one heart and life.

4. The decision about which is the New Testament church will influence our daily living for God, our spiritual identity, our worship, and our spiritual service.

5. Acts 2:41–47; 5:11; 7:38; and 8:1, 3 show that the New Testament church began on the Day of Pentecost.

6. Major departures from God's Word began in the second century A.D. These departures culminated in the seventh

century with the rise of the Catholic Church and the addition of the pope and a complicated hierarchy. Other denominations began to spring up in the sixteenth century.

7. Individual Christians compose the body of Christ.

8. Any name other than one found in the New Testament does not identify a group as the New Testament church.

9. Yes, Christians today should follow the approved practices of the New Testament church which were established according to the commands of God.

SPECIAL WORDS FOR GOD'S PEOPLE
(questions for Chapter 13 are found on page 168)

1. God was Israel's king, the head of the government and head of their religion. Israel was a "theocracy" (a God-ruled nation).

2. King Saul was to be the servant of Jehovah. His authority was to be limited by the law of Moses.

3. According to Daniel's prophecy, the coming kingdom would be special. It would be an eternal kingdom which would have a nature beyond that of all other kingdoms.

4. Through the guidance of the Holy Spirit, the word "kingdom" was gradually replaced with the word "church." This word use shows how the kingly role of Christ over people's hearts creates the church.

5. Paul was in the kingdom of God but looked forward to entering into the heavenly kingdom. Faithful Christians are under the spiritual rule of Christ now, but will enter into a fuller and closer relationship with God, Christ, and the Holy Spirit in eternity.

6. The word "church" is used 114 times in the New Testament. We cannot understand Christ's way of salvation without understanding the use of this important word in the New Testament. (See Appendix 3 on page 279.)

7. The word "church" commonly meant an assembly, as in Acts 19:25.

8. The word "church" in the New Testament does not always mean a religious or "called out" assembly.

THE DIVINE DESIGNATIONS
OF THE CHURCH

(questions for Chapter 14 are found on page 182)

1. Jesus is the King (head), and members of the church are citizens of His spiritual kingdom.
2. Christ founded the church, purchased it, owns it, and serves as its head. The church may also be viewed as "the church of God."
3. Specific designations for the church were given by God. They fulfill a divine purpose, and we should use them.
4. When we refer to the church as the Bible does, we set ourselves on the right track to become what God intended for us to be.
5. Christians are God's family. At their conversion, God adopts people as His children, giving them family privileges and making them heirs of eternal life with Christ.
6. A "Christian" is a follower of Christ who tries to live as Jesus taught His followers to live.
7. Paul said, "For me to live is Christ, and to die is gain."
8. At conversion, one is adopted as God's child. He or she has an eternal inheritance, as well as the strength and support of God's earthly family. God is the Father, Jesus is the elder Brother, and all Christians are brothers and sisters in Christ.
9. The word "disciple" appears in the New Testament 238 times.
10. A disciple is one who commits himself to someone greater than he and continually learns from the greater one. He is a listener, a learner, and an understudy.
11. "Saints" are set apart for God. A person becomes a "saint," set apart for God, when he or she becomes a Christian. A saint is called with a holy calling, lives in holy conduct, and seeks to appear before God on the last day "holy and blameless and beyond reproach." (See Colossians 1:22.)

CHRIST, THE HEAD OF THE CHURCH

(questions for Chapter 15 are found on page 190)

1. Leadership which is not out in front leading is not true leadership.

2. Jesus leads the church by His law. (See Ephesians 1:21, 23; Colossians 1:18, 19.)
3. Christ will reign as head of the church until the end of time.
4. Jesus became our perfect Savior by living a perfect life and by His obedience to God the Father.
5. We become what we behold. Christians look to the life of Christ as a model of how to live. He ever leads them with His perfect life.
6. We should follow Christ's example of humility and service.
7. Christians "wash each other's feet" by serving one another in whatever way is needed.

HOW DO YOU ENTER THE CHURCH?
(questions for Chapter 16 are found on page 199)

1. The priceless worth of the Lord's church is shown by its divine origin, its precious cost, and the great value placed upon it.
2. Yes, the conditions of the Great Commission are binding upon us today. These are in effect until the end of the world (Matthew 28:18–20).
3. We cannot be saved as the thief on the cross was saved because the thief died under the old law. Now that Christ has died for us, we must obey His Great Commission.
4. In order to become a member of the church today, one must believe, repent, confess Christ, and be baptized (Acts 2:38, 47).
5. Men do not add the saved to the Lord's church; God alone does that.
6. When someone does what was done in the Book of Acts to become a Christian, God will do for him what He did for those who obeyed His will in the Book of Acts.
7. By obeying the gospel the same way people did in Acts 2, one can be sure that he is in Christ's church. He can be sure because the promises of God are sure.
8. Yes, when the Lord's conditions of salvation are corrupted, great damage is done. No one can take seriously Jesus' commission without obeying these conditions and seeing their significance in the Lord's plan.

THE UNITY OF THE CHURCH
(questions for Chapter 17 are found on page 210)

1. Unity is pleasant because it promotes faith in Christ. It is good because Christ prayed for it.
2. Before His crucifixion, Christ prayed for the unity of believers.
3. Paul pleaded for unity in the very name of Jesus Christ.
4. Christians have become one with Christ and one with each other, like the members of one family.
5. When one is baptized into Christ, he or she becomes one with other Christians.
6. The church has oneness in teaching and belief. Unity is given by the Holy Spirit to everyone who enters the body of Christ, but the way to keep that unity is for each Christian to obey the teachings of the Scriptures.
7. Submission to the will of Christ produces unity.
8. Unity in teaching comes from each Christian's concern for obeying the Bible, while unity in day-to-day living comes from concern for each other. The church needs both.
9. To keep unity, Christians must consider brothers and sisters with love and grace. Each should devalue his own opinions and wishes, doing nothing from selfishness.

ETERNAL REWARD AND PUNISHMENT
(questions for Chapter 18 are found on page 226)

1. While God is loving, kind, and forbearing, He is also a God of wrath and vengeance. God is both kind and severe.
2. The wicked will continue to be punished without end throughout eternity. Revelation 14:11 says their torment goes on "forever and ever."
3. Those who are sent to hell will be separated from God, living with the devil and his angels, tormented in fire and brimstone, in outer darkness, and suffering God's vengeance.
4. Paul described those who will be punished as people who have stubborn and unrepentant hearts, do not know God, and do not obey the truth.
5. Our greatest goal should be to reach heaven and escape the horrors of hell.

6. Those under the old law were promised the land of Canaan, with long life and prosperity. Christians are promised a place forever in heaven.
7. "Heaven" refers to three different realms; (1) the sky where the clouds are and the birds fly; (2) the universe filled with the stars and constellations; and (3) God's dwelling place.
8. We will not have the sun, moon, or a lamp because God will be our light. We will not need physical food, for we will have access to the tree of life.
9. Those who do the will of God will go to heaven.

REPENTANCE
(questions for Chapter 19 are found on page 239)

1. After his death, the rich man's priorities changed. He became concerned for his soul's condition and for the spiritual condition of his brothers.
2. "Repentance" is a cornerstone word because only those who have repented can become Christians. In fact, the door of eternal life is only opened by true repentance.
3. Judas' regret (Matthew 27:3) demonstrates that repentance is more than mere regret. Judas regretted that he had betrayed Jesus, but he did not repent.
4. Godly sorrow precedes and produces repentance. Godly sorrow is a part of the process, but it is not repentance itself.
5. Saul made a resolute change of will that clearly showed his repentance. He stopped persecuting the church of Christ and committed his whole life to Jesus.
6. Paul commended the Thessalonians because in their repentance "they had turned to God from idols to serve a living and true God" (1 Thessalonians 1:9). They demonstrated that repentance is not only turning from sin, but also a turning to God.
7. Repentance is more than just confession of sins in that there must also be a turning from sin and a turning to Christ. Some think that confession of sins to another person is repentance. Acknowledging our sin is important (James 5:16), but there must also be abandonment of sinful practices.

8. The goodness of God, the promise of reward, and the fear of punishment are three scriptural incentives for repentance.

WHAT WILL YOU DO WITH JESUS?
(questions for Chapter 20 are found on page 258)

1. Since Jesus is the only way to heaven, our response to Him will determine where we will spend eternity.
2. Infants and small children do not need to be baptized because they do not understand what sin is.
3. Baptism is for the remission, or forgiveness, of sins.
4. To identify the New Testament church, ask, "Are they trying to be the New Testament church?"; "Do they partake of the Lord's Supper each Sunday?"; "Do they sing without instrumental accompaniment?"; "Do they pray in Jesus' name?"; "Do they give of their means each Sunday?"; "How are they organized?"; "Do they have an earthly headquarters?"; "What is their mission?"
5. Romans 6:4 teaches that baptism is a burial in water.
6. A good way to summarize the life of a Christian is to say that he has been baptized into Christ and is a follower of Christ.
7. A Christian stays close to the Word of God so that he can imitate Christ's faithful obedience to God.
8. Each Sunday, or Lord's Day, Christians worship together by singing, praying, studying God's Word, partaking of the Lord's Supper, and giving of their money.
9. In creating the Lord's Supper, Jesus used unleavened bread and the fruit of the vine, or grape juice.
10. In order to become a Christian and live as a Christian, you should (1) come to Christ, (2) begin living for Him, (3) worship with other Christians regularly, and (4) begin serving others.

Appendix 2

Study Helps for Accurately Handling The Word of Truth

"Be diligent to present yourself approved to God as a workman who does not need to be ashamed, handling accurately the word of truth" (2 Timothy 2:15).

It is very important to handle the word of truth (the Bible) accurately. Among other things, this means to understand the difference between the Old Testament and the New Testament. The Old Testament is the shadow, while the New Testament is the reality (Hebrews 10:1). The Old Testament has been "nailed to the cross," and the New Testament is the law now spiritually binding (Colossians 2:14). The Old Testament is valuable for examples and to demonstrate how God always keeps His promises (1 Corinthians 10:6). God's promises are made in the Old Testament and fulfilled in the New Testament. (Study the chart on page 274.)

ACCURATELY HANDLING THE WORD OF TRUTH
2 Timothy 2:15

Old Testament	New Testament
PROMISES MADE	**PROMISES FULFILLED**
(Genesis 3:15; 12:3)	

1. Kingdom To Be
   Established
   (Daniel 2:44)

   Mark 9:1; Acts 1:8; 2:1–4;
   Luke 22:29, 30;
   1 Corinthians 11:23

2. Lord's House To Be
   Built (Isaiah 2:2, 3)

   Hebrews 10:21;
   1 Timothy 3:15

   Will be in "last days"   Acts 2:16, 17; Hebrews 1:1, 2
   Will begin in Jerusalem   Luke 24:46, 47; Acts 1:4–8
   All nations admitted   Acts 2:9; Romans 1:16

3. Christ Will Be King
   (Jeremiah 23:5, 6)

   Matthew 28:18;
   Acts 2:29–33

4. New Covenant Binding
   (Jeremiah 31:31)

   Matthew 16:18, 19;
   Acts 2:36–38;
   Hebrews 9:15–17

5. Holy Spirit To Be Given
   (Joel 2:28)

   Acts 2:16–21

**All promises made concerning the church
are fulfilled in Acts 2, which records the events
of one day, the Day of Pentecost.**

Every Scripture speaking of the kingdom
BEFORE Acts 2 speaks of it as being
in the **FUTURE** (Isaiah 2:2–4;
Micah 4:1, 2; Daniel 2:44;
Matthew 3:1, 2; 6:9, 10;
16:18; Mark 9:1).

ACTS 2: PENTECOST

Every Scripture
speaking of the kingdom
AFTER Acts 2 speaks of it as being
in **EXISTENCE** (Acts 2:47; Colossians 1:13, 14).

HOW TO ORGANIZE A NEW CONGREGATION ACCORDING TO THE BIBLE

As an Independent Body—Every congregation of the Lord's church is a separate, independent unit. Never is one congregation over another congregation. There is no organization of churches, nor is there any other organization larger than the local congregation.

As the Body of Christ—In the Bible the church is called "the body of Christ." In this figure of speech we see that Christ is the "head of the body" (Colossians 1:18; Ephesians 1:22). As each member of the physical body has a particular function, so it is with the body of Christ. No member of the church is more important than another. All have their places and contribute to the well-being of the whole body, the church.

With Jesus as the Only Head—Christ is the "head of the church" and as such has all authority (Matthew 28:18). No one is permitted to change the structure of the church in any way, for no one has the authority to do so.

Under the Leadership of Elders—As the local congregation increases in number and spiritual maturity, men from the congregation should be appointed to serve as elders. These men are to be selected by the congregation itself; they are not self-appointed. Elders are also called "shepherds" and serve as guardians of the flock (1 Peter 5:1–5). Qualifications for elders are found in 1 Timothy 3:1–8 and Titus 1:5–8. The church may be established without elders or deacons being appointed. It must exist without them at first, for those who serve in these capacities must be well qualified through years of experience.

With Deacons Appointed to Serve—Men are also appointed to the office of deacons to serve the congregation. They serve under the elders (Philippians 1:1; Acts 20:28). Their qualifications are found in 1 Timothy 3:8–13.

THE CHRISTIAN MAN

In many ways, Christian men have the same responsibilities that Christian women have. Both are to attend church services faithfully (Hebrews 10:25), to be liberal in giving (1 Corinthians 16:2), to lead pure lives (James 1:27), to evangelize (Matthew 28:19, 20), to study the Bible (2 Timothy 2:15; see Acts 17:11), and to grow spiritually (1 Peter 2:2).

What the Christian Man Is Not To Do:

1. He is not to abuse his wife and children (Ephesians 5:25–31; 1 Peter 3:7; 1 Thessalonians 2:11).

2. He is not to be violent (Romans 12:18).

3. He is not to be promiscuous (1 Corinthians 6:18, 19).

4. He is not to seek pleasure (2 Timothy 3:4; Titus 3:3).

5. He is not to be unfeeling or unemotional (Luke 22:62; John 11:35; Acts 20:37).

What the Christian Man Is To Do:

1. He is responsible for leadership in the Lord's church (1 Timothy 2:8–15; 1 Corinthians 14:33, 36).

2. He is to lead his family lovingly (Ephesians 5:21–33; Colossians 3:18–21; 1 Peter 3:1–6; 1 Corinthians 11:2–5).

3. He is to provide for the spiritual and physical needs of his family (1 Timothy 5:8).

4. He is to make sure that his children are reared properly (Ephesians 6:4).

NEW TESTAMENT "ROLE MODELS" FOR MEN

1. All Christian men should aspire to meet the qualifications given for leaders in the church. (See page 278.)

2. They should be servant-leaders, like Jesus (Luke 22:27).

3. Like Barnabas, men can be generous with financial gifts and encouraging words (Acts 4:36, 37).

4. Like Philemon, men can open their homes to fellow Christians (Philemon 2) and can set aside personal differences to do what is best for the brethren (Philemon 10–20).

THE CHRISTIAN WOMAN

What the Christian Woman Cannot Scripturally Do:

1. She is restricted from exercising leadership in the assembly of the church (1 Corinthians 14:34, 35; see 14:19, 23, 26, 28). Preachers speak in the assembly, so Christian women are not to serve as preachers.

2. She is restricted from having authority over men; therefore, she cannot serve as an elder or a deacon (1 Timothy 2:12; 3:2).

3. She is restricted from appearing to reject the authority of her husband (1 Corinthians 11).

What the Christian Woman Can Scripturally Do:

1. She is not restricted from leading in activities in which she will not have authority over men.

2. She is not restricted from teaching other women or children. In some situations she may teach, or help to teach, men (Acts 18:24–28; Titus 2:4).

3. She is not restricted from doing personal work, from leading individuals to Christ.

4. She is not restricted from working for the church, even receiving pay, in any job that is scripturally right for her to do.

NEW TESTAMENT "ROLE MODELS" FOR WOMEN

1. Women accompanied Jesus and helped to support Him financially in His teaching (Matthew 27:55; Luke 8:1–3).

2. Mary, the sister of Lazarus, listened to the Lord's word, seated at His feet (Luke 10:39, 42).

3. Mary Magdalene was a devoted follower of Jesus, eager to tell others about the risen Lord (John 20:1–18).

4. Dorcas, or Tabitha, did "deeds of kindness and charity" (Acts 9:36).

5. Phoebe was "a servant of the church," a helper to Paul (Romans 16:1, 2).

6. Priscilla was a faithful wife, an apostle's fellow worker, and a missionary. With her husband, she hosted the church in her own home. (See Romans 16:3–5; Acts 18:1–3, 24–28.)

WHAT ELDERS ARE TO BE,
ALL CHRISTIANS ARE TO BE

Elders	Characteristic	All Christians
1 Timothy 3:2	Above reproach (blameless)	1 Timothy 5:7; 6:14
1 Timothy 3:2	Temperate (vigilant)	1 Peter 1:13; 4:7; 5:8
1 Timothy 3:2	Prudent (sensible; sober)	Titus 2:2, 5; Romans 12:3
1 Timothy 3:2	Hospitable	Romans 12:13; Hebrews 13:2
1 Timothy 3:2	Able to teach	Hebrews 5:12
1 Timothy 3:3	Not addicted to wine (no drunkard)	Titus 2:3; Ephesians 5:18
1 Timothy 3:3	Gentle (patient)	Philippians 4:5; Colossians 3:13; Titus 3:2
1 Timothy 3:3	Uncontentious (not quarrelsome; not a brawler)	James 4:2; 2 Timothy 2:24
1 Timothy 3:3	No lover of money	1 Timothy 6:10; 2 Timothy 3:2
1 Timothy 3:4	Having submissive, respectful children	Ephesians 6:1–4
1 Timothy 3:7	Well thought of by outsiders	1 Peter 2:12–16
Titus 1:8	Just (upright)	Colossians 4:1
Titus 1:8	Devout (holy)	Ephesians 4:24; 1 Timothy 2:8
Titus 1:8	Self-controlled (temperate)	Galatians 5:23

Elders do have three qualifications which are not required of all Christians. The elder is to be the "husband of one wife," must have "children who believe," and is not to be "a new convert" (1 Timothy 3:2, 6; Titus 1:6). (While the married Christian is to have one spouse only, an unmarried man or woman may also become a Christian.)

Appendix 3

The Words "Church" And "Churches" In the New Testament

For a better understanding of the nature of the New Testament church, study carefully the different contexts in which the words "church" and "churches" are used. First, the word "church" is used to mean a secular assembly called together for a special purpose or one which just occurs. (See Acts 19:32, 39, 41.) Second, it is used in a universal sense in reference to all of God's people. (See Matthew 16:18.) Third, it is used in reference to the saved of a specific racial background. (See Romans 16:4.) Fourth, it is used in reference to the churches of a given general area. (See Galatians 1:2 and Acts 9:31.) Fifth, the word is used as a reference to a specific group of Christians worshiping together. (See 1 Corinthians 1:2 and Colossians 4:16.) Sixth, it is used in reference to the assembly of Christians for worship and study. (See 1 Corinthians 11:18.)

Study carefully the use the Holy Spirit made of the words "church" and "churches" in the New Testament. The numbers in parentheses indicate *the number of times* the word or expression appears.

"Church" (79)

Matthew (3)—16:18; 18:17 (twice).

Acts (21)—2:47 (the KJV has "church," but manuscript evidence is poor for its appearance in Acts 2:47); 5:11; 7:38 (the word "congregation" is from *ekklesia* ["church"]); 8:1; 8:3; 9:31; 11:22; 11:26; 12:1; 12:5; 13:1; 14:23; 14:27; 15:3; 15:4; 15:22; 18:22; 19:32 (the word "assembly" is from *ekklesia* ["church"]); 19:39 (the word "assembly" is from *ekklesia* ["church"]); 19:40, 41 (the word "assembly" is from *ekklesia* ["church"]); 20:17; 20:28.

Romans (3)—16:1; 16:5; 16:23.

1 Corinthians (16)—1:2; 4:17; 6:4; 10:32; 11:18; 11:22; 12:28; 14:4; 14:5; 14:12; 14:19; 14:23; 14:28; 14:35; 15:9; 16:19.

2 Corinthians (1)—1:1.

Galatians (1)—1:13.

Ephesians (9)—1:22; 3:10; 3:21; 5:23; 5:24; 5:25; 5:27; 5:29; 5:32.

Philippians (2)—3:6; 4:15.

Colossians (4)—1:18; 1:24; 4:15; 4:16.

1 Thessalonians (1)—1:1.

2 Thessalonians (1)—1:1.

1 Timothy (3)—3:5; 3:15; 5:16.

Philemon (1)—2.

Hebrews (2)—2:12; 12:23.

James (1)—5:14.

3 John (3)—6; 9; 10.

Revelation (7)—2:1; 2:8; 2:12; 2:18; 3:1; 3:7; 3:14.

"Churches" (35)

Acts (2)—15:41; 16:5.

Romans (2)—16:4; 16:16.

1 Corinthians (6)—7:17; 11:16; 14:33; 14:34; 16:1; 16:19.

2 Corinthians (8)—8:1; 8:18; 8:19; 8:23; 8:24; 11:8; 11:28; 12:13.

Galatians (2)—1:2; 1:22.

1 Thessalonians (1)—2:14.

2 Thessalonians (1)—1:4.

Revelation (13)—1:4; 1:11; 1:20 (twice); 2:7, 11, 17, 29; 3:6, 13, 22; 2:23; 22:16.

Appendix 4

The Words "Kingdom" And "Kingdoms" In the New Testament

The basic meaning of the word "kingdom" in the New Testament is "rule, power, or sovereignty." The kingdom of God, therefore, is the rule or sovereignty of God.

The word "kingdom" appears in about six different contexts in the New Testament. First, the word is used in reference to an earthly, political rule. (See Matthew 4:8.) Second, it is used in reference to the kingdom of Israel. (See Matthew 8:12.) Third, it is used in reference to the power or rule of God. (See Matthew 12:28.) Fourth, it is used in reference to the church, the special rule of God on earth today. (See Matthew 11:11; 16:18; John 3:5; Colossians 1:13.) Fifth, it is used in reference to heaven as the eternal kingdom of God. (See Luke 13:28.) Sixth, it is used of Satan's realm of dominion. (See Matthew 12:26.)

Matthew predominantly used the phrase "kingdom of heaven." Mark, Luke, and John used, without exception, the phrase "kingdom of God." The two phrases obviously have the same meaning.

Study carefully the use the Holy Spirit made of the word "kingdom" in the New Testament. The numbers in parentheses indicate *the number of times* that particular word or expression appears.

"A kingdom" (2)

Luke (1)—22:29, 30.
Hebrews (1)—12:28.

"The kingdom" (11)

Matthew (4)—6:13 (the last sentence of this verse is not found in most reliable manuscripts); 8:12; 13:19; 13:38; 25:34.
Mark (1)—11:10.
Luke (1)—12:32.
Acts (2)—1:6; 20:25.
1 Corinthians (1)—15:24.
James (1)—2:5.
Revelation (1)—1:9.

"Kingdom of heaven" (31)

Matthew (31)—3:2; 4:17; 5:3; 5:10; 5:19 (twice); 5:20; 7:21; 8:11; 11:11; 11:12; 13:11; 13:24; 13:31; 13:33; 13:44; 13:45; 13:47; 13:52; 16:19; 18:1; 18:3; 18:4; 18:23; 19:12; 19:14; 19:23; 20:1; 22:2; 23:13; 25:1.

"The gospel of the kingdom" (3)

Matthew (3)—4:23; 9:35; 24:14.

"Kingdom of God" (67)

Matthew (4)—12:28; 19:24; 21:31; 21:43.
Mark (14)—1:15; 4:11; 4:26; 4:30; 9:1; 9:47; 10:14; 10:15; 10:23; 10:24; 10:25; 12:34; 14:25; 15:43.
Luke (32)—4:43; 6:20; 7:28; 8:1; 8:10; 9:2; 9:11; 9:27; 9:60; 9:62; 10:9; 10:11; 11:20; 13:18; 13:20; 13:28; 13:29; 14:15; 16:16; 17:20 (twice); 17:21; 18:16; 18:17; 18:24; 18:25; 18:29, 30; 19:11; 21:31; 22:16; 22:18; 23:50, 51.
John (2)—3:3; 3:5.

Acts (6)—1:3; 8:12; 14:22; 19:8; 28:23; 28:31.
Romans (1)—14:17.
1 Corinthians (4)—4:20; 6:9; 6:10; 15:50.
Galatians (1)—5:21.
Colossians (1)—4:11.
2 Thessalonians (1)—1:5.
Revelation (1)—12:10.

Kingdom of Christ (15)

Matthew (3)—13:41; 16:28; 20:21.
Luke (3)—1:33; 22:30; 23:42.
John (3)—18:36 (three times).
Colossians (1)—1:13.
2 Timothy (2)—4:1; 4:18.
Hebrews (1)—1:8.
2 Peter (1)—1:11.
Revelation (1)—11:15.

The Father's kingdom (7)

Matthew (4)—6:10; 6:33; 13:43; 26:29.
Luke (2)—11:2; 12:31.
1 Thessalonians (1)—2:12.

"The kingdom of Christ and God" (1)

Ephesians (1)—5:5.

Earthly "kingdom" or "kingdoms" (20)

Matthew (4)—4:8; 12:25; 24:7 (twice).
Mark (5)—3:24 (twice); 6:23; 13:8 (twice).
Luke (6)—4:5; 11:17; 19:12; 19:15; 21:10 (twice).
Hebrews (1)—11:33.
Revelation (4)—11:15; 17:12; 17:17; 17:18 (the Greek text has "a
    kingdom over the kings of the earth").

Satan's kingdom (3)

Matthew (1)—12:26.
Luke (1)—11:18.
Revelation (1)—16:10.

Appendix 5

A Survey
Of the Old Testament

As we begin reading the Bible, it does not take us long to see who is the hero of the Bible. "In the beginning God . . ." (Genesis 1:1). The Bible is the story, not so much of man, but of God—a God who acts in history, a God who plans for our redemption, a God who has a part in our lives as He did in the lives of the people of old.

The story begins in Genesis 1 with the creation: "In the beginning God created the heavens and the earth. . . . Then God said, 'Let there be light'; and there was light" (Genesis 1:1, 3). God created the firmament and separated the waters above from the waters below. God caused the dry land to appear, and He brought forth the vegetation: the trees, plants, flowers, and grass. And God put the sun, moon, and stars in their places, the sun to rule the day, and the moon, the night. Then He made the air and the sea creatures (Genesis 1:6–23). On the sixth day He made the land animals, and then He said, "Let Us make man in Our image" (Genesis 1:26). God created man in His own image, and from man He took the rib, literally the side piece, and made a woman. He said she is "a helper suitable for him" (Genesis 2:18) and brought her unto the man. Genesis 2:24 says, "For this cause a man shall leave his father and his mother, and shall cleave to his wife; and they shall become one flesh."

It was not long until the beauty and the purity of their existence in the Garden of Eden were marred by the sin of eating the forbidden fruit. A curse came upon them, and death came upon all mankind. Man and woman were driven from the garden. Soon after that, a child was born named Cain and another one named Abel. Cain killed his brother Abel because God had respect unto Abel's sacrifice and did not have respect unto Cain's. Cain was jealous and hated his brother for it. (See Genesis 3:1—4:8.)

Man continued to get worse until finally the Lord was sorry that He had even made man and said, "The end of all flesh has come before Me" (Genesis 6:13). Only one family found favor in the sight of God, the family of Noah. Noah and his wife and Shem, Ham, and Japheth and their wives all entered the ark to be saved from the flood that God would send upon the earth. Two of every unclean animal and seven pairs of the clean animals were brought into the ark, and God shut the door. It rained for forty days and nights, and the fountains of the deep were opened. All flesh upon the earth was destroyed. (See Genesis 6:9—7:24.)

The generations continued, and they became worse and worse. They tried to build the Tower of Babel, and God confounded their language so that they could not complete it. (See Genesis 11:1–9.) Then we come to one particular man who would become a most important person in the genealogy of our Lord, Abraham.

About 2000 B.C. came the word of God to Abraham in Ur of the Chaldees: "Go forth from your country, and from your relatives and from your father's house, to the land which I will show you" (Genesis 12:1). Then He said, "And in you all the families of the earth will be blessed" (Genesis 12:3). This is the first definite reference to Christ in the Old Testament.

Abraham, Sarah, Lot, Abraham's father, and a number of others left Ur of the Chaldees and journeyed northwest till they came to Haran and settled there. After the death of Terah, his father, Abraham moved down into the Promised Land at the age of seventy-five. He sojourned there. During this time he was separated from Lot, and he went into Egypt briefly and came back. During this time, God said that he would have a son, even though he and Sarah were past the age of having children. (See Genesis 11:31—13:1.)

One evening God told him to look up into the sky to see if he could count the stars. Of course, he could not. God said, "So shall your descendants be" (Genesis 15:5). Abraham believed God, and it was reckoned to him for righteousness. Twenty-five years after the promise had been given to him at the age of seventy-five, when Abraham was one hun-dred and his wife Sarah was ninety, the child Isaac was born. (See Genesis 21:1–7.)

The child of promise grew up and became a young man. One day God told Abraham to take Isaac unto the place that He would show him in the land of Moriah and there offer him as a burnt offering. Without even wincing, Abraham took his son and was willing to sacrifice him; but an angel of God stopped his hand and said, "Do not stretch out your hand against the lad, and do nothing to him; for now I know that you fear God, since you have not withheld your son, your only son, from Me" (Genesis 22:12). God later told him, "And in you and your descendants shall all the families of the earth be blessed" (Genesis 28:14b).

Isaac found a wife from the land of Paddan-aram. He married his cousin Rebekah. They had sons named Jacob and Esau. Jacob was the child of promise. He married Rachel and Leah; and they had twelve sons, four by the handmaidens and eight by the wives. The favorite of these sons was Joseph. The brothers hated Joseph and sold him into Egypt. (See Genesis 24—37.)

Joseph was sold into the hands of Potiphar. When he was accused of making advances against Potiphar's wife, he was cast into prison. In the prison he interpreted the dreams of the butler and the baker. Two years later, he interpreted the dream of Pharaoh. Pharaoh had dreamed that seven healthy cows came out of the Nile River and seven gaunt cows ate them. Then seven good ears of grain were devoured by seven bad ears. By this, Joseph predicted seven years of plenty followed by seven years of famine. He sent for all of his family to come to Egypt. They came and settled in Goshen. Thus they were spared from the famine. (See Genesis 39—46.)

The children of Israel lived in the land of Egypt for four hundred years or more. There arose a Pharaoh who knew not Joseph, and he oppressed the children of Israel greatly. He tried to wear them out by making their service hard in making bricks for his building projects. (See Exodus 1.) The children of Israel cried unto God for deliverance.

A man from the tribe of Levi had a child who was later named Moses. Little Moses was placed in the bulrushes in the Nile River, and Pharaoh's daughter found him there. She even paid Moses' mother to take care of her own child. (See Exodus 2.)

At the age of forty, Moses left the land after he had killed an Egyptian. Moses fled to the land of Horeb, the land of Sinai. There he kept the flock of his father-in-law, Jethro, for forty years. At the age of eighty, he observed a bush that was burning. He went up to see why it was not consumed and heard the Lord say, "Do not come near here; remove your sandals from your feet, for the place on which you are standing is holy ground. . . . I am the God of your father, the God of Abraham, the God of Isaac, and the God of Jacob" (Exodus 3:5, 6). Then God said to Moses, "Therefore, come now, and I will send you to Pharaoh, so that you may bring My people, the sons of Israel, out of Egypt"; ". . . you shall worship God at this mountain" (Exodus 3:10, 12).

After much persuasion, Moses went. When Moses returned to Egypt, Pharaoh would not listen to him, but even made the work harder for God's people. Ultimately, with the help of his brother, Aaron, Moses, through the power of God, brought ten plagues upon the Egyptians: the water turned into blood, the frogs, the lice, the flies, the murrain on the cattle, the boils and the blains, the hail, the locusts, darkness, and the death of the firstborn. The Passover lamb was killed, and the blood was put on the doorposts and the lintels of the Israelites' houses. God said, "For I will go through the land of Egypt on that night, and will strike down all the firstborn in the land of Egypt, both man and beast; and against all the gods of Egypt I will execute judgments—I am the LORD. The blood shall be a sign for you on the houses where you live; and when I see the blood I will pass over you, and no plague will befall you to destroy you when I strike the land of Egypt" (Exodus 12:12, 13). All the firstborn in Pharaoh's house and in all Egypt died, but those who had the blood on the doorposts and the lintels of their houses were spared. A great cry went throughout Egypt that night.

All the children of Israel gathered their materials and journeyed eastward toward the Red Sea. Pharaoh came after them shortly thereafter. They saw Pharaoh coming and cried unto Moses, "Is it because there were no graves in Egypt that you have taken us away to die in the wilderness?" (Exodus 14:11). Moses said, "Do not fear! Stand by and see the salvation of the LORD" (Exodus 14:13). The Lord told Moses to stretch the rod over the water. He did, and the waters parted. The children of Israel marched through on dry land. Pharaoh and his army came in behind them. Moses raised his hand over the waters, the waves returned, and Pharaoh and his army perished in the Red Sea. About 600,000 men of war (close to 3,000,000 people in all) came out of Egypt on that day. (See Numbers 1:46.)

They journeyed southeastward toward Mount Sinai. They ran out of water, and Moses brought water from the rock to the waters of Rephidim. They were attacked by the Amalekites. By the hand of Moses and the help of the Lord, Joshua defeated the Amalekites. (See Exodus 17.) Finally, after three months' journey, they arrived at the foot of Mount Sinai.

They saw the smoke billow from the mount and heard the thunder of God and saw the lightning flash. The voice of God spoke to them:

I am the LORD your God, who brought you out of the land of Egypt, out of the house of slavery.

You shall have no other gods before Me.

You shall not make for yourself an idol, or any likeness of what is in heaven above or on the earth beneath or in the water under the earth. You shall not worship them or serve them. . . .

You shall not take the name of the LORD your God in vain. . . .

Remember the sabbath day, to keep it holy. . . .

Honor your father and your mother, that your days may be prolonged in the land which the LORD your God gives you.

You shall not murder.

You shall not commit adultery.

You shall not steal.

You shall not bear false witness. . . .

You shall not covet . . . (Exodus 20:2–17).[1]

Moses went up on the mountain and stayed there forty days, where he received instructions from God regarding the building of the tabernacle and the Jewish system of worship. (See Exodus 24:18—31:18.)

During these forty days, the children of Israel became impatient and asked Aaron, "Come, make us a god who will go before us; as for this Moses, the man who brought us up from the land of Egypt, we do not know what has become of him" (Exodus 32:1). Aaron took their gold and from it fashioned the calf,

---

[1]These are the Ten Commandments referred to on the next page.

and they worshiped the golden calf.

When Moses came down from the mountain and saw what they had done, he broke the tables of stone on which the Ten Commandments were written. He burned the calf and ground it into powder, scattered it on the water, and made them drink it. (See Exodus 32:15–20.)

Moses returned to the mountain and stayed forty more days. Then he came down with the instructions for the tabernacle. There, at the foot of Mount Sinai, they built the tabernacle. It was a movable structure with tents laid over the boards. A veil divided it into a holy place and a most holy place. The ark of the covenant, the most holy piece of furniture, was in the most holy place. The table of showbread, the lamp-stand, and the altar of incense were in the holy place. The brass altar and the brazen laver were outside. Aaron was ordained as high priest. His four sons, Eleazar, Ithamar, Nadab, and Abihu, were the priests who served with him. Their robes and their garments were made, and the worship was set up. The cloud from the Lord descended, symbolizing His presence there. (See Exodus 33—40.)

They stayed at the foot of Mount Sinai for eleven months. One day that cloud moved and headed northeastward, and the Lord said, "You have stayed long enough at this mountain" (Deuteronomy 1:6). They were told to go northward, so they journeyed toward Kadesh-barnea. (See Numbers 10:11, 12.)

On the way they complained, and a fire of the Lord devoured some of them. They lusted when the quail were sent, and many of them died. The place was called "Graves of Lusting," Kibroth-hattaavah (Numbers 11:34).

They came to Kadesh-barnea. From there they sent twelve spies; two of them were Caleb and Joshua. They went into Canaan and came back, bringing a sample of the fruit. It was a cluster of grapes so large that it took two men to carry it on a pole. They said, "It is a good land, but it is a land that devours its inhabitants. They have cities with walls that reach to heaven. There are giants in the land, and we're as grasshoppers in our own sight, and so were we in their sight." However, Caleb and Joshua stilled the people and said, "We're well able to overtake it. The Lord will give us the land." The people did not believe the report of the two and said, "We cannot take it. Let us choose a captain and go back to Egypt." Because of their unbelief, they wandered for forty years in the wilderness. For every day they were gone, the people had a year of wandering. (See Numbers 13; 14.)

During this time Korah, Dathan, and Abiram rebelled against Moses and Aaron, and the ground opened up and swallowed them. Moses was told to speak to a rock and bring forth water; and he, in his anger, said, "Listen now, you rebels; shall we bring forth water for you out of this rock?" (Numbers 20:10), and he struck it. God said, "Because you have not believed Me, . . . you shall not bring this assembly into the land which I have given them" (Numbers 20:12). At this time the fiery serpents were sent among them because they had complained and murmured against the Lord. Also at this time Balaam was brought over to bring a curse upon Israel by Balak, the son of Moab, because the Moabites feared this horde of Israelites who had already defeated Sihon and Og and had taken possession of the east side of the Jordan River. (See Numbers 21; 22.)

At the age of 120, Moses died on Mount Nebo. First, God showed him all the land and all the beautiful hillside and the valleys and then said, "I have let you see it with your eyes, but you shall not go over there" (Deuteronomy 34:4b). Moses died and was buried, and Joshua was chosen to be his successor (Deuteronomy 34:5; Joshua 1:1–9).

Joshua led the children of Israel across the Jordan River. As the priests stood there holding the ark of the covenant in the waters of the Jordan, the waters were cut off, and the people marched over on dry land. The first city to be taken was Jericho. The children of Israel marched around it once a day for six days and seven times on the seventh day. Then they blew the trumpets and shouted, and all the city was destroyed. Rahab and her family were saved because she had befriended the two spies. (See Joshua 1—6.)

From about 1400 to 1350 B.C., the land was taken from the Canaanites. During this time Israel cut through the middle of the land, from Jericho in the east to Ai and Bethel, which divided the land in two. They defeated the southern confederacy of the Canaanites and then the northern confederacy of the Canaanites. This was the day that Joshua commanded the sun to stand still. God listened to the voice of a man, and the sun stayed in its course. (See Joshua 7—11.)

All the land was divided among the Israelites. The tabernacle was set up at Shiloh as a religious center at that time. The Levites were put in forty-eight different cities, and the cities of refuge were arranged so the manslayers could flee to them for safety.

Joshua died. The children of Israel served God all the days of Joshua and all the days of the elders who outlived Joshua. (See Joshua 13—24.)

During a period from about 1350 to 1050 B.C., we have a recurring cycle: (1) The children of Israel did evil in the sight of the Lord. (2) They were sold into the hand of their enemies. (3) They cried to the Lord for help. (4) God sent them a deliverer known as a judge. Then the cycle would begin again. They would sin again, get in trouble again, cry for help again, and be delivered again.

These were the days of Othniel, Ehud, and Shamgar. Deborah, along with the help of Barak (and I might add Jael), defeated Sisera and his armies; Gideon defeated the Midianites with three hundred men; Jephthah made the rash vow and, it seems, may have offered his daughter as a sacrifice; and Samson began the defeat of the Philistines. During these days, Ruth lived. She came from Moab and gleaned in the fields of Boaz and ended up becoming his wife and the great-grandmother of David. The last of the judges were Eli and Samuel. These were dark days for the children of Israel. (See Judges 1—16; Ruth 1—4; 1 Samuel 1—7.)

The people tired of being ruled by the judges and said, "Appoint a king for us to judge us like all the nations" (1 Samuel 8:5). God said to Samuel, "Listen to the voice of the people in regard to all that they say to you, for they have not rejected you, but they have rejected Me from being king over them" (1 Samuel 8:7). So it was that their first king, Saul, from the land of Benjamin, was anointed over the land of Israel; and the period of the judges ended. (See 1 Samuel 9; 10.)

From about 1050 to 930 B.C., we have the period known as the United Kingdom. Saul reigned for forty years. He disobeyed the Lord by not destroying the Amalekites as he should have. Samuel told him, "The LORD has rejected you from being king" (1 Samuel 15:26). God had chosen for Him a new king, a man after His own heart. Samuel was sent to the house of Jesse in Bethlehem, and there he anointed David to be the next king. (See 1 Samuel 11—16.)

David first reigned in Hebron and then moved to Jerusalem. His capital became Jerusalem when it was taken from the Jebusites. The ark of the covenant was brought there, and Jerusalem was made not only the political center, but also the religious center of the land (2 Samuel 2:1–4; 5; 6). David wanted to build a temple for the Lord, but the Lord said, "No. You are a man of blood. You can't do it. You don't make Me a house. I will make you a house. One of these days when you are dead, I'll raise up your son who will build a house for Me" (see 2 Samuel 7:8–13). That was a prophecy of Solomon, to be sure; but there was more to it than that. It was a prophecy that the Messiah would come through David (Hebrews 1:5).

David was not perfect. He committed a grievous sin in the matter with Bathsheba, killing Uriah and taking her for his own wife, and his family paid for his sins. Nathan himself had given David God's message: "Now therefore, the sword shall never depart from your house, because you have despised Me . . ." (2 Samuel 12:10). Amnon, David's son, raped his own sister. Another son, Absalom, had Amnon killed. Then Absalom rebelled against his father and would have taken the kingdom and the life of his father if he had been able to do so. His rebellion was put down. Near the end of David's life, Adonijah decided he would be the king, and his rebellion was put down. Solomon was finally proclaimed as king. (See 2 Samuel 13—19; 1 Kings 1; 2.)

Solomon reigned from about 970 to 930 B.C. He was the last of the three kings of the United Kingdom—Saul, David, and Solomon. With the help of Hiram, king of Tyre, in the land of Phoenicia, Solomon built the temple of the Lord in Jerusalem. Solomon was asked in a dream what he would have. Of all the things he could have chosen, he chose wisdom. He became the wisest of all, and his proverbs and his songs were legendary. (See 1 Kings 5—10.)

During the time of David and Solomon, most of the psalms were written and the proverbs were collected. Ecclesiastes and the Song of Solomon and likely even the Book of Job were written at this time, though Job probably lived before the days of Abraham. The wisdom and the poetic literature were very prominent at this time.

Solomon committed a great sin in marrying the women of the nations around them which God had forbidden (1 Kings 11). His going after the gods of these foreign women led to the division of the kingdom. When Solomon died, his son Rehoboam was asked to lighten the load of his father. Solomon had practically bankrupted the country to have the splendor that he enjoyed; but Rehoboam followed the advice of the young men, who told him to say, "My little finger is thicker than my father's loins! Whereas my father loaded you with a heavy yoke, I will add to your yoke; my father disciplined you with whips, but I will discipline you with scorpions" (1 Kings 12:10, 11). Because of this, the kingdom split.

Ten tribes went north and formed the kingdom of Israel, or Ephraim, as it was called. Later it was called Samaria. They appointed Jeroboam to be their king. Rehoboam, the son of Solomon, was left with only two tribes, Judah and Benjamin. Many of the Levites moved south. There were not any good kings in the north. Jeroboam is always known as the one who made Israel to sin. When he died, his son, Nadab, followed him, and then Nadab was killed. The whole family of Jeroboam was killed by a man named Baasha. Baasha was followed by his son, Elah. All of his family was killed by Zimri. He lasted only seven days as king and then was killed by Omri, who moved the capital of the north to Samaria. Omri was the father of Ahab, who took Jezebel to be his wife. (See 1 Kings 12—16.)

During these days, Elijah spoke against Ahab and condemned him for his sins. The contest on Mount Carmel occurred, and the fire came down from heaven and burned up the sacrifice prepared for God. Ahab was followed by Ahaziah and then Jehoram. Then Jehu came and destroyed the whole dynasty of Ahab. Jehu was followed by Jehoash, Jehoahaz, and Jeroboam II. (See 1 Kings 17—22; 2 Kings 9—14.)

In the days of Jeroboam II, two great prophets arose in the land of Israel, up in the north: Amos, the prophet of God's justice, and Hosea, the prophet of God's love. After Jeroboam II, there was a sharp decline. Zechariah and the whole family of Jehu were destroyed; Shallum was killed; Menahem paid a great tribute to Assyria just to stay alive; Pekahiah was killed, as was Hoshea. In 722 B.C., the Assyrians destroyed the northern kingdom and carried them

off into exile. The northern kingdom, as such, was
no more. (See 2 Kings 14—18.)

Meanwhile, in the southern kingdom, Rehoboam
was a wicked ruler. He was followed by Abijah, a
wicked king, who was followed by Asa, a good king,
and then Jehoshaphat, who was also a good king and
oddly enough a friend of Ahab's. Their children married each other. Jehoshaphat was followed by Jehoram, and then Ahaziah, who was also killed by Jehu.
(Jehu killed both the king of the south and the king
of the north.) (See 1 Kings 12—15; 22; 2 Kings 8; 9;
2 Chronicles 10—22.)

Then came a reign of terror. Jezebel's daughter,
Athaliah, the mother of Ahaziah, took over in the
south for about six years. Jehoash was put on the
throne at the age of seven; he was the only one left
in the line of David. Then little Jehoash was followed
by Amaziah, who was followed by Azariah, known
as Uzziah. He burned the incense in the temple, as
only a priest was authorized to do, and was smitten
with leprosy. In the year that Uzziah died, Isaiah saw
his vision and cried out, "Here am I. Send me!"
(Isaiah 6:8). He was followed by Jotham, Ahaz, and
Hezekiah. The prophet Micah prophesied in the days
of these men. (See 2 Kings 11—20; 2 Chronicles
22—32.)

The Assyrians in 722 B.C. had already taken the
northern kingdom. In 701 B.C., under Sennacherib,
they decided to take the southern kingdom, and they
would have if God had not intervened. They called
upon Hezekiah to surrender, and Isaiah sent a message from God to him saying, "God will save you."
Hezekiah took the letter demanding surrender to the
temple and spread it out before the Lord, as if to say,

"God, it's Yours. I can't do anything about it." One night the angel of the Lord slew 185,000 of the Assyrians; and when the people arose the next morning, dead men were all around them. The Assyrians left and never returned to threaten the southern kingdom. Hezekiah was given fifteen additional years to live because he petitioned God for it. (See Isaiah 36—38.)

After Hezekiah, one of the best kings, came his son, Manasseh, one of the worst kings. He reigned the longest and, without doubt, was the most wicked of all the kings of the south. He reigned for fifty-six years. (See 2 Kings 21; 2 Chronicles 33.)

Manasseh was followed by Amon, who was followed by Josiah, another good king. Under him, the temple was repaired. This is when the book of the law was found. We think it was the book of Deuteronomy. Josiah inaugurated a great reform about 621 B.C., called the Deuteronomic Reform. He was killed by Pharaoh Neco in 609 B.C., when he went out to attack the Egyptian army. He was followed by a series of weak kings who were mostly vassals, first to Egypt and then to Babylon: Jehoahaz, who lasted three months; Jehoiakim, who lasted eleven years; Jehoiachin, who lasted three months; and Zedekiah, who lasted eleven years. In 586 B.C., the southern kingdom came to an end. (See 2 Kings 21—24; 2 Chronicles 33—36.)

In 606 B.C., Nebuchadnezzar came the first time and carried away Daniel, Shadrach, Meshach, Abednego, and other choice young men to Babylon (see Daniel 1). In 597 B.C., he came again and carried away Ezekiel, Jehoiachin, and many other outstanding people (see Ezekiel 1:1–3). In 586 B.C., the wall was broken down after an eighteen-month siege. The temple was torched, the city was burned, and the people were led off into exile for seventy years (see Jeremiah 52).

These were the days of Zephaniah, who predicted that the day of the Lord would be a day of judgment upon the land.

These were the days of Jeremiah, who was called in the days of Josiah in 627 B.C., and preached till about 580 B.C., telling the people that resistance was useless, that God had decreed the fall of the kingdom. He was called "the weeping prophet."

These were the days of Ezekiel. He was carried off in 597 B.C. to Babylon to preach to the exiles by the river Chebar. He told them that Jerusalem would be destroyed and then gave them hope that one day God would bless them.

These were the days of Habakkuk, when the Jews were asking, "Lord, why are You letting the wicked Babylonians overrun us? I know we're bad, but we're not as bad as they are." The answer God gave to the prophet was, "You trust in Me, and I'll take care of the world. You take care of Habakkuk. The just will live by being faithful to Me."

These were the days of Nahum, who rejoiced over the fall of Nineveh, the capital of Assyria, in 612 B.C. The people did not rejoice for long because the scourge of Babylon soon succeeded it. These were the days of the exile.

The empire of Babylon fell in 539 B.C. Cyrus, the king of Persia, took Babylon. One of the first things he did was tell the captives to go home. Those who had been carried from their land were to go home and dwell in their cities and build temples. The children of Israel headed home about 538–37 B.C. (See Ezra 1:1–4.)

In 536 B.C., led by Zerubbabel, the people reached Palestine. A mongrel race of people had taken over the land. They were the Samaritans, who gave the Jews much trouble; but the children of Israel laid the foundation of the temple. Then again came opposition; but under the preaching of Haggai and Zechariah, they were encouraged to go ahead and get the temple underway, and so they did. In 516 B.C., exactly seventy years after it was destroyed, the temple was rebuilt. (See Ezra 3—6.)

Not long after that, Ezra appeared in Jerusalem. Under his leadership with a company of priests that he brought, the worship was restored. Then in 444 B.C., Nehemiah returned, and under his leadership the walls were built around the city. (See Ezra 7; Nehemiah 1—4.)

Shortly before that, Esther lived. King Ahasuerus had deposed Vashti from being queen, and Esther became his queen. It was she who saved her people, through the intervention of Mordecai, from the wicked plot of Haman. The Jews still celebrate a feast to commemorate this event, the Feast of Purim.

The Old Testament closes with the Book of Malachi. The temple had been rebuilt, the worship had been restored, and the people were back into their routine. Already, it was becoming commonplace. About 400 B.C., the prophet Malachi warned them that they were not to take God lightly. He ended with a promise: "But for you who fear My name, the sun of righteousness will rise with healing in its wings. . . . I am going to send you Elijah the prophet. . . . He will restore the hearts of the fathers to their children and the hearts of the children to their fathers . . ." (Malachi 4:2–6). The Old Testament ends on this note.

The Old Testament is not a complete book because the story was not over with the Book of Malachi. Many prophecies had been given to show that something better was coming. Abraham had been told, Isaac had been told, and Jacob had been told that their seed would bless all nations. The tribe of Judah was told that the scepter would never depart from them. The Son of Man/the Son of God would come through them. David was told that God would make of him a great family. The great prophets even more explicitly described God's theme of redemption which would be fulfilled some day; but the Old Testament ended, and that "some day" had not come.

Now the significance of all of the worship and the sacrifices in the Old Testament days can be seen because these point to the sacrifice of Christ. The kingdom that was predicted is His kingdom, His church; and the message is fulfilled in Jesus Christ.

The Old Testament, as well as the New Testament, is a story of a God who acted, of a God who planned, and of a God who took an interest in the lives of people and intervened in their lives and in their fortunes to accomplish His will among them. That is the God whom we can serve today.

TRUTH • FOR • TODAY
WORLD MISSION SCHOOL

We are glad that you have taken time to read these lessons. We hope you have reviewed the study guide at the end of the book and examined the New Testament. Our prayer is that you now desire to obey the gospel by being baptized into Christ. When you become a Christian, please write us at Truth for Today and let us know. If other Christians are meeting as the church of Christ in your city, please contact them. If you cannot find the church, you can begin one in your home (see Appendix 2). Notify us when you have fifteen or more Christians worshiping together, and we will send you materials for Bible classes and teaching. If you have further questions about the Bible, how to get to heaven, or how to live as a Christian, please contact us at the address below:

Truth for Today World Mission School
P.O. Box 2044
Searcy, AR 72145-2044

If you have access to a computer, you can e-mail us: **staff@biblecourses.com**.

Our website, **www.biblecourses.com**, offers additional Bible-study lessons that you can download.

May God bless you as you seek to do His will.

IN
SEARCH
OF THE LORD'S WAY ®

IN SEARCH OF THE LORD'S WAY television and radio program, now in its **28ᵗʰ year**, provides programming and information that can be used to help convert the non-Christian and strengthen the faith of the Christian. The intention of SEARCH is to spread the gospel message of Jesus Christ. Everything SEARCH does is designed to guide people to Christ and show them His way for mankind to live.

Mack Lyon is the founder and has been the only speaker on the SEARCH program from its beginning. He preaches the truth in love. He fearlessly yet calmly condemns the darkness of sin in every form. He believes and SAYS he believes that the Lord's way to be saved is the only way, and that the Lord's way to live this life is the very best way that has ever been introduced to the family of man. He believes that TO BE the best and only way, the Lord's way is different from the ways of men. He constantly points to the vast difference between Christianity as it is seen today and as it is revealed in the New Testament, and he preaches the need to return to the original.

For additional information, call SEARCH at 1-800-321-8633 or visit the SEARCH website at www.searchtv.org. To view a programming schedule, check the website for the current edition of **The Search Light.**

NEW TESTAMENT

NEW AMERICAN STANDARD BIBLE

What does God say about salvation?
Read Matthew 27:27-54 on page 25.

Foreword

Scriptural Promise

"The grass withers, the flower fades,
but the word of our God stands forever."
Isaiah 40:8

The New American Standard Bible has been produced with the conviction that the words of Scripture as originally penned in the Hebrew, Aramaic, and Greek were inspired by God. Since they are the eternal Word of God, the Holy Scriptures speak with fresh power to each generation, to give wisdom that leads to salvation, that men may serve Christ to the glory of God.

The Fourfold Aim
of
The Lockman Foundation

1. These publications shall be true to the original Hebrew, Aramaic, and Greek.
2. They shall be grammatically correct.
3. They shall be understandable.
4. They shall give the Lord Jesus Christ His proper place, the place which the Word gives Him; therefore, no work will ever be personalized.

Preface to The
New American Standard Bible

In the history of English Bible translations, the King James Version is the most prestigious. This time-honored version of 1611, itself a revision of the Bishops' Bible of 1568, became the basis for the English Revised Version appearing in 1881 (New Testament) and 1885 (Old Testament). The American counterpart of this last work was published in 1901 as the American Standard Version. The ASV, a product of both British and American scholarship, has been highly regarded for its scholarship and accuracy. Recognizing the values of the American Standard Version, The Lockman Foundation felt an urgency to preserve these and other lasting values of the ASV by incorporating recent discoveries of Hebrew and Greek textual sources and by rendering it into more current English. Therefore, in 1959 a new translation project was launched, based on the time-honored principles of translation of the ASV and KJV. The result is the New American Standard Bible.

Translation work for the NASB was begun in 1959. In the preparation of this work numerous other translations have been consulted along with the linguistic tools and literature of biblical scholarship. Decisions about English renderings were made by consensus of a team composed of educators and pastors. Subsequently, review and evaluation by other Hebrew and Greek scholars outside the Editorial Board were sought and carefully considered.

The Editorial Board has continued to function since publication of the complete Bible in 1971. This edition of the NASB represents revisions and refinements recommended over the last several years as well as thorough research based on modern English usage.

Principles of Translation

Modern English Usage: The attempt has been made to render the grammar and terminology in contemporary English. When it was felt that the word-for-word literalness was unacceptable to the modern reader, a change was made in the direction of a more current English idiom. In the instances where this has been done, the more literal rendering has been indicated in the notes. There are a few exceptions to this procedure. In particular, frequently "And" is not translated at the beginning of sentences because of differences in style between ancient and modern writing. Punctuation is a relatively modern invention, and ancient writers often linked most of their sentences with "and" or other connectives. Also, the Hebrew idiom "answered and said" is sometimes reduced to "answered" or "said" as demanded by the context. For current English the idiom "it came about that" has not been translated in the New Testament except when a major transition is needed.

Alternative Readings: In addition to the more literal renderings, notations have been made to include alternate translations, reading of variant manuscripts, and explanatory equivalents of the text. These notations have been used specifically to assist the reader in comprehending the terms used by the original author.

Greek Text: Consideration was given to the latest available manuscripts with a view to determining the best Greek text. In most instances the 26th edition of Eberhard Nestle's *Novum Testamentum Graece* was followed.

Greek Tenses: A careful distinction has been made in the treatment of the Greek aorist tense (usually translated as the English past, "He did") and the Greek imperfect tense (normally rendered either as English past progressive, "He was doing"; or, if inceptive, as "He began to do" or "He started to do"; or else if customary past, as "He used to do"). "Began" is italicized if it renders an imperfect tense, in order to distinguish it from the Greek verb for "begin." In some contexts the difference between the Greek imperfect and the English past is conveyed better by the choice of vocabulary or by other words in the context, and in such cases the Greek imperfect may be rendered as a simple past tense (e.g. "had an illness for many years" would be preferable to "was having an illness for many years" and would be understood in the same way).

On the other hand, not all aorists have been rendered as English pasts ("He did"), for some of them are clearly to be rendered as English perfects ("He has done"), or even as past perfects ("He had done"), judging from the context in which they occur. Such aorists have been rendered as perfects or past perfects in this translation.

As for the distinction between aorist and present imperatives, the translators have usually rendered these imperatives in the customary manner, rather than attempting any such fine distinction as "Begin to do!" (for the aorist imperative), or, "Continually do!" (for the present imperative).

As for sequence of tenses, the translators took care to follow English rules rather than Greek in translating Greek presents, imperfects, and aorists. Thus, where English says, "We knew that he was doing," Greek puts it, "We knew that he does"; similarly, "We knew that he had done" is the Greek, "We knew that he did." Likewise, the English, "When he had come, they met him," is represented in Greek by, "When he came, they met him." In all cases a consistent transfer has been made from the Greek tense in the subordinate clause to the appropriate tense in English.

In the rendering of negative questions introduced by the particle *mē* (which always expects the answer "No") the wording has been altered from a mere, "Will he not do this?" to a more accurate, "He will not do this, will he?"

The Lockman Foundation

Explanation of General Format

Footnotes at the bottom of the page refer to literal renderings, alternate translations, or explanations.

Paragraphs are designated by bold face verse numbers or letters.

Quotation Marks are used in the text in accordance with modern English usage.

"Thy," "Thee" and "Thou" are not used in this edition and have been rendered as "Your" and "You."

Personal Pronouns are capitalized when pertaining to Deity.

Italics are used in the text to indicate words which are not found in the original Hebrew, Aramaic, or Greek but implied by it. Italics are used in the footnotes to signify alternate readings for the text. Roman text in a footnote alternate reading is the same as italics in the Bible text.

Small Caps in the New Testament are used in the text to indicate Old Testament quotations or obvious references to Old Testament texts. Variations of Old Testament wording are found in New Testament citations depending on whether the New Testament writer translated from a Hebrew text, used existing Greek or Aramaic translations, or paraphrased the material. It should be noted that modern rules for the indication of direct quotation were not used in biblical times; thus, the ancient writer would use exact quotations or references to quotation without specific indication of such.

A **star** (*) is used to mark verbs that are historical presents in the Greek which have been translated with an English past tense in order to conform to modern usage. The translators recognized that in some contexts the present tense seems more unexpected and unjustified to the English reader than a past tense would have been. But Greek authors frequently used the present tense for the sake of heightened vividness, thereby transporting their readers in imagination to the actual scene at the time of occurrence. However, the translators felt that it would be wise to change these historical presents to English past tenses.

Abbreviations and Special Markings

Aram	= Aramaic
DSS	= Dead Sea Scrolls
Gr	= Greek translation of O.T. (Septuagint or LXX) or Greek text of N.T.
Heb	= Hebrew text, usually Masoretic
Lat	= Latin M.T.=Masoretic text
Syr	= Syriac
Lit	= A literal translation
Or	= An alternate translation justified by the Hebrew, Aramaic, or Greek
[ ]	= In text, brackets indicate words probably not in the original writings
[ ]	= In margin, brackets indicate references to a name, place, or thing similar to, but not identical with that in the text
cf	= compare
f, ff	= following verse or verses
mg	= Refers to a marginal reading on another verse
ms	= manuscript
mss	= manuscripts
v, vv	= verse, verses

The Books of the New Testament

THE GOSPEL ACCORDING TO MATTHEW

The Genealogy of Jesus the Messiah

1 The record of the genealogy of Jesus the Messiah, the son of David, the son of Abraham:

2 Abraham was the father of Isaac, Isaac the father of Jacob, and Jacob the father of ¹Judah and his brothers.

3 Judah was the father of Perez and Zerah by Tamar, Perez was the father of Hezron, and Hezron the father of Ram.

4 Ram was the father of Amminadab, Amminadab the father of Nahshon, and Nahshon the father of Salmon.

5 Salmon was the father of Boaz by Rahab, Boaz was the father of Obed by Ruth, and Obed the father of Jesse.

6 Jesse was the father of David the king.

David was the father of Solomon by ²Bathsheba who had been the wife of Uriah.

7 Solomon was the father of Rehoboam, Rehoboam the father of Abijah, and Abijah the father of Asa.

8 Asa was the father of Jehoshaphat, Jehoshaphat the father of Joram, and Joram the father of Uzziah.

9 Uzziah was the father of Jotham, Jotham the father of Ahaz, and Ahaz the father of Hezekiah.

10 Hezekiah was the father of Manasseh, Manasseh the father of Amon, and Amon the father of Josiah.

11 Josiah became the father of Jeconiah and his brothers, at the time of the deportation to Babylon.

12 After the deportation to Babylon: Jeconiah became the father of Shealtiel, and Shealtiel the father of Zerubbabel.

13 Zerubbabel was the father of Abihud, Abihud the father of Eliakim, and Eliakim the father of Azor.

14 Azor was the father of Zadok, Zadok the father of Achim, and Achim the father of Eliud.

15 Eliud was the father of Eleazar, Eleazar the father of Matthan, and Matthan the father of Jacob.

16 Jacob was the father of Joseph the husband of Mary, by whom Jesus was born, who is called the Messiah.

17 So all the generations from Abraham to David are fourteen generations; from David to the deportation to Babylon, fourteen generations; and from the deportation to Babylon to the Messiah, fourteen generations.

18 Now the birth of Jesus Christ was as follows: when His mother Mary had been betrothed to Joseph, before they came together she was found to be with child by the Holy Spirit.

19 And Joseph her husband, being a righteous man and not wanting to disgrace her, planned ³to send her away secretly.

20 But when he had considered this, behold, an angel of the Lord appeared to him in a dream, saying, "Joseph, son of David, do not be afraid to take Mary as your wife; for the Child who has been ⁴conceived in her is of the Holy Spirit.

21 "She will bear a Son; and you shall call His name Jesus, for He will save His people from their sins."

22 Now all this took place to fulfill what was spoken by the Lord through the prophet:

23 "BEHOLD, THE VIRGIN SHALL BE WITH CHILD AND SHALL BEAR A SON, AND THEY SHALL CALL HIS NAME IMMANUEL," which translated means, "GOD WITH US."

24 And Joseph awoke from his sleep and did as the angel of the Lord commanded him, and took *Mary* as his wife,

25 ⁵but kept her a virgin until she gave birth to a Son; and he called His name Jesus.

The Visit of the Magi

2 Now after Jesus was born in Bethlehem of Judea in the days of Herod the king, ⁶magi from the east arrived in Jerusalem, saying,

2 "Where is He who has been born King of the Jews? For we saw His star in the east and have come to worship Him."

3 When Herod the king heard *this*, he was troubled, and all Jerusalem with him.

4 Gathering together all the chief priests and scribes of the people, he inquired of them where the Messiah was to be born.

5 They said to him, "In Bethlehem of Judea; for this is what has been written by the prophet:

6 'AND YOU, BETHLEHEM, LAND OF JUDAH,
ARE BY NO MEANS LEAST AMONG THE LEADERS OF JUDAH;
FOR OUT OF YOU SHALL COME FORTH A RULER
WHO WILL SHEPHERD MY PEOPLE ISRAEL.' "

7 Then Herod secretly called the magi and determined from them the exact time the star appeared.

8 And he sent them to Bethlehem and said, "Go and search carefully for the Child; and when you have found *Him*, report to me, so that I too may come and worship Him."

9 After hearing the king, they went their way; and the star, which they had seen in the east, went on before them until it came and stood over *the place* where the Child was.

10 When they saw the star, they rejoiced exceedingly with great joy.

11 After coming into the house they saw the Child with Mary His mother; and they fell to the ground and worshiped Him. Then, opening their treasures, they presented to Him gifts of gold, frankincense, and myrrh.

12 And having been warned *by God* in a dream not to return to Herod, the magi left for their own country by another way.

---

1. Gr *Judas;* names of people in the Old Testament are given in their Old Testament form 2. Lit *her of Uriah* 3. Or *to divorce her* 4. Lit *begotten* 5. Lit *and was not knowing her* 6. A caste of wise men specializing in astronomy, astrology, and natural science

13 Now when they had gone, behold, an angel of the Lord *appeared to Joseph in a dream and said, "Get up! Take the Child and His mother and flee to Egypt, and remain there until I tell you; for Herod is going to search for the Child to destroy Him."

14 So Joseph got up and took the Child and His mother while it was still night, and left for Egypt.

15 He remained there until the death of Herod. *This was* to fulfill what had been spoken by the Lord through the prophet: "OUT OF EGYPT I CALLED MY SON."

16 Then when Herod saw that he had been tricked by the magi, he became very enraged, and sent and slew all the male children who were in Bethlehem and all its vicinity, from two years old and under, according to the time which he had determined from the magi.

17 Then what had been spoken through Jeremiah the prophet was fulfilled:

18 "A VOICE WAS HEARD IN RAMAH,
   WEEPING AND GREAT MOURNING,
   RACHEL WEEPING FOR HER CHILDREN;
   AND SHE REFUSED TO BE COMFORTED,
   BECAUSE THEY WERE NO MORE."

19 But when Herod died, behold, an angel of the Lord *appeared in a dream to Joseph in Egypt, and said,

20 "Get up, take the Child and His mother, and go into the land of Israel; for those who sought the Child's life are dead."

21 So Joseph got up, took the Child and His mother, and came into the land of Israel.

22 But when he heard that Archelaus was reigning over Judea in place of his father Herod, he was afraid to go there. Then after being warned *by God* in a dream, he left for the regions of Galilee,

23 and came and lived in a city called Nazareth. *This was* to fulfill what was spoken through the prophets: "He shall be called a Nazarene."

The Preaching of John the Baptist

3 Now in those days John the Baptist *came, preaching in the wilderness of Judea, saying,

2 "Repent, for the kingdom of heaven is at hand."

3 For this is the one referred to by Isaiah the prophet when he said,

"THE VOICE OF ONE CRYING IN THE WILDERNESS,
   'MAKE READY THE WAY OF THE LORD,
   MAKE HIS PATHS STRAIGHT!' "

4 Now John himself had a garment of camel's hair and a leather belt around his waist; and his food was locusts and wild honey.

5 Then Jerusalem was going out to him, and all Judea and all the district around the Jordan;

6 and they were being baptized by him in the Jordan River, as they confessed their sins.

7 But when he saw many of the Pharisees and Sadducees coming for baptism, he said to them, "You brood of vipers, who warned you to flee from the wrath to come?

8 "Therefore bear fruit in keeping with repentance;

9 and do not suppose that you can say to yourselves, 'We have Abraham for our father'; for I say to you that from these stones God is able to raise up children to Abraham.

10 "The axe is already laid at the root of the trees; therefore every tree that does not bear good fruit is cut down and thrown into the fire.

11 "As for me, I baptize you ¹with water for repentance, but He who is coming after me is mightier than I, and I am not fit to remove His sandals; He will baptize you with the Holy Spirit and fire.

12 "His winnowing fork is in His hand, and He will thoroughly clear His threshing floor; and He will gather His wheat into the barn, but He will burn up the chaff with unquenchable fire."

13 Then Jesus *arrived from Galilee at the Jordan *coming* to John, to be baptized by him.

14 But John tried to prevent Him, saying, "I have need to be baptized by You, and do You come to me?"

15 But Jesus answering said to him, "Permit *it* at this time; for in this way it is fitting for us to fulfill all righteousness." Then he *permitted Him.

16 After being baptized, Jesus came up immediately from the water; and behold, the heavens were opened, and he saw the Spirit of God descending as a dove *and* lighting on Him,

17 and behold, a voice out of the heavens said, "This is ²My beloved Son, in whom I am well-pleased."

The Temptation of Jesus

4 Then Jesus was led up by the Spirit into the wilderness to be tempted by the devil.

2 And after He had fasted forty days and forty nights, He ³then became hungry.

3 And the tempter came and said to Him, "If You are the Son of God, command that these stones become bread."

4 But He answered and said, "It is written, 'MAN SHALL NOT LIVE ON BREAD ALONE, BUT ON EVERY WORD THAT PROCEEDS OUT OF THE MOUTH OF GOD.' "

5 Then the devil *took Him into the holy city and had Him stand on the pinnacle of the temple,

6 and *said to Him, "If You are the Son of God, throw Yourself down; for it is written,

'HE WILL COMMAND HIS ANGELS CONCERNING YOU';
and
'ON *their* HANDS THEY WILL BEAR YOU UP,
   SO THAT YOU WILL NOT STRIKE YOUR FOOT
   AGAINST A STONE.' "

7 Jesus said to him, "On the other hand, it is written, 'YOU SHALL NOT PUT THE LORD YOUR GOD TO THE TEST.' "

8 Again, the devil *took Him to a very high mountain and *showed Him all the kingdoms of the world and their glory;

---

1. The Gr here can be translated *in, with* or *by* 2. Or *My Son, the Beloved* 3. Lit *later became; or afterward became*

9 and he said to Him, "All these things I will give You, if You fall down and worship me."

10 Then Jesus *said to him, "Go, Satan! For it is written, 'YOU SHALL WORSHIP THE LORD YOUR GOD, AND SERVE HIM ONLY.'"

11 Then the devil *left Him; and behold, angels came and *began to minister to Him.

12 Now when Jesus heard that John had been taken into custody, He withdrew into Galilee;

13 and leaving Nazareth, He came and settled in Capernaum, which is by the sea, in the region of Zebulun and Naphtali.

14 This was to fulfill what was spoken through Isaiah the prophet:

15 "THE LAND OF ZEBULUN AND THE LAND OF NAPHTALI,

BY THE WAY OF THE SEA, BEYOND THE JORDAN, GALILEE OF THE [1]GENTILES—

16 "THE PEOPLE WHO WERE SITTING IN DARKNESS SAW A GREAT LIGHT,

AND THOSE WHO WERE SITTING IN THE LAND AND SHADOW OF DEATH,

UPON THEM A LIGHT DAWNED."

17 From that time Jesus began to preach and say, "Repent, for the kingdom of heaven is at hand."

18 Now as Jesus was walking by the Sea of Galilee, He saw two brothers, Simon who was called Peter, and Andrew his brother, casting a net into the sea; for they were fishermen.

19 And He *said to them, "Follow Me, and I will make you fishers of men."

20 Immediately they left their nets and followed Him.

21 Going on from there He saw two other brothers, James the son of Zebedee, and John his brother, in the boat with Zebedee their father, mending their nets; and He called them.

22 Immediately they left the boat and their father, and followed Him.

23 Jesus was going throughout all Galilee, teaching in their synagogues and proclaiming the gospel of the kingdom, and healing every kind of disease and every kind of sickness among the people.

24 The news about Him spread throughout all Syria; and they brought to Him all who were ill, those suffering with various diseases and pains, demoniacs, epileptics, paralytics; and He healed them.

25 Large crowds followed Him from Galilee and the Decapolis and Jerusalem and Judea and from beyond the Jordan.

The Sermon on the Mount; The Beatitudes

5 When Jesus saw the crowds, He went up on the mountain; and after He sat down, His disciples came to Him.

2 He opened His mouth and began to teach them, saying,

3 "Blessed are the poor in spirit, for theirs is the kingdom of heaven.

4 "Blessed are those who mourn, for they shall be comforted.

5 "Blessed are the [2]gentle, for they shall inherit the earth.

6 "Blessed are those who hunger and thirst for righteousness, for they shall be satisfied.

7 "Blessed are the merciful, for they shall receive mercy.

8 "Blessed are the pure in heart, for they shall see God.

9 "Blessed are the peacemakers, for they shall be called sons of God.

10 "Blessed are those who have been persecuted for the sake of righteousness, for theirs is the kingdom of heaven.

11 "Blessed are you when people insult you and persecute you, and falsely say all kinds of evil against you because of Me.

12 "Rejoice and be glad, for your reward in heaven is great; for in the same way they persecuted the prophets who were before you.

13 "You are the salt of the earth; but if the salt has become tasteless, how can it be made salty again? It is no longer good for anything, except to be thrown out and trampled under foot by men.

14 "You are the light of the world. A city set on a hill cannot be hidden;

15 nor does anyone light a lamp and put it under a basket, but on the lampstand, and it gives light to all who are in the house.

16 "Let your light shine before men in such a way that they may see your good works, and glorify your Father who is in heaven.

17 "Do not think that I came to abolish the Law or the Prophets; I did not come to abolish but to fulfill.

18 "For truly I say to you, until heaven and earth pass away, not the smallest letter or stroke shall pass from the Law until all is accomplished.

19 "Whoever then annuls one of the least of these commandments, and teaches others to do the same, shall be called least in the kingdom of heaven; but whoever keeps and teaches them, he shall be called great in the kingdom of heaven.

20 "For I say to you that unless your righteousness surpasses that of the scribes and Pharisees, you will not enter the kingdom of heaven.

21 "You have heard that the ancients were told, 'YOU SHALL NOT COMMIT MURDER' and 'Whoever commits murder shall be [3]liable to the court.'

22 "But I say to you that everyone who is angry with his brother shall be guilty before the court; and whoever says to his brother, '[4]You good-for-nothing,' shall be guilty before [5]the supreme court; and whoever says, 'You fool,' shall be guilty enough to go into the [6]fiery hell.

23 "Therefore if you are presenting your offering at the altar, and there remember that your brother has something against you,

24 leave your offering there before the altar

---

1. Lit nations, usually non-Jewish 2. Or humble, meek 3. Or guilty before 4. Or empty-head; Gr Raka (Raca) fr Aram reqa
5. Lit the Sanhedrin 6. Lit Gehenna of fire

and go; first be reconciled to your brother, and then come and present your offering.

25 "Make friends quickly with your opponent at law while you are with him on the way, so that your opponent may not hand you over to the judge, and the judge to the officer, and you be thrown into prison.

26 "Truly I say to you, you will not come out of there until you have paid up the last [1]cent.

27 "You have heard that it was said, 'YOU SHALL NOT COMMIT ADULTERY';

28 but I say to you that everyone who looks at a woman with lust for her has already committed adultery with her in his heart.

29 "If your right eye makes you stumble, tear it out and throw it from you; for it is better for you to lose one of the parts of your body, than for your whole body to be thrown into hell.

30 "If your right hand makes you stumble, cut it off and throw it from you; for it is better for you to lose one of the parts of your body, than for your whole body to go into hell.

31 "It was said, 'WHOEVER SENDS HIS WIFE AWAY, LET HIM GIVE HER A CERTIFICATE OF DIVORCE';

32 but I say to you that everyone who divorces his wife, except for *the* reason of unchastity, makes her commit adultery; and whoever marries a divorced woman commits adultery.

33 "Again, you have heard that the ancients were told, 'YOU SHALL NOT MAKE FALSE VOWS, BUT SHALL FULFILL YOUR VOWS TO THE LORD.'

34 "But I say to you, make no oath at all, either by heaven, for it is the throne of God,

35 or by the earth, for it is the footstool of His feet, or by Jerusalem, for it is THE CITY OF THE GREAT KING.

36 "Nor shall you make an oath by your head, for you cannot make one hair white or black.

37 "But let your statement be, 'Yes, yes' *or* 'No, no'; anything beyond these is of evil.

38 "You have heard that it was said, 'AN EYE FOR AN EYE, AND A TOOTH FOR A TOOTH.'

39 "But I say to you, do not resist an evil person; but whoever slaps you on your right cheek, turn the other to him also.

40 "If anyone wants to sue you and take your [2]shirt, let him have your [3]coat also.

41 "Whoever forces you to go one mile, go with him two.

42 "Give to him who asks of you, and do not turn away from him who wants to borrow from you.

43 "You have heard that it was said, 'YOU SHALL LOVE YOUR NEIGHBOR and hate your enemy.'

44 "But I say to you, love your enemies and pray for those who persecute you,

45 so that you may be sons of your Father who is in heaven; for He causes His sun to rise on *the* evil and *the* good, and sends rain on *the* righteous and *the* unrighteous.

46 "For if you love those who love you, what reward do you have? Do not even the tax collectors do the same?

47 "If you greet only your brothers, what more are you doing *than others?* Do not even the Gentiles do the same?

48 "Therefore you are to be perfect, as your heavenly Father is perfect.

Giving to the Poor and Prayer

6 "Beware of practicing your righteousness before men to be noticed by them; otherwise you have no reward with your Father who is in heaven.

2 "So when you give to the poor, do not sound a trumpet before you, as the hypocrites do in the synagogues and in the streets, so that they may be honored by men. Truly I say to you, they have their reward in full.

3 "But when you give to the poor, do not let your left hand know what your right hand is doing,

4 so that your giving will be in secret; and your Father who sees *what is done* in secret will reward you.

5 "When you pray, you are not to be like the hypocrites; for they love to stand and pray in the synagogues and on the street corners so that they may be seen by men. Truly I say to you, they have their reward in full.

6 "But you, when you pray, go into your inner room, close your door and pray to your Father who is in secret, and your Father who sees *what is done* in secret will reward you.

7 "And when you are praying, do not use meaningless repetition as the Gentiles do, for they suppose that they will be heard for their many words.

8 "So do not be like them; for your Father knows what you need before you ask Him.

9 "Pray, then, in this way:
'Our Father who is in heaven,
Hallowed be Your name.

10 'Your kingdom come.
Your will be done,
On earth as it is in heaven.

11 'Give us this day our daily bread.

12 'And forgive us our debts, as we also have forgiven our debtors.

13 'And do not lead us into temptation, but deliver us from evil. [For Yours is the kingdom and the power and the glory forever. Amen.]'

14 "For if you forgive others for their transgressions, your heavenly Father will also forgive you.

15 "But if you do not forgive others, then your Father will not forgive your transgressions.

16 "Whenever you fast, do not put on a gloomy face as the hypocrites *do,* for they neglect their appearance so that they will be noticed by men when they are fasting. Truly I say to you, they have their reward in full.

17 "But you, when you fast, anoint your head and wash your face

18 so that your fasting will not be noticed by

---

1. Lit *quadrans* (equaling two mites); i.e. 1/64 of a daily wage 2. Lit *tunic;* i.e. a garment worn next to the body 3. Lit *cloak;* i.e. an outer garment

men, but by your Father who is in secret; and your Father who sees *what is done* in secret will reward you.

19 "Do not store up for yourselves treasures on earth, where moth and rust destroy, and where thieves break in and steal.

20 "But store up for yourselves treasures in heaven, where neither moth nor rust destroys, and where thieves do not break in or steal;

21 for where your treasure is, there your heart will be also.

22 "The eye is the lamp of the body; so then if your eye is clear, your whole body will be full of light.

23 "But if your eye is bad, your whole body will be full of darkness. If then the light that is in you is darkness, how great is the darkness!

24 "No one can serve two masters; for either he will hate the one and love the other, or he will be devoted to one and despise the other. You cannot serve God and ¹wealth.

25 "For this reason I say to you, do not be worried about your life, *as to* what you will eat or what you will drink; nor for your body, *as to* what you will put on. Is not life more than food, and the body more than clothing?

26 "Look at the birds of the air, that they do not sow, nor reap nor gather into barns, and *yet* your heavenly Father feeds them. Are you not worth much more than they?

27 "And who of you by being worried can add a *single* hour to his life?

28 "And why are you worried about clothing? Observe how the lilies of the field grow; they do not toil nor do they spin,

29 yet I say to you that not even Solomon in all his glory clothed himself like one of these.

30 "But if God so clothes the grass of the field, which is *alive* today and tomorrow is thrown into the furnace, *will He* not much more *clothe* you? You of little faith!

31 "Do not worry then, saying, 'What will we eat?' or 'What will we drink?' or 'What will we wear for clothing?'

32 "For the Gentiles eagerly seek all these things; for your heavenly Father knows that you need all these things.

33 "But seek first His kingdom and His righteousness, and all these things will be added to you.

34 "So do not worry about tomorrow; for tomorrow will care for itself. Each day has enough trouble of its own.

Judging Others

7 "Do not judge so that you will not be judged.

2 "For in the way you judge, you will be judged; and by your standard of measure, it will be measured to you.

3 "Why do you look at the speck that is in your brother's eye, but do not notice the log that is in your own eye?

4 "Or how can you say to your brother, 'Let me take the speck out of your eye,' and behold, the log is in your own eye?

5 "You hypocrite, first take the log out of your own eye, and then you will see clearly to take the speck out of your brother's eye.

6 "Do not give what is holy to dogs, and do not throw your pearls before swine, or they will trample them under their feet, and turn and tear you to pieces.

7 "Ask, and it will be given to you; seek, and you will find; knock, and it will be opened to you.

8 "For everyone who asks receives, and he who seeks finds, and to him who knocks it will be opened.

9 "Or what man is there among you who, when his son asks for a loaf, will give him a stone?

10 "Or if he asks for a fish, he will not give him a snake, will he?

11 "If you then, being evil, know how to give good gifts to your children, how much more will your Father who is in heaven give what is good to those who ask Him!

12 "In everything, therefore, treat people the same way you want them to treat you, for this is the Law and the Prophets.

13 "Enter through the narrow gate; for the gate is wide and the way is broad that leads to destruction, and there are many who enter through it.

14 "For the gate is small and the way is narrow that leads to life, and there are few who find it.

15 "Beware of the false prophets, who come to you in sheep's clothing, but inwardly are ravenous wolves.

16 "You will know them by their fruits. Grapes are not gathered from thorn *bushes* nor figs from thistles, are they?

17 "So every good tree bears good fruit, but the bad tree bears bad fruit.

18 "A good tree cannot produce bad fruit, nor can a bad tree produce good fruit.

19 "Every tree that does not bear good fruit is cut down and thrown into the fire.

20 "So then, you will know them by their fruits.

21 "Not everyone who says to Me, 'Lord, Lord,' will enter the kingdom of heaven, but he who does the will of My Father who is in heaven *will enter.*

22 "Many will say to Me on that day, 'Lord, Lord, did we not prophesy in Your name, and in Your name cast out demons, and in Your name perform many miracles?'

23 "And then I will declare to them, 'I never knew you; DEPART FROM ME, YOU WHO PRACTICE LAWLESSNESS.'

24 "Therefore everyone who hears these words of Mine and acts on them, may be compared to a wise man who built his house on the rock.

25 "And the rain fell, and the floods came, and the winds blew and slammed against that house; and *yet* it did not fall, for it had been founded on the rock.

26 "Everyone who hears these words of Mine and does not act on them, will be like a foolish man who built his house on the sand.

---

1. Gr *mamonas*, for Aram *mamon*(mammon); i.e. wealth, etc., personified as an object of worship

27 "The rain fell, and the floods came, and the winds blew and slammed against that house; and it fell—and great was its fall."

28 When Jesus had finished these words, the crowds were amazed at His teaching;

29 for He was teaching them as *one* having authority, and not as their scribes.

Jesus Cleanses a Leper; The Centurion's Faith

8 When Jesus came down from the mountain, large crowds followed Him.

2 And a leper came to Him and bowed down before Him, and said, "Lord, if You are willing, You can make me clean."

3 Jesus stretched out His hand and touched him, saying, "I am willing; be cleansed." And immediately his leprosy was cleansed.

4 And Jesus *said to him, "See that you tell no one; but go, show yourself to the priest and present the offering that Moses commanded, as a testimony to them."

5 And when Jesus entered Capernaum, a centurion came to Him, imploring Him,

6 and saying, "Lord, my servant is lying paralyzed at home, fearfully tormented."

7 Jesus *said to him, "I will come and heal him."

8 But the centurion said, "Lord, I am not worthy for You to come under my roof, but just say the word, and my servant will be healed.

9 "For I also am a man under authority, with soldiers under me; and I say to this one, 'Go!' and he goes, and to another, 'Come!' and he comes, and to my slave, 'Do this!' and he does *it*."

10 Now when Jesus heard *this*, He marveled and said to those who were following, "Truly I say to you, I have not found such great faith with anyone in Israel.

11 "I say to you that many will come from east and west, and ¹recline *at the table* with Abraham, Isaac and Jacob in the kingdom of heaven;

12 but the sons of the kingdom will be cast out into the outer darkness; in that place there will be weeping and gnashing of teeth."

13 And Jesus said to the centurion, "Go; it shall be done for you as you have believed." And the servant was healed that *very* moment.

14 When Jesus came into Peter's home, He saw his mother-in-law lying sick in bed with a fever.

15 He touched her hand, and the fever left her; and she got up and waited on Him.

16 When evening came, they brought to Him many who were demon-possessed; and He cast out the spirits with a word, and healed all who were ill.

17 This *was* to fulfill what was spoken through Isaiah the prophet: "HE HIMSELF TOOK OUR INFIRMITIES AND CARRIED AWAY OUR DISEASES."

18 Now when Jesus saw a crowd around Him, He gave orders to depart to the other side *of the sea*.

19 Then a scribe came and said to Him, "Teacher, I will follow You wherever You go."

20 Jesus *said to him, "The foxes have holes and the birds of the air *have* nests, but the Son of Man has nowhere to lay His head."

21 Another of the disciples said to Him, "Lord, permit me first to go and bury my father."

22 But Jesus *said to him, "Follow Me, and allow the dead to bury their own dead."

23 When He got into the boat, His disciples followed Him.

24 And behold, there arose a great storm on the sea, so that the boat was being covered with the waves; but Jesus Himself was asleep.

25 And they came to *Him* and woke Him, saying, "Save *us*, Lord; we are perishing!"

26 He *said to them, "Why are you afraid, you men of little faith?" Then He got up and rebuked the winds and the sea, and it became perfectly calm.

27 The men were amazed, and said, "What kind of a man is this, that even the winds and the sea obey Him?"

28 When He came to the other side into the country of the Gadarenes, two men who were demon-possessed met Him as they were coming out of the tombs. *They were* so extremely violent that no one could pass by that way.

29 And they cried out, saying, "What business do we have with each other, Son of God? Have You come here to torment us before the time?"

30 Now there was a herd of many swine feeding at a distance from them.

31 The demons *began* to entreat Him, saying, "If You *are going to* cast us out, send us into the herd of swine."

32 And He said to them, "Go!" And they came out and went into the swine, and the whole herd rushed down the steep bank into the sea and perished in the waters.

33 The herdsmen ran away, and went to the city and reported everything, including what had happened to the demoniacs.

34 And behold, the whole city came out to meet Jesus; and when they saw Him, they implored Him to leave their region.

A Paralytic Healed

9 Getting into a boat, Jesus crossed over *the sea* and came to His own city.

2 And they brought to Him a paralytic lying on a bed. Seeing their faith, Jesus said to the paralytic, "Take courage, son; your sins are forgiven."

3 And some of the scribes said to themselves, "This *fellow* blasphemes."

4 And Jesus knowing their thoughts said, "Why are you thinking evil in your hearts?

5 "Which is easier, to say, 'Your sins are forgiven,' or to say, 'Get up, and walk'?

6 "But so that you may know that the Son of Man has authority on earth to forgive sins"—then He *said to the paralytic, "Get up, pick up your bed and go home."

7 And he got up and went home.

---

1. **Or** *dine*

8 But when the crowds saw *this*, they were awestruck, and glorified God, who had given such authority to men.

9 As Jesus went on from there, He saw a man called Matthew, sitting in the tax collector's booth; and He *said to him, "Follow Me!" And he got up and followed Him.

10 Then it happened that as Jesus was reclining *at the table* in the house, behold, many tax collectors and sinners came and were dining with Jesus and His disciples.

11 When the Pharisees saw *this*, they said to His disciples, "Why is your Teacher eating with the tax collectors and sinners?"

12 But when Jesus heard *this*, He said, "*It is* not those who are healthy who need a physician, but those who are sick.

13 "But go and learn what this means: 'I DESIRE COMPASSION, [1]AND NOT SACRIFICE,' for I did not come to call the righteous, but sinners."

14 Then the disciples of John *came to Him, asking, "Why do we and the Pharisees fast, but Your disciples do not fast?"

15 And Jesus said to them, "The attendants of the bridegroom cannot mourn as long as the bridegroom is with them, can they? But the days will come when the bridegroom is taken away from them, and then they will fast.

16 "But no one puts a patch of unshrunk cloth on an old garment; for the patch pulls away from the garment, and a worse tear results.

17 "Nor do *people* put new wine into old wineskins; otherwise the wineskins burst, and the wine pours out and the wineskins are ruined; but they put new wine into fresh wineskins, and both are preserved."

18 While He was saying these things to them, a *synagogue* official came and bowed down before Him, and said, "My daughter has just died; but come and lay Your hand on her, and she will live."

19 Jesus got up and *began* to follow him, and *so did* His disciples.

20 And a woman who had been suffering from a hemorrhage for twelve years, came up behind Him and touched the fringe of His cloak;

21 for she was saying to herself, "If I only touch His garment, I will get well."

22 But Jesus turning and seeing her said, "Daughter, take courage; your faith has made you well." At once the woman was made well.

23 When Jesus came into the official's house, and saw the flute-players and the crowd in noisy disorder,

24 He said, "Leave; for the girl has not died, but is asleep." And they *began* laughing at Him.

25 But when the crowd had been sent out, He entered and took her by the hand, and the girl got up.

26 This news spread throughout all that land.

27 As Jesus went on from there, two blind men followed Him, crying out, "Have mercy on us, Son of David!"

28 When He entered the house, the blind men came up to Him, and Jesus *said to them, "Do you believe that I am able to do this?" They *said to Him, "Yes, Lord."

29 Then He touched their eyes, saying, "It shall be done to you according to your faith."

30 And their eyes were opened. And Jesus sternly warned them: "See that no one knows *about this!*"

31 But they went out and spread the news about Him throughout all that land.

32 As they were going out, a mute, demon-possessed man was brought to Him.

33 After the demon was cast out, the mute man spoke; and the crowds were amazed, *and were* saying, "Nothing like this has ever been seen in Israel."

34 But the Pharisees were saying, "He casts out the demons by the ruler of the demons."

35 Jesus was going through all the cities and villages, teaching in their synagogues and proclaiming the gospel of the kingdom, and healing every kind of disease and every kind of sickness.

36 Seeing the people, He felt compassion for them, because they were distressed and dispirited like sheep without a shepherd.

37 Then He *said to His disciples, "The harvest is plentiful, but the workers are few.

38 "Therefore beseech the Lord of the harvest to send out workers into His harvest."

The Twelve Disciples; Instructions for Service

10 Jesus summoned His twelve disciples and gave them authority over unclean spirits, to cast them out, and to heal every kind of disease and every kind of sickness.

2 Now the names of the twelve apostles are these: The first, Simon, who is called Peter, and Andrew his brother; and James the son of Zebedee, and John his brother;

3 Philip and Bartholomew; Thomas and Matthew the tax collector; James the son of Alphaeus, and Thaddaeus;

4 Simon the Zealot, and Judas Iscariot, the one who betrayed Him.

5 These twelve Jesus sent out after instructing them: "Do not go in *the* way of the Gentiles, and do not enter *any* city of the Samaritans;

6 but rather go to the lost sheep of the house of Israel.

7 "And as you go, preach, saying, 'The kingdom of heaven is at hand.'

8 "Heal *the* sick, raise *the* dead, cleanse *the* lepers, cast out demons. Freely you received, freely give.

9 "Do not acquire gold, or silver, or copper for your money belts,

10 or a bag for *your* journey, or even two coats, or sandals, or a staff; for the worker is worthy of his support.

11 "And whatever city or village you enter, inquire who is worthy in it, and stay at his house until you leave *that city*.

12 "As you enter the house, give it your greeting.

13 "If the house is worthy, give it your *blessing*

---

1. I.e. more than

of peace. But if it is not worthy, take back your *blessing of* peace.

14 "Whoever does not receive you, nor heed your words, as you go out of that house or that city, shake the dust off your feet.

15 "Truly I say to you, it will be more tolerable for *the* land of Sodom and Gomorrah in the day of judgment than for that city.

16 "Behold, I send you out as sheep in the midst of wolves; so be shrewd as serpents and innocent as doves.

17 "But beware of men, for they will hand you over to *the* courts and scourge you in their synagogues;

18 and you will even be brought before governors and kings for My sake, as a testimony to them and to the Gentiles.

19 "But when they hand you over, do not worry about how or what you are to say; for it will be given you in that hour what you are to say.

20 "For it is not you who speak, but *it is* the Spirit of your Father who speaks in you.

21 "Brother will betray brother to death, and a father *his* child; and children will rise up against parents and cause them to be put to death.

22 "You will be hated by all because of My name, but it is the one who has endured to the end who will be saved.

23 "But whenever they persecute you in one city, flee to the next; for truly I say to you, you will not finish *going through* the cities of Israel until the Son of Man comes.

24 "A disciple is not above his teacher, nor a slave above his master.

25 "It is enough for the disciple that he become like his teacher, and the slave like his master. If they have called the head of the house Beelzebul, how much more *will they malign* the members of his household!

26 "Therefore do not fear them, for there is nothing concealed that will not be revealed, or hidden that will not be known.

27 "What I tell you in the darkness, speak in the light; and what you hear *whispered* in *your* ear, proclaim upon the housetops.

28 "Do not fear those who kill the body but are unable to kill the soul; but rather fear Him who is able to destroy both soul and body in hell.

29 "Are not two sparrows sold for a ¹cent? And *yet* not one of them will fall to the ground apart from your Father.

30 "But the very hairs of your head are all numbered.

31 "So do not fear; you are more valuable than many sparrows.

32 "Therefore everyone who confesses Me before men, I will also confess him before My Father who is in heaven.

33 "But whoever denies Me before men, I will also deny him before My Father who is in heaven.

34 "Do not think that I came to bring peace on the earth; I did not come to bring peace, but a sword.

35 "For I came to SET A MAN AGAINST HIS FATHER, AND A DAUGHTER AGAINST HER MOTHER, AND A DAUGHTER-IN-LAW AGAINST HER MOTHER-IN-LAW;

36 and A MAN'S ENEMIES WILL BE THE MEMBERS OF HIS HOUSEHOLD.

37 "He who loves father or mother more than Me is not worthy of Me; and he who loves son or daughter more than Me is not worthy of Me.

38 "And he who does not take his cross and follow after Me is not worthy of Me.

39 "He who has found his life will lose it, and he who has lost his life for My sake will find it.

40 "He who receives you receives Me, and he who receives Me receives Him who sent Me.

41 "He who receives a prophet in *the* name of a prophet shall receive a prophet's reward; and he who receives a righteous man in the name of a righteous man shall receive a righteous man's reward.

42 "And whoever in the name of a disciple gives to one of these little ones even a cup of cold water to drink, truly I say to you, he shall not lose his reward."

John's Questions

11 When Jesus had finished giving instructions to His twelve disciples, He departed from there to teach and preach in their cities.

2 Now when John, while imprisoned, heard of the works of Christ, he sent *word* by his disciples

3 and said to Him, "Are You the Expected One, or shall we look for someone else?"

4 Jesus answered and said to them, "Go and report to John what you hear and see:

5 *the* BLIND RECEIVE SIGHT and *the* lame walk, *the* lepers are cleansed and *the* deaf hear, *the* dead are raised up, and *the* POOR HAVE THE GOSPEL PREACHED TO THEM.

6 "And blessed is he who does not take offense at Me."

7 As these men were going *away,* Jesus began to speak to the crowds about John, "What did you go out into the wilderness to see? A reed shaken by the wind?

8 "But what did you go out to see? A man dressed in soft *clothing?* Those who wear soft *clothing* are in kings' palaces!

9 "But what did you go out to see? A prophet? Yes, I tell you, and one who is more than a prophet.

10 "This is the one about whom it is written,

'BEHOLD, I SEND MY MESSENGER AHEAD OF YOU,
WHO WILL PREPARE YOUR WAY BEFORE YOU.'

11 "Truly I say to you, among those born of women there has not arisen *anyone* greater than John the Baptist! Yet the one who is least in the kingdom of heaven is greater than he.

12 "From the days of John the Baptist until now the kingdom of heaven suffers violence, and violent men take it by force.

---

1. Gr *assarion,* the smallest copper coin

13 "For all the prophets and the Law prophesied until John.

14 "And if you are willing to accept *it*, John himself is Elijah who was to come.

15 "He who has ears to hear, let him hear.

16 "But to what shall I compare this generation? It is like children sitting in the market places, who call out to the other *children*,

17 and say, 'We played the flute for you, and you did not dance; we sang a dirge, and you did not mourn.'

18 "For John came neither eating nor drinking, and they say, 'He has a demon!'

19 "The Son of Man came eating and drinking, and they say, 'Behold, a gluttonous man and a drunkard, a friend of tax collectors and sinners!' Yet wisdom is vindicated by her deeds."

20 Then He began to denounce the cities in which most of His miracles were done, because they did not repent.

21 "Woe to you, Chorazin! Woe to you, Bethsaida! For if the miracles had occurred in Tyre and Sidon which occurred in you, they would have repented long ago in sackcloth and ashes.

22 "Nevertheless I say to you, it will be more tolerable for Tyre and Sidon in *the* day of judgment than for you.

23 "And you, Capernaum, will not be exalted to heaven, will you? You will descend to Hades; for if the miracles had occurred in Sodom which occurred in you, it would have remained to this day.

24 "Nevertheless I say to you that it will be more tolerable for the land of Sodom in *the* day of judgment, than for you."

25 At that time Jesus said, "I praise You, Father, Lord of heaven and earth, that You have hidden these things from *the* wise and intelligent and have revealed them to infants.

26 "Yes, Father, for this way was well-pleasing in Your sight.

27 "All things have been handed over to Me by My Father; and no one knows the Son except the Father; nor does anyone know the Father except the Son, and anyone to whom the Son wills to reveal *Him*.

28 "Come to Me, all who are weary and heavy-laden, and I will give you rest.

29 "Take My yoke upon you and learn from Me, for I am gentle and humble in heart, and YOU WILL FIND REST FOR YOUR SOULS.

30 "For My yoke is easy and My burden is light."

Sabbath Questions

12 At that time Jesus went through the grainfields on the Sabbath, and His disciples became hungry and began to pick the heads *of grain* and eat.

2 But when the Pharisees saw *this*, they said to Him, "Look, Your disciples do what is not lawful to do on a Sabbath."

3 But He said to them, "Have you not read what David did when he became hungry, he and his companions,

4 how he entered the house of God, and they ate the consecrated bread, which was not lawful for him to eat nor for those with him, but for the priests alone?

5 "Or have you not read in the Law, that on the Sabbath the priests in the temple break the Sabbath and are innocent?

6 "But I say to you that something greater than the temple is here.

7 "But if you had known what this means, 'I DESIRE COMPASSION, AND NOT A SACRIFICE,' you would not have condemned the innocent.

8 "For the Son of Man is Lord of the Sabbath."

9 Departing from there, He went into their synagogue.

10 And a man *was there* whose hand was withered. And they questioned Jesus, asking, "Is it lawful to heal on the Sabbath?"—so that they might accuse Him.

11 And He said to them, "What man is there among you who has a sheep, and if it falls into a pit on the Sabbath, will he not take hold of it and lift it out?

12 "How much more valuable then is a man than a sheep! So then, it is lawful to do good on the Sabbath."

13 Then He *said to the man, "Stretch out your hand!" He stretched it out, and it was restored to normal, like the other.

14 But the Pharisees went out and conspired against Him, *as to* how they might destroy Him.

15 But Jesus, aware of *this*, withdrew from there. Many followed Him, and He healed them all,

16 and warned them not to tell who He was.

17 *This was* to fulfill what was spoken through Isaiah the prophet:

18 "BEHOLD, MY SERVANT WHOM I HAVE CHOSEN;
    MY BELOVED IN WHOM MY SOUL IS WELL-PLEASED;
    I WILL PUT MY SPIRIT UPON HIM,
    AND HE SHALL PROCLAIM JUSTICE TO THE GENTILES.

19 "HE WILL NOT QUARREL, NOR CRY OUT;
    NOR WILL ANYONE HEAR HIS VOICE IN THE STREETS.

20 "A BATTERED REED HE WILL NOT BREAK OFF,
    AND A SMOLDERING WICK HE WILL NOT PUT OUT,
    UNTIL HE LEADS JUSTICE TO VICTORY.

21 "AND IN HIS NAME THE GENTILES WILL HOPE."

22 Then a demon-possessed man *who was* blind and mute was brought to Jesus, and He healed him, so that the mute man spoke and saw.

23 All the crowds were amazed, and were saying, "This man cannot be the Son of David, can he?"

24 But when the Pharisees heard *this*, they said, "This man casts out demons only by Beelzebul the ruler of the demons."

25 And knowing their thoughts Jesus said to them, "Any kingdom divided against itself is laid waste; and any city or house divided against itself will not stand.

26 "If Satan casts out Satan, he is divided against himself; how then will his kingdom stand?

27 "If I by Beelzebul cast out demons, by whom do your sons cast *them* out? For this reason they will be your judges.

28 "But if I cast out demons by the Spirit of God, then the kingdom of God has come upon you.

29 "Or how can anyone enter the strong man's house and carry off his property, unless he first binds the strong *man?* And then he will plunder his house.

30 "He who is not with Me is against Me; and he who does not gather with Me scatters.

31 "Therefore I say to you, any sin and blasphemy shall be forgiven people, but blasphemy against the Spirit shall not be forgiven.

32 "Whoever speaks a word against the Son of Man, it shall be forgiven him; but whoever speaks against the Holy Spirit, it shall not be forgiven him, either in this age or in the *age* to come.

33 "Either make the tree good and its fruit good, or make the tree bad and its fruit bad; for the tree is known by its fruit.

34 "You brood of vipers, how can you, being evil, speak what is good? For the mouth speaks out of that which fills the heart.

35 "The good man brings out of *his* good treasure what is good; and the evil man brings out of *his* evil treasure what is evil.

36 "But I tell you that every careless word that people speak, they shall give an accounting for it in the day of judgment.

37 "For by your words you will be justified, and by your words you will be condemned."

38 Then some of the scribes and Pharisees said to Him, "Teacher, we want to see a sign from You."

39 But He answered and said to them, "An evil and adulterous generation craves for a sign; and *yet* no sign will be given to it but the sign of Jonah the prophet;

40 for just as Jonah was three days and three nights in the belly of the sea monster, so will the Son of Man be three days and three nights in the heart of the earth.

41 "The men of Nineveh will stand up with this generation at the judgment, and will condemn it because they repented at the preaching of Jonah; and behold, something greater than Jonah is here.

42 "*The* Queen of *the* South will rise up with this generation at the judgment and will condemn it, because she came from the ends of the earth to hear the wisdom of Solomon; and behold, something greater than Solomon is here.

43 "Now when the unclean spirit goes out of a man, it passes through waterless places seeking rest, and does not find *it.*

44 "Then it says, 'I will return to my house from which I came'; and when it comes, it finds *it* unoccupied, swept, and put in order.

45 "Then it goes and takes along with it seven other spirits more wicked than itself, and they go in and live there; and the last state of that man becomes worse than the first. That is the way it will also be with this evil generation."

46 While He was still speaking to the crowds, behold, His mother and brothers were standing outside, seeking to speak to Him.

47 Someone said to Him, "Behold, Your mother and Your brothers are standing outside seeking to speak to You."

48 But Jesus answered the one who was telling Him and said, "Who is My mother and who are My brothers?"

49 And stretching out His hand toward His disciples, He said, "Behold My mother and My brothers!

50 "For whoever does the will of My Father who is in heaven, he is My brother and sister and mother."

Jesus Teaches in Parables

13 That day Jesus went out of the house and was sitting by the sea.

2 And large crowds gathered to Him, so He got into a boat and sat down, and the whole crowd was standing on the beach.

3 And He spoke many things to them in parables, saying, "Behold, the sower went out to sow;

4 and as he sowed, some *seeds* fell beside the road, and the birds came and ate them up.

5 "Others fell on the rocky places, where they did not have much soil; and immediately they sprang up, because they had no depth of soil.

6 "But when the sun had risen, they were scorched; and because they had no root, they withered away.

7 "Others fell among the thorns, and the thorns came up and choked them out.

8 "And others fell on the good soil and *yielded a crop, some a hundredfold, some sixty, and some thirty.

9 "He who has ears, let him hear."

10 And the disciples came and said to Him, "Why do You speak to them in parables?"

11 Jesus answered them, "To you it has been granted to know the mysteries of the kingdom of heaven, but to them it has not been granted.

12 "For whoever has, to him *more* shall be given, and he will have an abundance; but whoever does not have, even what he has shall be taken away from him.

13 "Therefore I speak to them in parables; because while seeing they do not see, and while hearing they do not hear, nor do they understand.

14 "In their case the prophecy of Isaiah is being fulfilled, which says,

'You will keep on hearing, but will not understand;

YOU WILL KEEP ON SEEING, BUT WILL NOT PERCEIVE;
15 FOR THE HEART OF THIS PEOPLE HAS BECOME DULL,
WITH THEIR EARS THEY SCARCELY HEAR,
AND THEY HAVE CLOSED THEIR EYES,
OTHERWISE THEY WOULD SEE WITH THEIR EYES,
HEAR WITH THEIR EARS,
AND UNDERSTAND WITH THEIR HEART AND RETURN,
AND I WOULD HEAL THEM.'

16 "But blessed are your eyes, because they see; and your ears, because they hear.

17 "For truly I say to you that many prophets and righteous men desired to see what you see, and did not see *it*, and to hear what you hear, and did not hear *it*.

18 "Hear then the parable of the sower.

19 "When anyone hears the word of the kingdom and does not understand it, the evil *one* comes and snatches away what has been sown in his heart. This is the one on whom seed was sown beside the road.

20 "The one on whom seed was sown on the rocky places, this is the man who hears the word and immediately receives it with joy;

21 yet he has no *firm* root in himself, but is *only* temporary, and when affliction or persecution arises because of the word, immediately he falls away.

22 "And the one on whom seed was sown among the thorns, this is the man who hears the word, and the worry of the world and the deceitfulness of wealth choke the word, and it becomes unfruitful.

23 "And the one on whom seed was sown on the good soil, this is the man who hears the word and understands it; who indeed bears fruit and brings forth, some a hundredfold, some sixty, and some thirty."

24 Jesus presented another parable to them, saying, "The kingdom of heaven may be compared to a man who sowed good seed in his field.

25 "But while his men were sleeping, his enemy came and sowed [1]tares among the wheat, and went away.

26 "But when the wheat sprouted and bore grain, then the tares became evident also.

27 "The slaves of the landowner came and said to him, 'Sir, did you not sow good seed in your field? How then does it have tares?'

28 "And he said to them, 'An enemy has done this!' The slaves *said to him, 'Do you want us, then, to go and gather them up?'

29 "But he *said, 'No; for while you are gathering up the tares, you may uproot the wheat with them.

30 'Allow both to grow together until the harvest; and in the time of the harvest I will say to the reapers, "First gather up the tares and bind them in bundles to burn them up; but gather the wheat into my barn." ' "

31 He presented another parable to them,

saying, "The kingdom of heaven is like a mustard seed, which a man took and sowed in his field;

32 and this is smaller than all *other* seeds, but when it is full grown, it is larger than the garden plants and becomes a tree, so that THE BIRDS OF THE AIR come and NEST IN ITS BRANCHES."

33 He spoke another parable to them, "The kingdom of heaven is like leaven, which a woman took and hid in three pecks of flour until it was all leavened."

34 All these things Jesus spoke to the crowds in parables, and He did not speak to them without a parable.

35 *This was* to fulfill what was spoken through the prophet:
"I WILL OPEN MY MOUTH IN PARABLES;
I WILL UTTER THINGS HIDDEN SINCE THE FOUNDATION OF THE WORLD."

36 Then He left the crowds and went into the house. And His disciples came to Him and said, "Explain to us the parable of the tares of the field."

37 And He said, "The one who sows the good seed is the Son of Man,

38 and the field is the world; and *as for* the good seed, these are the sons of the kingdom; and the tares are the sons of the evil *one;*

39 and the enemy who sowed them is the devil, and the harvest is the end of the age; and the reapers are angels.

40 "So just as the tares are gathered up and burned with fire, so shall it be at the end of the age.

41 "The Son of Man will send forth His angels, and they will gather out of His kingdom all stumbling blocks, and those who commit lawlessness,

42 and will throw them into the furnace of fire; in that place there will be weeping and gnashing of teeth.

43 "Then THE RIGHTEOUS WILL SHINE FORTH AS THE SUN in the kingdom of their Father. He who has ears, let him hear.

44 "The kingdom of heaven is like a treasure hidden in the field, which a man found and hid *again;* and from joy over it he goes and sells all that he has and buys that field.

45 "Again, the kingdom of heaven is like a merchant seeking fine pearls,

46 and upon finding one pearl of great value, he went and sold all that he had and bought it.

47 "Again, the kingdom of heaven is like a dragnet cast into the sea, and gathering *fish* of every kind;

48 and when it was filled, they drew it up on the beach; and they sat down and gathered the good *fish* into containers, but the bad they threw away.

49 "So it will be at the end of the age; the angels will come forth and take out the wicked from among the righteous,

50 and will throw them into the furnace of

---

1. Or *darnel,* a weed resembling wheat

fire; in that place there will be weeping and gnashing of teeth.

51 "Have you understood all these things?" They *said to Him, "Yes."

52 And Jesus said to them, "Therefore every scribe who has become a disciple of the kingdom of heaven is like a head of a household, who brings out of his treasure things new and old."

53 When Jesus had finished these parables, He departed from there.

54 He came to His hometown and *began* teaching them in their synagogue, so that they were astonished, and said, "Where *did* this man *get* this wisdom and *these* miraculous powers?

55 "Is not this the carpenter's son? Is not His mother called Mary, and His brothers, James and Joseph and Simon and Judas?

56 "And His sisters, are they not all with us? Where then *did* this man *get* all these things?"

57 And they took offense at Him. But Jesus said to them, "A prophet is not without honor except in his hometown and in his *own* household."

58 And He did not do many miracles there because of their unbelief.

John the Baptist Beheaded

14 At that time Herod the tetrarch heard the news about Jesus,

2 and said to his servants, "This is John the Baptist; he has risen from the dead, and that is why miraculous powers are at work in him."

3 For when Herod had John arrested, he bound him and put him in prison because of Herodias, the wife of his brother Philip.

4 For John had been saying to him, "It is not lawful for you to have her."

5 Although Herod wanted to put him to death, he feared the crowd, because they regarded John as a prophet.

6 But when Herod's birthday came, the daughter of Herodias danced before *them* and pleased Herod,

7 so *much* that he promised with an oath to give her whatever she asked.

8 Having been prompted by her mother, she *said, "Give me here on a platter the head of John the Baptist."

9 Although he was grieved, the king commanded *it* to be given because of his oaths, and because of his dinner guests.

10 He sent and had John beheaded in the prison.

11 And his head was brought on a platter and given to the girl, and she brought it to her mother.

12 His disciples came and took away the body and buried it; and they went and reported to Jesus.

13 Now when Jesus heard *about John,* He withdrew from there in a boat to a secluded place by Himself; and when the people heard *of this,* they followed Him on foot from the cities.

14 When He went ashore, He saw a large crowd, and felt compassion for them and healed their sick.

15 When it was evening, the disciples came to Him and said, "This place is desolate and the hour is already late; so send the crowds away, that they may go into the villages and buy food for themselves."

16 But Jesus said to them, "They do not need to go away; you give them *something* to eat!"

17 They *said to Him, "We have here only five loaves and two fish."

18 And He said, "Bring them here to Me."

19 Ordering the people to sit down on the grass, He took the five loaves and the two fish, and looking up toward heaven, He blessed *the food,* and breaking the loaves He gave them to the disciples, and the disciples *gave them* to the crowds,

20 and they all ate and were satisfied. They picked up what was left over of the broken pieces, twelve full baskets.

21 There were about five thousand men who ate, besides women and children.

22 Immediately He made the disciples get into the boat and go ahead of Him to the other side, while He sent the crowds away.

23 After He had sent the crowds away, He went up on the mountain by Himself to pray; and when it was evening, He was there alone.

24 But the boat was already [1]a long distance from the land, battered by the waves; for the wind was contrary.

25 And in the [2]fourth watch of the night He came to them, walking on the sea.

26 When the disciples saw Him walking on the sea, they were terrified, and said, "It is a ghost!" And they cried out in fear.

27 But immediately Jesus spoke to them, saying, "Take courage, it is I; do not be afraid."

28 Peter said to Him, "Lord, if it is You, command me to come to You on the water."

29 And He said, "Come!" And Peter got out of the boat, and walked on the water and came toward Jesus.

30 But seeing the wind, he became frightened, and beginning to sink, he cried out, "Lord, save me!"

31 Immediately Jesus stretched out His hand and took hold of him, and *said to him, "You of little faith, why did you doubt?"

32 When they got into the boat, the wind stopped.

33 And those who were in the boat worshiped Him, saying, "You are certainly God's Son!"

34 When they had crossed over, they came to land at Gennesaret.

35 And when the men of that place recognized Him, they sent *word* into all that surrounding district and brought to Him all who were sick;

36 and they implored Him that they might just touch the fringe of His cloak; and as many as touched *it* were cured.

---

1. Lit *many stadia from;* a stadion was about 600 feet or about 182 meters   2. I.e. 3-6 a.m.

Tradition and Commandment

15 Then some Pharisees and scribes *came to Jesus from Jerusalem and said,

2 "Why do Your disciples break the tradition of the elders? For they do not wash their hands when they eat bread."

3 And He answered and said to them, "Why do you yourselves transgress the commandment of God for the sake of your tradition?

4 "For God said, 'HONOR YOUR FATHER AND MOTHER,' and, 'HE WHO SPEAKS EVIL OF FATHER OR MOTHER IS TO BE PUT TO DEATH.'

5 "But you say, 'Whoever says to *his* father or mother, "Whatever I have that would help you has been given to *God*,"

6 he is not to honor his father or his mother[1].' And *by this* you invalidated the word of God for the sake of your tradition.

7 "You hypocrites, rightly did Isaiah prophesy of you:

8 'THIS PEOPLE HONORS ME WITH THEIR LIPS,
BUT THEIR HEART IS FAR AWAY FROM ME.

9 'BUT IN VAIN DO THEY WORSHIP ME,
TEACHING AS DOCTRINES THE PRECEPTS OF MEN.' "

10 After Jesus called the crowd to Him, He said to them, "Hear and understand.

11 "*It is* not what enters into the mouth *that* defiles the man, but what proceeds out of the mouth, this defiles the man."

12 Then the disciples *came and *said to Him, "Do You know that the Pharisees were offended when they heard this statement?"

13 But He answered and said, "Every plant which My heavenly Father did not plant shall be uprooted.

14 "Let them alone; they are blind guides [2]of the blind. And if a blind man guides a blind man, both will fall into a pit."

15 Peter said to Him, "Explain the parable to us."

16 Jesus said, "Are you still lacking in understanding also?

17 "Do you not understand that everything that goes into the mouth passes into the stomach, and is eliminated?

18 "But the things that proceed out of the mouth come from the heart, and those defile the man.

19 "For out of the heart come evil thoughts, murders, adulteries, fornications, thefts, false witness, slanders.

20 "These are the things which defile the man; but to eat with unwashed hands does not defile the man."

21 Jesus went away from there, and withdrew into the district of Tyre and Sidon.

22 And a Canaanite woman from that region came out and *began* to cry out, saying, "Have mercy on me, Lord, Son of David; my daughter is cruelly demon-possessed."

23 But He did not answer her a word. And His disciples came and implored Him, saying, "Send her away, because she keeps shouting at us."

24 But He answered and said, "I was sent only to the lost sheep of the house of Israel."

25 But she came and *began* to bow down before Him, saying, "Lord, help me!"

26 And He answered and said, "It is not good to take the children's bread and throw it to the dogs."

27 But she said, "Yes, Lord; but even the dogs feed on the crumbs which fall from their masters' table."

28 Then Jesus said to her, "O woman, your faith is great; it shall be done for you as you wish." And her daughter was healed at once.

29 Departing from there, Jesus went along by the Sea of Galilee, and having gone up on the mountain, He was sitting there.

30 And large crowds came to Him, bringing with them *those who were* lame, crippled, blind, mute, and many others, and they laid them down at His feet; and He healed them.

31 So the crowd marveled as they saw the mute speaking, the crippled restored, and the lame walking, and the blind seeing; and they glorified the God of Israel.

32 And Jesus called His disciples to Him, and said, "I feel compassion for the people, because they have remained with Me now three days and have nothing to eat; and I do not want to send them away hungry, for they might faint on the way."

33 The disciples *said to Him, "Where would we get so many loaves in *this* desolate place to satisfy such a large crowd?"

34 And Jesus *said to them, "How many loaves do you have?" And they said, "Seven, and a few small fish."

35 And He directed the people to sit down on the ground;

36 and He took the seven loaves and the fish; and giving thanks, He broke them and started giving them to the disciples, and the disciples *gave them* to the people.

37 And they all ate and were satisfied, and they picked up what was left over of the broken pieces, seven large baskets full.

38 And those who ate were four thousand men, besides women and children.

39 And sending away the crowds, Jesus got into the boat and came to the region of Magadan.

Pharisees Test Jesus

16 The Pharisees and Sadducees came up, and testing Jesus, they asked Him to show them a sign from heaven.

2 But He replied to them, "When it is evening, you say, '*It will be* fair weather, for the sky is red.'

3 "And in the morning, '*There will be* a storm today, for the sky is red and threatening.' Do you know how to discern the appearance of the sky, but cannot *discern* the signs of the times?

4 "An evil and adulterous generation seeks after a sign; and a sign will not be given it, except the sign of Jonah." And He left them and went away.

---

1. I.e. by supporting them with it   2. Later mss add *of the blind*

5 And the disciples came to the other side of the sea, but they had forgotten to bring any bread.

6 And Jesus said to them, "Watch out and beware of the leaven of the Pharisees and Sadducees."

7 They began to discuss *this* among themselves, saying, "*He said that* because we did not bring *any* bread."

8 But Jesus, aware of this, said, "You men of little faith, why do you discuss among yourselves that you have no bread?

9 "Do you not yet understand or remember the five loaves of the five thousand, and how many baskets *full* you picked up?

10 "Or the seven loaves of the four thousand, and how many large baskets *full* you picked up?

11 "How is it that you do not understand that I did not speak to you concerning bread? But beware of the leaven of the Pharisees and Sadducees."

12 Then they understood that He did not say to beware of the leaven of bread, but of the teaching of the Pharisees and Sadducees.

13 Now when Jesus came into the district of Caesarea Philippi, He was asking His disciples, "Who do people say that the Son of Man is?"

14 And they said, "Some *say* John the Baptist; and others, Elijah; but still others, Jeremiah, or one of the prophets."

15 He *said to them, "But who do you say that I am?"

16 Simon Peter answered, "You are the Christ, the Son of the living God."

17 And Jesus said to him, "Blessed are you, Simon Barjona, because flesh and blood did not reveal *this* to you, but My Father who is in heaven.

18 "I also say to you that you are Peter, and upon this rock I will build My church; and the gates of Hades will not overpower it.

19 "I will give you the keys of the kingdom of heaven; and whatever you bind on earth shall have been bound in heaven, and whatever you loose on earth shall have been loosed in heaven."

20 Then He warned the disciples that they should tell no one that He was the Christ.

21 From that time Jesus began to show His disciples that He must go to Jerusalem, and suffer many things from the elders and chief priests and scribes, and be killed, and be raised up on the third day.

22 Peter took Him aside and began to rebuke Him, saying, "God forbid *it*, Lord! This shall never happen to You."

23 But He turned and said to Peter, "Get behind Me, Satan! You are a stumbling block to Me; for you are not setting your mind on God's interests, but man's."

24 Then Jesus said to His disciples, "If anyone wishes to come after Me, he must deny himself, and take up his cross and follow Me.

25 "For whoever wishes to save his life will lose it; but whoever loses his life for My sake will find it.

26 "For what will it profit a man if he gains the whole world and forfeits his soul? Or what will a man give in exchange for his soul?

27 "For the Son of Man is going to come in the glory of His Father with His angels, and WILL THEN REPAY EVERY MAN ACCORDING TO HIS DEEDS.

28 "Truly I say to you, there are some of those who are standing here who will not taste death until they see the Son of Man coming in His kingdom."

The Transfiguration

17 Six days later Jesus *took with Him Peter and James and John his brother, and *led them up on a high mountain by themselves.

2 And He was transfigured before them; and His face shone like the sun, and His garments became as white as light.

3 And behold, Moses and Elijah appeared to them, talking with Him.

4 Peter said to Jesus, "Lord, it is good for us to be here; if You wish, I will make three tabernacles here, one for You, and one for Moses, and one for Elijah."

5 While he was still speaking, a bright cloud overshadowed them, and behold, a voice out of the cloud said, "This is My beloved Son, with whom I am well-pleased; listen to Him!"

6 When the disciples heard *this*, they fell face down to the ground and were terrified.

7 And Jesus came to *them* and touched them and said, "Get up, and do not be afraid."

8 And lifting up their eyes, they saw no one except Jesus Himself alone.

9 As they were coming down from the mountain, Jesus commanded them, saying, "Tell the vision to no one until the Son of Man has risen from the dead."

10 And His disciples asked Him, "Why then do the scribes say that Elijah must come first?"

11 And He answered and said, "Elijah is coming and will restore all things;

12 but I say to you that Elijah already came, and they did not recognize him, but did to him whatever they wished. So also the Son of Man is going to suffer at their hands."

13 Then the disciples understood that He had spoken to them about John the Baptist.

14 When they came to the crowd, a man came up to Jesus, falling on his knees before Him and saying,

15 "Lord, have mercy on my son, for he is a lunatic and is very ill; for he often falls into the fire and often into the water.

16 "I brought him to Your disciples, and they could not cure him."

17 And Jesus answered and said, "You unbelieving and perverted generation, how long shall I be with you? How long shall I put up with you? Bring him here to Me."

18 And Jesus rebuked him, and the demon came out of him, and the boy was cured at once.

19 Then the disciples came to Jesus privately and said, "Why could we not drive it out?"

20 And He *said to them, "Because of the littleness of your faith; for truly I say to you, if you have faith the size of a mustard seed, you will say to this mountain, 'Move from here to there,' and it will move; and nothing will be impossible to you.

21 ["¹But this kind does not go out except by prayer and fasting."]

22 And while they were gathering together in Galilee, Jesus said to them, "The Son of Man is going to be delivered into the hands of men;

23 and they will kill Him, and He will be raised on the third day." And they were deeply grieved.

24 When they came to Capernaum, those who collected the ²two-drachma *tax* came to Peter and said, "Does your teacher not pay the ²two-drachma *tax?*"

25 He *said, "Yes." And when he came into the house, Jesus spoke to him first, saying, "What do you think, Simon? From whom do the kings of the earth collect customs or poll-tax, from their sons or from strangers?"

26 When Peter said, "From strangers," Jesus said to him, "Then the sons are exempt.

27 "However, so that we do not offend them, go to the sea and throw in a hook, and take the first fish that comes up; and when you open its mouth, you will find ³a shekel. Take that and give it to them for you and Me."

Rank in the Kingdom

18 At that time the disciples came to Jesus and said, "Who then is greatest in the kingdom of heaven?"

2 And He called a child to Himself and set him before them,

3 and said, "Truly I say to you, unless you are converted and become like children, you will not enter the kingdom of heaven.

4 "Whoever then humbles himself as this child, he is the greatest in the kingdom of heaven.

5 "And whoever receives one such child in My name receives Me;

6 but whoever causes one of these little ones who believe in Me to stumble, it would be better for him to have a heavy millstone hung around his neck, and to be drowned in the depth of the sea.

7 "Woe to the world because of *its* stumbling blocks! For it is inevitable that stumbling blocks come; but woe to that man through whom the stumbling block comes!

8 "If your hand or your foot causes you to stumble, cut it off and throw it from you; it is better for you to enter life crippled or lame, than to have two hands or two feet and be cast into the eternal fire.

9 "If your eye causes you to stumble, pluck it out and throw it from you. It is better for you to enter life with one eye, than to have two eyes and be cast into the fiery hell.

10 "See that you do not despise one of these little ones, for I say to you that their angels in heaven continually see the face of My Father who is in heaven.

11 ["⁴For the Son of Man has come to save that which was lost.]

12 "What do you think? If any man has a hundred sheep, and one of them has gone astray, does he not leave the ninety-nine on the mountains and go and search for the one that is straying?

13 "If it turns out that he finds it, truly I say to you, he rejoices over it more than over the ninety-nine which have not gone astray.

14 "So it is not *the* will of your Father who is in heaven that one of these little ones perish.

15 "If your brother sins⁵, go and show him his fault in private; if he listens to you, you have won your brother.

16 "But if he does not listen *to you*, take one or two more with you, so that BY THE MOUTH OF TWO OR THREE WITNESSES EVERY FACT MAY BE CONFIRMED.

17 "If he refuses to listen to them, tell it to the church; and if he refuses to listen even to the church, let him be to you as a Gentile and a tax collector.

18 "Truly I say to you, whatever you bind on earth shall have been bound in heaven; and whatever you loose on earth shall have been loosed in heaven.

19 "Again I say to you, that if two of you agree on earth about anything that they may ask, it shall be done for them by My Father who is in heaven.

20 "For where two or three have gathered together in My name, I am there in their midst."

21 Then Peter came and said to Him, "Lord, how often shall my brother sin against me and I forgive him? Up to seven times?"

22 Jesus *said to him, "I do not say to you, up to seven times, but up to seventy times seven.

23 "For this reason the kingdom of heaven may be compared to a king who wished to settle accounts with his slaves.

24 "When he had begun to settle *them*, one who owed him ⁶ten thousand talents was brought to him.

25 "But since he did not have *the means* to repay, his lord commanded him to be sold, along with his wife and children and all that he had, and repayment to be made.

26 "So the slave fell *to the ground* and prostrated himself before him, saying, 'Have patience with me and I will repay you everything.'

27 "And the lord of that slave felt compassion and released him and forgave him the debt.

28 "But that slave went out and found one of his fellow slaves who owed him a hundred

---

1. Early mss do not contain this v 2. Equivalent to two denarii or two days' wages, paid as a temple tax 3. Lit *standard coin,* which was a shekel 4. Early mss do not contain this v 5. Late mss add *against you* 6. A talent was worth more than fifteen years' wages of a laborer

¹denarii; and he seized him and *began* to choke *him*, saying, 'Pay back what you owe.'

29 "So his fellow slave fell *to the ground* and *began* to plead with him, saying, 'Have patience with me and I will repay you.'

30 "But he was unwilling and went and threw him in prison until he should pay back what was owed.

31 "So when his fellow slaves saw what had happened, they were deeply grieved and came and reported to their lord all that had happened.

32 "Then summoning him, his lord *said to him, 'You wicked slave, I forgave you all that debt because you pleaded with me.

33 'Should you not also have had mercy on your fellow slave, in the same way that I had mercy on you?'

34 "And his lord, moved with anger, handed him over to the torturers until he should repay all that was owed him.

35 "My heavenly Father will also do the same to you, if each of you does not forgive his brother from your heart."

Concerning Divorce

19 When Jesus had finished these words, He departed from Galilee and came into the region of Judea beyond the Jordan;

2 and large crowds followed Him, and He healed them there.

3 *Some* Pharisees came to Jesus, testing Him and asking, "Is it lawful *for a man* to divorce his wife for any reason at all?"

4 And He answered and said, "Have you not read that He who created *them* from the beginning MADE THEM MALE AND FEMALE,

5 and said, 'FOR THIS REASON A MAN SHALL LEAVE HIS FATHER AND MOTHER AND BE JOINED TO HIS WIFE, AND THE TWO SHALL BECOME ONE FLESH'?

6 "So they are no longer two, but one flesh. What therefore God has joined together, let no man separate."

7 They *said to Him, "Why then did Moses command to GIVE HER A CERTIFICATE OF DIVORCE AND SEND *her* AWAY?"

8 He *said to them, "Because of your hardness of heart Moses permitted you to divorce your wives; but from the beginning it has not been this way.

9 "And I say to you, whoever divorces his wife, except for immorality, and marries another woman commits adultery."

10 The disciples *said to Him, "If the relationship of the man with his wife is like this, it is better not to marry."

11 But He said to them, "Not all men *can* accept this statement, but *only* those to whom it has been given.

12 "For there are eunuchs who were born that way from their mother's womb; and there are eunuchs who were made eunuchs by men; and there are *also* eunuchs who made themselves eunuchs for the sake of the kingdom of heaven. He who is able to accept *this*, let him accept *it*."

13 Then *some* children were brought to Him so that He might lay His hands on them and pray; and the disciples rebuked them.

14 But Jesus said, "Let the children alone, and do not hinder them from coming to Me; for the kingdom of heaven belongs to such as these."

15 After laying His hands on them, He departed from there.

16 And someone came to Him and said, "Teacher, what good thing shall I do that I may obtain eternal life?"

17 And He said to him, "Why are you asking Me about what is good? There is *only* One who is good; but if you wish to enter into life, keep the commandments."

18 *Then* he *said to Him, "Which ones?" And Jesus said, "YOU SHALL NOT COMMIT MURDER; YOU SHALL NOT COMMIT ADULTERY; YOU SHALL NOT STEAL; YOU SHALL NOT BEAR FALSE WITNESS;

19 HONOR YOUR FATHER AND MOTHER; and YOU SHALL LOVE YOUR NEIGHBOR AS YOURSELF."

20 The young man *said to Him, "All these things I have kept; what am I still lacking?"

21 Jesus said to him, "If you wish to be complete, go *and* sell your possessions and give to *the* poor, and you will have treasure in heaven; and come, follow Me."

22 But when the young man heard this statement, he went away grieving; for he was one who owned much property.

23 And Jesus said to His disciples, "Truly I say to you, it is hard for a rich man to enter the kingdom of heaven.

24 "Again I say to you, it is easier for a camel to go through the eye of a needle, than for a rich man to enter the kingdom of God."

25 When the disciples heard *this*, they were very astonished and said, "Then who can be saved?"

26 And looking at *them* Jesus said to them, "With people this is impossible, but with God all things are possible."

27 Then Peter said to Him, "Behold, we have left everything and followed You; what then will there be for us?"

28 And Jesus said to them, "Truly I say to you, that you who have followed Me, in the regeneration when the Son of Man will sit on His glorious throne, you also shall sit upon twelve thrones, judging the twelve tribes of Israel.

29 "And everyone who has left houses or brothers or sisters or father or mother ²or children or farms for My name's sake, will receive many times as much, and will inherit eternal life.

30 "But many *who are* first will be last; and *the* last, first.

Laborers in the Vineyard

20 "For the kingdom of heaven is like a landowner who went out early in the morning to hire laborers for his vineyard.

2 "When he had agreed with the laborers

---

1. The denarius was a day's wages   2. One early ms adds *or wife*

for a ¹denarius for the day, he sent them into his vineyard.

3 "And he went out about the ²third hour and saw others standing idle in the market place;

4 and to those he said, 'You also go into the vineyard, and whatever is right I will give you.' And *so* they went.

5 "Again he went out about the ³sixth and the ninth hour, and did the same thing.

6 "And about the ⁴eleventh *hour* he went out and found others standing *around;* and he *said to them, 'Why have you been standing here idle all day long?'

7 "They *said to him, 'Because no one hired us.' He *said to them, 'You go into the vineyard too.'

8 "When evening came, the owner of the vineyard *said to his foreman, 'Call the laborers and pay them their wages, beginning with the last *group* to the first.'

9 "When those *hired* about the eleventh hour came, each one received a ¹denarius.

10 "When those *hired* first came, they thought that they would receive more; but each of them also received a denarius.

11 "When they received it, they grumbled at the landowner,

12 saying, 'These last men have worked *only* one hour, and you have made them equal to us who have borne the burden and the scorching heat of the day.'

13 "But he answered and said to one of them, 'Friend, I am doing you no wrong; did you not agree with me for a denarius?

14 'Take what is yours and go, but I wish to give to this last man the same as to you.

15 'Is it not lawful for me to do what I wish with what is my own? Or is your eye envious because I am generous?'

16 "So the last shall be first, and the first last."

17 As Jesus was about to go up to Jerusalem, He took the twelve *disciples* aside by themselves, and on the way He said to them,

18 "Behold, we are going up to Jerusalem; and the Son of Man will be delivered to the chief priests and scribes, and they will condemn Him to death,

19 and will hand Him over to the Gentiles to mock and scourge *Him,* and on the third day He will be raised up."

20 Then the mother of the sons of Zebedee came to Jesus with her sons, bowing down and making a request of Him.

21 And He said to her, "What do you wish?" She *said to Him, "Command that in Your kingdom these two sons of mine may sit one on Your right and one on Your left."

22 But Jesus answered, "You do not know what you are asking. Are you able to drink the cup that I am about to drink?" They *said to Him, "We are able."

23 He *said to them, "My cup you shall drink; but to sit on My right and on *My* left, this is not Mine to give, but it is for those for whom it has been prepared by My Father."

24 And hearing *this,* the ten became indignant with the two brothers.

25 But Jesus called them to Himself and said, "You know that the rulers of the Gentiles lord it over them, and *their* great men exercise authority over them.

26 "It is not this way among you, but whoever wishes to become great among you shall be your servant,

27 and whoever wishes to be first among you shall be your slave;

28 just as the Son of Man did not come to be served, but to serve, and to give His life a ransom for many."

29 As they were leaving Jericho, a large crowd followed Him.

30 And two blind men sitting by the road, hearing that Jesus was passing by, cried out, "Lord, have mercy on us, Son of David!"

31 The crowd sternly told them to be quiet, but they cried out all the more, "Lord, Son of David, have mercy on us!"

32 And Jesus stopped and called them, and said, "What do you want Me to do for you?"

33 They *said to Him, "Lord, *we want* our eyes to be opened."

34 Moved with compassion, Jesus touched their eyes; and immediately they regained their sight and followed Him.

The Triumphal Entry

21 When they had approached Jerusalem and had come to Bethphage, at the Mount of Olives, then Jesus sent two disciples,

2 saying to them, "Go into the village opposite you, and immediately you will find a donkey tied *there* and a colt with her; untie them and bring them to Me.

3 "If anyone says anything to you, you shall say, 'The Lord has need of them,' and immediately he will send them."

4 This took place to fulfill what was spoken through the prophet:

5 "SAY TO THE DAUGHTER OF ZION,
　'BEHOLD YOUR KING IS COMING TO YOU,
　GENTLE, AND MOUNTED ON A DONKEY,
　EVEN ON A COLT, THE FOAL OF A BEAST OF
　　BURDEN.' "

6 The disciples went and did just as Jesus had instructed them,

7 and brought the donkey and the colt, and laid their coats on them; and He sat on the coats.

8 Most of the crowd spread their coats in the road, and others were cutting branches from the trees and spreading them in the road.

9 The crowds going ahead of Him, and those who followed, were shouting,
　"Hosanna to the Son of David;
　BLESSED IS HE WHO COMES IN THE NAME OF
　　THE LORD;
　Hosanna in the highest!"

10 When He had entered Jerusalem, all the city was stirred, saying, "Who is this?"

11 And the crowds were saying, "This is the prophet Jesus, from Nazareth in Galilee."

---

1. The denarius was a day's wages 2. I.e. 9 a.m. 3. I.e. noon and 3 p.m. 4. I.e. 5 p.m.

12 And Jesus entered the temple and drove out all those who were buying and selling in the temple, and overturned the tables of the money changers and the seats of those who were selling doves.

13 And He *said to them, "It is written, 'MY HOUSE SHALL BE CALLED A HOUSE OF PRAYER'; but you are making it a ROBBERS' DEN."

14 And the blind and the lame came to Him in the temple, and He healed them.

15 But when the chief priests and the scribes saw the wonderful things that He had done, and the children who were shouting in the temple, "Hosanna to the Son of David," they became indignant

16 and said to Him, "Do You hear what these children are saying?" And Jesus *said to them, "Yes; have you never read, 'OUT OF THE MOUTH OF INFANTS AND NURSING BABIES YOU HAVE PREPARED PRAISE FOR YOURSELF'?"

17 And He left them and went out of the city to Bethany, and spent the night there.

18 Now in the morning, when He was returning to the city, He became hungry.

19 Seeing a lone fig tree by the road, He came to it and found nothing on it except leaves only; and He *said to it, "No longer shall there ever be any fruit from you." And at once the fig tree withered.

20 Seeing this, the disciples were amazed and asked, "How did the fig tree wither all at once?"

21 And Jesus answered and said to them, "Truly I say to you, if you have faith and do not doubt, you will not only do what was done to the fig tree, but even if you say to this mountain, 'Be taken up and cast into the sea,' it will happen.

22 "And all things you ask in prayer, believing, you will receive."

23 When He entered the temple, the chief priests and the elders of the people came to Him while He was teaching, and said, "By what authority are You doing these things, and who gave You this authority?"

24 Jesus said to them, "I will also ask you one thing, which if you tell Me, I will also tell you by what authority I do these things.

25 "The baptism of John was from what source, from heaven or from men?" And they began reasoning among themselves, saying, "If we say, 'From heaven,' He will say to us, 'Then why did you not believe him?'

26 "But if we say, 'From men,' we fear the people; for they all regard John as a prophet."

27 And answering Jesus, they said, "We do not know." He also said to them, "Neither will I tell you by what authority I do these things.

28 "But what do you think? A man had two sons, and he came to the first and said, 'Son, go work today in the vineyard.'

29 "And he answered, 'I will not'; but afterward he regretted it and went.

30 "The man came to the second and said the same thing; and he answered, 'I will, sir'; but he did not go.

31 "Which of the two did the will of his father?" They *said, "The first." Jesus *said to them, "Truly I say to you that the tax collectors and prostitutes will get into the kingdom of God before you.

32 "For John came to you in the way of righteousness and you did not believe him; but the tax collectors and prostitutes did believe him; and you, seeing this, did not even feel remorse afterward so as to believe him.

33 "Listen to another parable. There was a landowner who PLANTED A VINEYARD AND PUT A WALL AROUND IT AND DUG A WINE PRESS IN IT, AND BUILT A TOWER, and rented it out to vine-growers and went on a journey.

34 "When the harvest time approached, he sent his slaves to the vine-growers to receive his produce.

35 "The vine-growers took his slaves and beat one, and killed another, and stoned a third.

36 "Again he sent another group of slaves larger than the first; and they did the same thing to them.

37 "But afterward he sent his son to them, saying, 'They will respect my son.'

38 "But when the vine-growers saw the son, they said among themselves, 'This is the heir; come, let us kill him and seize his inheritance.'

39 "They took him, and threw him out of the vineyard and killed him.

40 "Therefore when the owner of the vineyard comes, what will he do to those vine-growers?"

41 They *said to Him, "He will bring those wretches to a wretched end, and will rent out the vineyard to other vine-growers who will pay him the proceeds at the proper seasons."

42 Jesus *said to them, "Did you never read in the Scriptures,

'THE STONE WHICH THE BUILDERS REJECTED,
THIS BECAME THE CHIEF CORNER stone;
THIS CAME ABOUT FROM THE LORD,
AND IT IS MARVELOUS IN OUR EYES'?

43 "Therefore I say to you, the kingdom of God will be taken away from you and given to a people, producing the fruit of it.

44 "And he who falls on this stone will be broken to pieces; but on whomever it falls, it will scatter him like dust."

45 When the chief priests and the Pharisees heard His parables, they understood that He was speaking about them.

46 When they sought to seize Him, they feared the people, because they considered Him to be a prophet.

Parable of the Marriage Feast

22 Jesus spoke to them again in parables, saying,

2 "The kingdom of heaven may be compared to a king who gave a wedding feast for his son.

3 "And he sent out his slaves to call those who had been invited to the wedding feast, and they were unwilling to come.

4 "Again he sent out other slaves saying, 'Tell those who have been invited, "Behold, I have prepared my dinner; my oxen and my fattened

livestock are *all* butchered and everything is ready; come to the wedding feast." '

5 "But they paid no attention and went their way, one to his own farm, another to his business,

6 and the rest seized his slaves and mistreated them and killed them.

7 "But the king was enraged, and he sent his armies and destroyed those murderers and set their city on fire.

8 "Then he *said to his slaves, 'The wedding is ready, but those who were invited were not worthy.

9 'Go therefore to the main highways, and as many as you find *there,* invite to the wedding feast.'

10 "Those slaves went out into the streets and gathered together all they found, both evil and good; and the wedding hall was filled with dinner guests.

11 "But when the king came in to look over the dinner guests, he saw a man there who was not dressed in wedding clothes,

12 and he *said to him, 'Friend, how did you come in here without wedding clothes?' And the man was speechless.

13 "Then the king said to the servants, 'Bind him hand and foot, and throw him into the outer darkness; in that place there will be weeping and gnashing of teeth.'

14 "For many are called, but few *are* chosen."

15 Then the Pharisees went and plotted together how they might trap Him in what He said.

16 And they *sent their disciples to Him, along with the Herodians, saying, "Teacher, we know that You are truthful and teach the way of God in truth, and defer to no one; for You are not partial to any.

17 "Tell us then, what do You think? Is it lawful to give a poll-tax to Caesar, or not?"

18 But Jesus perceived their malice, and said, "Why are you testing Me, you hypocrites?

19 "Show Me the coin *used* for the poll-tax." And they brought Him a denarius.

20 And He *said to them, "Whose likeness and inscription is this?"

21 They *said to Him, "Caesar's." Then He *said to them, "Then render to Caesar the things that are Caesar's; and to God the things that are God's."

22 And hearing *this,* they were amazed, and leaving Him, they went away.

23 On that day *some* Sadducees (who say there is no resurrection) came to Jesus and questioned Him,

24 asking, "Teacher, Moses said, 'IF A MAN DIES HAVING NO CHILDREN, HIS BROTHER AS NEXT OF KIN SHALL MARRY HIS WIFE, AND RAISE UP CHILDREN FOR HIS BROTHER.'

25 "Now there were seven brothers with us; and the first married and died, and having no children left his wife to his brother;

26 so also the second, and the third, down to the seventh.

27 "Last of all, the woman died.

28 "In the resurrection, therefore, whose wife of the seven will she be? For they all had *married* her."

29 But Jesus answered and said to them, "You are mistaken, not understanding the Scriptures nor the power of God.

30 "For in the resurrection they neither marry nor are given in marriage, but are like angels in heaven.

31 "But regarding the resurrection of the dead, have you not read what was spoken to you by God:

32 'I AM THE GOD OF ABRAHAM, AND THE GOD OF ISAAC, AND THE GOD OF JACOB'? He is not the God of the dead but of the living."

33 When the crowds heard *this,* they were astonished at His teaching.

34 But when the Pharisees heard that Jesus had silenced the Sadducees, they gathered themselves together.

35 One of them, [1]a lawyer, asked Him *a question,* testing Him,

36 "Teacher, which is the great commandment in the Law?"

37 And He said to him, " 'YOU SHALL LOVE THE LORD YOUR GOD WITH ALL YOUR HEART, AND WITH ALL YOUR SOUL, AND WITH ALL YOUR MIND.'

38 "This is the great and foremost commandment.

39 "The second is like it, 'YOU SHALL LOVE YOUR NEIGHBOR AS YOURSELF.'

40 "On these two commandments depend the whole Law and the Prophets."

41 Now while the Pharisees were gathered together, Jesus asked them a question:

42 "What do you think about the Christ, whose son is He?" They *said to Him, *"The son* of David."

43 He *said to them, "Then how does David in the Spirit call Him 'Lord,' saying,

44 'THE LORD SAID TO MY LORD,
    "SIT AT MY RIGHT HAND,
    UNTIL I PUT YOUR ENEMIES BENEATH YOUR
       FEET" '?

45 "If David then calls Him 'Lord,' how is He his son?"

46 No one was able to answer Him a word, nor did anyone dare from that day on to ask Him another question.

Pharisaism Exposed

23 Then Jesus spoke to the crowds and to His disciples,

2 saying: "The scribes and the Pharisees have seated themselves in the chair of Moses;

3 therefore all that they tell you, do and observe, but do not do according to their deeds; for they say *things* and do not do *them.*

4 "They tie up heavy burdens and lay them on men's shoulders, but they themselves are unwilling to move them with *so much as* a finger.

---

1. I.e. an expert in the Mosaic Law

5 "But they do all their deeds to be noticed by men; for they broaden their ¹phylacteries and lengthen the tassels *of their garments.*

6 "They love the place of honor at banquets and the chief seats in the synagogues,

7 and respectful greetings in the market places, and being called Rabbi by men.

8 "But do not be called Rabbi; for One is your Teacher, and you are all brothers.

9 "Do not call *anyone* on earth your father; for One is your Father, He who is in heaven.

10 "Do not be called leaders; for One is your Leader, *that is,* Christ.

11 "But the greatest among you shall be your servant.

12 "Whoever exalts himself shall be humbled; and whoever humbles himself shall be exalted.

13 "But woe to you, scribes and Pharisees, hypocrites, because you shut off the kingdom of heaven from people; for you do not enter in yourselves, nor do you allow those who are entering to go in.

14 ["²Woe to you, scribes and Pharisees, hypocrites, because you devour widows' houses, and for a pretense you make long prayers; therefore you will receive greater condemnation.]

15 "Woe to you, scribes and Pharisees, hypocrites, because you travel around on sea and land to make one proselyte; and when he becomes one, you make him twice as much a son of hell as yourselves.

16 "Woe to you, blind guides, who say, 'Whoever swears by the temple, *that* is nothing; but whoever swears by the gold of the temple is obligated.'

17 "You fools and blind men! Which is more important, the gold or the temple that sanctified the gold?

18 "And, 'Whoever swears by the altar, *that* is nothing, but whoever swears by the offering on it, he is obligated.'

19 "You blind men, which is more important, the offering, or the altar that sanctifies the offering?

20 "Therefore, whoever swears by the altar, swears *both* by the altar and by everything on it.

21 "And whoever swears by the temple, swears *both* by the temple and by Him who dwells within it.

22 "And whoever swears by heaven, swears *both* by the throne of God and by Him who sits upon it.

23 "Woe to you, scribes and Pharisees, hypocrites! For you tithe mint and dill and cummin, and have neglected the weightier provisions of the law: justice and mercy and faithfulness; but these are the things you should have done without neglecting the others.

24 "You blind guides, who strain out a gnat and swallow a camel!

25 "Woe to you, scribes and Pharisees, hypocrites! For you clean the outside of the cup and of the dish, but inside they are full of robbery and self-indulgence.

26 "You blind Pharisee, first clean the inside of the cup and of the dish, so that the outside of it may become clean also.

27 "Woe to you, scribes and Pharisees, hypocrites! For you are like whitewashed tombs which on the outside appear beautiful, but inside they are full of dead men's bones and all uncleanness.

28 "So you, too, outwardly appear righteous to men, but inwardly you are full of hypocrisy and lawlessness.

29 "Woe to you, scribes and Pharisees, hypocrites! For you build the tombs of the prophets and adorn the monuments of the righteous,

30 and say, 'If we had been *living* in the days of our fathers, we would not have been partners with them in *shedding* the blood of the prophets.'

31 "So you testify against yourselves, that you are sons of those who murdered the prophets.

32 "Fill up, then, the measure *of the guilt* of your fathers.

33 "You serpents, you brood of vipers, how will you escape the sentence of hell?

34 "Therefore, behold, I am sending you prophets and wise men and scribes; some of them you will kill and crucify, and some of them you will scourge in your synagogues, and persecute from city to city,

35 so that upon you may fall *the guilt of* all the righteous blood shed on earth, from the blood of righteous Abel to the blood of Zechariah, the son of Berechiah, whom you murdered between the temple and the altar.

36 "Truly I say to you, all these things will come upon this generation.

37 "Jerusalem, Jerusalem, who kills the prophets and stones those who are sent to her! How often I wanted to gather your children together, the way a hen gathers her chicks under her wings, and you were unwilling.

38 "Behold, your house is being left to you desolate!

39 "For I say to you, from now on you will not see Me until you say, 'BLESSED IS HE WHO COMES IN THE NAME OF THE LORD!' "

Signs of Christ's Return

24 Jesus came out from the temple and was going away when His disciples came up to point out the temple buildings to Him.

2 And He said to them, "Do you not see all these things? Truly I say to you, not one stone here will be left upon another, which will not be torn down."

3 As He was sitting on the Mount of Olives, the disciples came to Him privately, saying, "Tell us, when will these things happen, and what *will be* the sign of Your coming, and of the end of the age?"

4 And Jesus answered and said to them, "See to it that no one misleads you.

---

1. I.e. small cases containing Scripture texts worn on the left arm and forehead for religious purposes 2. This v not found in early mss

5 "For many will come in My name, saying, 'I am the Christ,' and will mislead many.

6 "You will be hearing of wars and rumors of wars. See that you are not frightened, for *those things* must take place, but *that* is not yet the end.

7 "For nation will rise against nation, and kingdom against kingdom, and in various places there will be famines and earthquakes.

8 "But all these things are *merely* the beginning of birth pangs.

9 "Then they will deliver you to tribulation, and will kill you, and you will be hated by all nations because of My name.

10 "At that time many will fall away and will betray one another and hate one another.

11 "Many false prophets will arise and will mislead many.

12 "Because lawlessness is increased, most people's love will grow cold.

13 "But the one who endures to the end, he will be saved.

14 "This gospel of the kingdom shall be preached in the whole world as a testimony to all the nations, and then the end will come.

15 "Therefore when you see the ABOMINATION OF DESOLATION which was spoken of through Daniel the prophet, standing in the holy place (let the reader understand),

16 then those who are in Judea must flee to the mountains.

17 "Whoever is on the housetop must not go down to get the things out that are in his house.

18 "Whoever is in the field must not turn back to get his cloak.

19 "But woe to those who are pregnant and to those who are nursing babies in those days!

20 "But pray that your flight will not be in the winter, or on a Sabbath.

21 "For then there will be a great tribulation, such as has not occurred since the beginning of the world until now, nor ever will.

22 "Unless those days had been cut short, no life would have been saved; but for the sake of the elect those days will be cut short.

23 "Then if anyone says to you, 'Behold, here is the Christ,' or 'There *He is*,' do not believe *him*.

24 "For false Christs and false prophets will arise and will show great signs and wonders, so as to mislead, if possible, even the elect.

25 "Behold, I have told you in advance.

26 "So if they say to you, 'Behold, He is in the wilderness,' do not go out, *or*, 'Behold, He is in the inner rooms,' do not believe *them*.

27 "For just as the lightning comes from the east and flashes even to the west, so will the coming of the Son of Man be.

28 "Wherever the corpse is, there the vultures will gather.

29 "But immediately after the tribulation of those days THE SUN WILL BE DARKENED, AND THE MOON WILL NOT GIVE ITS LIGHT, AND THE STARS WILL FALL from the sky, and the powers of the heavens will be shaken.

30 "And then the sign of the Son of Man will appear in the sky, and then all the tribes of the earth will mourn, and they will see the SON OF MAN COMING ON THE CLOUDS OF THE SKY with power and great glory.

31 "And He will send forth His angels with A GREAT TRUMPET and THEY WILL GATHER TOGETHER His elect from the four winds, from one end of the sky to the other.

32 "Now learn the parable from the fig tree: when its branch has already become tender and puts forth its leaves, you know that summer is near;

33 So, you too, when you see all these things, recognize that He is near, *right* at the door.

34 "Truly I say to you, this generation will not pass away until all these things take place.

35 "Heaven and earth will pass away, but My words will not pass away.

36 "But of that day and hour no one knows, not even the angels of heaven, nor the Son, but the Father alone.

37 "For the coming of the Son of Man will be just like the days of Noah.

38 "For as in those days before the flood they were eating and drinking, marrying and giving in marriage, until the day that Noah entered the ark,

39 and they did not understand until the flood came and took them all away; so will the coming of the Son of Man be.

40 "Then there will be two men in the field; one will be taken and one will be left.

41 "Two women *will be* grinding at the mill; one will be taken and one will be left.

42 "Therefore be on the alert, for you do not know which day your Lord is coming.

43 "But be sure of this, that if the head of the house had known at what time of the night the thief was coming, he would have been on the alert and would not have allowed his house to be broken into.

44 "For this reason you also must be ready; for the Son of Man is coming at an hour when you do not think *He will*.

45 "Who then is the faithful and sensible slave whom his master put in charge of his household to give them their food at the proper time?

46 "Blessed is that slave whom his master finds so doing when he comes.

47 "Truly I say to you that he will put him in charge of all his possessions.

48 "But if that evil slave says in his heart, 'My master is not coming for a long time,'

49 and begins to beat his fellow slaves and eat and drink with drunkards;

50 the master of that slave will come on a day when he does not expect *him* and at an hour which he does not know,

51 and will cut him in pieces and assign him a place with the hypocrites; in that place there will be weeping and gnashing of teeth.

Parable of Ten Virgins

25 "Then the kingdom of heaven will be comparable to ten virgins, who took their lamps and went out to meet the

bridegroom.

2 "Five of them were foolish, and five were prudent.

3 "For when the foolish took their lamps, they took no oil with them,

4 but the prudent took oil in flasks along with their lamps.

5 "Now while the bridegroom was delaying, they all got drowsy and *began* to sleep.

6 "But at midnight there was a shout, 'Behold, the bridegroom! Come out to meet him.'

7 "Then all those virgins rose and trimmed their lamps.

8 "The foolish said to the prudent, 'Give us some of your oil, for our lamps are going out.'

9 "But the prudent answered, 'No, there will not be enough for us and you *too;* go instead to the dealers and buy *some* for yourselves.'

10 "And while they were going away to make the purchase, the bridegroom came, and those who were ready went in with him to the wedding feast; and the door was shut.

11 "Later the other virgins also came, saying, 'Lord, lord, open up for us.'

12 "But he answered, 'Truly I say to you, I do not know you.'

13 "Be on the alert then, for you do not know the day nor the hour.

14 "For *it is* just like a man *about* to go on a journey, who called his own slaves and entrusted his possessions to them.

15 "To one he gave five talents, to another, two, and to another, one, each according to his own ability; and he went on his journey.

16 "Immediately the one who had received the five talents went and traded with them, and gained five more talents.

17 "In the same manner the one who *had received* the two *talents* gained two more.

18 "But he who received the one *talent* went away, and dug *a hole* in the ground and hid his master's money.

19 "Now after a long time the master of those slaves *came and *settled accounts with them.

20 "The one who had received the five talents came up and brought five more talents, saying, 'Master, you entrusted five talents to me. See, I have gained five more talents.'

21 "His master said to him, 'Well done, good and faithful slave. You were faithful with a few things, I will put you in charge of many things; enter into the joy of your master.'

22 "Also the one who *had received* the two talents came up and said, 'Master, you entrusted two talents to me. See, I have gained two more talents.'

23 "His master said to him, 'Well done, good and faithful slave. You were faithful with a few things, I will put you in charge of many things; enter into the joy of your master.'

24 "And the one also who had received the one talent came up and said, 'Master, I knew you to be a hard man, reaping where you did not sow and gathering where you scattered no *seed.*

25 'And I was afraid, and went away and hid your talent in the ground. See, you have what is yours.'

26 "But his master answered and said to him, 'You wicked, lazy slave, you knew that I reap where I did not sow and gather where I scattered no *seed.*

27 'Then you ought to have put my money in the bank, and on my arrival I would have received my *money* back with interest.

28 'Therefore take away the talent from him, and give it to the one who has the ten talents.'

29 "For to everyone who has, *more* shall be given, and he will have an abundance; but from the one who does not have, even what he does have shall be taken away.

30 "Throw out the worthless slave into the outer darkness; in that place there will be weeping and gnashing of teeth.

31 "But when the Son of Man comes in His glory, and all the angels with Him, then He will sit on His glorious throne.

32 "All the nations will be gathered before Him; and He will separate them from one another, as the shepherd separates the sheep from the goats;

33 and He will put the sheep on His right, and the goats on the left.

34 "Then the King will say to those on His right, 'Come, you who are blessed of My Father, inherit the kingdom prepared for you from the foundation of the world.

35 'For I was hungry, and you gave Me *something* to eat; I was thirsty, and you gave Me *something* to drink; I was a stranger, and you invited Me in;

36 naked, and you clothed Me; I was sick, and you visited Me; I was in prison, and you came to Me.'

37 "Then the righteous will answer Him, 'Lord, when did we see You hungry, and feed You, or thirsty, and give You *something* to drink?

38 'And when did we see You a stranger, and invite You in, or naked, and clothe You?

39 'When did we see You sick, or in prison, and come to You?'

40 "The King will answer and say to them, 'Truly I say to you, to the extent that you did it to one of these brothers of Mine, *even* the least *of them,* you did it to Me.'

41 "Then He will also say to those on His left, 'Depart from Me, accursed ones, into the eternal fire which has been prepared for the devil and his angels;

42 for I was hungry, and you gave Me *nothing* to eat; I was thirsty, and you gave Me nothing to drink;

43 I was a stranger, and you did not invite Me in; naked, and you did not clothe Me; sick, and in prison, and you did not visit Me.'

44 "Then they themselves also will answer, 'Lord, when did we see You hungry, or thirsty, or a stranger, or naked, or sick, or in prison, and did not take care of You?'

45 "Then He will answer them, 'Truly I say to you, to the extent that you did not do it to one of the least of these, you did not do it to Me.'

46 "These will go away into eternal punishment, but the righteous into eternal life."

The Plot to Kill Jesus

26 When Jesus had finished all these words, He said to His disciples,

2 "You know that after two days the Passover is coming, and the Son of Man is *to be* handed over for crucifixion."

3 Then the chief priests and the elders of the people were gathered together in the court of the high priest, named Caiaphas;

4 and they plotted together to seize Jesus by stealth and kill Him.

5 But they were saying, "Not during the festival, otherwise a riot might occur among the people."

6 Now when Jesus was in Bethany, at the home of Simon the leper,

7 a woman came to Him with an alabaster vial of very costly perfume, and she poured it on His head as He reclined *at the table.*

8 But the disciples were indignant when they saw *this,* and said, "Why this waste?

9 "For this *perfume* might have been sold for a high price and *the money* given to the poor."

10 But Jesus, aware of this, said to them, "Why do you bother the woman? For she has done a good deed to Me.

11 "For you always have the poor with you; but you do not always have Me.

12 "For when she poured this perfume on My body, she did it to prepare Me for burial.

13 "Truly I say to you, wherever this gospel is preached in the whole world, what this woman has done will also be spoken of in memory of her."

14 Then one of the twelve, named Judas Iscariot, went to the chief priests

15 and said, "What are you willing to give me to betray Him to you?" And they weighed out thirty pieces of silver to him.

16 From then on he *began* looking for a good opportunity to betray Jesus.

17 Now on the first *day* of Unleavened Bread the disciples came to Jesus and asked, "Where do You want us to prepare for You to eat the Passover?"

18 And He said, "Go into the city to a certain man, and say to him, 'The Teacher says, "My time is near; I *am* to keep the Passover at your house with My disciples." ' "

19 The disciples did as Jesus had directed them; and they prepared the Passover.

20 Now when evening came, Jesus was reclining *at the table* with the twelve disciples.

21 As they were eating, He said, "Truly I say to you that one of you will betray Me."

22 Being deeply grieved, they each one began to say to Him, "Surely not I, Lord?"

23 And He answered, "He who dipped his hand with Me in the bowl is the one who will betray Me.

24 "The Son of Man *is to* go, just as it is written of Him; but woe to that man by whom the Son of Man is betrayed! It would have been good for that man if he had not been born."

25 And Judas, who was betraying Him, said, "Surely it is not I, Rabbi?" Jesus *said to him, "You have said *it* yourself."

26 While they were eating, Jesus took *some* bread, and after a blessing, He broke *it* and gave *it* to the disciples, and said, "Take, eat; this is My body."

27 And when He had taken a cup and given thanks, He gave *it* to them, saying, "Drink from it, all of you;

28 for this is My blood of the covenant, which is poured out for many for forgiveness of sins.

29 "But I say to you, I will not drink of this fruit of the vine from now on until that day when I drink it new with you in My Father's kingdom."

30 After singing a hymn, they went out to the Mount of Olives.

31 Then Jesus *said to them, "You will all fall away because of Me this night, for it is written, 'I WILL STRIKE DOWN THE SHEPHERD, AND THE SHEEP OF THE FLOCK SHALL BE SCATTERED.'

32 "But after I have been raised, I will go ahead of you to Galilee."

33 But Peter said to Him, "*Even* though all may fall away because of You, I will never fall away."

34 Jesus said to him, "Truly I say to you that this *very* night, before a rooster crows, you will deny Me three times."

35 Peter *said to Him, "Even if I have to die with You, I will not deny You." All the disciples said the same thing too.

36 Then Jesus *came with them to a place called Gethsemane, and *said to His disciples, "Sit here while I go over there and pray."

37 And He took with Him Peter and the two sons of Zebedee, and began to be grieved and distressed.

38 Then He *said to them, "My soul is deeply grieved, to the point of death; remain here and keep watch with Me."

39 And He went a little beyond *them,* and fell on His face and prayed, saying, "My Father, if it is possible, let this cup pass from Me; yet not as I will, but as You will."

40 And He *came to the disciples and *found them sleeping, and *said to Peter, "So, you *men* could not keep watch with Me for one hour?

41 "Keep watching and praying that you may not enter into temptation; the spirit is willing, but the flesh is weak."

42 He went away again a second time and prayed, saying, "My Father, if this cannot pass away unless I drink it, Your will be done."

43 Again He came and found them sleeping, for their eyes were heavy.

44 And He left them again, and went away and prayed a third time, saying the same thing once more.

45 Then He *came to the disciples and *said to them, "Are you still sleeping and resting? Behold, the hour is at hand and the Son of Man is being betrayed into the hands of sinners.

46 "Get up, let us be going; behold, the one who betrays Me is at hand!"

blood shed for forgiveness of sins

His blood was shed in His death. Read John 19:34 on page 89.

He could have called legions of angels.

47 While He was still speaking, behold, Judas, one of the twelve, came up accompanied by a large crowd with swords and clubs, *who came* from the chief priests and elders of the people.

48 Now he who was betraying Him gave them a sign, saying, "Whomever I kiss, He is the one; seize Him."

49 Immediately Judas went to Jesus and said, "Hail, Rabbi!" and kissed Him.

50 And Jesus said to him, "Friend, *do* what you have come for." Then they came and laid hands on Jesus and seized Him.

51 And behold, one of those who were with Jesus reached and drew out his sword, and struck the slave of the high priest and cut off his ear.

52 Then Jesus *said to him, "Put your sword back into its place; for all those who take up the sword shall perish by the sword.

53 "Or do you think that I cannot appeal to My Father, and He will at once put at My disposal more than twelve 1legions of angels?

54 "How then will the Scriptures be fulfilled, *which say* that it must happen this way?"

55 At that time Jesus said to the crowds, "Have you come out with swords and clubs to arrest Me as *you would* against a robber? Every day I used to sit in the temple teaching and you did not seize Me.

56 "But all this has taken place to fulfill the Scriptures of the prophets." Then all the disciples left Him and fled.

57 Those who had seized Jesus led Him away to Caiaphas, the high priest, where the scribes and the elders were gathered together.

58 But Peter was following Him at a distance as far as the courtyard of the high priest, and entered in, and sat down with the officers to see the outcome.

59 Now the chief priests and the whole Council kept trying to obtain false testimony against Jesus, so that they might put Him to death.

60 They did not find *any,* even though many false witnesses came forward. But later on two came forward,

61 and said, "This man stated, 'I am able to destroy the temple of God and to rebuild it in three days.' "

62 The high priest stood up and said to Him, "Do You not answer? What is it that these men are testifying against You?"

63 But Jesus kept silent. And the high priest said to Him, "I adjure You by the living God, that You tell us whether You are the Christ, the Son of God."

64 Jesus *said to him, "You have said it *yourself;* nevertheless I tell you, hereafter you will see THE SON OF MAN SITTING AT THE RIGHT HAND OF POWER, and COMING ON THE CLOUDS OF HEAVEN."

65 Then the high priest tore his robes and said, "He has blasphemed! What further need do we have of witnesses? Behold, you have now heard the blasphemy;

66 what do you think?" They answered, "He deserves death!"

67 Then they spat in His face and beat Him with their fists; and others slapped Him,

68 and said, "Prophesy to us, You Christ; who is the one who hit You?"

69 Now Peter was sitting outside in the courtyard, and a servant-girl came to him and said, "You too were with Jesus the Galilean."

70 But he denied *it* before them all, saying, "I do not know what you are talking about."

71 When he had gone out to the gateway, another *servant-girl* saw him and *said to those who were there, "This man was with Jesus of Nazareth."

72 And again he denied *it* with an oath, "I do not know the man."

73 A little later the bystanders came up and said to Peter, "Surely you too are *one* of them; for even the way you talk gives you away."

74 Then he began to curse and swear, "I do not know the man!" And immediately a rooster crowed.

75 And Peter remembered the word which Jesus had said, "Before a rooster crows, you will deny Me three times." And he went out and wept bitterly.

Judas' Remorse

27 Now when morning came, all the chief priests and the elders of the people conferred together against Jesus to put Him to death;

2 and they bound Him, and led Him away and delivered Him to Pilate the governor.

3 Then when Judas, who had betrayed Him, saw that He had been condemned, he felt remorse and returned the thirty pieces of silver to the chief priests and elders,

4 saying, "I have sinned by betraying innocent blood." But they said, "What is that to us? See *to that* yourself!"

5 And he threw the pieces of silver into the temple sanctuary and departed; and he went away and hanged himself.

6 The chief priests took the pieces of silver and said, "It is not lawful to put them into the temple treasury, since it is the price of blood."

7 And they conferred together and with the money bought the Potter's Field as a burial place for strangers.

8 For this reason that field has been called the Field of Blood to this day.

9 Then that which was spoken through Jeremiah the prophet was fulfilled: "AND THEY TOOK THE THIRTY PIECES OF SILVER, THE PRICE OF THE ONE WHOSE PRICE HAD BEEN SET by the sons of Israel;

10 AND THEY GAVE THEM FOR THE POTTER'S FIELD, AS THE LORD DIRECTED ME."

11 Now Jesus stood before the governor, and the governor questioned Him, saying, "Are You the King of the Jews?" And Jesus said to him, "*It is as* you say."

12 And while He was being accused by the chief priests and elders, He did not answer.

---

1. A legion equaled 6,000 troops.

Why did He stay on the cross? Read John 15:13 on page 86.

13 Then Pilate *said to Him, "Do You not hear how many things they testify against You?"

14 And He did not answer him with regard to even a *single* charge, so the governor was quite amazed.

15 Now at *the* feast the governor was accustomed to release for the people *any* one prisoner whom they wanted.

16 At that time they were holding a notorious prisoner, called Barabbas.

17 So when the people gathered together, Pilate said to them, "Whom do you want me to release for you? Barabbas, or Jesus who is called Christ?"

18 For he knew that because of envy they had handed Him over.

19 While he was sitting on the judgment seat, his wife sent him *a message*, saying, "Have nothing to do with that righteous Man; for last night I suffered greatly in a dream because of Him."

20 But the chief priests and the elders persuaded the crowds to ask for Barabbas and to put Jesus to death.

21 But the governor said to them, "Which of the two do you want me to release for you?" And they said, "Barabbas."

22 Pilate *said to them, "Then what shall I do with Jesus who is called Christ?" They all *said, "Crucify Him!"

23 And he said, "Why, what evil has He done?" But they kept shouting all the more, saying, "Crucify Him!"

24 When Pilate saw that he was accomplishing nothing, but rather that a riot was starting, he took water and washed his hands in front of the crowd, saying, "I am innocent of this Man's blood; see *to that* yourselves."

25 And all the people said, "His blood shall be on us and on our children!"

26 Then he released Barabbas for them; but after having Jesus scourged, he handed Him over to be crucified.

27 Then the soldiers of the governor took Jesus into the Praetorium and gathered the whole *Roman* cohort around Him.

28 They stripped Him and put a scarlet robe on Him.

29 And after twisting together a crown of thorns, they put it on His head, and a reed in His right hand; and they knelt down before Him and mocked Him, saying, "Hail, King of the Jews!"

30 They spat on Him, and took the reed and *began* to beat Him on the head.

31 After they had mocked Him, they took the *scarlet* robe off Him and put His *own* garments back on Him, and led Him away to crucify Him.

32 As they were coming out, they found a man of Cyrene named Simon, whom they pressed into service to bear His cross.

33 And when they came to a place called Golgotha, which means Place of a Skull,

34 they gave Him wine to drink mixed with gall; and after tasting *it*, He was unwilling to drink.

35 And when they had crucified Him, they divided up His garments among themselves by casting lots.

36 And sitting down, they *began* to keep watch over Him there.

37 And above His head they put up the charge against Him which read, "THIS IS JESUS THE KING OF THE JEWS."

38 At that time two robbers *were crucified with Him, one on the right and one on the left.

39 And those passing by were hurling abuse at Him, wagging their heads

40 and saying, "You who *are going to* destroy the temple and rebuild it in three days, save Yourself! If You are the Son of God, come down from the cross."

41 In the same way the chief priests also, along with the scribes and elders, were mocking *Him* and saying,

42 "He saved others; He cannot save Himself. He is the King of Israel; let Him now come down from the cross, and we will believe in Him.

43 "HE TRUSTS IN GOD; LET GOD RESCUE *Him* now, IF HE DELIGHTS IN HIM; for He said, 'I am the Son of God.' "

44 The robbers who had been crucified with Him were also insulting Him with the same words.

45 Now from the [1]sixth hour darkness fell upon all the land until the [2]ninth hour.

46 About the ninth hour Jesus cried out with a loud voice, saying, "ELI, ELI, LAMA SABACHTHANI?" that is, "MY GOD, MY GOD, WHY HAVE YOU FORSAKEN ME?"

47 And some of those who were standing there, when they heard it, *began* saying, "This man is calling for Elijah."

48 Immediately one of them ran, and taking a sponge, he filled it with sour wine and put it on a reed, and gave Him a drink.

49 But the rest *of them* said, "Let us see whether Elijah will come to save Him."[3]

50 And Jesus cried out again with a loud voice, and yielded up His spirit.

51 And behold, the veil of the temple was torn in two from top to bottom; and the earth shook and the rocks were split.

52 The tombs were opened, and many bodies of the saints who had fallen asleep were raised;

53 and coming out of the tombs after His resurrection they entered the holy city and appeared to many.

54 Now the centurion, and those who were with him keeping guard over Jesus, when they saw the earthquake and the things that were happening, became very frightened and said, "Truly this was the Son of God!"

55 Many women were there looking on from a

1. I.e. noon 2. I.e. 3 p.m. 3. Some early mss read *And another took a spear and pierced His side, and there came out water and blood* (cf John 19:34)

Jesus could have resisted. Read Matthew 26:47-56 on page 24.

distance, who had followed Jesus from Galilee while ministering to Him.

56 Among them was Mary Magdalene, and Mary the mother of James and Joseph, and the mother of the sons of Zebedee.

57 When it was evening, there came a rich man from Arimathea, named Joseph, who himself had also become a disciple of Jesus.

58 This man went to Pilate and asked for the body of Jesus. Then Pilate ordered it to be given *to him.*

59 And Joseph took the body and wrapped it in a clean linen cloth,

60 and laid it in his own new tomb, which he had hewn out in the rock; and he rolled a large stone against the entrance of the tomb and went away.

61 And Mary Magdalene was there, and the other Mary, sitting opposite the grave.

62 Now on the next day, the day after the preparation, the chief priests and the Pharisees gathered together with Pilate,

63 and said, "Sir, we remember that when He was still alive that deceiver said, 'After three days I *am to* rise again.'

64 "Therefore, give orders for the grave to be made secure until the third day, otherwise His disciples may come and steal Him away and say to the people, 'He has risen from the dead,' and the last deception will be worse than the first."

65 Pilate said to them, "You have a guard; go, make it *as* secure as you know how."

66 And they went and made the grave secure, and along with the guard they set a seal on the stone.

Jesus Is Risen!

28 Now after the Sabbath, as it began to dawn toward the first *day* of the week, Mary Magdalene and the other Mary came to look at the grave.

2 And behold, a severe earthquake had occurred, for an angel of the Lord descended from heaven and came and rolled away the stone and sat upon it.

3 And his appearance was like lightning, and his clothing as white as snow.

4 The guards shook for fear of him and became like dead men.

5 The angel said to the women, "Do not be afraid; for I know that you are looking for Jesus who has been crucified.

6 "He is not here, for He has risen, just as He said. Come, see the place where He was lying.

7 "Go quickly and tell His disciples that He has risen from the dead; and behold, He is going ahead of you into Galilee, there you will see Him; behold, I have told you."

8 And they left the tomb quickly with fear and great joy and ran to report it to His disciples.

9 And behold, Jesus met them and greeted them. And they came up and took hold of His feet and worshiped Him.

10 Then Jesus *said to them, "Do not be afraid; go and take word to My brethren to leave for Galilee, and there they will see Me."

11 Now while they were on their way, some of the guard came into the city and reported to the chief priests all that had happened.

12 And when they had assembled with the elders and consulted together, they gave a large sum of money to the soldiers,

13 and said, "You are to say, 'His disciples came by night and stole Him away while we were asleep.'

14 "And if this should come to the governor's ears, we will win him over and keep you out of trouble."

15 And they took the money and did as they had been instructed; and this story was widely spread among the Jews, *and is* to this day.

16 But the eleven disciples proceeded to Galilee, to the mountain which Jesus had designated.

17 When they saw Him, they worshiped *Him;* but some were doubtful.

18 And Jesus came up and spoke to them, saying, "All authority has been given to Me in heaven and on earth.

19 "Go therefore and make disciples of all the nations, baptizing them in the name of the Father and the Son and the Holy Spirit,

20 teaching them to observe all that I commanded you; and lo, I am with you always, even to the end of the age."

THE GOSPEL ACCORDING TO MARK

Preaching of John the Baptist

1 The beginning of the gospel of Jesus Christ, the Son of God.

2 As it is written in Isaiah the prophet:
"BEHOLD, I SEND MY MESSENGER AHEAD OF YOU,
WHO WILL PREPARE YOUR WAY;

3 THE VOICE OF ONE CRYING IN THE WILDERNESS,
'MAKE READY THE WAY OF THE LORD,
MAKE HIS PATHS STRAIGHT.' "

4 John the Baptist appeared in the wilderness [1]preaching a baptism of repentance for the forgiveness of sins.

5 And all the country of Judea was going out to him, and all the people of Jerusalem; and they were being baptized by him in the Jordan River, confessing their sins.

6 John was clothed with camel's hair and *wore* a leather belt around his waist, and his diet was locusts and wild honey.

7 And he was preaching, and saying, "After me One is coming who is mightier than I, and I am not fit to stoop down and untie the thong of His sandals.

1. *Or* proclaiming

8 "I baptized you ¹with water; but He will baptize you ¹with the Holy Spirit."

9 In those days Jesus came from Nazareth in Galilee and was baptized by John in the Jordan.

10 Immediately coming up out of the water, He saw the heavens opening, and the Spirit like a dove descending upon Him;

11 and a voice came out of the heavens: "You are My beloved Son, in You I am well-pleased."

12 Immediately the Spirit *impelled Him *to go out into the wilderness.*

13 And He was in the wilderness forty days being tempted by Satan; and He was with the wild beasts, and the angels were ministering to Him.

14 Now after John had been taken into custody, Jesus came into Galilee, preaching the gospel of God,

15 and saying, "The time is fulfilled, and the kingdom of God is at hand; repent and believe in the gospel."

16 As He was going along by the Sea of Galilee, He saw Simon and Andrew, the brother of Simon, casting a net in the sea; for they were fishermen.

17 And Jesus said to them, "Follow Me, and I will make you become fishers of men."

18 Immediately they left their nets and followed Him.

19 Going on a little farther, He saw James the son of Zebedee, and John his brother, who were also in the boat mending the nets.

20 Immediately He called them; and they left their father Zebedee in the boat with the hired servants, and went away to follow Him.

21 They *went into Capernaum; and immediately on the Sabbath He entered the synagogue and *began to teach.*

22 They were amazed at His teaching; for He was teaching them as *one* having authority, and not as the scribes.

23 Just then there was a man in their synagogue with an unclean spirit; and he cried out,

24 saying, "What business do we have with each other, Jesus ²of Nazareth? Have You come to destroy us? I know who You are—the Holy One of God!"

25 And Jesus rebuked him, saying, "Be quiet, and come out of him!"

26 Throwing him into convulsions, the unclean spirit cried out with a loud voice and came out of him.

27 They were all amazed, so that they debated among themselves, saying, "What is this? A new teaching with authority! He commands even the unclean spirits, and they obey Him."

28 Immediately the news about Him spread everywhere into all the surrounding district of Galilee.

29 And immediately after they came out of the synagogue, they came into the house of Simon and Andrew, with James and John.

30 Now Simon's mother-in-law was lying sick with a fever; and immediately they *spoke to Jesus about her.

31 And He came to her and raised her up, taking her by the hand, and the fever left her, and she ³waited on them.

32 When evening came, after the sun had set, they *began* bringing to Him all who were ill and those who were demon-possessed.

33 And the whole city had gathered at the door.

34 And He healed many who were ill with various diseases, and cast out many demons; and He was not permitting the demons to speak, because they knew who He was.

35 In the early morning, while it was still dark, Jesus got up, left *the house,* and went away to a secluded place, and was praying there.

36 Simon and his companions searched for Him;

37 they found Him, and *said to Him, "Everyone is looking for You."

38 He *said to them, "Let us go somewhere else to the towns nearby, so that I may preach there also; for that is what I came for."

39 And He went into their synagogues throughout all Galilee, preaching and casting out the demons.

40 And a leper *came to Jesus, beseeching Him and falling on his knees before Him, and saying, "If You are willing, You can make me clean."

41 Moved with compassion, Jesus stretched out His hand and touched him, and *said to him, "I am willing; be cleansed."

42 Immediately the leprosy left him and he was cleansed.

43 And He sternly warned him and immediately sent him away,

44 and He *said to him, "See that you say nothing to anyone; but go, show yourself to the priest and offer for your cleansing what Moses commanded, as a testimony to them."

45 But he went out and began to proclaim it freely and to spread the news around, to such an extent that Jesus could no longer publicly enter a city, but ⁴stayed out in unpopulated areas; and they were coming to Him from everywhere.

The Paralytic Healed

2 When He had come back to Capernaum several days afterward, it was heard that He was at home.

2 And many were gathered together, so that there was no longer room, not even near the door; and He was speaking the word to them.

3 And they *came, bringing to Him a paralytic, carried by four men.

4 Being unable to get to Him because of the crowd, they removed the roof above Him; and when they had dug an opening, they let down the pallet on which the paralytic was lying.

5 And Jesus seeing their faith *said to the paralytic, "⁵Son, your sins are forgiven."

---

1. The Gr here can be translated *in, with* or *by* 2. Lit *the Nazarene* 3. Or *served* 4. Lit *was* 5. Lit *child*

6 But some of the scribes were sitting there and reasoning in their hearts,

7 "Why does this man speak that way? He is blaspheming; who can forgive sins but God alone?"

8 Immediately Jesus, aware in His spirit that they were reasoning that way within themselves, *said to them, "Why are you reasoning about these things in your hearts?

9 "Which is easier, to say to the paralytic, 'Your sins are forgiven'; or to say, 'Get up, and pick up your pallet and walk'?

10 "But so that you may know that the Son of Man has authority on earth to forgive sins"—He *said to the paralytic,

11 "I say to you, get up, pick up your pallet and go home."

12 And he got up and immediately picked up the pallet and went out in the sight of everyone, so that they were all amazed and were glorifying God, saying, "We have never seen anything like this."

13 And He went out again by the seashore; and all the people were coming to Him, and He was teaching them.

14 As He passed by, He saw Levi the son of Alphaeus sitting in the tax booth, and He *said to him, "Follow Me!" And he got up and followed Him.

15 And it *happened that He was reclining at the table in his house, and many tax collectors and sinners were dining with Jesus and His disciples; for there were many of them, and they were following Him.

16 When the scribes of the Pharisees saw that He was eating with the sinners and tax collectors, they said to His disciples, "Why is He eating and drinking with tax collectors and sinners?"

17 And hearing this, Jesus *said to them, "It is not those who are healthy who need a physician, but those who are sick;· I did not come to call the righteous, but sinners."

18 John's disciples and the Pharisees were fasting; and they *came and *said to Him, "Why do John's disciples and the disciples of the Pharisees fast, but Your disciples do not fast?"

19 And Jesus said to them, "While the bridegroom is with them, the attendants of the bridegroom cannot fast, can they? So long as they have the bridegroom with them, they cannot fast.

20 "But the days will come when the bridegroom is taken away from them, and then they will fast in that day.

21 "No one sews a patch of unshrunk cloth on an old garment; otherwise the patch pulls away from it, the new from the old, and a worse tear results.

22 "No one puts new wine into old wineskins; otherwise the wine will burst the skins, and the wine is lost and the skins as well; but one puts new wine into fresh wineskins.

23 And it happened that He was passing through the grainfields on the Sabbath, and His disciples began to make their way along while picking the heads of grain.

24 The Pharisees were saying to Him, "Look, why are they doing what is not lawful on the Sabbath?"

25 And He *said to them, "Have you never read what David did when he was in need and he and his companions became hungry;

26 how he entered the house of God in the time of Abiathar the high priest, and ate the consecrated bread, which is not lawful for anyone to eat except the priests, and he also gave it to those who were with him?"

27 Jesus said to them, "The Sabbath was made for man, and not man for the Sabbath.

28 "So the Son of Man is Lord even of the Sabbath."

Jesus Heals on the Sabbath

3 He entered again into a synagogue; and a man was there whose hand was withered.

2 They were watching Him to see if He would heal him on the Sabbath, so that they might accuse Him.

3 He *said to the man with the withered hand, "Get up and come forward!"

4 And He *said to them, "Is it lawful to do good or to do harm on the Sabbath, to save a life or to kill?" But they kept silent.

5 After looking around at them with anger, grieved at their hardness of heart, He *said to the man, "Stretch out your hand." And he stretched it out, and his hand was restored.

6 The Pharisees went out and immediately began conspiring with the Herodians against Him, as to how they might destroy Him.

7 Jesus withdrew to the sea with His disciples; and a great multitude from Galilee followed; and also from Judea,

8 and from Jerusalem, and from Idumea, and beyond the Jordan, and the vicinity of Tyre and Sidon, a great number of people heard of all that He was doing and came to Him.

9 And He told His disciples that a boat should stand ready for Him because of the crowd, so that they would not crowd Him;

10 for He had healed many, with the result that all those who had afflictions pressed around Him in order to touch Him.

11 Whenever the unclean spirits saw Him, they would fall down before Him and shout, "You are the Son of God!"

12 And He earnestly warned them not to tell who He was.

13 And He *went up on the mountain and *summoned those whom He Himself wanted, and they came to Him.

14 And He appointed twelve, so that they would be with Him and that He could send them out to preach,

15 and to have authority to cast out the demons.

16 And He appointed the twelve: Simon (to whom He gave the name Peter),

17 and James, the son of Zebedee, and John the brother of James (to them He gave the name Boanerges, which means, "Sons of Thunder");

18 and Andrew, and Philip, and Bartholomew, and Matthew, and Thomas, and James the son of Alphaeus, and Thaddaeus, and Simon the Zealot;

19 and Judas Iscariot, who betrayed Him.

20 And He *came ¹home, and the crowd *gathered again, to such an extent that they could not even eat a meal.

21 When His own ²people heard *of this*, they went out to take custody of Him; for they were saying, "He has lost His senses."

22 The scribes who came down from Jerusalem were saying, "He is possessed by Beelzebul," and "He casts out the demons by the ruler of the demons."

23 And He called them to Himself and began speaking to them in parables, "How can Satan cast out Satan?

24 "If a kingdom is divided against itself, that kingdom cannot stand.

25 "If a house is divided against itself, that house will not be able to stand.

26 "If Satan has risen up against himself and is divided, he cannot stand, but he is finished!

27 "But no one can enter the strong man's house and plunder his property unless he first binds the strong man, and then he will plunder his house.

28 "Truly I say to you, all sins shall be forgiven the sons of men, and whatever blasphemies they utter;

29 but whoever blasphemes against the Holy Spirit never has forgiveness, but is guilty of an eternal sin"—

30 because they were saying, "He has an unclean spirit."

31 Then His mother and His brothers *arrived, and standing outside they sent *word* to Him and called Him.

32 A crowd was sitting around Him, and they *said to Him, "Behold, Your mother and Your brothers are outside looking for You."

33 Answering them, He *said, "Who are My mother and My brothers?"

34 Looking about at those who were sitting around Him, He *said, "Behold My mother and My brothers!

35 "For whoever does the will of God, he is My brother and sister and mother."

Parable of the Sower and Soils

4 He began to teach again by the sea. And such a very large crowd gathered to Him that He got into a boat in the sea and sat down; and the whole crowd was by the sea on the land.

2 And He was teaching them many things in parables, and was saying to them in His teaching,

3 "Listen *to this!* Behold, the sower went out to sow;

4 as he was sowing, some *seed* fell beside the road, and the birds came and ate it up.

5 "Other *seed* fell on the rocky *ground* where it did not have much soil; and immediately it sprang up because it had no depth of soil.

6 "And after the sun had risen, it was scorched; and because it had no root, it withered away.

7 "Other *seed* fell among the thorns, and the thorns came up and choked it, and it yielded no crop.

8 "Other *seeds* fell into the good soil, and as they grew up and increased, they yielded a crop and produced thirty, sixty, and a hundredfold."

9 And He was saying, "He who has ears to hear, let him hear."

10 As soon as He was alone, His followers, along with the twelve, *began* asking Him *about* the parables.

11 And He was saying to them, "To you has been given the mystery of the kingdom of God, but those who are outside get everything in parables,

12 so that WHILE SEEING, THEY MAY SEE AND NOT PERCEIVE, AND WHILE HEARING, THEY MAY HEAR AND NOT UNDERSTAND, OTHERWISE THEY MIGHT RETURN AND BE FORGIVEN."

13 And He *said to them, "Do you not understand this parable? How will you understand all the parables?

14 "The sower sows the word.

15 "These are the ones who are beside the road where the word is sown; and when they hear, immediately Satan comes and takes away the word which has been sown in them.

16 "In a similar way these are the ones on whom seed was sown on the rocky *places*, who, when they hear the word, immediately receive it with joy;

17 and they have no *firm* root in themselves, but are *only* temporary; then, when affliction or persecution arises because of the word, immediately they fall away.

18 "And others are the ones on whom seed was sown among the thorns; these are the ones who have heard the word,

19 but the worries of the ³world, and the deceitfulness of riches, and the desires for other things enter in and choke the word, and it becomes unfruitful.

20 "And those are the ones on whom seed was sown on the good soil; and they hear the word and accept it and bear fruit, thirty, sixty, and a hundredfold."

21 And He was saying to them, "A lamp is not brought to be put under a basket, is it, or under a bed? Is it not *brought* to be put on the lampstand?

22 "For nothing is hidden, except to be revealed; nor has *anything* been secret, but that it would come to light.

23 "If anyone has ears to hear, let him hear."

24 And He was saying to them, "Take care what you listen to. By your standard of measure it will be measured to you; and more will be given you besides.

25 "For whoever has, to him *more* shall be given; and whoever does not have, even what he has shall be taken away from him."

---

1. Lit *into a house* 2. Or *kinsmen* 3. Or *age*

26 And He was saying, "The kingdom of God is like a man who casts seed upon the soil;

27 and he goes to bed at night and gets up by day, and the seed sprouts and grows—how, he himself does not know.

28 "The soil produces crops by itself; first the blade, then the head, then the mature grain in the head.

29 "But when the crop permits, he immediately puts in the sickle, because the harvest has come."

30 And He said, "How shall we ¹picture the kingdom of God, or by what parable shall we present it?

31 "*It is* like a mustard seed, which, when sown upon the soil, though it is smaller than all the seeds that are upon the soil,

32 yet when it is sown, it grows up and becomes larger than all the garden plants and forms large branches; so that THE BIRDS OF THE ²AIR can NEST UNDER ITS SHADE."

33 With many such parables He was speaking the word to them, so far as they were able to hear it;

34 and He did not speak to them without a parable; but He was explaining everything privately to His own disciples.

35 On that day, when evening came, He *said to them, "Let us go over to the other side."

36 Leaving the crowd, they *took Him along with them in the boat, just as He was; and other boats were with Him.

37 And there *arose a fierce gale of wind, and the waves were breaking over the boat so much that the boat was already filling up.

38 Jesus Himself was in the stern, asleep on the cushion; and they *woke Him and *said to Him, "Teacher, do You not care that we are perishing?"

39 And He got up and rebuked the wind and said to the sea, "Hush, be still." And the wind died down and it became perfectly calm.

40 And He said to them, "Why are you afraid? How is it that you have no faith?"

41 They became very much afraid and said to one another, "Who then is this, that even the wind and the sea obey Him?"

The Gerasene Demoniac

5 They came to the other side of the sea, into the country of the Gerasenes.

2 When He got out of the boat, immediately a man from the tombs with an unclean spirit met Him,

3 and he had his dwelling among the tombs. And no one was able to bind him anymore, even with a chain;

4 because he had often been bound with shackles and chains, and the chains had been torn apart by him and the shackles broken in pieces, and no one was strong enough to subdue him.

5 Constantly, night and day, he was screaming among the tombs and in the mountains, and gashing himself with stones.

6 Seeing Jesus from a distance, he ran up and bowed down before Him;

7 and shouting with a loud voice, he *said, "What business do we have with each other, Jesus, Son of the Most High God? I implore You by God, do not torment me!"

8 For He had been saying to him, "Come out of the man, you unclean spirit!"

9 And He was asking him, "What is your name?" And he *said to Him, "My name is Legion; for we are many."

10 And he *began to implore Him earnestly not to send them out of the country.

11 Now there was a large herd of swine feeding nearby on the mountain.

12 *The demons implored Him, saying, "Send us into the swine so that we may enter them."

13 Jesus gave them permission. And coming out, the unclean spirits entered the swine; and the herd rushed down the steep bank into the sea, about two thousand *of them;* and they were drowned in the sea.

14 Their herdsmen ran away and reported it in the city and in the country. And *the people* came to see what it was that had happened.

15 They *came to Jesus and *observed the man who had been demon-possessed sitting down, clothed and in his right mind, the very man who had had the "legion"; and they became frightened.

16 Those who had seen it described to them how it had happened to the demon-possessed man, and *all* about the swine.

17 And they began to implore Him to leave their region.

18 As He was getting into the boat, the man who had been demon-possessed was imploring Him that he might accompany Him.

19 And He did not let him, but He *said to him, "Go home to your people and report to them ³what great things the Lord has done for you, and *how* He had mercy on you."

20 And he went away and began to proclaim in Decapolis what great things Jesus had done for him; and everyone was amazed.

21 When Jesus had crossed over again in the boat to the other side, a large crowd gathered around Him; and so He stayed by the seashore.

22 One of the synagogue officials named Jairus *came up, and on seeing Him, *fell at His feet

23 and *implored Him earnestly, saying, "My little daughter is at the point of death; *please* come and lay Your hands on her, so that she will get well and live."

24 And He went off with him; and a large crowd was following Him and pressing in on Him.

25 A woman who had had a hemorrhage for twelve years,

26 and had endured much at the hands of many physicians, and had spent all that she had and was not helped at all, but rather had grown worse—

---

1. Lit *compare* 2. Or *sky* 3. Or *everything that*

27 after hearing about Jesus, she came up in the crowd behind *Him* and touched His cloak.

28 For she thought, "If I just touch His garments, I will get well."

29 Immediately the flow of her blood was dried up; and she felt in her body that she was healed of her affliction.

30 Immediately Jesus, perceiving in Himself that the power *proceeding* from Him had gone forth, turned around in the crowd and said, "Who touched My garments?"

31 And His disciples said to Him, "You see the crowd pressing in on You, and You say, 'Who touched Me?' "

32 And He looked around to see the woman who had done this.

33 But the woman fearing and trembling, aware of what had happened to her, came and fell down before Him and told Him the whole truth.

34 And He said to her, "Daughter, your faith has made you well; go in peace and be healed of your affliction."

35 While He was still speaking, they *came from the *house of* the synagogue official, saying, "Your daughter has died; why trouble the Teacher anymore?"

36 But Jesus, overhearing what was being spoken, *said to the synagogue official, "Do not be afraid *any longer*, only believe."

37 And He allowed no one to accompany Him, except Peter and James and John the brother of James.

38 They *came to the house of the synagogue official; and He *saw a commotion, and *people* loudly weeping and wailing.

39 And entering in, He *said to them, "Why make a commotion and weep? The child has not died, but is asleep."

40 They *began* laughing at Him. But putting them all out, He *took along the child's father and mother and His own companions, and *entered *the room* where the child was.

41 Taking the child by the hand, He *said to her, "Talitha kum!" (which translated means, "Little girl, I say to you, get up!").

42 Immediately the girl got up and *began* to walk, for she was twelve years old. And immediately they were completely astounded.

43 And He gave them strict orders that no one should know about this, and He said that *something* should be given her to eat.

Teaching at Nazareth

6 Jesus went out from there and *came into His hometown; and His disciples *followed Him.

2 When the Sabbath came, He began to teach in the synagogue; and the many listeners were astonished, saying, "Where did this man *get* these things, and what is *this* wisdom given to Him, and such miracles as these performed by His hands?

3 "Is not this the carpenter, the son of Mary, and brother of James and Joses and Judas and

Simon? Are not His sisters here with us?" And they took offense at Him.

4 Jesus said to them, "A prophet is not without honor except in his hometown and among his *own* relatives and in his *own* household."

5 And He could do no miracle there except that He laid His hands on a few sick people and healed them.

6 And He wondered at their unbelief.

And He was going around the villages teaching.

7 And He *summoned the twelve and began to send them out in pairs, and gave them authority over the unclean spirits;

8 and He instructed them that they should take nothing for *their* journey, except a mere staff—no bread, no bag, no money in their belt—

9 but *to* wear sandals; and He added, "Do not put on two ¹tunics."

10 And He said to them, "Wherever you enter a house, stay there until you leave town.

11 "Any place that does not receive you or listen to you, as you go out from there, shake the dust off the soles of your feet for a testimony against them."

12 They went out and preached that *men* should repent.

13 And they were casting out many demons and were anointing with oil many sick people and healing them.

14 And King Herod heard *of it*, for His name had become well known; and *people* were saying, "John the Baptist has risen from the dead, and that is why these miraculous powers are at work in Him."

15 But others were saying, "He is Elijah." And others were saying, "*He is* a prophet, like one of the prophets *of old.*"

16 But when Herod heard *of it*, he kept saying, "John, whom I beheaded, has risen!"

17 For Herod himself had sent and had John arrested and bound in prison on account of Herodias, the wife of his brother Philip, because he had married her.

18 For John had been saying to Herod, "It is not lawful for you to have your brother's wife."

19 Herodias had a grudge against him and wanted to put him to death and could not *do so;*

20 for Herod was afraid of John, knowing that he was a righteous and holy man, and he kept him safe. And when he heard him, he was very perplexed; but he used to enjoy listening to him.

21 A strategic day came when Herod on his birthday gave a banquet for his lords and military commanders and the leading men of Galilee;

22 and when the daughter of Herodias herself came in and danced, she pleased Herod and his dinner guests; and the king said to the girl, "Ask me for whatever you want and I will give it to you."

23 And he swore to her, "Whatever you ask of

---

1. Or *inner garments*

me, I will give it to you; up to half of my kingdom."

24 And she went out and said to her mother, "What shall I ask for?" And she said, "The head of John the Baptist."

25 Immediately she came in a hurry to the king and asked, saying, "I want you to give me at once the head of John the Baptist on a platter."

26 And although the king was very sorry, *yet* because of his oaths and because of his dinner guests, he was unwilling to refuse her.

27 Immediately the king sent an executioner and commanded *him* to bring *back* his head. And he went and had him beheaded in the prison,

28 and brought his head on a platter, and gave it to the girl; and the girl gave it to her mother.

29 When his disciples heard *about this,* they came and took away his body and laid it in a tomb.

30 The apostles *gathered together with Jesus; and they reported to Him all that they had done and taught.

31 And He *said to them, "Come away by yourselves to a secluded place and rest a while." (For there were many *people* coming and going, and they did not even have time to eat.)

32 They went away in the boat to a secluded place by themselves.

33 *The people* saw them going, and many recognized *them* and ran there together on foot from all the cities, and got there ahead of them.

34 When Jesus went ashore, He saw a large crowd, and He felt compassion for them because they were like sheep without a shepherd; and He began to teach them many things.

35 When it was already quite late, His disciples came to Him and said, "This place is desolate and it is already quite late;

36 send them away so that they may go into the surrounding countryside and villages and buy themselves something to eat."

37 But He answered them, "You give them *something* to eat!" And they *said to Him, "Shall we go and spend two hundred ¹denarii on bread and give them *something* to eat?"

38 And He *said to them, "How many loaves do you have? Go look!" And when they found out, they *said, "Five, and two fish."

39 And He commanded them all to sit down by groups on the green grass.

40 They sat down in groups of hundreds and of fifties.

41 And He took the five loaves and the two fish, and looking up toward heaven, He blessed *the food* and broke the loaves and He kept giving *them* to the disciples to set before them; and He divided up the two fish among them all.

42 They all ate and were satisfied,

43 and they picked up twelve full baskets of the broken pieces, and also of the fish.

44 There were five thousand men who ate the loaves.

---

1. The denarius was equivalent to one day's wage

45 Immediately Jesus made His disciples get into the boat and go ahead of *Him* to the other side to Bethsaida, while He Himself was sending the crowd away.

46 After bidding them farewell, He left for the mountain to pray.

47 When it was evening, the boat was in the middle of the sea, and He was alone on the land.

48 Seeing them straining at the oars, for the wind was against them, at about the fourth watch of the night He *came to them, walking on the sea; and He intended to pass by them.

49 But when they saw Him walking on the sea, they supposed that it was a ghost, and cried out;

50 for they all saw Him and were terrified. But immediately He spoke with them and *said to them, "Take courage; it is I, do not be afraid."

51 Then He got into the boat with them, and the wind stopped; and they were utterly astonished,

52 for they had not gained any insight from the *incident of* the loaves, but their heart was hardened.

53 When they had crossed over they came to land at Gennesaret, and moored to the shore.

54 When they got out of the boat, immediately *the people* recognized Him,

55 and ran about that whole country and began to carry here and there on their pallets those who were sick, to the place they heard He was.

56 Wherever He entered villages, or cities, or countryside, they were laying the sick in the market places, and imploring Him that they might just touch the fringe of His cloak; and as many as touched it were being cured.

Followers of Tradition

7 The Pharisees and some of the scribes gathered around Him when they had come from Jerusalem,

2 and had seen that some of His disciples were eating their bread with impure hands, that is, unwashed.

3 (For the Pharisees and all the Jews do not eat unless they carefully wash their hands, *thus* observing the traditions of the elders;

4 and *when they come* from the market place, they do not eat unless they cleanse themselves; and there are many other things which they have received in order to observe, such as the washing of cups and pitchers and copper pots.)

5 The Pharisees and the scribes *asked Him, "Why do Your disciples not walk according to the tradition of the elders, but eat their bread with impure hands?"

6 And He said to them, "Rightly did Isaiah prophesy of you hypocrites, as it is written:

'THIS PEOPLE HONORS ME WITH THEIR LIPS,
    BUT THEIR HEART IS FAR AWAY FROM ME.

7 'BUT IN VAIN DO THEY WORSHIP ME,

TEACHING AS DOCTRINES THE PRECEPTS OF MEN.'

8 "Neglecting the commandment of God, you hold to the tradition of men."

9 He was also saying to them, "You are experts at setting aside the commandment of God in order to keep your tradition.

10 "For Moses said, 'HONOR YOUR FATHER AND YOUR MOTHER'; and, 'HE WHO SPEAKS EVIL OF FATHER OR MOTHER, IS TO BE PUT TO DEATH';

11 but you say, 'If a man says to *his* father or *his* mother, whatever I have that would help you is Corban (that is to say, ¹given *to God*),'

12 you no longer permit him to do anything for *his* father or *his* mother;

13 *thus* invalidating the word of God by your tradition which you have handed down; and you do many things such as that."

14 After He called the crowd to Him again, He *began* saying to them, "Listen to Me, all of you, and understand:

15 there is nothing outside the man which can defile him if it goes into him; but the things which proceed out of the man are what defile the man.

16 ["²If anyone has ears to hear, let him hear."]

17 When he had left the crowd *and* entered the house, His disciples questioned Him about the parable.

18 And He *said to them, "Are you so lacking in understanding also? Do you not understand that whatever goes into the man from outside cannot defile him,

19 because it does not go into his heart, but into his stomach, and is eliminated?" (*Thus He* declared all foods clean.)

20 And He was saying, "That which proceeds out of the man, that is what defiles the man.

21 "For from within, out of the heart of men, proceed the evil thoughts, fornications, thefts, murders, adulteries,

22 deeds of coveting *and* wickedness, *as well as* deceit, sensuality, envy, slander, pride *and* foolishness.

23 "All these evil things proceed from within and defile the man."

24 Jesus got up and went away from there to the region of Tyre³. And when He had entered a house, He wanted no one to know *of it;* yet He could not escape notice.

25 But after hearing of Him, a woman whose little daughter had an unclean spirit immediately came and fell at His feet.

26 Now the woman was a ⁴Gentile, of the Syrophoenician race. And she kept asking Him to cast the demon out of her daughter.

27 And He was saying to her, "Let the children be satisfied first, for it is not good to take the children's bread and throw it to the dogs."

28 But she answered and *said to Him, "Yes, Lord, *but* even the dogs under the table feed on the children's crumbs."

29 And He said to her, "Because of this answer go; the demon has gone out of your daughter."

30 And going back to her home, she found the child lying on the bed, the demon having left.

31 Again He went out from the region of Tyre, and came through Sidon to the Sea of Galilee, within the region of Decapolis.

32 They *brought to Him one who was deaf and spoke with difficulty, and they *implored Him to lay His hand on him.

33 Jesus took him aside from the crowd, by himself, and put His fingers into his ears, and after spitting, He touched his tongue *with the saliva;*

34 and looking up to heaven with a deep sigh, He *said to him, "Ephphatha!" that is, "Be opened!"

35 And his ears were opened, and the impediment of his tongue was removed, and he *began* speaking plainly.

36 And He gave them orders not to tell anyone; but the more He ordered them, the more widely they continued to proclaim it.

37 They were utterly astonished, saying, "He has done all things well; He makes even the deaf to hear and the mute to speak."

Four Thousand Fed

8 In those days, when there was again a large crowd and they had nothing to eat, Jesus called His disciples and *said to them,

2 "I feel compassion for the people because they have remained with Me now three days and have nothing to eat.

3 "If I send them away hungry to their homes, they will faint on the way; and some of them have come from a great distance."

4 And His disciples answered Him, "Where will anyone be able *to find enough* bread here in *this* desolate place to satisfy these people?"

5 And He was asking them, "How many loaves do you have?" And they said, "Seven."

6 And He *directed the people to sit down on the ground; and taking the seven loaves, He gave thanks and broke them, and started giving them to His disciples to serve to them, and they served them to the people.

7 They also had a few small fish; and after He had blessed them, He ordered these to be served as well.

8 And they ate and were satisfied; and they picked up seven large baskets full of what was left over of the broken pieces.

9 About four thousand were *there;* and He sent them away.

10 And immediately He entered the boat with His disciples and came to the district of Dalmanutha.

11 The Pharisees came out and began to argue with Him, seeking from Him a sign from heaven, to test Him.

12 Sighing deeply in His spirit, He *said, "Why does this generation seek for a sign? Truly I say to you, no sign will be given to this generation."

---

1. Or *a gift*, i.e. *an offering*   2. Early mss do not contain this verse   3. Two early mss add *and Sidon*   4. Lit *Greek*

13 Leaving them, He again embarked and went away to the other side.

14 And they had forgotten to take bread, and did not have more than one loaf in the boat with them.

15 And He was giving orders to them, saying, "Watch out! Beware of the leaven of the Pharisees and the leaven of Herod."

16 They *began* to discuss with one another *the fact* that they had no bread.

17 And Jesus, aware of this, *said to them, "Why do you discuss *the fact* that you have no bread? Do you not yet see or understand? Do you have a hardened heart?

18 "HAVING EYES, DO YOU NOT SEE? AND HAVING EARS, DO YOU NOT HEAR? And do you not remember,

19 when I broke the five loaves for the five thousand, how many baskets full of broken pieces you picked up?" They *said to Him, "Twelve."

20 "When *I* broke the seven for the four thousand, how many large baskets full of broken pieces did you pick up?" And they *said to Him, "Seven."

21 And He was saying to them, "Do you not yet understand?"

22 And they *came to Bethsaida. And they *brought a blind man to Jesus and *implored Him to touch him.

23 Taking the blind man by the hand, He brought him out of the village; and after spitting on his eyes and laying His hands on him, He asked him, "Do you see anything?"

24 And he looked up and said, "I see men, for I see *them* like trees, walking around."

25 Then again He laid His hands on his eyes; and he looked intently and was restored, and *began* to see everything clearly.

26 And He sent him to his home, saying, "Do not even enter the village."

27 Jesus went out, along with His disciples, to the villages of Caesarea Philippi; and on the way He questioned His disciples, saying to them, "Who do people say that I am?"

28 They told Him, saying, "John the Baptist; and others *say* Elijah; but others, one of the prophets."

29 And He *continued* by questioning them, "But who do you say that I am?" Peter *answered and *said to Him, "You are the Christ."

30 And He warned them to tell no one about Him.

31 And He began to teach them that the Son of Man must suffer many things and be rejected by the elders and the chief priests and the scribes, and be killed, and after three days rise again.

32 And He was stating the matter plainly. And Peter took Him aside and began to rebuke Him.

33 But turning around and seeing His disciples, He rebuked Peter and *said, "Get behind Me, Satan; for you are not setting your mind on ¹God's interests, but man's."

34 And He summoned the crowd with His disciples, and said to them, "If anyone wishes to come after Me, he must deny himself, and take up his cross and follow Me.

35 "For whoever wishes to save his life will lose it, but whoever loses his life for My sake and the gospel's will save it.

36 "For what does it profit a man to gain the whole world, and forfeit his soul?

37 "For what will a man give in exchange for his soul?

38 "For whoever is ashamed of Me and My words in this adulterous and sinful generation, the Son of Man will also be ashamed of him when He comes in the glory of His Father with the holy angels."

The Transfiguration

9 And Jesus was saying to them, "Truly I say to you, there are some of those who are standing here who will not taste death until they see the kingdom of God after it has come with power."

2 Six days later, Jesus *took with Him Peter and James and John, and *brought them up on a high mountain by themselves. And He was transfigured before them;

3 and His garments became radiant and exceedingly white, as no launderer on earth can whiten them.

4 Elijah appeared to them along with Moses; and they were talking with Jesus.

5 Peter *said to Jesus, "Rabbi, it is good for us to be here; let us make three tabernacles, one for You, and one for Moses, and one for Elijah."

6 For he did not know what to answer; for they became terrified.

7 Then a cloud formed, overshadowing them, and a voice came out of the cloud, "This is My beloved Son, listen to Him!"

8 All at once they looked around and saw no one with them anymore, except Jesus alone.

9 As they were coming down from the mountain, He gave them orders not to relate to anyone what they had seen, until the Son of Man rose from the dead.

10 They seized upon that statement, discussing with one another what rising from the dead meant.

11 They asked Him, saying, "*Why is it* that the scribes say that Elijah must come first?"

12 And He said to them, "Elijah does first come and restore all things. And *yet* how is it written of the Son of Man that He will suffer many things and be treated with contempt?

13 "But I say to you that Elijah has indeed come, and they did to him whatever they wished, just as it is written of him."

14 When they came *back* to the disciples, they saw a large crowd around them, and *some* scribes arguing with them.

15 Immediately, when the entire crowd saw Him, they were amazed and *began* running up to greet Him.

16 And He asked them, "What are you discussing with them?"

---

1. Lit *the things of God*

17 And one of the crowd answered Him, "Teacher, I brought You my son, possessed with a spirit which makes him mute;

18 and whenever it seizes him, it slams him *to the ground* and he foams *at the mouth,* and grinds his teeth and stiffens out. I told Your disciples to cast it out, and they could not *do it.*"

19 And He *answered them and *said, "O unbelieving generation, how long shall I be with you? How long shall I put up with you? Bring him to Me!"

20 They brought the boy to Him. When he saw Him, immediately the spirit threw him into a convulsion, and falling to the ground, he *began* rolling around and foaming *at the mouth.*

21 And He asked his father, "How long has this been happening to him?" And he said, "From childhood.

22 "It has often thrown him both into the fire and into the water to destroy him. But if You can do anything, take pity on us and help us!"

23 And Jesus said to him, " 'If You can?' All things are possible to him who believes."

24 Immediately the boy's father cried out and said, "I do believe; help my unbelief."

25 When Jesus saw that a crowd was rapidly gathering, He rebuked the unclean spirit, saying to it, "You deaf and mute spirit, I command you, come out of him and do not enter him again."

26 After crying out and throwing him into terrible convulsions, it came out; and *the boy* became so much like a corpse that most *of them* said, "He is dead!"

27 But Jesus took him by the hand and raised him; and he got up.

28 When He came into *the* house, His disciples *began* questioning Him privately, "Why could we not drive it out?"

29 And He said to them, "This kind cannot come out by anything but prayer."

30 From there they went out and *began* to go through Galilee, and He did not want anyone to know *about it.*

31 For He was teaching His disciples and telling them, "The Son of Man is to be [1]delivered into the hands of men, and they will kill Him; and when He has been killed, He will rise three days later."

32 But they did not understand *this* statement, and they were afraid to ask Him.

33 They came to Capernaum; and when He was in the house, He *began* to question them, "What were you discussing on the way?"

34 But they kept silent, for on the way they had discussed with one another which *of them* was the greatest.

35 Sitting down, He called the twelve and *said to them, "If anyone wants to be first, he shall be last of all and servant of all."

36 Taking a child, He set him before them, and taking him in His arms, He said to them,

37 "Whoever receives one child like this in My name receives Me; and whoever receives Me does not receive Me, but Him who sent Me."

38 John said to Him, "Teacher, we saw someone casting out demons in Your name, and we tried to prevent him because he was not following us."

39 But Jesus said, "Do not hinder him, for there is no one who will perform a miracle in My name, and be able soon afterward to speak evil of Me.

40 "For he who is not against us is [2]for us.

41 "For whoever gives you a cup of water to drink because of your name as *followers* of Christ, truly I say to you, he will not lose his reward.

42 "Whoever causes one of these little ones who believe to stumble, it would be better for him if, with a heavy millstone hung around his neck, he had been cast into the sea.

43 "If your hand causes you to stumble, cut it off; it is better for you to enter life crippled, than, having your two hands, to go into hell, into the unquenchable fire,

44 [[3]where THEIR WORM DOES NOT DIE, AND THE FIRE IS NOT QUENCHED.]

45 "If your foot causes you to stumble, cut it off; it is better for you to enter life lame, than, having your two feet, to be cast into hell,

46 [[4]where THEIR WORM DOES NOT DIE, AND THE FIRE IS NOT QUENCHED.]

47 "If your eye causes you to stumble, throw it out; it is better for you to enter the kingdom of God with one eye, than, having two eyes, to be cast into hell,

48 where THEIR WORM DOES NOT DIE, AND THE FIRE IS NOT QUENCHED.

49 "For everyone will be salted with fire.

50 "Salt is good; but if the salt becomes unsalty, with what will you make it salty *again?* Have salt in yourselves, and be at peace with one another."

Jesus' Teaching about Divorce

10 Getting up, He *went from there to the region of Judea and beyond the Jordan; crowds *gathered around Him again, and, according to His custom, He once more *began* to teach them.

2 *Some* Pharisees came up to Jesus, testing Him, and *began* to question Him whether it was lawful for a man to divorce a wife.

3 And He answered and said to them, "What did Moses command you?"

4 They said, "Moses permitted *a man* TO WRITE A CERTIFICATE OF DIVORCE AND SEND *her* AWAY."

5 But Jesus said to them, "Because of your hardness of heart he wrote you this commandment.

6 "But from the beginning of creation, *God* MADE THEM MALE AND FEMALE.

7 "FOR THIS REASON A MAN SHALL LEAVE HIS FATHER AND MOTHER,[5]

8 AND THE TWO SHALL BECOME ONE FLESH; so they are no longer two, but one flesh.

---

1. Or *betrayed*   2. Or *on our side*   3. Vv 44 and 46, which are identical to v 48, are not found in the early mss   4. See v 44 note   5. Many late mss add *and shall cling to his wife*

9 "What therefore God has joined together, let no man separate."

10 In the house the disciples *began* questioning Him about this again.

11 And He *said to them, "Whoever divorces his wife and marries another woman commits adultery against her;

12 and if she herself divorces her husband and marries another man, she is committing adultery."

13 And they were bringing children to Him so that He might touch them; but the disciples rebuked them.

14 But when Jesus saw this, He was indignant and said to them, "Permit the children to come to Me; do not hinder them; for the kingdom of God belongs to such as these.

15 "Truly I say to you, whoever does not receive the kingdom of God like a child will not enter it *at all.*"

16 And He took them in His arms and *began* blessing them, laying His hands on them.

17 As He was setting out on a journey, a man ran up to Him and knelt before Him, and asked Him, "Good Teacher, what shall I do to inherit eternal life?"

18 And Jesus said to him, "Why do you call Me good? No one is good except God alone.

19 "You know the commandments, 'DO NOT MURDER, DO NOT COMMIT ADULTERY, DO NOT STEAL, DO NOT BEAR FALSE WITNESS, Do not defraud, HONOR YOUR FATHER AND MOTHER.' "

20 And he said to Him, "Teacher, I have kept all these things from my youth up."

21 Looking at him, Jesus felt a love for him and said to him, "One thing you lack: go and sell all you possess and give to the poor, and you will have treasure in heaven; and come, follow Me."

22 But at these words he was saddened, and he went away grieving, for he was one who owned much property.

23 And Jesus, looking around, *said to His disciples, "How hard it will be for those who are wealthy to enter the kingdom of God!"

24 The disciples were amazed at His words. But Jesus *answered again and *said to them, "Children, how hard it is to enter the kingdom of God!

25 "It is easier for a camel to go through the eye of a needle than for a rich man to enter the kingdom of God."

26 They were even more astonished and said to Him, "Then who can be saved?"

27 Looking at them, Jesus *said, "With people it is impossible, but not with God; for all things are possible with God."

28 Peter began to say to Him, "Behold, we have left everything and followed You."

29 Jesus said, "Truly I say to you, there is no one who has left house or brothers or sisters or mother or father or children or farms, for My sake and for the gospel's sake,

30 but that he will receive a hundred times as much now in the present age, houses and brothers and sisters and mothers and children and farms, along with persecutions; and in the age to come, eternal life.

31 "But many *who are* first will be last, and the last, first."

32 They were on the road going up to Jerusalem, and Jesus was walking on ahead of them; and they were amazed, and those who followed were fearful. And again He took the twelve aside and began to tell them what was going to happen to Him,

33 saying, "Behold, we are going up to Jerusalem, and the Son of Man will be ¹delivered to the chief priests and the scribes; and they will condemn Him to death and will hand Him over to the Gentiles.

34 "They will mock Him and spit on Him, and scourge Him and kill *Him,* and three days later He will rise again."

35 James and John, the two sons of Zebedee, *came up to Jesus, saying, "Teacher, we want You to do for us whatever we ask of You."

36 And He said to them, "What do you want Me to do for you?"

37 They said to Him, "Grant that we may sit, one on Your right and one on *Your* left, in Your glory."

38 But Jesus said to them, "You do not know what you are asking. Are you able to drink the cup that I drink, or to be baptized with the baptism with which I am baptized?"

39 They said to Him, "We are able." And Jesus said to them, "The cup that I drink you shall drink; and you shall be baptized with the baptism with which I am baptized.

40 "But to sit on My right or on *My* left, this is not Mine to give; but it is for those for whom it has been prepared."

41 Hearing *this,* the ten began to feel indignant with James and John.

42 Calling them to Himself, Jesus *said to them, "You know that those who are recognized as rulers of the Gentiles lord it over them; and their great men exercise authority over them.

43 "But it is not this way among you, but whoever wishes to become great among you shall be your servant;

44 and whoever wishes to be first among you shall be slave of all.

45 "For even the Son of Man did not come to be served, but to serve, and to give His life a ransom for many."

46 Then they *came to Jericho. And as He was leaving Jericho with His disciples and a large crowd, a blind beggar *named* Bartimaeus, the son of Timaeus, was sitting by the road.

47 When he heard that it was Jesus the Nazarene, he began to cry out and say, "Jesus, Son of David, have mercy on me!"

48 Many were sternly telling him to be quiet, but he kept crying out all the more, "Son of David, have mercy on me!"

49 And Jesus stopped and said, "Call him *here.*" So they *called the blind man, saying to

---

1. Or *betrayed*

him, "Take courage, stand up! He is calling for you."

50 Throwing aside his cloak, he jumped up and came to Jesus.

51 And answering him, Jesus said, "What do you want Me to do for you?" And the blind man said to Him, "¹Rabboni, I want to regain my sight!"

52 And Jesus said to him, "Go; your faith has made you well." Immediately he regained his sight and began following Him on the road.

The Triumphal Entry

11 As they *approached Jerusalem, at Bethphage and Bethany, near the Mount of Olives, He *sent two of His disciples,

2 and *said to them, "Go into the village opposite you, and immediately as you enter it, you will find a colt tied there, on which no one yet has ever sat; untie it and bring it here.

3 "If anyone says to you, 'Why are you doing this?' you say, 'The Lord has need of it'; and immediately he will send it back here."

4 They went away and found a colt tied at the door, outside in the street; and they *untied it.

5 Some of the bystanders were saying to them, "What are you doing, untying the colt?"

6 They spoke to them just as Jesus had told them, and they gave them permission.

7 They *brought the colt to Jesus and put their coats on it; and He sat on it.

8 And many spread their coats in the road, and others spread leafy branches which they had cut from the fields.

9 Those who went in front and those who followed were shouting:
"Hosanna!
BLESSED IS HE WHO COMES IN THE NAME OF THE LORD;

10 Blessed is the coming kingdom of our father David;
Hosanna in the highest!"

11 Jesus entered Jerusalem and came into the temple; and after looking around at everything, He left for Bethany with the twelve, since it was already late.

12 On the next day, when they had left Bethany, He became hungry.

13 Seeing at a distance a fig tree in leaf, He went to see if perhaps He would find anything on it; and when He came to it, He found nothing but leaves, for it was not the season for figs.

14 He said to it, "May no one ever eat fruit from you again!" And His disciples were listening.

15 Then they *came to Jerusalem. And He entered the temple and began to drive out those who were buying and selling in the temple, and overturned the tables of the money changers and the seats of those who were selling doves;

16 and He would not permit anyone to carry merchandise through the temple.

17 And He began to teach and say to them, "Is it not written, 'MY HOUSE SHALL BE CALLED A HOUSE OF PRAYER FOR ALL THE NATIONS'? But you have made it a ROBBERS' DEN."

18 The chief priests and the scribes heard this, and began seeking how to destroy Him; for they were afraid of Him, for the whole crowd was astonished at His teaching.

19 When evening came, they would go out of the city.

20 As they were passing by in the morning, they saw the fig tree withered from the roots up.

21 Being reminded, Peter *said to Him, "Rabbi, look, the fig tree which You cursed has withered."

22 And Jesus *answered saying to them, "Have faith in God.

23 "Truly I say to you, whoever says to this mountain, 'Be taken up and cast into the sea,' and does not doubt in his heart, but believes that what he says is going to happen, it will be granted him.

24 "Therefore I say to you, all things for which you pray and ask, believe that you have received them, and they will be granted you.

25 "Whenever you stand praying, forgive, if you have anything against anyone, so that your Father who is in heaven will also forgive you your transgressions.

26 ["²But if you do not forgive, neither will your Father who is in heaven forgive your transgressions."]

27 They *came again to Jerusalem. And as He was walking in the temple, the chief priests and the scribes and the elders *came to Him,

28 and began saying to Him, "By what authority are You doing these things, or who gave You this authority to do these things?"

29 And Jesus said to them, "I will ask you one question, and you answer Me, and then I will tell you by what authority I do these things.

30 "Was the baptism of John from heaven, or from men? Answer Me."

31 They began reasoning among themselves, saying, "If we say, 'From heaven,' He will say, 'Then why did you not believe him?'

32 "But shall we say, 'From men'?"—they were afraid of the people, for everyone considered John to have been a real prophet.

33 Answering Jesus, they *said, "We do not know." And Jesus *said to them, "Nor will I tell you by what authority I do these things."

Parable of the Vine-growers

12 And He began to speak to them in parables: "A man PLANTED A VINEYARD AND PUT A WALL AROUND IT, AND DUG A VAT UNDER THE WINE PRESS AND BUILT A TOWER, and rented it out to ³vine-growers and went on a journey.

2 "At the harvest time he sent a slave to the vine-growers, in order to receive some of the produce of the vineyard from the vine-growers.

3 "They took him, and beat him and sent him away empty-handed.

4 "Again he sent them another slave, and they wounded him in the head, and treated him shamefully.

---

1. I.e. My Master 2. Early mss do not contain this v 3. Or tenant farmers, also vv 2, 7, 9

5 "And he sent another, and that one they killed; and *so with* many others, beating some and killing others.

6 "He had one more *to send,* a beloved son; he sent him last *of all* to them, saying, 'They will respect my son.'

7 "But those vine-growers said to one another, 'This is the heir; come, let us kill him, and the inheritance will be ours!'

8 "They took him, and killed him and threw him out of the vineyard.

9 "What will the owner of the vineyard do? He will come and destroy the vine-growers, and will give the vineyard to others.

10 "Have you not even read this Scripture:

'THE STONE WHICH THE BUILDERS REJECTED, THIS BECAME THE CHIEF CORNER *stone;*

11 THIS CAME ABOUT FROM THE LORD, AND IT IS MARVELOUS IN OUR EYES'?"

12 And they were seeking to seize Him, and *yet* they feared the people, for they understood that He spoke the parable against them. And *so* they left Him and went away.

13 Then they *sent some of the Pharisees and Herodians to Him in order to trap Him in a statement.

14 They *came and *said to Him, "Teacher, we know that You are truthful and defer to no one; for You are not partial to any, but teach the way of God in truth. Is it lawful to pay a poll-tax to Caesar, or not?

15 "Shall we pay or shall we not pay?" But He, knowing their hypocrisy, said to them, "Why are you testing Me? Bring Me a ¹denarius to look at."

16 They brought *one.* And He *said to them, "Whose likeness and inscription is this?" And they said to Him, "Caesar's."

17 And Jesus said to them, "Render to Caesar the things that are Caesar's, and to God the things that are God's." And they were amazed at Him.

18 *Some* Sadducees (who say that there is no resurrection) *came to Jesus, and *began* questioning Him, saying,

19 "Teacher, Moses wrote for us that IF A MAN'S BROTHER DIES and leaves behind a wife AND LEAVES NO CHILD, HIS BROTHER SHOULD MARRY THE WIFE AND RAISE UP CHILDREN TO HIS BROTHER.

20 "There were seven brothers; and the first took a wife, and died leaving no children.

21 "The second one married her, and died leaving behind no children; and the third likewise;

22 and *so* all seven left no children. Last of all the woman died also.

23 "In the resurrection, ²when they rise again, which one's wife will she be? For all seven had married her."

24 Jesus said to them, "Is this not the reason you are mistaken, that you do not understand the Scriptures or the power of God?

25 "For when they rise from the dead, they neither marry nor are given in marriage, but are like angels in heaven.

26 "But regarding the fact that the dead rise again, have you not read in the book of Moses, in the *passage* about *the burning* bush, how God spoke to him, saying, 'I AM THE GOD OF ABRAHAM, AND THE GOD OF ISAAC, and the God of Jacob'?

27 "He is not the God of the dead, but of the living; you are greatly mistaken."

28 One of the scribes came and heard them arguing, and recognizing that He had answered them well, asked Him, "What commandment is the foremost of all?"

29 Jesus answered, "The foremost is, 'HEAR, O ISRAEL! THE LORD OUR GOD IS ONE LORD;

30 AND YOU SHALL LOVE THE LORD YOUR GOD WITH ALL YOUR HEART, AND WITH ALL YOUR SOUL, AND WITH ALL YOUR MIND, AND WITH ALL YOUR STRENGTH.'

31 "The second is this, 'YOU SHALL LOVE YOUR NEIGHBOR AS YOURSELF.' There is no other commandment greater than these."

32 The scribe said to Him, "Right, Teacher; You have truly stated that HE IS ONE, AND THERE IS NO ONE ELSE BESIDES HIM;

33 AND TO LOVE HIM WITH ALL THE HEART AND WITH ALL THE UNDERSTANDING AND WITH ALL THE STRENGTH, AND TO LOVE ONE'S NEIGHBOR AS HIMSELF, is much more than all burnt offerings and sacrifices."

34 When Jesus saw that he had answered intelligently, He said to him, "You are not far from the kingdom of God." After that, no one would venture to ask Him any more questions.

35 And Jesus *began* to say, as He taught in the temple, "How *is it that* the scribes say that the Christ is the son of David?

36 "David himself said in the Holy Spirit,

'THE LORD SAID TO MY LORD,

"SIT AT MY RIGHT HAND,

UNTIL I PUT YOUR ENEMIES BENEATH YOUR FEET." '

37 "David himself calls Him 'Lord'; so in what sense is He his son?" And the large crowd enjoyed listening to Him.

38 In His teaching He was saying: "Beware of the scribes who like to walk around in long robes, and *like* respectful greetings in the market places,

39 and chief seats in the synagogues and places of honor at banquets,

40 who devour widows' houses, and for appearance's sake offer long prayers; these will receive greater condemnation."

41 And He sat down opposite the treasury, and *began* observing how the people were putting money into the treasury; and many rich people were putting in large sums.

42 A poor widow came and put in two small copper coins, which amount to a cent.

43 Calling His disciples to Him, He said to them, "Truly I say to you, this poor widow put in more than all the contributors to the treasury;

---

1. The denarius was a day's wages 2. Early mss do not contain *when they rise again*

44 for they all put in out of their surplus, but she, out of her poverty, put in all she owned, all she had to live on."

Things to Come

13 As He was going out of the temple, one of His disciples *said to Him, "Teacher, behold ¹what wonderful stones and what wonderful buildings!"

2 And Jesus said to him, "Do you see these great buildings? Not one stone will be left upon another which will not be torn down."

3 As He was sitting on the Mount of Olives opposite the temple, Peter and James and John and Andrew were questioning Him privately,

4 "Tell us, when will these things be, and what *will be* the sign when all these things are going to be fulfilled?"

5 And Jesus began to say to them, "See to it that no one misleads you.

6 "Many will come in My name, saying, 'I am *He!'* and will mislead many.

7 "When you hear of wars and rumors of wars, do not be frightened; *those things* must take place; but *that is* not yet the end.

8 "For nation will rise up against nation, and kingdom against kingdom; there will be earthquakes in various places; there will *also* be famines. These things are *merely* the beginning of birth pangs.

9 "But be on your guard; for they will deliver you to *the* courts, and you will be flogged in *the* synagogues, and you will stand before governors and kings for My sake, as a testimony to them.

10 "The gospel must first be preached to all the nations.

11 "When they arrest you and hand you over, do not worry beforehand about what you are to say, but say whatever is given you in that hour; for it is not you who speak, but *it is* the Holy Spirit.

12 "Brother will betray brother to death, and a father *his* child; and children will rise up against parents and have them put to death.

13 "You will be hated by all because of My name, but the one who endures to the end, he will be saved.

14 "But when you see the ABOMINATION OF DESOLATION standing where it should not be (let the reader understand), then those who are in Judea must flee to the mountains.

15 "The one who is on the housetop must not go down, or go in to get anything out of his house;

16 and the one who is in the field must not turn back to get his coat.

17 "But woe to those who are pregnant and to those who are nursing babies in those days!

18 "But pray that it may not happen in the winter.

19 "For those days will be a *time of* tribulation such as has not occurred since the beginning of the creation which God created until now, and never will.

20 "Unless the Lord had shortened *those* days,

no life would have been saved; but for the sake of the elect, whom He chose, He shortened the days.

21 "And then if anyone says to you, 'Behold, here is the Christ'; or, 'Behold, *He is* there'; do not believe *him;*

22 for false Christs and false prophets will arise, and will show signs and wonders, in order to lead astray, if possible, the elect.

23 "But take heed; behold, I have told you everything in advance.

24 "But in those days, after that tribulation, THE SUN WILL BE DARKENED AND THE MOON WILL NOT GIVE ITS LIGHT,

25 AND THE STARS WILL BE FALLING from heaven, and the powers that are in the heavens will be shaken.

26 "Then they will see THE SON OF MAN COMING IN CLOUDS with great power and glory.

27 "And then He will send forth the angels, and will gather together His elect from the four winds, from the farthest end of the earth to the farthest end of heaven.

28 "Now learn the parable from the fig tree: when its branch has already become tender and puts forth its leaves, you know that summer is near.

29 "Even so, you too, when you see these things happening, recognize that He is near, *right* at the door.

30 "Truly I say to you, this ²generation will not pass away until all these things take place.

31 "Heaven and earth will pass away, but My words will not pass away.

32 "But of that day or hour no one knows, not even the angels in heaven, nor the Son, but the Father *alone.*

33 "Take heed, keep on the alert; for you do not know when the *appointed* time will come.

34 "*It is* like a man away on a journey, *who* upon leaving his house and putting his slaves in charge, *assigning* to each one his task, also commanded the doorkeeper to stay on the alert.

35 "Therefore, be on the alert—for you do not know when the master of the house is coming, whether in the evening, at midnight, or when the rooster crows, or in the morning—

36 in case he should come suddenly and find you asleep.

37 "What I say to you I say to all, 'Be on the alert!' "

Death Plot and Anointing

14 Now the Passover and Unleavened Bread were two days away; and the chief priests and the scribes were seeking how to seize Him by stealth and kill *Him;*

2 for they were saying, "Not during the festival, otherwise there might be a riot of the people."

3 While He was in Bethany at the home of Simon the leper, and reclining *at the table,* there came a woman with an alabaster vial of very costly perfume of pure nard; *and* she broke the vial and poured it over His head.

4 But some were indignantly *remarking* to

1. Lit *how great* 2. Or *race*

one another, "Why has this perfume been wasted?

5 "For this perfume might have been sold for over three hundred ¹denarii, and *the money* given to the poor." And they were scolding her.

6 But Jesus said, "Let her alone; why do you bother her? She has done a good deed to Me.

7 "For you always have the poor with you, and whenever you wish you can do good to them; but you do not always have Me.

8 "She has done what she could; she has anointed My body beforehand for the burial.

9 "Truly I say to you, wherever the gospel is preached in the whole world, what this woman has done will also be spoken of in memory of her."

10 Then Judas Iscariot, who was one of the twelve, went off to the chief priests in order to betray Him to them.

11 They were glad when they heard *this*, and promised to give him money. And he *began* seeking how to betray Him at an opportune time.

12 On the first day of Unleavened Bread, when the Passover *lamb* was being sacrificed, His disciples *said to Him, "Where do You want us to go and prepare for You to eat the Passover?"

13 And He *sent two of His disciples and *said to them, "Go into the city, and a man will meet you carrying a pitcher of water; follow him;

14 and wherever he enters, say to the owner of the house, 'The Teacher says, "Where is My guest room in which I may eat the Passover with My disciples?"'

15 "And he himself will show you a large upper room furnished *and* ready; prepare for us there."

16 The disciples went out and came to the city, and found *it* just as He had told them; and they prepared the Passover.

17 When it was evening He *came with the twelve.

18 As they were reclining *at the table* and eating, Jesus said, "Truly I say to you that one of you will betray Me—one who is eating with Me."

19 They began to be grieved and to say to Him one by one, "Surely not I?"

20 And He said to them, "*It is* one of the twelve, one who dips with Me in the bowl.

21 "For the Son of Man *is to* go just as it is written of Him; but woe to that man by whom the Son of Man is betrayed! *It would have been* good for that man if he had not been born."

22 While they were eating, He took *some* bread, and after a blessing He broke *it*, and gave *it* to them, and said, "Take *it;* this is My body."

23 And when He had taken a cup *and* given thanks, He gave *it* to them, and they all drank from it.

24 And He said to them, "This is My blood of the covenant, which is poured out for many.

25 "Truly I say to you, I will never again drink of the fruit of the vine until that day when I drink it new in the kingdom of God."

26 After singing a hymn, they went out to the Mount of Olives.

27 And Jesus *said to them, "You will all fall away, because it is written, 'I WILL STRIKE DOWN THE SHEPHERD, AND THE SHEEP SHALL BE SCATTERED.'

28 "But after I have been raised, I will go ahead of you to Galilee."

29 But Peter said to Him, "*Even though* all may fall away, yet I will not."

30 And Jesus *said to him, "Truly I say to you, that this very night, before a rooster crows twice, you yourself will deny Me three times."

31 But *Peter* kept saying insistently, "*Even* if I have to die with You, I will not deny You!" And they all were saying the same thing also.

32 They *came to a place named Gethsemane; and He *said to His disciples, "Sit here until I have prayed."

33 And He *took with Him Peter and James and John, and began to be very distressed and troubled.

34 And He *said to them, "My soul is deeply grieved to the point of death; remain here and keep watch."

35 And He went a little beyond *them*, and fell to the ground and *began* to pray that if it were possible, the hour might pass Him by.

36 And He was saying, "Abba! Father! All things are possible for You; remove this cup from Me; yet not what I will, but what You will."

37 And He *came and *found them sleeping, and *said to Peter, "Simon, are you asleep? Could you not keep watch for one hour?

38 "Keep watching and praying that you may not come into temptation; the spirit is willing, but the flesh is weak."

39 Again He went away and prayed, saying the same words.

40 And again He came and found them sleeping, for their eyes were very heavy; and they did not know what to answer Him.

41 And He *came the third time, and *said to them, "Are you still sleeping and resting? It is enough; the hour has come; behold, the Son of Man is being betrayed into the hands of sinners.

42 "Get up, let us be going; behold, the one who betrays Me is at hand!"

43 Immediately while He was still speaking, Judas, one of the twelve, *came up accompanied by a crowd with swords and clubs, *who were* from the chief priests and the scribes and the elders.

44 Now he who was betraying Him had given them a signal, saying, "Whomever I kiss, He is the one; seize Him and lead Him away under guard."

45 After coming, Judas immediately went to Him, saying, "Rabbi!" and kissed Him.

46 They laid hands on Him and seized Him.

47 But one of those who stood by drew his

---

1. The denarius was equivalent to a day's wages

sword, and struck the slave of the high priest and cut off his ear.

48 And Jesus said to them, "Have you come out with swords and clubs to arrest Me, as *you would* against a robber?

49 "Every day I was with you in the temple teaching, and you did not seize Me; but *this has taken place* to fulfill the Scriptures."

50 And they all left Him and fled.

51 A young man was following Him, wearing *nothing but* a linen sheet over *his* naked *body;* and they *seized him.

52 But he pulled free of the linen sheet and escaped naked.

53 They led Jesus away to the high priest; and all the chief priests and the elders and the scribes *gathered together.

54 Peter had followed Him at a distance, right into the courtyard of the high priest; and he was sitting with the officers and warming himself at the fire.

55 Now the chief priests and the whole ¹Council kept trying to obtain testimony against Jesus to put Him to death, and they were not finding any.

56 For many were giving false testimony against Him, but their testimony was not consistent.

57 Some stood up and *began* to give false testimony against Him, saying,

58 "We heard Him say, 'I will destroy this temple made with hands, and in three days I will build another made without hands.' "

59 Not even in this respect was their testimony consistent.

60 The high priest stood up *and came* forward and questioned Jesus, saying, "Do You not answer? What is it that these men are testifying against You?"

61 But He kept silent and did not answer. Again the high priest was questioning Him, and saying to Him, "Are You the Christ, the Son of the Blessed One?"

62 And Jesus said, "I am; and you shall see THE SON OF MAN SITTING AT THE RIGHT HAND OF POWER, and COMING WITH THE CLOUDS OF HEAVEN."

63 Tearing his clothes, the high priest *said, "What further need do we have of witnesses?

64 "You have heard the blasphemy; how does it seem to you?" And they all condemned Him to be deserving of death.

65 Some began to spit at Him, and to blindfold Him, and to beat Him with their fists, and to say to Him, "Prophesy!" And the officers received Him with slaps *in the face.*

66 As Peter was below in the courtyard, one of the servant-girls of the high priest *came,

67 and seeing Peter warming himself, she looked at him and *said, "You also were with Jesus the Nazarene."

68 But he denied *it,* saying, "I neither know nor understand what you are talking about." And he went out onto the porch.²

69 The servant-girl saw him, and began once more to say to the bystanders, "This is *one* of them!"

70 But again he denied it. And after a little while the bystanders were again saying to Peter, "Surely you are *one* of them, for you are a Galilean too."

71 But he began to curse and swear, "I do not know this man you are talking about!"

72 Immediately a rooster crowed a second time. And Peter remembered how Jesus had made the remark to him, "Before a rooster crows twice, you will deny Me three times." And he began to weep.

Jesus before Pilate

15 Early in the morning the chief priests with the elders and scribes and the whole ¹Council, immediately held a consultation; and binding Jesus, they led Him away and delivered Him to Pilate.

2 Pilate questioned Him, "Are You the King of the Jews?" And He *answered him, "*It is as you say.*"

3 The chief priests *began* to accuse Him harshly.

4 Then Pilate questioned Him again, saying, "Do You not answer? See how many charges they bring against You!"

5 But Jesus made no further answer; so Pilate was amazed.

6 Now at *the* feast he used to release for them *any* one prisoner whom they requested.

7 The man named Barabbas had been imprisoned with the insurrectionists who had committed murder in the insurrection.

8 The crowd went up and began asking him *to do* as he had been accustomed to do for them.

9 Pilate answered them, saying, "Do you want me to release for you the King of the Jews?"

10 For he was aware that the chief priests had handed Him over because of envy.

11 But the chief priests stirred up the crowd *to ask* him to release Barabbas for them instead.

12 Answering again, Pilate said to them, "Then what shall I do with Him whom you call the King of the Jews?"

13 They shouted back, "Crucify Him!"

14 But Pilate said to them, "Why, what evil has He done?" But they shouted all the more, "Crucify Him!"

15 Wishing to satisfy the crowd, Pilate released Barabbas for them, and after having Jesus scourged, he handed Him over to be crucified.

16 The soldiers took Him away into the palace (that is, the Praetorium), and they *called together the whole *Roman* ³cohort.

17 They *dressed Him up in purple, and after twisting a crown of thorns, they put it on Him;

18 and they began to acclaim Him, "Hail, King of the Jews!"

19 They kept beating His head with a ⁴reed, and spitting on Him, and kneeling and bowing before Him.

---

1. Or *Sanhedrin* 2. Later mss add *and a rooster crowed* 3. Or *battalion* 4. Or *staff* (made of a reed)

20 After they had mocked Him, they took the purple robe off Him and put His *own* garments on Him. And they *led Him out to crucify Him.

21 They *pressed into service a passer-by coming from the country, Simon of Cyrene (the father of Alexander and Rufus), to bear His cross.

22 Then they *brought Him to the place Golgotha, which is translated, Place of a Skull.

23 They tried to give Him wine mixed with myrrh; but He did not take it.

24 And they *crucified Him, and *divided up His garments among themselves, casting lots for them *to decide* what each man should take.

25 It was the ¹third hour when they crucified Him.

26 The inscription of the charge against Him read, "THE KING OF THE JEWS."

27 They *crucified two robbers with Him, one on His right and one on His left.

28 [²And the Scripture was fulfilled which says, "And He was numbered with transgressors."]

29 Those passing by were hurling abuse at Him, wagging their heads, and saying, "Ha! You who *are going to* destroy the temple and rebuild it in three days,

30 save Yourself, and come down from the cross!"

31 In the same way the chief priests also, along with the scribes, were mocking *Him* among themselves and saying, "He saved others; He cannot save Himself.

32 "Let *this* Christ, the King of Israel, now come down from the cross, so that we may see and believe!" Those who were crucified with Him were also insulting Him.

33 When the ³sixth hour came, darkness fell over the whole land until the ⁴ninth hour.

34 At the ninth hour Jesus cried out with a loud voice, "ELOI, ELOI, LAMA SABACHTHANI?" which is translated, "MY GOD, MY GOD, WHY HAVE YOU FORSAKEN ME?"

35 When some of the bystanders heard it, they *began* saying, "Behold, He is calling for Elijah."

36 Someone ran and filled a sponge with sour wine, put it on a reed, and gave Him a drink, saying, "Let us see whether Elijah will come to take Him down."

37 And Jesus uttered a loud cry, and breathed His last.

38 And the veil of the temple was torn in two from top to bottom.

39 When the centurion, who was standing right in front of Him, saw the way He breathed His last, he said, "Truly this man was the Son of God!"

40 There were also *some* women looking on from a distance, among whom *were* Mary Magdalene, and Mary the mother of James the Less and Joses, and Salome.

41 When He was in Galilee, they used to follow Him and minister to Him; and *there were* many other women who came up with Him to Jerusalem.

42 When evening had already come, because it was the preparation day, that is, the day before the Sabbath,

43 Joseph of Arimathea came, a prominent member of the Council, who himself was waiting for the kingdom of God; and he gathered up courage and went in before Pilate, and asked for the body of Jesus.

44 Pilate wondered if He was dead by this time, and summoning the centurion, he questioned him as to whether He was already dead.

45 And ascertaining this from the centurion, he granted the body to Joseph.

46 Joseph bought a linen cloth, took Him down, wrapped Him in the linen cloth and laid Him in a tomb which had been hewn out in the rock; and he rolled a stone against the entrance of the tomb.

47 Mary Magdalene and Mary the *mother* of Joses were looking on *to see* where He was laid.

The Resurrection

16 When the Sabbath was over, Mary Magdalene, and Mary the *mother* of James, and Salome, bought spices, so that they might come and anoint Him.

2 Very early on the first day of the week, they *came to the tomb when the sun had risen.

3 They were saying to one another, "Who will roll away the stone for us from the entrance of the tomb?"

4 Looking up, they *saw that the stone had been rolled away, although it was extremely large.

5 Entering the tomb, they saw a young man sitting at the right, wearing a white robe; and they were amazed.

6 And he *said to them, "Do not be amazed; you are looking for Jesus the Nazarene, who has been crucified. He has risen; He is not here; behold, *here is* the place where they laid Him.

7 "But go, tell His disciples and Peter, 'He is going ahead of you to Galilee; there you will see Him, just as He told you.' "

8 They went out and fled from the tomb, for trembling and astonishment had gripped them; and they said nothing to anyone, for they were afraid.

9 [⁵Now after He had risen early on the first day of the week, He first appeared to Mary Magdalene, from whom He had cast out seven demons.

10 She went and reported to those who had been with Him, while they were mourning and weeping.

11 When they heard that He was alive and had been seen by her, they refused to believe it.

12 After that, He appeared in a different form to two of them while they were walking along on their way to the country.

13 They went away and reported it to the others, but they did not believe them either.

14 Afterward He appeared to the eleven themselves as they were reclining *at the table;* and He reproached them for their unbelief and

---

1. I.e. 9 a.m. 2. Early mss do not contain this v 3. I.e. noon 4. I.e. 3 p.m. 5. Later mss add vv 9-20

hardness of heart, because they had not believed those who had seen Him after He had risen.

15 And He said to them, "Go into all the world and preach the gospel to all creation.

16 "He who has believed and has been baptized shall be saved; but he who has disbelieved shall be condemned.

17 "These signs will accompany those who have believed: in My name they will cast out demons, they will speak with new tongues;

18 they will pick up serpents, and if they drink any deadly *poison*, it will not hurt them;

they will lay hands on the sick, and they will recover."

19 So then, when the Lord Jesus had spoken to them, He was received up into heaven and sat down at the right hand of God.

20 And they went out and preached everywhere, while the Lord worked with them, and confirmed the word by the signs that followed.]

[¹*And they promptly reported all these instructions to Peter and his companions. And after that, Jesus Himself sent out through them from east to west the sacred and imperishable proclamation of eternal salvation.*]

THE GOSPEL ACCORDING TO LUKE

Introduction

1 Inasmuch as many have undertaken to compile an account of the things accomplished among us,

2 just as they were handed down to us by those who from the beginning were eyewitnesses and servants of the ²word,

3 it seemed fitting for me as well, having investigated everything carefully from the beginning, to write *it* out for you in consecutive order, most excellent Theophilus;

4 so that you may know the exact truth about the things you have been taught.

5 In the days of Herod, king of Judea, there was a priest named Zacharias, of the division of ³Abijah; and he had a wife ⁴from the daughters of Aaron, and her name was Elizabeth.

6 They were both righteous in the sight of God, walking blamelessly in all the commandments and requirements of the Lord.

7 But they had no child, because Elizabeth was barren, and they were both advanced in years.

8 Now it happened *that* while he was performing his priestly service before God in the *appointed* order of his division,

9 according to the custom of the priestly office, he was chosen by lot to enter the temple of the Lord and burn incense.

10 And the whole multitude of the people were in prayer outside at the hour of the incense offering.

11 And an angel of the Lord appeared to him, standing to the right of the altar of incense.

12 Zacharias was troubled when he saw *the angel*, and fear gripped him.

13 But the angel said to him, "Do not be afraid, Zacharias, for your petition has been heard, and your wife Elizabeth will bear you a son, and you will give him the name John.

14 "You will have joy and gladness, and many will rejoice at his birth.

15 "For he will be great in the sight of the Lord; and he will drink no wine or liquor, and he will be filled with the Holy Spirit while yet in his mother's womb.

16 "And he will turn many of the sons of Israel back to the Lord their God.

17 "It is he who will go *as a forerunner* before Him in the spirit and power of Elijah, TO TURN THE HEARTS OF THE FATHERS BACK TO THE CHILDREN, and the disobedient to the attitude of the righteous, so as to make ready a people prepared for the Lord."

18 Zacharias said to the angel, "How will I know this *for certain*? For I am an old man and my wife is advanced in years."

19 The angel answered and said to him, "I am Gabriel, who stands in the presence of God, and I have been sent to speak to you and to bring you this good news.

20 "And behold, you shall be silent and unable to speak until the day when these things take place, because you did not believe my words, which will be fulfilled in their proper time."

21 The people were waiting for Zacharias, and were wondering at his delay in the temple.

22 But when he came out, he was unable to speak to them; and they realized that he had seen a vision in the temple; and he kept making signs to them, and remained mute.

23 When the days of his priestly service were ended, he went back home.

24 After these days Elizabeth his wife became pregnant, and she kept herself in seclusion for five months, saying,

25 "This is the way the Lord has dealt with me in the days when He looked *with favor* upon *me*, to take away my disgrace among men."

26 Now in the sixth month the angel Gabriel was sent from God to a city in Galilee called Nazareth,

27 to a virgin engaged to a man whose name was Joseph, of the descendants of David; and the virgin's name was Mary.

28 And coming in, he said to her, "Greetings, favored one! The Lord *is* with you."

29 But she was very perplexed at *this* statement, and kept pondering what kind of salutation this was.

30 The angel said to her, "Do not be afraid, Mary; for you have found favor with God.

31 "And behold, you will conceive in your womb and bear a son, and you shall name Him Jesus.

32 "He will be great and will be called the Son

of the Most High; and the Lord God will give Him the throne of His father David;

33 and He will reign over the house of Jacob forever, and His kingdom will have no end."

34 Mary said to the angel, "How can this be, since I am a virgin?"

35 The angel answered and said to her, "The Holy Spirit will come upon you, and the power of the Most High will overshadow you; and for that reason the holy Child shall be called the Son of God.

36 "And behold, even your relative Elizabeth has also conceived a son in her old age; and she who was called barren is now in her sixth month.

37 "For nothing will be impossible with God."

38 And Mary said, "Behold, the ¹bondslave of the Lord; may it be done to me according to your word." And the angel departed from her.

39 Now at this time Mary arose and went in a hurry to the hill country, to a city of Judah,

40 and entered the house of Zacharias and greeted Elizabeth.

41 When Elizabeth heard Mary's greeting, the baby leaped in her womb; and Elizabeth was filled with the Holy Spirit.

42 And she cried out with a loud voice and said, "Blessed *are* you among women, and blessed *is* the fruit of your womb!

43 "And how has it *happened* to me, that the mother of my Lord would come to me?

44 "For behold, when the sound of your greeting reached my ears, the baby leaped in my womb for joy.

45 "And blessed *is* she who believed that there would be a fulfillment of what had been spoken to her by the Lord."

46 And Mary said:
"My soul exalts the Lord,

47 And my spirit has rejoiced in God my Savior.

48 "For He has had regard for the humble state of His bondslave;
For behold, from this time on all generations will count me blessed.

49 "For the Mighty One has done great things for me;
And holy is His name.

50 "AND HIS MERCY IS UPON GENERATION AFTER GENERATION
TOWARD THOSE WHO FEAR HIM.

51 "He has done mighty deeds with His arm;
He has scattered *those who were* proud in the thoughts of their heart.

52 "He has brought down rulers from *their* thrones,
And has exalted those who were humble.

53 "HE HAS FILLED THE HUNGRY WITH GOOD THINGS;
And sent away the rich empty-handed.

54 "He has given help to Israel His servant,
In remembrance of His mercy,

55 As He spoke to our fathers,
To Abraham and his descendants forever."

56 And Mary stayed with her about three months, and *then* returned to her home.

57 Now the time had come for Elizabeth to give birth, and she gave birth to a son.

58 Her neighbors and her relatives heard that the Lord had displayed His great mercy toward her; and they were rejoicing with her.

59 And it happened that on the eighth day they came to circumcise the child, and they were going to call him Zacharias, after his father.

60 But his mother answered and said, "No indeed; but he shall be called John."

61 And they said to her, "There is no one among your relatives who is called by that name."

62 And they made signs to his father, as to what he wanted him called.

63 And he asked for a tablet and wrote as follows, "His name is John." And they were all astonished.

64 And at once his mouth was opened and his tongue *loosed*, and he *began* to speak in praise of God.

65 Fear came on all those living around them; and all these matters were being talked about in all the hill country of Judea.

66 All who heard them kept them in mind, saying, "What then will this child turn out to be?" For the hand of the Lord was certainly with him.

67 And his father Zacharias was filled with the Holy Spirit, and prophesied, saying:

68 "Blessed *be* the Lord God of Israel,
For He has visited us and accomplished redemption for His people,

69 And has raised up a horn of salvation for us
In the house of David His servant—

70 As He spoke by the mouth of His holy prophets from of old—

71 Salvation FROM OUR ENEMIES,
And FROM THE HAND OF ALL WHO HATE US;

72 To show mercy toward our fathers,
And to remember His holy covenant,

73 The oath which He swore to Abraham our father,

74 To grant us that we, being rescued from the hand of our enemies,
Might serve Him without fear,

75 In holiness and righteousness before Him all our days.

76 "And you, child, will be called the prophet of the Most High;
For you will go on BEFORE THE LORD TO PREPARE HIS WAYS;

77 To give to His people *the* knowledge of salvation
By the forgiveness of their sins,

78 Because of the tender mercy of our God,
With which the Sunrise from on high will visit us,

79 TO SHINE UPON THOSE WHO SIT IN DARKNESS AND THE SHADOW OF DEATH,
To guide our feet into the way of peace."

---

1. I.e. female slave

80 And the child continued to grow and to become strong in spirit, and he lived in the deserts until the day of his public appearance to Israel.

Jesus' Birth in Bethlehem

2 Now in those days a decree went out from Caesar Augustus, that a census be taken of all [1]the inhabited earth.

2 This was the first census taken while [2]Quirinius was governor of Syria.

3 And everyone was on his way to register for the census, each to his own city.

4 Joseph also went up from Galilee, from the city of Nazareth, to Judea, to the city of David which is called Bethlehem, because he was of the house and family of David,

5 in order to register along with Mary, who was engaged to him, and was with child.

6 While they were there, the days were completed for her to give birth.

7 And she gave birth to her firstborn son; and she wrapped Him in cloths, and laid Him in a manger, because there was no room for them in the inn.

8 In the same region there were *some* shepherds staying out in the fields and keeping watch over their flock by night.

9 And an angel of the Lord suddenly stood before them, and the glory of the Lord shone around them; and they were terribly frightened.

10 But the angel said to them, "Do not be afraid; for behold, I bring you good news of great joy which will be for all the people;

11 for today in the city of David there has been born for you a Savior, who is [3]Christ the Lord.

12 "This *will be* a sign for you: you will find a baby wrapped in cloths and lying in a manger."

13 And suddenly there appeared with the angel a multitude of the heavenly host praising God and saying,

14 "Glory to God in the highest,
And on earth peace among men [4]with whom He is pleased."

15 When the angels had gone away from them into heaven, the shepherds *began* saying to one another, "Let us go straight to Bethlehem then, and see this thing that has happened which the Lord has made known to us."

16 So they came in a hurry and found their way to Mary and Joseph, and the baby as He lay in the manger.

17 When they had seen this, they made known the statement which had been told them about this Child.

18 And all who heard it wondered at the things which were told them by the shepherds.

19 But Mary treasured all these things, pondering them in her heart.

20 The shepherds went back, glorifying and praising God for all that they had heard and seen, just as had been told them.

21 And when eight days had passed, before His circumcision, His name was *then* called Jesus, the name given by the angel before He was conceived in the womb.

22 And when the days for their purification according to the law of Moses were completed, they brought Him up to Jerusalem to present Him to the Lord

23 (as it is written in the Law of the Lord, "EVERY *firstborn* MALE THAT OPENS THE WOMB SHALL BE CALLED HOLY TO THE LORD"),

24 and to offer a sacrifice according to what was said in the Law of the Lord, "A PAIR OF TURTLEDOVES OR TWO YOUNG PIGEONS."

25 And there was a man in Jerusalem whose name was Simeon; and this man was righteous and devout, looking for the consolation of Israel; and the Holy Spirit was upon him.

26 And it had been revealed to him by the Holy Spirit that he would not see death before he had seen the Lord's Christ.

27 And he came in the Spirit into the temple; and when the parents brought in the child Jesus, to carry out for Him the custom of the Law,

28 then he took Him into his arms, and blessed God, and said,

29 "Now Lord, You are releasing Your bond-servant to depart in peace,
According to Your word;

30 For my eyes have seen Your salvation,

31 Which You have prepared in the presence of all peoples,

32 A LIGHT OF REVELATION TO THE GENTILES,
And the glory of Your people Israel."

33 And His father and mother were amazed at the things which were being said about Him.

34 And Simeon blessed them and said to Mary His mother, "Behold, this *Child* is appointed for the fall and rise of many in Israel, and for a sign to be opposed—

35 and a sword will pierce even your own soul—to the end that thoughts from many hearts may be revealed."

36 And there was a prophetess, Anna the daughter of Phanuel, of the tribe of Asher. She was advanced in years and had lived with *her* husband seven years after her marriage,

37 and then as a widow to the age of eighty-four. She never left the temple, serving night and day with fastings and prayers.

38 At that very moment she came up and *began* giving thanks to God, and continued to speak of Him to all those who were looking for the redemption of Jerusalem.

39 When they had performed everything according to the Law of the Lord, they returned to Galilee, to their own city of Nazareth.

40 The Child continued to grow and become strong, increasing in wisdom; and the grace of God was upon Him.

41 Now His parents went to Jerusalem every year at the Feast of the Passover.

42 And when He became twelve, they went up *there* according to the custom of the Feast;

43 and as they were returning, after spending the full number of days, the boy Jesus stayed

---

1. I.e. the Roman empire 2. Gr *Kyrenios* 3. I.e. Messiah 4. Lit *of good pleasure; or of good will*

behind in Jerusalem. But His parents were unaware of it,

44 but supposed Him to be in the caravan, and went a day's journey; and they *began* looking for Him among their relatives and acquaintances.

45 When they did not find Him, they returned to Jerusalem looking for Him.

46 Then, after three days they found Him in the temple, sitting in the midst of the teachers, both listening to them and asking them questions.

47 And all who heard Him were amazed at His understanding and His answers.

48 When they saw Him, they were astonished; and His mother said to Him, "Son, why have You treated us this way? Behold, Your father and I have been anxiously looking for You."

49 And He said to them, "Why is it that you were looking for Me? Did you not know that I had to be in My Father's *house?*"

50 But they did not understand the statement which He had made to them.

51 And He went down with them and came to Nazareth, and He continued in subjection to them; and His mother treasured all *these* things in her heart.

52 And Jesus kept increasing in wisdom and stature, and in favor with God and men.

John the Baptist Preaches

3 Now in the fifteenth year of the reign of Tiberius Caesar, when Pontius Pilate was governor of Judea, and Herod was tetrarch of Galilee, and his brother Philip was tetrarch of the region of Ituraea and Trachonitis, and Lysanias was tetrarch of Abilene,

2 in the high priesthood of Annas and Caiaphas, the word of God came to John, the son of Zacharias, in the wilderness.

3 And he came into all the district around the Jordan, preaching a baptism of repentance for the forgiveness of sins;

4 as it is written in the book of the words of Isaiah the prophet,

"THE VOICE OF ONE CRYING IN THE WILDERNESS,
'MAKE READY THE WAY OF THE LORD,
MAKE HIS PATHS STRAIGHT.
5 'EVERY RAVINE WILL BE FILLED,
AND EVERY MOUNTAIN AND HILL WILL BE BROUGHT LOW;
THE CROOKED WILL BECOME STRAIGHT,
AND THE ROUGH ROADS SMOOTH;
6 AND ALL FLESH WILL SEE THE SALVATION OF GOD.' "

7 So he *began* saying to the crowds who were going out to be baptized by him, "You brood of vipers, who warned you to flee from the wrath to come?

8 "Therefore bear fruits in keeping with repentance, and do not begin to say to yourselves, 'We have Abraham for our father,' for I say to you that from these stones God is able to raise up children to Abraham.

9 "Indeed the axe is already laid at the root of the trees; so every tree that does not bear good fruit is cut down and thrown into the fire."

10 And the crowds were questioning him, saying, "Then what shall we do?"

11 And he would answer and say to them, "The man who has two tunics is to share with him who has none; and he who has food is to do likewise."

12 And *some* tax collectors also came to be baptized, and they said to him, "Teacher, what shall we do?"

13 And he said to them, "Collect no more than what you have been ordered to."

14 *Some* soldiers were questioning him, saying, "And *what about* us, what shall we do?" And he said to them, "Do not take money from anyone by force, or accuse *anyone* falsely, and be content with your wages."

15 Now while the people were in a state of expectation and all were wondering in their hearts about John, as to whether he was the Christ,

16 John answered and said to them all, "As for me, I baptize you with water; but One is coming who is mightier than I, and I am not fit to untie the thong of His sandals; He will baptize you with the Holy Spirit and fire.

17 "His winnowing fork is in His hand to thoroughly clear His threshing floor, and to gather the wheat into His barn; but He will burn up the chaff with unquenchable fire."

18 So with many other exhortations he preached the gospel to the people.

19 But when Herod the tetrarch was reprimanded by him because of Herodias, his brother's wife, and because of all the wicked things which Herod had done,

20 Herod also added this to them all: he locked John up in prison.

21 Now when all the people were baptized, Jesus was also baptized, and while He was praying, heaven was opened,

22 and the Holy Spirit descended upon Him in bodily form like a dove, and a voice came out of heaven, "You are My beloved Son, in You I am well-pleased."

23 When He began His ministry, Jesus Himself was about thirty years of age, being, as was supposed, the son of Joseph, the son of Eli,

24 the son of Matthat, the son of Levi, the son of Melchi, the son of Jannai, the son of Joseph,

25 the son of Mattathias, the son of Amos, the son of Nahum, the son of Hesli, the son of Naggai,

26 the son of Maath, the son of Mattathias, the son of Semein, the son of Josech, the son of Joda,

27 the son of Joanan, the son of Rhesa, the son of Zerubbabel, the son of Shealtiel, the son of Neri,

28 the son of Melchi, the son of Addi, the son of Cosam, the son of Elmadam, the son of Er,

29 the son of Joshua, the son of Eliezer, the son of Jorim, the son of Matthat, the son of Levi,

30 the son of Simeon, the son of Judah, the

son of Joseph, the son of Jonam, the son of Eliakim,

31 the son of Melea, the son of Menna, the son of Mattatha, the son of Nathan, the son of David,

32 the son of Jesse, the son of Obed, the son of Boaz, the son of Salmon, the son of Nahshon,

33 the son of Amminadab, the son of Admin, the son of Ram, the son of Hezron, the son of Perez, the son of Judah,

34 the son of Jacob, the son of Isaac, the son of Abraham, the son of Terah, the son of Nahor,

35 the son of Serug, the son of Reu, the son of Peleg, the son of Heber, the son of Shelah,

36 the son of Cainan, the son of Arphaxad, the son of Shem, the son of Noah, the son of Lamech,

37 the son of Methuselah, the son of Enoch, the son of Jared, the son of Mahalaleel, the son of Cainan,

38 the son of Enosh, the son of Seth, the son of Adam, the son of God.

The Temptation of Jesus

4 Jesus, full of the Holy Spirit, returned from the Jordan and was led around by the Spirit in the wilderness

2 for forty days, being tempted by the devil. And He ate nothing during those days, and when they had ended, He became hungry.

3 And the devil said to Him, "If You are the Son of God, tell this stone to become bread."

4 And Jesus answered him, "It is written, 'MAN SHALL NOT LIVE ON BREAD ALONE.' "

5 And he led Him up and showed Him all the kingdoms of the world in a moment of time.

6 And the devil said to Him, "I will give You all this domain and its glory; for it has been handed over to me, and I give it to whomever I wish.

7 "Therefore if You worship before me, it shall all be Yours."

8 Jesus answered him, "It is written, 'YOU SHALL WORSHIP THE LORD YOUR GOD AND SERVE HIM ONLY.' "

9 And he led Him to Jerusalem and had Him stand on the pinnacle of the temple, and said to Him, "If You are the Son of God, throw Yourself down from here;

10 for it is written,
'HE WILL COMMAND HIS ANGELS CONCERN-
    ING YOU TO GUARD YOU,'

11 and,
'ON their HANDS THEY WILL BEAR YOU UP,
SO THAT YOU WILL NOT STRIKE YOUR FOOT
    AGAINST A STONE.' "

12 And Jesus answered and said to him, "It is said, 'YOU SHALL NOT PUT THE LORD YOUR GOD TO THE TEST.' "

13 When the devil had finished every temptation, he left Him until an opportune time.

14 And Jesus returned to Galilee in the power of the Spirit, and news about Him spread through all the surrounding district.

15 And He began teaching in their synagogues and was praised by all.

16 And He came to Nazareth, where He had been brought up; and as was His custom, He entered the synagogue on the Sabbath, and stood up to read.

17 And the book of the prophet Isaiah was handed to Him. And He opened the book and found the place where it was written,

18 "THE SPIRIT OF THE LORD IS UPON ME,
    BECAUSE HE ANOINTED ME TO PREACH THE
        GOSPEL TO THE POOR.
    HE HAS SENT ME TO PROCLAIM RELEASE TO
        THE CAPTIVES,
    AND RECOVERY OF SIGHT TO THE BLIND,
    TO SET FREE THOSE WHO ARE OPPRESSED,

19 TO PROCLAIM THE FAVORABLE YEAR OF THE
        LORD."

20 And He closed the book, gave it back to the attendant and sat down; and the eyes of all in the synagogue were fixed on Him.

21 And He began to say to them, "Today this Scripture has been fulfilled in your hearing."

22 And all were speaking well of Him, and wondering at the gracious words which were falling from His lips; and they were saying, "Is this not Joseph's son?"

23 And He said to them, "No doubt you will quote this proverb to Me, 'Physician, heal yourself!' Whatever we heard was done at Capernaum, do here in your hometown as well.' "

24 And He said, "Truly I say to you, no prophet is welcome in his hometown.

25 "But I say to you in truth, there were many widows in Israel in the days of Elijah, when the sky was shut up for three years and six months, when a great famine came over all the land;

26 and yet Elijah was sent to none of them, but only to Zarephath, in the land of Sidon, to a woman who was a widow.

27 "And there were many lepers in Israel in the time of Elisha the prophet; and none of them was cleansed, but only Naaman the Syrian."

28 And all the people in the synagogue were filled with rage as they heard these things;

29 and they got up and drove Him out of the city, and led Him to the brow of the hill on which their city had been built, in order to throw Him down the cliff.

30 But passing through their midst, He went His way.

31 And He came down to Capernaum, a city of Galilee, and He was teaching them on the Sabbath;

32 and they were amazed at His teaching, for His message was with authority.

33 In the synagogue there was a man possessed by the spirit of an unclean demon, and he cried out with a loud voice,

34 "Let us alone! What business do we have with each other, Jesus of Nazareth? Have You come to destroy us? I know who You are—the Holy One of God!"

35 But Jesus rebuked him, saying, "Be quiet and come out of him!" And when the demon had thrown him down in the midst of the

people, he came out of him without doing him any harm.

36 And amazement came upon them all, and they *began* talking with one another saying, "What is this message? For with authority and power He commands the unclean spirits and they come out."

37 And the report about Him was spreading into every locality in the surrounding district.

38 Then He got up and *left* the synagogue, and entered Simon's home. Now Simon's mother-in-law was suffering from a high fever, and they asked Him to help her.

39 And standing over her, He rebuked the fever, and it left her; and she immediately got up and waited on them.

40 While the sun was setting, all those who had any *who were* sick with various diseases brought them to Him; and laying His hands on each one of them, He was healing them.

41 Demons also were coming out of many, shouting, "You are the Son of God!" But rebuking them, He would not allow them to speak, because they knew Him to be the Christ.

42 When day came, Jesus left and went to a secluded place; and the crowds were searching for Him, and came to Him and tried to keep Him from going away from them.

43 But He said to them, "I must preach the kingdom of God to the other cities also, for I was sent for this purpose."

44 So He kept on preaching in the synagogues of ¹Judea.

The First Disciples

5 Now it happened that while the crowd was pressing around Him and listening to the word of God, He was standing by the lake of Gennesaret;

2 and He saw two boats lying at the edge of the lake; but the fishermen had gotten out of them and were washing their nets.

3 And He got into one of the boats, which was Simon's, and asked him to put out a little way from the land. And He sat down and *began* teaching the people from the boat.

4 When He had finished speaking, He said to Simon, "Put out into the deep water and let down your nets for a catch."

5 Simon answered and said, "Master, we worked hard all night and caught nothing, but I will do as You say *and* let down the nets."

6 When they had done this, they enclosed a great quantity of fish, and their nets *began* to break;

7 so they signaled to their partners in the other boat for them to come and help them. And they came and filled both of the boats, so that they began to sink.

8 But when Simon Peter saw *that,* he fell down at Jesus' feet, saying, "Go away from me Lord, for I am a sinful man!"

9 For amazement had seized him and all his companions because of the catch of fish which they had taken;

10 and so also *were* James and John, sons of Zebedee, who were partners with Simon. And Jesus said to Simon, "Do not fear, from now on you will be catching men."

11 When they had brought their boats to land, they left everything and followed Him.

12 While He was in one of the cities, behold, *there was* a man covered with leprosy; and when he saw Jesus, he fell on his face and implored Him, saying, "Lord, if You are willing, You can make me clean."

13 And He stretched out His hand and touched him, saying, "I am willing; be cleansed." And immediately the leprosy left him.

14 And He ordered him to tell no one, "But go and show yourself to the priest and make an offering for your cleansing, just as Moses commanded, as a testimony to them."

15 But the news about Him was spreading even farther, and large crowds were gathering to hear *Him* and to be healed of their sicknesses.

16 But Jesus Himself would *often* slip away to the wilderness and pray.

17 One day He was teaching; and there were *some* Pharisees and teachers of the law sitting *there,* who had come from every village of Galilee and Judea and *from* Jerusalem; and the power of the Lord was *present* for Him to perform healing.

18 And *some* men *were* carrying on a bed a man who was paralyzed; and they were trying to bring him in and to set him down in front of Him.

19 But not finding any *way* to bring him in because of the crowd, they went up on the roof and let him down through the tiles with his stretcher, into the middle *of the crowd,* in front of Jesus.

20 Seeing their faith, He said, "Friend, your sins are forgiven you."

21 The scribes and the Pharisees began to reason, saying, "Who is this *man* who speaks blasphemies? Who can forgive sins, but God alone?"

22 But Jesus, aware of their reasonings, answered and said to them, "Why are you reasoning in your hearts?

23 "Which is easier, to say, 'Your sins have been forgiven you,' or to say, 'Get up and walk'?

24 "But, so that you may know that the Son of Man has authority on earth to forgive sins,"—He said to the paralytic—"I say to you, get up, and pick up your stretcher and go home."

25 Immediately he got up before them, and picked up what he had been lying on, and went home glorifying God.

26 They were all struck with astonishment and *began* glorifying God; and they were filled with fear, saying, "We have seen remarkable things today."

27 After that He went out and noticed a tax collector named Levi sitting in the tax booth, and He said to him, "Follow Me."

I. I.e. the country of the Jews (including Galilee)

28 And he left everything behind, and got up and *began* to follow Him.

29 And Levi gave a big reception for Him in his house; and there was a great crowd of tax collectors and other *people* who were reclining *at the table* with them.

30 The Pharisees and their scribes *began* grumbling at His disciples, saying, "Why do you eat and drink with the tax collectors and sinners?"

31 And Jesus answered and said to them, "*It is* not those who are well who need a physician, but those who are sick.

32 "I have not come to call the righteous but sinners to repentance."

33 And they said to Him, "The disciples of John often fast and offer prayers, the *disciples* of the Pharisees also do the same, but Yours eat and drink."

34 And Jesus said to them, "You cannot make the attendants of the bridegroom fast while the bridegroom is with them, can you?

35 "But *the* days will come; and when the bridegroom is taken away from them, then they will fast in those days."

36 And He was also telling them a parable: "No one tears a piece of cloth from a new garment and puts it on an old garment; otherwise he will both tear the new, and the piece from the new will not match the old.

37 "And no one puts new wine into old wineskins; otherwise the new wine will burst the skins and it will be spilled out, and the skins will be ruined.

38 "But new wine must be put into fresh wineskins.

39 "And no one, after drinking old *wine* wishes for new; for he says, 'The old is good *enough.*'"

Jesus Is Lord of the Sabbath

6 Now it happened that He was passing through *some* grainfields on a Sabbath; and His disciples were picking the heads of grain, rubbing them in their hands, and eating *the grain.*

2 But some of the Pharisees said, "Why do you do what is not lawful on the Sabbath?"

3 And Jesus answering them said, "Have you not even read what David did when he was hungry, he and those who were with him,

4 how he entered the house of God, and took and ate the [1]consecrated bread which is not lawful for any to eat except the priests alone, and gave it to his companions?"

5 And He was saying to them, "The Son of Man is Lord of the Sabbath."

6 On another Sabbath He entered the synagogue and was teaching; and there was a man whose right hand was withered.

7 The scribes and the Pharisees were watching Him closely *to see* if He healed on the Sabbath, so that they might find *reason* to accuse Him.

8 But He knew what they were thinking, and He said to the man with the withered hand,

"Get up and come forward!" And he got up and came forward.

9 And Jesus said to them, "I ask you, is it lawful to do good or to do harm on the Sabbath, to save a life or to destroy it?"

10 After looking around at them all, He said to him, "Stretch out your hand!" And he did *so;* and his hand was restored.

11 But they themselves were filled with rage, and discussed together what they might do to Jesus.

12 It was at this time that He went off to the mountain to pray, and He spent the whole night in prayer to God.

13 And when day came, He called His disciples to Him and chose twelve of them, whom He also named as apostles:

14 Simon, whom He also named Peter, and Andrew his brother; and James and John; and Philip and Bartholomew;

15 and Matthew and Thomas; James *the son* of Alphaeus, and Simon who was called the Zealot;

16 Judas *the son* of James, and Judas Iscariot, who became a traitor.

17 Jesus came down with them and stood on a level place; and *there was* a large crowd of His disciples, and a great throng of people from all Judea and Jerusalem and the coastal region of Tyre and Sidon,

18 who had come to hear Him and to be healed of their diseases; and those who were troubled with unclean spirits were being cured.

19 And all the people were trying to touch Him, for power was coming from Him and healing *them* all.

20 And turning His gaze toward His disciples, He *began* to say, "Blessed *are* you *who are* poor, for yours is the kingdom of God.

21 "Blessed *are* you who hunger now, for you shall be satisfied. Blessed *are* you who weep now, for you shall laugh.

22 "Blessed are you when men hate you, and ostracize you, and insult you, and scorn your name as evil, for the sake of the Son of Man.

23 "Be glad in that day and leap *for joy,* for behold, your reward is great in heaven. For in the same way their fathers used to treat the prophets.

24 "But woe to you who are rich, for you are receiving your comfort in full.

25 "Woe to you who are well-fed now, for you shall be hungry. Woe *to you* who laugh now, for you shall mourn and weep.

26 "Woe *to you* when all men speak well of you, for their fathers used to treat the false prophets in the same way.

27 "But I say to you who hear, love your enemies, do good to those who hate you,

28 bless those who curse you, pray for those who mistreat you.

29 "Whoever hits you on the cheek, offer him the other also; and whoever takes away your coat, do not withhold your shirt from him either.

---

1. Or *showbread;* lit *loaves of presentation*

30 "Give to everyone who asks of you, and whoever takes away what is yours, do not demand it back.

31 "Treat others the same way you want them to treat you.

32 "If you love those who love you, what credit is *that* to you? For even sinners love those who love them.

33 "If you do good to those who do good to you, what credit is *that* to you? For even sinners do the same.

34 "If you lend to those from whom you expect to receive, what credit is *that* to you? Even sinners lend to sinners in order to receive back the same *amount*.

35 "But love your enemies, and do good, and lend, expecting nothing in return; and your reward will be great, and you will be sons of the Most High; for He Himself is kind to ungrateful and evil *men*.

36 "Be merciful, just as your Father is merciful.

37 "Do not judge, and you will not be judged; and do not condemn, and you will not be condemned; pardon, and you will be pardoned.

38 "Give, and it will be given to you. They will pour into your lap a good measure—pressed down, shaken together, *and* running over. For by your standard of measure it will be measured to you in return."

39 And He also spoke a parable to them: "A blind man cannot guide a blind man, can he? Will they not both fall into a pit?

40 "A pupil is not above his teacher; but everyone, after he has been fully trained, will be like his teacher.

41 "Why do you look at the speck that is in your brother's eye, but do not notice the log that is in your own eye?

42 "Or how can you say to your brother, 'Brother, let me take out the speck that is in your eye,' when you yourself do not see the log that is in your own eye? You hypocrite, first take the log out of your own eye, and then you will see clearly to take out the speck that is in your brother's eye.

43 "For there is no good tree which produces bad fruit, nor, on the other hand, a bad tree which produces good fruit.

44 "For each tree is known by its own fruit. For men do not gather figs from thorns, nor do they pick grapes from a briar bush.

45 "The good man out of the good treasure of his heart brings forth what is good; and the evil *man* out of the evil *treasure* brings forth what is evil; for his mouth speaks from that which fills his heart.

46 "Why do you call Me, 'Lord, Lord,' and do not do what I say?

47 "Everyone who comes to Me and hears My words and acts on them, I will show you whom he is like:

48 he is like a man building a house, who dug deep and laid a foundation on the rock; and when a flood occurred, the torrent burst against that house and could not shake it, because it had been well built.

49 "But the one who has heard and has not acted *accordingly*, is like a man who built a house on the ground without any foundation; and the torrent burst against it and immediately it collapsed, and the ruin of that house was great."

Jesus Heals a Centurion's Servant

7 When He had completed all His discourse in the hearing of the people, He went to Capernaum.

2 And a centurion's slave, who was highly regarded by him, was sick and about to die.

3 When he heard about Jesus, he sent some Jewish elders asking Him to come and save the life of his slave.

4 When they came to Jesus, they earnestly implored Him, saying, "He is worthy for You to grant this to him;

5 for he loves our nation and it was he who built us our synagogue."

6 Now Jesus *started* on His way with them; and when He was not far from the house, the centurion sent friends, saying to Him, "Lord, do not trouble Yourself further, for I am not worthy for You to come under my roof;

7 for this reason I did not even consider myself worthy to come to You, but *just* say the word, and my servant will be healed.

8 "For I also am a man placed under authority, with soldiers under me; and I say to this one, 'Go!' and he goes, and to another, 'Come!' and he comes, and to my slave, 'Do this!' and he does it."

9 Now when Jesus heard this, He marveled at him, and turned and said to the crowd that was following Him, "I say to you, not even in Israel have I found such great faith."

10 When those who had been sent returned to the house, they found the slave in good health.

11 Soon afterwards He went to a city called Nain; and His disciples were going along with Him, accompanied by a large crowd.

12 Now as He approached the gate of the city, a dead man was being carried out, the only son of his mother, and she was a widow; and a sizeable crowd from the city was with her.

13 When the Lord saw her, He felt compassion for her, and said to her, "Do not weep."

14 And He came up and touched the coffin; and the bearers came to a halt. And He said, "Young man, I say to you, arise!"

15 The dead man sat up and began to speak. And *Jesus* gave him back to his mother.

16 Fear gripped them all, and they *began* glorifying God, saying, "A great prophet has arisen among us!" and, "God has visited His people!"

17 This report concerning Him went out all over Judea and in all the surrounding district.

18 The disciples of John reported to him about all these things.

19 Summoning two of his disciples, John sent them to the Lord, saying, "Are You the Expected One, or do we look for someone else?"

20 When the men came to Him, they said, "John the Baptist has sent us to You, to ask,

'Are You the Expected One, or do we look for someone else?' "

21 At that very time He cured many *people* of diseases and afflictions and evil spirits; and He gave sight to many *who were* blind.

22 And He answered and said to them, "Go and report to John what you have seen and heard: *the* BLIND RECEIVE SIGHT, *the* lame walk, *the* lepers are cleansed, and *the* deaf hear, *the* dead are raised up, *the* POOR HAVE THE GOSPEL PREACHED TO THEM.

23 "Blessed is he who does not take offense at Me."

24 When the messengers of John had left, He began to speak to the crowds about John, "What did you go out into the wilderness to see? A reed shaken by the wind?

25 "But what did you go out to see? A man dressed in soft clothing? Those who are splendidly clothed and live in luxury are *found* in royal palaces!

26 "But what did you go out to see? A prophet? Yes, I say to you, and one who is more than a prophet.

27 "This is the one about whom it is written,

'BEHOLD, I SEND MY MESSENGER AHEAD OF YOU,

WHO WILL PREPARE YOUR WAY BEFORE YOU.'

28 "I say to you, among those born of women there is no one greater than John; yet he who is least in the kingdom of God is greater than he."

29 When all the people and the tax collectors heard *this*, they acknowledged God's justice, having been baptized with the baptism of John.

30 But the Pharisees and the [1]lawyers rejected God's purpose for themselves, not having been baptized by John.

31 "To what then shall I compare the men of this generation, and what are they like?

32 "They are like children who sit in the market place and call to one another, and they say, 'We played the flute for you, and you did not dance; we sang a dirge, and you did not weep.'

33 "For John the Baptist has come eating no bread and drinking no wine, and you say, 'He has a demon!'

34 "The Son of Man has come eating and drinking, and you say, 'Behold, a gluttonous man and a drunkard, a friend of tax collectors and sinners!'

35 "Yet wisdom is vindicated by all her children."

36 Now one of the Pharisees was requesting Him to dine with him, and He entered the Pharisee's house and reclined *at the table*.

37 And there was a woman in the city who was a sinner; and when she learned that He was reclining *at the table* in the Pharisee's house, she brought an alabaster vial of perfume,

38 and standing behind *Him* at His feet, weeping, she began to wet His feet with her tears, and kept wiping them with the hair of her head, and kissing His feet and anointing them with the perfume.

39 Now when the Pharisee who had invited Him saw this, he said to himself, "If this man were a prophet He would know who and what sort of person this woman is who is touching Him, that she is a sinner."

40 And Jesus answered him, "Simon, I have something to say to you." And he replied, "Say it, Teacher."

41 "A moneylender had two debtors: one owed five hundred [2]denarii, and the other fifty.

42 "When they were unable to repay, he graciously forgave them both. So which of them will love him more?"

43 Simon answered and said, "I suppose the one whom he forgave more." And He said to him, "You have judged correctly."

44 Turning toward the woman, He said to Simon, "Do you see this woman? I entered your house; you gave Me no water for My feet, but she has wet My feet with her tears and wiped them with her hair.

45 "You gave Me no kiss; but she, since the time I came in, has not ceased to kiss My feet.

46 "You did not anoint My head with oil, but she anointed My feet with perfume.

47 "For this reason I say to you, her sins, which are many, have been forgiven, for she loved much; but he who is forgiven little, loves little."

48 Then He said to her, "Your sins have been forgiven."

49 Those who were reclining *at the table* with Him began to say to themselves, "Who is this *man* who even forgives sins?"

50 And He said to the woman, "Your faith has saved you; go in peace."

Ministering Women

8 Soon afterwards, He *began* going around from one city and village to another, proclaiming and preaching the kingdom of God. The twelve were with Him,

2 and *also* some women who had been healed of evil spirits and sicknesses: Mary who was called Magdalene, from whom seven demons had gone out,

3 and Joanna the wife of Chuza, Herod's steward, and Susanna, and many others who were contributing to their support out of their private means.

4 When a large crowd was coming together, and those from the various cities were journeying to Him, He spoke by way of a parable:

5 "The sower went out to sow his seed; and as he sowed, some fell beside the road, and it was trampled under foot and the birds of the air ate it up.

6 "Other *seed* fell on rocky *soil*, and as soon as it grew up, it withered away, because it had no moisture.

7 "Other *seed* fell among the thorns; and the thorns grew up with it and choked it out.

8 "Other *seed* fell into the good soil, and grew up, and produced a crop a hundred times as

---

1. I.e. experts in the Mosaic Law 2. The denarius was equivalent to a day's wages

great." As He said these things, He would call out, "He who has ears to hear, let him hear."

9 His disciples *began* questioning Him as to what this parable meant.

10 And He said, "To you it has been granted to know the mysteries of the kingdom of God, but to the rest *it is* in parables, so that SEEING THEY MAY NOT SEE, AND HEARING THEY MAY NOT UNDERSTAND.

11 "Now the parable is this: the seed is the word of God.

12 "Those beside the road are those who have heard; then the devil comes and takes away the word from their heart, so that they will not believe and be saved.

13 "Those on the rocky *soil are* those who, when they hear, receive the word with joy; and these have no *firm* root; they believe for a while, and in time of temptation fall away.

14 "The *seed* which fell among the thorns, these are the ones who have heard, and as they go on their way they are choked with worries and riches and pleasures of *this* life, and bring no fruit to maturity.

15 "But the *seed* in the good soil, these are the ones who have heard the word in an honest and good heart, and hold it fast, and bear fruit with perseverance.

16 "Now no one after lighting a lamp covers it over with a container, or puts it under a bed; but he puts it on a lampstand, so that those who come in may see the light.

17 "For nothing is hidden that will not become evident, nor *anything* secret that will not be known and come to light.

18 "So take care how you listen; for whoever has, to him *more* shall be given; and whoever does not have, even what he thinks he has shall be taken away from him."

19 And His mother and brothers came to Him, and they were unable to get to Him because of the crowd.

20 And it was reported to Him, "Your mother and Your brothers are standing outside, wishing to see You."

21 But He answered and said to them, "My mother and My brothers are these who hear the word of God and do it."

22 Now on one of *those* days Jesus and His disciples got into a boat, and He said to them, "Let us go over to the other side of the lake." So they launched out.

23 But as they were sailing along He fell asleep; and a fierce gale of wind descended on the lake, and they *began* to be swamped and to be in danger.

24 They came to Jesus and woke Him up, saying, "Master, Master, we are perishing!" And He got up and rebuked the wind and the surging waves, and they stopped, and it became calm.

25 And He said to them, "Where is your faith?" They were fearful and amazed, saying to one another, "Who then is this, that He commands even the winds and the water, and they obey Him?"

26 Then they sailed to the country of the Gerasenes, which is opposite Galilee.

27 And when He came out onto the land, He was met by a man from the city who was possessed with demons; and who had not put on any clothing for a long time, and was not living in a house, but in the tombs.

28 Seeing Jesus, he cried out and fell before Him, and said in a loud voice, "What business do we have with each other, Jesus, Son of the Most High God? I beg You, do not torment me."

29 For He had commanded the unclean spirit to come out of the man. For it had seized him many times; and he was bound with chains and shackles and kept under guard, and *yet* he would break his bonds and be driven by the demon into the desert.

30 And Jesus asked him, "What is your name?" And he said, "Legion"; for many demons had entered him.

31 They were imploring Him not to command them to go away into the abyss.

32 Now there was a herd of many swine feeding there on the mountain; and *the demons* implored Him to permit them to enter the swine. And He gave them permission.

33 And the demons came out of the man and entered the swine; and the herd rushed down the steep bank into the lake and was drowned.

34 When the herdsmen saw what had happened, they ran away and reported it in the city and *out* in the country.

35 *The people* went out to see what had happened; and they came to Jesus, and found the man from whom the demons had gone out, sitting down at the feet of Jesus, clothed and in his right mind; and they became frightened.

36 Those who had seen it reported to them how the man who was demon-possessed had been made well.

37 And all the people of the country of the Gerasenes and the surrounding district asked Him to leave them, for they were gripped with great fear; and He got into a boat and returned.

38 But the man from whom the demons had gone out was begging Him that he might accompany Him; but He sent him away, saying,

39 "Return to your house and describe what great things God has done for you." So he went away, proclaiming throughout the whole city what great things Jesus had done for him.

40 And as Jesus returned, the people welcomed Him, for they had all been waiting for Him.

41 And there came a man named Jairus, and he was an official of the synagogue; and he fell at Jesus' feet, and *began* to implore Him to come to his house;

42 for he had an only daughter, about twelve years old, and she was dying. But as He went, the crowds were pressing against Him.

43 And a woman who had a hemorrhage for twelve years, and could not be healed by anyone,

44 came up behind Him and touched the

fringe of His cloak, and immediately her hemorrhage stopped.

45 And Jesus said, "Who is the one who touched Me?" And while they were all denying it, Peter said, "Master, the people are crowding and pressing in on You."

46 But Jesus said, "Someone did touch Me, for I was aware that power had gone out of Me."

47 When the woman saw that she had not escaped notice, she came trembling and fell down before Him, and declared in the presence of all the people the reason why she had touched Him, and how she had been immediately healed.

48 And He said to her, "Daughter, your faith has made you well; go in peace."

49 While He was still speaking, someone *came from *the house of* the synagogue official, saying, "Your daughter has died; do not trouble the Teacher anymore."

50 But when Jesus heard *this,* He answered him, "Do not be afraid *any longer;* only believe, and she will be made well."

51 When He came to the house, He did not allow anyone to enter with Him, except Peter and John and James, and the girl's father and mother.

52 Now they were all weeping and lamenting for her; but He said, "Stop weeping, for she has not died, but is asleep."

53 And they *began* laughing at Him, knowing that she had died.

54 He, however, took her by the hand and called, saying, "Child, arise!"

55 And her spirit returned, and she got up immediately; and He gave orders for *something* to be given her to eat.

56 Her parents were amazed; but He instructed them to tell no one what had happened.

Ministry of the Twelve

9 And He called the twelve together, and gave them power and authority over all the demons and to heal diseases.

2 And He sent them out to proclaim the kingdom of God and to perform healing.

3 And He said to them, "Take nothing for *your* journey, neither a staff, nor a bag, nor bread, nor money; and do not *even* have two tunics apiece.

4 "Whatever house you enter, stay there until you leave that city.

5 "And as for those who do not receive you, as you go out from that city, shake the dust off your feet as a testimony against them."

6 Departing, they *began* going throughout the villages, preaching the gospel and healing everywhere.

7 Now Herod the tetrarch heard of all that was happening; and he was greatly perplexed, because it was said by some that John had risen from the dead,

8 and by some that Elijah had appeared, and by others that one of the prophets of old had risen again.

9 Herod said, "I myself had John beheaded; but who is this man about whom I hear such things?" And he kept trying to see Him.

10 When the apostles returned, they gave an account to Him of all that they had done. Taking them with Him, He withdrew by Himself to a city called Bethsaida.

11 But the crowds were aware of this and followed Him; and welcoming them, He *began* speaking to them about the kingdom of God and curing those who had need of healing.

12 Now the day was ending, and the twelve came and said to Him, "Send the crowd away, that they may go into the surrounding villages and countryside and find lodging and get something to eat; for here we are in a desolate place."

13 But He said to them, "You give them *something* to eat!" And they said, "We have no more than five loaves and two fish, unless perhaps we go and buy food for all these people."

14 (For there were about five thousand men.) And He said to His disciples, "Have them sit down *to eat* in groups of about fifty each."

15 They did so, and had them all sit down.

16 Then He took the five loaves and the two fish, and looking up to heaven, He blessed them, and broke *them,* and kept giving *them* to the disciples to set before the people.

17 And they all ate and were satisfied; and the broken pieces which they had left over were picked up, twelve baskets *full.*

18 And it happened that while He was praying alone, the disciples were with Him, and He questioned them, saying, "Who do the people say that I am?"

19 They answered and said, "John the Baptist, and others *say* Elijah; but others, that one of the prophets of old has risen again."

20 And He said to them, "But who do you say that I am?" And Peter answered and said, "The Christ of God."

21 But He warned them and instructed *them* not to tell this to anyone,

22 saying, "The Son of Man must suffer many things and be rejected by the elders and chief priests and scribes, and be killed and be raised up on the third day."

23 And He was saying to *them* all, "If anyone wishes to come after Me, he must deny himself, and take up his cross daily and follow Me.

24 "For whoever wishes to save his life will lose it, but whoever loses his life for My sake, he is the one who will save it.

25 "For what is a man profited if he gains the whole world, and loses or forfeits himself?

26 "For whoever is ashamed of Me and My words, the Son of Man will be ashamed of him when He comes in His glory, and *the glory* of the Father and of the holy angels.

27 "But I say to you truthfully, there are some of those standing here who will not taste death until they see the kingdom of God."

28 Some eight days after these sayings, He

took along Peter and John and James, and went up on the mountain to pray.

29 And while He was praying, the appearance of His face became different, and His clothing *became* white *and* gleaming.

30 And behold, two men were talking with Him; and they were Moses and Elijah,

31 who, appearing in glory, were speaking of His departure which He was about to accomplish at Jerusalem.

32 Now Peter and his companions had been overcome with sleep; but when they were fully awake, they saw His glory and the two men standing with Him.

33 And as these were leaving Him, Peter said to Jesus, "Master, it is good for us to be here; let us make three tabernacles: one for You, and one for Moses, and one for Elijah"—not realizing what he was saying.

34 While he was saying this, a cloud formed and *began* to overshadow them; and they were afraid as they entered the cloud.

35 Then a voice came out of the cloud, saying, "This is My Son, *My* Chosen One; listen to Him!"

36 And when the voice had spoken, Jesus was found alone. And they kept silent, and reported to no one in those days any of the things which they had seen.

37 On the next day, when they came down from the mountain, a large crowd met Him.

38 And a man from the crowd shouted, saying, "Teacher, I beg You to look at my son, for he is my only *boy,*

39 and a spirit seizes him, and he suddenly screams, and it throws him into a convulsion with foaming *at the mouth;* and only with difficulty does it leave him, mauling him *as it leaves.*

40 "I begged Your disciples to cast it out, and they could not."

41 And Jesus answered and said, "You unbelieving and perverted generation, how long shall I be with you and put up with you? Bring your son here."

42 While he was still approaching, the demon slammed him *to the ground* and threw him into a convulsion. But Jesus rebuked the unclean spirit, and healed the boy and gave him back to his father.

43 And they were all amazed at the greatness of God.

But while everyone was marveling at all that He was doing, He said to His disciples,

44 "Let these words sink into your ears; for the Son of Man is going to be delivered into the hands of men."

45 But they did not understand this statement, and it was concealed from them so that they would not perceive it; and they were afraid to ask Him about this statement.

46 An argument started among them as to which of them might be the greatest.

47 But Jesus, knowing what they were thinking in their heart, took a child and stood him by His side,

48 and said to them, "Whoever receives this child in My name receives Me, and whoever receives Me receives Him who sent Me; for the one who is least among all of you, this is the one who is great."

49 John answered and said, "Master, we saw someone casting out demons in Your name; and we tried to prevent him because he does not follow along with us."

50 But Jesus said to him, "Do not hinder *him;* for he who is not against you is for you."

51 When the days were approaching for His ascension, He was determined to go to Jerusalem;

52 and He sent messengers on ahead of Him, and they went and entered a village of the Samaritans to make arrangements for Him.

53 But they did not receive Him, because He was traveling toward Jerusalem.

54 When His disciples James and John saw *this,* they said, "Lord, do You want us to command fire to come down from heaven and consume them?"

55 But He turned and rebuked them, [and said, "You do not know what kind of spirit you are of;

56 for the Son of Man did not come to destroy men's lives, but to save them."] And they went on to another village.

57 As they were going along the road, someone said to Him, "I will follow You wherever You go."

58 And Jesus said to him, "The foxes have holes and the birds of the air *have* nests, but the Son of Man has nowhere to lay His head."

59 And He said to another, "Follow Me." But he said, "Lord, permit me first to go and bury my father."

60 But He said to him, "Allow the dead to bury their own dead; but as for you, go and proclaim everywhere the kingdom of God."

61 Another also said, "I will follow You, Lord; but first permit me to say good-bye to those at home."

62 But Jesus said to him, "No one, after putting his hand to the plow and looking back, is fit for the kingdom of God."

The Seventy Sent Out

10 Now after this the Lord appointed seventy others, and sent them in pairs ahead of Him to every city and place where He Himself was going to come.

2 And He was saying to them, "The harvest is plentiful, but the laborers are few; therefore beseech the Lord of the harvest to send out laborers into His harvest.

3 "Go; behold, I send you out as lambs in the midst of wolves.

4 "Carry no money belt, no bag, no shoes; and greet no one on the way.

5 "Whatever house you enter, first say, 'Peace *be* to this house.'

6 "If a man of peace is there, your peace will rest on him; but if not, it will return to you.

7 "Stay in that house, eating and drinking what they give you; for the laborer is worthy of

his wages. Do not keep moving from house to house.

8 "Whatever city you enter and they receive you, eat what is set before you;

9 and heal those in it who are sick, and say to them, 'The kingdom of God has come near to you.'

10 "But whatever city you enter and they do not receive you, go out into its streets and say,

11 'Even the dust of your city which clings to our feet we wipe off *in protest* against you; yet be sure of this, that the kingdom of God has come near.'

12 "I say to you, it will be more tolerable in that day for Sodom than for that city.

13 "Woe to you, Chorazin! Woe to you, Bethsaida! For if the miracles had been performed in Tyre and Sidon which occurred in you, they would have repented long ago, sitting in sackcloth and ashes.

14 "But it will be more tolerable for Tyre and Sidon in the judgment than for you.

15 "And you, Capernaum, will not be exalted to heaven, will you? You will be brought down to Hades!

16 "The one who listens to you listens to Me, and the one who rejects you rejects Me; and he who rejects Me rejects the One who sent Me."

17 The seventy returned with joy, saying, "Lord, even the demons are subject to us in Your name."

18 And He said to them, "I was watching Satan fall from heaven like lightning.

19 "Behold, I have given you authority to tread on serpents and scorpions, and over all the power of the enemy, and nothing will injure you.

20 "Nevertheless do not rejoice in this, that the spirits are subject to you, but rejoice that your names are recorded in heaven."

21 At that very time He rejoiced greatly in the Holy Spirit, and said, "I praise You, O Father, Lord of heaven and earth, that You have hidden these things from *the* wise and intelligent and have revealed them to infants. Yes, Father, for this way was well-pleasing in Your sight.

22 "All things have been handed over to Me by My Father, and no one knows who the Son is except the Father, and who the Father is except the Son, and anyone to whom the Son wills to reveal *Him*."

23 Turning to the disciples, He said privately, "Blessed *are* the eyes which see the things you see,

24 for I say to you, that many prophets and kings wished to see the things which you see, and did not see *them,* and to hear the things which you hear, and did not hear *them.*"

25 And a lawyer stood up and put Him to the test, saying, "Teacher, what shall I do to inherit eternal life?"

26 And He said to him, "What is written in the Law? How does it read to you?"

27 And he answered, "YOU SHALL LOVE THE LORD YOUR GOD WITH ALL YOUR HEART, AND WITH ALL YOUR SOUL, AND WITH ALL YOUR STRENGTH, AND WITH ALL YOUR MIND; AND YOUR NEIGHBOR AS YOURSELF."

28 And He said to him, "You have answered correctly; DO THIS AND YOU WILL LIVE."

29 But wishing to justify himself, he said to Jesus, "And who is my neighbor?"

30 Jesus replied and said, "A man was going down from Jerusalem to Jericho, and fell among robbers, and they stripped him and beat him, and went away leaving him half dead.

31 "And by chance a priest was going down on that road, and when he saw him, he passed by on the other side.

32 "Likewise a Levite also, when he came to the place and saw him, passed by on the other side.

33 "But a Samaritan, who was on a journey, came upon him; and when he saw him, he felt compassion,

34 and came to him and bandaged up his wounds, pouring oil and wine on *them;* and he put him on his own beast, and brought him to an inn and took care of him.

35 "On the next day he took out two [1]denarii and gave them to the innkeeper and said, 'Take care of him; and whatever more you spend, when I return I will repay you.'

36 "Which of these three do you think proved to be a neighbor to the man who fell into the robbers' *hands?*"

37 And he said, "The one who showed mercy toward him." Then Jesus said to him, "Go and do the same."

38 Now as they were traveling along, He entered a village; and a woman named Martha welcomed Him into her home.

39 She had a sister called Mary, who was seated at the Lord's feet, listening to His word.

40 But Martha was distracted with all her preparations; and she came up *to Him* and said, "Lord, do You not care that my sister has left me to do all the serving alone? Then tell her to help me."

41 But the Lord answered and said to her, "Martha, Martha, you are worried and bothered about so many things;

42 but *only* one thing is necessary, for Mary has chosen the good part, which shall not be taken away from her."

Instruction about Prayer

11 It happened that while Jesus was praying in a certain place, after He had finished, one of His disciples said to Him, "Lord, teach us to pray just as John also taught his disciples."

2 And He said to them, "When you pray, say: [2]Father, hallowed be Your name. Your kingdom come.

3 'Give us each day our daily bread.

4 'And forgive us our sins, For we ourselves also forgive everyone who is indebted to us.

---

1. **The denarius was equivalent to a day's wages** 2. **Later mss add phrases from Matt 6:9-13 to make the two passages closely similar**

And lead us not into temptation.' "

5 Then He said to them, "Suppose one of you has a friend, and goes to him at midnight and says to him, 'Friend, lend me three loaves;

6 for a friend of mine has come to me from a journey, and I have nothing to set before him';

7 and from inside he answers and says, 'Do not bother me; the door has already been shut and my children and I are in bed; I cannot get up and give you *anything*.'

8 "I tell you, even though he will not get up and give him *anything* because he is his friend, yet because of his persistence he will get up and give him as much as he needs.

9 "So I say to you, ask, and it will be given to you; seek, and you will find; knock, and it will be opened to you.

10 "For everyone who asks, receives; and he who seeks, finds; and to him who knocks, it will be opened.

11 "Now suppose one of you fathers is asked by his son for a fish; he will not give him a snake instead of a fish, will he?

12 "Or *if* he is asked for an egg, he will not give him a scorpion, will he?

13 "If you then, being evil, know how to give good gifts to your children, how much more will *your* heavenly Father give the Holy Spirit to those who ask Him?"

14 And He was casting out a demon, and it was mute; when the demon had gone out, the mute man spoke; and the crowds were amazed.

15 But some of them said, "He casts out demons by Beelzebul, the ruler of the demons."

16 Others, to test *Him*, were demanding of Him a sign from heaven.

17 But He knew their thoughts and said to them, "Any kingdom divided against itself is laid waste; and a house *divided* against itself falls.

18 "If Satan also is divided against himself, how will his kingdom stand? For you say that I cast out demons by Beelzebul.

19 "And if I by Beelzebul cast out demons, by whom do your sons cast them out? So they will be your judges.

20 "But if I cast out demons by the finger of God, then the kingdom of God has come upon you.

21 "When a strong *man*, fully armed, guards his own house, his possessions are undisturbed.

22 "But when someone stronger than he attacks him and overpowers him, he takes away from him all his armor on which he had relied and distributes his plunder.

23 "He who is not with Me is against Me; and he who does not gather with Me, scatters.

24 "When the unclean spirit goes out of a man, it passes through waterless places seeking rest, and not finding any, it says, 'I will return to my house from which I came.'

25 "And when it comes, it finds it swept and put in order.

26 "Then it goes and takes *along* seven other spirits more evil than itself, and they go in and live there; and the last state of that man becomes worse than the first."

27 While Jesus was saying these things, one of the women in the crowd raised her voice and said to Him, "Blessed is the womb that bore You and the breasts at which You nursed."

28 But He said, "On the contrary, blessed are those who hear the word of God and observe it."

29 As the crowds were increasing, He began to say, "This generation is a wicked generation; it seeks for a sign, and *yet* no sign will be given to it but the sign of Jonah.

30 "For just as Jonah became a sign to the Ninevites, so will the Son of Man be to this generation.

31 "The Queen of the South will rise up with the men of this generation at the judgment and condemn them, because she came from the ends of the earth to hear the wisdom of Solomon; and behold, something greater than Solomon is here.

32 "The men of Nineveh will stand up with this generation at the judgment and condemn it, because they repented at the preaching of Jonah; and behold, something greater than Jonah is here.

33 "No one, after lighting a lamp, puts it away in a cellar nor under a basket, but on the lampstand, so that those who enter may see the light.

34 "The eye is the lamp of your body; when your eye is clear, your whole body also is full of light; but when it is bad, your body also is full of darkness.

35 "Then watch out that the light in you is not darkness.

36 "If therefore your whole body is full of light, with no dark part in it, it will be wholly illumined, as when the lamp illumines you with its rays."

37 Now when He had spoken, a Pharisee *asked Him to have lunch with him; and He went in, and reclined *at the table.*

38 When the Pharisee saw it, he was surprised that He had not first ceremonially washed before the meal.

39 But the Lord said to him, "Now you Pharisees clean the outside of the cup and of the platter; but inside of you, you are full of robbery and wickedness.

40 "You foolish ones, did not He who made the outside make the inside also?

41 "But give that which is within as charity, and then all things are clean for you.

42 "But woe to you Pharisees! For you pay tithe of mint and rue and every *kind of* garden herb, and *yet* disregard justice and the love of God; but these are the things you should have done without neglecting the others.

43 "Woe to you Pharisees! For you love the chief seats in the synagogues and the respectful greetings in the market places.

44 "Woe to you! For you are like concealed tombs, and the people who walk over *them* are unaware *of it.*"

45 One of the [1]lawyers *said to Him in reply, "Teacher, when You say this, You insult us too."

46 But He said, "Woe to you lawyers as well! For you weigh men down with burdens hard to bear, while you yourselves will not even touch the burdens with one of your fingers.

47 "Woe to you! For you build the tombs of the prophets, and *it was* your fathers *who* killed them.

48 "So you are witnesses and approve the deeds of your fathers; because it was they who killed them, and you build *their tombs.*

49 "For this reason also the wisdom of God said, 'I will send to them prophets and apostles, and *some* of them they will kill and *some* they will persecute,

50 so that the blood of all the prophets, shed since the foundation of the world, may be charged against this generation,

51 from the blood of Abel to the blood of Zechariah, who was killed between the altar and the house *of God;* yes, I tell you, it shall be charged against this generation.'

52 "Woe to you lawyers! For you have taken away the key of knowledge; you yourselves did not enter, and you hindered those who were entering."

53 When He left there, the scribes and the Pharisees began to be very hostile and to question Him closely on many subjects,

54 plotting against Him to catch *Him* in something He might say.

God Knows and Cares

12 Under these circumstances, after so many thousands of people had gathered together that they were stepping on one another, He began saying to His disciples first *of all,* "Beware of the leaven of the Pharisees, which is hypocrisy.

2 "But there is nothing covered up that will not be revealed, and hidden that will not be known.

3 "Accordingly, whatever you have said in the dark will be heard in the light, and what you have whispered in the inner rooms will be proclaimed upon the housetops.

4 "I say to you, My friends, do not be afraid of those who kill the body and after that have no more that they can do.

5 "But I will warn you whom to fear: fear the One who, after He has killed, has authority to cast into hell; yes, I tell you, fear Him!

6 "Are not five sparrows sold for two cents? Yet not one of them is forgotten before God.

7 "Indeed, the very hairs of your head are all numbered. Do not fear; you are more valuable than many sparrows.

8 "And I say to you, everyone who confesses Me before men, the Son of Man will confess him also before the angels of God;

9 but he who denies Me before men will be denied before the angels of God.

10 "And everyone who speaks a word against the Son of Man, it will be forgiven him; but he who blasphemes against the Holy Spirit, it will not be forgiven him.

11 "When they bring you before the synagogues and the rulers and the authorities, do not worry about how or what you are to speak in your defense, or what you are to say;

12 for the Holy Spirit will teach you in that very hour what you ought to say."

13 Someone in the crowd said to Him, "Teacher, tell my brother to divide the *family* inheritance with me."

14 But He said to him, "Man, who appointed Me a judge or arbitrator over you?"

15 Then He said to them, "Beware, and be on your guard against every form of greed; for not *even* when one has an abundance does his life consist of his possessions."

16 And He told them a parable, saying, "The land of a rich man was very productive.

17 "And he began reasoning to himself, saying, 'What shall I do, since I have no place to store my crops?'

18 "Then he said, 'This is what I will do: I will tear down my barns and build larger ones, and there I will store all my grain and my goods.

19 'And I will say to my soul, "Soul, you have many goods laid up for many years *to come;* take your ease, eat, drink *and* be merry." '

20 "But God said to him, 'You fool! This *very* night your soul is required of you; and *now* who will own what you have prepared?'

21 "So is the man who stores up treasure for himself, and is not rich toward God."

22 And He said to His disciples, "For this reason I say to you, do not worry about *your* life, *as to* what you will eat; nor for your body, *as to* what you will put on.

23 "For life is more than food, and the body more than clothing.

24 "Consider the ravens, for they neither sow nor reap; they have no storeroom nor barn, and *yet* God feeds them; how much more valuable you are than the birds!

25 "And which of you by worrying can add a *single* [2]hour to his [3]life's span?

26 "If then you cannot do even a very little thing, why do you worry about other matters?

27 "Consider the lilies, how they grow: they neither toil nor spin; but I tell you, not even Solomon in all his glory clothed himself like one of these.

28 "But if God so clothes the grass in the field, which is *alive* today and tomorrow is thrown into the furnace, how much more *will He clothe* you? You men of little faith!

29 "And do not seek what you will eat and what you will drink, and do not keep worrying.

30 "For all these things the nations of the world eagerly seek; but your Father knows that you need these things.

31 "But seek His kingdom, and these things will be added to you.

32 "Do not be afraid, little flock, for your Father has chosen gladly to give you the kingdom.

---

1. I.e. experts in the Mosaic Law 2. Lit *cubit* (approx 18 in.) 3. Or *height*

33 "Sell your possessions and give to charity; make yourselves money belts which do not wear out, an unfailing treasure in heaven, where no thief comes near nor moth destroys.

34 "For where your treasure is, there your heart will be also.

35 "Be dressed in readiness, and *keep* your lamps lit.

36 "Be like men who are waiting for their master when he returns from the wedding feast, so that they may immediately open *the door* to him when he comes and knocks.

37 "Blessed are those slaves whom the master will find on the alert when he comes; truly I say to you, that he will gird himself *to serve*, and have them recline *at the table*, and will come up and wait on them.

38 "Whether he comes in the ¹second watch, or even in the ²third, and finds *them* so, blessed are those *slaves*.

39 "But be sure of this, that if the head of the house had known at what hour the thief was coming, he would not have allowed his house to be broken into.

40 "You too, be ready; for the Son of Man is coming at an hour that you do not expect."

41 Peter said, "Lord, are You addressing this parable to us, or to everyone *else* as well?"

42 And the Lord said, "Who then is the faithful and sensible steward, whom his master will put in charge of his servants, to give them their rations at the proper time?

43 "Blessed is that slave whom his master finds so doing when he comes.

44 "Truly I say to you that he will put him in charge of all his possessions.

45 "But if that slave says in his heart, 'My master will be a long time in coming,' and begins to beat the slaves, *both* men and women, and to eat and drink and get drunk;

46 the master of that slave will come on a day when he does not expect *him* and at an hour he does not know, and will cut him in pieces, and assign him a place with the unbelievers.

47 "And that slave who knew his master's will and did not get ready or act in accord with his will, will receive many lashes,

48 but the one who did not know *it*, and committed deeds worthy of a flogging, will receive but few. From everyone who has been given much, much will be required; and to whom they entrusted much, of him they will ask all the more.

49 "I have come to cast fire upon the earth; and how I wish it were already kindled!

50 "But I have a baptism to undergo, and how distressed I am until it is accomplished!

51 "Do you suppose that I came to grant peace on earth? I tell you, no, but rather division;

52 for from now on five *members* in one household will be divided, three against two and two against three.

53 "They will be divided, father against son and son against father, mother against daughter and daughter against mother, mother-in-law against daughter-in-law and daughter-in-law against mother-in-law."

54 And He was also saying to the crowds, "When you see a cloud rising in the west, immediately you say, 'A shower is coming,' and so it turns out.

55 "And when *you see* a south wind blowing, you say, 'It will be a hot day,' and it turns out *that way.*

56 "You hypocrites! You know how to analyze the appearance of the earth and the sky, but why do you not analyze this present time?

57 "And why do you not even on your own initiative judge what is right?

58 "For while you are going with your opponent to appear before the magistrate, on *your* way *there* make an effort to settle with him, so that he may not drag you before the judge, and the judge turn you over to the officer, and the officer throw you into prison.

59 "I say to you, you will not get out of there until you have paid the very last cent."

Call to Repent

13 Now on the same occasion there were some present who reported to Him about the Galileans whose blood Pilate had mixed with their sacrifices.

2 And Jesus said to them, "Do you suppose that these Galileans were *greater* sinners than all *other* Galileans because they suffered this *fate?*

3 "I tell you, no, but unless you repent, you will all likewise perish.

4 "Or do you suppose that those eighteen on whom the tower in Siloam fell and killed them were *worse* culprits than all the men who live in Jerusalem?

5 "I tell you, no, but unless you repent, you will all likewise perish."

6 And He *began* telling this parable: "A man had a fig tree which had been planted in his vineyard; and he came looking for fruit on it and did not find any.

7 "And he said to the vineyard-keeper, 'Behold, for three years I have come looking for fruit on this fig tree without finding any. Cut it down! Why does it even use up the ground?'

8 "And he answered and said to him, 'Let it alone, sir, for this year too, until I dig around it and put in fertilizer;

9 and if it bears fruit next year, *fine;* but if not, cut it down.' "

10 And He was teaching in one of the synagogues on the Sabbath.

11 And there was a woman who for eighteen years had had a sickness caused by a spirit; and she was bent double, and could not straighten up at all.

12 When Jesus saw her, He called her over and said to her, "Woman, you are freed from your sickness."

13 And He laid His hands on her; and immediately she was made erect again and *began* glorifying God.

14 But the synagogue official, indignant

---

1. I.e. 9 p.m. to midnight 2. I.e. midnight to 3 a.m.

because Jesus had healed on the Sabbath, *began* saying to the crowd in response, "There are six days in which work should be done; so come during them and get healed, and not on the Sabbath day."

15 But the Lord answered him and said, "You hypocrites, does not each of you on the Sabbath untie his ox or his donkey from the stall and lead him away to water *him?*

16 "And this woman, a daughter of Abraham as she is, whom Satan has bound for eighteen long years, should she not have been released from this bond on the Sabbath day?"

17 As He said this, all His opponents were being humiliated; and the entire crowd was rejoicing over all the glorious things being done by Him.

18 So He was saying, "What is the kingdom of God like, and to what shall I compare it?

19 "It is like a mustard seed, which a man took and threw into his own garden; and it grew and became a tree, and THE BIRDS OF THE AIR NESTED IN ITS BRANCHES."

20 And again He said, "To what shall I compare the kingdom of God?

21 "It is like leaven, which a woman took and hid in three pecks of flour until it was all leavened."

22 And He was passing through from one city and village to another, teaching, and proceeding on His way to Jerusalem.

23 And someone said to Him, "Lord, are there *just* a few who are being saved?" And He said to them,

24 "Strive to enter through the narrow door; for many, I tell you, will seek to enter and will not be able.

25 "Once the head of the house gets up and shuts the door, and you begin to stand outside and knock on the door, saying, 'Lord, open up to us!' then He will answer and say to you, 'I do not know where you are from.'

26 "Then you will begin to say, 'We ate and drank in Your presence, and You taught in our streets';

27 and He will say, 'I tell you, I do not know where you are from; DEPART FROM ME, ALL YOU EVILDOERS.'

28 "In that place there will be weeping and gnashing of teeth when you see Abraham and Isaac and Jacob and all the prophets in the kingdom of God, but yourselves being thrown out.

29 "And they will come from east and west and from north and south, and will recline *at the table* in the kingdom of God.

30 "And behold, *some* are last who will be first and *some* are first who will be last."

31 Just at that time some Pharisees approached, saying to Him, "Go away, leave here, for Herod wants to kill You."

32 And He said to them, "Go and tell that fox, 'Behold, I cast out demons and perform cures today and tomorrow, and the third *day* I reach My goal.'

33 "Nevertheless I must journey on today and tomorrow and the next *day;* for it cannot be that a prophet would perish outside of Jerusalem.

34 "O Jerusalem, Jerusalem, *the city* that kills the prophets and stones those sent to her! How often I wanted to gather your children together, just as a hen *gathers* her brood under her wings, and you would not *have it!*

35 "Behold, your house is left to you *desolate;* and I say to you, you will not see Me until *the time* comes when you say, 'BLESSED IS HE WHO COMES IN THE NAME OF THE LORD!'"

Jesus Heals on the Sabbath

14 It happened that when He went into the house of one of the leaders of the Pharisees on *the* Sabbath to eat bread, they were watching Him closely.

2 And there in front of Him was a man suffering from dropsy.

3 And Jesus answered and spoke to the lawyers and Pharisees, saying, "Is it lawful to heal on the Sabbath, or not?"

4 But they kept silent. And He took hold of him and healed him, and sent him away.

5 And He said to them, "Which one of you will have a son or an ox fall into a well, and will not immediately pull him out on a Sabbath day?"

6 And they could make no reply to this.

7 And He *began* speaking a parable to the invited guests when He noticed how they had been picking out the places of honor *at the table,* saying to them,

8 "When you are invited by someone to a wedding feast, do not take the place of honor, for someone more distinguished than you may have been invited by him,

9 and he who invited you both will come and say to you, 'Give *your* place to this man,' and then in disgrace you proceed to occupy the last place.

10 "But when you are invited, go and recline at the last place, so that when the one who has invited you comes, he may say to you, 'Friend, move up higher'; then you will have honor in the sight of all who are at the table with you.

11 "For everyone who exalts himself will be humbled, and he who humbles himself will be exalted."

12 And He also went on to say to the one who had invited Him, "When you give a luncheon or a dinner, do not invite your friends or your brothers or your relatives or rich neighbors, otherwise they may also invite you in return and *that* will be your repayment.

13 "But when you give a reception, invite *the* poor, *the* crippled, *the* lame, *the* blind,

14 and you will be blessed, since they do not have *the means* to repay you; for you will be repaid at the resurrection of the righteous."

15 When one of those who were reclining *at the table* with Him heard this, he said to Him, "Blessed is everyone who will eat bread in the kingdom of God!"

16 But He said to him, "A man was giving a big dinner, and he invited many;

17 and at the dinner hour he sent his slave to

say to those who had been invited, 'Come; for everything is ready now.'

18 "But they all alike began to make excuses. The first one said to him, 'I have bought a piece of land and I need to go out and look at it; please consider me excused.'

19 "Another one said, 'I have bought five yoke of oxen, and I am going to try them out; please consider me excused.'

20 "Another one said, 'I have married a wife, and for that reason I cannot come.'

21 "And the slave came *back* and reported this to his master. Then the head of the household became angry and said to his slave, 'Go out at once into the streets and lanes of the city and bring in here the poor and crippled and blind and lame.'

22 "And the slave said, 'Master, what you commanded has been done, and still there is room.'

23 "And the master said to the slave, 'Go out into the highways and along the hedges, and compel *them* to come in, so that my house may be filled.

24 'For I tell you, none of those men who were invited shall taste of my dinner.' "

25 Now large crowds were going along with Him; and He turned and said to them,

26 "If anyone comes to Me, and does not ¹hate his own father and mother and wife and children and brothers and sisters, yes, and even his own life, he cannot be My disciple.

27 "Whoever does not carry his own cross and come after Me cannot be My disciple.

28 "For which one of you, when he wants to build a tower, does not first sit down and calculate the cost to see if he has enough to complete it?

29 "Otherwise, when he has laid a foundation and is not able to finish, all who observe it begin to ridicule him,

30 saying, 'This man began to build and was not able to finish.'

31 "Or what king, when he sets out to meet another king in battle, will not first sit down and consider whether he is strong enough with ten thousand *men* to encounter the one coming against him with twenty thousand?

32 "Or else, while the other is still far away, he sends a delegation and asks for terms of peace.

33 "So then, none of you can be My disciple who does not give up all his own possessions.

34 "Therefore, salt is good; but if even salt has become tasteless, with what will it be seasoned?

35 "It is useless either for the soil or for the manure pile; it is thrown out. He who has ears to hear, let him hear."

The Lost Sheep

15 Now all the tax collectors and the sinners were coming near Him to listen to Him.

2 Both the Pharisees and the scribes *began* to grumble, saying, "This man receives sinners and eats with them."

3 So He told them this parable, saying,

---

1. I.e. by comparison of his love for Me

4 "What man among you, if he has a hundred sheep and has lost one of them, does not leave the ninety-nine in the open pasture and go after the one which is lost until he finds it?

5 "When he has found it, he lays it on his shoulders, rejoicing.

6 "And when he comes home, he calls together his friends and his neighbors, saying to them, 'Rejoice with me, for I have found my sheep which was lost!'

7 "I tell you that in the same way, there will be *more* joy in heaven over one sinner who repents than over ninety-nine righteous persons who need no repentance.

8 "Or what woman, if she has ten silver coins and loses one coin, does not light a lamp and sweep the house and search carefully until she finds it?

9 "When she has found it, she calls together her friends and neighbors, saying, 'Rejoice with me, for I have found the coin which I had lost!'

10 "In the same way, I tell you, there is joy in the presence of the angels of God over one sinner who repents."

11 And He said, "A man had two sons.

12 "The younger of them said to his father, 'Father, give me the share of the estate that falls to me.' So he divided his wealth between them.

13 "And not many days later, the younger son gathered everything together and went on a journey into a distant country, and there he squandered his estate with loose living.

14 "Now when he had spent everything, a severe famine occurred in that country, and he began to be impoverished.

15 "So he went and hired himself out to one of the citizens of that country, and he sent him into his fields to feed swine.

16 "And he would have gladly filled his stomach with the pods that the swine were eating, and no one was giving *anything* to him.

17 "But when he came to his senses, he said, 'How many of my father's hired men have more than enough bread, but I am dying here with hunger!

18 'I will get up and go to my father, and will say to him, "Father, I have sinned against heaven, and in your sight;

19 I am no longer worthy to be called your son; make me as one of your hired men." '

20 "So he got up and came to his father. But while he was still a long way off, his father saw him and felt compassion *for him*, and ran and embraced him and kissed him.

21 "And the son said to him, 'Father, I have sinned against heaven and in your sight; I am no longer worthy to be called your son.'

22 "But the father said to his slaves, 'Quickly bring out the best robe and put it on him, and put a ring on his hand and sandals on his feet;

23 and bring the fattened calf, kill it, and let us eat and celebrate;

24 for this son of mine was dead and has come to life again; he was lost and has been found.' And they began to celebrate.

25 "Now his older son was in the field, and when he came and approached the house, he heard music and dancing.

26 "And he summoned one of the servants and *began* inquiring what these things could be.

27 "And he said to him, 'Your brother has come, and your father has killed the fattened calf because he has received him back safe and sound.'

28 "But he became angry and was not willing to go in; and his father came out and *began* pleading with him.

29 "But he answered and said to his father, 'Look! For so many years I have been serving you and I have never neglected a command of yours; and *yet* you have never given me a young goat, so that I might celebrate with my friends;

30 but when this son of yours came, who has devoured your wealth with prostitutes, you killed the fattened calf for him.'

31 "And he said to him, 'Son, you have always been with me, and all that is mine is yours.

32 'But we had to celebrate and rejoice, for this brother of yours was dead and *has begun* to live, and *was* lost and has been found.' "

The Unrighteous Steward

16 Now He was also saying to the disciples, "There was a rich man who had a manager, and this *manager* was reported to him as squandering his possessions.

2 "And he called him and said to him, 'What is this I hear about you? Give an accounting of your management, for you can no longer be manager.'

3 "The manager said to himself, 'What shall I do, since my master is taking the management away from me? I am not strong enough to dig; I am ashamed to beg.

4 'I know what I shall do, so that when I am removed from the management people will welcome me into their homes.'

5 "And he summoned each one of his master's debtors, and he *began* saying to the first, 'How much do you owe my master?'

6 "And he said, 'A hundred measures of oil.' And he said to him, 'Take your bill, and sit down quickly and write fifty.'

7 "Then he said to another, 'And how much do you owe?' And he said, 'A hundred measures of wheat.' He *said to him, 'Take your bill, and write eighty.'

8 "And his master praised the unrighteous manager because he had acted shrewdly; for the sons of this age are more shrewd in relation to their own kind than the sons of light.

9 "And I say to you, make friends for yourselves by means of the ¹wealth of unrighteousness, so that when it fails, they will receive you into the eternal dwellings.

10 "He who is faithful in a very little thing is faithful also in much; and he who is unrighteous in a very little thing is unrighteous also in much.

11 "Therefore if you have not been faithful in the *use of* unrighteous wealth, who will entrust the true *riches* to you?

12 "And if you have not been faithful in *the use of* that which is another's, who will give you that which is your own?

13 "No servant can serve two masters; for either he will hate the one and love the other, or else he will be devoted to one and despise the other. You cannot serve God and wealth."

14 Now the Pharisees, who were lovers of money, were listening to all these things and were scoffing at Him.

15 And He said to them, "You are those who justify yourselves in the sight of men, but God knows your hearts; for that which is highly esteemed among men is detestable in the sight of God.

16 "The Law and the Prophets *were proclaimed* until John; since that time the gospel of the kingdom of God has been preached, and everyone is forcing his way into it.

17 "But it is easier for heaven and earth to pass away than for one stroke of a letter of the Law to fail.

18 "Everyone who divorces his wife and marries another commits adultery, and he who marries one who is divorced from a husband commits adultery.

19 "Now there was a rich man, and he habitually dressed in purple and fine linen, joyously living in splendor every day.

20 "And a poor man named Lazarus was laid at his gate, covered with sores,

21 and longing to be fed with the *crumbs* which were falling from the rich man's table; besides, even the dogs were coming and licking his sores.

22 "Now the poor man died and was carried away by the angels to Abraham's bosom; and the rich man also died and was buried.

23 "In Hades he lifted up his eyes, being in torment, and *saw Abraham far away and Lazarus in his bosom.

24 "And he cried out and said, 'Father Abraham, have mercy on me, and send Lazarus so that he may dip the tip of his finger in water and cool off my tongue, for I am in agony in this flame.'

25 "But Abraham said, 'Child, remember that during your life you received your good things, and likewise Lazarus bad things; but now he is being comforted here, and you are in agony.

26 'And besides all this, between us and you there is a great chasm fixed, so that those who wish to come over from here to you will not be able, and *that* none may cross over from there to us.'

27 "And he said, 'Then I beg you, father, that you send him to my father's house—

28 for I have five brothers—in order that he may warn them, so that they will not also come to this place of torment.'

29 "But Abraham *said, 'They have Moses and the Prophets; let them hear them.'

30 "But he said, 'No, father Abraham, but if

---

1. Gr *mamonas*, for Aram *mamon*(mammon); i.e. wealth, etc., personified as an object of worship

someone goes to them from the dead, they will repent!'

31 "But he said to him, 'If they do not listen to Moses and the Prophets, they will not be persuaded even if someone rises from the dead.' "

Instructions

17 He said to His disciples, "It is inevitable that stumbling blocks come, but woe to him through whom they come!

2 "It would be better for him if a millstone were hung around his neck and he were thrown into the sea, than that he would cause one of these little ones to stumble.

3 "Be on your guard! If your brother sins, rebuke him; and if he repents, forgive him.

4 "And if he sins against you seven times a day, and returns to you seven times, saying, 'I repent,' forgive him."

5 The apostles said to the Lord, "Increase our faith!"

6 And the Lord said, "If you had faith like a mustard seed, you would say to this mulberry tree, 'Be uprooted and be planted in the sea²; and it would obey you.

7 "Which of you, having a slave plowing or tending sheep, will say to him when he has come in from the field, 'Come immediately and sit down to eat'?

8 "But will he not say to him, 'Prepare something for me to eat, and *properly* clothe yourself and serve me while I eat and drink; and afterward you may eat and drink'?

9 "He does not thank the slave because he did the things which were commanded, does he?

10 "So you too, when you do all the things which are commanded you, say, 'We are unworthy slaves; we have done *only* that which we ought to have done.' "

11 While He was on the way to Jerusalem, He was passing between Samaria and Galilee.

12 As He entered a village, ten leprous men who stood at a distance met Him;

13 and they raised their voices, saying, "Jesus, Master, have mercy on us!"

14 When He saw them, He said to them, "Go and show yourselves to the priests." And as they were going, they were cleansed.

15 Now one of them, when he saw that he had been healed, turned back, glorifying God with a loud voice,

16 and he fell on his face at His feet, giving thanks to Him. And he was a Samaritan.

17 Then Jesus answered and said, "Were there not ten cleansed? But the nine—where are they?

18 "Was no one found who returned to give glory to God, except this foreigner?"

19 And He said to him, "Stand up and go; your faith ¹has made you well."

20 Now having been questioned by the Pharisees as to when the kingdom of God was coming, He answered them and said, "The kingdom of God is not coming with signs to be observed;

21 nor will they say, 'Look, here *it is!*' or, 'There *it is!*' For behold, the kingdom of God is in your midst."

22 And He said to the disciples, "The days will come when you will long to see one of the days of the Son of Man, and you will not see it.

23 "They will say to you, 'Look there! Look here!' Do not go away, and do not run after *them.*

24 "For just like the lightning, when it flashes out of one part of the sky, shines to the other part of the sky, so will the Son of Man be in His day.

25 "But first He must suffer many things and be rejected by this generation.

26 "And just as it happened in the days of Noah, so it will be also in the days of the Son of Man:

27 they were eating, they were drinking, they were marrying, they were being given in marriage, until the day that Noah entered the ark, and the flood came and destroyed them all.

28 "It was the same as happened in the days of Lot: they were eating, they were drinking, they were buying, they were selling, they were planting, they were building;

29 but on the day that Lot went out from Sodom it rained fire and brimstone from heaven and destroyed them all.

30 "It will be just the same on the day that the Son of Man is revealed.

31 "On that day, the one who is on the housetop and whose goods are in the house must not go down to take them out; and likewise the one who is in the field must not turn back.

32 "Remember Lot's wife.

33 "Whoever seeks to keep his life will lose it, and whoever loses *his life* will preserve it.

34 "I tell you, on that night there will be two in one bed; one will be taken and the other will be left.

35 "There will be two women grinding at the same place; one will be taken and the other will be left.

36 [²Two men will be in the field; one will be taken and the other will be left."]

37 And answering they *said to Him, "Where, Lord?" And He said to them, "Where the body *is,* there also the vultures will be gathered."

Parables on Prayer

18 Now He was telling them a parable to show that at all times they ought to pray and not to lose heart,

2 saying, "In a certain city there was a judge who did not fear God and did not respect man.

3 "There was a widow in that city, and she kept coming to him, saying, 'Give me legal protection from my opponent.'

4 "For a while he was unwilling; but afterward he said to himself, 'Even though I do not fear God nor respect man,

5 yet because this widow bothers me, I will give her legal protection, otherwise by continually coming she will wear me out.' "

---

1. Lit *has saved you*   2. Early mss do not contain this v

6 And the Lord said, "Hear what the unrighteous judge *said;

7 now, will not God bring about justice for His elect who cry to Him day and night, and will He delay long over them?

8 "I tell you that He will bring about justice for them quickly. However, when the Son of Man comes, will He find faith on the earth?"

9 And He also told this parable to some people who trusted in themselves that they were righteous, and viewed others with contempt:

10 "Two men went up into the temple to pray, one a Pharisee and the other a tax collector.

11 "The Pharisee stood and was praying this to himself: 'God, I thank You that I am not like other people: swindlers, unjust, adulterers, or even like this tax collector.

12 'I fast twice a week; I pay tithes of all that I get.'

13 "But the tax collector, standing some distance away, was even unwilling to lift up his eyes to heaven, but was beating his breast, saying, 'God, be merciful to me, the sinner!'

14 "I tell you, this man went to his house justified rather than the other; for everyone who exalts himself will be humbled, but he who humbles himself will be exalted."

15 And they were bringing even their babies to Him so that He would touch them, but when the disciples saw it, they *began* rebuking them.

16 But Jesus called for them, saying, "Permit the children to come to Me, and do not hinder them, for the kingdom of God belongs to such as these.

17 "Truly I say to you, whoever does not receive the kingdom of God like a child will not enter it *at all*."

18 A ruler questioned Him, saying, "Good Teacher, what shall I do to inherit eternal life?"

19 And Jesus said to him, "Why do you call Me good? No one is good except God alone.

20 "You know the commandments, 'DO NOT COMMIT ADULTERY, DO NOT MURDER, DO NOT STEAL, DO NOT BEAR FALSE WITNESS, HONOR YOUR FATHER AND MOTHER.' "

21 And he said, "All these things I have kept from *my* youth."

22 When Jesus heard *this*, He said to him, "One thing you still lack; sell all that you possess and distribute it to the poor, and you shall have treasure in heaven; and come, follow Me."

23 But when he had heard these things, he became very sad, for he was extremely rich.

24 And Jesus looked at him and said, "How hard it is for those who are wealthy to enter the kingdom of God!

25 "For it is easier for a camel to go through the eye of a needle than for a rich man to enter the kingdom of God."

26 They who heard it said, "Then who can be saved?"

27 But He said, "The things that are impossible with people are possible with God."

28 Peter said, "Behold, we have left our own *homes* and followed You."

29 And He said to them, "Truly I say to you, there is no one who has left house or wife or brothers or parents or children, for the sake of the kingdom of God,

30 who will not receive many times as much at this time and in the age to come, eternal life."

31 Then He took the twelve aside and said to them, "Behold, we are going up to Jerusalem, and all things which are written through the prophets about the Son of Man will be accomplished.

32 "For He will be handed over to the Gentiles, and will be mocked and mistreated and spit upon,

33 and after they have scourged Him, they will kill Him; and the third day He will rise again."

34 But the disciples understood none of these things, and *the meaning of* this statement was hidden from them, and they did not comprehend the things that were said.

35 As Jesus was approaching Jericho, a blind man was sitting by the road begging.

36 Now hearing a crowd going by, he *began* to inquire what this was.

37 They told him that Jesus of Nazareth was passing by.

38 And he called out, saying, "Jesus, Son of David, have mercy on me!"

39 Those who led the way were sternly telling him to be quiet; but he kept crying out all the more, "Son of David, have mercy on me!"

40 And Jesus stopped and commanded that he be brought to Him; and when he came near, He questioned him,

41 "What do you want Me to do for you?" And he said, "Lord, I want to regain my sight!"

42 And Jesus said to him, "Receive your sight; your faith has made you well."

43 Immediately he regained his sight and *began* following Him, glorifying God; and when all the people saw it, they gave praise to God.

Zaccheus Converted

19 He entered Jericho and was passing through.

2 And there was a man called by the name of Zaccheus; he was a chief tax collector and he was rich.

3 Zaccheus was trying to see who Jesus was, and was unable because of the crowd, for he was small in stature.

4 So he ran on ahead and climbed up into a sycamore tree in order to see Him, for He was about to pass through that way.

5 When Jesus came to the place, He looked up and said to him, "Zaccheus, hurry and come down, for today I must stay at your house."

6 And he hurried and came down and received Him gladly.

7 When they saw it, they all *began* to grumble, saying, "He has gone to be the guest of a man who is a sinner."

8 Zaccheus stopped and said to the Lord, "Behold, Lord, half of my possessions I will give

to the poor, and if I have defrauded anyone of anything, I will give back four times as much."

9 And Jesus said to him, "Today salvation has come to this house, because he, too, is a son of Abraham.

10 "For the Son of Man has come to seek and to save that which was lost."

11 While they were listening to these things, Jesus went on to tell a parable, because He was near Jerusalem, and they supposed that the kingdom of God was going to appear immediately.

12 So He said, "A nobleman went to a distant country to receive a kingdom for himself, and *then* return.

13 "And he called ten of his slaves, and gave them ten ¹minas and said to them, 'Do business *with this* until I come *back*.'

14 "But his citizens hated him and sent a delegation after him, saying, 'We do not want this man to reign over us.'

15 "When he returned, after receiving the kingdom, he ordered that these slaves, to whom he had given the money, be called to him so that he might know what business they had done.

16 "The first appeared, saying, 'Master, your mina has made ten minas more.'

17 "And he said to him, 'Well done, good slave, because you have been faithful in a very little thing, you are to be in authority over ten cities.'

18 "The second came, saying, 'Your mina, master, has made five minas.'

19 "And he said to him also, 'And you are to be over five cities.'

20 "Another came, saying, 'Master, here is your mina, which I kept put away in a handkerchief;

21 for I was afraid of you, because you are an exacting man; you take up what you did not lay down and reap what you did not sow.'

22 "He *said to him, 'By your own words I will judge you, you worthless slave. Did you know that I am an exacting man, taking up what I did not lay down and reaping what I did not sow?

23 'Then why did you not put my money in the bank, and having come, I would have collected it with interest?'

24 "Then he said to the bystanders, 'Take the mina away from him and give it to the one who has the ten minas.'

25 "And they said to him, 'Master, he has ten minas *already*.'

26 "I tell you that to everyone who has, more shall be given, but from the one who does not have, even what he does have shall be taken away.

27 "But these enemies of mine, who did not want me to reign over them, bring them here and slay them in my presence."

28 After He had said these things, He was going on ahead, going up to Jerusalem.

29 When He approached Bethphage and Bethany, near the mount that is called Olivet, He sent two of the disciples,

30 saying, "Go into the village ahead of *you;*

there, as you enter, you will find a colt tied on which no one yet has ever sat; untie it and bring it *here.*

31 "If anyone asks you, 'Why are you untying it?' you shall say, 'The Lord has need of it.' "

32 So those who were sent went away and found it just as He had told them.

33 As they were untying the colt, its owners said to them, "Why are you untying the colt?"

34 They said, "The Lord has need of it."

35 They brought it to Jesus, and they threw their coats on the colt and put Jesus *on it.*

36 As He was going, they were spreading their coats on the road.

37 As soon as He was approaching, near the descent of the Mount of Olives, the whole crowd of the disciples began to praise God joyfully with a loud voice for all the miracles which they had seen,

38 shouting:

"BLESSED IS THE KING WHO COMES IN THE NAME OF THE LORD;

Peace in heaven and glory in the highest!"

39 Some of the Pharisees in the crowd said to Him, "Teacher, rebuke Your disciples."

40 But Jesus answered, "I tell you, if these become silent, the stones will cry out!"

41 When He approached *Jerusalem*, He saw the city and wept over it,

42 saying, "If you had known in this day, even you, the things which make for peace! But now they have been hidden from your eyes.

43 "For the days will come upon you when your enemies will throw up a barricade against you, and surround you and hem you in on every side,

44 and they will level you to the ground and your children within you, and they will not leave in you one stone upon another, because you did not recognize the time of your visitation."

45 Jesus entered the temple and began to drive out those who were selling,

46 saying to them, "It is written, 'AND MY HOUSE SHALL BE A HOUSE OF PRAYER,' but you have made it a ROBBERS' DEN."

47 And He was teaching daily in the temple; but the chief priests and the scribes and the leading men among the people were trying to destroy Him,

48 and they could not find anything that they might do, for all the people were hanging on to every word He said.

Jesus' Authority Questioned

20 On one of the days while He was teaching the people in the temple and preaching the gospel, the chief priests and the scribes with the elders confronted *Him,*

2 and they spoke, saying to Him, "Tell us by what authority You are doing these things, or who is the one who gave You this authority?"

3 Jesus answered and said to them, "I will also ask you a question, and you tell Me:

4 "Was the baptism of John from heaven or from men?"

1. A mina is equal to about 100 days' wages

5 They reasoned among themselves, saying, "If we say, 'From heaven,' He will say, 'Why did you not believe him?'

6 "But if we say, 'From men,' all the people will stone us to death, for they are convinced that John was a prophet."

7 So they answered that they did not know where *it came* from.

8 And Jesus said to them, "Nor will I tell you by what authority I do these things."

9 And He began to tell the people this parable: "A man planted a vineyard and rented it out to vine-growers, and went on a journey for a long time.

10 "At the *harvest* time he sent a slave to the vine-growers, so that they would give him *some* of the produce of the vineyard; but the vine-growers beat him and sent him away empty-handed.

11 "And he proceeded to send another slave; and they beat him also and treated him shamefully and sent him away empty-handed.

12 "And he proceeded to send a third; and this one also they wounded and cast out.

13 "The owner of the vineyard said, 'What shall I do? I will send my beloved son; perhaps they will respect him.'

14 "But when the vine-growers saw him, they reasoned with one another, saying, 'This is the heir; let us kill him so that the inheritance will be ours.'

15 "So they threw him out of the vineyard and killed him. What, then, will the owner of the vineyard do to them?

16 "He will come and destroy these vine-growers and will give the vineyard to others." When they heard it, they said, "May it never be!"

17 But Jesus looked at them and said, "What then is this that is written:

'THE STONE WHICH THE BUILDERS REJECTED,
THIS BECAME THE CHIEF CORNER *stone*'?

18 "Everyone who falls on that stone will be broken to pieces; but on whomever it falls, it will scatter him like dust."

19 The scribes and the chief priests tried to lay hands on Him that very hour, and they feared the people; for they understood that He spoke this parable against them.

20 So they watched Him, and sent spies who pretended to be righteous, in order that they might catch Him in some statement, so that they *could* deliver Him to the rule and the authority of the governor.

21 They questioned Him, saying, "Teacher, we know that You speak and teach correctly, and You are not partial to any, but teach the way of God in truth.

22 "Is it lawful for us to pay taxes to Caesar, or not?"

23 But He detected their trickery and said to them,

24 "Show Me a ¹denarius. Whose likeness and inscription does it have?" They said, "Caesar's."

25 And He said to them, "Then render to Caesar the things that are Caesar's, and to God the things that are God's."

26 And they were unable to catch Him in a saying in the presence of the people; and being amazed at His answer, they became silent.

27 Now there came to Him some of the Sadducees (who say that there is no resurrection),

28 and they questioned Him, saying, "Teacher, Moses wrote for us that IF A MAN'S BROTHER DIES, having a wife, AND HE IS CHILDLESS, HIS BROTHER SHOULD MARRY THE WIFE AND RAISE UP CHILDREN TO HIS BROTHER.

29 "Now there were seven brothers; and the first took a wife and died childless;

30 and the second

31 and the third married her; and in the same way all seven died, leaving no children.

32 "Finally the woman died also.

33 "In the resurrection therefore, which one's wife will she be? For all seven had married her."

34 Jesus said to them, "The sons of this age marry and are given in marriage,

35 but those who are considered worthy to attain to that age and the resurrection from the dead, neither marry nor are given in marriage;

36 for they cannot even die anymore, because they are like angels, and are sons of God, being sons of the resurrection.

37 "But that the dead are raised, even Moses showed, in the *passage about the burning* bush, where he calls the Lord THE GOD OF ABRAHAM, AND THE GOD OF ISAAC, AND THE GOD OF JACOB.

38 "Now He is not the God of the dead but of the living; for all live to Him."

39 Some of the scribes answered and said, "Teacher, You have spoken well."

40 For they did not have courage to question Him any longer about anything.

41 Then He said to them, "How *is it that* they say ²the Christ is David's son?

42 "For David himself says in the book of Psalms,

'THE LORD SAID TO MY LORD,
"SIT AT MY RIGHT HAND,

43 UNTIL I MAKE YOUR ENEMIES A FOOTSTOOL FOR YOUR FEET." '

44 "Therefore David calls Him 'Lord,' and how is He his son?"

45 And while all the people were listening, He said to the disciples,

46 "Beware of the scribes, who like to walk around in long robes, and love respectful greetings in the market places, and chief seats in the synagogues and places of honor at banquets,

47 who devour widows' houses, and for appearance's sake offer long prayers. These will receive greater condemnation."

The Widow's Gift

21 And He looked up and saw the rich putting their gifts into the treasury.

2 And He saw a poor widow putting in two small copper coins.

---

1. The denarius was a day's wages 2. I.e. the Messiah

3 And He said, "Truly I say to you, this poor widow put in more than all *of them;*

4 for they all out of their surplus put into the offering; but she out of her poverty put in all that she had to live on."

5 And while some were talking about the temple, that it was adorned with beautiful stones and votive gifts, He said,

6 "*As for* these things which you are looking at, the days will come in which there will not be left one stone upon another which will not be torn down."

7 They questioned Him, saying, "Teacher, when therefore will these things happen? And what *will be* the sign when these things are about to take place?"

8 And He said, "See to it that you are not misled; for many will come in My name, saying, 'I am *He*,' and, 'The time is near.' Do not go after them.

9 "When you hear of wars and disturbances, do not be terrified; for these things must take place first, but the end *does* not *follow* immediately."

10 Then He continued by saying to them, "Nation will rise against nation and kingdom against kingdom,

11 and there will be great earthquakes, and in various places plagues and famines; and there will be terrors and great signs from heaven.

12 "But before all these things, they will lay their hands on you and will persecute you, delivering you to the synagogues and prisons, bringing you before kings and governors for My name's sake.

13 "It will lead to an opportunity for your testimony.

14 "So make up your minds not to prepare beforehand to defend yourselves;

15 for I will give you utterance and wisdom which none of your opponents will be able to resist or refute.

16 "But you will be betrayed even by parents and brothers and relatives and friends, and they will put *some* of you to death,

17 and you will be hated by all because of My name.

18 "Yet not a hair of your head will perish.

19 "By your endurance you will gain your lives.

20 "But when you see Jerusalem surrounded by armies, then recognize that her desolation is near.

21 "Then those who are in Judea must flee to the mountains, and those who are in the midst of the city must leave, and those who are in the country must not enter the city;

22 because these are days of vengeance, so that all things which are written will be fulfilled.

23 "Woe to those who are pregnant and to those who are nursing babies in those days; for there will be great distress upon the land and wrath to this people;

24 and they will fall by the edge of the sword, and will be led captive into all the nations; and Jerusalem will be trampled under foot by the Gentiles until the times of the Gentiles are fulfilled.

25 "There will be signs in sun and moon and stars, and on the earth dismay among nations, in perplexity at the roaring of the sea and the waves,

26 men fainting from fear and the expectation of the things which are coming upon the world; for the powers of the heavens will be shaken.

27 "Then they will see THE SON OF MAN COMING IN A CLOUD with power and great glory.

28 "But when these things begin to take place, straighten up and lift up your heads, because your redemption is drawing near."

29 Then He told them a parable: "Behold the fig tree and all the trees;

30 as soon as they put forth *leaves*, you see it and know for yourselves that summer is now near.

31 "So you also, when you see these things happening, recognize that the kingdom of God is near.

32 "Truly I say to you, this generation will not pass away until all things take place.

33 "Heaven and earth will pass away, but My words will not pass away.

34 "Be on guard, so that your hearts will not be weighted down with dissipation and drunkenness and the worries of life, and that day will not come on you suddenly like a trap;

35 for it will come upon all those who dwell on the face of the earth.

36 "But keep on the alert at all times, praying that you may have strength to escape all these things that are about to take place, and to stand before the Son of Man."

37 Now during the day He was teaching in the temple, but at evening He would go out and spend the night on the mount that is called Olivet.

38 And all the people would get up early in the morning *to come* to Him in the temple to listen to Him.

Preparing the Passover

22 Now the Feast of Unleavened Bread, which is called the Passover, was approaching.

2 The chief priests and the scribes were seeking how they might put Him to death; for they were afraid of the people.

3 And Satan entered into Judas who was called Iscariot, belonging to the number of the twelve.

4 And he went away and discussed with the chief priests and officers how he might betray Him to them.

5 They were glad and agreed to give him money.

6 So he consented, and *began* seeking a good opportunity to betray Him to them apart from the crowd.

7 Then came the *first* day of Unleavened Bread on which the Passover *lamb* had to be sacrificed.

8 And Jesus sent Peter and John, saying,

"Go and prepare the Passover for us, so that we may eat it."

9 They said to Him, "Where do You want us to prepare it?"

10 And He said to them, "When you have entered the city, a man will meet you carrying a pitcher of water; follow him into the house that he enters.

11 "And you shall say to the owner of the house, 'The Teacher says to you, "Where is the guest room in which I may eat the Passover with My disciples?" '

12 "And he will show you a large, furnished upper room; prepare it there."

13 And they left and found *everything* just as He had told them; and they prepared the Passover.

14 When the hour had come, He reclined *at the table*, and the apostles with Him.

15 And He said to them, "I have earnestly desired to eat this Passover with you before I suffer;

16 for I say to you, I shall never again eat it until it is fulfilled in the kingdom of God."

17 And when He had taken a cup *and* given thanks, He said, "Take this and share it among yourselves;

18 for I say to you, I will not drink of the fruit of the vine from now on until the kingdom of God comes."

19 And when He had taken *some* bread *and* given thanks, He broke it and gave it to them, saying, "This is My body which is given for you; do this in remembrance of Me."

20 And in the same way *He took* the cup after they had eaten, saying, "This cup which is poured out for you is the new covenant in My blood.

21 "But behold, the hand of the one betraying Me is with Mine on the table.

22 "For indeed, the Son of Man is going as it has been determined; but woe to that man by whom He is betrayed!"

23 And they began to discuss among themselves which one of them it might be who was going to do this thing.

24 And there arose also a dispute among them *as to* which one of them was regarded to be greatest.

25 And He said to them, "The kings of the Gentiles lord it over them; and those who have authority over them are called 'Benefactors.'

26 "But *it is* not this way with you, but the one who is the greatest among you must become like the youngest, and the leader like the servant.

27 "For who is greater, the one who reclines *at the table* or the one who serves? Is it not the one who reclines *at the table*? But I am among you as the one who serves.

28 "You are those who have stood by Me in My trials;

29 and just as My Father has granted Me a kingdom, I grant you

30 that you may eat and drink at My table in My kingdom, and you will sit on thrones judging the twelve tribes of Israel.

31 "Simon, Simon, behold, Satan has demanded *permission* to sift you like wheat;

32 but I have prayed for you, that your faith may not fail; and you, when once you have turned again, strengthen your brothers."

33 But he said to Him, "Lord, with You I am ready to go both to prison and to death!"

34 And He said, "I say to you, Peter, the rooster will not crow today until you have denied three times that you know Me."

35 And He said to them, "When I sent you out without money belt and bag and sandals, you did not lack anything, did you?" They said, "*No*, nothing."

36 And He said to them, "But now, whoever has a money belt is to take it along, likewise also a bag, and whoever has no sword is to sell his coat and buy one.

37 "For I tell you that this which is written must be fulfilled in Me, 'AND HE WAS NUMBERED WITH TRANSGRESSORS'; for that which refers to Me has *its* fulfillment."

38 They said, "Lord, look, here are two swords." And He said to them, "It is enough."

39 And He came out and proceeded as was His custom to the Mount of Olives; and the disciples also followed Him.

40 When He arrived at the place, He said to them, "Pray that you may not enter into temptation."

41 And He withdrew from them about a stone's throw, and He knelt down and *began* to pray,

42 saying, "Father, if You are willing, remove this cup from Me; yet not My will, but Yours be done."

43 Now an angel from heaven appeared to Him, strengthening Him.

44 And being in agony He was praying very fervently; and His sweat became like drops of blood, falling down upon the ground.

45 When He rose from prayer, He came to the disciples and found them sleeping from sorrow,

46 and said to them, "Why are you sleeping? Get up and pray that you may not enter into temptation."

47 While He was still speaking, behold, a crowd *came*, and the one called Judas, one of the twelve, was preceding them; and he approached Jesus to kiss Him.

48 But Jesus said to him, "Judas, are you betraying the Son of Man with a kiss?"

49 When those who were around Him saw what was going to happen, they said, "Lord, shall we strike with the sword?"

50 And one of them struck the slave of the high priest and cut off his right ear.

51 But Jesus answered and said, "Stop! No more of this." And He touched his ear and healed him.

52 Then Jesus said to the chief priests and officers of the temple and elders who had come against Him, "Have you come out with swords and clubs as you would against a robber?

53 "While I was with you daily in the temple, you did not lay hands on Me; but this hour and the power of darkness are yours."

54 Having arrested Him, they led Him *away* and brought Him to the house of the high priest; but Peter was following at a distance.

55 After they had kindled a fire in the middle of the courtyard and had sat down together, Peter was sitting among them.

56 And a servant-girl, seeing him as he sat in the firelight and looking intently at him, said, "This man was with Him too."

57 But he denied *it*, saying, "Woman, I do not know Him."

58 A little later, another saw him and said, "You are *one* of them too!" But Peter said, "Man, I am not!"

59 After about an hour had passed, another man *began* to insist, saying, "Certainly this man also was with Him, for he is a Galilean too."

60 But Peter said, "Man, I do not know what you are talking about." Immediately, while he was still speaking, a rooster crowed.

61 The Lord turned and looked at Peter. And Peter remembered the word of the Lord, how He had told him, "Before a rooster crows today, you will deny Me three times."

62 And he went out and wept bitterly.

63 Now the men who were holding Jesus in custody were mocking Him and beating Him,

64 and they blindfolded Him and were asking Him, saying, "Prophesy, who is the one who hit You?"

65 And they were saying many other things against Him, blaspheming.

66 When it was day, the 1Council of elders of the people assembled, both chief priests and scribes, and they led Him away to their council *chamber,* saying,

67 "If You are the Christ, tell us." But He said to them, "If I tell you, you will not believe;

68 and if I ask a question, you will not answer.

69 "But from now on THE SON OF MAN WILL BE SEATED AT THE RIGHT HAND of the power of GOD."

70 And they all said, "Are You the Son of God, then?" And He said to them, "Yes, I am."

71 Then they said, "What further need do we have of testimony? For we have heard it ourselves from His own mouth."

Jesus before Pilate

23 Then the whole body of them got up and brought Him before Pilate.

2 And they began to accuse Him, saying, "We found this man misleading our nation and forbidding to pay taxes to Caesar, and saying that He Himself is Christ, a King."

3 So Pilate asked Him, saying, "Are You the King of the Jews?" And He answered him and said, "*It is as* you say."

4 Then Pilate said to the chief priests and the crowds, "I find no guilt in this man."

5 But they kept on insisting, saying, "He stirs up the people, teaching all over Judea, starting from Galilee even as far as this place."

6 When Pilate heard it, he asked whether the man was a Galilean.

7 And when he learned that He belonged to Herod's jurisdiction, he sent Him to Herod, who himself also was in Jerusalem at that time.

8 Now Herod was very glad when he saw Jesus; for he had wanted to see Him for a long time, because he had been hearing about Him and was hoping to see some sign performed by Him.

9 And he questioned Him at some length; but He answered him nothing.

10 And the chief priests and the scribes were standing there, accusing Him vehemently.

11 And Herod with his soldiers, after treating Him with contempt and mocking Him, dressed Him in a gorgeous robe and sent Him back to Pilate.

12 Now Herod and Pilate became friends with one another that very day; for before they had been enemies with each other.

13 Pilate summoned the chief priests and the rulers and the people,

14 and said to them, "You brought this man to me as one who incites the people to rebellion, and behold, having examined Him before you, I have found no guilt in this man regarding the charges which you make against Him.

15 "No, nor has Herod, for he sent Him back to us; and behold, nothing deserving death has been done by Him.

16 "Therefore I will punish Him and release Him."

17 [2Now he was obliged to release to them at the feast one prisoner.]

18 But they cried out all together, saying, "Away with this man, and release for us Barabbas!"

19 (He was one who had been thrown into prison for an insurrection made in the city, and for murder.)

20 Pilate, wanting to release Jesus, addressed them again,

21 but they kept on calling out, saying, "Crucify, crucify Him!"

22 And he said to them the third time, "Why, what evil has this man done? I have found in Him no guilt *demanding* death; therefore I will punish Him and release Him."

23 But they were insistent, with loud voices asking that He be crucified. And their voices *began* to prevail.

24 And Pilate pronounced sentence that their demand be granted.

25 And he released the man they were asking for who had been thrown into prison for insurrection and murder, but he delivered Jesus to their will.

26 When they led Him away, they seized a man, Simon of Cyrene, coming in from the country, and placed on him the cross to carry behind Jesus.

27 And following Him was a large crowd of the people, and of women who were mourning and lamenting Him.

---

1. Or *Sanhedrin* 2. Early mss do not contain this v

28 But Jesus turning to them said, "Daughters of Jerusalem, stop weeping for Me, but weep for yourselves and for your children.

29 "For behold, the days are coming when they will say, 'Blessed are the barren, and the wombs that never bore, and the breasts that never nursed.'

30 "Then they will begin TO SAY TO THE MOUNTAINS, 'FALL ON US,' AND TO THE HILLS, 'COVER US.'

31 "For if they do these things when the tree is green, what will happen when it is dry?"

32 Two others also, who were criminals, were being led away to be put to death with Him.

33 When they came to the place called The Skull, there they crucified Him and the criminals, one on the right and the other on the left.

34 But Jesus was saying, "Father, forgive them; for they do not know what they are doing." And they cast lots, dividing up His garments among themselves.

35 And the people stood by, looking on. And even the rulers were sneering at Him, saying, "He saved others; let Him save Himself if this is the Christ of God, His Chosen One."

36 The soldiers also mocked Him, coming up to Him, offering Him sour wine,

37 and saying, "If You are the King of the Jews, save Yourself!"

38 Now there was also an inscription above Him, "THIS IS THE KING OF THE JEWS."

39 One of the criminals who were hanged *there* was hurling abuse at Him, saying, "Are You not the Christ? Save Yourself and us!"

40 But the other answered, and rebuking him said, "Do you not even fear God, since you are under the same sentence of condemnation?

41 "And we indeed *are suffering* justly, for we are receiving what we deserve for our deeds; but this man has done nothing wrong."

42 And he was saying, "Jesus, remember me when You come in Your kingdom!"

43 And He said to him, "Truly I say to you, today you shall be with Me in Paradise."

44 It was now about [1]the sixth hour, and darkness fell over the whole land until [2]the ninth hour,

45 because the sun was obscured; and the veil of the temple was torn in two.

46 And Jesus, crying out with a loud voice, said, "Father, INTO YOUR HANDS I COMMIT MY SPIRIT." Having said this, He breathed His last.

47 Now when the centurion saw what had happened, he *began* praising God, saying, "Certainly this man was innocent."

48 And all the crowds who came together for this spectacle, when they observed what had happened, *began* to return, beating their breasts.

49 And all His acquaintances and the women who accompanied Him from Galilee were standing at a distance, seeing these things.

50 And a man named Joseph, who was a member of the Council, a good and righteous man

51 (he had not consented to their plan and action), *a man* from Arimathea, a city of the Jews, who was waiting for the kingdom of God;

52 this man went to Pilate and asked for the body of Jesus.

53 And he took it down and wrapped it in a linen cloth, and laid Him in a tomb cut into the rock, where no one had ever lain.

54 It was the preparation day, and the Sabbath was about to begin.

55 Now the women who had come with Him out of Galilee followed, and saw the tomb and how His body was laid.

56 Then they returned and prepared spices and perfumes.

And on the Sabbath they rested according to the commandment.

The Resurrection

24 But on the first day of the week, at early dawn, they came to the tomb bringing the spices which they had prepared.

2 And they found the stone rolled away from the tomb,

3 but when they entered, they did not find the body of the Lord Jesus.

4 While they were perplexed about this, behold, two men suddenly stood near them in dazzling clothing;

5 and as *the women* were terrified and bowed their faces to the ground, *the men* said to them, "Why do you seek the living One among the dead?

6 "He is not here, but He has risen. Remember how He spoke to you while He was still in Galilee,

7 saying that the Son of Man must be delivered into the hands of sinful men, and be crucified, and the third day rise again."

8 And they remembered His words,

9 and returned from the tomb and reported all these things to the eleven and to all the rest.

10 Now they were Mary Magdalene and Joanna and Mary the *mother* of James; also the other women with them were telling these things to the apostles.

11 But these words appeared to them as nonsense, and they would not believe them.

12 But Peter got up and ran to the tomb; stooping and looking in, he *saw the linen wrappings only; and he went away to his home, marveling at what had happened.

13 And behold, two of them were going that very day to a village named Emmaus, which was [3]about seven miles from Jerusalem.

14 And they were talking with each other about all these things which had taken place.

15 While they were talking and discussing, Jesus Himself approached and *began* traveling with them.

16 But their eyes were prevented from recognizing Him.

17 And He said to them, "What are these words that you are exchanging with one

---

1. I.e. noon   2. I.e. 3 p.m.   3. Lit *60 stadia;* one stadion was about 600 ft

another as you are walking?" And they stood still, looking sad.

18 One *of them*, named Cleopas, answered and said to Him, "Are You the only one visiting Jerusalem and unaware of the things which have happened here in these days?"

19 And He said to them, "What things?" And they said to Him, "The things about Jesus the Nazarene, who was a prophet mighty in deed and word in the sight of God and all the people,

20 and how the chief priests and our rulers delivered Him to the sentence of death, and crucified Him.

21 "But we were hoping that it was He who was going to redeem Israel. Indeed, besides all this, it is the third day since these things happened.

22 "But also some women among us amazed us. When they were at the tomb early in the morning,

23 and did not find His body, they came, saying that they had also seen a vision of angels who said that He was alive.

24 "Some of those who were with us went to the tomb and found it just exactly as the women also had said; but Him they did not see."

25 And He said to them, "O foolish men and slow of heart to believe in all that the prophets have spoken!

26 "Was it not necessary for the Christ to suffer these things and to enter into His glory?"

27 Then beginning with Moses and with all the prophets, He explained to them the things concerning Himself in all the Scriptures.

28 And they approached the village where they were going, and He acted as though He were going farther.

29 But they urged Him, saying, "Stay with us, for it is *getting* toward evening, and the day is now nearly over." So He went in to stay with them.

30 When He had reclined *at the table* with them, He took the bread and blessed *it*, and breaking *it*, He *began* giving *it* to them.

31 Then their eyes were opened and they recognized Him; and He vanished from their sight.

32 They said to one another, "Were not our hearts burning within us while He was speaking to us on the road, while He was explaining the Scriptures to us?"

33 And they got up that very hour and returned to Jerusalem, and found gathered together the eleven and those who were with them,

34 saying, "The Lord has really risen and has appeared to Simon."

35 They *began* to relate their experiences on the road and how He was recognized by them in the breaking of the bread.

36 While they were telling these things, He Himself stood in their midst and *said to them, "Peace be to you."

37 But they were startled and frightened and thought that they were seeing a spirit.

38 And He said to them, "Why are you troubled, and why do doubts arise in your hearts?

39 "See My hands and My feet, that it is I Myself; touch Me and see, for a spirit does not have flesh and bones as you see that I have."

40 And when He had said this, He showed them His hands and His feet.

41 While they still could not believe *it* because of their joy and amazement, He said to them, "Have you anything here to eat?"

42 They gave Him a piece of a broiled fish;

43 and He took it and ate *it* before them.

44 Now He said to them, "These are My words which I spoke to you while I was still with you, that all things which are written about Me in the Law of Moses and the Prophets and the Psalms must be fulfilled."

45 Then He opened their minds to understand the Scriptures,

46 and He said to them, "Thus it is written, that the Christ would suffer and rise again from the dead the third day,

47 and that repentance for forgiveness of sins would be proclaimed in His name to all the nations, beginning from Jerusalem.

48 "You are witnesses of these things.

49 "And behold, I am sending forth the promise of My Father upon you; but you are to stay in the city until you are clothed with power from on high."

50 And He led them out as far as Bethany, and He lifted up His hands and blessed them.

51 While He was blessing them, He parted from them and was carried up into heaven.

52 And they, after worshiping Him, returned to Jerusalem with great joy,

53 and were continually in the temple praising God.

THE GOSPEL ACCORDING TO JOHN

The Deity of Jesus Christ

1 In the beginning was the Word, and the Word was with God, and the Word was God.

2 He was in the beginning with God.

3 All things came into being through Him, and apart from Him nothing came into being that has come into being.

4 In Him was life, and the life was the Light of men.

5 The Light shines in the darkness, and the darkness did not ¹comprehend it.

6 There ²came a man sent from God, whose name was John.

7 He came as a witness, to testify about the Light, so that all might believe through him.

8 He was not the Light, but *he came* to testify about the Light.

9 There was the true Light ³which, coming into the world, enlightens every man.

10 He was in the world, and the world was made through Him, and the world did not know Him.

11 He came to His ⁴own, and those who were His own did not receive Him.

12 But as many as received Him, to them He gave the right to become children of God, *even* to those who believe in His name,

13 who were born, not of blood nor of the will of the flesh nor of the will of man, but of God.

14 And the Word became flesh, and dwelt among us, and we saw His glory, glory as of the only begotten from the Father, full of grace and truth.

15 John *testified about Him and cried out, saying, "This was He of whom I said, 'He who comes after me has a higher rank than I, for He existed before me.' "

16 For of His fullness we have all received, and grace upon grace.

17 For the Law was given through Moses; grace and truth were realized through Jesus Christ.

18 No one has seen God at any time; the only begotten God who is in the bosom of the Father, He has explained *Him.*

19 This is the testimony of John, when the Jews sent to him priests and Levites from Jerusalem to ask him, "Who are you?"

20 And he confessed and did not deny, but confessed, "I am not the Christ."

21 They asked him, "What then? Are you Elijah?" And he *said, "I am not." "Are you the Prophet?" And he answered, "No."

22 Then they said to him, "Who are you, so that we may give an answer to those who sent us? What do you say about yourself?"

23 He said, "I am a VOICE OF ONE CRYING IN THE WILDERNESS, 'MAKE STRAIGHT THE WAY OF THE LORD,' as Isaiah the prophet said."

24 Now they had been sent from the Pharisees.

25 They asked him, and said to him, "Why then are you baptizing, if you are not the Christ, nor Elijah, nor the Prophet?"

26 John answered them saying, "I baptize ⁵in water, *but* among you stands One whom you do not know.

27 "*It is* He who comes after me, the thong of whose sandal I am not worthy to untie."

28 These things took place in Bethany beyond the Jordan, where John was baptizing.

29 The next day he *saw Jesus coming to him and *said, "Behold, the Lamb of God who takes away the sin of the world!

30 "This is He on behalf of whom I said, 'After me comes a Man who has a higher rank than I, for He existed before me.'

31 "I did not recognize Him, but so that He might be manifested to Israel, I came baptizing ⁵in water."

32 John testified saying, "I have seen the Spirit descending as a dove out of heaven, and He remained upon Him.

33 "I did not recognize Him, but He who sent me to baptize ⁵in water said to me, 'He upon whom you see the Spirit descending and remaining upon Him, this is the One who baptizes in the Holy Spirit.'

34 "I myself have seen, and have testified that this is the Son of God."

35 Again the next day John was standing with two of his disciples,

36 and he looked at Jesus as He walked, and *said, "Behold, the Lamb of God!"

37 The two disciples heard him speak, and they followed Jesus.

38 And Jesus turned and saw them following, and *said to them, "What do you seek?" They said to Him, "Rabbi (which translated means Teacher), where are You staying?"

39 He *said to them, "Come, and you will see." So they came and saw where He was staying; and they stayed with Him that day, for it was about the ⁶tenth hour.

40 One of the two who heard John *speak* and followed Him, was Andrew, Simon Peter's brother.

41 He *found first his own brother Simon and *said to him, "We have found the Messiah" (which translated means Christ).

42 He brought him to Jesus. Jesus looked at him and said, "You are Simon the son of John; you shall be called Cephas" (which is translated Peter).

43 The next day He purposed to go into Galilee, and He *found Philip. And Jesus *said to him, "Follow Me."

44 Now Philip was from Bethsaida, of the city of Andrew and Peter.

45 Philip *found Nathanael and *said to him, "We have found Him of whom Moses in the Law and *also* the Prophets wrote—Jesus of Nazareth, the son of Joseph."

---

1. Or *overpower* 2. Or *came into being* 3. Or *which enlightens every person coming into the world* 4. Or *own things, possessions, domain* 5. The Gr here can be translated *in, with* or *by* 6. Perhaps 10 a.m. (Roman time)

Jesus is the only way to God. Read John 14:6 on page 85.

46 Nathanael said to him, "Can any good thing come out of Nazareth?" Philip *said to him, "Come and see."

47 Jesus saw Nathanael coming to Him, and *said of him, "Behold, an Israelite indeed, in whom there is no deceit!"

48 Nathanael *said to Him, "How do You know me?" Jesus answered and said to him, "Before Philip called you, when you were under the fig tree, I saw you."

49 Nathanael answered Him, "Rabbi, You are the Son of God; You are the King of Israel."

50 Jesus answered and said to him, "Because I said to you that I saw you under the fig tree, do you believe? You will see greater things than these."

51 And He *said to him, "Truly, truly, I say to you, you will see the heavens opened and the angels of God ascending and descending on the Son of Man."

Miracle at Cana

2 On the third day there was a wedding in Cana of Galilee, and the mother of Jesus was there;

2 and both Jesus and His disciples were invited to the wedding.

3 When the wine ran out, the mother of Jesus *said to Him, "They have no wine."

4 And Jesus *said to her, "Woman, what does that have to do with us? My hour has not yet come."

5 His mother *said to the servants, "Whatever He says to you, do it."

6 Now there were six stone waterpots set there for the Jewish custom of purification, containing twenty or thirty gallons each.

7 Jesus *said to them, "Fill the waterpots with water." So they filled them up to the brim.

8 And He *said to them, "Draw *some* out now and take it to the ¹headwaiter." So they took it *to him.*

9 When the headwaiter tasted the water which had become wine, and did not know where it came from (but the servants who had drawn the water knew), the headwaiter *called the bridegroom,

10 and *said to him, "Every man serves the good wine first, and when *the people* have drunk freely, *then he serves* the poorer *wine; but* you have kept the good wine until now."

11 This beginning of *His* signs Jesus did in Cana of Galilee, and manifested His glory, and His disciples believed in Him.

12 After this He went down to Capernaum, He and His mother and *His* brothers and His disciples; and they stayed there a few days.

13 The Passover of the Jews was near, and Jesus went up to Jerusalem.

14 And He found in the temple those who were selling oxen and sheep and doves, and the money changers seated *at their tables.*

15 And He made a scourge of cords, and drove *them* all out of the temple, with the sheep and the oxen; and He poured out the coins of the money changers and overturned their tables;

16 and to those who were selling the doves He said, "Take these things away; stop making My Father's house a place of business."

17 His disciples remembered that it was written, "ZEAL FOR YOUR HOUSE WILL CONSUME ME."

18 The Jews then said to Him, "What sign do You show us as your authority for doing these things?"

19 Jesus answered them, "Destroy this temple, and in three days I will raise it up."

20 The Jews then said, "It took forty-six years to build this temple, and will You raise it up in three days?"

21 But He was speaking of the temple of His body.

22 So when He was raised from the dead, His disciples remembered that He said this; and they believed the Scripture and the word which Jesus had spoken.

23 Now when He was in Jerusalem at the Passover, during the feast, many believed in His name, observing His signs which He was doing.

24 But Jesus, on His part, was not entrusting Himself to them, for He knew all men,

25 and because He did not need anyone to testify concerning man, for He Himself knew what was in man.

The New Birth

3 Now there was a man of the Pharisees, named Nicodemus, a ruler of the Jews;

2 this man came to Jesus by night and said to Him, "Rabbi, we know that You have come from God *as* a teacher; for no one can do these signs that You do unless God is with him."

3 Jesus answered and said to him, "Truly, truly, I say to you, unless one is born again he cannot see the kingdom of God."

4 Nicodemus *said to Him, "How can a man be born when he is old? He cannot enter a second time into his mother's womb and be born, can he?"

5 Jesus answered, "Truly, truly, I say to you, unless one is born of water and the Spirit he cannot enter into the kingdom of God.

6 "That which is born of the flesh is flesh, and that which is born of the Spirit is spirit.

7 "Do not be amazed that I said to you, 'You must be born again.'

8 "The wind blows where it wishes and you hear the sound of it, but do not know where it comes from and where it is going; so is everyone who is born of the Spirit."

9 Nicodemus said to Him, "How can these things be?"

10 Jesus answered and said to him, "Are you the teacher of Israel and do not understand these things?

11 "Truly, truly, I say to you, we speak of what we know and testify of what we have seen, and you do not accept our testimony.

---

1. Or *steward*

the Son of God

12 "If I told you earthly things and you do not believe, how will you believe if I tell you heavenly things?

13 "No one has ascended into heaven, but He who descended from heaven: the Son of Man.

14 "As Moses lifted up the serpent in the wilderness, even so must the Son of Man be lifted up;

15 so that whoever [1]believes will in Him have eternal life.

16 "For God so loved the world, that He gave His only begotten Son, that whoever believes in Him shall not perish, but have eternal life.

17 "For God did not send the Son into the world to judge the world, but that the world might be saved through Him.

18 "He who believes in Him is not judged; he who does not believe has been judged already, because he has not believed in the name of the only begotten Son of God.

19 "This is the judgment, that the Light has come into the world, and men loved the darkness rather than the Light, for their deeds were evil.

20 "For everyone who does evil hates the Light, and does not come to the Light for fear that his deeds will be exposed.

21 "But he who practices the truth comes to the Light, so that his deeds may be manifested as having been wrought in God."

22 After these things Jesus and His disciples came into the land of Judea, and there He was spending time with them and baptizing.

23 John also was baptizing in Aenon near Salim, because there was much water there; and *people* were coming and were being baptized—

24 for John had not yet been thrown into prison.

25 Therefore there arose a discussion on the part of John's disciples with a Jew about purification.

26 And they came to John and said to him, "Rabbi, He who was with you beyond the Jordan, to whom you have testified, behold, He is baptizing and all are coming to Him."

27 John answered and said, "A man can receive nothing unless it has been given him from heaven.

28 "You yourselves are my witnesses that I said, 'I am not the Christ,' but, 'I have been sent ahead of Him.'

29 "He who has the bride is the bridegroom; but the friend of the bridegroom, who stands and hears him, rejoices greatly because of the bridegroom's voice. So this joy of mine has been made full.

30 "He must increase, but I must decrease.

31 "He who comes from above is above all; he who is of the earth is from the earth and speaks of the earth. He who comes from heaven is above all.

32 "What He has seen and heard, of that He testifies; and no one receives His testimony.

33 "He who has received His testimony has set his seal to *this*, that God is true.

34 "For He whom God has sent speaks the words of God; for He gives the Spirit without measure.

35 "The Father loves the Son and has given all things into His hand.

36 "He who believes in the Son has eternal life; but he who does not obey the Son will not see life, but the wrath of God abides on him."

Jesus Goes to Galilee

4 Therefore when the Lord knew that the Pharisees had heard that Jesus was making and baptizing more disciples than John

2 (although Jesus Himself was not baptizing, but His disciples were),

3 He left Judea and went away again into Galilee.

4 And He had to pass through Samaria.

5 So He *came to a city of Samaria called Sychar, near the parcel of ground that Jacob gave to his son Joseph;

6 and Jacob's well was there. So Jesus, being wearied from His journey, was sitting thus by the well. It was about [2]the sixth hour.

7 There *came a woman of Samaria to draw water. Jesus *said to her, "Give Me a drink."

8 For His disciples had gone away into the city to buy food.

9 Therefore the Samaritan woman *said to Him, "How is it that You, being a Jew, ask me for a drink since I am a Samaritan woman?" (For Jews have no dealings with Samaritans.)

10 Jesus answered and said to her, "If you knew the gift of God, and who it is who says to you, 'Give Me a drink,' you would have asked Him, and He would have given you living water."

11 She *said to Him, "Sir, You have nothing to draw with and the well is deep; where then do You get that living water?

12 "You are not greater than our father Jacob, are You, who gave us the well, and drank of it himself and his sons and his cattle?"

13 Jesus answered and said to her, "Everyone who drinks of this water will thirst again;

14 but whoever drinks of the water that I will give him shall never thirst; but the water that I will give him will become in him a well of water springing up to eternal life."

15 The woman *said to Him, "Sir, give me this water, so I will not be thirsty nor come all the way here to draw."

16 He *said to her, "Go, call your husband and come here."

17 The woman answered and said, "I have no husband." Jesus *said to her, "You have correctly said, 'I have no husband';

18 for you have had five husbands, and the one whom you now have is not your husband; this you have said truly."

19 The woman *said to Him, "Sir, I perceive that You are a prophet.

20 "Our fathers worshiped in this mountain,

1. Or *believes in Him will have eternal life* 2. Perhaps 6 p.m. Roman time or noon Jewish time

and you *people* say that in Jerusalem is the place where men ought to worship."

21 Jesus *said to her, "Woman, believe Me, an hour is coming when neither in this mountain nor in Jerusalem will you worship the Father.

22 "You worship what you do not know; we worship what we know, for salvation is from the Jews.

23 "But an hour is coming, and now is, when the true worshipers will worship the Father in spirit and truth; for such people the Father seeks to be His worshipers.

24 "God is spirit, and those who worship Him must worship in spirit and truth."

25 The woman *said to Him, "I know that Messiah is coming (He who is called Christ); when that One comes, He will declare all things to us."

26 Jesus *said to her, "I who speak to you am He."

27 At this point His disciples came, and they were amazed that He had been speaking with a woman, yet no one said, "What do You seek?" or, "Why do You speak with her?"

28 So the woman left her waterpot, and went into the city and *said to the men,

29 "Come, see a man who told me all the things that I *have* done; this is not the Christ, is it?"

30 They went out of the city, and were coming to Him.

31 Meanwhile the disciples were urging Him, saying, "Rabbi, eat."

32 But He said to them, "I have food to eat that you do not know about."

33 So the disciples were saying to one another, "No one brought Him *anything* to eat, did he?"

34 Jesus *said to them, "My food is to do the will of Him who sent Me and to accomplish His work.

35 "Do you not say, 'There are yet four months, and *then* comes the harvest'? Behold, I say to you, lift up your eyes and look on the fields, that they are white for harvest.

36 "Already he who reaps is receiving wages and is gathering fruit for life eternal; so that he who sows and he who reaps may rejoice together.

37 "For in this *case* the saying is true, 'One sows and another reaps.'

38 "I sent you to reap that for which you have not labored; others have labored and you have entered into their labor."

39 From that city many of the Samaritans believed in Him because of the word of the woman who testified, "He told me all the things that I *have* done."

40 So when the Samaritans came to Jesus, they were asking Him to stay with them; and He stayed there two days.

41 Many more believed because of His word;

42 and they were saying to the woman, "It is no longer because of what you said that we believe, for we have heard for ourselves and know that this One is indeed the Savior of the world."

43 After the two days He went forth from there into Galilee.

44 For Jesus Himself testified that a prophet has no honor in his own country.

45 So when He came to Galilee, the Galileans received Him, having seen all the things that He did in Jerusalem at the feast; for they themselves also went to the feast.

46 Therefore He came again to Cana of Galilee where He had made the water wine. And there was a royal official whose son was sick at Capernaum.

47 When he heard that Jesus had come out of Judea into Galilee, he went to Him and was imploring *Him* to come down and heal his son; for he was at the point of death.

48 So Jesus said to him, "Unless you *people* see signs and wonders, you *simply* will not believe."

49 The royal official *said to Him, "Sir, come down before my child dies."

50 Jesus *said to him, "Go; your son lives." The man believed the word that Jesus spoke to him and started off.

51 As he was now going down, *his* slaves met him, saying that his son was living.

52 So he inquired of them the hour when he began to get better. Then they said to him, "Yesterday at the ¹seventh hour the fever left him."

53 So the father knew that *it was* at that hour in which Jesus said to him, "Your son lives"; and he himself believed and his whole household.

54 This is again a second sign that Jesus performed when He had come out of Judea into Galilee.

The Healing at Bethesda

5 After these things there was a feast of the Jews, and Jesus went up to Jerusalem.

2 Now there is in Jerusalem by the sheep *gate* a pool, which is called in Hebrew Bethesda, having five porticoes.

3 In these lay a multitude of those who were sick, blind, lame, and withered, [²waiting for the moving of the waters;

4 for an angel of the Lord went down at certain seasons into the pool and stirred up the water; whoever then first, after the stirring up of the water, stepped in was made well from whatever disease with which he was afflicted.]

5 A man was there who had been ill for thirty-eight years.

6 When Jesus saw him lying *there*, and knew that he had already been a long time *in that condition*, He *said to him, "Do you wish to get well?"

7 The sick man answered Him, "Sir, I have no man to put me into the pool when the water is stirred up, but while I am coming, another steps down before me."

8 Jesus *said to him, "Get up, pick up your pallet and walk."

9 Immediately the man became well, and picked up his pallet and *began* to walk.

---

1. Perhaps 7 p.m. Roman time or 1 p.m. Jewish time   2. Early mss do not contain the remainder of v 3, nor v 4

Now it was the Sabbath on that day.

10 So the Jews were saying to the man who was cured, "It is the Sabbath, and it is not permissible for you to carry your pallet."

11 But he answered them, "He who made me well was the one who said to me, 'Pick up your pallet and walk.' "

12 They asked him, "Who is the man who said to you, 'Pick up *your pallet* and walk'?"

13 But the man who was healed did not know who it was, for Jesus had slipped away while there was a crowd in *that* place.

14 Afterward Jesus *found him in the temple and said to him, "Behold, you have become well; do not sin anymore, so that nothing worse happens to you."

15 The man went away, and told the Jews that it was Jesus who had made him well.

16 For this reason the Jews were persecuting Jesus, because He was doing these things on the Sabbath.

17 But He answered them, "My Father is working until now, and I Myself am working."

18 For this reason therefore the Jews were seeking all the more to kill Him, because He not only was breaking the Sabbath, but also was calling God His own Father, making Himself equal with God.

19 Therefore Jesus answered and was saying to them, "Truly, truly, I say to you, the Son can do nothing of Himself, unless *it is* something He sees the Father doing; for whatever the Father does, these things the Son also does in like manner.

20 "For the Father loves the Son, and shows Him all things that He Himself is doing; and *the Father* will show Him greater works than these, so that you will marvel.

21 "For just as the Father raises the dead and gives them life, even so the Son also gives life to whom He wishes.

22 "For not even the Father judges anyone, but He has given all judgment to the Son,

23 so that all will honor the Son even as they honor the Father. He who does not honor the Son does not honor the Father who sent Him.

24 "Truly, truly, I say to you, he who hears My word, and believes Him who sent Me, has eternal life, and does not come into judgment, but has passed out of death into life.

25 "Truly, truly, I say to you, an hour is coming and now is, when the dead will hear the voice of the Son of God, and those who hear will live.

26 "For just as the Father has life in Himself, even so He gave to the Son also to have life in Himself;

27 and He gave Him authority to execute judgment, because He is *the* Son of Man.

28 "Do not marvel at this; for an hour is coming, in which all who are in the tombs will hear His voice,

29 and will come forth; those who did the good *deeds* to a resurrection of life, those who committed the evil *deeds* to a resurrection of judgment.

30 "I can do nothing on My own initiative. As I hear, I judge; and My judgment is just, because I do not seek My own will, but the will of Him who sent Me.

31 "If I *alone* testify about Myself, My testimony is not true.

32 "There is another who testifies of Me, and I know that the testimony which He gives about Me is true.

33 "You have sent to John, and he has testified to the truth.

34 "But the testimony which I receive is not from man, but I say these things so that you may be saved.

35 "He was the lamp that was burning and was shining and you were willing to rejoice for a while in his light.

36 "But the testimony which I have is greater than *the testimony of* John; for the works which the Father has given Me to accomplish—the very works that I do—testify about Me, that the Father has sent Me.

37 "And the Father who sent Me, He has testified of Me. You have neither heard His voice at any time nor seen His form.

38 "You do not have His word abiding in you, for you do not believe Him whom He sent.

39 "¹You search the Scriptures because you think that in them you have eternal life; it is these that testify about Me;

40 and you are unwilling to come to Me so that you may have life.

41 "I do not receive glory from men;

42 but I know you, that you do not have the love of God in yourselves.

43 "I have come in My Father's name, and you do not receive Me; if another comes in his own name, you will receive him.

44 "How can you believe, when you receive glory from one another and you do not seek the glory that is from the *one and* only God?

45 "Do not think that I will accuse you before the Father; the one who accuses you is Moses, in whom you have set your hope.

46 "For if you believed Moses, you would believe Me, for he wrote about Me.

47 "But if you do not believe his writings, how will you believe My words?"

Five Thousand Fed

6 After these things Jesus went away to the other side of the Sea of Galilee (or Tiberias).

2 A large crowd followed Him, because they saw the signs which He was performing on those who were sick.

3 Then Jesus went up on the mountain, and there He sat down with His disciples.

4 Now the Passover, the feast of the Jews, was near.

5 Therefore Jesus, lifting up His eyes and seeing that a large crowd was coming to Him, *said to Philip, "Where are we to buy bread, so that these may eat?"

6 This He was saying to test him, for He Himself knew what He was intending to do.

---

1. Or (a command) *Search the Scriptures!*

7 Philip answered Him, "Two hundred ¹denarii worth of bread is not sufficient for them, for everyone to receive a little."

8 One of His disciples, Andrew, Simon Peter's brother, *said to Him,

9 "There is a lad here who has five barley loaves and two fish, but what are these for so many people?"

10 Jesus said, "Have the people sit down." Now there was much grass in the place. So the men sat down, in number about five thousand.

11 Jesus then took the loaves, and having given thanks, He distributed to those who were seated; likewise also of the fish as much as they wanted.

12 When they were filled, He *said to His disciples, "Gather up the leftover fragments so that nothing will be lost."

13 So they gathered them up, and filled twelve baskets with fragments from the five barley loaves which were left over by those who had eaten.

14 Therefore when the people saw the sign which He had performed, they said, "This is truly the Prophet who is to come into the world."

15 So Jesus, perceiving that they were intending to come and take Him by force to make Him king, withdrew again to the mountain by Himself alone.

16 Now when evening came, His disciples went down to the sea,

17 and after getting into a boat, they *started to* cross the sea to Capernaum. It had already become dark, and Jesus had not yet come to them.

18 The sea *began* to be stirred up because a strong wind was blowing.

19 Then, when they had rowed about three or four miles, they *saw Jesus walking on the sea and drawing near to the boat; and they were frightened.

20 But He *said to them, "It is I; do not be afraid."

21 So they were willing to receive Him into the boat, and immediately the boat was at the land to which they were going.

22 The next day the crowd that stood on the other side of the sea saw that there was no other small boat there, except one, and that Jesus had not entered with His disciples into the boat, but *that* His disciples had gone away alone.

23 There came other small boats from Tiberias near to the place where they ate the bread after the Lord had given thanks.

24 So when the crowd saw that Jesus was not there, nor His disciples, they themselves got into the small boats, and came to Capernaum seeking Jesus.

25 When they found Him on the other side of the sea, they said to Him, "Rabbi, when did You get here?"

26 Jesus answered them and said, "Truly, truly, I say to you, you seek Me, not because you saw signs, but because you ate of the loaves and were filled.

27 "Do not work for the food which perishes, but for the food which endures to eternal life, which the Son of Man will give to you, for on Him the Father, God, has set His seal."

28 Therefore they said to Him, "What shall we do, so that we may work the works of God?"

29 Jesus answered and said to them, "This is the work of God, that you believe in Him whom He has sent."

30 So they said to Him, "What then do You do for a sign, so that we may see, and believe You? What work do You perform?

31 "Our fathers ate the manna in the wilderness; as it is written, 'HE GAVE THEM BREAD OUT OF HEAVEN TO EAT.' "

32 Jesus then said to them, "Truly, truly, I say to you, it is not Moses who has given you the bread out of heaven, but it is My Father who gives you the true bread out of heaven.

33 "For the bread of God is ²that which comes down out of heaven, and gives life to the world."

34 Then they said to Him, "Lord, always give us this bread."

35 Jesus said to them, "I am the bread of life; he who comes to Me will not hunger, and he who believes in Me will never thirst.

36 "But I said to you that you have seen Me, and yet do not believe.

37 "All that the Father gives Me will come to Me, and the one who comes to Me I will certainly not cast out.

38 "For I have come down from heaven, not to do My own will, but the will of Him who sent Me.

39 "This is the will of Him who sent Me, that of all that He has given Me I lose nothing, but raise it up on the last day.

40 "For this is the will of My Father, that everyone who beholds the Son and believes in Him will have eternal life, and I Myself will raise him up on the last day."

41 Therefore the Jews were grumbling about Him, because He said, "I am the bread that came down out of heaven."

42 They were saying, "Is not this Jesus, the son of Joseph, whose father and mother we know? How does He now say, 'I have come down out of heaven'?"

43 Jesus answered and said to them, "Do not grumble among yourselves.

44 "No one can come to Me unless the Father who sent Me draws him; and I will raise him up on the last day.

45 "It is written in the prophets, 'AND THEY SHALL ALL BE TAUGHT OF GOD.' Everyone who has heard and learned from the Father, comes to Me.

46 "Not that anyone has seen the Father, except the One who is from God; He has seen the Father.

47 "Truly, truly, I say to you, he who believes has eternal life.

---

1. The denarius was equivalent to a day's wages 2. Or *He who comes*

48 "I am the bread of life.

49 "Your fathers ate the manna in the wilderness, and they died.

50 "This is the bread which comes down out of heaven, so that one may eat of it and not die.

51 "I am the living bread that came down out of heaven; if anyone eats of this bread, he will live forever; and the bread also which I will give for the life of the world is My flesh."

52 Then the Jews *began* to argue with one another, saying, "How can this man give us *His* flesh to eat?"

53 So Jesus said to them, "Truly, truly, I say to you, unless you eat the flesh of the Son of Man and drink His blood, you have no life in yourselves.

54 "He who eats My flesh and drinks My blood has eternal life, and I will raise him up on the last day.

55 "For My flesh is true food, and My blood is true drink.

56 "He who eats My flesh and drinks My blood abides in Me, and I in him.

57 "As the living Father sent Me, and I live because of the Father, so he who eats Me, he also will live because of Me.

58 "This is the bread which came down out of heaven; not as the fathers ate and died; he who eats this bread will live forever."

59 These things He said in the synagogue as He taught in Capernaum.

60 Therefore many of His disciples, when they heard *this* said, "This is a difficult statement; who can listen to it?"

61 But Jesus, conscious that His disciples grumbled at this, said to them, "Does this cause you to stumble?

62 "*What* then if you see the Son of Man ascending to where He was before?

63 "It is the Spirit who gives life; the flesh profits nothing; the words that I have spoken to you are spirit and are life.

64 "But there are some of you who do not believe." For Jesus knew from the beginning who they were who did not believe, and who it was that would betray Him.

65 And He was saying, "For this reason I have said to you, that no one can come to Me unless it has been granted him from the Father."

66 As a result of this many of His disciples withdrew and were not walking with Him anymore.

67 So Jesus said to the twelve, "You do not want to go away also, do you?"

68 Simon Peter answered Him, "Lord, to whom shall we go? You have words of eternal life.

69 "We have believed and have come to know that You are the Holy One of God."

70 Jesus answered them, "Did I Myself not choose you, the twelve, and *yet* one of you is a devil?"

71 Now He meant Judas *the son* of Simon Iscariot, for he, one of the twelve, was going to betray Him.

Jesus Teaches at the Feast

7 After these things Jesus was walking in Galilee, for He was unwilling to walk in Judea because the Jews were seeking to kill Him.

2 Now the feast of the Jews, the Feast of Booths, was near.

3 Therefore His brothers said to Him, "Leave here and go into Judea, so that Your disciples also may see Your works which You are doing.

4 "For no one does anything in secret when he himself seeks to be *known* publicly. If You do these things, show Yourself to the world."

5 For not even His brothers were believing in Him.

6 So Jesus *said to them, "My time is not yet here, but your time is always opportune.

7 "The world cannot hate you, but it hates Me because I testify of it, that its deeds are evil.

8 "Go up to the feast yourselves; I do not go up to this feast because My time has not yet fully come."

9 Having said these things to them, He stayed in Galilee.

10 But when His brothers had gone up to the feast, then He Himself also went up, not publicly, but as if, in secret.

11 So the Jews were seeking Him at the feast and were saying, "Where is He?"

12 There was much grumbling among the crowds concerning Him; some were saying, "He is a good man"; others were saying, "No, on the contrary, He leads the people astray."

13 Yet no one was speaking openly of Him for fear of the Jews.

14 But when it was now the midst of the feast Jesus went up into the temple, and *began to* teach.

15 The Jews then were astonished, saying, "How has this man become learned, having never been educated?"

16 So Jesus answered them and said, "My teaching is not Mine, but His who sent Me.

17 "If anyone is willing to do His will, he will know of the teaching, whether it is of God or *whether* I speak from Myself.

18 "He who speaks from himself seeks his own glory; but He who is seeking the glory of the One who sent Him, He is true, and there is no unrighteousness in Him.

19 "Did not Moses give you the Law, and *yet* none of you carries out the Law? Why do you seek to kill Me?"

20 The crowd answered, "You have a demon! Who seeks to kill You?"

21 Jesus answered them, "I did one deed, and you all marvel.

22 "For this reason Moses has given you circumcision (not because it is from Moses, but from the fathers), and on *the* Sabbath you circumcise a man.

23 "If a man receives circumcision on *the* Sabbath so that the Law of Moses will not be broken, are you angry with Me because I made an entire man well on *the* Sabbath?

24 "Do not judge according to appearance, but judge with righteous judgment."

25 So some of the people of Jerusalem were saying, "Is this not the man whom they are seeking to kill?

26 "Look, He is speaking publicly, and they are saying nothing to Him. The rulers do not really know that this is the Christ, do they?

27 "However, we know where this man is from; but whenever the Christ may come, no one knows where He is from."

28 Then Jesus cried out in the temple, teaching and saying, "You both know Me and know where I am from; and I have not come of Myself, but He who sent Me is true, whom you do not know.

29 "I know Him, because I am from Him, and He sent Me."

30 So they were seeking to seize Him; and no man laid his hand on Him, because His hour had not yet come.

31 But many of the crowd believed in Him; and they were saying, "When the Christ comes, He will not perform more signs than those which this man has, will He?"

32 The Pharisees heard the crowd muttering these things about Him, and the chief priests and the Pharisees sent officers to seize Him.

33 Therefore Jesus said, "For a little while longer I am with you, then I go to Him who sent Me.

34 "You will seek Me, and will not find Me; and where I am, you cannot come."

35 The Jews then said to one another, "Where does this man intend to go that we will not find Him? He is not intending to go to the Dispersion among the Greeks, and teach the Greeks, is He?

36 "What is this statement that He said, 'You will seek Me, and will not find Me; and where I am, you cannot come'?"

37 Now on the last day, the great *day* of the feast, Jesus stood and cried out, saying, "If anyone is thirsty, let him come to Me and drink.

38 "He who believes in Me, as the Scripture said, 'From his innermost being will flow rivers of living water.' "

39 But this He spoke of the Spirit, whom those who believed in Him were to receive; for the Spirit was not yet *given,* because Jesus was not yet glorified.

40 *Some* of the people therefore, when they heard these words, were saying, "This certainly is the Prophet."

41 Others were saying, "This is the Christ." Still others were saying, "Surely the Christ is not going to come from Galilee, is He?

42 "Has not the Scripture said that the Christ comes from the descendants of David, and from Bethlehem, the village where David was?"

43 So a division occurred in the crowd because of Him.

44 Some of them wanted to seize Him, but no one laid hands on Him.

45 The officers then came to the chief priests and Pharisees, and they said to them, "Why did you not bring Him?"

46 The officers answered, "Never has a man spoken the way this man speaks."

47 The Pharisees then answered them, "You have not also been led astray, have you?

48 "No one of the rulers or Pharisees has believed in Him, has he?

49 "But this crowd which does not know the Law is accursed."

50 Nicodemus (he who came to Him before, being one of them) *said to them,

51 "Our Law does not judge a man unless it first hears from him and knows what he is doing, does it?"

52 They answered him, "You are not also from Galilee, are you? Search, and see that no prophet arises out of Galilee."

53 [¹Everyone went to his home.

The Adulterous Woman

8 But Jesus went to the Mount of Olives. 2 Early in the morning He came again into the temple, and all the people were coming to Him; and He sat down and *began* to teach them.

3 The scribes and the Pharisees *brought a woman caught in adultery, and having set her in the center *of the court,*

4 they *said to Him, "Teacher, this woman has been caught in adultery, in the very act.

5 "Now in the Law Moses commanded us to stone such women; what then do You say?"

6 They were saying this, testing Him, so that they might have grounds for accusing Him. But Jesus stooped down and with His finger wrote on the ground.

7 But when they persisted in asking Him, He straightened up, and said to them, "He who is without sin among you, let him *be the* first to throw a stone at her."

8 Again He stooped down and wrote on the ground.

9 When they heard it, they *began* to go out one by one, beginning with the older ones, and He was left alone, and the woman, where she was, in the center *of the court.*

10 Straightening up, Jesus said to her, "Woman, where are they? Did no one condemn you?"

11 She said, "No one, Lord." And Jesus said, "I do not condemn you, either. Go. From now on sin no more."]

12 Then Jesus again spoke to them, saying, "I am the Light of the world; he who follows Me will not walk in the darkness, but will have the Light of life."

13 So the Pharisees said to Him, "You are testifying about Yourself; Your testimony is not true."

14 Jesus answered and said to them, "Even if I testify about Myself, My testimony is true, for I know where I came from and where I am going; but you do not know where I come from or where I am going.

---

1. Later mss add the story of the adulterous woman, numbering it as John 7:53-8:11

15 "You judge according to the flesh; I am not judging anyone.

16 "But even if I do judge, My judgment is true; for I am not alone *in it,* but I and the Father who sent Me.

17 "Even in your law it has been written that the testimony of two men is true.

18 "I am He who testifies about Myself, and the Father who sent Me testifies about Me."

19 So they were saying to Him, "Where is Your Father?" Jesus answered, "You know neither Me nor My Father; if you knew Me, you would know My Father also."

20 These words He spoke in the treasury, as He taught in the temple; and no one seized Him, because His hour had not yet come.

21 Then He said again to them, "I go away, and you will seek Me, and will die in your sin; where I am going, you cannot come."

22 So the Jews were saying, "Surely He will not kill Himself, will He, since He says, 'Where I am going, you cannot come'?"

23 And He was saying to them, "You are from below, I am from above; you are of this world, I am not of this world.

24 "Therefore I said to you that you will die in your sins; for unless you believe that I am *He,* you will die in your sins."

25 So they were saying to Him, "Who are You?" Jesus said to them, "What have I been saying to you *from* the beginning?

26 "I have many things to speak and to judge concerning you, but He who sent Me is true; and the things which I heard from Him, these I speak to the world."

27 They did not realize that He had been speaking to them about the Father.

28 So Jesus said, "When you lift up the Son of Man, then you will know that I am *He,* and I do nothing on My own initiative, but I speak these things as the Father taught Me.

29 "And He who sent Me is with Me; He has not left Me alone, for I always do the things that are pleasing to Him."

30 As He spoke these things, many came to believe in Him.

31 So Jesus was saying to those Jews who had believed Him, "If you continue in My word, *then* you are truly disciples of Mine;

32 and you will know the truth, and the truth will make you free."

33 They answered Him, "We are Abraham's descendants and have never yet been enslaved to anyone; how is it that You say, 'You will become free'?"

34 Jesus answered them, "Truly, truly, I say to you, everyone who commits sin is the slave of sin.

35 "The slave does not remain in the house forever; the son does remain forever.

36 "So if the Son makes you free, you will be free indeed.

37 "I know that you are Abraham's descendants; yet you seek to kill Me, because My word has no place in you.

38 "I speak the things which I have seen with *My* Father; therefore you also do the things which you heard from *your* father."

39 They answered and said to Him, "Abraham is our father." Jesus *said to them, "If you are Abraham's children, do the deeds of Abraham.

40 "But as it is, you are seeking to kill Me, a man who has told you the truth, which I heard from God; this Abraham did not do.

41 "You are doing the deeds of your father." They said to Him, "We were not born of fornication; we have one Father: God."

42 Jesus said to them, "If God were your Father, you would love Me, for I proceeded forth and have come from God, for I have not even come on My own initiative, but He sent Me.

43 "Why do you not understand what I am saying? *It is* because you cannot hear My word.

44 "You are of *your* father the devil, and you want to do the desires of your father. He was a murderer from the beginning, and does not stand in the truth because there is no truth in him. Whenever he speaks a lie, he speaks from his own *nature,* for he is a liar and the father of lies.

45 "But because I speak the truth, you do not believe Me.

46 "Which one of you convicts Me of sin? If I speak truth, why do you not believe Me?

47 "He who is of God hears the words of God; for this reason you do not hear *them,* because you are not of God."

48 The Jews answered and said to Him, "Do we not say rightly that You are a Samaritan and have a demon?"

49 Jesus answered, "I do not have a demon; but I honor My Father, and you dishonor Me.

50 "But I do not seek My glory; there is One who seeks and judges.

51 "Truly, truly, I say to you, if anyone keeps My word he will never see death."

52 The Jews said to Him, "Now we know that You have a demon. Abraham died, and the prophets *also;* and You say, 'If anyone keeps My word, he will never taste of death.'

53 "Surely You are not greater than our father Abraham, who died? The prophets died too; whom do You make Yourself out *to be?*"

54 Jesus answered, "If I glorify Myself, My glory is nothing; it is My Father who glorifies Me, of whom you say, 'He is our God';

55 and you have not come to know Him, but I know Him; and if I say that I do not know Him, I will be a liar like you, but I do know Him and keep His word.

56 "Your father Abraham rejoiced to see My day, and he saw *it* and was glad."

57 So the Jews said to Him, "You are not yet fifty years old, and have You seen Abraham?"

58 Jesus said to them, "Truly, truly, I say to you, before Abraham was born, I am."

59 Therefore they picked up stones to throw at Him, but Jesus hid Himself and went out of the temple.

Healing the Man Born Blind

9 As He passed by, He saw a man blind from birth.

2 And His disciples asked Him, "Rabbi, who sinned, this man or his parents, that he would be born blind?"

3 Jesus answered, "*It was* neither *that* this man sinned, nor his parents; but *it was* so that the works of God might be displayed in him.

4 "We must work the works of Him who sent Me as long as it is day; night is coming when no one can work.

5 "While I am in the world, I am the Light of the world."

6 When He had said this, He spat on the ground, and made clay of the spittle, and applied the clay to his eyes,

7 and said to him, "Go, wash in the pool of Siloam" (which is translated, Sent). So he went away and washed, and came *back* seeing.

8 Therefore the neighbors, and those who previously saw him as a beggar, were saying, "Is not this the one who used to sit and beg?"

9 Others were saying, "This is he," *still* others were saying, "No, but he is like him." He kept saying, "I am the one."

10 So they were saying to him, "How then were your eyes opened?"

11 He answered, "The man who is called Jesus made clay, and anointed my eyes, and said to me, 'Go to Siloam and wash'; so I went away and washed, and I received sight."

12 They said to him, "Where is He?" He *said, "I do not know."

13 They *brought to the Pharisees the man who was formerly blind.

14 Now it was a Sabbath on the day when Jesus made the clay and opened his eyes.

15 Then the Pharisees also were asking him again how he received his sight. And he said to them, "He applied clay to my eyes, and I washed, and I see."

16 Therefore some of the Pharisees were saying, "This man is not from God, because He does not keep the Sabbath." But others were saying, "How can a man who is a sinner perform such signs?" And there was a division among them.

17 So they *said to the blind man again, "What do you say about Him, since He opened your eyes?" And he said, "He is a prophet."

18 The Jews then did not believe *it* of him, that he had been blind and had received sight, until they called the parents of the very one who had received his sight,

19 and questioned them, saying, "Is this your son, who you say was born blind? Then how does he now see?"

20 His parents answered them and said, "We know that this is our son, and that he was born blind;

21 but how he now sees, we do not know; or who opened his eyes, we do not know. Ask him; he is of age, he will speak for himself."

22 His parents said this because they were afraid of the Jews; for the Jews had already agreed that if anyone confessed Him to be Christ, he was to be put out of the synagogue.

23 For this reason his parents said, "He is of age; ask him."

24 So a second time they called the man who had been blind, and said to him, "Give glory to God; we know that this man is a sinner."

25 He then answered, "Whether He is a sinner, I do not know; one thing I do know, that though I was blind, now I see."

26 So they said to him, "What did He do to you? How did He open your eyes?"

27 He answered them, "I told you already and you did not listen; why do you want to hear *it* again? You do not want to become His disciples too, do you?"

28 They reviled him and said, "You are His disciple, but we are disciples of Moses.

29 "We know that God has spoken to Moses, but as for this man, we do not know where He is from."

30 The man answered and said to them, "Well, here is an amazing thing, that you do not know where He is from, and *yet* He opened my eyes.

31 "We know that God does not hear sinners; but if anyone is God-fearing and does His will, He hears him.

32 "Since the beginning of time it has never been heard that anyone opened the eyes of a person born blind.

33 "If this man were not from God, He could do nothing."

34 They answered him, "You were born entirely in sins, and are you teaching us?" So they put him out.

35 Jesus heard that they had put him out, and finding him, He said, "Do you believe in the Son of Man?"

36 He answered, "Who is He, Lord, that I may believe in Him?"

37 Jesus said to him, "You have both seen Him, and He is the one who is talking with you."

38 And he said, "Lord, I believe." And he worshiped Him.

39 And Jesus said, "For judgment I came into this world, so that those who do not see may see, and that those who see may become blind."

40 Those of the Pharisees who were with Him heard these things and said to Him, "We are not blind too, are we?"

41 Jesus said to them, "If you were blind, you would have no sin; but since you say, 'We see,' your sin remains.

Parable of the Good Shepherd

10 "Truly, truly, I say to you, he who does not enter by the door into the fold of the sheep, but climbs up some other way, he is a thief and a robber.

2 "But he who enters by the door is a shepherd of the sheep.

3 "To him the doorkeeper opens, and the sheep hear his voice, and he calls his own sheep by name and leads them out.

4 "When he puts forth all his own, he goes

ahead of them, and the sheep follow him because they know his voice.

5 "A stranger they simply will not follow, but will flee from him, because they do not know the voice of strangers."

6 This figure of speech Jesus spoke to them, but they did not understand what those things were which He had been saying to them.

7 So Jesus said to them again, "Truly, truly, I say to you, I am the door of the sheep.

8 "All who came before Me are thieves and robbers, but the sheep did not hear them.

9 "I am the door; if anyone enters through Me, he will be saved, and will go in and out and find pasture.

10 "The thief comes only to steal and kill and destroy; I came that they may have life, and have it abundantly.

11 "I am the good shepherd; the good shepherd lays down His life for the sheep.

12 "He who is a hired hand, and not a shepherd, who is not the owner of the sheep, sees the wolf coming, and leaves the sheep and flees, and the wolf snatches them and scatters them.

13 "He flees because he is a hired hand and is not concerned about the sheep.

14 "I am the good shepherd, and I know My own and My own know Me,

15 even as the Father knows Me and I know the Father; and I lay down My life for the sheep.

16 "I have other sheep, which are not of this fold; I must bring them also, and they will hear My voice; and they will become one flock with one shepherd.

17 "For this reason the Father loves Me, because I lay down My life so that I may take it again.

18 "No one has taken it away from Me, but I lay it down on My own initiative. I have authority to lay it down, and I have authority to take it up again. This commandment I received from My Father."

19 A division occurred again among the Jews because of these words.

20 Many of them were saying, "He has a demon and is insane. Why do you listen to Him?"

21 Others were saying, "These are not the sayings of one demon-possessed. A demon cannot open the eyes of the blind, can he?"

22 At that time the Feast of the Dedication took place at Jerusalem;

23 it was winter, and Jesus was walking in the temple in the portico of Solomon.

24 The Jews then gathered around Him, and were saying to Him, "How long will You keep us in suspense? If You are the Christ, tell us plainly."

25 Jesus answered them, "I told you, and you do not believe; the works that I do in My Father's name, these testify of Me.

26 "But you do not believe because you are not of My sheep.

27 "My sheep hear My voice, and I know them, and they follow Me;

28 and I give eternal life to them, and they will never perish; and no one will snatch them out of My hand.

29 "¹My Father, who has given them to Me, is greater than all; and no one is able to snatch them out of the Father's hand.

30 "I and the Father are one."

31 The Jews picked up stones again to stone Him.

32 Jesus answered them, "I showed you many good works from the Father; for which of them are you stoning Me?"

33 The Jews answered Him, "For a good work we do not stone You, but for blasphemy; and because You, being a man, make Yourself out to be God."

34 Jesus answered them, "Has it not been written in your Law, 'I SAID, YOU ARE GODS'?

35 "If he called them gods, to whom the word of God came (and the Scripture cannot be broken),

36 do you say of Him, whom the Father sanctified and sent into the world, 'You are blaspheming,' because I said, 'I am the Son of God'?

37 "If I do not do the works of My Father, do not believe Me;

38 but if I do them, though you do not believe Me, believe the works, so that you may know and understand that the Father is in Me, and I in the Father."

39 Therefore they were seeking again to seize Him, and He eluded their grasp.

40 And He went away again beyond the Jordan to the place where John was first baptizing, and He was staying there.

41 Many came to Him and were saying, "While John performed no sign, yet everything John said about this man was true."

42 Many believed in Him there.

The Death and Resurrection of Lazarus

11 Now a certain man was sick, Lazarus of Bethany, the village of Mary and her sister Martha.

2 It was the Mary who anointed the Lord with ointment, and wiped His feet with her hair, whose brother Lazarus was sick.

3 So the sisters sent word to Him, saying, "Lord, behold, he whom You love is sick."

4 But when Jesus heard this, He said, "This sickness is not to end in death, but for the glory of God, so that the Son of God may be glorified by it."

5 Now Jesus loved Martha and her sister and Lazarus.

6 So when He heard that he was sick, He then stayed two days longer in the place where He was.

7 Then after this He *said to the disciples, "Let us go to Judea again."

8 The disciples *said to Him, "Rabbi, the Jews were just now seeking to stone You, and are You going there again?"

---

1. One early ms reads *What My Father has given Me is greater than all*

9 Jesus answered, "Are there not twelve hours in the day? If anyone walks in the day, he does not stumble, because he sees the light of this world.

10 "But if anyone walks in the night, he stumbles, because the light is not in him."

11 This He said, and after that He *said to them, "Our friend Lazarus has fallen asleep; but I go, so that I may awaken him out of sleep."

12 The disciples then said to Him, "Lord, if he has fallen asleep, he will recover."

13 Now Jesus had spoken of his death, but they thought that He was speaking of literal sleep.

14 So Jesus then said to them plainly, "Lazarus is dead,

15 and I am glad for your sakes that I was not there, so that you may believe; but let us go to him."

16 Therefore Thomas, who is called Didymus, said to his fellow disciples, "Let us also go, so that we may die with Him."

17 So when Jesus came, He found that he had already been in the tomb four days.

18 Now Bethany was near Jerusalem, about two miles off;

19 and many of the Jews had come to Martha and Mary, to console them concerning their brother.

20 Martha therefore, when she heard that Jesus was coming, went to meet Him, but Mary stayed at the house.

21 Martha then said to Jesus, "Lord, if You had been here, my brother would not have died.

22 "Even now I know that whatever You ask of God, God will give You."

23 Jesus *said to her, "Your brother will rise again."

24 Martha *said to Him, "I know that he will rise again in the resurrection on the last day."

25 Jesus said to her, "I am the resurrection and the life; he who believes in Me will live even if he dies,

26 and everyone who lives and believes in Me will never die. Do you believe this?"

27 She *said to Him, "Yes, Lord; I have believed that You are the Christ, the Son of God, even He who comes into the world."

28 When she had said this, she went away and called Mary her sister, saying secretly, "The Teacher is here and is calling for you."

29 And when she heard it, she *got up quickly and was coming to Him.

30 Now Jesus had not yet come into the village, but was still in the place where Martha met Him.

31 Then the Jews who were with her in the house, and consoling her, when they saw that Mary got up quickly and went out, they followed her, supposing that she was going to the tomb to weep there.

32 Therefore, when Mary came where Jesus was, she saw Him, and fell at His feet, saying to Him, "Lord, if You had been here, my brother would not have died."

33 When Jesus therefore saw her weeping, and the Jews who came with her also weeping, He was deeply moved in spirit and was troubled,

34 and said, "Where have you laid him?" They *said to Him, "Lord, come and see."

35 Jesus wept.

36 So the Jews were saying, "See how He loved him!"

37 But some of them said, "Could not this man, who opened the eyes of the blind man, have kept this man also from dying?"

38 So Jesus, again being deeply moved within, *came to the tomb. Now it was a cave, and a stone was lying against it.

39 Jesus *said, "Remove the stone." Martha, the sister of the deceased, *said to Him, "Lord, by this time there will be a stench, for he has been dead four days."

40 Jesus *said to her, "Did I not say to you that if you believe, you will see the glory of God?"

41 So they removed the stone. Then Jesus raised His eyes, and said, "Father, I thank You that You have heard Me.

42 "I knew that You always hear Me; but because of the people standing around I said it, so that they may believe that You sent Me."

43 When He had said these things, He cried out with a loud voice, "Lazarus, come forth."

44 The man who had died came forth, bound hand and foot with wrappings, and his face was wrapped around with a cloth. Jesus *said to them, "Unbind him, and let him go."

45 Therefore many of the Jews who came to Mary, and saw what He had done, believed in Him.

46 But some of them went to the Pharisees and told them the things which Jesus had done.

47 Therefore the chief priests and the Pharisees convened a council, and were saying, "What are we doing? For this man is performing many signs.

48 "If we let Him go on like this, all men will believe in Him, and the Romans will come and take away both our place and our nation."

49 But one of them, Caiaphas, who was high priest that year, said to them, "You know nothing at all,

50 nor do you take into account that it is expedient for you that one man die for the people, and that the whole nation not perish."

51 Now he did not say this on his own initiative, but being high priest that year, he prophesied that Jesus was going to die for the nation,

52 and not for the nation only, but in order that He might also gather together into one the children of God who are scattered abroad.

53 So from that day on they planned together to kill Him.

54 Therefore Jesus no longer continued to walk publicly among the Jews, but went away from there to the country near the wilderness, into a city called Ephraim; and there He stayed with the disciples.

55 Now the Passover of the Jews was near, and many went up to Jerusalem out of the country before the Passover to purify themselves.

56 So they were seeking for Jesus, and were saying to one another as they stood in the temple, "What do you think; that He will not come to the feast at all?"

57 Now the chief priests and the Pharisees had given orders that if anyone knew where He was, he was to report it, so that they might seize Him.

Mary Anoints Jesus

12 Jesus, therefore, six days before the Passover, came to Bethany where Lazarus was, whom Jesus had raised from the dead.

2 So they made Him a supper there, and Martha was serving; but Lazarus was one of those reclining *at the table* with Him.

3 Mary then took a pound of very costly perfume of pure nard, and anointed the feet of Jesus and wiped His feet with her hair; and the house was filled with the fragrance of the perfume.

4 But Judas Iscariot, one of His disciples, who was intending to betray Him, *said,

5 "Why was this perfume not sold for ¹three hundred denarii and given to poor *people?*"

6 Now he said this, not because he was concerned about the poor, but because he was a thief, and as he had the money box, he used to pilfer what was put into it.

7 Therefore Jesus said, "Let her alone, so that she may keep ²it for the day of My burial.

8 "For you always have the poor with you, but you do not always have Me."

9 The large crowd of the Jews then learned that He was there; and they came, not for Jesus' sake only, but that they might also see Lazarus, whom He raised from the dead.

10 But the chief priests planned to put Lazarus to death also;

11 because on account of him many of the Jews were going away and were believing in Jesus.

12 On the next day the large crowd who had come to the feast, when they heard that Jesus was coming to Jerusalem,

13 took the branches of the palm trees and went out to meet Him, and *began* to shout, "Hosanna! BLESSED IS HE WHO COMES IN THE NAME OF THE LORD, even the King of Israel."

14 Jesus, finding a young donkey, sat on it; as it is written,

15 "FEAR NOT, DAUGHTER OF ZION; BEHOLD, YOUR KING IS COMING, SEATED ON A DONKEY'S COLT."

16 These things His disciples did not understand at the first; but when Jesus was glorified, then they remembered that these things were written of Him, and that they had done these things to Him.

17 So the people, who were with Him when He called Lazarus out of the tomb and raised him from the dead, continued to testify *about Him.*

18 For this reason also the people went and met Him, because they heard that He had performed this sign.

19 So the Pharisees said to one another, "You see that you are not doing any good; look, the world has gone after Him."

20 Now there were some Greeks among those who were going up to worship at the feast;

21 these then came to Philip, who was from Bethsaida of Galilee, and *began to* ask him, saying, "Sir, we wish to see Jesus."

22 Philip *came and *told Andrew; Andrew and Philip *came and *told Jesus.

23 And Jesus *answered them, saying, "The hour has come for the Son of Man to be glorified.

24 "Truly, truly, I say to you, unless a grain of wheat falls into the earth and dies, it remains alone; but if it dies, it bears much fruit.

25 "He who loves his life loses it, and he who hates his life in this world will keep it to life eternal.

26 "If anyone serves Me, he must follow Me; and where I am, there My servant will be also; if anyone serves Me, the Father will honor him.

27 "Now My soul has become troubled; and what shall I say, 'Father, save Me from this hour'? But for this purpose I came to this hour.

28 "Father, glorify Your name." Then a voice came out of heaven: "I have both glorified it, and will glorify it again."

29 So the crowd *of people* who stood by and heard it were saying that it had thundered; others were saying, "An angel has spoken to Him."

30 Jesus answered and said, "This voice has not come for My sake, but for your sakes.

31 "Now judgment is upon this world; now the ruler of this world will be cast out.

32 "And I, if I am lifted up from the earth, will draw all men to Myself."

33 But He was saying this to indicate the kind of death by which He was to die.

34 The crowd then answered Him, "We have heard out of the Law that the Christ is to remain forever; and how can You say, 'The Son of Man must be lifted up'? Who is this Son of Man?"

35 So Jesus said to them, "For a little while longer the Light is among you. Walk while you have the Light, so that darkness will not overtake you; he who walks in the darkness does not know where he goes.

36 "While you have the Light, believe in the Light, so that you may become sons of Light."

These things Jesus spoke, and He went away and hid Himself from them.

37 But though He had performed so many signs before them, *yet* they were not believing in Him.

38 *This was* to fulfill the word of Isaiah the prophet which he spoke: "LORD, WHO HAS

---

1. Equivalent to 11 months' wages   2. I.e. the custom of preparing the body for burial

BELIEVED OUR REPORT? AND TO WHOM HAS THE ARM OF THE LORD BEEN REVEALED?"

39 For this reason they could not believe, for Isaiah said again,

40 "HE HAS BLINDED THEIR EYES AND HE HARDENED THEIR HEART, SO THAT THEY WOULD NOT SEE WITH THEIR EYES AND PERCEIVE WITH THEIR HEART, AND BE CONVERTED AND I HEAL THEM."

41 These things Isaiah said because he saw His glory, and he spoke of Him.

42 Nevertheless many even of the rulers believed in Him, but because of the Pharisees they were not confessing *Him*, for fear that they would be put out of the synagogue;

43 for they loved the approval of men rather than the approval of God.

44 And Jesus cried out and said, "He who believes in Me, does not believe in Me but in Him who sent Me.

45 "He who sees Me sees the One who sent Me.

46 "I have come *as* Light into the world, so that everyone who believes in Me will not remain in darkness.

47 "If anyone hears My sayings and does not keep them, I do not judge him; for I did not come to judge the world, but to save the world.

48 "He who rejects Me and does not receive My sayings, has one who judges him; the word I spoke is what will judge him at the last day.

49 "For I did not speak on My own initiative, but the Father Himself who sent Me has given Me a commandment *as to* what to say and what to speak.

50 "I know that His commandment is eternal life; therefore the things I speak, I speak just as the Father has told Me."

The Lord's Supper

13 Now before the Feast of the Passover, Jesus knowing that His hour had come that He would depart out of this world to the Father, having loved His own who were in the world, He loved them to the end.

2 During supper, the devil having already put into the heart of Judas Iscariot, *the son* of Simon, to betray Him,

3 *Jesus*, knowing that the Father had given all things into His hands, and that He had come forth from God and was going back to God,

4 *got up from supper, and *laid aside His garments; and taking a towel, He girded Himself.

5 Then He *poured water into the basin, and began to wash the disciples' feet and to wipe them with the towel with which He was girded.

6 So He *came to Simon Peter. He *said to Him, "Lord, do You wash my feet?"

7 Jesus answered and said to him, "What I do you do not realize now, but you will understand hereafter."

8 Peter *said to Him, "Never shall You wash my feet!" Jesus answered him, "If I do not wash you, you have no part with Me."

9 Simon Peter *said to Him, "Lord, *then* wash not only my feet, but also my hands and my head."

10 Jesus *said to him, "He who has bathed needs only to wash his feet, but is completely clean; and you are clean, but not all *of you*."

11 For He knew the one who was betraying Him; for this reason He said, "Not all of you are clean."

12 So when He had washed their feet, and taken His garments and reclined *at the table* again, He said to them, "Do you know what I have done to you?

13 "You call Me Teacher and Lord; and you are right, for *so* I am.

14 "If I then, the Lord and the Teacher, washed your feet, you also ought to wash one another's feet.

15 "For I gave you an example that you also should do as I did to you.

16 "Truly, truly, I say to you, a slave is not greater than his master, nor *is* one who is sent greater than the one who sent him.

17 "If you know these things, you are blessed if you do them.

18 "I do not speak of all of you. I know the ones I have chosen; but *it is* that the Scripture may be fulfilled, 'HE WHO EATS MY BREAD HAS LIFTED UP HIS HEEL AGAINST ME.'

19 "From now on I am telling you before *it* comes to pass, so that when it does occur, you may believe that I am He.

20 "Truly, truly, I say to you, he who receives whomever I send receives Me; and he who receives Me receives Him who sent Me."

21 When Jesus had said this, He became troubled in spirit, and testified and said, "Truly, truly, I say to you, that one of you will betray Me."

22 The disciples *began* looking at one another, at a loss *to know* of which one He was speaking.

23 There was reclining on Jesus' bosom one of His disciples, whom Jesus loved.

24 So Simon Peter *gestured to him, and *said to him, "Tell *us* who it is of whom He is speaking."

25 He, leaning back thus on Jesus' bosom, *said to Him, "Lord, who is it?"

26 Jesus then *answered, "That is the one for whom I shall dip the morsel and give it to him." So when He had dipped the morsel, He *took and *gave it to Judas, *the son* of Simon Iscariot.

27 After the morsel, Satan then entered into him. Therefore Jesus *said to him, "What you do, do quickly."

28 Now no one of those reclining *at the table* knew for what purpose He had said this to him.

29 For some were supposing, because Judas had the money box, that Jesus was saying to him, "Buy the things we have need of for the feast"; or else, that he should give something to the poor.

30 So after receiving the morsel he went out immediately; and it was night.

31 Therefore when he had gone out, Jesus *said, "Now is the Son of Man glorified, and God is glorified in Him;

32 if God is glorified in Him, God will also

glorify Him in Himself, and will glorify Him immediately.

33 "Little children, I am with you a little while longer. You will seek Me; and as I said to the Jews, now I also say to you, 'Where I am going, you cannot come.'

34 "A new commandment I give to you, that you love one another, even as I have loved you, that you also love one another.

35 "By this all men will know that you are My disciples, if you have love for one another."

36 Simon Peter *said to Him, "Lord, where are You going?" Jesus answered, "Where I go, you cannot follow Me now; but you will follow later."

37 Peter *said to Him, "Lord, why can I not follow You right now? I will lay down my life for You."

38 Jesus *answered, "Will you lay down your life for Me? Truly, truly, I say to you, a rooster will not crow until you deny Me three times.

Jesus Comforts His Disciples

14 "Do not let your heart be troubled; [1]believe in God, believe also in Me.

2 "In My Father's house are many dwelling places; if it were not so, I would have told you; for I go to prepare a place for you.

3 "If I go and prepare a place for you, I will come again and receive you to Myself, that where I am, *there* you may be also.

4 "And you know the way where I am going."

5 Thomas *said to Him, "Lord, we do not know where You are going, how do we know the way?"

6 Jesus *said to him, "I am the way, and the truth, and the life; no one comes to the Father but through Me.

Jesus is the way.

7 "If you had known Me, you would have known My Father also; from now on you know Him, and have seen Him."

8 Philip *said to Him, "Lord, show us the Father, and it is enough for us."

9 Jesus *said to him, "Have I been so long with you, and *yet* you have not come to know Me, Philip? He who has seen Me has seen the Father; how *can* you say, 'Show us the Father'?

10 "Do you not believe that I am in the Father, and the Father is in Me? The words that I say to you I do not speak on My own initiative, but the Father abiding in Me does His works.

11 "Believe Me that I am in the Father and the Father is in Me; otherwise believe because of the works themselves.

12 "Truly, truly, I say to you, he who believes in Me, the works that I do, he will do also; and greater *works* than these he will do; because I go to the Father.

13 "Whatever you ask in My name, that will I do, so that the Father may be glorified in the Son.

14 "If you ask Me anything in My name, I will do *it*.

15 "If you love Me, you will keep My commandments.

16 "I will ask the Father, and He will give you another Helper, that He may be with you forever;

17 *that is* the Spirit of truth, whom the world cannot receive, because it does not see Him or know Him, *but* you know Him because He abides with you and will be in you.

18 "I will not leave you as orphans; I will come to you.

19 "After a little while the world will no longer see Me, but you *will* see Me; because I live, you will live also.

20 "In that day you will know that I am in My Father, and you in Me, and I in you.

21 "He who has My commandments and keeps them is the one who loves Me; and he who loves Me will be loved by My Father, and I will love him and will disclose Myself to him."

22 Judas (not Iscariot) *said to Him, "Lord, what then has happened that You are going to disclose Yourself to us and not to the world?"

23 Jesus answered and said to him, "If anyone loves Me, he will keep My word; and My Father will love him, and We will come to him and make Our abode with him.

24 "He who does not love Me does not keep My words; and the word which you hear is not Mine, but the Father's who sent Me.

25 "These things I have spoken to you while abiding with you.

26 "But the Helper, the Holy Spirit, whom the Father will send in My name, He will teach you all things, and bring to your remembrance all that I said to you.

27 "Peace I leave with you; My peace I give to you; not as the world gives do I give to you. Do not let your heart be troubled, nor let it be fearful.

28 "You heard that I said to you, 'I go away, and I will come to you.' If you loved Me, you would have rejoiced because I go to the Father, for the Father is greater than I.

29 "Now I have told you before it happens, so that when it happens, you may believe.

30 "I will not speak much more with you, for the ruler of the world is coming, and he has nothing in Me;

31 but so that the world may know that I love the Father, I do exactly as the Father commanded Me. Get up, let us go from here.

Jesus Is the Vine—Followers Are Branches

15 "I am the true vine, and My Father is the vinedresser.

2 "Every branch in Me that does not bear fruit, He takes away; and every *branch* that bears fruit, He [2]prunes it so that it may bear more fruit.

3 "You are already clean because of the word which I have spoken to you.

4 "Abide in Me, and I in you. As the branch cannot bear fruit of itself unless it abides in the vine, so neither *can* you unless you abide in Me.

5 "I am the vine, you are the branches; he who abides in Me and I in him, he bears much fruit, for apart from Me you can do nothing.

6 "If anyone does not abide in Me, he is

1. Or *you believe in God* 2. Lit *cleans;* used to describe pruning

Jesus died on the cross for your sins. Read 1 Peter 2:21-24 on page 181.

thrown away as a branch and dries up; and they gather them, and cast them into the fire and they are burned.

7 "If you abide in Me, and My words abide in you, ask whatever you wish, and it will be done for you.

8 "My Father is glorified by this, that you bear much fruit, and *so* prove to be My disciples.

9 "Just as the Father has loved Me, I have also loved you; abide in My love.

10 "If you keep My commandments, you will abide in My love; just as I have kept My Father's commandments and abide in His love.

11 "These things I have spoken to you so that My joy may be in you, and *that* your joy may be made full.

12 "This is My commandment, that you love one another, just as I have loved you.

13 "Greater love has no one than this, that one lay down his life for his friends.

14 "You are My friends if you do what I command you.

15 "No longer do I call you slaves, for the slave does not know what his master is doing; but I have called you friends, for all things that I have heard from My Father I have made known to you.

16 "You did not choose Me but I chose you, and appointed you that you would go and bear fruit, and *that* your fruit would remain, so that whatever you ask of the Father in My name He may give to you.

17 "This I command you, that you love one another.

18 "If the world hates you, you know that it has hated Me before *it hated* you.

19 "If you were of the world, the world would love its own; but because you are not of the world, but I chose you out of the world, because of this the world hates you.

20 "Remember the word that I said to you, 'A slave is not greater than his master.' If they persecuted Me, they will also persecute you; if they kept My word, they will keep yours also.

21 "But all these things they will do to you for My name's sake, because they do not know the One who sent Me.

22 "If I had not come and spoken to them, they would not have sin, but now they have no excuse for their sin.

23 "He who hates Me hates My Father also.

24 "If I had not done among them the works which no one else did, they would not have sin; but now they have both seen and hated Me and My Father as well.

25 "But *they have done this* to fulfill the word that is written in their Law, 'THEY HATED ME WITHOUT A CAUSE.'

26 "When the Helper comes, whom I will send to you from the Father, *that is* the Spirit of truth who proceeds from the Father, He will testify about Me,

27 and you *will* testify also, because you have been with Me from the beginning.

Jesus' Warning

16 "These things I have spoken to you so that you may be kept from stumbling.

2 "They will make you outcasts from the synagogue, but an hour is coming for everyone who kills you to think that he is offering service to God.

3 "These things they will do because they have not known the Father or Me.

4 "But these things I have spoken to you, so that when their hour comes, you may remember that I told you of them. These things I did not say to you at the beginning, because I was with you.

5 "But now I am going to Him who sent Me; and none of you asks Me, 'Where are You going?'

6 "But because I have said these things to you, sorrow has filled your heart.

7 "But I tell you the truth, it is to your advantage that I go away; for if I do not go away, the Helper will not come to you; but if I go, I will send Him to you.

8 "And He, when He comes, will convict the world concerning sin and righteousness and judgment;

9 concerning sin, because they do not believe in Me;

10 and concerning righteousness, because I go to the Father and you no longer see Me;

11 and concerning judgment, because the ruler of this world has been judged.

12 "I have many more things to say to you, but you cannot bear *them* now.

13 "But when He, the Spirit of truth, comes, He will guide you into all the truth; for He will not speak on His own initiative, but whatever He hears, He will speak; and He will disclose to you what is to come.

14 "He will glorify Me, for He will take of Mine and will disclose *it* to you.

15 "All things that the Father has are Mine; therefore I said that He takes of Mine and will disclose *it* to you.

16 "A little while, and you will no longer see Me; and again a little while, and you will see Me."

17 *Some* of His disciples then said to one another, "What is this thing He is telling us, 'A little while, and you will not see Me; and again a little while, and you will see Me'; and, 'because I go to the Father'?"

18 So they were saying, "What is this that He says, 'A little while'? We do not know what He is talking about."

19 Jesus knew that they wished to question Him, and He said to them, "Are you deliberating together about this, that I said, 'A little while, and you will not see Me, and again a little while, and you will see Me'?

20 "Truly, truly, I say to you, that you will weep and lament, but the world will rejoice; you will grieve, but your grief will be turned into joy.

21 "Whenever a woman is in labor she has pain, because her hour has come; but when she gives birth to the child, she no longer

Jesus was not just a man. Read John 3:16 on page 73.

no greater love

remembers the anguish because of the joy that a child has been born into the world.

22 "Therefore you too have grief now; but I will see you again, and your heart will rejoice, and no one *will* take your joy away from you.

23 "In that day you will not question Me about anything. Truly, truly, I say to you, if you ask the Father for anything in My name, He will give it to you.

24 "Until now you have asked for nothing in My name; ask and you will receive, so that your joy may be made full.

25 "These things I have spoken to you in figurative language; an hour is coming when I will no longer speak to you in figurative language, but will tell you plainly of the Father.

26 "In that day you will ask in My name, and I do not say to you that I will request of the Father on your behalf;

27 for the Father Himself loves you, because you have loved Me and have believed that I came forth from the Father.

28 "I came forth from the Father and have come into the world; I am leaving the world again and going to the Father."

29 His disciples *said, "Lo, now You are speaking plainly and are not using a figure of speech.

30 "Now we know that You know all things, and have no need for anyone to question You; by this we believe that You came from God."

31 Jesus answered them, "Do you now believe?

32 "Behold, an hour is coming, and has *already* come, for you to be scattered, each to his own *home*, and to leave Me alone; and *yet* I am not alone, because the Father is with Me.

33 "These things I have spoken to you, so that in Me you may have peace. In the world you have tribulation, but take courage; I have overcome the world."

The High Priestly Prayer

17 Jesus spoke these things; and lifting up His eyes to heaven, He said, "Father, the hour has come; glorify Your Son, that the Son may glorify You,

2 even as You gave Him authority over all flesh, that to all whom You have given Him, He may give eternal life.

3 "This is eternal life, that they may know You, the only true God, and Jesus Christ whom You have sent.

4 "I glorified You on the earth, having accomplished the work which You have given Me to do.

5 "Now, Father, glorify Me together with Yourself, with the glory which I had with You before the world was.

6 "I have manifested Your name to the men whom You gave Me out of the world; they were Yours and You gave them to Me, and they have kept Your word.

7 "Now they have come to know that everything You have given Me is from You;

8 for the words which You gave Me I have given to them; and they received *them* and truly

understood that I came forth from You, and they believed that You sent Me.

9 "I ask on their behalf; I do not ask on behalf of the world, but of those whom You have given Me; for they are Yours;

10 and all things that are Mine are Yours, and Yours are Mine; and I have been glorified in them.

11 "I am no longer in the world; and *yet* they themselves are in the world, and I come to You. Holy Father, keep them in Your name, *the name* which You have given Me, that they may be one even as We *are.*

12 "While I was with them, I was keeping them in Your name which You have given Me; and I guarded them and not one of them perished but the son of perdition, so that the Scripture would be fulfilled.

13 "But now I come to You; and these things I speak in the world so that they may have My joy made full in themselves.

14 "I have given them Your word; and the world has hated them, because they are not of the world, even as I am not of the world.

15 "I do not ask You to take them out of the world, but to keep them from the evil *one.*

16 "They are not of the world, even as I am not of the world.

17 "Sanctify them in the truth; Your word is truth.

18 "As You sent Me into the world, I also have sent them into the world.

19 "For their sakes I sanctify Myself, that they themselves also may be sanctified in truth.

20 "I do not ask on behalf of these alone, but for those also who believe in Me through their word;

21 that they may all be one; even as You, Father, *are* in Me and I in You, that they also may be in Us, so that the world may believe that You sent Me.

22 "The glory which You have given Me I have given to them, that they may be one, just as We are one;

23 I in them and You in Me, that they may be perfected in unity, so that the world may know that You sent Me, and loved them, even as You have loved Me.

24 "Father, I desire that they also, whom You have given Me, be with Me where I am, so that they may see My glory which You have given Me, for You loved Me before the foundation of the world.

25 "O righteous Father, although the world has not known You, yet I have known You; and these have known that You sent Me;

26 and I have made Your name known to them, and will make it known, so that the love with which You loved Me may be in them, and I in them."

Judas Betrays Jesus

18 When Jesus had spoken these words, He went forth with His disciples over the ravine of the Kidron, where there was a garden, in which He entered with His disciples.

2 Now Judas also, who was betraying Him,

knew the place, for Jesus had often met there with His disciples.

3 Judas then, having received the *Roman* cohort and officers from the chief priests and the Pharisees, *came there with lanterns and torches and weapons.

4 So Jesus, knowing all the things that were coming upon Him, went forth and *said to them, "Whom do you seek?"

5 They answered Him, "Jesus the Nazarene." He *said to them, "I am *He.*" And Judas also, who was betraying Him, was standing with them.

6 So when He said to them, "I am *He,*" they drew back and fell to the ground.

7 Therefore He again asked them, "Whom do you seek?" And they said, "Jesus the Nazarene."

8 Jesus answered, "I told you that I am *He;* so if you seek Me, let these go their way,"

9 to fulfill the word which He spoke, "Of those whom You have given Me I lost not one."

10 Simon Peter then, having a sword, drew it and struck the high priest's slave, and cut off his right ear; and the slave's name was Malchus.

11 So Jesus said to Peter, "Put the sword into the sheath; the cup which the Father has given Me, shall I not drink it?"

12 So the *Roman* cohort and the commander and the officers of the Jews, arrested Jesus and bound Him,

13 and led Him to Annas first; for he was father-in-law of Caiaphas, who was high priest that year.

14 Now Caiaphas was the one who had advised the Jews that it was expedient for one man to die on behalf of the people.

15 Simon Peter was following Jesus, and *so was* another disciple. Now that disciple was known to the high priest, and entered with Jesus into the court of the high priest,

16 but Peter was standing at the door outside. So the other disciple, who was known to the high priest, went out and spoke to the doorkeeper, and brought Peter in.

17 Then the slave-girl who kept the door *said to Peter, "You are not also *one* of this man's disciples, are you?" He *said, "I am not."

18 Now the slaves and the officers were standing *there,* having made a charcoal fire, for it was cold and they were warming themselves; and Peter was also with them, standing and warming himself.

19 The high priest then questioned Jesus about His disciples, and about His teaching.

20 Jesus answered him, "I have spoken openly to the world; I always taught in synagogues and in the temple, where all the Jews come together; and I spoke nothing in secret.

21 "Why do you question Me? Question those who have heard what I spoke to them; they know what I said."

22 When He had said this, one of the officers standing nearby struck Jesus, saying, "Is that the way You answer the high priest?"

23 Jesus answered him, "If I have spoken wrongly, testify of the wrong; but if rightly, why do you strike Me?"

24 So Annas sent Him bound to Caiaphas the high priest.

25 Now Simon Peter was standing and warming himself. So they said to him, "You are not also *one* of His disciples, are you?" He denied *it,* and said, "I am not."

26 One of the slaves of the high priest, being a relative of the one whose ear Peter cut off, *said, "Did I not see you in the garden with Him?"

27 Peter then denied *it* again, and immediately a rooster crowed.

28 Then they *led Jesus from Caiaphas into the [1]Praetorium, and it was early; and they themselves did not enter into the Praetorium so that they would not be defiled, but might eat the Passover.

29 Therefore Pilate went out to them and *said, "What accusation do you bring against this Man?"

30 They answered and said to him, "If this Man were not an evildoer, we would not have delivered Him to you."

31 So Pilate said to them, "Take Him yourselves, and judge Him according to your law." The Jews said to him, "We are not permitted to put anyone to death,"

32 to fulfill the word of Jesus which He spoke, signifying by what kind of death He was about to die.

33 Therefore Pilate entered again into the Praetorium, and summoned Jesus and said to Him, "Are You the King of the Jews?"

34 Jesus answered, "Are you saying this on your own initiative, or did others tell you about Me?"

35 Pilate answered, "I am not a Jew, am I? Your own nation and the chief priests delivered You to me; what have You done?"

36 Jesus answered, "My kingdom is not of this world. If My kingdom were of this world, then My servants would be fighting so that I would not be handed over to the Jews; but as it is, My kingdom is not [2]of this realm."

37 Therefore Pilate said to Him, "So You are a king?" Jesus answered, "You say *correctly* that I am a king. For this I have been born, and for this I have come into the world, to testify to the truth. Everyone who is of the truth hears My voice."

38 Pilate *said to Him, "What is truth?" And when he had said this, he went out again to the Jews and *said to them, "I find no guilt in Him.

39 "But you have a custom that I release someone for you at the Passover; do you wish then that I release for you the King of the Jews?"

40 So they cried out again, saying, "Not this

---

1. **I.e. governor's official residence**   2. **Lit** *from here*

Man, but Barabbas." Now Barabbas was a robber.

19 Pilate then took Jesus and scourged Him.

2 And the soldiers twisted together a crown of thorns and put it on His head, and put a purple robe on Him;

3 and they *began* to come up to Him and say, "Hail, King of the Jews!" and to give Him slaps *in the face.*

4 Pilate came out again and *said to them, "Behold, I am bringing Him out to you so that you may know that I find no guilt in Him."

5 Jesus then came out, wearing the crown of thorns and the purple robe. *Pilate* *said to them, "Behold, the Man!"

6 So when the chief priests and the officers saw Him, they cried out saying, "Crucify, crucify!" Pilate *said to them, "Take Him yourselves and crucify Him, for I find no guilt in Him."

7 The Jews answered him, "We have a law, and by that law He ought to die because He made Himself out *to be* the Son of God."

8 Therefore when Pilate heard this statement, he was *even* more afraid;

9 and he entered into the ¹Praetorium again and *said to Jesus, "Where are You from?" But Jesus gave him no answer.

10 So Pilate *said to Him, "You do not speak to me? Do You not know that I have authority to release You, and I have authority to crucify You?"

11 Jesus answered, "You would have no authority over Me, unless it had been given you from above; for this reason he who delivered Me to you has *the* greater sin."

12 As a result of this Pilate made efforts to release Him, but the Jews cried out saying, "If you release this Man, you are no friend of Caesar; everyone who makes himself out *to be* a king opposes Caesar."

13 Therefore when Pilate heard these words, he brought Jesus out, and sat down on the judgment seat at a place called The Pavement, but in Hebrew, Gabbatha.

14 Now it was the day of preparation for the Passover; it was about the ²sixth hour. And he *said to the Jews, "Behold, your King!"

15 So they cried out, "Away with *Him,* away with *Him,* crucify Him!" Pilate *said to them, "Shall I crucify your King?" The chief priests answered, "We have no king but Caesar."

16 So he then handed Him over to them to be crucified.

17 They took Jesus, therefore, and He went out, bearing His own cross, to the place called the Place of a Skull, which is called in Hebrew, Golgotha.

18 There they crucified Him, and with Him two other men, one on either side, and Jesus in between.

19 Pilate also wrote an inscription and put it

on the cross. It was written, "JESUS THE NAZARENE, THE KING OF THE JEWS."

20 Therefore many of the Jews read this inscription, for the place where Jesus was crucified was near the city; and it was written in Hebrew, Latin *and* in Greek.

21 So the chief priests of the Jews were saying to Pilate, "Do not write, 'The King of the Jews'; but that He said, 'I am King of the Jews.' "

22 Pilate answered, "What I have written I have written."

23 Then the soldiers, when they had crucified Jesus, took His outer garments and made four parts, a part to every soldier and *also* the ³tunic; now the tunic was seamless, woven in one piece.

24 So they said to one another, "Let us not tear it, but cast lots for it, *to decide* whose it shall be"; *this was* to fulfill the Scripture: "THEY DIVIDED MY OUTER GARMENTS AMONG THEM, AND FOR MY CLOTHING THEY CAST LOTS."

25 Therefore the soldiers did these things.

But standing by the cross of Jesus were His mother, and His mother's sister, Mary the *wife* of Clopas, and Mary Magdalene.

26 When Jesus then saw His mother, and the disciple whom He loved standing nearby, He *said to His mother, "Woman, behold, your son!"

27 Then He *said to the disciple, "Behold, your mother!" From that hour the disciple took her into his own *household.*

28 After this, Jesus, knowing that all things had already been accomplished, to fulfill the Scripture, *said, "I am thirsty."

29 A jar full of sour wine was standing there; so they put a sponge full of the sour wine upon *a branch of* hyssop and brought it up to His mouth.

30 Therefore when Jesus had received the sour wine, He said, "It is finished!" And He bowed His head and gave up His spirit.

31 Then the Jews, because it was the day of preparation, so that the bodies would not remain on the cross on the Sabbath (for that Sabbath was a high day), asked Pilate that their legs might be broken, and *that* they might be taken away.

32 So the soldiers came, and broke the legs of the first man and of the other who was crucified with Him;

33 but coming to Jesus, when they saw that He was already dead, they did not break His legs.

34 But one of the soldiers pierced His side with a spear, and immediately blood and water came out.

35 And he who has seen has testified, and his testimony is true; and he knows that he is telling the truth, so that you also may believe.

36 For these things came to pass to fulfill the Scripture, "NOT A BONE OF HIM SHALL BE BROKEN."

37 And again another Scripture says, "THEY SHALL LOOK ON HIM WHOM THEY PIERCED."

38 After these things Joseph of Arimathea,

---

1. I.e. governor's official residence 2. Perhaps 6 a.m. 3. Gr *khiton,* the garment worn next to the skin

being a disciple of Jesus, but a secret *one* for fear of the Jews, asked Pilate that he might take away the body of Jesus; and Pilate granted permission. So he came and took away His body.

39 Nicodemus, who had first come to Him by night, also came, bringing a mixture of myrrh and aloes, about a hundred pounds *weight*.

40 So they took the body of Jesus and bound it in linen wrappings with the spices, as is the burial custom of the Jews.

41 Now in the place where He was crucified there was a garden, and in the garden a new tomb in which no one had yet been laid.

42 Therefore because of the Jewish day of preparation, since the tomb was nearby, they laid Jesus there.

The Empty Tomb

20 Now on the first *day* of the week Mary Magdalene *came early to the tomb, while it *was still dark, and *saw the stone *already* taken away from the tomb.

2 So she *ran and *came to Simon Peter and to the other disciple whom Jesus loved, and *said to them, "They have taken away the Lord out of the tomb, and we do not know where they have laid Him."

3 So Peter and the other disciple went forth, and they were going to the tomb.

4 The two were running together; and the other disciple ran ahead faster than Peter and came to the tomb first;

5 and stooping and looking in, he *saw the linen wrappings lying *there;* but he did not go in.

6 And so Simon Peter also *came, following him, and entered the tomb; and he *saw the linen wrappings lying *there,*

7 and the face-cloth which had been on His head, not lying with the linen wrappings, but rolled up in a place by itself.

8 So the other disciple who had first come to the tomb then also entered, and he saw and believed.

9 For as yet they did not understand the Scripture, that He must rise again from the dead.

10 So the disciples went away again to their own homes.

11 But Mary was standing outside the tomb weeping; and so, as she wept, she stooped and looked into the tomb;

12 and she *saw two angels in white sitting, one at the head and one at the feet, where the body of Jesus had been lying.

13 And they *said to her, "Woman, why are you weeping?" She *said to them, "Because they have taken away my Lord, and I do not know where they have laid Him."

14 When she had said this, she turned around and *saw Jesus standing *there,* and did not know that it was Jesus.

15 Jesus *said to her, "Woman, why are you weeping? Whom are you seeking?" Supposing Him to be the gardener, she *said to Him, "Sir,

if you have carried Him away, tell me where you have laid Him, and I will take Him away."

16 Jesus *said to her, "Mary!" She turned and *said to Him in Hebrew, "Rabboni!" (which means, Teacher).

17 Jesus *said to her, "Stop clinging to Me, for I have not yet ascended to the Father; but go to My brethren and say to them, 'I ascend to My Father and your Father, and My God and your God.' "

18 Mary Magdalene *came, announcing to the disciples, "I have seen the Lord," and *that* He had said these things to her.

19 So when it was evening on that day, the first *day* of the week, and when the doors were shut where the disciples were, for fear of the Jews, Jesus came and stood in their midst and *said to them, "Peace *be* with you."

20 And when He had said this, He showed them both His hands and His side. The disciples then rejoiced when they saw the Lord.

21 So Jesus said to them again, "Peace *be* with you; as the Father has sent Me, I also send you."

22 And when He had said this, He breathed on them and *said to them, "Receive the Holy Spirit.

23 "If you forgive the sins of any, *their sins* have been forgiven them; if you retain the *sins* of any, they have been retained."

24 But Thomas, one of the twelve, called Didymus, was not with them when Jesus came.

25 So the other disciples were saying to him, "We have seen the Lord!" But he said to them, "Unless I see in His hands the imprint of the nails, and put my finger into the place of the nails, and put my hand into His side, I will not believe."

26 After eight days His disciples were again inside, and Thomas with them. Jesus *came, the doors having been shut, and stood in their midst and said, "Peace *be* with you."

27 Then He *said to Thomas, "Reach here with your finger, and see My hands; and reach here your hand and put it into My side; and do not be unbelieving, but believing."

28 Thomas answered and said to Him, "My Lord and my God!"

29 Jesus *said to him, "Because you have seen Me, have you believed? Blessed *are* they who did not see, and *yet* believed."

30 Therefore many other signs Jesus also performed in the presence of the disciples, which are not written in this book;

31 but these have been written so that you may believe that Jesus is the Christ, the Son of God; and that believing you may have life in His name.

Jesus Appears at the Sea of Galilee

21 After these things Jesus manifested Himself again to the disciples at the Sea of Tiberias, and He manifested *Himself* in this way.

2 Simon Peter, and Thomas called Didymus, and Nathanael of Cana in Galilee, and the *sons*

of Zebedee, and two others of His disciples were together.

3 Simon Peter *said to them, "I am going fishing." They *said to him, "We will also come with you." They went out and got into the boat; and that night they caught nothing.

4 But when the day was now breaking, Jesus stood on the beach; yet the disciples did not know that it was Jesus.

5 So Jesus *said to them, "Children, you do not have any fish, do you?" They answered Him, "No."

6 And He said to them, "Cast the net on the right-hand side of the boat and you will find a catch." So they cast, and then they were not able to haul it in because of the great number of fish.

7 Therefore that disciple whom Jesus loved *said to Peter, "It is the Lord." So when Simon Peter heard that it was the Lord, he put his outer garment on (for he was stripped for work), and threw himself into the sea.

8 But the other disciples came in the little boat, for they were not far from the land, but about one hundred yards away, dragging the net full of fish.

9 So when they got out on the land, they *saw a charcoal fire already laid and fish placed on it, and bread.

10 Jesus *said to them, "Bring some of the fish which you have now caught."

11 Simon Peter went up and drew the net to land, full of large fish, a hundred and fifty-three; and although there were so many, the net was not torn.

12 Jesus *said to them, "Come and have breakfast." None of the disciples ventured to question Him, "Who are You?" knowing that it was the Lord.

13 Jesus *came and *took the bread and *gave it to them, and the fish likewise.

14 This is now the third time that Jesus was manifested to the disciples, after He was raised from the dead.

15 So when they had finished breakfast, Jesus *said to Simon Peter, "Simon, son of John, do you love Me more than these?" He *said to Him, "Yes, Lord; You know that I love You." He *said to him, "Tend My lambs."

16 He *said to him again a second time, "Simon, son of John, do you love Me?" He *said to Him, "Yes, Lord; You know that I love You." He *said to him, "Shepherd My sheep."

17 He *said to him the third time, "Simon, son of John, do you love Me?" Peter was grieved because He said to him the third time, "Do you love Me?" And he said to Him, "Lord, You know all things; You know that I love You." Jesus *said to him, "Tend My sheep.

18 "Truly, truly, I say to you, when you were younger, you used to gird yourself and walk wherever you wished; but when you grow old, you will stretch out your hands and someone else will gird you, and bring you where you do not wish to go."

19 Now this He said, signifying by what kind of death he would glorify God. And when He had spoken this, He *said to him, "Follow Me!"

20 Peter, turning around, *saw the disciple whom Jesus loved following them; the one who also had leaned back on His bosom at the supper and said, "Lord, who is the one who betrays You?"

21 So Peter seeing him *said to Jesus, "Lord, and what about this man?"

22 Jesus *said to him, "If I want him to remain until I come, what is that to you? You follow Me!"

23 Therefore this saying went out among the brethren that that disciple would not die; yet Jesus did not say to him that he would not die, but only, "If I want him to remain until I come, what is that to you?"

24 This is the disciple who is testifying to these things and wrote these things, and we know that his testimony is true.

25 And there are also many other things which Jesus did, which if they *were written in detail, I suppose that even the world itself *would not contain the books that *would be written.

THE ACTS OF THE APOSTLES

Introduction

1 The first account I composed, Theophilus, about all that Jesus began to do and teach,

2 until the day when He was taken up to heaven, after He had by the Holy Spirit given orders to the apostles whom He had chosen.

3 To these He also presented Himself alive after His suffering, by many convincing proofs, appearing to them over a period of forty days and speaking of the things concerning the kingdom of God.

4 Gathering them together, He commanded them not to leave Jerusalem, but to wait for what the Father had promised, "Which," He said, "you heard of from Me;

5 for John baptized with water, but you will be baptized with the Holy Spirit not many days from now."

6 So when they had come together, they were asking Him, saying, "Lord, is it at this time You are restoring the kingdom to Israel?"

7 He said to them, "It is not for you to know times or epochs which the Father has fixed by His own authority;

8 but you will receive power when the Holy Spirit has come upon you; and you shall be My witnesses both in Jerusalem, and in all Judea and Samaria, and even to the remotest part of the earth."

9 And after He had said these things, He was lifted up while they were looking on, and a cloud received Him out of their sight.

10 And as they were gazing intently into the sky while He was going, behold, two men in white clothing stood beside them.

11 They also said, "Men of Galilee, why do

you stand looking into the sky? This Jesus, who has been taken up from you into heaven, will come in just the same way as you have watched Him go into heaven."

12 Then they returned to Jerusalem from the mount called Olivet, which is near Jerusalem, a Sabbath day's journey away.

13 When they had entered *the city*, they went up to the upper room where they were staying; that is, Peter and John and James and Andrew, Philip and Thomas, Bartholomew and Matthew, James *the son* of Alphaeus, and Simon the Zealot, and Judas *the son* of James.

14 These all with one mind were continually devoting themselves to prayer, along with *the* women, and Mary the mother of Jesus, and with His brothers.

15 At this time Peter stood up in the midst of the brethren (a gathering of about one hundred and twenty persons was there together), and said,

16 "Brethren, the Scripture had to be fulfilled, which the Holy Spirit foretold by the mouth of David concerning Judas, who became a guide to those who arrested Jesus.

17 "For he was counted among us and received his share in this ministry."

18 (Now this man acquired a field with the price of his wickedness, and falling headlong, he burst open in the middle and all his intestines gushed out.

19 And it became known to all who were living in Jerusalem; so that in their own language that field was called Hakeldama, that is, Field of Blood.)

20 "For it is written in the book of Psalms,
'LET HIS HOMESTEAD BE MADE DESOLATE,
    AND LET NO ONE DWELL IN IT';
and,
'LET ANOTHER MAN TAKE HIS OFFICE.'

21 "Therefore it is necessary that of the men who have accompanied us all the time that the Lord Jesus went in and out among us—

22 beginning with the baptism of John until the day that He was taken up from us—one of these *must* become a witness with us of His resurrection."

23 So they put forward two men, Joseph called Barsabbas (who was also called Justus), and Matthias.

24 And they prayed and said, "You, Lord, who know the hearts of all men, show which one of these two You have chosen

25 to occupy this ministry and apostleship from which Judas turned aside to go to his own place."

26 And they drew lots for them, and the lot fell to Matthias; and he was added to the eleven apostles.

The Day of Pentecost

2 When the day of Pentecost had come, they were all together in one place.

2 And suddenly there came from heaven a noise like a violent rushing wind, and it filled the whole house where they were sitting.

3 And there appeared to them tongues as of fire distributing themselves, and they rested on each one of them.

4 And they were all filled with the Holy Spirit and began to speak with other tongues, as the Spirit was giving them utterance.

5 Now there were Jews living in Jerusalem, devout men from every nation under heaven.

6 And when this sound occurred, the crowd came together, and were bewildered because each one of them was hearing them speak in his own language.

7 They were amazed and astonished, saying, "Why, are not all these who are speaking Galileans?

8 "And how is it that we each hear *them* in our own language to which we were born?

9 "Parthians and Medes and Elamites, and residents of Mesopotamia, Judea and Cappadocia, Pontus and Asia,

10 Phrygia and Pamphylia, Egypt and the districts of Libya around Cyrene, and visitors from Rome, both Jews and ¹proselytes,

11 Cretans and Arabs—we hear them in our *own* tongues speaking of the mighty deeds of God."

12 And they all continued in amazement and great perplexity, saying to one another, "What does this mean?"

13 But others were mocking and saying, "They are full of sweet wine."

14 But Peter, taking his stand with the eleven, raised his voice and declared to them: "Men of Judea and all you who live in Jerusalem, let this be known to you and give heed to my words.

15 "For these men are not drunk, as you suppose, for it is *only* the ²third hour of the day;

16 but this is what was spoken of through the prophet Joel:

17 'AND IT SHALL BE IN THE LAST DAYS,' God says,
'THAT I WILL POUR FORTH OF MY SPIRIT ON
    ALL MANKIND;
AND YOUR SONS AND YOUR DAUGHTERS
    SHALL PROPHESY,
AND YOUR YOUNG MEN SHALL SEE VISIONS,
AND YOUR OLD MEN SHALL DREAM DREAMS;
18 EVEN ON MY BONDSLAVES, BOTH MEN AND
    WOMEN,
I WILL IN THOSE DAYS POUR FORTH OF MY
    SPIRIT
And they shall prophesy.
19 'AND I WILL GRANT WONDERS IN THE SKY
    ABOVE
AND SIGNS ON THE EARTH BELOW,
BLOOD, AND FIRE, AND VAPOR OF SMOKE.
20 'THE SUN WILL BE TURNED INTO DARKNESS
AND THE MOON INTO BLOOD,
BEFORE THE GREAT AND GLORIOUS DAY OF
    THE LORD SHALL COME.
21 'AND IT SHALL BE THAT EVERYONE WHO
    CALLS ON THE NAME OF THE LORD WILL BE
    SAVED.'
22 "Men of Israel, listen to these words: Jesus the Nazarene, a man attested to you by God

---

1. I.e. Gentile converts to Judaism 2. I.e. 9 a.m.

with miracles and wonders and signs which God performed through Him in your midst, just as you yourselves know—

23 this *Man*, delivered over by the predetermined plan and foreknowledge of God, you nailed to a cross by the hands of godless men and put *Him* to death.

24 "But God raised Him up again, putting an end to the agony of death, since it was impossible for Him to be held in its power.

25 "For David says of Him,

'I SAW THE LORD ALWAYS IN MY PRESENCE;
FOR HE IS AT MY RIGHT HAND, SO THAT I
WILL NOT BE SHAKEN.

26 'THEREFORE MY HEART WAS GLAD AND MY
TONGUE EXULTED;
MOREOVER MY FLESH ALSO WILL LIVE IN
HOPE;

27 BECAUSE YOU WILL NOT ABANDON MY SOUL
TO HADES,
NOR ALLOW YOUR HOLY ONE TO UNDERGO
DECAY.

28 'YOU HAVE MADE KNOWN TO ME THE WAYS OF
LIFE;
YOU WILL MAKE ME FULL OF GLADNESS WITH
YOUR PRESENCE.'

29 "Brethren, I may confidently say to you regarding the patriarch David that he both died and was buried, and his tomb is with us to this day.

30 "And so, because he was a prophet and knew that GOD HAD SWORN TO HIM WITH AN OATH TO SEAT *one* OF HIS DESCENDANTS ON HIS THRONE,

31 he looked ahead and spoke of the resurrection of [1]the Christ, that HE WAS NEITHER ABANDONED TO HADES, NOR DID His flesh SUFFER DECAY.

32 "This Jesus God raised up again, to which we are all witnesses.

33 "Therefore having been exalted to the right hand of God, and having received from the Father the promise of the Holy Spirit, He has poured forth this which you both see and hear.

34 "For it was not David who ascended into heaven, but he himself says:

'THE LORD SAID TO MY LORD,
"SIT AT MY RIGHT HAND,

35 UNTIL I MAKE YOUR ENEMIES A FOOTSTOOL
FOR YOUR FEET." '

36 "Therefore let all the house of Israel know for certain that God has made Him both Lord and Christ—this Jesus whom you crucified."

37 Now when they heard *this*, they were pierced to the heart, and said to Peter and the rest of the apostles, "Brethren, what shall we do?"

38 Peter *said* to them, "Repent, and each of you be baptized in the name of Jesus Christ for the forgiveness of your sins; and you will receive the gift of the Holy Spirit.

39 "For the promise is for you and your children and for all who are far off, as many as the Lord our God will call to Himself."

40 And with many other words he solemnly testified and kept on exhorting them, saying, "Be saved from this perverse generation!"

41 So then, those who had received his word were baptized; and that day there were added about three thousand [2]souls.

42 They were continually devoting themselves to the apostles' teaching and to fellowship, to the breaking of bread and to prayer.

43 Everyone kept feeling a sense of awe; and many wonders and signs were taking place through the apostles.

44 And all those who had believed [3]were together and had all things in common;

45 and they *began* selling their property and possessions and were sharing them with all, as anyone might have need.

46 Day by day continuing with one mind in the temple, and breaking bread from house to house, they were taking their meals together with gladness and sincerity of heart,

47 praising God and having favor with all the people. And the Lord was adding to their number day by day those who were being saved.

Healing the Lame Beggar

3 Now Peter and John were going up to the temple at the [4]ninth *hour,* the hour of prayer.

2 And a man who had been lame from his mother's womb was being carried along, whom they used to set down every day at the gate of the temple which is called Beautiful, in order to beg [5]alms of those who were entering the temple.

3 When he saw Peter and John about to go into the temple, he *began* asking to receive alms.

4 But Peter, along with John, fixed his gaze on him and said, "Look at us!"

5 And he *began* to give them his attention, expecting to receive something from them.

6 But Peter said, "I do not possess silver and gold, but what I do have I give to you: In the name of Jesus Christ the Nazarene—walk!"

7 And seizing him by the right hand, he raised him up; and immediately his feet and his ankles were strengthened.

8 With a leap he stood upright and *began* to walk; and he entered the temple with them, walking and leaping and praising God.

9 And all the people saw him walking and praising God;

10 and they were taking note of him as being the one who used to sit at the Beautiful Gate of the temple to *beg* alms, and they were filled with wonder and amazement at what had happened to him.

11 While he was clinging to Peter and John, all the people ran together to them at the so-called portico of Solomon, full of amazement.

12 But when Peter saw *this,* he replied to the people, "Men of Israel, why are you amazed at this, or why do you gaze at us, as if by our own power or piety we had made him walk?

13 "The God of Abraham, Isaac and Jacob, the

[side note:] His blood forgives when we believe, repent, and are baptized.

1. I.e. the Messiah 2. I.e. persons 3. One early ms does not contain *were* and *and* 4. I.e. 3 p.m. 5. Or *a gift of charity*

God of our fathers, has glorified His servant Jesus, *the one* whom you delivered and disowned in the presence of Pilate, when he had decided to release Him.

14 "But you disowned the Holy and Righteous One and asked for a murderer to be granted to you,

15 but put to death the Prince of life, *the one* whom God raised from the dead, *a fact* to which we are witnesses.

16 "And on the basis of faith in His name, *it is* the name of Jesus which has strengthened this man whom you see and know; and the faith which *comes* through Him has given him this perfect health in the presence of you all.

17 "And now, brethren, I know that you acted in ignorance, just as your rulers did also.

18 "But the things which God announced beforehand by the mouth of all the prophets, that His Christ would suffer, He has thus fulfilled.

19 "Therefore repent and return, so that your sins may be wiped away, in order that times of refreshing may come from the presence of the Lord;

20 and that He may send Jesus, the Christ appointed for you,

21 whom heaven must receive until *the* period of restoration of all things about which God spoke by the mouth of His holy prophets from ancient time.

22 "Moses said, 'THE LORD GOD WILL RAISE UP FOR YOU A PROPHET LIKE ME FROM YOUR BRETHREN; TO HIM YOU SHALL GIVE HEED to everything He says to you.

23 'And it will be that every soul that does not heed that prophet shall be utterly destroyed from among the people.'

24 "And likewise, all the prophets who have spoken, from Samuel and *his* successors onward, also announced these days.

25 "It is you who are the sons of the prophets and of the covenant which God made with your fathers, saying to Abraham, 'AND IN YOUR SEED ALL THE FAMILIES OF THE EARTH SHALL BE BLESSED.'

26 "For you first, God raised up His Servant and sent Him to bless you by turning every one *of you* from your wicked ways."

Peter and John Arrested

4 As they were speaking to the people, the priests and the captain of the temple *guard* and the Sadducees came up to them,

2 being greatly disturbed because they were teaching the people and proclaiming in Jesus the resurrection from the dead.

3 And they laid hands on them and put them in jail until the next day, for it was already evening.

4 But many of those who had heard the message believed; and the number of the men came to be about five thousand.

5 On the next day, their rulers and elders and scribes were gathered together in Jerusalem;

6 and Annas the high priest *was there,* and Caiaphas and John and Alexander, and all who were of high-priestly descent.

7 When they had placed them in the center, they *began to* inquire, "By what power, or in what name, have you done this?"

8 Then Peter, filled with the Holy Spirit, said to them, "Rulers and elders of the people,

9 if we are on trial today for a benefit done to a sick man, as to how this man has been made well,

10 let it be known to all of you and to all the people of Israel, that by the name of Jesus Christ the Nazarene, whom you crucified, whom God raised from the dead—by this *name* this man stands here before you in good health.

11 "He is the STONE WHICH WAS REJECTED by you, THE BUILDERS, *but* WHICH BECAME THE CHIEF CORNER *stone.*

12 "And there is salvation in no one else; for there is no other name under heaven that has been given among men by which we must be saved."

13 Now as they observed the confidence of Peter and John and understood that they were uneducated and untrained men, they were amazed, and *began* to recognize them as having been with Jesus.

14 And seeing the man who had been healed standing with them, they had nothing to say in reply.

15 But when they had ordered them to leave the Council, they *began* to confer with one another,

16 saying, "What shall we do with these men? For the fact that a noteworthy miracle has taken place through them is apparent to all who live in Jerusalem, and we cannot deny it.

17 "But so that it will not spread any further among the people, let us warn them to speak no longer to any man in this name."

18 And when they had summoned them, they commanded them not to speak or teach at all in the name of Jesus.

19 But Peter and John answered and said to them, "Whether it is right in the sight of God to give heed to you rather than to God, you be the judge;

20 for we cannot stop speaking about what we have seen and heard."

21 When they had threatened them further, they let them go (finding no basis on which to punish them) on account of the people, because they were all glorifying God for what had happened;

22 for the man was more than forty years old on whom this miracle of healing had been performed.

23 When they had been released, they went to their own *companions* and reported all that the chief priests and the elders had said to them.

24 And when they heard *this,* they lifted their voices to God with one accord and said, "O Lord, it is You who MADE THE HEAVEN AND THE EARTH AND THE SEA, AND ALL THAT IS IN THEM,

25 who by the Holy Spirit, *through* the mouth of our father David Your servant, said,

'WHY DID THE ¹GENTILES RAGE,
AND THE PEOPLES DEVISE FUTILE THINGS?
26 'THE KINGS OF THE EARTH TOOK THEIR
STAND,
AND THE RULERS WERE GATHERED
TOGETHER
AGAINST THE LORD AND AGAINST HIS
CHRIST.'
27 "For truly in this city there were gathered together against Your holy servant Jesus, whom You anointed, both Herod and Pontius Pilate, along with the Gentiles and the peoples of Israel,
28 to do whatever Your hand and Your purpose predestined to occur.
29 "And now, Lord, take note of their threats, and grant that Your bond-servants may speak Your word with all confidence,
30 while You extend Your hand to heal, and signs and wonders take place through the name of Your holy servant Jesus."
31 And when they had prayed, the place where they had gathered together was shaken, and they were all filled with the Holy Spirit and *began* to speak the word of God with boldness.
32 And the congregation of those who believed were of one heart and soul; and not one *of them* claimed that anything belonging to him was his own, but all things were common property to them.
33 And with great power the apostles were giving testimony to the resurrection of the Lord Jesus, and abundant grace was upon them all.
34 For there was not a needy person among them, for all who were owners of land or houses would sell them and bring the proceeds of the sales
35 and lay them at the apostles' feet, and they would be distributed to each as any had need.
36 Now Joseph, a Levite of Cyprian birth, who was also called Barnabas by the apostles (which translated means Son of Encouragement),
37 and who owned a tract of land, sold it and brought the money and laid it at the apostles' feet.

Fate of Ananias and Sapphira

5 But a man named Ananias, with his wife Sapphira, sold a piece of property,
2 and kept back *some* of the price for himself, with his wife's full knowledge, and bringing a portion of it, he laid it at the apostles' feet.
3 But Peter said, "Ananias, why has Satan filled your heart to lie to the Holy Spirit and to keep back *some* of the price of the land?
4 "While it remained *unsold*, did it not remain your own? And after it was sold, was it not under your control? Why is it that you have conceived this deed in your heart? You have not lied to men but to God."
5 And as he heard these words, Ananias fell down and breathed his last; and great fear came over all who heard of it.

6 The young men got up and covered him up, and after carrying him out, they buried him.
7 Now there elapsed an interval of about three hours, and his wife came in, not knowing what had happened.
8 And Peter responded to her, "Tell me whether you sold the land for such and such a price?" And she said, "Yes, that was the price."
9 Then Peter *said* to her, "Why is it that you have agreed together to put the Spirit of the Lord to the test? Behold, the feet of those who have buried your husband are at the door, and they will carry you out *as well*."
10 And immediately she fell at his feet and breathed her last, and the young men came in and found her dead, and they carried her out and buried her beside her husband.
11 And great fear came over the whole church, and over all who heard of these things.
12 At the hands of the apostles many signs and wonders were taking place among the people; and they were all with one accord in Solomon's portico.
13 But none of the rest dared to associate with them; however, the people held them in high esteem.
14 And all the more believers in the Lord, multitudes of men and women, were constantly added to *their number*,
15 to such an extent that they even carried the sick out into the streets and laid them on cots and pallets, so that when Peter came by at least his shadow might fall on any one of them.
16 Also the people from the cities in the vicinity of Jerusalem were coming together, bringing people who were sick ²or afflicted with unclean spirits, and they were all being healed.
17 But the high priest rose up, along with all his associates (that is the sect of the Sadducees), and they were filled with jealousy.
18 They laid hands on the apostles and put them in a public jail.
19 But during the night an angel of the Lord opened the gates of the prison, and taking them out he said,
20 "Go, stand and speak to the people in the temple the whole message of this Life."
21 Upon hearing *this*, they entered into the temple about daybreak and *began* to teach.
Now when the high priest and his associates came, they called the Council together, even all the Senate of the sons of Israel, and sent *orders* to the prison house for them to be brought.
22 But the officers who came did not find them in the prison; and they returned and reported back,
23 saying, "We found the prison house locked quite securely and the guards standing at the doors; but when we had opened up, we found no one inside."
24 Now when the captain of the temple *guard* and the chief priests heard these words, they were greatly perplexed about them as to what would come of this.
25 But someone came and reported to them,

---

1. Or *nations* 2. Lit *and*

"The men whom you put in prison are standing in the temple and teaching the people!"

26 Then the captain went along with the officers and *proceeded* to bring them *back* without violence (for they were afraid of the people, that they might be stoned).

27 When they had brought them, they stood them before the Council. The high priest questioned them,

28 saying, "We gave you strict orders not to continue teaching in this name, and yet, you have filled Jerusalem with your teaching and intend to bring this man's blood upon us."

29 But Peter and the apostles answered, "We must obey God rather than men.

30 "The God of our fathers raised up Jesus, whom you had put to death by hanging Him on a cross.

31 "He is the one whom God exalted to His right hand as a Prince and a Savior, to grant repentance to Israel, and forgiveness of sins.

32 "And we are witnesses [1]of these things; and *so is* the Holy Spirit, whom God has given to those who obey Him."

33 But when they heard this, they were cut to the quick and intended to kill them.

34 But a Pharisee named Gamaliel, a teacher of the Law, respected by all the people, stood up in the Council and gave orders to put the men outside for a short time.

35 And he said to them, "Men of Israel, take care what you propose to do with these men.

36 "For some time ago Theudas rose up, claiming to be somebody, and a group of about four hundred men joined up with him. But he was killed, and all who followed him were dispersed and came to nothing.

37 "After this man, Judas of Galilee rose up in the days of the census and drew away *some* people after him; he too perished, and all those who followed him were scattered.

38 "So in the present case, I say to you, stay away from these men and let them alone, for if this plan or action is of men, it will be overthrown;

39 but if it is of God, you will not be able to overthrow them; or else you may even be found fighting against God."

40 They took his advice; and after calling the apostles in, they flogged them and ordered them not to speak in the name of Jesus, and *then* released them.

41 So they went on their way from the presence of the Council, rejoicing that they had been considered worthy to suffer shame for *His* name.

42 And every day, in the temple and from house to house, they kept right on teaching and preaching Jesus *as* the Christ.

Choosing of the Seven

6 Now at this time while the disciples were increasing *in number*, a complaint arose on the part of the [2]Hellenistic *Jews* against the *native* Hebrews, because their widows were being overlooked in the daily serving *of food.*

2 So the twelve summoned the congregation of the disciples and said, "It is not desirable for us to neglect the word of God in order to serve tables.

3 "Therefore, brethren, select from among you seven men of good reputation, full of the Spirit and of wisdom, whom we may put in charge of this task.

4 "But we will devote ourselves to prayer and to the ministry of the word."

5 The statement found approval with the whole congregation; and they chose Stephen, a man full of faith and of the Holy Spirit, and Philip, Prochorus, Nicanor, Timon, Parmenas and Nicolas, a [3]proselyte from Antioch.

6 And these they brought before the apostles; and after praying, they laid their hands on them.

7 The word of God kept on spreading; and the number of the disciples continued to increase greatly in Jerusalem, and a great many of the priests were becoming obedient to the faith.

8 And Stephen, full of grace and power, was performing great wonders and signs among the people.

9 But some men from what was called the Synagogue of the Freedmen, *including* both Cyrenians and Alexandrians, and some from Cilicia and Asia, rose up and argued with Stephen.

10 But they were unable to cope with the wisdom and the Spirit with which he was speaking.

11 Then they secretly induced men to say, "We have heard him speak blasphemous words against Moses and *against* God."

12 And they stirred up the people, the elders and the scribes, and they came up to him and dragged him away and brought him before the Council.

13 They put forward false witnesses who said, "This man incessantly speaks against this holy place and the Law;

14 for we have heard him say that this Nazarene, Jesus, will destroy this place and alter the customs which Moses handed down to us."

15 And fixing their gaze on him, all who were sitting in the Council saw his face like the face of an angel.

Stephen's Defense

7 The high priest said, "Are these things so?" 2 And he said, "Hear me, brethren and fathers! The God of glory appeared to our father Abraham when he was in Mesopotamia, before he lived in Haran,

3 and said to him, 'LEAVE YOUR COUNTRY AND YOUR RELATIVES, AND COME INTO THE LAND THAT I WILL SHOW YOU.'

4 "Then he left the land of the Chaldeans and settled in Haran. From there, after his father

---

1. One early ms adds *in Him* 2. Jews who adopted the Gr language and much of Gr culture throughout acculturation 3. I.e. a Gentile convert to Judaism

died, *God* had him move to this country in which you are now living.

5 "But He gave him no inheritance in it, not even a foot of ground, and *yet*, even when he had no child, He promised that HE WOULD GIVE IT TO HIM AS A POSSESSION, AND TO HIS DESCENDANTS AFTER HIM.

6 "But God spoke to this effect, that his DESCENDANTS WOULD BE ALIENS IN A FOREIGN LAND, AND THAT THEY WOULD BE ENSLAVED AND MISTREATED FOR FOUR HUNDRED YEARS.

7 " 'AND WHATEVER NATION TO WHICH THEY WILL BE IN BONDAGE I MYSELF WILL JUDGE,' said God, 'AND AFTER THAT THEY WILL COME OUT AND ¹SERVE ME IN THIS PLACE.'

8 "And He gave him the covenant of circumcision; and so *Abraham* became the father of Isaac, and circumcised him on the eighth day; and Isaac *became the father of* Jacob, and Jacob *of* the twelve patriarchs.

9 "The patriarchs became jealous of Joseph and sold him into Egypt. *Yet* God was with him,

10 and rescued him from all his afflictions, and granted him favor and wisdom in the sight of Pharaoh, king of Egypt, and he made him governor over Egypt and all his household.

11 "Now a famine came over all Egypt and Canaan, and great affliction *with it,* and our fathers could find no food.

12 "But when Jacob heard that there was grain in Egypt, he sent our fathers *there* the first time.

13 "On the second *visit* Joseph made himself known to his brothers, and Joseph's family was disclosed to Pharaoh.

14 "Then Joseph sent *word* and invited Jacob his father and all his relatives to come to him, seventy-five persons *in all.*

15 "And Jacob went down to Egypt and *there* he and our fathers died.

16 "*From there* they were removed to Shechem and laid in the tomb which Abraham had purchased for a sum of money from the sons of Hamor in Shechem.

17 "But as the time of the promise was approaching which God had assured to Abraham, the people increased and multiplied in Egypt,

18 until THERE AROSE ANOTHER KING OVER EGYPT WHO KNEW NOTHING ABOUT JOSEPH.

19 "It was he who took shrewd advantage of our race and mistreated our fathers so that they would expose their infants and they would not survive.

20 "It was at this time that Moses was born; and he was lovely in the sight of God, and he was nurtured three months in his father's home.

21 "And after he had been set outside, Pharaoh's daughter took him away and nurtured him as her own son.

22 "Moses was educated in all the learning of the Egyptians, and he was a man of power in words and deeds.

23 "But when he was approaching the age of

forty, it entered his mind to visit his brethren, the sons of Israel.

24 "And when he saw one *of them* being treated unjustly, he defended him and took vengeance for the oppressed by striking down the Egyptian.

25 "And he supposed that his brethren understood that God was granting them deliverance through him, but they did not understand.

26 "On the following day he appeared to them as they were fighting together, and he tried to reconcile them in peace, saying, 'Men, you are brethren, why do you injure one another?'

27 "But the one who was injuring his neighbor pushed him away, saying, 'WHO MADE YOU A RULER AND JUDGE OVER US?

28 'YOU DO NOT MEAN TO KILL ME AS YOU KILLED THE EGYPTIAN YESTERDAY, DO YOU?'

29 "At this remark, MOSES FLED AND BECAME AN ALIEN IN THE LAND OF MIDIAN, where he became the father of two sons.

30 "After forty years had passed, AN ANGEL APPEARED TO HIM IN THE WILDERNESS OF MOUNT Sinai, IN THE FLAME OF A BURNING THORN BUSH.

31 "When Moses saw it, he marveled at the sight; and as he approached to look *more* closely, there came the voice of the Lord:

32 'I AM THE GOD OF YOUR FATHERS, THE GOD OF ABRAHAM AND ISAAC AND JACOB.' Moses shook with fear and would not venture to look.

33 "BUT THE LORD SAID TO HIM, 'TAKE OFF THE SANDALS FROM YOUR FEET, FOR THE PLACE ON WHICH YOU ARE STANDING IS HOLY GROUND.

34 'I HAVE CERTAINLY SEEN THE OPPRESSION OF MY PEOPLE IN EGYPT AND HAVE HEARD THEIR GROANS, AND I HAVE COME DOWN TO RESCUE THEM; COME NOW, AND I WILL SEND YOU TO EGYPT.'

35 "This Moses whom they disowned, saying, 'WHO MADE YOU A RULER AND A JUDGE?' is the one whom God sent *to be* both a ruler and a deliverer with the help of the angel who appeared to him in the thorn bush.

36 "This man led them out, performing wonders and signs in the land of Egypt and in the Red Sea and in the wilderness for forty years.

37 "This is the Moses who said to the sons of Israel, 'GOD WILL RAISE UP FOR YOU A PROPHET LIKE ME FROM YOUR BRETHREN.'

38 "This is the one who was in the congregation in the wilderness together with the angel who was speaking to him on Mount Sinai, and *who was* with our fathers; and he received living oracles to pass on to you.

39 "Our fathers were unwilling to be obedient to him, but repudiated him and in their hearts turned back to Egypt,

40 SAYING TO AARON, 'MAKE FOR US GODS WHO WILL GO BEFORE US; FOR THIS MOSES WHO LED US OUT OF THE LAND OF EGYPT—WE DO NOT KNOW WHAT HAPPENED TO HIM.'

41 "At that time they made a calf and brought

---

1. Or *worship*

a sacrifice to the idol, and were rejoicing in the works of their hands.

42 "But God turned away and delivered them up to serve the host of heaven; as it is written in the book of the prophets, 'IT WAS NOT TO ME THAT YOU OFFERED VICTIMS AND SACRIFICES FORTY YEARS IN THE WILDERNESS, WAS IT, O HOUSE OF ISRAEL?

43 'YOU ALSO TOOK ALONG THE TABERNACLE OF MOLOCH AND THE STAR OF THE GOD ROMPHA, THE IMAGES WHICH YOU MADE TO WORSHIP. I ALSO WILL REMOVE YOU BEYOND BABYLON.'

44 "Our fathers had the tabernacle of testimony in the wilderness, just as He who spoke to Moses directed *him* to make it according to the pattern which he had seen.

45 "And having received it in their turn, our fathers brought it in with Joshua upon dispossessing the nations whom God drove out before our fathers, until the time of David.

46 "*David* found favor in God's sight, and asked that he might find a dwelling place for the ¹God of Jacob.

47 "But it was Solomon who built a house for Him.

48 "However, the Most High does not dwell in *houses* made by *human* hands; as the prophet says:

49 'HEAVEN IS MY THRONE,
  AND EARTH IS THE FOOTSTOOL OF MY FEET;
  WHAT KIND OF HOUSE WILL YOU BUILD FOR
    ME?' says the Lord,
  'OR WHAT PLACE IS THERE FOR MY REPOSE?
50 'WAS IT NOT MY HAND WHICH MADE ALL
    THESE THINGS?'

51 "You men who are stiff-necked and uncircumcised in heart and ears are always resisting the Holy Spirit; you are doing just as your fathers did.

52 "Which one of the prophets did your fathers not persecute? They killed those who had previously announced the coming of the Righteous One, whose betrayers and murderers you have now become;

53 you who received the law as ordained by angels, and *yet* did not keep it."

54 Now when they heard this, they were cut to the quick, and they *began* gnashing their teeth at him.

55 But being full of the Holy Spirit, he gazed intently into heaven and saw the glory of God, and Jesus standing at the right hand of God;

56 and he said, "Behold, I see the heavens opened up and the Son of Man standing at the right hand of God."

57 But they cried out with a loud voice, and covered their ears and rushed at him with one impulse.

58 When they had driven him out of the city, they *began* stoning *him;* and the witnesses laid aside their robes at the feet of a young man named Saul.

59 They went on stoning Stephen as he called on the *Lord* and said, "Lord Jesus, receive my spirit!"

60 Then falling on his knees, he cried out with a loud voice, "Lord, do not hold this sin against them!" Having said this, he fell asleep.

Saul Persecutes the Church

8 Saul was in hearty agreement with putting him to death.

And on that day a great persecution began against the church in Jerusalem, and they were all scattered throughout the regions of Judea and Samaria, except the apostles.

2 *Some* devout men buried Stephen, and made loud lamentation over him.

3 But Saul *began* ravaging the church, entering house after house, and dragging off men and women, he would put them in prison.

4 Therefore, those who had been scattered went about preaching the word.

5 Philip went down to the city of Samaria and *began* proclaiming Christ to them.

6 The crowds with one accord were giving attention to what was said by Philip, as they heard and saw the signs which he was performing.

7 For *in the case of* many who had unclean spirits, they were coming out *of them* shouting with a loud voice; and many who had been paralyzed and lame were healed.

8 So there was much rejoicing in that city.

9 Now there was a man named Simon, who formerly was practicing magic in the city and astonishing the people of Samaria, claiming to be someone great;

10 and they all, from smallest to greatest, were giving attention to him, saying, "This man is what is called the Great Power of God."

11 And they were giving him attention because he had for a long time astonished them with his magic arts.

12 But when they believed Philip preaching the good news about the kingdom of God and the name of Jesus Christ, they were being baptized, men and women alike.

13 Even Simon himself believed; and after being baptized, he continued on with Philip, and as he observed signs and great miracles taking place, he was constantly amazed.

14 Now when the apostles in Jerusalem heard that Samaria had received the word of God, they sent them Peter and John,

15 who came down and prayed for them that they might receive the Holy Spirit.

16 For He had not yet fallen upon any of them; they had simply been baptized in the name of the Lord Jesus.

17 Then they *began* laying their hands on them, and they were receiving the Holy Spirit.

18 Now when Simon saw that the Spirit was bestowed through the laying on of the apostles' hands, he offered them money,

19 saying, "Give this authority to me as well, so that everyone on whom I lay my hands may receive the Holy Spirit."

20 But Peter said to him, "May your silver perish with you, because you thought you could obtain the gift of God with money!

---

1. The earliest mss read *house* instead of *God;* the Septuagint reads *God*

21 "You have no part or portion in this matter, for your heart is not right before God.

22 "Therefore repent of this wickedness of yours, and pray the Lord that, if possible, the intention of your heart may be forgiven you.

23 "For I see that you are in the gall of bitterness and in the bondage of iniquity."

24 But Simon answered and said, "Pray to the Lord for me yourselves, so that nothing of what you have said may come upon me."

25 So, when they had solemnly testified and spoken the word of the Lord, they started back to Jerusalem, and were preaching the gospel to many villages of the Samaritans.

26 But an angel of the Lord spoke to Philip saying, "Get up and go south to the road that descends from Jerusalem to Gaza." (This is a desert *road*.)

27 So he got up and went; and there was an Ethiopian eunuch, a court official of Candace, queen of the Ethiopians, who was in charge of all her treasure; and he had come to Jerusalem to worship,

28 and he was returning and sitting in his chariot, and was reading the prophet Isaiah.

29 Then the Spirit said to Philip, "Go up and join this chariot."

30 Philip ran up and heard him reading Isaiah the prophet, and said, "Do you understand what you are reading?"

31 And he said, "Well, how could I, unless someone guides me?" And he invited Philip to come up and sit with him.

32 Now the passage of Scripture which he was reading was this:

"HE WAS LED AS A SHEEP TO SLAUGHTER;
AND AS A LAMB BEFORE ITS SHEARER IS SILENT,
SO HE DOES NOT OPEN HIS MOUTH.

33 "IN HUMILIATION HIS JUDGMENT WAS TAKEN AWAY;
WHO WILL RELATE HIS GENERATION?
FOR HIS LIFE IS REMOVED FROM THE EARTH."

34 The eunuch answered Philip and said, "Please *tell me*, of whom does the prophet say this? Of himself or of someone else?"

35 Then Philip opened his mouth, and beginning from this Scripture he preached Jesus to him.

36 As they went along the road they came to some water; and the eunuch *said, "Look! Water! What prevents me from being baptized?"

37 [¹And Philip said, "If you believe with all your heart, you may." And he answered and said, "I believe that Jesus Christ is the Son of God."]

38 And he ordered the chariot to stop; and they both went down into the water, Philip as well as the eunuch, and he baptized him.

39 When they came up out of the water, the Spirit of the Lord snatched Philip away; and the eunuch no longer saw him, but went on his way rejoicing.

40 But Philip found himself at Azotus, and as he passed through he kept preaching the gospel to all the cities until he came to Caesarea.

The Conversion of Saul

9 Now Saul, still breathing threats and murder against the disciples of the Lord, went to the high priest,

2 and asked for letters from him to the synagogues at Damascus, so that if he found any belonging to the Way, both men and women, he might bring them bound to Jerusalem.

3 As he was traveling, it happened that he was approaching Damascus, and suddenly a light from heaven flashed around him;

4 and he fell to the ground and heard a voice saying to him, "Saul, Saul, why are you persecuting Me?"

5 And he said, "Who are You, Lord?" And He *said*, "I am Jesus whom you are persecuting,

6 but get up and enter the city, and it will be told you what you must do."

7 The men who traveled with him stood speechless, hearing the voice but seeing no one.

8 Saul got up from the ground, and though his eyes were open, he could see nothing; and leading him by the hand, they brought him into Damascus.

9 And he was three days without sight, and neither ate nor drank.

10 Now there was a disciple at Damascus named Ananias; and the Lord said to him in a vision, "Ananias." And he said, "Here I am, Lord."

11 And the Lord *said* to him, "Get up and go to the street called Straight, and inquire at the house of Judas for a man from Tarsus named Saul, for he is praying,

12 and he has seen ²in a vision a man named Ananias come in and lay his hands on him, so that he might regain his sight."

13 But Ananias answered, "Lord, I have heard from many about this man, how much harm he did to Your saints at Jerusalem;

14 and here he has authority from the chief priests to bind all who call on Your name."

15 But the Lord said to him, "Go, for he is a chosen ³instrument of Mine, to bear My name before the Gentiles and kings and the sons of Israel;

16 for I will show him how much he must suffer for My name's sake."

17 So Ananias departed and entered the house, and after laying his hands on him said, "Brother Saul, the Lord Jesus, who appeared to you on the road by which you were coming, has sent me so that you may regain your sight and be filled with the Holy Spirit."

18 And immediately there fell from his eyes something like scales, and he regained his sight, and he got up and was baptized;

19 and he took food and was strengthened.
Now for several days he was with the disciples who were at Damascus,

20 and immediately he *began* to proclaim

---

1. Early mss do not contain this v   2. A few early mss do not contain *in a vision*   3. Or *vessel*

The Ethiopian was immersed in water upon his confession of faith in Jesus.
How about you?

Jesus in the synagogues, saying, "He is the Son of God."

21 All those hearing him continued to be amazed, and were saying, "Is this not he who in Jerusalem destroyed those who called on this name, and *who* had come here for the purpose of bringing them bound before the chief priests?"

22 But Saul kept increasing in strength and confounding the Jews who lived at Damascus by proving that this *Jesus* is the Christ.

23 When many days had elapsed, the Jews plotted together to do away with him,

24 but their plot became known to Saul. They were also watching the gates day and night so that they might put him to death;

25 but his disciples took him by night and let him down through *an opening in* the wall, lowering him in a large basket.

26 When he came to Jerusalem, he was trying to associate with the disciples; but they were all afraid of him, not believing that he was a disciple.

27 But Barnabas took hold of him and brought him to the apostles and described to them how he had seen the Lord on the road, and that He had talked to him, and how at Damascus he had spoken out boldly in the name of Jesus.

28 And he was with them, moving about freely in Jerusalem, speaking out boldly in the name of the Lord.

29 And he was talking and arguing with the Hellenistic *Jews;* but they were attempting to put him to death.

30 But when the brethren learned *of it,* they brought him down to Caesarea and sent him away to Tarsus.

31 So the church throughout all Judea and Galilee and Samaria enjoyed peace, being built up; and going on in the fear of the Lord and in the comfort of the Holy Spirit, it continued to increase.

32 Now as Peter was traveling through all *those regions,* he came down also to the saints who lived at Lydda.

33 There he found a man named Aeneas, who had been bedridden eight years, for he was paralyzed.

34 Peter said to him, "Aeneas, Jesus Christ heals you; get up and make your bed." Immediately he got up.

35 And all who lived at Lydda and Sharon saw him, and they turned to the Lord.

36 Now in Joppa there was a disciple named Tabitha (which translated *in Greek* is called Dorcas); this woman was abounding with deeds of kindness and charity which she continually did.

37 And it happened at that time that she fell sick and died; and when they had washed her body, they laid it in an upper room.

38 Since Lydda was near Joppa, the disciples, having heard that Peter was there, sent two

men to him, imploring him, "Do not delay in coming to us."

39 So Peter arose and went with them. When he arrived, they brought him into the upper room; and all the widows stood beside him, weeping and showing all the [1]tunics and garments that Dorcas used to make while she was with them.

40 But Peter sent them all out and knelt down and prayed, and turning to the body, he said, "Tabitha, arise." And she opened her eyes, and when she saw Peter, she sat up.

41 And he gave her his hand and raised her up; and calling the saints and widows, he presented her alive.

42 It became known all over Joppa, and many believed in the Lord.

43 And Peter stayed many days in Joppa with a tanner *named* Simon.

Cornelius' Vision

10 Now *there was* a man at Caesarea named Cornelius, a centurion of what was called the Italian [2]cohort,

2 a devout man and one who feared God with all his household, and gave many [3]alms to the *Jewish* people and prayed to God continually.

3 About the [4]ninth hour of the day he clearly saw in a vision an angel of God who had *just* come in and said to him, "Cornelius!"

4 And fixing his gaze on him and being much alarmed, he said, "What is it, Lord?" And he said to him, "Your prayers and [5]alms have ascended as a memorial before God.

5 "Now dispatch *some* men to Joppa and send for a man *named* Simon, who is also called Peter;

6 he is staying with a tanner *named* Simon, whose house is by the sea."

7 When the angel who was speaking to him had left, he summoned two of his servants and a devout soldier of those who were his personal attendants,

8 and after he had explained everything to them, he sent them to Joppa.

9 On the next day, as they were on their way and approaching the city, Peter went up on the housetop about the [6]sixth hour to pray.

10 But he became hungry and was desiring to eat; but while they were making preparations, he fell into a trance;

11 and he *saw the sky opened up, and an [7]object like a great sheet coming down, lowered by four corners to the ground,

12 and there were in it all *kinds of* four-footed animals and [8]crawling creatures of the earth and birds of the air.

13 A voice came to him, "Get up, Peter, kill and eat!"

14 But Peter said, "By no means, Lord, for I have never eaten anything unholy and unclean."

15 Again a voice *came* to him a second time,

---

1. Or *inner garments* 2. Or *battalion* 3. Or *gifts of charity* 4. I.e. 3 p.m. 5. Or *deeds of charity* 6. I.e. noon 7. Or *vessel* 8. Or *reptiles*

"What God has cleansed, no *longer* consider unholy."

16 This happened three times, and immediately the object was taken up into the sky.

17 Now while Peter was greatly perplexed in mind as to what the vision which he had seen might be, behold, the men who had been sent by Cornelius, having asked directions for Simon's house, appeared at the gate;

18 and calling out, they were asking whether Simon, who was also called Peter, was staying there.

19 While Peter was reflecting on the vision, the Spirit said to him, "Behold, three men are looking for you.

20 "But get up, go downstairs and accompany them without misgivings, for I have sent them Myself."

21 Peter went down to the men and said, "Behold, I am the one you are looking for; what is the reason for which you have come?"

22 They said, "Cornelius, a centurion, a righteous and God-fearing man well spoken of by the entire nation of the Jews, was *divinely* directed by a holy angel to send for you *to come* to his house and hear a message from you."

23 So he invited them in and gave them lodging.

And on the next day he got up and went away with them, and some of the brethren from Joppa accompanied him.

24 On the following day he entered Caesarea. Now Cornelius was waiting for them and had called together his relatives and close friends.

25 When Peter entered, Cornelius met him, and fell at his feet and worshiped *him*.

26 But Peter raised him up, saying, "Stand up; I too am *just* a man."

27 As he talked with him, he entered and *found many people assembled.

28 And he said to them, "You yourselves know how unlawful it is for a man who is a Jew to associate with a foreigner or to visit him; and *yet* God has shown me that I should not call any man unholy or unclean.

29 "That is why I came without even raising any objection when I was sent for. So I ask for what reason you have sent for me."

30 Cornelius said, "Four days ago to this hour, I was praying in my house during the [1]ninth hour; and behold, a man stood before me in shining garments,

31 and he *said, 'Cornelius, your prayer has been heard and your alms have been remembered before God.

32 'Therefore send to Joppa and invite Simon, who is also called Peter, to come to you; he is staying at the house of Simon *the* tanner by the sea.'

33 "So I sent for you immediately, and you have been kind enough to come. Now then, we are all here present before God to hear all that you have been commanded by the Lord."

34 Opening his mouth, Peter said:

"I most certainly understand *now* that God is not one to show partiality,

35 but in every nation the man who fears Him and does what is right is welcome to Him.

36 "The word which He sent to the sons of Israel, preaching peace through Jesus Christ (He is Lord of all)—

37 you yourselves know the thing which took place throughout all Judea, starting from Galilee, after the baptism which John proclaimed.

38 "*You know of* Jesus of Nazareth, how God anointed Him with the Holy Spirit and with power, and *how* He went about doing good and healing all who were oppressed by the devil, for God was with Him.

39 "We are witnesses of all the things He did both in the land of the Jews and in Jerusalem. They also put Him to death by hanging Him on a cross.

40 "God raised Him up on the third day and granted that He become visible,

41 not to all the people, but to witnesses who were chosen beforehand by God, *that is,* to us who ate and drank with Him after He arose from the dead.

42 "And He ordered us to preach to the people, and solemnly to testify that this is the One who has been appointed by God as Judge of the living and the dead.

43 "Of Him all the prophets bear witness that through His name everyone who believes in Him receives forgiveness of sins."

44 While Peter was still speaking these words, the Holy Spirit fell upon all those who were listening to the message.

45 All the circumcised believers who came with Peter were amazed, because the gift of the Holy Spirit had been poured out on the Gentiles also.

46 For they were hearing them speaking with tongues and exalting God. Then Peter answered,

47 "Surely no one can refuse the water for these to be baptized who have received the Holy Spirit just as we *did,* can he?"

48 And he ordered them to be baptized in the name of Jesus Christ. Then they asked him to stay on for a few days.

Peter Reports at Jerusalem

11 Now the apostles and the brethren who were throughout Judea heard that the Gentiles also had received the word of God.

2 And when Peter came up to Jerusalem, those who were circumcised took issue with him,

3 saying, "You went to uncircumcised men and ate with them."

4 But Peter began *speaking* and *proceeded* to explain to them in orderly sequence, saying,

5 "I was in the city of Joppa praying; and in a trance I saw a vision, an object coming down like a great sheet lowered by four corners from the sky; and it came right down to me,

6 and when I had fixed my gaze on it and

1. I.e. 3 to 4 p.m.

was observing it I saw the four-footed animals of the earth and the wild beasts and the ¹crawling creatures and the birds of the air.

7 "I also heard a voice saying to me, 'Get up, Peter; kill and eat.'

8 "But I said, 'By no means, Lord, for nothing unholy or unclean has ever entered my mouth.'

9 "But a voice from heaven answered a second time, 'What God has cleansed, no longer consider unholy.'

10 "This happened three times, and everything was drawn back up into the sky.

11 "And behold, at that moment three men appeared at the house in which we were *staying*, having been sent to me from Caesarea.

12 "The Spirit told me to go with them without misgivings. These six brethren also went with me and we entered the man's house.

13 "And he reported to us how he had seen the angel standing in his house, and saying, 'Send to Joppa and have Simon, who is also called Peter, brought here;

14 and he will speak words to you by which you will be saved, you and all your household.'

15 "And as I began to speak, the Holy Spirit fell upon them just as *He did* upon us at the beginning.

16 "And I remembered the word of the Lord, how He used to say, 'John baptized with water, but you will be baptized with the Holy Spirit.'

17 "Therefore if God gave to them the same gift as *He gave* to us also after believing in the Lord Jesus Christ, who was I that I could stand in God's way?"

18 When they heard this, they quieted down and glorified God, saying, "Well then, God has granted to the Gentiles also the repentance *that leads* to life."

19 So then those who were scattered because of the persecution that occurred in connection with Stephen made their way to Phoenicia and Cyprus and Antioch, speaking the word to no one except to Jews alone.

20 But there were some of them, men of Cyprus and Cyrene, who came to Antioch and *began* speaking to the ²Greeks also, preaching the Lord Jesus.

21 And the hand of the Lord was with them, and a large number who believed turned to the Lord.

22 The news about them reached the ears of the church at Jerusalem, and they sent Barnabas off to Antioch.

23 Then when he arrived and witnessed the grace of God, he rejoiced and *began* to encourage them all with resolute heart to remain *true* to the Lord;

24 for he was a good man, and full of the Holy Spirit and of faith. And considerable numbers were brought to the Lord.

25 And he left for Tarsus to look for Saul;

26 and when he had found him, he brought him to Antioch. And for an entire year they met with the church and taught considerable

numbers; and the disciples were first called Christians in Antioch.

27 Now at this time some prophets came down from Jerusalem to Antioch.

28 One of them named Agabus stood up and *began* to indicate by the Spirit that there would certainly be a great famine all over the world. And this took place in the *reign* of Claudius.

29 And in the proportion that any of the disciples had means, each of them determined to send *a contribution* for the relief of the brethren living in Judea.

30 And this they did, sending it in charge of Barnabas and Saul to the elders.

Peter's Arrest and Deliverance

12 Now about that time Herod the king laid hands on some who belonged to the church in order to mistreat them.

2 And he had James the brother of John put to death with a sword.

3 When he saw that it pleased the Jews, he proceeded to arrest Peter also. Now it was during the days of Unleavened Bread.

4 When he had seized him, he put him in prison, delivering him to four squads of soldiers to guard him, intending after the Passover to bring him out before the people.

5 So Peter was kept in the prison, but prayer for him was being made fervently by the church to God.

6 On the very night when Herod was about to bring him forward, Peter was sleeping between two soldiers, bound with two chains, and guards in front of the door were watching over the prison.

7 And behold, an angel of the Lord suddenly appeared and a light shone in the cell; and he struck Peter's side and woke him up, saying, "Get up quickly." And his chains fell off his hands.

8 And the angel said to him, "Gird yourself and put on your sandals." And he did so. And he *said to him, "Wrap your cloak around you and follow me."

9 And he went out and continued to follow, and he did not know that what was being done by the angel was real, but thought he was seeing a vision.

10 When they had passed the first and second guard, they came to the iron gate that leads into the city, which opened for them by itself; and they went out and went along one street, and immediately the angel departed from him.

11 When Peter came to himself, he said, "Now I know for sure that the Lord has sent forth His angel and rescued me from the hand of Herod and from all that the Jewish people were expecting."

12 And when he realized *this*, he went to the house of Mary, the mother of John who was also called Mark, where many were gathered together and were praying.

13 When he knocked at the door of the gate, a servant-girl named Rhoda came to answer.

14 When she recognized Peter's voice, because

---

1. Or *reptiles* 2. Lit *Hellenists*; people who lived by Greek customs and culture

of her joy she did not open the gate, but ran in and announced that Peter was standing in front of the gate.

15 They said to her, "You are out of your mind!" But she kept insisting that it was so. They kept saying, "It is his angel."

16 But Peter continued knocking; and when they had opened *the door*, they saw him and were amazed.

17 But motioning to them with his hand to be silent, he described to them how the Lord had led him out of the prison. And he said, "Report these things to James and the brethren." Then he left and went to another place.

18 Now when day came, there was no small disturbance among the soldiers *as to* what could have become of Peter.

19 When Herod had searched for him and had not found him, he examined the guards and ordered that they be led away *to execution*. Then he went down from Judea to Caesarea and was spending time there.

20 Now he was very angry with the people of Tyre and Sidon; and with one accord they came to him, and having won over Blastus the king's chamberlain, they were asking for peace, because their country was fed by the king's country.

21 On an appointed day Herod, having put on his royal apparel, took his seat on the rostrum and *began* delivering an address to them.

22 The people kept crying out, "The voice of a god and not of a man!"

23 And immediately an angel of the Lord struck him because he did not give God the glory, and he was eaten by worms and died.

24 But the word of the Lord continued to grow and to be multiplied.

25 And Barnabas and Saul returned from Jerusalem when they had fulfilled their mission, taking along with *them* John, who was also called Mark.

First Missionary Journey

13 Now there were at Antioch, in the church that was *there*, prophets and teachers: Barnabas, and Simeon who was called Niger, and Lucius of Cyrene, and Manaen who had been brought up with Herod the tetrarch, and Saul.

2 While they were ministering to the Lord and fasting, the Holy Spirit said, "Set apart for Me Barnabas and Saul for the work to which I have called them."

3 Then, when they had fasted and prayed and laid their hands on them, they sent them away.

4 So, being sent out by the Holy Spirit, they went down to Seleucia and from there they sailed to Cyprus.

5 When they reached Salamis, they *began* to proclaim the word of God in the synagogues of the Jews; and they also had John as their helper.

6 When they had gone through the whole island as far as Paphos, they found a magician, a Jewish false prophet whose name was Bar-Jesus,

7 who was with the proconsul, Sergius Paulus, a man of intelligence. This man summoned Barnabas and Saul and sought to hear the word of God.

8 But Elymas the magician (for so his name is translated) was opposing them, seeking to turn the proconsul away from the faith.

9 But Saul, who was also *known as* Paul, filled with the Holy Spirit, fixed his gaze on him,

10 and said, "You who are full of all deceit and fraud, you son of the devil, you enemy of all righteousness, will you not cease to make crooked the straight ways of the Lord?

11 "Now, behold, the hand of the Lord is upon you, and you will be blind and not see the sun for a time." And immediately a mist and a darkness fell upon him, and he went about seeking those who would lead him by the hand.

12 Then the proconsul believed when he saw what had happened, being amazed at the teaching of the Lord.

13 Now Paul and his companions put out to sea from Paphos and came to Perga in Pamphylia; but John left them and returned to Jerusalem.

14 But going on from Perga, they arrived at Pisidian Antioch, and on the Sabbath day they went into the synagogue and sat down.

15 After the reading of the Law and the Prophets the synagogue officials sent to them, saying, "Brethren, if you have any word of exhortation for the people, say it."

16 Paul stood up, and motioning with his hand said,

"Men of Israel, and you who fear God, listen:

17 "The God of this people Israel chose our fathers and made the people great during their stay in the land of Egypt, and with an uplifted arm He led them out from it.

18 "For a period of about forty years He put up with them in the wilderness.

19 "When He had destroyed seven nations in the land of Canaan, He distributed their land as an inheritance—*all of which took* about four hundred and fifty years.

20 "After these things He gave *them* judges until Samuel the prophet.

21 "Then they asked for a king, and God gave them Saul the son of Kish, a man of the tribe of Benjamin, for forty years.

22 "After He had removed him, He raised up David to be their king, concerning whom He also testified and said, 'I HAVE FOUND DAVID the son of Jesse, A MAN AFTER MY HEART, who will do all My will.'

23 "From the descendants of this man, according to promise, God has brought to Israel a Savior, Jesus,

24 after John had proclaimed before His coming a baptism of repentance to all the people of Israel.

25 "And while John was completing his course, he kept saying, 'What do you suppose that I

am? I am not *He*. But behold, one is coming after me the sandals of whose feet I am not worthy to untie.'

26 "Brethren, sons of Abraham's family, and those among you who fear God, to us the message of this salvation has been sent.

27 "For those who live in Jerusalem, and their rulers, recognizing neither Him nor the utterances of the prophets which are read every Sabbath, fulfilled *these* by condemning *Him*.

28 "And though they found no ground for *putting Him to* death, they asked Pilate that He be executed.

29 "When they had carried out all that was written concerning Him, they took Him down from the cross and laid Him in a tomb.

30 "But God raised Him from the dead;

31 and for many days He appeared to those who came up with Him from Galilee to Jerusalem, the very ones who are now His witnesses to the people.

32 "And we preach to you the good news of the promise made to the fathers,

33 that God has fulfilled this *promise* to our children in that He raised up Jesus, as it is also written in the second Psalm, 'YOU ARE MY SON; TODAY I HAVE BEGOTTEN YOU.'

34 "*As for the fact* that He raised Him up from the dead, no longer to return to decay, He has spoken in this way: 'I WILL GIVE YOU THE HOLY and SURE *blessings* OF DAVID.'

35 "Therefore He also says in another *Psalm*, 'YOU WILL NOT ALLOW YOUR HOLY ONE TO UNDERGO DECAY.'

36 "For David, after he had served the purpose of God in his own generation, fell asleep, and was laid among his fathers and underwent decay;

37 but He whom God raised did not undergo decay.

38 "Therefore let it be known to you, brethren, that through Him forgiveness of sins is proclaimed to you,

39 and through Him everyone who believes is freed from all things, from which you could not be freed through the Law of Moses.

40 "Therefore take heed, so that the thing spoken of in the Prophets may not come upon *you*:

41 'BEHOLD, YOU SCOFFERS, AND MARVEL, AND PERISH;
FOR I AM ACCOMPLISHING A WORK IN YOUR DAYS,
A WORK WHICH YOU WILL NEVER BELIEVE, THOUGH SOMEONE SHOULD DESCRIBE IT TO YOU.' "

42 As Paul and Barnabas were going out, the people kept begging that these things might be spoken to them the next Sabbath.

43 Now when *the meeting of* the synagogue had broken up, many of the Jews and of the God-fearing proselytes followed Paul and Barnabas, who, speaking to them, were urging them to continue in the grace of God.

44 The next Sabbath nearly the whole city assembled to hear the word of the Lord.

45 But when the Jews saw the crowds, they were filled with jealousy and *began* contradicting the things spoken by Paul, and were blaspheming.

46 Paul and Barnabas spoke out boldly and said, "It was necessary that the word of God be spoken to you first; since you repudiate it and judge yourselves unworthy of eternal life, behold, we are turning to the Gentiles.

47 "For so the Lord has commanded us,
'I HAVE PLACED YOU AS A LIGHT FOR THE GENTILES,
THAT YOU MAY BRING SALVATION TO THE END OF THE EARTH.' "

48 When the Gentiles heard this, they *began* rejoicing and glorifying the word of the Lord; and as many as had been appointed to eternal life believed.

49 And the word of the Lord was being spread through the whole region.

50 But the Jews incited the devout women of prominence and the leading men of the city, and instigated a persecution against Paul and Barnabas, and drove them out of their district.

51 But they shook off the dust of their feet *in protest* against them and went to Iconium.

52 And the disciples were continually filled with joy and with the Holy Spirit.

Acceptance and Opposition

14 In Iconium they entered the synagogue of the Jews together, and spoke in such a manner that a large number of people believed, both of Jews and of Greeks.

2 But the Jews who disbelieved stirred up the minds of the Gentiles and embittered them against the brethren.

3 Therefore they spent a long time *there* speaking boldly *with reliance* upon the Lord, who was testifying to the word of His grace, granting that signs and wonders be done by their hands.

4 But the people of the city were divided; and some sided with the Jews, and some with the apostles.

5 And when an attempt was made by both the Gentiles and the Jews with their rulers, to mistreat and to stone them,

6 they became aware of it and fled to the cities of Lycaonia, Lystra and Derbe, and the surrounding region;

7 and there they continued to preach the gospel.

8 At Lystra a man was sitting who had no strength in his feet, lame from his mother's womb, who had never walked.

9 This man was listening to Paul as he spoke, who, when he had fixed his gaze on him and had seen that he had faith to be made well,

10 said with a loud voice, "Stand upright on your feet." And he leaped up and *began* to walk.

11 When the crowds saw what Paul had done, they raised their voice, saying in the Lycaonian language, "The gods have become like men and have come down to us."

12 And they *began* calling Barnabas, Zeus,

and Paul, Hermes, because he was the chief speaker.

13 The priest of Zeus, whose *temple* was just outside the city, brought oxen and garlands to the gates, and wanted to offer sacrifice with the crowds.

14 But when the apostles Barnabas and Paul heard of it, they tore their robes and rushed out into the crowd, crying out

15 and saying, "Men, why are you doing these things? We are also men of the same nature as you, and preach the gospel to you that you should turn from these ¹vain things to a living God, WHO MADE THE HEAVEN AND THE EARTH AND THE SEA AND ALL THAT IS IN THEM.

16 "In the generations gone by He permitted all the nations to go their own ways;

17 and yet He did not leave Himself without witness, in that He did good and gave you rains from heaven and fruitful seasons, satisfying your hearts with food and gladness."

18 *Even* saying these things, with difficulty they restrained the crowds from offering sacrifice to them.

19 But Jews came from Antioch and Iconium, and having won over the crowds, they stoned Paul and dragged him out of the city, supposing him to be dead.

20 But while the disciples stood around him, he got up and entered the city. The next day he went away with Barnabas to Derbe.

21 After they had preached the gospel to that city and had made many disciples, they returned to Lystra and to Iconium and to Antioch,

22 strengthening the souls of the disciples, encouraging them to continue in the faith, and *saying*, "Through many tribulations we must enter the kingdom of God."

23 When they had appointed elders for them in every church, having prayed with fasting, they commended them to the Lord in whom they had believed.

24 They passed through Pisidia and came into Pamphylia.

25 When they had spoken the word in Perga, they went down to Attalia.

26 From there they sailed to Antioch, from which they had been commended to the grace of God for the work that they had accomplished.

27 When they had arrived and gathered the church together, they *began* to report all things that God had done with them and how He had opened a door of faith to the Gentiles.

28 And they spent a long time with the disciples.

The Council at Jerusalem

15 Some men came down from Judea and *began* teaching the brethren, "Unless you are circumcised according to the custom of Moses, you cannot be saved."

2 And when Paul and Barnabas had great dissension and debate with them, *the brethren* determined that Paul and Barnabas and some

---

1. I.e. idols

others of them should go up to Jerusalem to the apostles and elders concerning this issue.

3 Therefore, being sent on their way by the church, they were passing through both Phoenicia and Samaria, describing in detail the conversion of the Gentiles, and were bringing great joy to all the brethren.

4 When they arrived at Jerusalem, they were received by the church and the apostles and the elders, and they reported all that God had done with them.

5 But some of the sect of the Pharisees who had believed stood up, saying, "It is necessary to circumcise them and to direct them to observe the Law of Moses."

6 The apostles and the elders came together to look into this matter.

7 After there had been much debate, Peter stood up and said to them, "Brethren, you know that in the early days God made a choice among you, that by my mouth the Gentiles would hear the word of the gospel and believe.

8 "And God, who knows the heart, testified to them giving them the Holy Spirit, just as He also did to us;

9 and He made no distinction between us and them, cleansing their hearts by faith.

10 "Now therefore why do you put God to the test by placing upon the neck of the disciples a yoke which neither our fathers nor we have been able to bear?

11 "But we believe that we are saved through the grace of the Lord Jesus, in the same way as they also are."

12 All the people kept silent, and they were listening to Barnabas and Paul as they were relating what signs and wonders God had done through them among the Gentiles.

13 After they had stopped speaking, James answered, saying, "Brethren, listen to me.

14 "Simeon has related how God first concerned Himself about taking from among the Gentiles a people for His name.

15 "With this the words of the Prophets agree, just as it is written,

16 'AFTER THESE THINGS I will return,
AND I WILL REBUILD THE TABERNACLE OF DAVID WHICH HAS FALLEN,
AND I WILL REBUILD ITS RUINS,
AND I WILL RESTORE IT,

17 SO THAT THE REST OF MANKIND MAY SEEK THE LORD,
AND ALL THE GENTILES WHO ARE CALLED BY MY NAME,'

18 SAYS THE LORD, WHO MAKES THESE THINGS KNOWN FROM LONG AGO.

19 "Therefore it is my judgment that we do not trouble those who are turning to God from among the Gentiles,

20 but that we write to them that they abstain from things contaminated by idols and from fornication and from what is strangled and from blood.

21 "For Moses from ancient generations has in

every city those who preach him, since he is read in the synagogues every Sabbath."

22 Then it seemed good to the apostles and the elders, with the whole church, to choose men from among them to send to Antioch with Paul and Barnabas—Judas called Barsabbas, and Silas, leading men among the brethren,

23 and they sent this letter by them,

"The apostles and the brethren who are elders, to the brethren in Antioch and Syria and Cilicia who are from the Gentiles, greetings.

24 "Since we have heard that some of our number to whom we gave no instruction have disturbed you with *their* words, unsettling your souls,

25 it seemed good to us, having become of one mind, to select men to send to you with our beloved Barnabas and Paul,

26 men who have risked their lives for the name of our Lord Jesus Christ.

27 "Therefore we have sent Judas and Silas, who themselves will also report the same things by word *of mouth.*

28 "For it seemed good to the Holy Spirit and to us to lay upon you no greater burden than these essentials:

29 that you abstain from things sacrificed to idols and from blood and from things strangled and from fornication; if you keep yourselves free from such things, you will do well. Farewell."

30 So when they were sent away, they went down to Antioch; and having gathered the congregation together, they delivered the letter.

31 When they had read it, they rejoiced because of its encouragement.

32 Judas and Silas, also being prophets themselves, encouraged and strengthened the brethren with a lengthy message.

33 After they had spent time *there,* they were sent away from the brethren in peace to those who had sent them out.

34 [¹But it seemed good to Silas to remain there.]

35 But Paul and Barnabas stayed in Antioch, teaching and preaching with many others also, the word of the Lord.

36 After some days Paul said to Barnabas, "Let us return and visit the brethren in every city in which we proclaimed the word of the Lord, *and see* how they are."

37 Barnabas wanted to take John, called Mark, along with them also.

38 But Paul kept insisting that they should not take him along who had deserted them in Pamphylia and had not gone with them to the work.

39 And there occurred such a sharp disagreement that they separated from one another, and Barnabas took Mark with him and sailed away to Cyprus.

40 But Paul chose Silas and left, being committed by the brethren to the grace of the Lord.

41 And he was traveling through Syria and Cilicia, strengthening the churches.

The Macedonian Vision

16 Paul came also to Derbe and to Lystra. And a disciple was there, named Timothy, the son of a Jewish woman who was a believer, but his father was a Greek,

2 and he was well spoken of by the brethren who were in Lystra and Iconium.

3 Paul wanted this man to go with him; and he took him and circumcised him because of the Jews who were in those parts, for they all knew that his father was a Greek.

4 Now while they were passing through the cities, they were delivering the decrees which had been decided upon by the apostles and elders who were in Jerusalem, for them to observe.

5 So the churches were being strengthened in the faith, and were increasing in number daily.

6 They passed through the Phrygian and Galatian region, having been forbidden by the Holy Spirit to speak the word in Asia;

7 and after they came to Mysia, they were trying to go into Bithynia, and the Spirit of Jesus did not permit them;

8 and passing by Mysia, they came down to Troas.

9 A vision appeared to Paul in the night: a man of Macedonia was standing and appealing to him, and saying, "Come over to Macedonia and help us."

10 When he had seen the vision, immediately we sought to go into Macedonia, concluding that God had called us to preach the gospel to them.

11 So putting out to sea from Troas, we ran a straight course to Samothrace, and on the day following to Neapolis;

12 and from there to Philippi, which is a leading city of the district of Macedonia, a *Roman* colony; and we were staying in this city for some days.

13 And on the Sabbath day we went outside the gate to a riverside, where we were supposing that there would be a place of prayer; and we sat down and began speaking to the women who had assembled.

14 A woman named Lydia, from the city of Thyatira, a seller of purple fabrics, a worshiper of God, was listening; and the Lord opened her heart to respond to the things spoken by Paul.

15 And when she and her household had been baptized, she urged us, saying, "If you have judged me to be faithful to the Lord, come into my house and stay." And she prevailed upon us.

16 It happened that as we were going to the place of prayer, a slave-girl having a spirit of divination met us, who was bringing her masters much profit by fortune-telling.

17 Following after Paul and us, she kept crying out, saying, "These men are bond-servants of the Most High God, who are proclaiming to you the way of salvation."

18 She continued doing this for many days.

---

1. Early mss do not contain this v

But Paul was greatly annoyed, and turned and said to the spirit, "I command you in the name of Jesus Christ to come out of her!" And it came out at that very moment.

19 But when her masters saw that their hope of profit was gone, they seized Paul and Silas and dragged them into the market place before the authorities,

20 and when they had brought them to the chief magistrates, they said, "These men are throwing our city into confusion, being Jews,

21 and are proclaiming customs which it is not lawful for us to accept or to observe, being Romans."

22 The crowd rose up together against them, and the chief magistrates tore their robes off them and proceeded to order *them* to be beaten with rods.

23 When they had struck them with many blows, they threw them into prison, commanding the jailer to guard them securely;

24 and he, having received such a command, threw them into the inner prison and fastened their feet in the stocks.

25 But about midnight Paul and Silas were praying and singing hymns of praise to God, and the prisoners were listening to them;

26 and suddenly there came a great earthquake, so that the foundations of the prison house were shaken; and immediately all the doors were opened and everyone's chains were unfastened.

27 When the jailer awoke and saw the prison doors opened, he drew his sword and was about to kill himself, supposing that the prisoners had escaped.

28 But Paul cried out with a loud voice, saying, "Do not harm yourself, for we are all here!"

29 And he called for lights and rushed in, and trembling with fear he fell down before Paul and Silas,

30 and after he brought them out, he said, "Sirs, what must I do to be saved?"

31 They said, "Believe in the Lord Jesus, and you will be saved, you and your household."

32 And they spoke the word of the Lord to him together with all who were in his house.

33 And he took them that *very* hour of the night and washed their wounds, and immediately he was baptized, he and all his *household.*

34 And he brought them into his house and set food before them, and rejoiced greatly, having believed in God with his whole household.

35 Now when day came, the chief magistrates sent their policemen, saying, "Release those men."

36 And the jailer reported these words to Paul, *saying,* "The chief magistrates have sent to release you. Therefore come out now and go in peace."

37 But Paul said to them, "They have beaten us in public without trial, men who are

Romans, and have thrown us into prison; and now are they sending us away secretly? No indeed! But let them come themselves and bring us out."

38 The policemen reported these words to the chief magistrates. They were afraid when they heard that they were Romans,

39 and they came and appealed to them, and when they had brought them out, they kept begging them to leave the city.

40 They went out of the prison and entered the house of Lydia, and when they saw the brethren, they encouraged them and departed.

Paul at Thessalonica

17 Now when they had traveled through Amphipolis and Apollonia, they came to Thessalonica, where there was a synagogue of the Jews.

2 And according to Paul's custom, he went to them, and for three Sabbaths reasoned with them from the Scriptures,

3 explaining and giving evidence that the Christ had to suffer and rise again from the dead, and *saying,* "This Jesus whom I am proclaiming to you is the Christ."

4 And some of them were persuaded and joined Paul and Silas, along with a large number of the God-fearing Greeks and a number of the leading women.

5 But the Jews, becoming jealous and taking along some wicked men from the market place, formed a mob and set the city in an uproar; and attacking the house of Jason, they were seeking to bring them out to the people.

6 When they did not find them, they *began* dragging Jason and some brethren before the city authorities, shouting, "These men who have upset ¹the world have come here also;

7 and Jason has welcomed them, and they all act contrary to the decrees of Caesar, saying that there is another king, Jesus."

8 They stirred up the crowd and the city authorities who heard these things.

9 And when they had received a pledge from Jason and the others, they released them.

10 The brethren immediately sent Paul and Silas away by night to Berea, and when they arrived, they went into the synagogue of the Jews.

11 Now these were more noble-minded than those in Thessalonica, for they received the word with great eagerness, examining the Scriptures daily *to see* whether these things were so.

12 Therefore many of them believed, along with a number of prominent Greek women and men.

13 But when the Jews of Thessalonica found out that the word of God had been proclaimed by Paul in Berea also, they came there as well, agitating and stirring up the crowds.

14 Then immediately the brethren sent Paul out to go as far as the sea; and Silas and Timothy remained there.

15 Now those who escorted Paul brought him

---

1. Lit *the inhabited earth*

as far as Athens; and receiving a command for Silas and Timothy to come to him as soon as possible, they left.

16 Now while Paul was waiting for them at Athens, his spirit was being provoked within him as he was observing the city full of idols.

17 So he was reasoning in the synagogue with the Jews and the God-fearing *Gentiles*, and in the market place every day with those who happened to be present.

18 And also some of the Epicurean and Stoic philosophers were conversing with him. Some were saying, "What would this idle babbler wish to say?" Others, "He seems to be a proclaimer of strange deities,"—because he was preaching Jesus and the resurrection.

19 And they took him and brought him to the Areopagus, saying, "May we know what this new teaching is which you are proclaiming?

20 "For you are bringing some strange things to our ears; so we want to know what these things mean."

21 (Now all the Athenians and the strangers visiting there used to spend their time in nothing other than telling or hearing something new.)

22 So Paul stood in the midst of the Areopagus and said, "Men of Athens, I observe that you are very religious in all respects.

23 "For while I was passing through and examining the objects of your worship, I also found an altar with this inscription, 'TO AN UNKNOWN GOD.' Therefore what you worship in ignorance, this I proclaim to you.

24 "The God who made the world and all things in it, since He is Lord of heaven and earth, does not dwell in temples made with hands;

25 nor is He served by human hands, as though He needed anything, since He Himself gives to all *people* life and breath and all things;

26 and He made from one *man* every nation of mankind to live on all the face of the earth, having determined *their* appointed times and the boundaries of their habitation,

27 that they would seek God, if perhaps they might grope for Him and find Him, though He is not far from each one of us;

28 for in Him we live and move and exist, as even some of your own poets have said, 'For we also are His children.'

29 "Being then the children of God, we ought not to think that the Divine Nature is like gold or silver or stone, an image formed by the art and thought of man.

30 "Therefore having overlooked the times of ignorance, God is now declaring to men that all *people* everywhere should repent,

31 because He has fixed a day in which He will judge the world in righteousness through a Man whom He has appointed, having furnished proof to all men by raising Him from the dead."

32 Now when they heard of the resurrection of the dead, some *began* to sneer, but others said, "We shall hear you again concerning this."

33 So Paul went out of their midst.

34 But some men joined him and believed, among whom also were Dionysius the Areopagite and a woman named Damaris and others with them.

Paul at Corinth

18 After these things he left Athens and went to Corinth.

2 And he found a Jew named Aquila, a native of Pontus, having recently come from Italy with his wife Priscilla, because Claudius had commanded all the Jews to leave Rome. He came to them,

3 and because he was of the same trade, he stayed with them and they were working, for by trade they were tent-makers.

4 And he was reasoning in the synagogue every Sabbath and trying to persuade Jews and Greeks.

5 But when Silas and Timothy came down from Macedonia, Paul *began* devoting himself completely to the word, solemnly testifying to the Jews that Jesus was the Christ.

6 But when they resisted and blasphemed, he shook out his garments and said to them, "Your blood *be* on your own heads! I am clean. From now on I will go to the Gentiles."

7 Then he left there and went to the house of a man named Titius Justus, a worshiper of God, whose house was next to the synagogue.

8 Crispus, the leader of the synagogue, believed in the Lord with all his household, and many of the Corinthians when they heard were believing and being baptized.

9 And the Lord said to Paul in the night by a vision, "Do not be afraid *any longer*, but go on speaking and do not be silent;

10 for I am with you, and no man will attack you in order to harm you, for I have many people in this city."

11 And he settled *there* a year and six months, teaching the word of God among them.

12 But while Gallio was proconsul of Achaia, the Jews with one accord rose up against Paul and brought him before the judgment seat,

13 saying, "This man persuades men to worship God contrary to the law."

14 But when Paul was about to open his mouth, Gallio said to the Jews, "If it were a matter of wrong or of vicious crime, O Jews, it would be reasonable for me to put up with you;

15 but if there are questions about words and names and your own law, look after it yourselves; I am unwilling to be a judge of these matters."

16 And he drove them away from the judgment seat.

17 And they all took hold of Sosthenes, the leader of the synagogue, and *began* beating him in front of the judgment seat. But Gallio was not concerned about any of these things.

18 Paul, having remained many days longer, took leave of the brethren and put out to sea for Syria, and with him were Priscilla and Aquila. In Cenchrea he had his hair cut, for he was keeping a vow.

19 They came to Ephesus, and he left them there. Now he himself entered the synagogue and reasoned with the Jews.

20 When they asked him to stay for a longer time, he did not consent,

21 but taking leave of them and saying, "I will return to you again if God wills," he set sail from Ephesus.

22 When he had landed at Caesarea, he went up and greeted the church, and went down to Antioch.

23 And having spent some time *there*, he left and passed successively through the Galatian region and Phrygia, strengthening all the disciples.

24 Now a Jew named Apollos, an Alexandrian by birth, an eloquent man, came to Ephesus; and he was mighty in the Scriptures.

25 This man had been instructed in the way of the Lord; and being fervent in spirit, he was speaking and teaching accurately the things concerning Jesus, being acquainted only with the baptism of John;

26 and he began to speak out boldly in the synagogue. But when Priscilla and Aquila heard him, they took him aside and explained to him the way of God more accurately.

27 And when he wanted to go across to Achaia, the brethren encouraged him and wrote to the disciples to welcome him; and when he had arrived, he greatly helped those who had believed through grace,

28 for he powerfully refuted the Jews in public, demonstrating by the Scriptures that Jesus was the Christ.

Paul at Ephesus

19 It happened that while Apollos was at Corinth, Paul passed through the upper country and came to Ephesus, and found some disciples.

2 He said to them, "Did you receive the Holy Spirit when you believed?" And they *said* to him, "No, we have not even heard whether there is a Holy Spirit."

3 And he said, "Into what then were you baptized?" And they said, "Into John's baptism."

4 Paul said, "John baptized with the baptism of repentance, telling the people to believe in Him who was coming after him, that is, in Jesus."

5 When they heard this, they were baptized in the name of the Lord Jesus.

6 And when Paul had laid his hands upon them, the Holy Spirit came on them, and they *began* speaking with tongues and prophesying.

7 There were in all about twelve men.

8 And he entered the synagogue and continued speaking out boldly for three months, reasoning and persuading *them* about the kingdom of God.

9 But when some were becoming hardened and disobedient, speaking evil of the Way before the people, he withdrew from them and took away the disciples, reasoning daily in the school of Tyrannus.

10 This took place for two years, so that all who lived in Asia heard the word of the Lord, both Jews and Greeks.

11 God was performing extraordinary miracles by the hands of Paul,

12 so that handkerchiefs or aprons were even carried from his body to the sick, and the diseases left them and the evil spirits went out.

13 But also some of the Jewish exorcists, who went from place to place, attempted to name over those who had the evil spirits the name of the Lord Jesus, saying, "I adjure you by Jesus whom Paul preaches."

14 Seven sons of one Sceva, a Jewish chief priest, were doing this.

15 And the evil spirit answered and said to them, "I recognize Jesus, and I know about Paul, but who are you?"

16 And the man, in whom was the evil spirit, leaped on them and subdued all of them and overpowered them, so that they fled out of that house naked and wounded.

17 This became known to all, both Jews and Greeks, who lived in Ephesus; and fear fell upon them all and the name of the Lord Jesus was being magnified.

18 Many also of those who had believed kept coming, confessing and disclosing their practices.

19 And many of those who practiced magic brought their books together and *began* burning them in the sight of everyone; and they counted up the price of them and found it fifty thousand pieces of silver.

20 So the word of the Lord was growing mightily and prevailing.

21 Now after these things were finished, Paul purposed in the Spirit to go to Jerusalem after he had passed through Macedonia and Achaia, saying, "After I have been there, I must also see Rome."

22 And having sent into Macedonia two of those who ministered to him, Timothy and Erastus, he himself stayed in Asia for a while.

23 About that time there occurred no small disturbance concerning the Way.

24 For a man named Demetrius, a silversmith, who made silver shrines of Artemis, was bringing no little business to the craftsmen;

25 these he gathered together with the workmen of similar *trades,* and said, "Men, you know that our prosperity depends upon this business.

26 "You see and hear that not only in Ephesus, but in almost all of Asia, this Paul has persuaded and turned away a considerable number of people, saying that gods made with hands are no gods *at all.*

27 "Not only is there danger that this trade of ours fall into disrepute, but also that the temple of the great goddess Artemis be regarded as worthless and that she whom all of Asia and the world worship will even be dethroned from her magnificence."

28 When they heard *this* and were filled with

rage, they *began* crying out, saying, "Great is Artemis of the Ephesians!"

29 The city was filled with the confusion, and they rushed with one accord into the theater, dragging along Gaius and Aristarchus, Paul's traveling companions from Macedonia.

30 And when Paul wanted to go into the assembly, the disciples would not let him.

31 Also some of the ¹Asiarchs who were friends of his sent to him and repeatedly urged him not to venture into the theater.

32 So then, some were shouting one thing and some another, for the assembly was in confusion and the majority did not know for what reason they had come together.

33 Some of the crowd concluded *it was* Alexander, since the Jews had put him forward; and having motioned with his hand, Alexander was intending to make a defense to the assembly.

34 But when they recognized that he was a Jew, a *single* outcry arose from them all as they shouted for about two hours, "Great is Artemis of the Ephesians!"

35 After quieting the crowd, the town clerk *said, "Men of Ephesus, what man is there after all who does not know that the city of the Ephesians is guardian of the temple of the great Artemis and of the *image* which fell down from heaven?

36 "So, since these are undeniable facts, you ought to keep calm and to do nothing rash.

37 "For you have brought these men *here* who are neither robbers of temples nor blasphemers of our goddess.

38 "So then, if Demetrius and the craftsmen who are with him have a complaint against any man, the courts are in session and proconsuls are *available*; let them bring charges against one another.

39 "But if you want anything beyond this, it shall be settled in the lawful assembly.

40 "For indeed we are in danger of being accused of a riot in connection with today's events, since there is no *real* cause *for it*, and in this connection we will be unable to account for this disorderly gathering."

41 After saying this he dismissed the assembly.

Paul in Macedonia and Greece

20 After the uproar had ceased, Paul sent for the disciples, and when he had exhorted them and taken his leave of them, he left to go to Macedonia.

2 When he had gone through those districts and had given them much exhortation, he came to Greece.

3 And *there* he spent three months, and when a plot was formed against him by the Jews as he was about to set sail for Syria, he decided to return through Macedonia.

4 And he was accompanied by Sopater of Berea, *the son* of Pyrrhus, and by Aristarchus and Secundus of the Thessalonians, and Gaius

of Derbe, and Timothy, and Tychicus and Trophimus of Asia.

5 But these had gone on ahead and were waiting for us at Troas.

6 We sailed from Philippi after the days of Unleavened Bread, and came to them at Troas within five days; and there we stayed seven days.

7 On the first day of the week, when we were gathered together to break bread, Paul *began* talking to them, intending to leave the next day, and he prolonged his message until midnight.

8 There were many lamps in the upper room where we were gathered together.

9 And there was a young man named Eutychus sitting on the window sill, sinking into a deep sleep; and as Paul kept on talking, he was overcome by sleep and fell down from the third floor and was picked up dead.

10 But Paul went down and fell upon him, and after embracing him, he said, "Do not be troubled, for his life is in him."

11 When he had gone *back* up and had broken the bread and eaten, he talked with them a long while until daybreak, and then left.

12 They took away the boy alive, and were greatly comforted.

13 But we, going ahead to the ship, set sail for Assos, intending from there to take Paul on board; for so he had arranged it, intending himself to go by land.

14 And when he met us at Assos, we took him on board and came to Mitylene.

15 Sailing from there, we arrived the following day opposite Chios; and the next day we crossed over to Samos; and the day following we came to Miletus.

16 For Paul had decided to sail past Ephesus so that he would not have to spend time in Asia; for he was hurrying to be in Jerusalem, if possible, on the day of Pentecost.

17 From Miletus he sent to Ephesus and called to him the elders of the church.

18 And when they had come to him, he said to them,

"You yourselves know, from the first day that I set foot in Asia, how I was with you the whole time,

19 serving the Lord with all humility and with tears and with trials which came upon me through the plots of the Jews;

20 how I did not shrink from declaring to you anything that was profitable, and teaching you publicly and from house to house,

21 solemnly testifying to both Jews and Greeks of repentance toward God and faith in our Lord Jesus Christ.

22 "And now, behold, bound by the Spirit, I am on my way to Jerusalem, not knowing what will happen to me there,

23 except that the Holy Spirit solemnly testifies to me in every city, saying that bonds and afflictions await me.

24 "But I do not consider my life of any account as dear to myself, so that I may finish

---

1. I.e. political or religious officials of the province of Asia

my course and the ministry which I received from the Lord Jesus, to testify solemnly of the gospel of the grace of God.

25 "And now, behold, I know that all of you, among whom I went about preaching the kingdom, will no longer see my face.

26 "Therefore, I testify to you this day that I am innocent of the blood of all men.

27 "For I did not shrink from declaring to you the whole purpose of God.

28 "Be on guard for yourselves and for all the flock, among which the Holy Spirit has made you overseers, to shepherd the church of God which He purchased with His own blood.

29 "I know that after my departure savage wolves will come in among you, not sparing the flock;

30 and from among your own selves men will arise, speaking perverse things, to draw away the disciples after them.

31 "Therefore be on the alert, remembering that night and day for a period of three years I did not cease to admonish each one with tears.

32 "And now I commend you to God and to the word of His grace, which is able to build you up and to give you the inheritance among all those who are sanctified.

33 "I have coveted no one's silver or gold or clothes.

34 "You yourselves know that these hands ministered to my own needs and to the men who were with me.

35 "In everything I showed you that by working hard in this manner you must help the weak and remember the words of the Lord Jesus, that He Himself said, 'It is more blessed to give than to receive.' "

36 When he had said these things, he knelt down and prayed with them all.

37 And they began to weep aloud and embraced Paul, and repeatedly kissed him,

38 grieving especially over the word which he had spoken, that they would not see his face again. And they were accompanying him to the ship.

Paul Sails from Miletus

21 When we had parted from them and had set sail, we ran a straight course to Cos and the next day to Rhodes and from there to Patara;

2 and having found a ship crossing over to Phoenicia, we went aboard and set sail.

3 When we came in sight of Cyprus, leaving it on the left, we kept sailing to Syria and landed at Tyre; for there the ship was to unload its cargo.

4 When we came in sight of the disciples, we stayed there seven days; and they kept telling Paul through the Spirit not to set foot in Jerusalem.

5 When our days there were ended, we left and started on our journey, while they all, with wives and children, escorted us until we were out of the city. After kneeling down on the beach and praying, we said farewell to one another.

6 Then we went on board the ship, and they returned home again.

7 When we had finished the voyage from Tyre, we arrived at Ptolemais, and after greeting the brethren, we stayed with them for a day.

8 On the next day we left and came to Caesarea, and entering the house of Philip the evangelist, who was one of the seven, we stayed with him.

9 Now this man had four virgin daughters who were prophetesses.

10 As we were staying there for some days, a prophet named Agabus came down from Judea.

11 And coming to us, he took Paul's belt and bound his own feet and hands, and said, "This is what the Holy Spirit says: 'In this way the Jews at Jerusalem will bind the man who owns this belt and deliver him into the hands of the Gentiles.' "

12 When we had heard this, we as well as the local residents began begging him not to go up to Jerusalem.

13 Then Paul answered, "What are you doing, weeping and breaking my heart? For I am ready not only to be bound, but even to die at Jerusalem for the name of the Lord Jesus."

14 And since he would not be persuaded, we fell silent, remarking, "The will of the Lord be done!"

15 After these days we got ready and started on our way up to Jerusalem.

16 Some of the disciples from Caesarea also came with us, taking us to Mnason of Cyprus, a disciple of long standing with whom we were to lodge.

17 After we arrived in Jerusalem, the brethren received us gladly.

18 And the following day Paul went in with us to James, and all the elders were present.

19 After he had greeted them, he began to relate one by one the things which God had done among the Gentiles through his ministry.

20 And when they heard it they began glorifying God; and they said to him, "You see, brother, how many thousands there are among the Jews of those who have believed, and they are all zealous for the Law;

21 and they have been told about you, that you are teaching all the Jews who are among the Gentiles to forsake Moses, telling them not to circumcise their children nor to walk according to the customs.

22 "What, then, is to be done? They will certainly hear that you have come.

23 "Therefore do this that we tell you. We have four men who are under a vow;

24 take them and purify yourself along with them, and pay their expenses so that they may shave their heads; and all will know that there is nothing to the things which they have been told about you, but that you yourself also walk orderly, keeping the Law.

25 "But concerning the Gentiles who have believed, we wrote, having decided that they

should abstain from meat sacrificed to idols and from blood and from what is strangled and from fornication."

26 Then Paul took the men, and the next day, purifying himself along with them, went into the temple giving notice of the completion of the days of purification, until the sacrifice was offered for each one of them.

27 When the seven days were almost over, the Jews from Asia, upon seeing him in the temple, *began* to stir up all the crowd and laid hands on him,

28 crying out, "Men of Israel, come to our aid! This is the man who preaches to all men everywhere against our people and the Law and this place; and besides he has even brought Greeks into the temple and has defiled this holy place."

29 For they had previously seen Trophimus the Ephesian in the city with him, and they supposed that Paul had brought him into the temple.

30 Then all the city was provoked, and the people rushed together, and taking hold of Paul they dragged him out of the temple, and immediately the doors were shut.

31 While they were seeking to kill him, a report came up to the ¹commander of the *Roman* cohort that all Jerusalem was in confusion.

32 At once he took along *some* soldiers and centurions and ran down to them; and when they saw the commander and the soldiers, they stopped beating Paul.

33 Then the commander came up and took hold of him, and ordered him to be bound with two chains; and he *began* asking who he was and what he had done.

34 But among the crowd some were shouting one thing *and* some another, and when he could not find out the facts because of the uproar, he ordered him to be brought into the barracks.

35 When he got to the stairs, he was carried by the soldiers because of the violence of the mob;

36 for the multitude of the people kept following them, shouting, "Away with him!"

37 As Paul was about to be brought into the barracks, he said to the commander, "May I say something to you?" And he *said, "Do you know Greek?

38 "Then you are not the Egyptian who some time ago stirred up a revolt and led the four thousand men of the Assassins out into the wilderness?"

39 But Paul said, "I am a Jew of Tarsus in Cilicia, a citizen of no insignificant city; and I beg you, allow me to speak to the people."

40 When he had given him permission, Paul, standing on the stairs, motioned to the people with his hand; and when there was a great hush, he spoke to them in the Hebrew dialect, saying,

1. I.e. chiliarch, in command of one thousand troops

Paul's Defense before the Jews

22 "Brethren and fathers, hear my defense which I now *offer* to you."

2 And when they heard that he was addressing them in the Hebrew dialect, they became even more quiet; and he *said,

3 "I am a Jew, born in Tarsus of Cilicia, but brought up in this city, educated under Gamaliel, strictly according to the law of our fathers, being zealous for God just as you all are today.

4 "I persecuted this Way to the death, binding and putting both men and women into prisons,

5 as also the high priest and all the Council of the elders can testify. From them I also received letters to the brethren, and started off for Damascus in order to bring even those who were there to Jerusalem as prisoners to be punished.

6 "But it happened that as I was on my way, approaching Damascus about noontime, a very bright light suddenly flashed from heaven all around me,

7 and I fell to the ground and heard a voice saying to me, 'Saul, Saul, why are you persecuting Me?'

8 "And I answered, 'Who are You, Lord?' And He said to me, 'I am Jesus the Nazarene, whom you are persecuting.'

9 "And those who were with me saw the light, to be sure, but did not understand the voice of the One who was speaking to me.

10 "And I said, 'What shall I do, Lord?' And the Lord said to me, 'Get up and go on into Damascus, and there you will be told of all that has been appointed for you to do.'

11 "But since I could not see because of the brightness of that light, I was led by the hand by those who were with me and came into Damascus.

12 "A certain Ananias, a man who was devout by the standard of the Law, *and* well spoken of by all the Jews who lived there,

13 came to me, and standing near said to me, 'Brother Saul, receive your sight!' And at that very time I looked up at him.

14 "And he said, 'The God of our fathers has appointed you to know His will and to see the Righteous One and to hear an utterance from His mouth.

15 'For you will be a witness for Him to all men of what you have seen and heard.

16 'Now why do you delay? Get up and be baptized, and wash away your sins, calling on His name.'

17 "It happened when I returned to Jerusalem and was praying in the temple, that I fell into a trance,

18 and I saw Him saying to me, 'Make haste, and get out of Jerusalem quickly, because they will not accept your testimony about Me.'

19 "And I said, 'Lord, they themselves understand that in one synagogue after another I used to imprison and beat those who believed in You.

Wash away your sins.

Your sins are washed away when you are baptized. Do you believe in Jesus? Do you want a new life? Then why delay? Get up and be buried with Christ in baptism! For an example of an Ethiopian obeying the gospel, read Acts 8:26-39 on page 99.

20 'And when the blood of Your witness Stephen was being shed, I also was standing by approving, and watching out for the coats of those who were slaying him.'

21 "And He said to me, 'Go! For I will send you far away to the Gentiles.' "

22 They listened to him up to this statement, and *then* they raised their voices and said, "Away with such a fellow from the earth, for he should not be allowed to live!"

23 And as they were crying out and throwing off their cloaks and tossing dust into the air,

24 the ¹commander ordered him to be brought into the barracks, stating that he should be examined by scourging so that he might find out the reason why they were shouting against him that way.

25 But when they stretched him out with thongs, Paul said to the centurion who was standing by, "Is it lawful for you to scourge a man who is a Roman and uncondemned?"

26 When the centurion heard *this*, he went to the commander and told him, saying, "What are you about to do? For this man is a Roman."

27 The commander came and said to him, "Tell me, are you a Roman?" And he said, "Yes."

28 The commander answered, "I acquired this citizenship with a large sum of money." And Paul said, "But I was actually born *a citizen*."

29 Therefore those who were about to examine him immediately let go of him; and the commander also was afraid when he found out that he was a Roman, and because he had put him in chains.

30 But on the next day, wishing to know for certain why he had been accused by the Jews, he released him and ordered the chief priests and all the Council to assemble, and brought Paul down and set him before them.

Paul before the Council

23 Paul, looking intently at the Council, said, "Brethren, I have lived my life with a perfectly good conscience before God up to this day."

2 The high priest Ananias commanded those standing beside him to strike him on the mouth.

3 Then Paul said to him, "God is going to strike you, you whitewashed wall! Do you sit to try me according to the Law, and in violation of the Law order me to be struck?"

4 But the bystanders said, "Do you revile God's high priest?"

5 And Paul said, "I was not aware, brethren, that he was high priest; for it is written, 'YOU SHALL NOT SPEAK EVIL OF A RULER OF YOUR PEOPLE.' "

6 But perceiving that one group were Sadducees and the other Pharisees, Paul *began* crying out in the Council, "Brethren, I am a Pharisee, a son of Pharisees; I am on trial for the hope and resurrection of the dead!"

7 As he said this, there occurred a dissension between the Pharisees and Sadducees, and the assembly was divided.

8 For the Sadducees say that there is no resurrection, nor an angel, nor a spirit, but the Pharisees acknowledge them all.

9 And there occurred a great uproar; and some of the scribes of the Pharisaic party stood up and *began* to argue heatedly, saying, "We find nothing wrong with this man; suppose a spirit or an angel has spoken to him?"

10 And as a great dissension was developing, the ¹commander was afraid Paul would be torn to pieces by them and ordered the troops to go down and take him away from them by force, and bring him into the barracks.

11 But on the night *immediately* following, the Lord stood at his side and said, "Take courage; for as you have solemnly witnessed to My cause at Jerusalem, so you must witness at Rome also."

12 When it was day, the Jews formed a conspiracy and bound themselves under an oath, saying that they would neither eat nor drink until they had killed Paul.

13 There were more than forty who formed this plot.

14 They came to the chief priests and the elders and said, "We have bound ourselves under a solemn oath to taste nothing until we have killed Paul.

15 "Now therefore, you and the Council notify the commander to bring him down to you, as though you were going to determine his case by a more thorough investigation; and we for our part are ready to slay him before he comes near *the place*."

16 But the son of Paul's sister heard of their ambush, and he came and entered the barracks and told Paul.

17 Paul called one of the centurions to him and said, "Lead this young man to the commander, for he has something to report to him."

18 So he took him and led him to the commander and *said, "Paul the prisoner called me to him and asked me to lead this young man to you since he has something to tell you."

19 The commander took him by the hand and stepping aside, *began* to inquire of him privately, "What is it that you have to report to me?"

20 And he said, "The Jews have agreed to ask you to bring Paul down tomorrow to the Council, as though they were going to inquire somewhat more thoroughly about him.

21 "So do not listen to them, for more than forty of them are lying in wait for him who have bound themselves under a curse not to eat or drink until they slay him; and now they are ready and waiting for the promise from you."

22 So the commander let the young man go, instructing him, "Tell no one that you have notified me of these things."

23 And he called to him two of the centurions and said, "Get two hundred soldiers ready by ²the third hour of the night to proceed to

---

1. I.e. chiliarch, in command of one thousand troops   2. I.e. 9 p.m.

Caesarea, with seventy horsemen and two hundred spearmen."

24 *They were* also to provide mounts to put Paul on and bring him safely to Felix the governor.

25 And he wrote a letter having this form:

26 "Claudius Lysias, to the most excellent governor Felix, greetings.

27 "When this man was arrested by the Jews and was about to be slain by them, I came up to them with the troops and rescued him, having learned that he was a Roman.

28 "And wanting to ascertain the charge for which they were accusing him, I brought him down to their Council;

29 and I found him to be accused over questions about their Law, but under no accusation deserving death or imprisonment.

30 "When I was informed that there would be a plot against the man, I sent him to you at once, also instructing his accusers to bring charges against him before you."

31 So the soldiers, in accordance with their orders, took Paul and brought him by night to Antipatris.

32 But the next day, leaving the horsemen to go on with him, they returned to the barracks.

33 When these had come to Caesarea and delivered the letter to the governor, they also presented Paul to him.

34 When he had read it, he asked from what province he was, and when he learned that he was from Cilicia,

35 he said, "I will give you a hearing after your accusers arrive also," giving orders for him to be kept in Herod's ¹Praetorium.

Paul before Felix

24 After five days the high priest Ananias came down with some elders, with an attorney *named* Tertullus, and they brought charges to the governor against Paul.

2 After *Paul* had been summoned, Tertullus began to accuse him, saying *to the governor,*

"Since we have through you attained much peace, and since by your providence reforms are being carried out for this nation,

3 we acknowledge *this* in every way and everywhere, most excellent Felix, with all thankfulness.

4 "But, that I may not weary you any further, I beg you to grant us, by your kindness, a brief hearing.

5 "For we have found this man a real pest and a fellow who stirs up dissension among all the Jews throughout ²the world, and a ringleader of the sect of the Nazarenes.

6 "And he even tried to desecrate the temple; and then we arrested him. [³We wanted to judge him according to our own Law.

7 "But Lysias the commander came along, and with much violence took him out of our hands,

8 ordering his accusers to come before you.]

By examining him yourself concerning all these matters you will be able to ascertain the things of which we accuse him."

9 The Jews also joined in the attack, asserting that these things were so.

10 When the governor had nodded for him to speak, Paul responded:

"Knowing that for many years you have been a judge to this nation, I cheerfully make my defense,

11 since you can take note of the fact that no more than twelve days ago I went up to Jerusalem to worship.

12 "Neither in the temple, nor in the synagogues, nor in the city *itself* did they find me carrying on a discussion with anyone or causing a riot.

13 "Nor can they prove to you *the charges* of which they now accuse me.

14 "But this I admit to you, that according to the Way which they call a sect I do serve the God of our fathers, believing everything that is in accordance with the Law and that is written in the Prophets;

15 having a hope in God, which these men cherish themselves, that there shall certainly be a resurrection of both the righteous and the wicked.

16 "In view of this, I also do my best to maintain always a blameless conscience *both* before God and before men.

17 "Now after several years I came to bring ⁴alms to my nation and to present offerings;

18 in which they found me *occupied* in the temple, having been purified, without *any* crowd or uproar. But *there were* some Jews from Asia—

19 who ought to have been present before you and to make accusation, if they should have anything against me.

20 "Or else let these men themselves tell what misdeed they found when I stood before the Council,

21 other than for this one statement which I shouted out while standing among them, 'For the resurrection of the dead I am on trial before you today.'"

22 But Felix, having a more exact knowledge about the Way, put them off, saying, "When Lysias the ⁵commander comes down, I will decide your case."

23 Then he gave orders to the centurion for him to be kept in custody and *yet* have *some* freedom, and not to prevent any of his friends from ministering to him.

24 But some days later Felix arrived with Drusilla, his wife who was a Jewess, and sent for Paul and heard him *speak* about faith in Christ Jesus.

25 But as he was discussing righteousness, self-control and the judgment to come, Felix became frightened and said, "Go away for the present, and when I find time I will summon you."

1. I.e. governor's official residence 2. Lit *the inhabited earth* 3. The early mss do not contain the remainder of v 6, v 7, nor the first part of v 8 4. Or *gifts to charity* 5. I.e. chiliarch, in command of one thousand troops

26 At the same time too, he was hoping that money would be given him by Paul; therefore he also used to send for him quite often and converse with him.

27 But after two years had passed, Felix was succeeded by Porcius Festus, and wishing to do the Jews a favor, Felix left Paul imprisoned.

Paul before Festus

25 Festus then, having arrived in the province, three days later went up to Jerusalem from Caesarea.

2 And the chief priests and the leading men of the Jews brought charges against Paul, and they were urging him,

3 requesting a concession against Paul, that he might have him brought to Jerusalem (*at the same time*, setting an ambush to kill him on the way).

4 Festus then answered that Paul was being kept in custody at Caesarea and that he himself was about to leave shortly.

5 "Therefore," he *said, "let the influential men among you go there with me, and if there is anything wrong about the man, let them prosecute him."

6 After he had spent not more than eight or ten days among them, he went down to Caesarea, and on the next day he took his seat on the tribunal and ordered Paul to be brought.

7 After Paul arrived, the Jews who had come down from Jerusalem stood around him, bringing many and serious charges against him which they could not prove,

8 while Paul said in his own defense, "I have committed no offense either against the Law of the Jews or against the temple or against Caesar."

9 But Festus, wishing to do the Jews a favor, answered Paul and said, "Are you willing to go up to Jerusalem and stand trial before me on these *charges?*"

10 But Paul said, "I am standing before Caesar's tribunal, where I ought to be tried. I have done no wrong to *the* Jews, as you also very well know.

11 "If, then, I am a wrongdoer and have committed anything worthy of death, I do not refuse to die; but if none of those things is *true* of which these men accuse me, no one can hand me over to them. I appeal to Caesar."

12 Then when Festus had conferred with his council, he answered, "You have appealed to Caesar, to Caesar you shall go."

13 Now when several days had elapsed, King Agrippa and Bernice arrived at Caesarea and paid their respects to Festus.

14 While they were spending many days there, Festus laid Paul's case before the king, saying, "There is a man who was left as a prisoner by Felix;

15 and when I was at Jerusalem, the chief priests and the elders of the Jews brought charges against him, asking for a sentence of condemnation against him.

16 "I answered them that it is not the custom of the Romans to hand over any man before the accused meets his accusers face to face and has an opportunity to make his defense against the charges.

17 "So after they had assembled here, I did not delay, but on the next day took my seat on the tribunal and ordered the man to be brought before me.

18 "When the accusers stood up, they *began* bringing charges against him not of such crimes as I was expecting,

19 but they *simply* had some points of disagreement with him about their own religion and about a dead man, Jesus, whom Paul asserted to be alive.

20 "Being at a loss how to investigate such matters, I asked whether he was willing to go to Jerusalem and there stand trial on these matters.

21 "But when Paul appealed to be held in custody for [1]the Emperor's decision, I ordered him to be kept in custody until I send him to Caesar."

22 Then Agrippa *said* to Festus, "I also would like to hear the man myself." "Tomorrow," he *said, "you shall hear him."

23 So, on the next day when Agrippa came together with Bernice amid great pomp, and entered the auditorium [2]accompanied by the commanders and the prominent men of the city, at the command of Festus, Paul was brought in.

24 Festus *said, "King Agrippa, and all you gentlemen here present with us, you see this man about whom all the people of the Jews appealed to me, both at Jerusalem and here, loudly declaring that he ought not to live any longer.

25 "But I found that he had committed nothing worthy of death; and since he himself appealed to the Emperor, I decided to send him.

26 "Yet I have nothing definite about him to write to my lord. Therefore I have brought him before you *all* and especially before you, King Agrippa, so that after the investigation has taken place, I may have something to write.

27 "For it seems absurd to me in sending a prisoner, not to indicate also the charges against him."

Paul's Defense before Agrippa

26 Agrippa said to Paul, "You are permitted to speak for yourself." Then Paul stretched out his hand and *proceeded* to make his defense:

2 "In regard to all the things of which I am accused by the Jews, I consider myself fortunate, King Agrippa, that I am about to make my defense before you today;

3 especially because you are an expert in all customs and questions among *the* Jews; therefore I beg you to listen to me patiently.

4 "So then, all Jews know my manner of life from my youth up, which from the beginning was spent among my *own* nation and at Jerusalem;

5 since they have known about me for a long

---

1. Lit *the Augustus'* (in this case Nero)   2. Lit *and with*

time, if they are willing to testify, that I lived *as* a Pharisee according to the strictest sect of our religion.

6 "And now I am standing trial for the hope of the promise made by God to our fathers;

7 *the promise* to which our twelve tribes hope to attain, as they earnestly serve *God* night and day. And for this hope, O King, I am being accused by Jews.

8 "Why is it considered incredible among you *people* if God does raise the dead?

9 "So then, I thought to myself that I had to do many things hostile to the name of Jesus of Nazareth.

10 "And this is just what I did in Jerusalem; not only did I lock up many of the saints in prisons, having received authority from the chief priests, but also when they were being put to death I cast my vote against them.

11 "And as I punished them often in all the synagogues, I tried to force them to blaspheme; and being furiously enraged at them, I kept pursuing them even to foreign cities.

12 "While so engaged as I was journeying to Damascus with the authority and commission of the chief priests,

13 at midday, O King, I saw on the way a light from heaven, brighter than the sun, shining all around me and those who were journeying with me.

14 "And when we had all fallen to the ground, I heard a voice saying to me in the Hebrew dialect, 'Saul, Saul, why are you persecuting Me? It is hard for you to kick against the goads.'

15 "And I said, 'Who are You, Lord?' And the Lord said, 'I am Jesus whom you are persecuting.

16 'But get up and stand on your feet; for this purpose I have appeared to you, to appoint you a minister and a witness not only to the things which you have seen, but also to the things in which I will appear to you;

17 rescuing you from the *Jewish* people and from the Gentiles, to whom I am sending you,

18 to open their eyes so that they may turn from darkness to light and from the dominion of Satan to God, that they may receive forgiveness of sins and an inheritance among those who have been sanctified by faith in Me.'

19 "So, King Agrippa, I did not prove disobedient to the heavenly vision,

20 but *kept* declaring both to those of Damascus first, and *also* at Jerusalem and *then* throughout all the region of Judea, and *even* to the Gentiles, that they should repent and turn to God, performing deeds appropriate to repentance.

21 "For this reason *some* Jews seized me in the temple and tried to put me to death.

22 "So, having obtained help from God, I stand to this day testifying both to small and great, stating nothing but what the Prophets and Moses said was going to take place;

23 that the Christ was to suffer, *and* that by reason of *His* resurrection from the dead He would be the first to proclaim light both to the *Jewish* people and to the Gentiles."

24 While *Paul* was saying this in his defense, Festus *said in a loud voice, "Paul, you are out of your mind! *Your* great learning is driving you mad."

25 But Paul *said, "I am not out of my mind, most excellent Festus, but I utter words of sober truth.

26 "For the king knows about these matters, and I speak to him also with confidence, since I am persuaded that none of these things escape his notice; for this has not been done in a corner.

27 "King Agrippa, do you believe the Prophets? I know that you do."

28 Agrippa *replied to Paul, "In a short time you will persuade me to become a Christian."

29 And Paul *said, "I would wish to God, that whether in a short or long time, not only you, but also all who hear me this day, might become such as I am, except for these chains."

30 The king stood up and the governor and Bernice, and those who were sitting with them,

31 and when they had gone aside, they *began* talking to one another, saying, "This man is not doing anything worthy of death or imprisonment."

32 And Agrippa said to Festus, "This man might have been set free if he had not appealed to Caesar."

Paul Is Sent to Rome

27 When it was decided that we would sail for Italy, they proceeded to deliver Paul and some other prisoners to a centurion of the Augustan [1]cohort named Julius.

2 And embarking in an Adramyttian ship, which was about to sail to the regions along the coast of Asia, we put out to sea accompanied by Aristarchus, a Macedonian of Thessalonica.

3 The next day we put in at Sidon; and Julius treated Paul with consideration and allowed him to go to his friends and receive care.

4 From there we put out to sea and sailed under the shelter of Cyprus because the winds were contrary.

5 When we had sailed through the sea along the coast of Cilicia and Pamphylia, we landed at Myra in Lycia.

6 There the centurion found an Alexandrian ship sailing for Italy, and he put us aboard it.

7 When we had sailed slowly for a good many days, and with difficulty had arrived off Cnidus, since the wind did not permit us *to go* farther, we sailed under the shelter of Crete, off Salmone;

8 and with difficulty sailing past it we came to a place called Fair Havens, near which was the city of Lasea.

9 When considerable time had passed and the voyage was now dangerous, since even the [2]fast was already over, Paul *began* to admonish them,

10 and said to them, "Men, I perceive that the

---

1. Or *battalion* 2. I.e. Day of Atonement in September or October, which was a dangerous time of year for navigation

voyage will certainly be with damage and great loss, not only of the cargo and the ship, but also of our lives."

11 But the centurion was more persuaded by the pilot and the captain of the ship than by what was being said by Paul.

12 Because the harbor was not suitable for wintering, the majority reached a decision to put out to sea from there, if somehow they could reach Phoenix, a harbor of Crete, facing southwest and northwest, and spend the winter there.

13 When a moderate south wind came up, supposing that they had attained their purpose, they weighed anchor and *began* sailing along Crete, close *inshore.*

14 But before very long there rushed down from the land a violent wind, called [1]Euraquilo;

15 and when the ship was caught *in it* and could not face the wind, we gave way *to it* and let ourselves be driven along.

16 Running under the shelter of a small island called Clauda, we were scarcely able to get the *ship's* boat under control.

17 After they had hoisted it up, they used supporting cables in undergirding the ship; and fearing that they might run aground on *the shallows* of Syrtis, they let down the sea anchor and in this way let themselves be driven along.

18 The next day as we were being violently storm-tossed, they began to jettison the cargo;

19 and on the third day they threw the ship's tackle overboard with their own hands.

20 Since neither sun nor stars appeared for many days, and no small storm was assailing *us,* from then on all hope of our being saved was gradually abandoned.

21 When they had gone a long time without food, then Paul stood up in their midst and said, "Men, you ought to have followed my advice and not to have set sail from Crete and incurred this damage and loss.

22 "Yet now I urge you to keep up your courage, for there will be no loss of life among you, but *only* of the ship.

23 "For this very night an angel of the God to whom I belong and whom I serve stood before me,

24 saying, 'Do not be afraid, Paul; you must stand before Caesar; and behold, God has granted you all those who are sailing with you.'

25 "Therefore, keep up your courage, men, for I believe God that it will turn out exactly as I have been told.

26 "But we must run aground on a certain island."

27 But when the fourteenth night came, as we were being driven about in the Adriatic Sea, about midnight the sailors *began* to surmise that they were approaching some land.

28 They took soundings and found *it to be* twenty fathoms; and a little farther on they took another sounding and found *it to be* fifteen fathoms.

29 Fearing that we might run aground

somewhere on the rocks, they cast four anchors from the stern and wished for daybreak.

30 But as the sailors were trying to escape from the ship and had let down the *ship's* boat into the sea, on the pretense of intending to lay out anchors from the bow,

31 Paul said to the centurion and to the soldiers, "Unless these men remain in the ship, you yourselves cannot be saved."

32 Then the soldiers cut away the ropes of the *ship's* boat and let it fall away.

33 Until the day was about to dawn, Paul was encouraging them all to take some food, saying, "Today is the fourteenth day that you have been constantly watching and going without eating, having taken nothing.

34 "Therefore I encourage you to take some food, for this is for your preservation, for not a hair from the head of any of you will perish."

35 Having said this, he took bread and gave thanks to God in the presence of all, and he broke it and began to eat.

36 All of them were encouraged and they themselves also took food.

37 All of us in the ship were two hundred and seventy-six persons.

38 When they had eaten enough, they *began* to lighten the ship by throwing out the wheat into the sea.

39 When day came, they could not recognize the land; but they did observe a bay with a beach, and they resolved to drive the ship onto it if they could.

40 And casting off the anchors, they left them in the sea while at the same time they were loosening the ropes of the rudders; and hoisting the foresail to the wind, they were heading for the beach.

41 But striking a reef where two seas met, they ran the vessel aground; and the prow stuck fast and remained immovable, but the stern *began* to be broken up by the force *of the waves.*

42 The soldiers' plan was to kill the prisoners, so that none *of them* would swim away and escape;

43 but the centurion, wanting to bring Paul safely through, kept them from their intention, and commanded that those who could swim should jump overboard first and get to land,

44 and the rest *should follow,* some on planks, and others on various things from the ship. And so it happened that they all were brought safely to land.

Safe at Malta

28 When they had been brought safely through, then we found out that the island was called Malta.

2 The natives showed us extraordinary kindness; for because of the rain that had set in and because of the cold, they kindled a fire and received us all.

3 But when Paul had gathered a bundle of sticks and laid them on the fire, a viper came out because of the heat and fastened itself on his hand.

1. I.e. a northeaster

4 When the natives saw the creature hanging from his hand, they *began* saying to one another, "Undoubtedly this man is a murderer, and though he has been saved from the sea, justice has not allowed him to live."

5 However he shook the creature off into the fire and suffered no harm.

6 But they were expecting that he was about to swell up or suddenly fall down dead. But after they had waited a long time and had seen nothing unusual happen to him, they changed their minds and *began* to say that he was a god.

7 Now in the neighborhood of that place were lands belonging to the leading man of the island, named Publius, who welcomed us and entertained us courteously three days.

8 And it happened that the father of Publius was lying *in bed* afflicted with *recurrent* fever and dysentery; and Paul went in *to see* him and after he had prayed, he laid his hands on him and healed him.

9 After this had happened, the rest of the people on the island who had diseases were coming to him and getting cured.

10 They also honored us with many marks of respect; and when we were setting sail, they supplied *us* with all we needed.

11 At the end of three months we set sail on an Alexandrian ship which had wintered at the island, and which had the Twin Brothers for its figurehead.

12 After we put in at Syracuse, we stayed there for three days.

13 From there we sailed around and arrived at Rhegium, and a day later a south wind sprang up, and on the second day we came to Puteoli.

14 There we found *some* brethren, and were invited to stay with them for seven days; and thus we came to Rome.

15 And the brethren, when they heard about us, came from there as far as the Market of Appius and Three Inns to meet us; and when Paul saw them, he thanked God and took courage.

16 When we entered Rome, Paul was allowed to stay by himself, with the soldier who was guarding him.

17 After three days Paul called together those who were the leading men of the Jews, and when they came together, he *began* saying to them, "Brethren, though I had done nothing against our people or the customs of our fathers, yet I was delivered as a prisoner from Jerusalem into the hands of the Romans.

18 "And when they had examined me, they were willing to release me because there was no ground for putting me to death.

19 "But when the Jews objected, I was forced to appeal to Caesar, not that I had any accusation against my nation.

20 "For this reason, therefore, I requested to see you and to speak with you, for I am wearing this chain for the sake of the hope of Israel."

21 They said to him, "We have neither received letters from Judea concerning you, nor have any of the brethren come here and reported or spoken anything bad about you.

22 "But we desire to hear from you what your views are; for concerning this sect, it is known to us that it is spoken against everywhere."

23 When they had set a day for Paul, they came to him at his lodging in large numbers; and he was explaining to them by solemnly testifying about the kingdom of God and trying to persuade them concerning Jesus, from both the Law of Moses and from the Prophets, from morning until evening.

24 Some were being persuaded by the things spoken, but others would not believe.

25 And when they did not agree with one another, they *began* leaving after Paul had spoken one *parting* word, "The Holy Spirit rightly spoke through Isaiah the prophet to your fathers,

26 saying,

'GO TO THIS PEOPLE AND SAY,
"YOU WILL KEEP ON HEARING, BUT WILL NOT UNDERSTAND;
AND YOU WILL KEEP ON SEEING, BUT WILL NOT PERCEIVE;

27 FOR THE HEART OF THIS PEOPLE HAS BECOME DULL,
AND WITH THEIR EARS THEY SCARCELY HEAR,
AND THEY HAVE CLOSED THEIR EYES;
OTHERWISE THEY MIGHT SEE WITH THEIR EYES,
AND HEAR WITH THEIR EARS,
AND UNDERSTAND WITH THEIR HEART AND RETURN,
AND I WOULD HEAL THEM." ' '

28 "Therefore let it be known to you that this salvation of God has been sent to the Gentiles; they will also listen."

29 [¹When he had spoken these words, the Jews departed, having a great dispute among themselves.]

30 And he stayed two full years in his own rented quarters and was welcoming all who came to him,

31 preaching the kingdom of God and teaching concerning the Lord Jesus Christ with all openness, unhindered.

---

1. Early mss do not contain this v

THE LETTER OF PAUL TO THE ROMANS

The Gospel Exalted

1 Paul, a bond-servant of Christ Jesus, called *as* an apostle, set apart for the gospel of God,

2 which He promised beforehand through His prophets in the holy Scriptures,

3 concerning His Son, who was born of a descendant of David according to the flesh,

4 who was declared the Son of God with power [1]by the resurrection from the dead, according to the Spirit of holiness, Jesus Christ our Lord,

5 through whom we have received grace and apostleship to bring about *the* obedience of faith among all the Gentiles for His name's sake,

6 among whom you also are the called of Jesus Christ;

7 to all who are beloved of God in Rome, called *as* saints: Grace to you and peace from God our Father and the Lord Jesus Christ.

8 First, I thank my God through Jesus Christ for you all, because your faith is being proclaimed throughout the whole world.

9 For God, whom I serve in my spirit in the *preaching of the* gospel of His Son, is my witness *as to* how unceasingly I make mention of you,

10 always in my prayers making request, if perhaps now at last by the will of God I may succeed in coming to you.

11 For I long to see you so that I may impart some spiritual gift to you, that you may be established;

12 that is, that I may be encouraged together with you *while* among you, each of us by the other's faith, both yours and mine.

13 I do not want you to be unaware, brethren, that often I have planned to come to you (and have been prevented so far) so that I may obtain some fruit among you also, even as among the rest of the Gentiles.

14 I am [2]under obligation both to Greeks and to barbarians, both to the wise and to the foolish.

15 So, for my part, I am eager to preach the gospel to you also who are in Rome.

16 For I am not ashamed of the gospel, for it is the power of God for salvation to everyone who believes, to the Jew first and also to the Greek.

17 For in it *the* righteousness of God is revealed from faith to faith; as it is written, "BUT THE RIGHTEOUS *man* SHALL LIVE BY FAITH."

18 For the wrath of God is revealed from heaven against all ungodliness and unrighteousness of men who suppress the truth in unrighteousness,

19 because that which is known about God is evident within them; for God made it evident to them.

20 For since the creation of the world His invisible attributes, His eternal power and divine nature, have been clearly seen, being

understood through what has been made, so that they are without excuse.

21 For even though they knew God, they did not [3]honor Him as God or give thanks, but they became futile in their speculations, and their foolish heart was darkened.

22 Professing to be wise, they became fools,

23 and exchanged the glory of the incorruptible God for an image in the form of corruptible man and of birds and four-footed animals and [4]crawling creatures.

24 Therefore God gave them over in the lusts of their hearts to impurity, so that their bodies would be dishonored among them.

25 For they exchanged the truth of God for a lie, and worshiped and served the creature rather than the Creator, who is blessed forever. Amen.

26 For this reason God gave them over to degrading passions; for their women exchanged the natural function for that which is unnatural,

27 and in the same way also the men abandoned the natural function of the woman and burned in their desire toward one another, men with men committing indecent acts and receiving in their own persons the due penalty of their error.

28 And just as they did not see fit to acknowledge God any longer, God gave them over to a depraved mind, to do those things which are not proper,

29 being filled with all unrighteousness, wickedness, greed, evil; full of envy, murder, strife, deceit, malice; *they are* gossips,

30 slanderers, haters of God, insolent, arrogant, boastful, inventors of evil, disobedient to parents,

31 without understanding, untrustworthy, unloving, unmerciful;

32 and although they know the ordinance of God, that those who practice such things are worthy of death, they not only do the same, but also give hearty approval to those who practice them.

The Impartiality of God

2 Therefore you have no excuse, everyone of you who passes judgment, for in that which you judge another, you condemn yourself; for you who judge practice the same things.

2 And we know that the judgment of God rightly falls upon those who practice such things.

3 But do you suppose this, O man, when you pass judgment on those who practice such things and do the same *yourself*, that you will escape the judgment of God?

4 Or do you think lightly of the riches of His kindness and tolerance and patience, not knowing that the kindness of God leads you to repentance?

5 But because of your stubbornness and

---

1. Or *as a result of* 2. Lit *debtor* 3. Lit *glorify* 4. Or *reptiles*

unrepentant heart you are storing up wrath for yourself in the day of wrath and revelation of the righteous judgment of God,

6 who WILL RENDER TO EACH PERSON ACCORDING TO HIS DEEDS:

7 to those who by perseverance in doing good seek for glory and honor and immortality, eternal life;

8 but to those who are selfishly ambitious and do not obey the truth, but obey unrighteousness, wrath and indignation.

9 *There will be* tribulation and distress for every soul of man who does evil, of the Jew first and also of the Greek,

10 but glory and honor and peace to everyone who does good, to the Jew first and also to the Greek.

11 For there is no partiality with God.

12 For all who have sinned without the Law will also perish without the Law, and all who have sinned under the Law will be judged by the Law;

13 for *it is* not the hearers of the Law *who* are just before God, but the doers of the Law will be justified.

14 For when Gentiles who do not have the Law do instinctively the things of the Law, these, not having the Law, are a law to themselves,

15 in that they show the work of the Law written in their hearts, their conscience bearing witness and their thoughts alternately accusing or else defending them,

16 on the day when, according to my gospel, God will judge the secrets of men through Christ Jesus.

17 But if you bear the name "Jew" and rely upon the Law and boast in God,

18 and know *His* will and approve the things that are essential, being instructed out of the Law,

19 and are confident that you yourself are a guide to the blind, a light to those who are in darkness,

20 a corrector of the foolish, a teacher of the immature, having in the Law the embodiment of knowledge and of the truth,

21 you, therefore, who teach another, do you not teach yourself? You who preach that one shall not steal, do you steal?

22 You who say that one should not commit adultery, do you commit adultery? You who abhor idols, do you rob temples?

23 You who boast in the Law, through your breaking the Law, do you dishonor God?

24 For "THE NAME OF GOD IS BLASPHEMED AMONG THE GENTILES BECAUSE OF YOU," just as it is written.

25 For indeed circumcision is of value if you practice the Law; but if you are a transgressor of the Law, your circumcision has become uncircumcision.

26 So if the uncircumcised man keeps the requirements of the Law, will not his uncircumcision be regarded as circumcision?

27 And he who is physically uncircumcised, if he keeps the Law, will he not judge you who though having the letter *of the Law* and circumcision are a transgressor of the Law?

28 For he is not a Jew who is one outwardly, nor is circumcision that which is outward in the flesh.

29 But he is a Jew who is one inwardly; and circumcision is that which is of the heart, by the Spirit, not by the letter; and his praise is not from men, but from God.

All the World Guilty

3 Then what advantage has the Jew? Or what is the benefit of circumcision?

2 Great in every respect. First of all, that they were entrusted with the oracles of God.

3 What then? If some did not believe, their unbelief will not nullify the faithfulness of God, will it?

4 May it never be! Rather, let God be found true, though every man *be found* a liar, as it is written,

"THAT YOU MAY BE JUSTIFIED IN YOUR WORDS,
AND PREVAIL WHEN YOU ARE JUDGED."

5 But if our unrighteousness demonstrates the righteousness of God, what shall we say? The God who inflicts wrath is not unrighteous, is He? (I am speaking in human terms.)

6 May it never be! For otherwise, how will God judge the world?

7 But if through my lie the truth of God abounded to His glory, why am I also still being judged as a sinner?

8 And why not *say* (as we are slanderously reported and as some claim that we say), "Let us do evil that good may come"? Their condemnation is just.

9 What then? Are we better than they? Not at all; for we have already charged that both Jews and Greeks are all under sin;

10 as it is written,
"THERE IS NONE RIGHTEOUS, NOT EVEN ONE;

11 THERE IS NONE WHO UNDERSTANDS,
THERE IS NONE WHO SEEKS FOR GOD;

12 ALL HAVE TURNED ASIDE, TOGETHER THEY HAVE BECOME USELESS;
THERE IS NONE WHO DOES GOOD,
THERE IS NOT EVEN ONE."

13 "THEIR THROAT IS AN OPEN GRAVE,
WITH THEIR TONGUES THEY KEEP DECEIVING,"
"THE POISON OF ASPS IS UNDER THEIR LIPS";

14 "WHOSE MOUTH IS FULL OF CURSING AND BITTERNESS";

15 "THEIR FEET ARE SWIFT TO SHED BLOOD,

16 DESTRUCTION AND MISERY ARE IN THEIR PATHS,

17 AND THE PATH OF PEACE THEY HAVE NOT KNOWN."

18 "THERE IS NO FEAR OF GOD BEFORE THEIR EYES."

19 Now we know that whatever the Law says, it speaks to those who are under the Law, so that every mouth may be closed and all the world may become accountable to God;

20 because by the works of the Law no flesh

will be justified in His sight; for through the Law *comes* the knowledge of sin.

21 But now apart from the Law *the* righteousness of God has been manifested, being witnessed by the Law and the Prophets,

22 even *the* righteousness of God through faith in Jesus Christ for all those who believe; for there is no distinction;

23 for all have sinned and fall short of the glory of God,

24 being justified as a gift by His grace through the redemption which is in Christ Jesus;

25 whom God displayed publicly as a propitiation in His blood through faith. *This was* to demonstrate His righteousness, because in the forbearance of God He passed over the sins previously committed;

26 for the demonstration, *I say*, of His righteousness at the present time, so that He would be just and the justifier of the one who has faith in Jesus.

27 Where then is boasting? It is excluded. By what kind of law? Of works? No, but by a law of faith.

28 For we maintain that a man is justified by faith apart from works of the Law.

29 Or is God *the God* of Jews only? Is He not *the God* of Gentiles also? Yes, of Gentiles also,

30 since indeed God who will justify the circumcised by faith and the uncircumcised through faith is one.

31 Do we then nullify the Law through faith? May it never be! On the contrary, we establish the Law.

Justification by Faith Evidenced in Old Testament

4 What then shall we say that Abraham, our forefather according to the flesh, has found?

2 For if Abraham was justified by works, he has something to boast about, but not before God.

3 For what does the Scripture say? "ABRAHAM BELIEVED GOD, AND IT WAS CREDITED TO HIM AS RIGHTEOUSNESS."

4 Now to the one who works, his wage is not credited as a favor, but as what is due.

5 But to the one who does not work, but believes in Him who justifies the ungodly, his faith is credited as righteousness,

6 just as David also speaks of the blessing on the man to whom God credits righteousness apart from works:

7 "BLESSED ARE THOSE WHOSE LAWLESS DEEDS HAVE BEEN FORGIVEN,
AND WHOSE SINS HAVE BEEN COVERED.

8 "BLESSED IS THE MAN WHOSE SIN THE LORD WILL NOT TAKE INTO ACCOUNT."

9 Is this blessing then on the circumcised, or on the uncircumcised also? For we say, "FAITH WAS CREDITED TO ABRAHAM AS RIGHTEOUSNESS."

10 How then was it credited? While he was circumcised, or uncircumcised? Not while circumcised, but while uncircumcised;

11 and he received the sign of circumcision, a seal of the righteousness of the faith which he had while uncircumcised, so that he might be the father of all who believe without being circumcised, that righteousness might be credited to them,

12 and the father of circumcision to those who not only are of the circumcision, but who also follow in the steps of the faith of our father Abraham which he had while uncircumcised.

13 For the promise to Abraham or to his descendants that he would be heir of the world was not through the Law, but through the righteousness of faith.

14 For if those who are of the Law are heirs, faith is made void and the promise is nullified;

15 for the Law brings about wrath, but where there is no law, there also is no violation.

16 For this reason *it is* by faith, in order that *it may be* in accordance with grace, so that the promise will be guaranteed to all the descendants, not only to those who are of the Law, but also to those who are of the faith of Abraham, who is the father of us all,

17 (as it is written, "A FATHER OF MANY NATIONS HAVE I MADE YOU") in the presence of Him whom he believed, *even* God, who gives life to the dead and calls into being that which does not exist.

18 In hope against hope he believed, so that he might become a father of many nations according to that which had been spoken, "SO SHALL YOUR DESCENDANTS BE."

19 Without becoming weak in faith he contemplated his own body, now as good as dead since he was about a hundred years old, and the deadness of Sarah's womb;

20 yet, with respect to the promise of God, he did not waver in unbelief but grew strong in faith, giving glory to God,

21 and being fully assured that what God had promised, He was able also to perform.

22 Therefore IT WAS ALSO CREDITED TO HIM AS RIGHTEOUSNESS.

23 Now not for his sake only was it written that it was credited to him,

24 but for our sake also, to whom it will be credited, as those who believe in Him who raised Jesus our Lord from the dead,

25 *He* who was delivered over because of our transgressions, and was raised because of our justification.

Results of Justification

5 Therefore, having been justified by faith, we have peace with God through our Lord Jesus Christ,

2 through whom also we have obtained our introduction by faith into this grace in which we stand; and we exult in hope of the glory of God.

3 And not only this, but we also exult in our tribulations, knowing that tribulation brings about perseverance;

4 and perseverance, proven character; and proven character, hope;

5 and hope does not disappoint, because the love of God has been poured out within our

hearts through the Holy Spirit who was given to us.

6 For while we were still helpless, at the right time Christ died for the ungodly.

7 For one will hardly die for a righteous man; though perhaps for the good man someone would dare even to die.

8 But God demonstrates His own love toward us, in that while we were yet sinners, Christ died for us.

9 Much more then, having now been justified by His blood, we shall be saved from the wrath of God through Him.

10 For if while we were enemies we were reconciled to God through the death of His Son, much more, having been reconciled, we shall be saved by His life.

11 And not only this, but we also exult in God through our Lord Jesus Christ, through whom we have now received the reconciliation.

12 Therefore, just as through one man sin entered into the world, and death through sin, and so death spread to all men, because all sinned—

13 for until the Law sin was in the world, but sin is not imputed when there is no law.

14 Nevertheless death reigned from Adam until Moses, even over those who had not sinned in the likeness of the offense of Adam, who is a ¹type of Him who was to come.

15 But the free gift is not like the transgression. For if by the transgression of the one the many died, much more did the grace of God and the gift by the grace of the one Man, Jesus Christ, abound to the many.

16 The gift is not like *that which came* through the one who sinned; for on the one hand the judgment *arose* from one *transgression* resulting in condemnation, but on the other hand the free gift *arose* from many transgressions resulting in justification.

17 For if by the transgression of the one, death reigned through the one, much more those who receive the abundance of grace and of the gift of righteousness will reign in life through the One, Jesus Christ.

18 So then as through one transgression there resulted condemnation to all men, even so through one act of righteousness there resulted justification of life to all men.

19 For as through the one man's disobedience the many were made sinners, even so through the obedience of the One the many will be made righteous.

20 The Law came in so that the transgression would increase; but where sin increased, grace abounded all the more,

21 so that, as sin reigned in death, even so grace would reign through righteousness to eternal life through Jesus Christ our Lord.

Believers Are Dead to Sin, Alive to God

6 What shall we say then? Are we to continue in sin so that grace may increase?

2 May it never be! How shall we who died to sin still live in it?

3 Or do you not know that all of us who have been baptized into Christ Jesus have been baptized into His death?

4 Therefore we have been buried with Him through baptism into death, so that as Christ was raised from the dead through the glory of the Father, so we too might walk in newness of life.

5 For if we have become united with *Him* in the likeness of His death, certainly we shall also be *in the likeness* of His resurrection,

6 knowing this, that our old self was crucified with *Him*, in order that our body of sin might be done away with, so that we would no longer be slaves to sin;

7 for he who has died is freed from sin.

8 Now if we have died with Christ, we believe that we shall also live with Him,

9 knowing that Christ, having been raised from the dead, is never to die again; death no longer is master over Him.

10 For the death that He died, He died to sin once for all; but the life that He lives, He lives to God.

11 Even so consider yourselves to be dead to sin, but alive to God in Christ Jesus.

12 Therefore do not let sin reign in your mortal body so that you obey its lusts,

13 and do not go on presenting the members of your body to sin *as* instruments of unrighteousness; but present yourselves to God as those alive from the dead, and your members *as* instruments of righteousness to God.

14 For sin shall not be master over you, for you are not under law but under grace.

15 What then? Shall we sin because we are not under law but under grace? May it never be!

16 Do you not know that when you present yourselves to someone *as* slaves for obedience, you are slaves of the one whom you obey, either of sin resulting in death, or of obedience resulting in righteousness?

17 But thanks be to God that though you were slaves of sin, you became obedient from the heart to that form of teaching to which you were committed,

18 and having been freed from sin, you became slaves of righteousness.

19 I am speaking in human terms because of the weakness of your flesh. For just as you presented your members as slaves to impurity and to lawlessness, resulting in *further* lawlessness, so now present your members as slaves to righteousness, resulting in sanctification.

20 For when you were slaves of sin, you were free in regard to righteousness.

21 Therefore what benefit were you then deriving from the things of which you are now ashamed? For the outcome of those things is death.

22 But now having been freed from sin and enslaved to God, you derive your benefit,

---

1. Or *foreshadowing*

The blood of Jesus forgives your sins when you repent and are baptized.
Read Acts 2:36-39 on page 93.

resulting in sanctification, and the outcome, eternal life.

23 For the wages of sin is death, but the free gift of God is eternal life in Christ Jesus our Lord.

Believers United to Christ

7 Or do you not know, brethren (for I am speaking to those who know the law), that the law has jurisdiction over a person as long as he lives?

2 For the married woman is bound by law to her husband while he is living; but if her husband dies, she is released from the law concerning the husband.

3 So then, if while her husband is living she is joined to another man, she shall be called an adulteress; but if her husband dies, she is free from the law, so that she is not an adulteress though she is joined to another man.

4 Therefore, my brethren, you also were made to die to the Law through the body of Christ, so that you might be joined to another, to Him who was raised from the dead, in order that we might bear fruit for God.

5 For while we were in the flesh, the sinful passions, which were *aroused* by the Law, were at work in the members of our body to bear fruit for death.

6 But now we have been released from the Law, having died to that by which we were bound, so that we serve in newness of the ¹Spirit and not in oldness of the letter.

7 What shall we say then? Is the Law sin? May it never be! On the contrary, I would not have come to know sin except through the Law; for I would not have known about coveting if the Law had not said, "YOU SHALL NOT COVET."

8 But sin, taking opportunity through the commandment, produced in me coveting of every kind; for apart from the Law sin *is* dead.

9 I was once alive apart from the Law; but when the commandment came, sin became alive and I died;

10 and this commandment, which was to result in life, proved to result in death for me;

11 for sin, taking an opportunity through the commandment, deceived me and through it killed me.

12 So then, the Law is holy, and the commandment is holy and righteous and good.

13 Therefore did that which is good become *a cause of* death for me? May it never be! Rather it was sin, in order that it might be shown to be sin by effecting my death through that which is good, so that through the commandment sin would become utterly sinful.

14 For we know that the Law is spiritual, but I am of flesh, sold into bondage to sin.

15 For what I am doing, I do not understand; for I am not practicing what I *would* like to do, but I am doing the very thing I hate.

16 But if I do the very thing I do not want to *do,* I agree with the Law, *confessing* that the Law is good.

17 So now, no longer am I the one doing it, but sin which dwells in me.

18 For I know that nothing good dwells in me, that is, in my flesh; for the willing is present in me, but the doing of the good *is* not.

19 For the good that I want, I do not do, but I practice the very evil that I do not want.

20 But if I am doing the very thing I do not want, I am no longer the one doing it, but sin which dwells in me.

21 I find then the principle that evil is present in me, the one who wants to do good.

22 For I joyfully concur with the law of God in the inner man,

23 but I see a different law in the members of my body, waging war against the law of my mind and making me a prisoner of the law of sin which is in my members.

24 Wretched man that I am! Who will set me free from the body of this death?

25 Thanks be to God through Jesus Christ our Lord! So then, on the one hand I myself with my mind am serving the law of God, but on the other, with my flesh the law of sin.

Deliverance from Bondage

8 Therefore there is now no condemnation for those who are in Christ Jesus.

2 For the law of the Spirit of life in Christ Jesus has set you free from the law of sin and of death.

3 For what the Law could not do, weak as it was through the flesh, God *did:* sending His own Son in the likeness of sinful flesh and *as an offering* for sin, He condemned sin in the flesh,

4 so that the requirement of the Law might be fulfilled in us, who do not walk according to the flesh but according to the Spirit.

5 For those who are according to the flesh set their minds on the things of the flesh, but those who are according to the Spirit, the things of the Spirit.

6 For the mind set on the flesh is death, but the mind set on the Spirit is life and peace,

7 because the mind set on the flesh is hostile toward God; for it does not subject itself to the law of God, for it is not even able *to do so,*

8 and those who are in the flesh cannot please God.

9 However, you are not in the flesh but in the Spirit, if indeed the Spirit of God dwells in you. But if anyone does not have the Spirit of Christ, he does not belong to Him.

10 If Christ is in you, though the body is dead because of sin, yet the spirit is alive because of righteousness.

11 But if the Spirit of Him who raised Jesus from the dead dwells in you, He who raised Christ Jesus from the dead will also give life to your mortal bodies ²through His Spirit who dwells in you.

12 So then, brethren, we are under obligation, not to the flesh, to live according to the flesh—

13 for if you are living according to the flesh, you must die; but if by the Spirit you are

---

1. Or *spirit* 2. One early ms reads *because of*

putting to death the deeds of the body, you will live.

14 For all who are being led by the Spirit of God, these are sons of God.

15 For you have not received a spirit of slavery leading to fear again, but you have received a spirit of adoption as sons by which we cry out, "Abba! Father!"

16 The Spirit Himself testifies with our spirit that we are children of God,

17 and if children, heirs also, heirs of God and fellow heirs with Christ, if indeed we suffer with *Him* so that we may also be glorified with *Him*.

18 For I consider that the sufferings of this present time are not worthy to be compared with the glory that is to be revealed to us.

19 For the anxious longing of the creation waits eagerly for the revealing of the sons of God.

20 For the creation was subjected to futility, not willingly, but because of Him who subjected it, ¹in hope

21 that the creation itself also will be set free from its slavery to corruption into the freedom of the glory of the children of God.

22 For we know that the whole creation groans and suffers the pains of childbirth together until now.

23 And not only this, but also we ourselves, having the first fruits of the Spirit, even we ourselves groan within ourselves, waiting eagerly for *our* adoption as sons, the redemption of our body.

24 For in hope we have been saved, but hope that is seen is not hope; for who hopes for what he *already* sees?

25 But if we hope for what we do not see, with perseverance we wait eagerly for it.

26 In the same way the Spirit also helps our weakness; for we do not know how to pray as we should, but the Spirit Himself intercedes for *us* with groanings too deep for words;

27 and He who searches the hearts knows what the mind of the Spirit is, because He intercedes for the saints according to *the will of* God.

28 And we know that ²God causes all things to work together for good to those who love God, to those who are called according to *His* purpose.

29 For those whom He foreknew, He also predestined *to become* conformed to the image of His Son, so that He would be the firstborn among many brethren;

30 and these whom He predestined, He also called; and these whom He called, He also justified; and these whom He justified, He also glorified.

31 What then shall we say to these things? If God *is* for us, who *is* against us?

32 He who did not spare His own Son, but delivered Him over for us all, how will He not also with Him freely give us all things?

33 Who will bring a charge against God's elect? God is the one who justifies;

34 who is the one who condemns? Christ Jesus is He who died, yes, rather who was ³raised, who is at the right hand of God, who also intercedes for us.

35 Who will separate us from the love of ⁴Christ? Will tribulation, or distress, or persecution, or famine, or nakedness, or peril, or sword?

36 Just as it is written,

"FOR YOUR SAKE WE ARE BEING PUT TO
   DEATH ALL DAY LONG;
WE WERE CONSIDERED AS SHEEP TO BE
   SLAUGHTERED."

37 But in all these things we overwhelmingly conquer through Him who loved us.

38 For I am convinced that neither death, nor life, nor angels, nor principalities, nor things present, nor things to come, nor powers,

39 nor height, nor depth, nor any other created thing, will be able to separate us from the love of God, which is in Christ Jesus our Lord.

Solicitude for Israel

9 I am telling the truth in Christ, I am not lying, my conscience testifies with me in the Holy Spirit,

2 that I have great sorrow and unceasing grief in my heart.

3 For I could wish that I myself were accursed, *separated* from Christ for the sake of my brethren, my kinsmen according to the flesh,

4 who are Israelites, to whom belongs the adoption as sons, and the glory and the covenants and the giving of the Law and the *temple* service and the promises,

5 whose are the fathers, and from whom is the Christ according to the flesh, who is over all, God blessed forever. Amen.

6 But *it is* not as though the word of God has failed. For they are not all Israel who are *descended* from Israel;

7 nor are they all children because they are Abraham's descendants, but: "THROUGH ISAAC YOUR DESCENDANTS WILL BE NAMED."

8 That is, it is not the children of the flesh who are children of God, but the children of the promise are regarded as descendants.

9 For this is the word of promise: "AT THIS TIME I WILL COME, AND SARAH SHALL HAVE A SON."

10 And not only this, but there was Rebekah also, when she had conceived *twins* by one man, our father Isaac;

11 for though *the twins* were not yet born and had not done anything good or bad, so that God's purpose according to *His* choice would stand, not because of works but because of Him who calls,

12 it was said to her, "THE OLDER WILL SERVE THE YOUNGER."

---

1. Or *in hope; because the creation*   2. One early ms reads *all things work together for good*   3. One early ms reads *raised from the dead*   4. Two early mss read *God*

13 Just as it is written, "JACOB I LOVED, BUT ESAU I HATED."

14 What shall we say then? There is no injustice with God, is there? May it never be!

15 For He says to Moses, "I WILL HAVE MERCY ON WHOM I HAVE MERCY, AND I WILL HAVE COMPASSION ON WHOM I HAVE COMPASSION."

16 So then it *does* not *depend* on the man who wills or the man who runs, but on God who has mercy.

17 For the Scripture says to Pharaoh, "FOR THIS VERY PURPOSE I RAISED YOU UP, TO DEMONSTRATE MY POWER IN YOU, AND THAT MY NAME MIGHT BE PROCLAIMED THROUGHOUT THE WHOLE EARTH."

18 So then He has mercy on whom He desires, and He hardens whom He desires.

19 You will say to me then, "Why does He still find fault? For who resists His will?"

20 On the contrary, who are you, O man, who answers back to God? The thing molded will not say to the molder, "Why did you make me like this," will it?

21 Or does not the potter have a right over the clay, to make from the same lump one vessel for honorable use and another for common use?

22 What if God, although willing to demonstrate His wrath and to make His power known, endured with much patience vessels of wrath prepared for destruction?

23 And *He did so* to make known the riches of His glory upon vessels of mercy, which He prepared beforehand for glory,

24 *even* us, whom He also called, not from among Jews only, but also from among Gentiles.

25 As He says also in Hosea,

"I WILL CALL THOSE WHO WERE NOT MY
    PEOPLE, 'MY PEOPLE,'
AND HER WHO WAS NOT BELOVED,
    'BELOVED.' "

26 "AND IT SHALL BE THAT IN THE PLACE WHERE
    IT WAS SAID TO THEM, 'YOU ARE NOT MY
    PEOPLE,'
THERE THEY SHALL BE CALLED SONS OF THE
    LIVING GOD."

27 Isaiah cries out concerning Israel, "THOUGH THE NUMBER OF THE SONS OF ISRAEL BE LIKE THE SAND OF THE SEA, IT IS THE REMNANT THAT WILL BE SAVED;

28 FOR THE LORD WILL EXECUTE HIS WORD ON THE EARTH, THOROUGHLY AND QUICKLY."

29 And just as Isaiah foretold,

"UNLESS THE LORD OF SABAOTH HAD LEFT TO
    US A POSTERITY,
WE WOULD HAVE BECOME LIKE SODOM, AND
    WOULD HAVE RESEMBLED GOMORRAH."

30 What shall we say then? That Gentiles, who did not pursue righteousness, attained righteousness, even the righteousness which is by faith;

31 but Israel, pursuing a law of righteousness, did not arrive at *that* law.

32 Why? Because *they did* not *pursue it* by faith, but as though *it were* by works. They stumbled over the stumbling stone,

33 just as it is written,

"BEHOLD, I LAY IN ZION A STONE OF
    STUMBLING AND A ROCK OF OFFENSE,
AND HE WHO BELIEVES IN HIM WILL NOT BE
    DISAPPOINTED."

The Word of Faith Brings Salvation

10 Brethren, my heart's desire and my prayer to God for them is for *their* salvation.

2 For I testify about them that they have a zeal for God, but not in accordance with knowledge.

3 For not knowing about God's righteousness and seeking to establish their own, they did not subject themselves to the righteousness of God.

4 For Christ is the end of the law for righteousness to everyone who believes.

5 For Moses writes that the man who practices the righteousness which is based on law shall live by that righteousness.

6 But the righteousness based on faith speaks as follows: "DO NOT SAY IN YOUR HEART, 'WHO WILL ASCEND INTO HEAVEN?' (that is, to bring Christ down),

7 or 'WHO WILL DESCEND INTO THE ABYSS?' (that is, to bring Christ up from the dead)."

8 But what does it say? "THE WORD IS NEAR YOU, IN YOUR MOUTH AND IN YOUR HEART"—that is, the word of faith which we are preaching,

9 that if you confess with your mouth Jesus *as* Lord, and believe in your heart that God raised Him from the dead, you will be saved;

10 for with the heart a person believes, resulting in righteousness, and with the mouth he confesses, resulting in salvation.

11 For the Scripture says, "WHOEVER BELIEVES IN HIM WILL NOT BE DISAPPOINTED."

12 For there is no distinction between Jew and Greek; for the same *Lord* is Lord of all, abounding in riches for all who call on Him;

13 for "WHOEVER WILL CALL ON THE NAME OF THE LORD WILL BE SAVED."

14 How then will they call on Him in whom they have not believed? How will they believe in Him whom they have not heard? And how will they hear without a preacher?

15 How will they preach unless they are sent? Just as it is written, "HOW BEAUTIFUL ARE THE FEET OF THOSE WHO BRING GOOD NEWS OF GOOD THINGS!"

16 However, they did not all heed the good news; for Isaiah says, "LORD, WHO HAS BELIEVED OUR REPORT?"

17 So faith *comes* from hearing, and hearing by the word of Christ.

18 But I say, surely they have never heard, have they? Indeed they have;

"THEIR VOICE HAS GONE OUT INTO ALL THE
    EARTH,
AND THEIR WORDS TO THE ENDS OF THE
    WORLD."

19 But I say, surely Israel did not know, did they? First Moses says,

"I WILL MAKE YOU JEALOUS BY THAT WHICH IS
    NOT A NATION,

BY A NATION WITHOUT UNDERSTANDING
WILL I ANGER YOU."

20 And Isaiah is very bold and says,
"I WAS FOUND BY THOSE WHO DID NOT SEEK
ME,
I BECAME MANIFEST TO THOSE WHO DID NOT
ASK FOR ME."

21 But as for Israel He says, "ALL THE DAY
LONG I HAVE STRETCHED OUT MY HANDS TO A
DISOBEDIENT AND OBSTINATE PEOPLE,"

Israel Is Not Cast Away

11 I say then, God has not rejected His
people, has He? May it never be! For I
too am an Israelite, a descendant of Abraham,
of the tribe of Benjamin.

2 God has not rejected His people whom He
foreknew. Or do you not know what the
Scripture says in *the passage about* Elijah, how
he pleads with God against Israel?

3 "Lord, THEY HAVE KILLED YOUR PROPHETS,
THEY HAVE TORN DOWN YOUR ALTARS, AND I
ALONE AM LEFT, AND THEY ARE SEEKING MY
LIFE."

4 But what is the divine response to him? "I
HAVE KEPT for Myself SEVEN THOUSAND MEN
WHO HAVE NOT BOWED THE KNEE TO BAAL."

5 In the same way then, there has also come
to be at the present time a remnant according to
God's gracious choice.

6 But if it is by grace, it is no longer on the
basis of works, otherwise grace is no longer
grace.

7 What then? What Israel is seeking, it has
not obtained, but those who were chosen
obtained it, and the rest were hardened;

8 just as it is written,
"GOD GAVE THEM A SPIRIT OF STUPOR,
EYES TO SEE NOT AND EARS TO HEAR NOT,
DOWN TO THIS VERY DAY."

9 And David says,
"LET THEIR TABLE BECOME A SNARE AND A
TRAP,
AND A STUMBLING BLOCK AND A
RETRIBUTION TO THEM.

10 "LET THEIR EYES BE DARKENED TO SEE NOT,
AND BEND THEIR BACKS FOREVER."

11 I say then, they did not stumble so as to
fall, did they? May it never be! But by their
transgression salvation *has come* to the
Gentiles, to make them jealous.

12 Now if their transgression is riches for the
world and their failure is riches for the Gentiles,
how much more will their fulfillment be!

13 But I am speaking to you who are Gentiles.
Inasmuch then as I am an apostle of Gentiles, I
magnify my ministry,

14 if somehow I might move to jealousy my
fellow countrymen and save some of them.

15 For if their rejection is the reconciliation of
the world, what will *their* acceptance be but life
from the dead?

16 If the first piece *of dough* is holy, the lump
is also; and if the root is holy, the branches are
too.

17 But if some of the branches were broken
off, and you, being a wild olive, were grafted in

among them and became partaker with them of
the rich root of the olive tree,

18 do not be arrogant toward the branches;
but if you are arrogant, *remember that* it is not
you who supports the root, but the root *supports*
you.

19 You will say then, "Branches were broken
off so that I might be grafted in."

20 Quite right, they were broken off for their
unbelief, but you stand by your faith. Do not be
conceited, but fear;

21 for if God did not spare the natural
branches, He will not spare you, either.

22 Behold then the kindness and severity of
God; to those who fell, severity, but to you,
God's kindness, if you continue in His kindness;
otherwise you also will be cut off.

23 And they also, if they do not continue in
their unbelief, will be grafted in, for God is able
to graft them in again.

24 For if you were cut off from what is by
nature a wild olive tree, and were grafted
contrary to nature into a cultivated olive tree,
how much more will these who are the natural
branches be grafted into their own olive tree?

25 For I do not want you, brethren, to be
uninformed of this mystery—so that you will
not be wise in your own estimation—that a
partial hardening has happened to Israel until
the fullness of the Gentiles has come in;

26 and so all Israel will be saved; just as it is
written,
"THE DELIVERER WILL COME FROM ZION,
HE WILL REMOVE UNGODLINESS FROM
JACOB."

27 "THIS IS MY COVENANT WITH THEM,
WHEN I TAKE AWAY THEIR SINS."

28 From the standpoint of the gospel they are
enemies for your sake, but from the standpoint
of God's choice they are beloved for the sake of
the fathers;

29 for the gifts and the calling of God are
irrevocable.

30 For just as you once were disobedient to
God, but now have been shown mercy because
of their disobedience,

31 so these also now have been disobedient,
that because of the mercy shown to you they
also may now be shown mercy.

32 For God has shut up all in disobedience so
that He may show mercy to all.

33 Oh, the depth of the riches both of the
wisdom and knowledge of God! How
unsearchable are His judgments and
unfathomable His ways!

34 For WHO HAS KNOWN THE MIND OF THE
LORD, OR WHO BECAME HIS COUNSELOR?

35 Or WHO HAS FIRST GIVEN TO HIM THAT IT
MIGHT BE PAID BACK TO HIM AGAIN?

36 For from Him and through Him and to
Him are all things. To Him *be* the glory forever.
Amen.

Dedicated Service

12 Therefore I urge you, brethren, by the
mercies of God, to present your bodies a
living and holy sacrifice, acceptable to God,

which is your spiritual service of worship.

2 And do not be conformed to this world, but be transformed by the renewing of your mind, so that you may prove what the will of God is, that which is good and acceptable and perfect.

3 For through the grace given to me I say to everyone among you not to think more highly of himself than he ought to think; but to think so as to have sound judgment, as God has allotted to each a measure of faith.

4 For just as we have many members in one body and all the members do not have the same function,

5 so we, who are many, are one body in Christ, and individually members one of another.

6 Since we have gifts that differ according to the grace given to us, *each of us is to exercise them accordingly:* if prophecy, according to the proportion of his faith;

7 if service, in his serving; or he who teaches, in his teaching;

8 or he who exhorts, in his exhortation; he who gives, with [1]liberality; he who leads, with diligence; he who shows mercy, with cheerfulness.

9 Let love *be* without hypocrisy. Abhor what is evil; cling to what is good.

10 *Be* devoted to one another in brotherly love; give preference to one another in honor;

11 not lagging behind in diligence, fervent in spirit, serving the Lord;

12 rejoicing in hope, persevering in tribulation, devoted to prayer,

13 contributing to the needs of the saints, practicing hospitality.

14 Bless those who persecute [2]you; bless and do not curse.

15 Rejoice with those who rejoice, and weep with those who weep.

16 Be of the same mind toward one another; do not be haughty in mind, but associate with the lowly. Do not be wise in your own estimation.

17 Never pay back evil for evil to anyone. Respect what is right in the sight of all men.

18 If possible, so far as it depends on you, be at peace with all men.

19 Never take your own revenge, beloved, but leave room for the wrath *of God,* for it is written, "VENGEANCE IS MINE, I WILL REPAY," says the Lord.

20 "BUT IF YOUR ENEMY IS HUNGRY, FEED HIM, AND IF HE IS THIRSTY, GIVE HIM A DRINK; FOR IN SO DOING YOU WILL HEAP BURNING COALS ON HIS HEAD."

21 Do not be overcome by evil, but overcome evil with good.

Be Subject to Government

13 Every person is to be in subjection to the governing authorities. For there is no authority except from God, and those which exist are established by God.

2 Therefore whoever resists authority has opposed the ordinance of God; and they who have opposed will receive condemnation upon themselves.

3 For rulers are not a cause of fear for good behavior, but for evil. Do you want to have no fear of authority? Do what is good and you will have praise from the same;

4 for it is a minister of God to you for good. But if you do what is evil, be afraid; for it does not bear the sword for nothing; for it is a minister of God, an avenger who brings wrath on the one who practices evil.

5 Therefore it is necessary to be in subjection, not only because of wrath, but also for conscience' sake.

6 For because of this you also pay taxes, for *rulers* are servants of God, devoting themselves to this very thing.

7 Render to all what is due them: tax to whom tax *is due;* custom to whom custom; fear to whom fear; honor to whom honor.

8 Owe nothing to anyone except to love one another; for he who loves his neighbor has fulfilled *the* law.

9 For this, "YOU SHALL NOT COMMIT ADULTERY, YOU SHALL NOT MURDER, YOU SHALL NOT STEAL, YOU SHALL NOT COVET," and if there is any other commandment, it is summed up in this saying, "YOU SHALL LOVE YOUR NEIGHBOR AS YOURSELF."

10 Love does no wrong to a neighbor; therefore love is the fulfillment of *the* law.

11 *Do* this, knowing the time, that it is already the hour for you to awaken from sleep; for now [3]salvation is nearer to us than when we believed.

12 The night is almost gone, and the day is near. Therefore let us lay aside the deeds of darkness and put on the armor of light.

13 Let us behave properly as in the day, not in carousing and drunkenness, not in sexual promiscuity and sensuality, not in strife and jealousy.

14 But put on the Lord Jesus Christ, and make no provision for the flesh in regard to *its* lusts.

Principles of Conscience

14 Now accept the one who is weak in faith, *but not for the purpose of* passing judgment on his opinions.

2 One person has faith that he may eat all things, but he who is weak eats vegetables *only.*

3 The one who eats is not to regard with contempt the one who does not eat, and the one who does not eat is not to judge the one who eats, for God has accepted him.

4 Who are you to judge the servant of another? To his own master he stands or falls; and he will stand, for the Lord is able to make him stand.

5 One person regards one day above another; another regards every day *alike.* Each person must be fully convinced in his own mind.

6 He who observes the day, observes it for the Lord, and he who eats, does so for the Lord, for he gives thanks to God; and he who eats not, for

---

1. Or *simplicity*   2. Two early mss do not contain *you*   3. Or *our salvation is nearer than when*

the Lord he does not eat, and gives thanks to God.

7 For not one of us lives for himself, and not one dies for himself;

8 for if we live, we live for the Lord, or if we die, we die for the Lord; therefore whether we live or die, we are the Lord's.

9 For to this end Christ died and lived again, that He might be Lord both of the dead and of the living.

10 But you, why do you judge your brother? Or you again, why do you regard your brother with contempt? For we will all stand before the judgment seat of God.

11 For it is written,

"AS I LIVE, SAYS THE LORD, EVERY KNEE SHALL BOW TO ME,

AND EVERY TONGUE SHALL GIVE PRAISE TO GOD."

12 So then each one of us will give an account of himself to God.

13 Therefore let us not judge one another anymore, but rather determine this—not to put an obstacle or a stumbling block in a brother's way.

14 I know and am convinced in the Lord Jesus that nothing is unclean in itself; but to him who thinks anything to be unclean, to him it is unclean.

15 For if because of food your brother is hurt, you are no longer walking according to love. Do not destroy with your food him for whom Christ died.

16 Therefore do not let what is for you a good thing be spoken of as evil;

17 for the kingdom of God is not eating and drinking, but righteousness and peace and joy in the Holy Spirit.

18 For he who in this *way* serves Christ is acceptable to God and approved by men.

19 So then [1]we pursue the things which make for peace and the building up of one another.

20 Do not tear down the work of God for the sake of food. All things indeed are clean, but they are evil for the man who eats and gives offense.

21 It is good not to eat meat or to drink wine, or *to do anything* by which your brother stumbles.

22 The faith which you have, have as your own conviction before God. Happy is he who does not condemn himself in what he approves.

23 But he who doubts is condemned if he eats, because *his eating is* not from faith; and whatever is not from faith is sin.

Self-denial on Behalf of Others

15 Now we who are strong ought to bear the weaknesses of those without strength and not *just* please ourselves.

2 Each of us is to please his neighbor for his good, to his edification.

3 For even Christ did not please Himself; but

1. Later mss read *let us pursue*

as it is written, "THE REPROACHES OF THOSE WHO REPROACHED YOU FELL ON ME."

4 For whatever was written in earlier times was written for our instruction, so that through perseverance and the encouragement of the Scriptures we might have hope.

5 Now may the God who gives perseverance and encouragement grant you to be of the same mind with one another according to Christ Jesus,

6 so that with one accord you may with one voice glorify the God and Father of our Lord Jesus Christ.

7 Therefore, accept one another, just as Christ also accepted us to the glory of God.

8 For I say that Christ has become a servant to the circumcision on behalf of the truth of God to confirm the promises *given* to the fathers,

9 and for the Gentiles to glorify God for His mercy; as it is written,

"THEREFORE I WILL GIVE PRAISE TO YOU AMONG THE GENTILES,

AND I WILL SING TO YOUR NAME."

10 Again he says,

"REJOICE, O GENTILES, WITH HIS PEOPLE."

11 And again,

"PRAISE THE LORD ALL YOU GENTILES,

AND LET ALL THE PEOPLES PRAISE HIM."

12 Again Isaiah says,

"THERE SHALL COME THE ROOT OF JESSE,

AND HE WHO ARISES TO RULE OVER THE GENTILES,

IN HIM SHALL THE GENTILES HOPE."

13 Now may the God of hope fill you with all joy and peace in believing, so that you will abound in hope by the power of the Holy Spirit.

14 And concerning you, my brethren, I myself also am convinced that you yourselves are full of goodness, filled with all knowledge and able also to admonish one another.

15 But I have written very boldly to you on some points so as to remind you again, because of the grace that was given me from God,

16 to be a minister of Christ Jesus to the Gentiles, ministering as a priest the gospel of God, so that *my* offering of the Gentiles may become acceptable, sanctified by the Holy Spirit.

17 Therefore in Christ Jesus I have found reason for boasting in things pertaining to God.

18 For I will not presume to speak of anything except what Christ has accomplished through me, resulting in the obedience of the Gentiles by word and deed,

19 in the power of signs and wonders, in the power of the Spirit; so that from Jerusalem and round about as far as Illyricum I have fully preached the gospel of Christ.

20 And thus I aspired to preach the gospel, not where Christ was *already* named, so that I would not build on another man's foundation;

21 but as it is written,
"THEY WHO HAD NO NEWS OF HIM SHALL SEE,
AND THEY WHO HAVE NOT HEARD SHALL
UNDERSTAND."
22 For this reason I have often been prevented from coming to you;
23 but now, with no further place for me in these regions, and since I have had for many years a longing to come to you
24 whenever I go to Spain—for I hope to see you in passing, and to be helped on my way there by you, when I have first enjoyed your company for a while—
25 but now, I am going to Jerusalem serving the saints.
26 For Macedonia and Achaia have been pleased to make a contribution for the poor among the saints in Jerusalem.
27 Yes, they were pleased *to do so,* and they are indebted to them. For if the Gentiles have shared in their spiritual things, they are indebted to minister to them also in material things.
28 Therefore, when I have finished this, and have put my seal on this fruit of theirs, I will go on by way of you to Spain.
29 I know that when I come to you, I will come in the fullness of the blessing of Christ.
30 Now I urge you, brethren, by our Lord Jesus Christ and by the love of the Spirit, to strive together with me in your prayers to God for me,
31 that I may be rescued from those who are disobedient in Judea, and *that* my service for Jerusalem may prove acceptable to the saints;
32 so that I may come to you in joy by the will of God and find *refreshing* rest in your company.
33 Now the God of peace be with you all. Amen.

Greetings and Love Expressed

16 I commend to you our sister Phoebe, who is a servant of the church which is at Cenchrea;
2 that you receive her in the Lord in a manner worthy of the saints, and that you help her in whatever matter she may have need of you; for she herself has also been a helper of many, and of myself as well.
3 Greet Prisca and Aquila, my fellow workers in Christ Jesus,
4 who for my life risked their own necks, to whom not only do I give thanks, but also all the churches of the Gentiles;
5 also *greet* the church that is in their house. Greet Epaenetus, my beloved, who is the first convert to Christ from Asia.
6 Greet Mary, who has worked hard for you.
7 Greet Andronicus and Junias, my kinsmen and my fellow prisoners, who are outstanding among the apostles, who also were in Christ before me.
8 Greet Ampliatus, my beloved in the Lord.
9 Greet Urbanus, our fellow worker in Christ, and Stachys my beloved.
10 Greet Apelles, the approved in Christ. Greet those who are of the *household* of Aristobulus.
11 Greet Herodion, my kinsman. Greet those of the *household* of Narcissus, who are in the Lord.
12 Greet Tryphaena and Tryphosa, workers in the Lord. Greet Persis the beloved, who has worked hard in the Lord.
13 Greet Rufus, a choice man in the Lord, also his mother and mine.
14 Greet Asyncritus, Phlegon, Hermes, Patrobas, Hermas and the brethren with them.
15 Greet Philologus and Julia, Nereus and his sister, and Olympas, and all the saints who are with them.
16 Greet one another with a holy kiss. All the churches of Christ greet you.
17 Now I urge you, brethren, keep your eye on those who cause dissensions and hindrances contrary to the teaching which you learned, and turn away from them.
18 For such men are slaves, not of our Lord Christ but of their own appetites; and by their smooth and flattering speech they deceive the hearts of the unsuspecting.
19 For the report of your obedience has reached to all; therefore I am rejoicing over you, but I want you to be wise in what is good, and innocent in what is evil.
20 The God of peace will soon crush Satan under your feet.
The grace of our Lord Jesus be with you.
21 Timothy my fellow worker greets you, and *so do* Lucius and Jason and Sosipater, my kinsmen.
22 I, Tertius, who write this letter, greet you in the Lord.
23 Gaius, host to me and to the whole church, greets you. Erastus, the city treasurer greets you, and Quartus, the brother.
24 [¹The grace of our Lord Jesus Christ be with you all. Amen.]
25 Now to Him who is able to establish you according to my gospel and the preaching of Jesus Christ, according to the revelation of the mystery which has been kept secret for long ages past,
26 but now is manifested, and by the Scriptures of the prophets, according to the commandment of the eternal God, has been made known to all the nations, *leading* to obedience of faith;
27 to the only wise God, through Jesus Christ, be the glory forever. Amen.

---

1. Early mss do not contain this v

THE FIRST LETTER OF PAUL TO THE CORINTHIANS

Appeal to Unity

1 Paul, called *as* an apostle of Jesus Christ by the will of God, and Sosthenes our brother,

2 To the church of God which is at Corinth, to those who have been sanctified in Christ Jesus, saints by calling, with all who in every place call on the name of our Lord Jesus Christ, their *Lord* and ours:

3 Grace to you and peace from God our Father and the Lord Jesus Christ.

4 I thank ¹my God always concerning you for the grace of God which was given you in Christ Jesus,

5 that in everything you were enriched in Him, in all speech and all knowledge,

6 even as the testimony concerning Christ was confirmed in you,

7 so that you are not lacking in any gift, awaiting eagerly the revelation of our Lord Jesus Christ,

8 who will also confirm you to the end, blameless in the day of our Lord Jesus Christ.

9 God is faithful, through whom you were called into fellowship with His Son, Jesus Christ our Lord.

10 Now I exhort you, brethren, by the name of our Lord Jesus Christ, that you all agree and that there be no divisions among you, but that you be made complete in the same mind and in the same judgment.

11 For I have been informed concerning you, my brethren, by Chloe's *people*, that there are quarrels among you.

12 Now I mean this, that each one of you is saying, "I am of Paul," and "I of Apollos," and "I of Cephas," and "I of Christ."

13 Has Christ been divided? Paul was not crucified for you, was he? Or were you baptized in the name of Paul?

14 ²I thank God that I baptized none of you except Crispus and Gaius,

15 so that no one would say you were baptized in my name.

16 Now I did baptize also the household of Stephanas; beyond that, I do not know whether I baptized any other.

17 For Christ did not send me to baptize, but to preach the gospel, not in cleverness of speech, so that the cross of Christ would not be made void.

18 For the word of the cross is foolishness to those who are perishing, but to us who are being saved it is the power of God.

19 For it is written,

"I WILL DESTROY THE WISDOM OF THE WISE,
AND THE CLEVERNESS OF THE CLEVER I WILL
SET ASIDE."

20 Where is the wise man? Where is the scribe? Where is the debater of this age? Has not God made foolish the wisdom of the world?

21 For since in the wisdom of God the world through its wisdom did not *come to* know God,

God was well-pleased through the foolishness of the message preached to save those who believe.

22 For indeed Jews ask for signs and Greeks search for wisdom;

23 but we preach ³Christ crucified, to Jews a stumbling block and to Gentiles foolishness,

24 but to those who are the called, both Jews and Greeks, Christ the power of God and the wisdom of God.

25 Because the foolishness of God is wiser than men, and the weakness of God is stronger than men.

26 For consider your calling, brethren, that there were not many wise according to the flesh, not many mighty, not many noble;

27 but God has chosen the foolish things of the world to shame the wise, and God has chosen the weak things of the world to shame the things which are strong,

28 and the base things of the world and the despised God has chosen, the things that are not, so that He may nullify the things that are,

29 so that no man may boast before God.

30 But by His doing you are in Christ Jesus, who became to us wisdom from God, and righteousness and sanctification, and redemption,

31 so that, just as it is written, "LET HIM WHO BOASTS, BOAST IN THE LORD."

Paul's Reliance upon the Spirit

2 And when I came to you, brethren, I did not come with superiority of speech or of wisdom, proclaiming to you the ⁴testimony of God.

2 For I determined to know nothing among you except Jesus Christ, and Him crucified.

3 I was with you in weakness and in fear and in much trembling,

4 and my message and my preaching were not in persuasive words of wisdom, but in demonstration of the Spirit and of power,

5 so that your faith would not rest on the wisdom of men, but on the power of God.

6 Yet we do speak wisdom among those who are mature; a wisdom, however, not of this age nor of the rulers of this age, who are passing away;

7 but we speak God's wisdom in a mystery, the hidden *wisdom* which God predestined before the ages to our glory;

8 *the wisdom* which none of the rulers of this age has understood; for if they had understood it they would not have crucified the Lord of glory;

9 but just as it is written,

"THINGS WHICH EYE HAS NOT SEEN AND EAR
HAS NOT HEARD,
AND *which* HAVE NOT ENTERED THE HEART
OF MAN,
ALL THAT GOD HAS PREPARED FOR THOSE
WHO LOVE HIM."

1. Two early mss do not contain *my* 2. Two early mss read *I give thanks that* 3. I.e. Messiah 4. One early ms reads *mystery*

10 ¹For to us God revealed *them* through the Spirit; for the Spirit searches all things, even the depths of God.

11 For who among men knows the *thoughts* of a man except the spirit of the man which is in him? Even so the *thoughts* of God no one knows except the Spirit of God.

12 Now we have received, not the spirit of the world, but the Spirit who is from God, so that we may know the things freely given to us by God,

13 which things we also speak, not in words taught by human wisdom, but in those taught by the Spirit, combining spiritual *thoughts* with spiritual *words*.

14 But a natural man does not accept the things of the Spirit of God, for they are foolishness to him; and he cannot understand them, because they are spiritually appraised.

15 But he who is spiritual appraises all things, yet he himself is appraised by no one.

16 For WHO HAS KNOWN THE MIND OF THE LORD, THAT HE WILL INSTRUCT HIM? But we have the mind of Christ.

Foundations for Living

3 And I, brethren, could not speak to you as to spiritual men, but as to men of flesh, as to infants in Christ.

2 I gave you milk to drink, not solid food; for you were not yet able *to receive it*. Indeed, even now you are not yet able,

3 for you are still fleshly. For since there is jealousy and strife among you, are you not fleshly, and are you not walking like mere men?

4 For when one says, "I am of Paul," and another, "I am of Apollos," are you not *mere* men?

5 What then is Apollos? And what is Paul? Servants through whom you believed, even as the Lord gave *opportunity* to each one.

6 I planted, Apollos watered, but God was causing the growth.

7 So then neither the one who plants nor the one who waters is anything, but God who causes the growth.

8 Now he who plants and he who waters are one; but each will receive his own reward according to his own labor.

9 For we are God's fellow workers; you are God's field, God's building.

10 According to the grace of God which was given to me, like a wise master builder I laid a foundation, and another is building on it. But each man must be careful how he builds on it.

11 For no man can lay a foundation other than the one which is laid, which is Jesus Christ.

12 Now if any man builds on the foundation with gold, silver, precious stones, wood, hay, straw,

13 each man's work will become evident; for the day will show it because it is *to be* revealed with fire, and the fire itself will test the quality of each man's work.

14 If any man's work which he has built on it remains, he will receive a reward.

15 If any man's work is burned up, he will suffer loss; but he himself will be saved, yet so as through fire.

16 Do you not know that you are a temple of God and *that* the Spirit of God dwells in you?

17 If any man destroys the temple of God, God will destroy him, for the temple of God is holy, and that is what you are.

18 Let no man deceive himself. If any man among you thinks that he is wise in this age, he must become foolish, so that he may become wise.

19 For the wisdom of this world is foolishness before God. For it is written, "*He is* THE ONE WHO CATCHES THE WISE IN THEIR CRAFTINESS";

20 and again, "THE LORD KNOWS THE REASONINGS of the wise, THAT THEY ARE USELESS."

21 So then let no one boast in men. For all things belong to you,

22 whether Paul or Apollos or Cephas or the world or life or death or things present or things to come; all things belong to you,

23 and you belong to Christ; and Christ belongs to God.

Servants of Christ

4 Let a man regard us in this manner, as servants of Christ and stewards of the mysteries of God.

2 In this case, moreover, it is required of stewards that one be found trustworthy.

3 But to me it is a very small thing that I may be examined by you, or by *any* human court; in fact, I do not even examine myself.

4 For I am conscious of nothing against myself, yet I am not by this acquitted; but the one who examines me is the Lord.

5 Therefore do not go on passing judgment before ²the time, *but wait* until the Lord comes who will both bring to light the things hidden in the darkness and disclose the motives of *men's* hearts; and then each man's praise will come to him from God.

6 Now these things, brethren, I have figuratively applied to myself and Apollos for your sakes, so that in us you may learn not to exceed what is written, so that no one of you will become arrogant in behalf of one against the other.

7 For who regards you as superior? What do you have that you did not receive? And if you did receive it, why do you boast as if you had not received it?

8 You are already filled, you have already become rich, you have become kings without us; and indeed, *I* wish that you had become kings so that we also might reign with you.

9 For, I think, God has exhibited us apostles last of all, as men condemned to death; because we have become a spectacle to the world, both to angels and to men.

10 We are fools for Christ's sake, but you are prudent in Christ; we are weak, but you are

---

1. One early ms reads *But* 2. I.e. the appointed time of judgment

strong; you are distinguished, but we are without honor.

11 To this present hour we are both hungry and thirsty, and are poorly clothed, and are roughly treated, and are homeless;

12 and we toil, working with our own hands; when we are reviled, we bless; when we are persecuted, we endure;

13 when we are slandered, we try to conciliate; we have become as the scum of the world, the dregs of all things, *even* until now.

14 I do not write these things to shame you, but to admonish you as my beloved children.

15 For if you were to have countless tutors in Christ, yet *you would* not *have* many fathers, for in Christ Jesus I became your father through the gospel.

16 Therefore I exhort you, be imitators of me.

17 For this reason I have sent to you Timothy, who is my beloved and faithful child in the Lord, and he will remind you of my ways which are in Christ, just as I teach everywhere in every church.

18 Now some have become arrogant, as though I were not coming to you.

19 But I will come to you soon, if the Lord wills, and I shall find out, not the words of those who are arrogant but their power.

20 For the kingdom of God does not consist in words but in power.

21 What do you desire? Shall I come to you with a rod, or with love and a spirit of gentleness?

Immorality Rebuked

5 It is actually reported that there is immorality among you, and immorality of such a kind as does not exist even among the Gentiles, that someone has his father's wife.

2 You have become arrogant and have not mourned instead, so that the one who had done this deed would be removed from your midst.

3 For I, on my part, though absent in body but present in spirit, have already judged him who has so committed this, as though I were present.

4 In the name of our Lord Jesus, when you are assembled, and I with you in spirit, with the power of our Lord Jesus,

5 I *have decided* to deliver such a one to Satan for the destruction of his flesh, so that his spirit may be saved in the day of the Lord [1]Jesus.

6 Your boasting is not good. Do you not know that a little leaven leavens the whole lump *of dough?*

7 Clean out the old leaven so that you may be a new lump, just as you are *in fact* unleavened. For Christ our Passover also has been sacrificed.

8 Therefore let us celebrate the feast, not with old leaven, nor with the leaven of malice and wickedness, but with the unleavened bread of sincerity and truth.

9 I wrote you in my letter not to associate with immoral people;

10 I *did* not at all *mean* with the immoral people of this world, or with the covetous and swindlers, or with idolaters, for then you would have to go out of the world.

11 But actually, I wrote to you not to associate with any so-called brother if he is an immoral person, or covetous, or an idolater, or a reviler, or a drunkard, or a swindler—not even to eat with such a one.

12 For what have I to do with judging outsiders? Do you not judge those who are within *the church?*

13 But those who are outside, God judges. REMOVE THE WICKED MAN FROM AMONG YOURSELVES.

Lawsuits Discouraged

6 Does any one of you, when he has a case against his neighbor, dare to go to law before the unrighteous and not before the saints?

2 Or do you not know that the saints will judge the world? If the world is judged by you, are you not competent *to constitute* the smallest law courts?

3 Do you not know that we will judge angels? How much more matters of this life?

4 So if you have law courts dealing with matters of this life, do you appoint them as judges who are of no account in the church?

5 I say *this* to your shame. *Is it* so, *that* there is not among you one wise man who will be able to decide between his brethren,

6 but brother goes to law with brother, and that before unbelievers?

7 Actually, then, it is already a defeat for you, that you have lawsuits with one another. Why not rather be wronged? Why not rather be defrauded?

8 On the contrary, you yourselves wrong and defraud. *You do* this even to *your* brethren.

9 Or do you not know that the unrighteous will not inherit the kingdom of God? Do not be deceived; neither fornicators, nor idolaters, nor adulterers, nor [2]effeminate, nor homosexuals,

10 nor thieves, nor *the* covetous, nor drunkards, nor revilers, nor swindlers, will inherit the kingdom of God.

11 Such were some of you; but you were washed, but you were sanctified, but you were justified in the name of the Lord Jesus Christ and in the Spirit of our God.

12 All things are lawful for me, but not all things are profitable. All things are lawful for me, but I will not be mastered by anything.

13 Food is for the stomach and the stomach is for food, but God will do away with both of them. Yet the body is not for immorality, but for the Lord, and the Lord is for the body.

14 Now God has not only raised the Lord, but will also raise us up through His power.

15 Do you not know that your bodies are members of Christ? Shall I then take away the members of Christ and make them members of a prostitute? May it never be!

16 Or do you not know that the one who joins

washed, sanctified, justified

---

1. Two early mss do not contain *Jesus* 2. **I.e. effeminate by perversion**

How can you experience this washing? Read Hebrews 5:8, 9 on page 171.

himself to a prostitute is one body *with her?* For He says, "THE TWO SHALL BECOME ONE FLESH."

17 But the one who joins himself to the Lord is one spirit *with Him.*

18 Flee immorality. Every *other* sin that a man commits is outside the body, but the immoral man sins against his own body.

19 Or do you not know that your body is a temple of the Holy Spirit who is in you, whom you have from God, and that you are not your own?

20 For you have been bought with a price: therefore glorify God in your body.

Teaching on Marriage

7 Now concerning the things about which you wrote, it is good for a man not to touch a woman.

2 But because of immoralities, each man is to have his own wife, and each woman is to have her own husband.

3 The husband must fulfill his duty to his wife, and likewise also the wife to her husband.

4 The wife does not have authority over her own body, but the husband *does;* and likewise also the husband does not have authority over his own body, but the wife *does.*

5 Stop depriving one another, except by agreement for a time, so that you may devote yourselves to prayer, and come together again so that Satan will not tempt you because of your lack of self-control.

6 But this I say by way of concession, not of command.

7 ¹Yet I wish that all men were even as I myself am. However, each man has his own gift from God, one in this manner, and another in that.

8 But I say to the unmarried and to widows that it is good for them if they remain even as I.

9 But if they do not have self-control, let them marry; for it is better to marry than to burn *with passion.*

10 But to the married I give instructions, not I, but the Lord, that the wife should not leave her husband

11 (but if she does leave, she must remain unmarried, or else be reconciled to her husband), and that the husband should not divorce his wife.

12 But to the rest I say, not the Lord, that if any brother has a wife who is an unbeliever, and she consents to live with him, he must not divorce her.

13 And a woman who has an unbelieving husband, and he consents to live with her, she must not send her husband away.

14 For the unbelieving husband is sanctified through his wife, and the unbelieving wife is sanctified through her believing husband; for otherwise your children are unclean, but now they are holy.

15 Yet if the unbelieving one leaves, let him leave; the brother or the sister is not under bondage in such *cases,* but God has called ²us to peace.

16 For how do you know, O wife, whether you will save your husband? Or how do you know, O husband, whether you will save your wife?

17 Only, as the Lord has assigned to each one, as God has called each, in this manner let him walk. And so I direct in all the churches.

18 Was any man called *when he was already* circumcised? He is not to become uncircumcised. Has anyone been called in uncircumcision? He is not to be circumcised.

19 Circumcision is nothing, and uncircumcision is nothing, but *what matters is* the keeping of the commandments of God.

20 Each man must remain in that condition in which he was called.

21 Were you called while a slave? Do not worry about it; but if you are able also to become free, rather do that.

22 For he who was called in the Lord while a slave, is the Lord's freedman; likewise he who was called while free, is Christ's slave.

23 You were bought with a price; do not become slaves of men.

24 Brethren, each one is to remain with God in that *condition* in which he was called.

25 Now concerning virgins I have no command of the Lord, but I give an opinion as one who by the mercy of the Lord is trustworthy.

26 I think then that this is good in view of the present distress, that it is good for a man to remain as he is.

27 Are you bound to a wife? Do not seek to be released. Are you released from a wife? Do not seek a wife.

28 But if you marry, you have not sinned; and if a virgin marries, she has not sinned. Yet such will have trouble in this life, and I am trying to spare you.

29 But this I say, brethren, the time has been shortened, so that from now on those who have wives should be as though they had none;

30 and those who weep, as though they did not weep; and those who rejoice, as though they did not rejoice; and those who buy, as though they did not possess;

31 and those who use the world, as though they did not make full use of it; for the form of this world is passing away.

32 But I want you to be free from concern. One who is unmarried is concerned about the things of the Lord, how he may please the Lord;

33 but one who is married is concerned about the things of the world, how he may please his wife,

34 and *his interests* are divided. The woman who is unmarried, and the virgin, is concerned about the things of the Lord, that she may be holy both in body and spirit; but one who is married is concerned about the things of the world, how she may please her husband.

35 This I say for your own benefit; not to put a restraint upon you, but to promote what is appropriate and *to secure* undistracted devotion to the Lord.

---

1. One early ms reads *For*   2. One early ms reads *you*

36 But if any man thinks that he is acting unbecomingly toward his virgin *daughter,* if she is past her youth, and if it must be so, let him do what he wishes, he does not sin; let her marry.

37 But he who stands firm in his heart, being under no constraint, but has authority over his own will, and has decided this in his own heart, to keep his own virgin *daughter,* he will do well.

38 So then both he who gives his own virgin *daughter* in marriage does well, and he who does not give her in marriage will do better.

39 A wife is bound as long as her husband lives; but if her husband is dead, she is free to be married to whom she wishes, only in the Lord.

40 But in my opinion she is happier if she remains as she is; and I think that I also have the Spirit of God.

Take Care with Your Liberty

8 Now concerning things sacrificed to idols, we know that we all have knowledge. Knowledge makes arrogant, but love edifies.

2 If anyone supposes that he knows anything, he has not yet known as he ought to know;

3 but if anyone loves God, he is known by Him.

4 Therefore concerning the eating of things sacrificed to idols, we know that ¹there is no such thing as an idol in the world, and that there is no God but one.

5 For even if there are so-called gods whether in heaven or on earth, as indeed there are many gods and many lords,

6 yet for us there is *but* one God, the Father, from whom are all things and we *exist* for Him; and one Lord, Jesus Christ, by whom are all things, and we *exist* through Him.

7 However not all men have this knowledge; but some, being accustomed to the idol until now, eat *food* as if it were sacrificed to an idol; and their conscience being weak is defiled.

8 But food will not commend us to God; we are neither the worse if we do not eat, nor the better if we do eat.

9 But take care that this liberty of yours does not somehow become a stumbling block to the weak.

10 For if someone sees you, who have knowledge, dining in an idol's temple, will not his conscience, if he is weak, be strengthened to eat things sacrificed to idols?

11 For through your knowledge he who is weak is ruined, the brother for whose sake Christ died.

12 And so, by sinning against the brethren and wounding their conscience when it is weak, you sin against Christ.

13 Therefore, if food causes my brother to stumble, I will never eat meat again, so that I will not cause my brother to stumble.

Paul's Use of Liberty

9 Am I not free? Am I not an apostle? Have I not seen Jesus our Lord? Are you not my work in the Lord?

2 If to others I am not an apostle, at least I am to you; for you are the seal of my apostleship in the Lord.

3 My defense to those who examine me is this:

4 Do we not have a right to eat and drink?

5 Do we not have a right to take along a believing wife, even as the rest of the apostles and the brothers of the Lord and Cephas?

6 Or do only Barnabas and I not have a right to refrain from working?

7 Who at any time serves as a soldier at his own expense? Who plants a vineyard and does not eat the fruit of it? Or who tends a flock and does not use the milk of the flock?

8 I am not speaking these things according to human judgment, am I? Or does not the Law also say these things?

9 For it is written in the Law of Moses, "You SHALL NOT MUZZLE THE OX WHILE HE IS THRESHING." God is not concerned about oxen, is He?

10 Or is He speaking altogether for our sake? Yes, for our sake it was written, because the plowman ought to plow in hope, and the thresher *to thresh* in hope of sharing *the crops.*

11 If we sowed spiritual things in you, is it too much if we reap material things from you?

12 If others share the right over you, do we not more? Nevertheless, we did not use this right, but we endure all things so that we will cause no hindrance to the gospel of Christ.

13 Do you not know that those who perform sacred services eat the *food* of the temple, *and* those who attend regularly to the altar have their share from the altar?

14 So also the Lord directed those who proclaim the gospel to get their living from the gospel.

15 But I have used none of these things. And I am not writing these things so that it will be done so in my case; for it would be better for me to die than have any man make my boast an empty one.

16 For if I preach the gospel, I have nothing to boast of, for I am under compulsion; for woe is me if I do not preach the gospel.

17 For if I do this voluntarily, I have a reward; but if against my will, I have a stewardship entrusted to me.

18 What then is my reward? That, when I preach the gospel, I may offer the gospel without charge, so as not to make full use of my right in the gospel.

19 For though I am free from all *men,* I have made myself a slave to all, so that I may win more.

20 To the Jews I became as a Jew, so that I might win Jews; to those who are under the Law, as under the Law though not being myself under the Law, so that I might win those who are under the Law;

21 to those who are without law, as without law, though not being without the law of God but under the law of Christ, so that I might win those who are without law.

---

1. Lit *nothing is an idol in the world;* i.e. an idol has no real existence

22 To the weak I became weak, that I might win the weak; I have become all things to all men, so that I may by all means save some.

23 I do all things for the sake of the gospel, so that I may become a fellow partaker of it.

24 Do you not know that those who run in a race all run, but *only* one receives the prize? Run in such a way that you may win.

25 Everyone who competes in the games exercises self-control in all things. They then *do it* to receive a perishable wreath, but we an imperishable.

26 Therefore I run in such a way, as not without aim; I box in such a way, as not beating the air;

27 but I discipline my body and make it my slave, so that, after I have preached to others, I myself will not be disqualified.

Avoid Israel's Mistakes

10 For I do not want you to be unaware, brethren, that our fathers were all under the cloud and all passed through the sea;

2 and all were baptized into Moses in the cloud and in the sea;

3 and all ate the same spiritual food;

4 and all drank the same spiritual drink, for they were drinking from a spiritual rock which followed them; and the rock was Christ.

5 Nevertheless, with most of them God was not well-pleased; for they were laid low in the wilderness.

6 Now these things happened as examples for us, so that we would not crave evil things as they also craved.

7 Do not be idolaters, as some of them were; as it is written, "THE PEOPLE SAT DOWN TO EAT AND DRINK, AND STOOD UP TO PLAY."

8 Nor let us act immorally, as some of them did, and twenty-three thousand fell in one day.

9 Nor let us try the Lord, as some of them did, and were destroyed by the serpents.

10 Nor grumble, as some of them did, and were destroyed by the destroyer.

11 Now these things happened to them as an example, and they were written for our instruction, upon whom the ends of the ages have come.

12 Therefore let him who thinks he stands take heed that he does not fall.

13 No temptation has overtaken you but such as is common to man; and God is faithful, who will not allow you to be tempted beyond what you are able, but with the temptation will provide the way of escape also, so that you will be able to endure it.

14 Therefore, my beloved, flee from idolatry.

15 I speak as to wise men; you judge what I say.

16 Is not the cup of blessing which we bless a sharing in the blood of Christ? Is not the bread which we break a sharing in the body of Christ?

17 Since there is one bread, we who are many are one body; for we all partake of the one bread.

18 Look at the nation Israel; are not those who eat the sacrifices sharers in the altar?

19 What do I mean then? That a thing sacrificed to idols is anything, or that an idol is anything?

20 *No,* but *I say* that the things which the Gentiles sacrifice, they sacrifice to demons and not to God; and I do not want you to become sharers in demons.

21 You cannot drink the cup of the Lord and the cup of demons; you cannot partake of the table of the Lord and the table of demons.

22 Or do we provoke the Lord to jealousy? We are not stronger than He, are we?

23 All things are lawful, but not all things are profitable. All things are lawful, but not all things edify.

24 Let no one seek his own *good,* but that of his neighbor.

25 Eat anything that is sold in the meat market without asking questions for conscience' sake;

26 FOR THE EARTH IS THE LORD'S, AND ALL IT CONTAINS.

27 If one of the unbelievers invites you and you want to go, eat anything that is set before you without asking questions for conscience' sake.

28 But if anyone says to you, "This is meat sacrificed to idols," do not eat *it,* for the sake of the one who informed *you,* and for conscience' sake;

29 I mean not your own conscience, but the other *man's;* for why is my freedom judged by another's conscience?

30 If I partake with thankfulness, why am I slandered concerning that for which I give thanks?

31 Whether, then, you eat or drink or whatever you do, do all to the glory of God.

32 Give no offense either to Jews or to Greeks or to the church of God;

33 just as I also please all men in all things, not seeking my own profit but the *profit* of the many, so that they may be saved.

Christian Order

11 Be imitators of me, just as I also am of Christ.

2 Now I praise you because you remember me in everything and hold firmly to the traditions, just as I delivered them to you.

3 But I want you to understand that Christ is the head of every man, and the man is the head of a woman, and God is the head of Christ.

4 Every man who has *something* on his head while praying or prophesying disgraces his head.

5 But every woman who has her head uncovered while praying or prophesying disgraces her head, for she is one and the same as the woman whose head is shaved.

6 For if a woman does not cover her head, let her also have her hair cut off; but if it is disgraceful for a woman to have her hair cut off or her head shaved, let her cover her head.

7 For a man ought not to have his head covered, since he is the image and glory of God; but the woman is the glory of man.

8 For man does not originate from woman, but woman from man;

9 for indeed man was not created for the woman's sake, but woman for the man's sake.

10 Therefore the woman ought to have *a symbol of* authority on her head, because of the angels.

11 However, in the Lord, neither is woman independent of man, nor is man independent of woman.

12 For as the woman originates from the man, so also the man *has his birth* through the woman; and all things originate from God.

13 Judge for yourselves: is it proper for a woman to pray to God *with her head* uncovered?

14 Does not even nature itself teach you that if a man has long hair, it is a dishonor to him,

15 but if a woman has long hair, it is a glory to her? For her hair is given to her for a covering.

16 But if one is inclined to be contentious, we have no other practice, nor have the churches of God.

17 But in giving this instruction, I do not praise you, because you come together not for the better but for the worse.

18 For, in the first place, when you come together as a church, I hear that divisions exist among you; and in part I believe it.

19 For there must also be factions among you, so that those who are approved may become evident among you.

20 Therefore when you meet together, it is not to eat the Lord's Supper,

21 for in your eating each one takes his own supper first; and one is hungry and another is drunk.

22 What! Do you not have houses in which to eat and drink? Or do you despise the church of God and shame those who have nothing? What shall I say to you? Shall I praise you? In this I will not praise you.

23 For I received from the Lord that which I also delivered to you, that the Lord Jesus in the night in which He was betrayed took bread;

24 and when He had given thanks, He broke it and said, "This is My body, which is for you; do this in remembrance of Me."

25 In the same way *He took* the cup also after supper, saying, "This cup is the new covenant in My blood; do this, as often as you drink *it,* in remembrance of Me."

26 For as often as you eat this bread and drink the cup, you proclaim the Lord's death until He comes.

27 Therefore whoever eats the bread or drinks the cup of the Lord in an unworthy manner, shall be guilty of the body and the blood of the Lord.

28 But a man must examine himself, and in so doing he is to eat of the bread and drink of the cup.

29 For he who eats and drinks, eats and drinks judgment to himself if he does not judge the body rightly.

30 For this reason many among you are weak and sick, and a number sleep.

31 But if we judged ourselves rightly, we would not be judged.

32 But when we are judged, we are disciplined by the Lord so that we will not be condemned along with the world.

33 So then, my brethren, when you come together to eat, wait for one another.

34 If anyone is hungry, let him eat at home, so that you will not come together for judgment. The remaining matters I will arrange when I come.

The Use of Spiritual Gifts

12 Now concerning spiritual *gifts,* brethren, I do not want you to be unaware.

2 You know that when you were pagans, *you were* led astray to the mute idols, however you were led.

3 Therefore I make known to you that no one speaking by the Spirit of God says, "Jesus is accursed"; and no one can say, "Jesus is Lord," except by the Holy Spirit.

4 Now there are varieties of gifts, but the same Spirit.

5 And there are varieties of ministries, and the same Lord.

6 There are varieties of effects, but the same God who works all things in all *persons.*

7 But to each one is given the manifestation of the Spirit for the common good.

8 For to one is given the word of wisdom through the Spirit, and to another the word of knowledge according to the same Spirit;

9 to another faith by the same Spirit, and to another gifts of healing by the one Spirit,

10 and to another the effecting of miracles, and to another prophecy, and to another the distinguishing of spirits, to another *various* kinds of tongues, and to another the interpretation of tongues.

11 But one and the same Spirit works all these things, distributing to each one individually just as He wills.

12 For even as the body is one and *yet* has many members, and all the members of the body, though they are many, are one body, so also is Christ.

13 For by one Spirit we were all baptized into one body, whether Jews or Greeks, whether slaves or free, and we were all made to drink of one Spirit.

14 For the body is not one member, but many.

15 If the foot says, "Because I am not a hand, I am not *a part* of the body," it is not for this reason any the less *a part* of the body.

16 And if the ear says, "Because I am not an eye, I am not *a part* of the body," it is not for this reason any the less *a part* of the body.

17 If the whole body were an eye, where would the hearing be? If the whole were hearing, where would the sense of smell be?

18 But now God has placed the members, each one of them, in the body, just as He desired.

19 If they were all one member, where would the body be?

20 But now there are many members, but one body.

21 And the eye cannot say to the hand, "I have no need of you"; or again the head to the feet, "I have no need of you."

22 On the contrary, it is much truer that the members of the body which seem to be weaker are necessary;

23 and those *members* of the body which we deem less honorable, on these we bestow more abundant honor, and our less presentable members become much more presentable,

24 whereas our more presentable members have no need *of it.* But God has *so* composed the body, giving more abundant honor to that *member* which lacked,

25 so that there may be no division in the body, but *that* the members may have the same care for one another.

26 And if one member suffers, all the members suffer with it; if *one* member is honored, all the members rejoice with it.

27 Now you are Christ's body, and individually members of it.

28 And God has appointed in the church, first apostles, second prophets, third teachers, then miracles, then gifts of healings, helps, administrations, *various* kinds of tongues.

29 All are not apostles, are they? All are not prophets, are they? All are not teachers, are they? All are not *workers of* miracles, are they?

30 All do not have gifts of healings, do they? All do not speak with tongues, do they? All do not interpret, do they?

31 But earnestly desire the greater gifts. And I show you a still more excellent way.

The Excellence of Love

13 If I speak with the tongues of men and of angels, but do not have love, I have become a noisy gong or a clanging cymbal.

2 If I have *the gift of* prophecy, and know all mysteries and all knowledge; and if I have all faith, so as to remove mountains, but do not have love, I am nothing.

3 And if I give all my possessions to feed *the poor,* and if I surrender my body [1]to be burned, but do not have love, it profits me nothing.

4 Love is patient, love is kind *and* is not jealous; love does not brag *and* is not arrogant,

5 does not act unbecomingly; it does not seek its own, is not provoked, does not take into account a wrong *suffered,*

6 does not rejoice in unrighteousness, but rejoices with the truth;

7 bears all things, believes all things, hopes all things, endures all things.

8 Love never fails; but if *there are gifts of* prophecy, they will be done away; if *there are* tongues, they will cease; if *there is* knowledge, it will be done away.

9 For we know in part and we prophesy in part;

10 but when the perfect comes, the partial will be done away.

11 When I was a child, I used to speak like a child, think like a child, reason like a child; when I became a man, I did away with childish things.

12 For now we see in a mirror dimly, but then face to face; now I know in part, but then I will know fully just as I also have been fully known.

13 But now faith, hope, love, abide these three; but the greatest of these is love.

Prophecy a Superior Gift

14 Pursue love, yet desire earnestly spiritual *gifts,* but especially that you may prophesy.

2 For one who speaks in a tongue does not speak to men but to God; for no one understands, but in *his* spirit he speaks mysteries.

3 But one who prophesies speaks to men for edification and exhortation and consolation.

4 One who speaks in a tongue edifies himself; but one who prophesies edifies the church.

5 Now I wish that you all spoke in tongues, but *even* more that you would prophesy; and greater is one who prophesies than one who speaks in tongues, unless he interprets, so that the church may receive edifying.

6 But now, brethren, if I come to you speaking in tongues, what will I profit you unless I speak to you either by way of revelation or of knowledge or of prophecy or of teaching?

7 Yet *even* lifeless things, either flute or harp, in producing a sound, if they do not produce a distinction in the tones, how will it be known what is played on the flute or on the harp?

8 For if the bugle produces an indistinct sound, who will prepare himself for battle?

9 So also you, unless you utter by the tongue speech that is clear, how will it be known what is spoken? For you will be speaking into the air.

10 There are, perhaps, a great many kinds of languages in the world, and no *kind* is without meaning.

11 If then I do not know the meaning of the language, I will be to the one who speaks a barbarian, and the one who speaks will be a barbarian to me.

12 So also you, since you are zealous of spiritual *gifts,* seek to abound for the edification of the church.

13 Therefore let one who speaks in a tongue pray that he may interpret.

14 For if I pray in a tongue, my spirit prays, but my mind is unfruitful.

15 What is *the outcome* then? I will pray with the spirit and I will pray with the mind also; I will sing with the spirit and I will sing with the mind also.

16 Otherwise if you bless in the spirit *only,* how will the one who fills the place of the ungifted say the "Amen" at your giving of thanks, since he does not know what you are saying?

1. Early mss read *that I may boast*

17 For you are giving thanks well enough, but the other person is not edified.

18 I thank God, I speak in tongues more than you all;

19 however, in the church I desire to speak five words with my mind so that I may instruct others also, rather than ten thousand words in a tongue.

20 Brethren, do not be children in your thinking; yet in evil be infants, but in your thinking be mature.

21 In the Law it is written, "BY MEN OF STRANGE TONGUES AND BY THE LIPS OF STRANGERS I WILL SPEAK TO THIS PEOPLE, AND EVEN SO THEY WILL NOT LISTEN TO ME," says the Lord.

22 So then tongues are for a sign, not to those who believe but to unbelievers; but prophecy is for a sign, not to unbelievers but to those who believe.

23 Therefore if the whole church assembles together and all speak in tongues, and ungifted men or unbelievers enter, will they not say that you are mad?

24 But if all prophesy, and an unbeliever or an ungifted man enters, he is convicted by all, he is called to account by all;

25 the secrets of his heart are disclosed; and so he will fall on his face and worship God, declaring that God is certainly among you.

26 What is the outcome then, brethren? When you assemble, each one has a psalm, has a teaching, has a revelation, has a tongue, has an interpretation. Let all things be done for edification.

27 If anyone speaks in a tongue, it should be by two or at the most three, and each in turn, and one must interpret;

28 but if there is no interpreter, he must keep silent in the church; and let him speak to himself and to God.

29 Let two or three prophets speak, and let the others pass judgment.

30 But if a revelation is made to another who is seated, the first one must keep silent.

31 For you can all prophesy one by one, so that all may learn and all may be exhorted;

32 and the spirits of prophets are subject to prophets;

33 for God is not a God of confusion but of peace, as in all the churches of the saints.

34 The women are to keep silent in the churches; for they are not permitted to speak, but are to subject themselves, just as the Law also says.

35 If they desire to learn anything, let them ask their own husbands at home; for it is improper for a woman to speak in church.

36 Was it from you that the word of God first went forth? Or has it come to you only?

37 If anyone thinks he is a prophet or spiritual, let him recognize that the things which I write to you are the Lord's commandment.

38 But if anyone does not recognize this, he [1]is not recognized.

39 Therefore, my brethren, desire earnestly to prophesy, and do not forbid to speak in tongues.

40 But all things must be done properly and in an orderly manner.

The Fact of Christ's Resurrection

15 Now I make known to you, brethren, the gospel which I preached to you, which also you received, in which also you stand,

2 by which also you are saved, if you hold fast the word which I preached to you, unless you believed in vain.

3 For I delivered to you as of first importance what I also received, that Christ died for our sins according to the Scriptures,

4 and that He was buried, and that He was raised on the third day according to the Scriptures,

5 and that He appeared to Cephas, then to the twelve.

6 After that He appeared to more than five hundred brethren at one time, most of whom remain until now, but some have fallen asleep;

7 then He appeared to James, then to all the apostles;

8 and last of all, as to one untimely born, He appeared to me also.

9 For I am the least of the apostles, and not fit to be called an apostle, because I persecuted the church of God.

10 But by the grace of God I am what I am, and His grace toward me did not prove vain; but I labored even more than all of them, yet not I, but the grace of God with me.

11 Whether then it was I or they, so we preach and so you believed.

12 Now if Christ is preached, that He has been raised from the dead, how do some among you say that there is no resurrection of the dead?

13 But if there is no resurrection of the dead, not even Christ has been raised;

14 and if Christ has not been raised, then our preaching is vain, your faith also is vain.

15 Moreover we are even found to be false witnesses of God, because we testified against God that He raised [2]Christ, whom He did not raise, if in fact the dead are not raised.

16 For if the dead are not raised, not even Christ has been raised;

17 and if Christ has not been raised, your faith is worthless; you are still in your sins.

18 Then those also who have fallen asleep in Christ have perished.

19 If we have hoped in Christ in this life only, we are of all men most to be pitied.

20 But now Christ has been raised from the dead, the first fruits of those who are asleep.

21 For since by a man came death, by a man also came the resurrection of the dead.

22 For as in Adam all die, so also in Christ all will be made alive.

23 But each in his own order: Christ the first fruits, after that those who are Christ's at His coming,

gospel - death - burial - resurrection

---

1. Two early mss read is not to be recognized   2. I.e. the Messiah

24 then *comes* the end, when He hands over the kingdom to the God and Father, when He has abolished all rule and all authority and power.

25 For He must reign until He has put all His enemies under His feet.

26 The last enemy that will be abolished is death.

27 For HE HAS PUT ALL THINGS IN SUBJECTION UNDER HIS FEET. But when He says, "All things are put in subjection," it is evident that He is excepted who put all things in subjection to Him.

28 When all things are subjected to Him, then the Son Himself also will be subjected to the One who subjected all things to Him, so that God may be all in all.

29 Otherwise, what will those do who are baptized for the dead? If the dead are not raised at all, why then are they baptized for them?

30 Why are we also in danger every hour?

31 I affirm, brethren, by the boasting in you which I have in Christ Jesus our Lord, I die daily.

32 If from human motives I fought with wild beasts at Ephesus, what does it profit me? If the dead are not raised, LET US EAT AND DRINK, FOR TOMORROW WE DIE.

33 Do not be deceived: "Bad company corrupts good morals."

34 Become sober-minded as you ought, and stop sinning; for some have no knowledge of God. I speak *this* to your shame.

35 But someone will say, "How are the dead raised? And with what kind of body do they come?"

36 You fool! That which you sow does not come to life unless it dies;

37 and that which you sow, you do not sow the body which is to be, but a bare grain, perhaps of wheat or of something else.

38 But God gives it a body just as He wished, and to each of the seeds a body of its own.

39 All flesh is not the same flesh, but there is one *flesh* of men, and another flesh of beasts, and another flesh of birds, and another of fish.

40 There are also heavenly bodies and earthly bodies, but the glory of the heavenly is one, and the *glory* of the earthly is another.

41 There is one glory of the sun, and another glory of the moon, and another glory of the stars; for star differs from star in glory.

42 So also is the resurrection of the dead. It is sown a perishable *body*, it is raised an imperishable *body;*

43 it is sown in dishonor, it is raised in glory; it is sown in weakness, it is raised in power;

44 it is sown a natural body, it is raised a spiritual body. If there is a natural body, there is also a spiritual *body.*

45 So also it is written, "The first MAN, Adam, BECAME A LIVING SOUL." The last Adam *became* a life-giving spirit.

46 However, the spiritual is not first, but the natural; then the spiritual.

47 The first man is from the earth, earthy; the second man is from heaven.

48 As is the earthy, so also are those who are earthy; and as is the heavenly, so also are those who are heavenly.

49 Just as we have borne the image of the earthy, [1]we will also bear the image of the heavenly.

50 Now I say this, brethren, that flesh and blood cannot inherit the kingdom of God; nor does the perishable inherit the imperishable.

51 Behold, I tell you a mystery; we will not all sleep, but we will all be changed,

52 in a moment, in the twinkling of an eye, at the last trumpet; for the trumpet will sound, and the dead will be raised imperishable, and we will be changed.

53 For this perishable must put on the imperishable, and this mortal must put on immortality.

54 But when this perishable will have put on the imperishable, and this mortal will have put on immortality, then will come about the saying that is written, "DEATH IS SWALLOWED UP in victory.

55 "O DEATH, WHERE IS YOUR VICTORY? O DEATH, WHERE IS YOUR STING?"

56 The sting of death is sin, and the power of sin is the law;

57 but thanks be to God, who gives us the victory through our Lord Jesus Christ.

58 Therefore, my beloved brethren, be steadfast, immovable, always abounding in the work of the Lord, knowing that your toil is not *in* vain in the Lord.

Instructions and Greetings

16 Now concerning the collection for the saints, as I directed the churches of Galatia, so do you also.

2 On the first day of every week each one of you is to put aside and save, as he may prosper, so that no collections be made when I come.

3 When I arrive, whomever you may approve, I will send them with letters to carry your gift to Jerusalem;

4 and if it is fitting for me to go also, they will go with me.

5 But I will come to you after I go through Macedonia, for I am going through Macedonia;

6 and perhaps I will stay with you, or even spend the winter, so that you may send me on my way wherever I may go.

7 For I do not wish to see you now *just* in passing; for I hope to remain with you for some time, if the Lord permits.

8 But I will remain in Ephesus until Pentecost;

9 for a wide door for effective *service* has opened to me, and there are many adversaries.

10 Now if Timothy comes, see that he is with you without cause to be afraid, for he is doing the Lord's work, as I also am.

11 So let no one despise him. But send him on his way in peace, so that he may come to me; for I expect him with the brethren.

---

1. Two early mss read *let us also*

12 But concerning Apollos our brother, I encouraged him greatly to come to you with the brethren; and it was not at all *his* desire to come now, but he will come when he has opportunity.

13 Be on the alert, stand firm in the faith, act like men, be strong.

14 Let all that you do be done in love.

15 Now I urge you, brethren (you know the household of Stephanas, that they were the first fruits of Achaia, and that they have devoted themselves for ministry to the saints),

16 that you also be in subjection to such men and to everyone who helps in the work and labors.

17 I rejoice over the coming of Stephanas and Fortunatus and Achaicus, because they have supplied what was lacking on your part.

18 For they have refreshed my spirit and yours. Therefore acknowledge such men.

19 The churches of Asia greet you. Aquila and Prisca greet you heartily in the Lord, with the church that is in their house.

20 All the brethren greet you. Greet one another with a holy kiss.

21 The greeting is in my own hand—Paul.

22 If anyone does not love the Lord, he is to be accursed. Maranatha.

23 The grace of the Lord Jesus be with you.

24 My love be with you all in Christ Jesus. Amen.

THE SECOND LETTER OF PAUL TO THE CORINTHIANS

Introduction

1 Paul, an apostle of Christ Jesus by the will of God, and Timothy *our* brother,

To the church of God which is at Corinth with all the saints who are throughout Achaia:

2 Grace to you and peace from God our Father and the Lord Jesus Christ.

3 Blessed *be* the God and Father of our Lord Jesus Christ, the Father of mercies and God of all comfort,

4 who comforts us in all our affliction so that we will be able to comfort those who are in any affliction with the comfort with which we ourselves are comforted by God.

5 For just as the sufferings of Christ are ours in abundance, so also our comfort is abundant through Christ.

6 But if we are afflicted, it is for your comfort and salvation; or if we are comforted, it is for your comfort, which is effective in the patient enduring of the same sufferings which we also suffer;

7 and our hope for you is firmly grounded, knowing that as you are sharers of our sufferings, so also you are *sharers* of our comfort.

8 For we do not want you to be unaware, brethren, of our affliction which came *to us* in Asia, that we were burdened excessively, beyond our strength, so that we despaired even of life;

9 indeed, we had the sentence of death within ourselves so that we would not trust in ourselves, but in God who raises the dead;

10 who delivered us from so great a *peril of* death, and will deliver *us*, He on whom we have set our hope. And He will yet deliver us,

11 you also joining in helping us through your prayers, so that thanks may be given by many persons on our behalf for the favor bestowed on us through *the prayers of* many.

12 For our proud confidence is this: the testimony of our conscience, that in holiness and godly sincerity, not in fleshly wisdom but in the grace of God, we have conducted ourselves in the world, and especially toward you.

13 For we write nothing else to you than what you read and understand, and I hope you will understand until the end;

14 just as you also partially did understand us, that we are your reason to be proud as you also are ours, in the day of our Lord Jesus.

15 In this confidence I intended at first to come to you, so that you might twice receive a blessing;

16 that is, to pass your way into Macedonia, and again from Macedonia to come to you, and by you to be helped on my journey to Judea.

17 Therefore, I was not vacillating when I intended to do this, was I? Or what I purpose, do I purpose according to the flesh, so that with me there will be yes, yes and no, no *at the same time?*

18 But as God is faithful, our word to you is not yes and no.

19 For the Son of God, Christ Jesus, who was preached among you by us—by me and Silvanus and Timothy—was not yes and no, but is yes in Him.

20 For as many as are the promises of God, in Him they are yes; therefore also through Him is our Amen to the glory of God through us.

21 Now He who establishes us with you in Christ and anointed us is God,

22 who also sealed us and gave *us* the Spirit in our hearts as a pledge.

23 But I call God as witness to my soul, that to spare you I did not come again to Corinth.

24 Not that we lord it over your faith, but are workers with you for your joy; for in your faith you are standing firm.

Reaffirm Your Love

2 But I determined this for my own sake, that I would not come to you in sorrow again.

2 For if I cause you sorrow, who then makes me glad but the one whom I made sorrowful?

3 This is the very thing I wrote you, so that when I came, I would not have sorrow from those who ought to make me rejoice; having confidence in you all that my joy would be *the joy* of you all.

4 For out of much affliction and anguish of heart I wrote to you with many tears; not so that you would be made sorrowful, but that you might know the love which I have especially for you.

5 But if any has caused sorrow, he has caused

sorrow not to me, but in some degree—in order not to say too much—to all of you.

6 Sufficient for such a one is this punishment which *was inflicted* by the majority,

7 so that on the contrary you should rather forgive and comfort *him*, otherwise such a one might be overwhelmed by excessive sorrow.

8 Wherefore I urge you to reaffirm *your* love for him.

9 For to this end also I wrote, so that I might put you to the test, whether you are obedient in all things.

10 But one whom you forgive anything, I *forgive* also; for indeed what I have forgiven, if I have forgiven anything, *I did it* for your sakes in the presence of Christ,

11 so that no advantage would be taken of us by Satan, for we are not ignorant of his schemes.

12 Now when I came to Troas for the gospel of Christ and when a door was opened for me in the Lord,

13 I had no rest for my spirit, not finding Titus my brother; but taking my leave of them, I went on to Macedonia.

14 But thanks be to God, who always leads us in triumph in Christ, and manifests through us the sweet aroma of the knowledge of Him in every place.

15 For we are a fragrance of Christ to God among those who are being saved and among those who are perishing;

16 to the one an aroma from death to death, to the other an aroma from life to life. And who is adequate for these things?

17 For we are not like many, [1]peddling the word of God, but as from sincerity, but as from God, we speak in Christ in the sight of God.

Ministers of a New Covenant

3 Are we beginning to commend ourselves again? Or do we need, as some, letters of commendation to you or from you?

2 You are our letter, written in our hearts, known and read by all men;

3 being manifested that you are a letter of Christ, cared for by us, written not with ink but with the Spirit of the living God, not on tablets of stone but on tablets of human hearts.

4 Such confidence we have through Christ toward God.

5 Not that we are adequate in ourselves to consider anything as *coming* from ourselves, but our adequacy is from God,

6 who also made us adequate *as* servants of a new covenant, not of the letter but of the Spirit; for the letter kills, but the Spirit gives life.

7 But if the ministry of death, in letters engraved on stones, came with glory, so that the sons of Israel could not look intently at the face of Moses because of the glory of his face, fading *as* it was,

8 how will the ministry of the Spirit fail to be even more with glory?

9 For if the ministry of condemnation has glory, much more does the ministry of righteousness abound in glory.

10 For indeed what had glory, in this case has no glory because of the glory that surpasses *it*.

11 For if that which fades away *was* with glory, much more that which remains *is* in glory.

12 Therefore having such a hope, we use great boldness in *our* speech,

13 and *are* not like Moses, *who* used to put a veil over his face so that the sons of Israel would not look intently at the end of what was fading away.

14 But their minds were hardened; for until this very day at the reading of the old covenant the same veil remains unlifted, because it is removed in Christ.

15 But to this day whenever Moses is read, a veil lies over their heart;

16 but whenever a person turns to the Lord, the veil is taken away.

17 Now the Lord is the Spirit, and where the Spirit of the Lord is, *there* is liberty.

18 But we all, with unveiled face, beholding as in a mirror the glory of the Lord, are being transformed into the same image from glory to glory, just as from the Lord, the Spirit.

Paul's Apostolic Ministry

4 Therefore, since we have this ministry, as we received mercy, we do not lose heart,

2 but we have renounced the things hidden because of shame, not walking in craftiness or adulterating the word of God, but by the manifestation of truth commending ourselves to every man's conscience in the sight of God.

3 And even if our gospel is veiled, it is veiled to those who are perishing,

4 in whose case the god of this world has blinded the minds of the unbelieving so that they might not see the light of the gospel of the glory of Christ, who is the image of God.

5 For we do not preach ourselves but Christ Jesus as Lord, and ourselves as your bond-servants for Jesus' sake.

6 For God, who said, "Light shall shine out of darkness," is the One who has shone in our hearts to give the Light of the knowledge of the glory of God in the face of Christ.

7 But we have this treasure in earthen vessels, so that the surpassing greatness of the power will be of God and not from ourselves;

8 *we are* afflicted in every way, but not crushed; perplexed, but not despairing;

9 persecuted, but not forsaken; struck down, but not destroyed;

10 always carrying about in the body the dying of Jesus, so that the life of Jesus also may be manifested in our body.

11 For we who live are constantly being delivered over to death for Jesus' sake, so that the life of Jesus also may be manifested in our mortal flesh.

12 So death works in us, but life in you.

13 But having the same spirit of faith, according to what is written, "I BELIEVED,

---

1. Or *corrupting*

THEREFORE I SPOKE," we also believe, therefore we also speak,

14 knowing that He who raised the Lord Jesus will raise us also with Jesus and will present us with you.

15 For all things *are* for your sakes, so that the grace which is spreading to more and more people may cause the giving of thanks to abound to the glory of God.

16 Therefore we do not lose heart, but though our outer man is decaying, yet our inner man is being renewed day by day.

17 For momentary, light affliction is producing for us an eternal weight of glory far beyond all comparison,

18 while we look not at the things which are seen, but at the things which are not seen; for the things which are seen are temporal, but the things which are not seen are eternal.

The Temporal and Eternal

5 For we know that if the earthly tent which is our house is torn down, we have a building from God, a house not made with hands, eternal in the heavens.

2 For indeed in this *house* we groan, longing to be clothed with our dwelling from heaven,

3 inasmuch as we, having put it on, will not be found naked.

4 For indeed while we are in this tent, we groan, being burdened, because we do not want to be unclothed but to be clothed, so that what is mortal will be swallowed up by life.

5 Now He who prepared us for this very purpose is God, who gave to us the Spirit as a pledge.

6 Therefore, being always of good courage, and knowing that while we are at home in the body we are absent from the Lord—

7 for we walk by faith, not by sight—

8 we are of good courage, I say, and prefer rather to be absent from the body and to be at home with the Lord.

9 Therefore we also have as our ambition, whether at home or absent, to be pleasing to Him.

10 For we must all appear before the judgment seat of Christ, so that each one may be recompensed for his deeds in the body, according to what he has done, whether good or bad.

11 Therefore, knowing the fear of the Lord, we persuade men, but we are made manifest to God; and I hope that we are made manifest also in your consciences.

12 We are not again commending ourselves to you but *are* giving you an occasion to be proud of us, so that you will have *an answer* for those who take pride in appearance and not in heart.

13 For if we are beside ourselves, it is for God; if we are of sound mind, it is for you.

14 For the love of Christ controls us, having concluded this, that one died for all, therefore all died;

15 and He died for all, so that they who live might no longer live for themselves, but for Him who died and rose again on their behalf.

16 Therefore from now on we recognize no one according to the flesh; even though we have known Christ according to the flesh, yet now we know *Him in this way* no longer.

17 Therefore if anyone is in Christ, *he is* a new creature; the old things passed away; behold, new things have come.

18 Now all *these* things are from God, who reconciled us to Himself through Christ and gave us the ministry of reconciliation,

19 namely, that God was in Christ reconciling the world to Himself, not counting their trespasses against them, and He has committed to us the word of reconciliation.

20 Therefore, we are ambassadors for Christ, as though God were making an appeal through us; we beg you on behalf of Christ, be reconciled to God.

21 He made Him who knew no sin *to be* sin on our behalf, so that we might become the righteousness of God in Him.

Their Ministry Commended

6 And working together *with Him*, we also urge you not to receive the grace of God in vain—

2 for He says,

"AT THE ACCEPTABLE TIME I LISTENED TO YOU,
AND ON THE DAY OF SALVATION I HELPED YOU."

Behold, now is "THE ACCEPTABLE TIME," behold, now is "THE DAY OF SALVATION"—

3 giving no cause for offense in anything, so that the ministry will not be discredited,

4 but in everything commending ourselves as servants of God, in much endurance, in afflictions, in hardships, in distresses,

5 in beatings, in imprisonments, in tumults, in labors, in sleeplessness, in hunger,

6 in purity, in knowledge, in patience, in kindness, in the Holy Spirit, in genuine love,

7 in the word of truth, in the power of God; by the weapons of righteousness for the right hand and the left,

8 by glory and dishonor, by evil report and good report; *regarded* as deceivers and yet true;

9 as unknown yet well-known, as dying yet behold, we live; as punished yet not put to death,

10 as sorrowful yet always rejoicing, as poor yet making many rich, as having nothing yet possessing all things.

11 Our mouth has spoken freely to you, O Corinthians, our heart is opened wide.

12 You are not restrained by us, but you are restrained in your own affections.

13 Now in a like exchange—I speak as to children—open wide *to us* also.

14 Do not be bound together with unbelievers; for what partnership have righteousness and lawlessness, or what fellowship has light with darkness?

15 Or what harmony has Christ with Belial, or what has a believer in common with an unbeliever?

16 Or what agreement has the temple of God

with idols? For we are the temple of the living God; just as God said,

"I WILL DWELL IN THEM AND WALK AMONG THEM;
AND I WILL BE THEIR GOD, AND THEY SHALL BE MY PEOPLE.

17 "Therefore, COME OUT FROM THEIR MIDST AND BE SEPARATE," says the Lord.

"AND DO NOT TOUCH WHAT IS UNCLEAN;
And I will welcome you.

18 "And I will be a father to you,
And you shall be sons and daughters to Me,"

Says the Lord Almighty.

Paul Reveals His Heart

7 Therefore, having these promises, beloved, let us cleanse ourselves from all defilement of flesh and spirit, perfecting holiness in the fear of God.

2 Make room for us *in your hearts;* we wronged no one, we corrupted no one, we took advantage of no one.

3 I do not speak to condemn you, for I have said before that you are in our hearts to die together and to live together.

4 Great is my confidence in you; great is my boasting on your behalf. I am filled with comfort; I am overflowing with joy in all our affliction.

5 For even when we came into Macedonia our flesh had no rest, but we were afflicted on every side: conflicts without, fears within.

6 But God, who comforts the depressed, comforted us by the coming of Titus;

7 and not only by his coming, but also by the comfort with which he was comforted in you, as he reported to us your longing, your mourning, your zeal for me; so that I rejoiced even more.

8 For though I caused you sorrow by my letter, I do not regret it; though I did regret it—*for* I see that that letter caused you sorrow, though only for a while—

9 I now rejoice, not that you were made sorrowful, but that you were made sorrowful to *the point of* repentance; for you were made sorrowful according to *the will of* God, so that you might not suffer loss in anything through us.

10 For the sorrow that is according to *the will* *of* God produces a repentance without regret, *leading* to salvation, but the sorrow of the world produces death.

11 For behold what earnestness this very thing, this godly sorrow, has produced in you: what vindication of yourselves, what indignation, what fear, what longing, what zeal, what avenging of wrong! In everything you demonstrated yourselves to be innocent in the matter.

12 So although I wrote to you, *it was* not for the sake of the offender nor for the sake of the one offended, but that your earnestness on our behalf might be made known to you in the sight of God.

13 For this reason we have been comforted.

And besides our comfort, we rejoiced even much more for the joy of Titus, because his spirit has been refreshed by you all.

14 For if in anything I have boasted to him about you, I was not put to shame; but as we spoke all things to you in truth, so also our boasting before Titus proved to be *the* truth.

15 His affection abounds all the more toward you, as he remembers the obedience of you all, how you received him with fear and trembling.

16 I rejoice that in everything I have confidence in you.

Great Generosity

8 Now, brethren, we *wish to* make known to you the grace of God which has been given in the churches of Macedonia,

2 that in a great ordeal of affliction their abundance of joy and their deep poverty overflowed in the wealth of their liberality.

3 For I testify that according to their ability, and beyond their ability, *they gave* of their own accord,

4 begging us with much urging for the favor of participation in the support of the saints,

5 and *this,* not as we had expected, but they first gave themselves to the Lord and to us by the will of God.

6 So we urged Titus that as he had previously made a beginning, so he would also complete in you this gracious work as well.

7 But just as you abound in everything, in faith and utterance and knowledge and in all earnestness and in the [1]love we inspired in you, *see* that you abound in this gracious work also.

8 I am not speaking *this* as a command, but as proving through the earnestness of others the sincerity of your love also.

9 For you know the grace of our Lord Jesus Christ, that though He was rich, yet for your sake He became poor, so that you through His poverty might become rich.

10 I give *my* opinion in this matter, for this is to your advantage, who were the first to begin a year ago not only to do *this,* but also to desire *to do it.*

11 But now finish doing it also, so that just as *there was* the readiness to desire it, so *there may be* also the completion of it by your ability.

12 For if the readiness is present, it is acceptable according to what *a person* has, not according to what he does not have.

13 For *this* is not for the ease of others *and* for your affliction, but by way of equality—

14 at this present time your abundance *being* *a supply* for their need, so that their abundance also may become *a supply* for your need, that there may be equality;

15 as it is written, "HE WHO *gathered* MUCH DID NOT HAVE TOO MUCH, AND HE WHO *gathered* LITTLE HAD NO LACK."

16 But thanks be to God who puts the same earnestness on your behalf in the heart of Titus.

17 For he not only accepted our appeal, but being himself very earnest, he has gone to you of his own accord.

---

1. Lit *love from us in you;* one early ms reads *your love for us*

Godly sorrow brings change.

There is a solution. Read 1 Corinthians 6:9-11 on page 132.

18 We have sent along with him the brother whose fame in *the things of* the gospel *has* spread through all the churches;

19 and not only *this*, but he has also been appointed by the churches to travel with us in this gracious work, which is being administered by us for the glory of the Lord Himself, and *to show* our readiness,

20 taking precaution so that no one will discredit us in our administration of this generous gift;

21 for we have regard for what is honorable, not only in the sight of the Lord, but also in the sight of men.

22 We have sent with them our brother, whom we have often tested and found diligent in many things, but now even more diligent because of *his* great confidence in you.

23 As for Titus, *he is* my partner and fellow worker among you; as for our brethren, *they are* messengers of the churches, a glory to Christ.

24 Therefore openly before the churches, show them the proof of your love and of our reason for boasting about you.

God Gives Most

9 For it is superfluous for me to write to you about this ministry to the saints;

2 for I know your readiness, of which I boast about you to the Macedonians, *namely*, that Achaia has been prepared since last year, and your zeal has stirred up most of them.

3 But I have sent the brethren, in order that our boasting about you may not be made empty in this case, so that, as I was saying, you may be prepared;

4 otherwise if any Macedonians come with me and find you unprepared, we—not to speak of you—will be put to shame by this confidence.

5 So I thought it necessary to urge the brethren that they would go on ahead to you and arrange beforehand your previously promised bountiful gift, so that the same would be ready as a bountiful gift and not affected by covetousness.

6 Now this *I say*, he who sows sparingly will also reap sparingly, and he who sows bountifully will also reap bountifully.

7 Each one *must do* just as he has purposed in his heart, not grudgingly or under compulsion, for God loves a cheerful giver.

8 And God is able to make all grace abound to you, so that always having all sufficiency in everything, you may have an abundance for every good deed;

9 as it is written,

"HE SCATTERED ABROAD, HE GAVE TO THE POOR,

HIS RIGHTEOUSNESS ENDURES FOREVER."

10 Now He who supplies seed to the sower and bread for food will supply and multiply your seed for sowing and increase the harvest of your righteousness;

11 you will be enriched in everything for all liberality, which through us is producing thanksgiving to God.

12 For the ministry of this service is not only fully supplying the needs of the saints, but is also overflowing through many thanksgivings to God.

13 Because of the proof given by this ministry, they will glorify God for *your* obedience to your confession of the gospel of Christ and for the liberality of your contribution to them and to all,

14 while they also, by prayer on your behalf, yearn for you because of the surpassing grace of God in you.

15 Thanks be to God for His indescribable gift!

Paul Describes Himself

10 Now I, Paul, myself urge you by the meekness and gentleness of Christ—I who am meek when face to face with you, but bold toward you when absent!

2 I ask that when I am present I *need* not be bold with the confidence with which I propose to be courageous against some, who regard us as if we walked according to the flesh.

3 For though we walk in the flesh, we do not war according to the flesh,

4 for the weapons of our warfare are not of the flesh, but divinely powerful for the destruction of fortresses.

5 *We are* destroying speculations and every lofty thing raised up against the knowledge of God, and *we are* taking every thought captive to the obedience of Christ,

6 and we are ready to punish all disobedience, whenever your obedience is complete.

7 You are looking at things as they are outwardly. If anyone is confident in himself that he is Christ's, let him consider this again within himself, that just as he is Christ's, so also are we.

8 For even if I boast somewhat further about our authority, which the Lord gave for building you up and not for destroying you, I will not be put to shame,

9 I do not wish to seem as if I would terrify you by my letters.

10 For they say, "His letters are weighty and strong, but his personal presence is unimpressive and his speech contemptible."

11 Let such a person consider this, that what we are in word by letters when absent, such persons *we are* also in deed when present.

12 For we are not bold to class or compare ourselves with some of those who commend themselves; but when they measure themselves by themselves and compare themselves with themselves, they are without understanding.

13 But we will not boast beyond *our* measure, but within the measure of the sphere which God apportioned to us as a measure, to reach even as far as you.

14 For we are not overextending ourselves, as if we did not reach to you, for we were the first to come even as far as you in the gospel of Christ;

15 not boasting beyond *our* measure, *that is*, in other men's labors, but with the hope that as

your faith grows, we will be, within our sphere, enlarged even more by you,

16 so as to preach the gospel even to the regions beyond you, *and* not to boast in what has been accomplished in the sphere of another.

17 But HE WHO BOASTS IS TO BOAST IN THE LORD.

18 For it is not he who commends himself that is approved, but he whom the Lord commends.

Paul Defends His Apostleship

11 I wish that you would bear with me in a little foolishness; but indeed you are bearing with me.

2 For I am jealous for you with a godly jealousy; for I betrothed you to one husband, so that to Christ I might present you *as* a pure virgin.

3 But I am afraid that, as the serpent deceived Eve by his craftiness, your minds will be led astray from the simplicity and purity *of devotion* to Christ.

4 For if one comes and preaches another Jesus whom we have not preached, or you receive a different spirit which you have not received, or a different gospel which you have not accepted, you bear *this* beautifully.

5 For I consider myself not in the least inferior to the most eminent apostles.

6 But even if I am unskilled in speech, yet I am not *so* in knowledge; in fact, in every way we have made *this* evident to you in all things.

7 Or did I commit a sin in humbling myself so that you might be exalted, because I preached the gospel of God to you without charge?

8 I robbed other churches by taking wages *from them* to serve you;

9 and when I was present with you and was in need, I was not a burden to anyone; for when the brethren came from Macedonia they fully supplied my need, and in everything I kept myself from being a burden to you, and will continue to do so.

10 As the truth of Christ is in me, this boasting of mine will not be stopped in the regions of Achaia.

11 Why? Because I do not love you? God knows *I do!*

12 But what I am doing I will continue to do, so that I may cut off opportunity from those who desire an opportunity to be regarded just as we are in the matter about which they are boasting.

13 For such men are false apostles, deceitful workers, disguising themselves as apostles of Christ.

14 No wonder, for even Satan disguises himself as an angel of light.

15 Therefore it is not surprising if his servants also disguise themselves as servants of righteousness, whose end will be according to their deeds.

16 Again I say, let no one think me foolish; but if *you do,* receive me even as foolish, so that I also may boast a little.

17 What I am saying, I am not saying as the Lord would, but as in foolishness, in this confidence of boasting.

18 Since many boast according to the flesh, I will boast also.

19 For you, being *so* wise, tolerate the foolish gladly.

20 For you tolerate it if anyone enslaves you, anyone devours you, anyone takes advantage of you, anyone exalts himself, anyone hits you in the face.

21 To *my* shame I *must* say that we have been weak *by comparison.*

But in whatever respect anyone *else* is bold—I speak in foolishness—I am just as bold myself.

22 Are they Hebrews? So am I. Are they Israelites? So am I. Are they descendants of Abraham? So am I.

23 Are they servants of Christ?—I speak as if insane—I more so; in far more labors, in far more imprisonments, beaten times without number, often in danger of death.

24 Five times I received from the Jews thirty-nine *lashes.*

25 Three times I was beaten with rods, once I was stoned, three times I was shipwrecked, a night and a day I have spent in the deep.

26 *I have been* on frequent journeys, in dangers from rivers, dangers from robbers, dangers from *my* countrymen, dangers from the Gentiles, dangers in the city, dangers in the wilderness, dangers on the sea, dangers among false brethren;

27 *I have been* in labor and hardship, through many sleepless nights, in hunger and thirst, often without food, in cold and exposure.

28 Apart from *such* external things, there is the daily pressure on me *of* concern for all the churches.

29 Who is weak without my being weak? Who is led into sin without my intense concern?

30 If I have to boast, I will boast of what pertains to my weakness.

31 The God and Father of the Lord Jesus, He who is blessed forever, knows that I am not lying.

32 In Damascus the ethnarch under Aretas the king was guarding the city of the Damascenes in order to seize me,

33 and I was let down in a basket through a window in the wall, and *so* escaped his hands.

Paul's Vision

12 Boasting is necessary, though it is not profitable; but I will go on to visions and revelations of the Lord.

2 I know a man in Christ who fourteen years ago—whether in the body I do not know, or out of the body I do not know, God knows—such a man was caught up to the third heaven.

3 And I know how such a man—whether in the body or apart from the body I do not know, God knows—

4 was caught up into Paradise and heard inexpressible words, which a man is not permitted to speak.

5 On behalf of such a man I will boast; but on

my own behalf I will not boast, except in regard to *my* weaknesses.

6 For if I do wish to boast I will not be foolish, for I will be speaking the truth; but I refrain *from this,* so that no one will credit me with more than he sees *in* me or hears from me.

7 Because of the surpassing greatness of the revelations, for this reason, to keep me from exalting myself, there was given me a thorn in the flesh, a messenger of Satan to torment me—to keep me from exalting myself!

8 Concerning this I implored the Lord three times that it might leave me.

9 And He has said to me, "My grace is sufficient for you, for power is perfected in weakness." Most gladly, therefore, I will rather boast about my weaknesses, so that the power of Christ may dwell in me.

10 Therefore I am well content with weaknesses, with insults, with distresses, with persecutions, with difficulties, for Christ's sake; for when I am weak, then I am strong.

11 I have become foolish; you yourselves compelled me. Actually I should have been commended by you, for in no respect was I inferior to the most eminent apostles, even though I am a nobody.

12 The signs of a true apostle were performed among you with all perseverance, by signs and wonders and miracles.

13 For in what respect were you treated as inferior to the rest of the churches, except that I myself did not become a burden to you? Forgive me this wrong!

14 Here for this third time I am ready to come to you, and I will not be a burden to you; for I do not seek what is yours, but you; for children are not responsible to save up for *their* parents, but parents for *their* children.

15 I will most gladly spend and be expended for your souls. If I love you more, am I to be loved less?

16 But be that as it may, I did not burden you myself; nevertheless, crafty fellow that I am, I took you in by deceit.

17 *Certainly* I have not taken advantage of you through any of those whom I have sent to you, have I?

18 I urged Titus *to go,* and I sent the brother with him. Titus did not take any advantage of you, did he? Did we not conduct ourselves in the same spirit *and walk* in the same steps?

19 All this time you have been thinking that we are defending ourselves to you. *Actually,* it is in the sight of God that we have been speaking in Christ; and all for your upbuilding, beloved.

20 For I am afraid that perhaps when I come I

may find you to be not what I wish and may be found by you to be not what you wish; that perhaps *there will be* strife, jealousy, angry tempers, disputes, slanders, gossip, arrogance, disturbances;

21 I am afraid that when I come again my God may humiliate me before you, and I may mourn over many of those who have sinned in the past and not repented of the impurity, immorality and sensuality which they have practiced.

Examine Yourselves

13 This is the third time I am coming to you. EVERY FACT IS TO BE CONFIRMED BY THE TESTIMONY OF TWO OR THREE WITNESSES.

2 I have previously said when present the second time, and though now absent I say in advance to those who have sinned in the past and to all the rest *as well,* that if I come again I will not spare *anyone,*

3 since you are seeking for proof of the Christ who speaks in me, and who is not weak toward you, but mighty in you.

4 For indeed He was crucified because of weakness, yet He lives because of the power of God. For we also are weak [1]in Him, yet we will live with Him because of the power of God *directed* toward you.

5 Test yourselves *to see* if you are in the faith; examine yourselves! Or do you not recognize this about yourselves, that Jesus Christ is in you—unless indeed you fail the test?

6 But I trust that you will realize that we ourselves do not fail the test.

7 Now we pray to God that you do no wrong; not that we ourselves may appear approved, but that you may do what is right, even though we may appear unapproved.

8 For we can do nothing against the truth, but *only* for the truth.

9 For we rejoice when we ourselves are weak but you are strong; this we also pray for, that you be made complete.

10 For this reason I am writing these things while absent, so that when present I *need* not use severity, in accordance with the authority which the Lord gave me for building up and not for tearing down.

11 Finally, brethren, rejoice, be made complete, be comforted, be like-minded, live in peace; and the God of love and peace will be with you.

12 Greet one another with a holy kiss.

13 All the saints greet you.

14 The grace of the Lord Jesus Christ, and the love of God, and the fellowship of the Holy Spirit, be with you all.

---

1. **One early ms reads** *with Him*

THE LETTER OF PAUL TO THE GALATIANS

Introduction

1 Paul, an apostle (not *sent* from men nor through the agency of man, but through Jesus Christ and God the Father, who raised Him from the dead),

2 and all the brethren who are with me, To the churches of Galatia:

3 Grace to you and peace from God our Father and the Lord Jesus Christ,

4 who gave Himself for our sins so that He might rescue us from this present evil age, according to the will of our God and Father,

5 to whom *be* the glory forevermore. Amen.

6 I am amazed that you are so quickly deserting Him who called you by the grace of Christ, for a different gospel;

7 which is *really* not another; only there are some who are disturbing you and want to distort the gospel of Christ.

8 But even if we, or an angel from heaven, should preach to you a gospel contrary to what we have preached to you, he is to be accursed!

9 As we have said before, so I say again now, if any man is preaching to you a gospel contrary to what you received, he is to be accursed!

10 For am I now seeking the favor of men, or of God? Or am I striving to please men? If I were still trying to please men, I would not be a bond-servant of Christ.

11 For I would have you know, brethren, that the gospel which was preached by me is not according to man.

12 For I neither received it from man, nor was I taught it, but *I received it* through a revelation of Jesus Christ.

13 For you have heard of my former manner of life in Judaism, how I used to persecute the church of God beyond measure and tried to destroy it;

14 and I was advancing in Judaism beyond many of my contemporaries among my countrymen, being more extremely zealous for my ancestral traditions.

15 But when God, who had set me apart *even* from my mother's womb and called me through His grace, was pleased

16 to reveal His Son in me so that I might preach Him among the Gentiles, I did not immediately consult with flesh and blood,

17 nor did I go up to Jerusalem to those who were apostles before me; but I went away to Arabia, and returned once more to Damascus.

18 Then three years later I went up to Jerusalem to become acquainted with Cephas, and stayed with him fifteen days.

19 But I did not see any other of the apostles except James, the Lord's brother.

20 (Now in what I am writing to you, I assure you before God that I am not lying.)

21 Then I went into the regions of Syria and Cilicia.

22 I was *still* unknown by sight to the churches of Judea which were in Christ;

23 but only, they kept hearing, "He who once persecuted us is now preaching the faith which he once tried to destroy."

24 And they were glorifying God because of me.

The Council at Jerusalem

2 Then after an interval of fourteen years I went up again to Jerusalem with Barnabas, taking Titus along also.

2 It was because of a revelation that I went up; and I submitted to them the gospel which I preach among the Gentiles, but *I did so* in private to those who were of reputation, for fear that I might be running, or had run, in vain.

3 But not even Titus, who was with me, though he was a Greek, was compelled to be circumcised.

4 But *it was* because of the false brethren secretly brought in, who had sneaked in to spy out our liberty which we have in Christ Jesus, in order to bring us into bondage.

5 But we did not yield in subjection to them for even an hour, so that the truth of the gospel would remain with you.

6 But from those who were of high reputation (what they were makes no difference to me; God shows no partiality)—well, those who were of reputation contributed nothing to me.

7 But on the contrary, seeing that I had been entrusted with the gospel to the uncircumcised, just as Peter *had been* to the circumcised

8 (for He who effectually worked for Peter in *his* apostleship to the circumcised effectually worked for me also to the Gentiles),

9 and recognizing the grace that had been given to me, James and Cephas and John, who were reputed to be pillars, gave to me and Barnabas the right hand of fellowship, so that we *might go* to the Gentiles and they to the circumcised.

10 *They* only *asked* us to remember the poor—the very thing I also was eager to do.

11 But when Cephas came to Antioch, I opposed him to his face, because he stood condemned.

12 For prior to the coming of certain men from James, he used to eat with the Gentiles; but when they came, he *began* to withdraw and hold himself aloof, fearing the party of the circumcision.

13 The rest of the Jews joined him in hypocrisy, with the result that even Barnabas was carried away by their hypocrisy.

14 But when I saw that they were not straightforward about the truth of the gospel, I said to Cephas in the presence of all, "If you, being a Jew, live like the Gentiles and not like the Jews, how *is it that* you compel the Gentiles to live like Jews?

15 "We *are* Jews by nature and not sinners from among the Gentiles;

16 nevertheless knowing that a man is not justified by the works of the Law but through faith in Christ Jesus, even we have believed in

Christ Jesus, so that we may be justified by faith in Christ and not by the works of the Law; since by the works of the Law no flesh will be justified.

17 "But if, while seeking to be justified in Christ, we ourselves have also been found sinners, is Christ then a minister of sin? May it never be!

18 "For if I rebuild what I have *once* destroyed, I prove myself to be a transgressor.

19 "For through the Law I died to the Law, so that I might live to God.

20 "I have been crucified with Christ; and it is no longer I who live, but Christ lives in me; and the *life* which I now live in the flesh I live by faith in the Son of God, who loved me and gave Himself up for me.

21 "I do not nullify the grace of God, for if righteousness *comes* through the Law, then Christ died needlessly."

Faith Brings Righteousness

3 You foolish Galatians, who has bewitched you, before whose eyes Jesus Christ was publicly portrayed *as* crucified?

2 This is the only thing I want to find out from you: did you receive the Spirit by the works of the Law, or by hearing with faith?

3 Are you so foolish? Having begun by the Spirit, are you now being perfected by the flesh?

4 Did you suffer so many things in vain—if indeed it was in vain?

5 So then, does He who provides you with the Spirit and works miracles among you, do it by the works of the Law, or by hearing with faith?

6 Even so Abraham BELIEVED GOD, AND IT WAS RECKONED TO HIM AS RIGHTEOUSNESS.

7 Therefore, be sure that it is those who are of faith who are sons of Abraham.

8 The Scripture, foreseeing that God would justify the Gentiles by faith, preached the gospel beforehand to Abraham, *saying*, "ALL THE NATIONS WILL BE BLESSED IN YOU."

9 So then those who are of faith are blessed with Abraham, the believer.

10 For as many as are of the works of the Law are under a curse; for it is written, "CURSED IS EVERYONE WHO DOES NOT ABIDE BY ALL THINGS WRITTEN IN THE BOOK OF THE LAW, TO PERFORM THEM."

11 Now that no one is justified by the Law before God is evident; for, "THE RIGHTEOUS MAN SHALL LIVE BY FAITH."

12 However, the Law is not of faith; on the contrary, "HE WHO PRACTICES THEM SHALL LIVE BY THEM."

13 Christ redeemed us from the curse of the Law, having become a curse for us—for it is written, "CURSED IS EVERYONE WHO HANGS ON A TREE"—

14 in order that in Christ Jesus the blessing of Abraham might come to the Gentiles, so that we would receive the promise of the Spirit through faith.

15 Brethren, I speak in terms of human relations: even though it is *only* a man's covenant, yet when it has been ratified, no one sets it aside or adds conditions to it.

16 Now the promises were spoken to Abraham and to his seed. He does not say, "And to seeds," as *referring* to many, but *rather* to one, "And to your seed," that is, Christ.

17 What I am saying is this: the Law, which came four hundred and thirty years later, does not invalidate a covenant previously ratified by God, so as to nullify the promise.

18 For if the inheritance is based on law, it is no longer based on a promise; but God has granted it to Abraham by means of a promise.

19 Why the Law then? It was added because of transgressions, having been ordained through angels by the agency of a mediator, until the seed would come to whom the promise had been made.

20 Now a mediator is not for one *party only*; whereas God is *only* one.

21 Is the Law then contrary to the promises of God? May it never be! For if a law had been given which was able to impart life, then righteousness would indeed have been based on law.

22 But the Scripture has shut up everyone under sin, so that the promise by faith in Jesus Christ might be given to those who believe.

23 But before faith came, we were kept in custody under the law, being shut up to the faith which was later to be revealed.

24 Therefore the Law has become our tutor *to lead us* to Christ, so that we may be justified by faith.

25 But now that faith has come, we are no longer under a tutor.

26 For you are all sons of God through faith in Christ Jesus.

27 For all of you who were baptized into Christ have clothed yourselves with Christ.

28 There is neither Jew nor Greek, there is neither slave nor free man, there is neither male nor female; for you are all one in Christ Jesus.

29 And if you belong to Christ, then you are Abraham's descendants, heirs according to promise.

Sonship in Christ

4 Now I say, as long as the heir is a child, he does not differ at all from a slave although he is owner of everything,

2 but he is under guardians and managers until the date set by the father.

3 So also we, while we were children, were held in bondage under the elemental things of the world.

4 But when the fullness of the time came, God sent forth His Son, born of a woman, born under the Law,

5 so that He might redeem those who were under the Law, that we might receive the adoption as sons.

6 Because you are sons, God has sent forth the Spirit of His Son into our hearts, crying, "Abba! Father!"

7 Therefore you are no longer a slave, but a son; and if a son, then an heir through God.

8 However at that time, when you did not know God, you were slaves to those which by nature are no gods.

9 But now that you have come to know God, or rather to be known by God, how is it that you turn back again to the weak and worthless elemental things, to which you desire to be enslaved all over again?

10 You observe days and months and seasons and years.

11 I fear for you, that perhaps I have labored over you in vain.

12 I beg of you, brethren, become as I *am*, for I also *have become* as you *are*. You have done me no wrong;

13 but you know that it was because of a bodily illness that I preached the gospel to you the first time;

14 and that which was a trial to you in my bodily condition you did not despise or loathe, but you received me as an angel of God, as Christ Jesus *Himself*.

15 Where then is that sense of blessing you had? For I bear you witness that, if possible, you would have plucked out your eyes and given them to me.

16 So have I become your enemy by telling you the truth?

17 They eagerly seek you, not commendably, but they wish to shut you out so that you will seek them.

18 But it is good always to be eagerly sought in a commendable manner, and not only when I am present with you.

19 My children, with whom I am again in labor until Christ is formed in you—

20 but I could wish to be present with you now and to change my tone, for I am perplexed about you.

21 Tell me, you who want to be under law, do you not listen to the law?

22 For it is written that Abraham had two sons, one by the bondwoman and one by the free woman.

23 But the son by the bondwoman was born according to the flesh, and the son by the free woman through the promise.

24 This is allegorically speaking, for these *women* are two covenants: one *proceeding* from Mount Sinai bearing children who are to be slaves; she is Hagar.

25 Now this Hagar is Mount Sinai in Arabia and corresponds to the present Jerusalem, for she is in slavery with her children.

26 But the Jerusalem above is free; she is our mother.

27 For it is written,

"REJOICE, BARREN WOMAN WHO DOES NOT BEAR;
BREAK FORTH AND SHOUT, YOU WHO ARE NOT IN LABOR;
FOR MORE NUMEROUS ARE THE CHILDREN OF THE DESOLATE
THAN OF THE ONE WHO HAS A HUSBAND."

28 And you brethren, like Isaac, are children of promise.

29 But as at that time he who was born according to the flesh persecuted him *who was born* according to the Spirit, so it is now also.

30 But what does the Scripture say?

"CAST OUT THE BONDWOMAN AND HER SON,
FOR THE SON OF THE BONDWOMAN SHALL NOT BE AN HEIR WITH THE SON OF THE FREE WOMAN."

31 So then, brethren, we are not children of a bondwoman, but of the free woman.

Walk by the Spirit

5 It was for freedom that Christ set us free; therefore keep standing firm and do not be subject again to a yoke of slavery.

2 Behold I, Paul, say to you that if you receive circumcision, Christ will be of no benefit to you.

3 And I testify again to every man who receives circumcision, that he is under obligation to keep the whole Law.

4 You have been severed from Christ, you who are seeking to be justified by law; you have fallen from grace.

5 For we through the Spirit, by faith, are waiting for the hope of righteousness.

6 For in Christ Jesus neither circumcision nor uncircumcision means anything, but faith working through love.

7 You were running well; who hindered you from obeying the truth?

8 This persuasion *did* not *come* from Him who calls you.

9 A little leaven leavens the whole lump *of dough.*

10 I have confidence in you in the Lord that you will adopt no other view; but the one who is disturbing you will bear his judgment, whoever he is.

11 But I, brethren, if I still preach circumcision, why am I still persecuted? Then the stumbling block of the cross has been abolished.

12 I wish that those who are troubling you would even mutilate themselves.

13 For you were called to freedom, brethren; only *do* not *turn* your freedom into an opportunity for the flesh, but through love serve one another.

14 For the whole Law is fulfilled in one word, in the *statement*, "YOU SHALL LOVE YOUR NEIGHBOR AS YOURSELF."

15 But if you bite and devour one another, take care that you are not consumed by one another.

16 But I say, walk by the Spirit, and you will not carry out the desire of the flesh.

17 For the flesh sets its desire against the Spirit, and the Spirit against the flesh; for these are in opposition to one another, so that you may not do the things that you please.

18 But if you are led by the Spirit, you are not under the Law.

19 Now the deeds of the flesh are evident, which are: immorality, impurity, sensuality,

20 idolatry, sorcery, enmities, strife, jealousy,

outbursts of anger, disputes, dissensions, factions,

21 envying, drunkenness, carousing, and things like these, of which I forewarn you, just as I have forewarned you, that those who practice such things will not inherit the kingdom of God.

22 But the fruit of the Spirit is love, joy, peace, patience, kindness, goodness, faithfulness,

23 gentleness, self-control; against such things there is no law.

24 Now those who belong to Christ Jesus have crucified the flesh with its passions and desires.

25 If we live by the Spirit, let us also walk by the Spirit.

26 Let us not become boastful, challenging one another, envying one another.

Bear One Another's Burdens

6 Brethren, even if anyone is caught in any trespass, you who are spiritual, restore such a one in a spirit of gentleness; *each one* looking to yourself, so that you too will not be tempted.

2 Bear one another's burdens, and thereby fulfill the law of Christ.

3 For if anyone thinks he is something when he is nothing, he deceives himself.

4 But each one must examine his own work, and then he will have *reason for* boasting in regard to himself alone, and not in regard to another.

5 For each one will bear his own load.

6 The one who is taught the word is to share all good things with the one who teaches *him*.

7 Do not be deceived, God is not mocked; for whatever a man sows, this he will also reap.

8 For the one who sows to his own flesh will from the flesh reap corruption, but the one who sows to the Spirit will from the Spirit reap eternal life.

9 Let us not lose heart in doing good, for in due time we will reap if we do not grow weary.

10 So then, while we have opportunity, let us do good to all people, and especially to those who are of the household of the faith.

11 See with what large letters I am writing to you with my own hand.

12 Those who desire to make a good showing in the flesh try to compel you to be circumcised, simply so that they will not be persecuted for the cross of Christ.

13 For those who [1]are circumcised do not even keep the Law themselves, but they desire to have you circumcised so that they may boast in your flesh.

14 But may it never be that I would boast, except in the cross of our Lord Jesus Christ, through which the world has been crucified to me, and I to the world.

15 For neither is circumcision anything, nor uncircumcision, but a new creation.

16 And those who will walk by this rule, peace and mercy *be* upon them, and upon the Israel of God.

17 From now on let no one cause trouble for me, for I bear on my body the brand-marks of Jesus.

18 The grace of our Lord Jesus Christ be with your spirit, brethren. Amen.

THE LETTER OF PAUL TO THE EPHESIANS

The Blessings of Redemption

1 Paul, an apostle of Christ Jesus by the will of God,

To the saints who are [2]at Ephesus and *who are* faithful in Christ Jesus:

2 Grace to you and peace from God our Father and the Lord Jesus Christ.

3 Blessed *be* the God and Father of our Lord Jesus Christ, who has blessed us with every spiritual blessing in the heavenly *places* in Christ,

4 just as He chose us in Him before the foundation of the world, that we would be holy and blameless before [3]Him. In love

5 He predestined us to adoption as sons through Jesus Christ to Himself, according to the kind intention of His will,

6 to the praise of the glory of His grace, which He freely bestowed on us in the Beloved.

7 In Him we have redemption through His blood, the forgiveness of our trespasses, according to the riches of His grace

8 which He lavished on us. In all wisdom and insight

9 He made known to us the mystery of His will, according to His kind intention which He purposed in Him

10 with a view to an administration suitable to the fullness of the times, *that is,* the summing up of all things in Christ, things in the heavens and things on the earth. In Him

11 also we have obtained an inheritance, having been predestined according to His purpose who works all things after the counsel of His will,

12 to the end that we who were the first to hope in [4]Christ would be to the praise of His glory.

13 In Him, you also, after listening to the message of truth, the gospel of your salvation—having also believed, you were sealed in Him with the Holy Spirit of promise,

14 who is given as a pledge of our inheritance, with a view to the redemption of *God's own* possession, to the praise of His glory.

15 For this reason I too, having heard of the faith in the Lord Jesus which *exists* among you and [5]your love for all the saints,

16 do not cease giving thanks for you, while making mention *of you* in my prayers;

17 that the God of our Lord Jesus Christ, the Father of glory, may give to you a spirit of wisdom and of revelation in the knowledge of Him.

---

1. Two early mss read *have been* 2. Three early mss do not contain *at Ephesus* 3. Or *Him, in love* 4. I.e. the Messiah
5. Three early mss do not contain *your love*

18 *I pray that* the eyes of your heart may be enlightened, so that you will know what is the hope of His calling, what are the riches of the glory of His inheritance in the saints,

19 and what is the surpassing greatness of His power toward us who believe. *These are* in accordance with the working of the strength of His might

20 which He brought about in Christ, when He raised Him from the dead and seated Him at His right hand in the heavenly *places,*

21 far above all rule and authority and power and dominion, and every name that is named, not only in this age but also in the one to come.

22 And He put all things in subjection under His feet, and gave Him as head over all things to the church,

23 which is His body, the fullness of Him who fills all in all.

Made Alive in Christ

2 And you were dead in your trespasses and sins,

2 in which you formerly walked according to the course of this world, according to the prince of the power of the air, of the spirit that is now working in the sons of disobedience.

3 Among them we too all formerly lived in the lusts of our flesh, indulging the desires of the flesh and of the mind, and were by nature children of wrath, even as the rest.

4 But God, being rich in mercy, because of His great love with which He loved us,

5 even when we were dead in our transgressions, made us alive together [1]with Christ (by grace you have been saved),

6 and raised us up with Him, and seated us with Him in the heavenly *places* in Christ Jesus,

7 so that in the ages to come He might show the surpassing riches of His grace in kindness toward us in Christ Jesus.

8 For by grace you have been saved through faith; and that not of yourselves, *it is* the gift of God;

9 not as a result of works, so that no one may boast.

10 For we are His workmanship, created in Christ Jesus for good works, which God prepared beforehand so that we would walk in them.

11 Therefore remember that formerly you, the Gentiles in the flesh, who are called "Uncircumcision" by the so-called "Circumcision," *which is* performed in the flesh by human hands—

12 *remember* that you were at that time separate from Christ, excluded from the commonwealth of Israel, and strangers to the covenants of promise, having no hope and without God in the world.

13 But now in Christ Jesus you who formerly were far off have been brought near by the blood of Christ.

14 For He Himself is our peace, who made both *groups into* one and broke down the barrier of the dividing wall,

15 by abolishing in His flesh the enmity, *which is* the Law of commandments *contained* in ordinances, so that in Himself He might make the two into one new man, *thus* establishing peace,

16 and might reconcile them both in one body to God through the cross, by it having put to death the enmity.

17 AND HE CAME AND PREACHED PEACE TO YOU WHO WERE FAR AWAY, AND PEACE TO THOSE WHO WERE NEAR;

18 for through Him we both have our access in one Spirit to the Father.

19 So then you are no longer strangers and aliens, but you are fellow citizens with the saints, and are of God's household,

20 having been built on the foundation of the apostles and prophets, Christ Jesus Himself being the corner *stone,*

21 in whom the whole building, being fitted together, is growing into a holy temple in the Lord,

22 in whom you also are being built together into a dwelling of God in the Spirit.

Paul's Stewardship

3 For this reason I, Paul, the prisoner of Christ Jesus for the sake of you Gentiles—

2 if indeed you have heard of the stewardship of God's grace which was given to me for you;

3 that by revelation there was made known to me the mystery, as I wrote before in brief.

4 By referring to this, when you read you can understand my insight into the mystery of Christ,

5 which in other generations was not made known to the sons of men, as it has now been revealed to His holy apostles and prophets in the Spirit;

6 *to be specific,* that the Gentiles are fellow heirs and fellow members of the body, and fellow partakers of the promise in Christ Jesus through the gospel,

7 of which I was made a minister, according to the gift of God's grace which was given to me according to the working of His power.

8 To me, the very least of all saints, this grace was given, to preach to the Gentiles the unfathomable riches of Christ,

9 and to bring to light what is the administration of the mystery which for ages has been hidden in God who created all things;

10 so that the manifold wisdom of God might now be made known through the church to the rulers and the authorities in the heavenly *places.*

11 *This was* in accordance with the eternal purpose which He carried out in Christ Jesus our Lord,

12 in whom we have boldness and confident access through faith in Him.

13 Therefore I ask you not to lose heart at my tribulations on your behalf, for they are your glory.

---

1. Two early mss read *in Christ*

14 For this reason I bow my knees before the Father,

15 from whom every family in heaven and on earth derives its name,

16 that He would grant you, according to the riches of His glory, to be strengthened with power through His Spirit in the inner man,

17 so that Christ may dwell in your hearts through faith; *and* that you, being rooted and grounded in love,

18 may be able to comprehend with all the saints what is the breadth and length and height and depth,

19 and to know the love of Christ which surpasses knowledge, that you may be filled up to all the fullness of God.

20 Now to Him who is able to do far more abundantly beyond all that we ask or think, according to the power that works within us,

21 to Him *be* the glory in the church and in Christ Jesus to all generations forever and ever. Amen.

Unity of the Spirit

4 Therefore I, the prisoner of the Lord, implore you to walk in a manner worthy of the calling which you have been called,

2 with all humility and gentleness, with patience, showing tolerance for one another in love,

3 being diligent to preserve the unity of the Spirit in the bond of peace.

4 *There is* one body and one Spirit, just as also you were called in one hope of your calling;

5 one Lord, one faith, one baptism,

6 one God and Father of all who is over all and through all and in all.

7 But to each one of us grace was given according to the measure of Christ's gift.

8 Therefore it says,

"WHEN HE ASCENDED ON HIGH,
HE LED CAPTIVE A HOST OF CAPTIVES,
AND HE GAVE GIFTS TO MEN."

9 (Now this *expression,* "He ascended," what does it mean except that He also had descended into the lower parts of the earth?

10 He who descended is Himself also He who ascended far above all the heavens, so that He might fill all things.)

11 And He gave some *as* apostles, and some *as* prophets, and some *as* evangelists, and some *as* pastors and teachers,

12 for the equipping of the saints for the work of service, to the building up of the body of Christ;

13 until we all attain to the unity of the faith, and of the knowledge of the Son of God, to a mature man, to the measure of the stature which belongs to the fullness of Christ.

14 As a result, we are no longer to be children, tossed here and there by waves and carried about by every wind of doctrine, by the trickery of men, by craftiness in deceitful scheming;

15 but speaking the truth in love, we are to grow up in all *aspects* into Him who is the head, *even* Christ,

16 from whom the whole body, being fitted and held together by what every joint supplies, according to the proper working of each individual part, causes the growth of the body for the building up of itself in love.

17 So this I say, and affirm together with the Lord, that you walk no longer just as the Gentiles also walk, in the futility of their mind,

18 being darkened in their understanding, excluded from the life of God because of the ignorance that is in them, because of the hardness of their heart;

19 and they, having become callous, have given themselves over to sensuality for the practice of every kind of impurity with greediness.

20 But you did not learn Christ in this way,

21 if indeed you have heard Him and have been taught in Him, just as truth is in Jesus,

22 that, in reference to your former manner of life, you lay aside the old self, which is being corrupted in accordance with the lusts of deceit,

23 and that you be renewed in the spirit of your mind,

24 and put on the new self, which in *the likeness* of God has been created in righteousness and holiness of the truth.

25 Therefore, laying aside falsehood, SPEAK TRUTH EACH ONE *of you* WITH HIS NEIGHBOR, for we are members of one another.

26 BE ANGRY, AND *yet* DO NOT SIN; do not let the sun go down on your anger,

27 and do not give the devil an opportunity.

28 He who steals must steal no longer; but rather he must labor, performing with his own hands what is good, so that he will have *something* to share with one who has need.

29 Let no unwholesome word proceed from your mouth, but only such *a word* as is good for edification according to the need *of the moment,* so that it will give grace to those who hear.

30 Do not grieve the Holy Spirit of God, by whom you were sealed for the day of redemption.

31 Let all bitterness and wrath and anger and clamor and slander be put away from you, along with all malice.

32 Be kind to one another, tender-hearted, forgiving each other, just as God in Christ also has forgiven [1]you.

Be Imitators of God

5 Therefore be imitators of God, as beloved children;

2 and walk in love, just as Christ also loved [2]you and gave Himself up for us, an offering and a sacrifice to God as a fragrant aroma.

3 But immorality or any impurity or greed must not even be named among you, as is proper among saints;

4 and *there must be no* filthiness and silly talk, or coarse jesting, which are not fitting, but rather giving of thanks.

5 For this you know with certainty, that no immoral or impure person or covetous man,

---

1. Two early mss read *us*　2. One early ms reads *us*

who is an idolater, has an inheritance in the kingdom of Christ and God.

6 Let no one deceive you with empty words, for because of these things the wrath of God comes upon the sons of disobedience.

7 Therefore do not be partakers with them;

8 for you were formerly darkness, but now you are Light in the Lord; walk as children of Light

9 (for the fruit of the Light *consists* in all goodness and righteousness and truth),

10 trying to learn what is pleasing to the Lord.

11 Do not participate in the unfruitful deeds of darkness, but instead even expose them;

12 for it is disgraceful even to speak of the things which are done by them in secret.

13 But all things become visible when they are exposed by the light, for everything that becomes visible is light.

14 For this reason it says,
"Awake, sleeper,
And arise from the dead,
And Christ will shine on you."

15 Therefore be careful how you walk, not as unwise men but as wise,

16 making the most of your time, because the days are evil.

17 So then do not be foolish, but understand what the will of the Lord is.

18 And do not get drunk with wine, for that is dissipation, but be filled with the Spirit,

19 speaking to one another in psalms and hymns and spiritual songs, singing and making melody with your heart to the Lord;

20 always giving thanks for all things in the name of our Lord Jesus Christ to God, even the Father;

21 and be subject to one another in the fear of Christ.

22 Wives, *be subject* to your own husbands, as to the Lord.

23 For the husband is the head of the wife, as Christ also is the head of the church, He Himself *being* the Savior of the body.

24 But as the church is subject to Christ, so also the wives *ought to be* to their husbands in everything.

25 Husbands, love your wives, just as Christ also loved the church and gave Himself up for her,

26 so that He might sanctify her, having cleansed her by the washing of water with the word,

27 that He might present to Himself the church in all her glory, having no spot or wrinkle or any such thing; but that she would be holy and blameless.

28 So husbands ought also to love their own wives as their own bodies. He who loves his own wife loves himself;

29 for no one ever hated his own flesh, but nourishes and cherishes it, just as Christ also *does* the church,

30 because we are members of His body.

31 FOR THIS REASON A MAN SHALL LEAVE HIS FATHER AND MOTHER AND SHALL BE JOINED TO HIS WIFE, AND THE TWO SHALL BECOME ONE FLESH.

32 This mystery is great; but I am speaking with reference to Christ and the church.

33 Nevertheless, each individual among you also is to love his own wife even as himself, and the wife must *see to it* that she respects her husband.

Family Relationships

6 Children, obey your parents in the Lord, for this is right.

2 HONOR YOUR FATHER AND MOTHER (which is the first commandment with a promise),

3 SO THAT IT MAY BE WELL WITH YOU, AND THAT YOU MAY LIVE LONG ON THE EARTH.

4 Fathers, do not provoke your children to anger, but bring them up in the discipline and instruction of the Lord.

5 Slaves, be obedient to those who are your masters according to the flesh, with fear and trembling, in the sincerity of your heart, as to Christ;

6 not by way of eyeservice, as men-pleasers, but as slaves of Christ, doing the will of God from the heart.

7 With good will render service, as to the Lord, and not to men,

8 knowing that whatever good thing each one does, this he will receive back from the Lord, whether slave or free.

9 And masters, do the same things to them, and give up threatening, knowing that both their Master and yours is in heaven, and there is no partiality with Him.

10 Finally, be strong in the Lord and in the strength of His might.

11 Put on the full armor of God, so that you will be able to stand firm against the schemes of the devil.

12 For our struggle is not against flesh and blood, but against the rulers, against the powers, against the world forces of this darkness, against the spiritual *forces* of wickedness in the heavenly *places*.

13 Therefore, take up the full armor of God, so that you will be able to resist in the evil day, and having done everything, to stand firm.

14 Stand firm therefore, HAVING GIRDED YOUR LOINS WITH TRUTH, and HAVING PUT ON THE BREASTPLATE OF RIGHTEOUSNESS,

15 and having shod YOUR FEET WITH THE PREPARATION OF THE GOSPEL OF PEACE;

16 in addition to all, taking up the shield of faith with which you will be able to extinguish all the flaming arrows of the evil *one*.

17 And take THE HELMET OF SALVATION, and the sword of the Spirit, which is the word of God.

18 With all prayer and petition pray at all times in the Spirit, and with this in view, be on the alert with all perseverance and petition for all the saints,

19 and *pray* on my behalf, that utterance may be given to me in the opening of my mouth, to make known with boldness the mystery of the gospel,

20 for which I am an ambassador in chains; that [1]in *proclaiming* it I may speak boldly, as I ought to speak.

21 But that you also may know about my circumstances, how I am doing, Tychicus, the beloved brother and faithful minister in the Lord, will make everything known to you.

22 I have sent him to you for this very purpose, so that you may know about us, and that he may comfort your hearts.

23 Peace be to the brethren, and love with faith, from God the Father and the Lord Jesus Christ.

24 Grace be with all those who love our Lord Jesus Christ with incorruptible *love.*

THE LETTER OF PAUL TO THE PHILIPPIANS

Thanksgiving

1 Paul and Timothy, bond-servants of Christ Jesus,

To all the saints in Christ Jesus who are in Philippi, including the overseers and deacons:

2 Grace to you and peace from God our Father and the Lord Jesus Christ.

3 I thank my God in all my remembrance of you,

4 always offering prayer with joy in my every prayer for you all,

5 in view of your participation in the gospel from the first day until now.

6 *For I am* confident of this very thing, that He who began a good work in you will perfect it until the day of Christ Jesus.

7 For it is only right for me to feel this way about you all, because I have you in my heart, since both in my imprisonment and in the defense and confirmation of the gospel, you all are partakers of grace with me.

8 For God is my witness, how I long for you all with the affection of Christ Jesus.

9 And this I pray, that your love may abound still more and more in real knowledge and all discernment,

10 so that you may approve the things that are excellent, in order to be sincere and blameless until the day of Christ;

11 having been filled with the fruit of righteousness which *comes* through Jesus Christ, to the glory and praise of God.

12 Now I want you to know, brethren, that my circumstances have turned out for the greater progress of the gospel,

13 so that my imprisonment in *the cause of* Christ has become well known throughout the whole [2]praetorian guard and to everyone else,

14 and that most of the brethren, trusting in the Lord because of my imprisonment, have far more courage to speak the word of God without fear.

15 Some, to be sure, are preaching Christ even from envy and strife, but some also from good will;

16 the latter *do it* out of love, knowing that I am appointed for the defense of the gospel;

17 the former proclaim Christ out of selfish ambition rather than from pure motives, thinking to cause me distress in my imprisonment.

18 What then? Only that in every way, whether in pretense or in truth, Christ is proclaimed; and in this I rejoice.

Yes, and I will rejoice,

19 for I know that this will turn out for my deliverance through your prayers and the provision of the Spirit of Jesus Christ,

20 according to my earnest expectation and hope, that I will not be put to shame in anything, but *that* with all boldness, Christ will even now, as always, be exalted in my body, whether by life or by death.

21 For to me, to live is Christ and to die is gain.

22 But if *I am* to live *on* in the flesh, this *will mean* fruitful labor for me; and I do not know which to choose.

23 But I am hard-pressed from both *directions,* having the desire to depart and be with Christ, for *that* is very much better;

24 yet to remain on in the flesh is more necessary for your sake.

25 Convinced of this, I know that I will remain and continue with you all for your progress and joy in the faith,

26 so that your proud confidence in me may abound in Christ Jesus through my coming to you again.

27 Only conduct yourselves in a manner worthy of the gospel of Christ, so that whether I come and see you or remain absent, I will hear of you that you are standing firm in one spirit, with one mind striving together for the faith of the gospel;

28 in no way alarmed by *your* opponents—which is a sign of destruction for them, but of salvation for you, and that *too,* from God.

29 For to you it has been granted for Christ's sake, not only to believe in Him, but also to suffer for His sake,

30 experiencing the same conflict which you saw in me, and now hear *to be* in me.

Be Like Christ

2 Therefore if there is any encouragement in Christ, if there is any consolation of love, if there is any fellowship of the Spirit, if any affection and compassion,

2 make my joy complete by being of the same mind, maintaining the same love, united in spirit, intent on one purpose.

3 Do nothing from selfishness or empty conceit, but with humility of mind regard one another as more important than yourselves;

4 do not *merely* look out for your own personal interests, but also for the interests of others.

---

1. Two early mss read *I may speak it boldly* 2. Or *governor's palace*

5 Have this attitude in yourselves which was also in Christ Jesus,

6 who, although He existed in the form of God, did not regard equality with God a thing to be grasped,

7 but [1]emptied Himself, taking the form of a bond-servant, *and* being made in the likeness of men.

8 Being found in appearance as a man, He humbled Himself by becoming obedient to the point of death, even death on a cross.

9 For this reason also, God highly exalted Him, and bestowed on Him the name which is above every name,

10 so that at the name of Jesus EVERY KNEE WILL BOW, of those who are in heaven and on earth and under the earth,

11 and that every tongue will confess that Jesus Christ is Lord, to the glory of God the Father.

12 So then, my beloved, just as you have always obeyed, not as in my presence only, but now much more in my absence, work out your salvation with fear and trembling;

13 for it is God who is at work in you, both to will and to work for *His* good pleasure.

14 Do all things without grumbling or disputing;

15 so that you will prove yourselves to be blameless and innocent, children of God above reproach in the midst of a crooked and perverse generation, among whom you appear as lights in the world,

16 holding fast the word of life, so that in the day of Christ I will have reason to glory because I did not run in vain nor toil in vain.

17 But even if I am being poured out as a drink offering upon the sacrifice and service of your faith, I rejoice and share my joy with you all.

18 You too, *I urge you,* rejoice in the same way and share your joy with me.

19 But I hope in the Lord Jesus to send Timothy to you shortly, so that I also may be encouraged when I learn of your condition.

20 For I have no one *else* of kindred spirit who will genuinely be concerned for your welfare.

21 For they all seek after their own interests, not those of Christ Jesus.

22 But you know of his proven worth, that he served with me in the furtherance of the gospel like a child *serving* his father.

23 Therefore I hope to send him immediately, as soon as I see how things *go* with me;

24 and I trust in the Lord that I myself also will be coming shortly.

25 But I thought it necessary to send to you Epaphroditus, my brother and fellow worker and fellow soldier, who is also your messenger and minister to my need;

26 because he was longing [2]for you all and was distressed because you had heard that he was sick.

27 For indeed he was sick to the point of death, but God had mercy on him, and not on

him only but also on me, so that I would not have sorrow upon sorrow.

28 Therefore I have sent him all the more eagerly so that when you see him again you may rejoice and I may be less concerned *about you.*

29 Receive him then in the Lord with all joy, and hold men like him in high regard;

30 because he came close to death for the work of Christ, risking his life to complete what was deficient in your service to me.

The Goal of Life

3 Finally, my brethren, rejoice in the Lord. To write the same things *again* is no trouble to me, and it is a safeguard for you.

2 Beware of the dogs, beware of the evil workers, beware of the false circumcision;

3 for we are the *true* circumcision, who worship in the Spirit of God and glory in Christ Jesus and put no confidence in the flesh,

4 although I myself might have confidence even in the flesh. If anyone else has a mind to put confidence in the flesh, I far more:

5 circumcised the eighth day, of the nation of Israel, of the tribe of Benjamin, a Hebrew of Hebrews; as to the Law, a Pharisee;

6 as to zeal, a persecutor of the church; as to the righteousness which is in the Law, found blameless.

7 But whatever things were gain to me, those things I have counted as loss for the sake of Christ.

8 More than that, I count all things to be loss in view of the surpassing value of knowing Christ Jesus my Lord, for whom I have suffered the loss of all things, and count them but rubbish so that I may gain Christ,

9 and may be found in Him, not having a righteousness of my own derived from *the* Law, but that which is through faith in Christ, the righteousness which *comes* from God on the basis of faith,

10 that I may know Him and the power of His resurrection and the fellowship of His sufferings, being conformed to His death;

11 in order that I may attain to the resurrection from the dead.

12 Not that I have already obtained *it* or have already become perfect, but I press on so that I may lay hold of that for which also I was laid hold of by Christ Jesus.

13 Brethren, I do not regard myself as having laid hold of *it* yet; but one thing *I do:* forgetting what *lies* behind and reaching forward to what *lies* ahead,

14 I press on toward the goal for the prize of the upward call of God in Christ Jesus.

15 Let us therefore, as many as are perfect, have this attitude; and if in anything you have a different attitude, God will reveal that also to you;

16 however, let us keep living by that same *standard* to which we have attained.

17 Brethren, join in following my example,

1. I.e. laid aside His privileges 2. One early ms reads *to see you all*

and observe those who walk according to the pattern you have in us.

18 For many walk, of whom I often told you, and now tell you even weeping, *that they are* enemies of the cross of Christ,

19 whose end is destruction, whose god is *their* appetite, and *whose* glory is in their shame, who set their minds on earthly things.

20 For our citizenship is in heaven, from which also we eagerly wait for a Savior, the Lord Jesus Christ;

21 who will transform the body of our humble state into conformity with the body of His glory, by the exertion of the power that He has even to subject all things to Himself.

Think of Excellence

4 Therefore, my beloved brethren whom I long *to see*, my joy and crown, in this way stand firm in the Lord, my beloved.

2 I urge Euodia and I urge Syntyche to live in harmony in the Lord.

3 Indeed, true companion, I ask you also to help these women who have shared my struggle in *the cause of* the gospel, together with Clement also and the rest of my fellow workers, whose names are in the book of life.

4 Rejoice in the Lord always; again I will say, rejoice!

5 Let your gentle *spirit* be known to all men. The Lord is near.

6 Be anxious for nothing, but in everything by prayer and supplication with thanksgiving let your requests be made known to God.

7 And the peace of God, which surpasses all comprehension, will guard your hearts and your minds in Christ Jesus.

8 Finally, brethren, whatever is true, whatever is honorable, whatever is right, whatever is pure, whatever is lovely, whatever is of good repute, if there is any excellence and if anything worthy of praise, dwell on these things.

9 The things you have learned and received and heard and seen in me, practice these things, and the God of peace will be with you.

10 But I rejoiced in the Lord greatly, that now at last you have revived your concern for me; indeed, you were concerned *before*, but you lacked opportunity.

11 Not that I speak from want, for I have learned to be content in whatever circumstances I am.

12 I know how to get along with humble means, and I also know how to live in prosperity; in any and every circumstance I have learned the secret of being filled and going hungry, both of having abundance and suffering need.

13 I can do all things through Him who strengthens me.

14 Nevertheless, you have done well to share *with me* in my affliction.

15 You yourselves also know, Philippians, that at the first preaching of the gospel, after I left Macedonia, no church shared with me in the matter of giving and receiving but you alone;

16 for even in Thessalonica you sent *a gift* more than once for my needs.

17 Not that I seek the gift itself, but I seek for the profit which increases to your account.

18 But I have received everything in full and have an abundance; I am amply supplied, having received from Epaphroditus what you have sent, a fragrant aroma, an acceptable sacrifice, well-pleasing to God.

19 And my God will supply all your needs according to His riches in glory in Christ Jesus.

20 Now to our God and Father *be* the glory forever and ever. Amen.

21 Greet every saint in Christ Jesus. The brethren who are with me greet you.

22 All the saints greet you, especially those of Caesar's household.

23 The grace of the Lord Jesus Christ be with your spirit.

THE LETTER OF PAUL TO THE COLOSSIANS

Thankfulness for Spiritual Attainments

1 Paul, an apostle of Jesus Christ by the will of God, and Timothy our brother,

2 To the saints and faithful brethren in Christ *who are* at Colossae: Grace to you and peace from God our Father.

3 We give thanks to God, the Father of our Lord Jesus Christ, praying always for you,

4 since we heard of your faith in Christ Jesus and the love which you have for all the saints;

5 because of the hope laid up for you in heaven, of which you previously heard in the word of truth, the gospel

6 which has come to you, just as in all the world also it is constantly bearing fruit and increasing, even as *it has been doing* in you also since the day you heard *of it* and understood the grace of God in truth;

7 just as you learned *it* from Epaphras, our beloved fellow bond-servant, who is a faithful servant of Christ on our behalf,

8 and he also informed us of your love in the Spirit.

9 For this reason also, since the day we heard *of it*, we have not ceased to pray for you and to ask that you may be filled with the knowledge of His will in all spiritual wisdom and understanding,

10 so that you will walk in a manner worthy of the Lord, to please *Him* in all respects, bearing fruit in every good work and increasing in the knowledge of God;

11 strengthened with all power, according to His glorious might, for the attaining of all steadfastness and patience; joyously

12 giving thanks to the Father, who has qualified us to share in the inheritance of the saints in Light.

13 For He rescued us from the domain of darkness, and transferred us to the kingdom of His beloved Son,

14 in whom we have redemption, the forgiveness of sins.

15 He is the image of the invisible God, the firstborn of all creation.

16 For by Him all things were created, *both* in the heavens and on earth, visible and invisible, whether thrones or dominions or rulers or authorities—all things have been created through Him and for Him.

17 He is before all things, and in Him all things hold together.

18 He is also head of the body, the church; and He is the beginning, the firstborn from the dead, so that He Himself will come to have first place in everything.

19 For it was the *Father's* good pleasure for all the fullness to dwell in Him,

20 and through Him to reconcile all things to Himself, having made peace through the blood of His cross; through Him, *I say*, whether things on earth or things in heaven.

21 And although you were formerly alienated and hostile in mind, *engaged* in evil deeds,

22 yet He has now reconciled you in His fleshly body through death, in order to present you before Him holy and blameless and beyond reproach—

23 if indeed you continue in the faith firmly established and steadfast, and not moved away from the hope of the gospel that you have heard, which was proclaimed in all creation under heaven, and of which I, Paul, was made a minister.

24 Now I rejoice in my sufferings for your sake, and in my flesh I do my share on behalf of His body, which is the church, in filling up what is lacking in Christ's afflictions.

25 Of *this church* I was made a minister according to the stewardship from God bestowed on me for your benefit, so that I might fully carry out the *preaching of* the word of God,

26 *that is,* the mystery which has been hidden from the *past* ages and generations, but has now been manifested to His saints,

27 to whom God willed to make known what is the riches of the glory of this mystery among the Gentiles, which is Christ in you, the hope of glory.

28 We proclaim Him, admonishing every man and teaching every man with all wisdom, so that we may present every man complete in Christ.

29 For this purpose also I labor, striving according to His power, which mightily works within me.

You Are Built Up in Christ

2 For I want you to know how great a struggle I have on your behalf and for those who are at Laodicea, and for all those who have not personally seen my face,

2 that their hearts may be encouraged, having been knit together in love, and *attaining* to all the wealth that comes from the full assurance of understanding, *resulting* in a true

knowledge of God's mystery, *that is,* Christ *Himself,*

3 in whom are hidden all the treasures of wisdom and knowledge.

4 I say this so that no one will delude you with persuasive argument.

5 For even though I am absent in body, nevertheless I am with you in spirit, rejoicing to see your good discipline and the stability of your faith in Christ.

6 Therefore as you have received Christ Jesus the Lord, *so* walk in Him,

7 having been firmly rooted *and now* being built up in Him and established [1]in your faith, just as you were instructed, *and* overflowing with gratitude.

8 See to it that no one takes you captive through philosophy and empty deception, according to the tradition of men, according to the elementary principles of the world, rather than according to Christ.

9 For in Him all the fullness of Deity dwells in bodily form,

10 and in Him you have been made complete, and He is the head over all rule and authority;

11 and in Him you were also circumcised with a circumcision made without hands, in the removal of the body of the flesh by the circumcision of Christ;

12 having been buried with Him in baptism, in which you were also raised up with Him through faith in the working of God, who raised Him from the dead.

13 When you were dead in your transgressions and the uncircumcision of your flesh, He made you alive together with Him, having forgiven us all our transgressions,

14 having canceled out the certificate of debt consisting of decrees against us, which was hostile to us; and He has taken it out of the way, having nailed it to the cross.

15 When He had disarmed the rulers and authorities, He made a public display of them, having triumphed over them through Him.

16 Therefore no one is to act as your judge in regard to food or drink or in respect to a festival or a new moon or a Sabbath day—

17 things which are a *mere* shadow of what is to come; but the substance belongs to Christ.

18 Let no one keep defrauding you of your prize by delighting in self-abasement and the worship of the angels, taking his stand on *visions* he has seen, inflated without cause by his fleshly mind,

19 and not holding fast to the head, from whom the entire body, being supplied and held together by the joints and ligaments, grows with a growth which is from God.

20 If you have died with Christ to the elementary principles of the world, why, as if you were living in the world, do you submit yourself to decrees, such as,

21 "Do not handle, do not taste, do not touch!"

22 (which all *refer to* things destined to perish

---

1. Or *by*

with use)—in accordance with the commandments and teachings of men?

23 These are matters which have, to be sure, the appearance of wisdom in self-made religion and self-abasement and severe treatment of the body, *but are* of no value against fleshly indulgence.

Put On the New Self

3 Therefore if you have been raised up with Christ, keep seeking the things above, where Christ is, seated at the right hand of God.

2 Set your mind on the things above, not on the things that are on earth.

3 For you have died and your life is hidden with Christ in God.

4 When Christ, who is our life, is revealed, then you also will be revealed with Him in glory.

5 Therefore consider the members of your earthly body as dead to immorality, impurity, passion, evil desire, and greed, which amounts to idolatry.

6 For it is because of these things that the wrath of God will come [1]upon the sons of disobedience,

7 and in them you also once walked, when you were living in them.

8 But now you also, put them all aside: anger, wrath, malice, slander, *and* abusive speech from your mouth.

9 Do not lie to one another, since you laid aside the old self with its *evil* practices,

10 and have put on the new self who is being renewed to a true knowledge according to the image of the One who created him—

11 *a renewal* in which there is no *distinction between* Greek and Jew, circumcised and uncircumcised, barbarian, Scythian, slave and freeman, but Christ is all, and in all.

12 So, as those who have been chosen of God, holy and beloved, put on a heart of compassion, kindness, humility, gentleness and patience;

13 bearing with one another, and forgiving each other, whoever has a complaint against anyone; just as the Lord forgave you, so also should you.

14 Beyond all these things *put on* love, which is the perfect bond of unity.

15 Let the peace of Christ rule in your hearts, to which indeed you were called in one body; and be thankful.

16 Let the word of [2]Christ richly dwell within you, with all wisdom teaching and admonishing one another with psalms *and* hymns *and* spiritual songs, singing with thankfulness in your hearts to God.

17 Whatever you do in word or deed, *do* all in the name of the Lord Jesus, giving thanks through Him to God the Father.

18 Wives, be subject to your husbands, as is fitting in the Lord.

19 Husbands, love your wives and do not be embittered against them.

20 Children, be obedient to your parents in all things, for this is well-pleasing to the Lord.

21 Fathers, do not exasperate your children, so that they will not lose heart.

22 Slaves, in all things obey those who are your masters on earth, not with external service, as those who *merely* please men, but with sincerity of heart, fearing the Lord.

23 Whatever you do, do your work heartily, as for the Lord rather than for men,

24 knowing that from the Lord you will receive the reward of the inheritance. It is the Lord Christ whom you serve.

25 For he who does wrong will receive the consequences of the wrong which he has done, and that without partiality.

Fellow Workers

4 Masters, grant to your slaves justice and fairness, knowing that you too have a Master in heaven.

2 Devote yourselves to prayer, keeping alert in it with *an attitude of* thanksgiving;

3 praying at the same time for us as well, that God will open up to us a door for the word, so that we may speak forth the mystery of Christ, for which I have also been imprisoned;

4 that I may make it clear in the way I ought to speak.

5 Conduct yourselves with wisdom toward outsiders, making the most of the opportunity.

6 Let your speech always be with grace, *as though* seasoned with salt, so that you will know how you should respond to each person.

7 As to all my affairs, Tychicus, *our* beloved brother and faithful servant and fellow bond-servant in the Lord, will bring you information.

8 *For* I have sent him to you for this very purpose, that you may know about our circumstances and that he may encourage your hearts;

9 and with him Onesimus, *our* faithful and beloved brother, who is one of your *number.* They will inform you about the whole situation here.

10 Aristarchus, my fellow prisoner, sends you his greetings; and *also* Barnabas' cousin Mark (about whom you received instructions; if he comes to you, welcome him);

11 and *also* Jesus who is called Justus; these are the only fellow workers for the kingdom of God who are from the circumcision, and they have proved to be an encouragement to me.

12 Epaphras, who is one of your number, a bondslave of Jesus Christ, sends you his greetings, always laboring earnestly for you in his prayers, that you may stand perfect and fully assured in all the will of God.

13 For I testify for him that he has a deep concern for you and for those who are in Laodicea and Hierapolis.

14 Luke, the beloved physician, sends you his greetings, and *also* Demas.

15 Greet the brethren who are in Laodicea and also [3]Nympha and the church that is in her house.

---

1. Two early mss do not contain *upon the sons of disobedience* 2. One early ms reads *the Lord* 3. Or *Nymphas* (masc)

16 When this letter is read among you, have it also read in the church of the Laodiceans; and you, for your part read my letter *that is coming* from Laodicea.

17 Say to Archippus, "Take heed to the ministry which you have received in the Lord, that you may fulfill it."

18 I, Paul, write this greeting with my own hand. Remember my imprisonment. Grace be with you.

THE FIRST LETTER OF PAUL TO THE THESSALONIANS

Thanksgiving for These Believers

1 Paul and Silvanus and Timothy,
To the church of the Thessalonians in God the Father and the Lord Jesus Christ: Grace to you and peace.

2 We give thanks to God always for all of you, making mention *of you* in our prayers;

3 constantly bearing in mind your work of faith and labor of love and steadfastness of hope in our Lord Jesus Christ in the presence of our God and Father,

4 knowing, brethren beloved by God, *His* choice of you;

5 for our gospel did not come to you in word only, but also in power and in the Holy Spirit and with full conviction; just as you know what kind of men we proved to be among you for your sake.

6 You also became imitators of us and of the Lord, having received the word in much tribulation with the joy of the Holy Spirit,

7 so that you became an example to all the believers in Macedonia and in Achaia.

8 For the word of the Lord has sounded forth from you, not only in Macedonia and Achaia, but also in every place your faith toward God has gone forth, so that we have no need to say anything.

9 For they themselves report about us what kind of a reception we had with you, and how you turned to God from idols to serve a living and true God,

10 and to wait for His Son from heaven, whom He raised from the dead, *that is* Jesus, who rescues us from the wrath to come.

Paul's Ministry

2 For you yourselves know, brethren, that our coming to you was not in vain,

2 but after we had already suffered and been mistreated in Philippi, as you know, we had the boldness in our God to speak to you the gospel of God amid much opposition.

3 For our exhortation does not *come* from error or impurity or by way of deceit;

4 but just as we have been approved by God to be entrusted with the gospel, so we speak, not as pleasing men, but God who examines our hearts.

5 For we never came with flattering speech, as you know, nor with a pretext for greed—God is witness—

6 nor did we seek glory from men, either from you or from others, even though as apostles of Christ we might have asserted our authority.

7 But we proved to be ¹gentle among you, as a nursing *mother* tenderly cares for her own children.

8 Having so fond an affection for you, we were well-pleased to impart to you not only the gospel of God but also our own lives, because you had become very dear to us.

9 For you recall, brethren, our labor and hardship, *how* working night and day so as not to be a burden to any of you, we proclaimed to you the gospel of God.

10 You are witnesses, and *so is* God, how devoutly and uprightly and blamelessly we behaved toward you believers;

11 just as you know how we *were* exhorting and encouraging and imploring each one of you as a father *would* his own children,

12 so that you would walk in a manner worthy of the God who calls you into His own kingdom and glory.

13 For this reason we also constantly thank God that when you received the word of God which you heard from us, you accepted *it* not *as* the word of men, but *for* what it really is, the word of God, which also performs its work in you who believe.

14 For you, brethren, became imitators of the churches of God in Christ Jesus that are in Judea, for you also endured the same sufferings at the hands of your own countrymen, even as they *did* from the Jews,

15 who both killed the Lord Jesus and the prophets, and drove us out. They are not pleasing to God, but hostile to all men,

16 hindering us from speaking to the Gentiles so that they may be saved; with the result that they always fill up the measure of their sins. But wrath has come upon them ²to the utmost.

17 But we, brethren, having been taken away from you for a short while—in person, not in spirit—were all the more eager with great desire to see your face.

18 For we wanted to come to you—I, Paul, more than once—and *yet* Satan hindered us.

19 For who is our hope or joy or crown of exultation? Is it not even you, in the presence of our Lord Jesus at His coming?

20 For you are our glory and joy.

Encouragement of Timothy's Visit

3 Therefore when we could endure *it* no longer, we thought it best to be left behind at Athens alone,

2 and we sent Timothy, our brother and God's fellow worker in the gospel of Christ, to strengthen and encourage you as to your faith,

3 so that no one would be disturbed by these afflictions; for you yourselves know that we have been destined for this.

---

1. Three early mss read *babes* 2. Or *forever* or *altogether*; lit *to the end*

4 For indeed when we were with you, we *kept* telling you in advance that we were going to suffer affliction; and so it came to pass, as you know.

5 For this reason, when I could endure *it* no longer, I also sent to find out about your faith, for fear that the tempter might have tempted you, and our labor would be in vain.

6 But now that Timothy has come to us from you, and has brought us good news of your faith and love, and that you always think kindly of us, longing to see us just as we also long to see you,

7 for this reason, brethren, in all our distress and affliction we were comforted about you through your faith;

8 for now we *really* live, if you stand firm in the Lord.

9 For what thanks can we render to God for you in return for all the joy with which we rejoice before our God on your account,

10 as we night and day keep praying most earnestly that we may see your face, and may complete what is lacking in your faith?

11 Now may our God and Father Himself and Jesus our Lord direct our way to you;

12 and may the Lord cause you to increase and abound in love for one another, and for all people, just as we also *do* for you;

13 so that He may establish your hearts without blame in holiness before our God and Father at the coming of our Lord Jesus with all His saints.

Sanctification and Love

4 Finally then, brethren, we request and exhort you in the Lord Jesus, that as you received from us *instruction* as to how you ought to walk and please God (just as you actually do ¹walk), that you excel still more.

2 For you know what commandments we gave you ²by *the authority of* the Lord Jesus.

3 For this is the will of God, your sanctification; *that is,* that you abstain from sexual immorality;

4 that each of you know how to possess his own ³vessel in sanctification and honor,

5 not in lustful passion, like the Gentiles who do not know God;

6 *and* that no man transgress and defraud his brother in the matter because the Lord is *the* avenger in all these things, just as we also told you before and solemnly warned *you.*

7 For God has not called us for the purpose of impurity, but in sanctification.

8 So, he who rejects *this* is not rejecting man but the God who gives His Holy Spirit to you.

9 Now as to the love of the brethren, you have no need for *anyone* to write to you, for you yourselves are taught by God to love one another;

10 for indeed you do practice it toward all the brethren who are in all Macedonia. But we urge you, brethren, to excel still more,

11 and to make it your ambition to lead a quiet life and attend to your own business and work with your hands, just as we commanded you,

12 so that you will behave properly toward outsiders and not be in any need.

13 But we do not want you to be uninformed, brethren, about those who are asleep, so that you will not grieve as do the rest who have no hope.

14 For if we believe that Jesus died and rose again, even so God will bring with Him those who have fallen asleep in Jesus.

15 For this we say to you by the word of the Lord, that we who are alive and remain until the coming of the Lord, will not precede those who have fallen asleep.

16 For the Lord Himself will descend from heaven with a shout, with the voice of *the* archangel and with the trumpet of God, and the dead in Christ will rise first.

17 Then we who are alive and remain will be caught up together with them in the clouds to meet the Lord in the air, and so we shall always be with the Lord.

18 Therefore comfort one another with these words.

The Day of the Lord

5 Now as to the times and the epochs, brethren, you have no need of anything to be written to you.

2 For you yourselves know full well that the day of the Lord will come just like a thief in the night.

3 While they are saying, "Peace and safety!" then destruction will come upon them suddenly like labor pains upon a woman with child, and they will not escape.

4 But you, brethren, are not in darkness, that the day would overtake you like a thief;

5 for you are all sons of light and sons of day. We are not of night nor of darkness;

6 so then let us not sleep as others do, but let us be alert and ⁴sober.

7 For those who sleep do their sleeping at night, and those who get drunk get drunk at night.

8 But since we are of *the* day, let us be ⁴sober, having put on the breastplate of faith and love, and as a helmet, the hope of salvation.

9 For God has not destined us for wrath, but for obtaining salvation through our Lord Jesus Christ,

10 who died for us, so that whether we are awake or asleep, we will live together with Him.

11 Therefore encourage one another and build up one another, just as you also are doing.

12 But we request of you, brethren, that you appreciate those who diligently labor among you, and have charge over you in the Lord and give you instruction,

13 and that you esteem them very highly in love because of their work. Live in peace with one another.

14 We urge you, brethren, admonish the unruly, encourage the fainthearted, help the weak, be patient with everyone.

---

1. Or *conduct yourselves*   2. Lit *through the Lord*   3. I.e. body; or wife   4. Or *self-controlled*

15 See that no one repays another with evil for evil, but always seek after that which is good for one another and for all people.

16 Rejoice always;

17 pray without ceasing;

18 in everything give thanks; for this is God's will for you in Christ Jesus.

19 Do not quench the Spirit;

20 do not despise prophetic [1]utterances.

21 But examine everything *carefully;* hold fast to that which is good;

22 abstain from every [2]form of evil.

23 Now may the God of peace Himself sanctify you entirely; and may your spirit and soul and body be preserved complete, without blame at the coming of our Lord Jesus Christ.

24 Faithful is He who calls you, and He also will bring it to pass.

25 Brethren, pray for us[3].

26 Greet all the brethren with a holy kiss.

27 I adjure you by the Lord to have this letter read to all the brethren.

28 The grace of our Lord Jesus Christ be with you.

THE SECOND LETTER OF PAUL TO THE THESSALONIANS

Thanksgiving for Faith and Perseverance

1 Paul and Silvanus and Timothy,
To the church of the Thessalonians in God our Father and the Lord Jesus Christ:

2 Grace to you and peace from God the Father and the Lord Jesus Christ.

3 We ought always to give thanks to God for you, brethren, as is *only* fitting, because your faith is greatly enlarged, and the love of each one of you toward one another grows *ever* greater;

4 therefore, we ourselves speak proudly of you among the churches of God for your perseverance and faith in the midst of all your persecutions and afflictions which you endure.

5 *This is* a plain indication of God's righteous judgment so that you will be considered worthy of the kingdom of God, for which indeed you are suffering.

6 For after all it is *only* just for God to repay with affliction those who afflict you,

7 and *to give* relief to you who are afflicted and to us as well when the Lord Jesus will be revealed from heaven with His mighty angels in flaming fire,

8 dealing out retribution to those who do not know God and to those who do not obey the gospel of our Lord Jesus.

9 These will pay the penalty of eternal destruction, away from the presence of the Lord and from the glory of His power,

10 when He comes to be glorified in His saints on that day, and to be marveled at among all who have believed—for our testimony to you was believed.

11 To this end also we pray for you always, that our God will count you worthy of your calling, and fulfill every desire for goodness and the work of faith with power,

12 so that the name of our Lord Jesus will be glorified in you, and you in Him, according to the grace of our God and *the* Lord Jesus Christ.

Man of Lawlessness

2 Now we request you, brethren, with regard to the coming of our Lord Jesus Christ and our gathering together to Him,

2 that you not be quickly shaken from your composure or be disturbed either by a spirit or a message or a letter as if from us, to the effect that the day of the Lord has come.

3 Let no one in any way deceive you, for *it will not come* unless the [4]apostasy comes first, and the man of lawlessness is revealed, the son of destruction,

4 who opposes and exalts himself above every so-called god or object of worship, so that he takes his seat in the temple of God, displaying himself as being God.

5 Do you not remember that while I was still with you, I was telling you these things?

6 And you know what restrains him now, so that in his time he will be revealed.

7 For the mystery of lawlessness is already at work; only he who now restrains *will do so* until he is taken out of the way.

8 Then that lawless one will be revealed whom the Lord will slay with the breath of His mouth and bring to an end by the appearance of His coming;

9 *that is,* the one whose coming is in accord with the activity of Satan, with all power and signs and false wonders,

10 and with all the deception of wickedness for those who perish, because they did not receive the love of the truth so as to be saved.

11 For this reason God will send upon them a deluding influence so that they will believe what is false,

12 in order that they all may be judged who did not believe the truth, but took pleasure in wickedness.

13 But we should always give thanks to God for you, brethren beloved by the Lord, because God has chosen you [5]from the beginning for salvation through sanctification by the Spirit and faith in the truth.

14 It was for this He called you through our gospel, that you may gain the glory of our Lord Jesus Christ.

15 So then, brethren, stand firm and hold to the traditions which you were taught, whether by word *of mouth* or by letter from us.

16 Now may our Lord Jesus Christ Himself and God our Father, who has loved us and given us eternal comfort and good hope by grace,

17 comfort and strengthen your hearts in every good work and word.

---

1. Or *gifts* 2. Or *appearance* 3. Two early mss add *also* 4. Or *falling away* from the faith 5. One early ms reads *first fruits*

What is the gospel? Read 1 Corinthians 15:1-7 on page 138.

Exhortation

3 Finally, brethren, pray for us that the word of the Lord will spread rapidly and be glorified, just as *it did* also with you;

2 and that we will be rescued from perverse and evil men; for not all have faith.

3 But the Lord is faithful, and He will strengthen and protect you from the evil *one.*

4 We have confidence in the Lord concerning you, that you are doing and will *continue to* do what we command.

5 May the Lord direct your hearts into the love of God and into the steadfastness of Christ.

6 Now we command you, brethren, in the name of our Lord Jesus Christ, that you keep away from every brother who leads an unruly life and not according to the tradition which you received from us.

7 For you yourselves know how you ought to follow our example, because we did not act in an undisciplined manner among you,

8 nor did we eat anyone's bread without paying for it, but with labor and hardship we *kept* working night and day so that we would not be a burden to any of you;

9 not because we do not have the right *to* use

this, but in order to offer ourselves as a model for you, so that you would follow our example.

10 For even when we were with you, we used to give you this order: if anyone is not willing to work, then he is not to eat, either.

11 For we hear that some among you are leading an undisciplined life, doing no work at all, but acting like busybodies.

12 Now such persons we command and exhort in the Lord Jesus Christ to work in quiet fashion and eat their own bread.

13 But as for you, brethren, do not grow weary of doing good.

14 If anyone does not obey our instruction in this letter, take special note of that person and do not associate with him, so that he will be put to shame.

15 *Yet* do not regard him as an enemy, but admonish him as a brother.

16 Now may the Lord of peace Himself continually grant you peace in every circumstance. The Lord be with you all!

17 I, Paul, write this greeting with my own hand, and this is a distinguishing mark in every letter; this is the way I write.

18 The grace of our Lord Jesus Christ be with you all.

THE FIRST LETTER OF PAUL TO TIMOTHY

Misleadings in Doctrine and Living

1 Paul, an apostle of Christ Jesus according to the commandment of God our Savior, and of Christ Jesus, *who is* our hope,

2 To Timothy, *my* true child in *the* faith: Grace, mercy *and* peace from God the Father and Christ Jesus our Lord.

3 As I urged you upon my departure for Macedonia, remain on at Ephesus so that you may instruct certain men not to teach strange doctrines,

4 nor to pay attention to myths and endless genealogies, which give rise to mere speculation rather than *furthering* the administration of God which is by faith.

5 But the goal of our instruction is love from a pure heart and a good conscience and a sincere faith.

6 For some men, straying from these things, have turned aside to fruitless discussion,

7 wanting to be teachers of the Law, even though they do not understand either what they are saying or the matters about which they make confident assertions.

8 But we know that the Law is good, if one uses it lawfully,

9 realizing the fact that law is not made for a righteous person, but for those who are lawless and rebellious, for the ungodly and sinners, for the unholy and profane, for those who kill their fathers or mothers, for murderers

10 and immoral men and homosexuals and kidnappers and liars and perjurers, and whatever else is contrary to sound teaching,

11 according to the glorious gospel of the blessed God, with which I have been entrusted.

12 I thank Christ Jesus our Lord, who has

strengthened me, because He considered me faithful, putting me into service,

13 even though I was formerly a blasphemer and a persecutor and a violent aggressor. Yet I was shown mercy because I acted ignorantly in unbelief;

14 and the grace of our Lord was more than abundant, with the faith and love which are *found* in Christ Jesus.

15 It is a trustworthy statement, deserving full acceptance, that Christ Jesus came into the world to save sinners, among whom I am foremost *of all.*

16 Yet for this reason I found mercy, so that in me as the foremost, Jesus Christ might demonstrate His perfect patience as an example for those who would believe in Him for eternal life.

17 Now to the King eternal, immortal, invisible, the only God, *be* honor and glory forever and ever. Amen.

18 This command I entrust to you, Timothy, *my* son, in accordance with the prophecies previously made concerning you, that by them you fight the good fight,

19 keeping faith and a good conscience, which some have rejected and suffered shipwreck in regard to their faith.

20 Among these are Hymenaeus and Alexander, whom I have handed over to Satan, so that they will be taught not to blaspheme.

A Call to Prayer

2 First of all, then, I urge that entreaties *and* prayers, petitions *and* thanksgivings, be made on behalf of all men,

2 for kings and all who are in authority, so

that we may lead a tranquil and quiet life in all godliness and dignity.

3 This is good and acceptable in the sight of God our Savior,

4 who desires all men to be saved and to come to the knowledge of the truth.

5 For there is one God, *and* one mediator also between God and men, *the* man Christ Jesus,

6 who gave Himself as a ransom for all, the testimony *given* at the proper time.

7 For this I was appointed a preacher and an apostle (I am telling the truth, I am not lying) as a teacher of the Gentiles in faith and truth.

8 Therefore I want the men in every place to pray, lifting up holy hands, without wrath and dissension.

9 Likewise, *I want* women to adorn themselves with proper clothing, modestly and discreetly, not with braided hair and gold or pearls or costly garments,

10 but rather by means of good works, as is proper for women making a claim to godliness.

11 A woman must quietly receive instruction with entire submissiveness.

12 But I do not allow a woman to teach or exercise authority over a man, but to remain quiet.

13 For it was Adam who was first created, *and* then Eve.

14 And *it was* not Adam *who* was deceived, but the woman being deceived, fell into transgression.

15 But *women* will be preserved through the bearing of children if they continue in faith and love and sanctity with self-restraint.

Overseers and Deacons

3 It is a trustworthy statement: if any man aspires to the office of overseer, it is a fine work he desires *to do.*

2 An overseer, then, must be above reproach, the husband of one wife, temperate, prudent, respectable, hospitable, able to teach,

3 not addicted to wine or pugnacious, but gentle, peaceable, free from the love of money.

4 *He must be* one who manages his own household well, keeping his children under control with all dignity

5 (but if a man does not know how to manage his own household, how will he take care of the church of God?),

6 *and* not a new convert, so that he will not become conceited and fall into the condemnation incurred by the devil.

7 And he must have a good reputation with those outside *the church,* so that he will not fall into reproach and the snare of the devil.

8 Deacons likewise *must be* men of dignity, not double-tongued, or addicted to much wine or fond of sordid gain,

9 *but* holding to the mystery of the faith with a clear conscience.

10 These men must also first be tested; then let them serve as deacons if they are beyond reproach.

11 Women *must* likewise *be* dignified, not malicious gossips, but temperate, faithful in all things.

12 Deacons must be husbands of *only* one wife, *and* good managers of *their* children and their own households.

13 For those who have served well as deacons obtain for themselves a high standing and great confidence in the faith that is in Christ Jesus.

14 I am writing these things to you, hoping to come to you before long;

15 but in case I am delayed, *I write* so that you will know how one ought to conduct himself in the household of God, which is the church of the living God, the pillar and support of the truth.

16 By common confession, great is the mystery of godliness:

He who was revealed in the flesh,
Was vindicated in the Spirit,
Seen by angels,
Proclaimed among the nations,
Believed on in the world,
Taken up in glory.

Apostasy

4 But the Spirit explicitly says that in later times some will fall away from the faith, paying attention to deceitful spirits and doctrines of demons,

2 by means of the hypocrisy of liars seared in their own conscience as with a branding iron,

3 *men* who forbid marriage *and* advocate abstaining from foods which God has created to be gratefully shared in by those who believe and know the truth.

4 For everything created by God is good, and nothing is to be rejected if it is received with gratitude;

5 for it is sanctified by means of the word of God and prayer.

6 In pointing out these things to the brethren, you will be a good servant of Christ Jesus, *constantly* nourished on the words of the faith and of the sound doctrine which you have been following.

7 But have nothing to do with worldly fables fit only for old women. On the other hand, discipline yourself for the purpose of godliness;

8 for bodily discipline is only of little profit, but godliness is profitable for all things, since it holds promise for the present life and *also* for the *life* to come.

9 It is a trustworthy statement deserving full acceptance.

10 For it is for this we labor and strive, because we have fixed our hope on the living God, who is the Savior of all men, especially of believers.

11 Prescribe and teach these things.

12 Let no one look down on your youthfulness, but *rather* in speech, conduct, love, faith *and* purity, show yourself an example of those who believe.

13 Until I come, give attention to the *public* reading *of Scripture,* to exhortation and teaching.

14 Do not neglect the spiritual gift within you,

which was bestowed on you through prophetic utterance with the laying on of hands by the presbytery.

15 Take pains with these things; be *absorbed* in them, so that your progress will be evident to all.

16 Pay close attention to yourself and to your teaching; persevere in these things, for as you do this you will ensure salvation both for yourself and for those who hear you.

Honor Widows

5 Do not sharply rebuke an older man, but *rather* appeal to *him* as a father, *to* the younger men as brothers,

2 the older women as mothers, *and* the younger women as sisters, in all purity.

3 Honor widows who are widows indeed;

4 but if any widow has children or grandchildren, they must first learn to practice piety in regard to their own family and to make some return to their parents; for this is acceptable in the sight of God.

5 Now she who is a widow indeed and who has been left alone, has fixed her hope on God and continues in entreaties and prayers night and day.

6 But she who gives herself to wanton pleasure is dead even while she lives.

7 Prescribe these things as well, so that they may be above reproach.

8 But if anyone does not provide for his own, and especially for those of his household, he has denied the faith and is worse than an unbeliever.

9 A widow is to be put on the list only if she is not less than sixty years old, *having been* the wife of one man,

10 having a reputation for good works; *and* if she has brought up children, if she has shown hospitality to strangers, if she has washed the saints' feet, if she has assisted those in distress, *and* if she has devoted herself to every good work.

11 But refuse *to put* younger widows *on the list*, for when they feel sensual desires in disregard of Christ, they want to get married,

12 *thus* incurring condemnation, because they have set aside their previous pledge.

13 At the same time they also learn *to be* idle, as they go around from house to house; and not merely idle, but also gossips and busybodies, talking about things not proper *to mention.*

14 Therefore, I want younger *widows* to get married, bear children, keep house, *and* give the enemy no occasion for reproach;

15 for some have already turned aside to follow Satan.

16 If any woman who is a believer has *dependent* widows, she must assist them and the church must not be burdened, so that it may assist those who are widows indeed.

17 The elders who rule well are to be considered worthy of double honor, especially those who work hard at preaching and teaching.

18 For the Scripture says, "YOU SHALL NOT MUZZLE THE OX WHILE HE IS THRESHING," and "The laborer is worthy of his wages."

19 Do not receive an accusation against an elder except on the basis of two or three witnesses.

20 Those who continue in sin, rebuke in the presence of all, so that the rest also will be fearful *of sinning.*

21 I solemnly charge you in the presence of God and of Christ Jesus and of *His* chosen angels, to maintain these *principles* without bias, doing nothing in a *spirit of* partiality.

22 Do not lay hands upon anyone *too* hastily and thereby share *responsibility for* the sins of others; keep yourself free from sin.

23 No longer drink water *exclusively,* but use a little wine for the sake of your stomach and your frequent ailments.

24 The sins of some men are quite evident, going before them to judgment; for others, their *sins* follow after.

25 Likewise also, deeds that are good are quite evident, and those which are otherwise cannot be concealed.

Instructions to Those Who Minister

6 All who are under the yoke as slaves are to regard their own masters as worthy of all honor so that the name of God and *our* doctrine will not be spoken against.

2 Those who have believers as their masters must not be disrespectful to them because they are brethren, but must serve them all the more, because those who partake of the benefit are believers and beloved. Teach and preach these *principles.*

3 If anyone advocates a different doctrine and does not agree with sound words, those of our Lord Jesus Christ, and with the doctrine conforming to godliness,

4 he is conceited *and* understands nothing; but he has a morbid interest in controversial questions and disputes about words, out of which arise envy, strife, abusive language, evil suspicions,

5 and constant friction between men of depraved mind and deprived of the truth, who suppose that godliness is a means of gain.

6 But godliness *actually* is a means of great gain when accompanied by contentment.

7 For we have brought nothing into the world, so we cannot take anything out of it either.

8 If we have food and covering, with these we shall be content.

9 But those who want to get rich fall into temptation and a snare and many foolish and harmful desires which plunge men into ruin and destruction.

10 For the love of money is a root of all sorts of evil, and some by longing for it have wandered away from the faith and pierced themselves with many griefs.

11 But flee from these things, you man of God, and pursue righteousness, godliness, faith, love, perseverance *and* gentleness.

12 Fight the good fight of faith; take hold of

the eternal life to which you were called, and you made the good confession in the presence of many witnesses.

13 I charge you in the presence of God, who gives life to all things, and of Christ Jesus, who testified the good confession before Pontius Pilate,

14 that you keep the commandment without stain or reproach until the appearing of our Lord Jesus Christ,

15 which He will bring about at the proper time—He who is the blessed and only Sovereign, the King of kings and Lord of lords,

16 who alone possesses immortality and dwells in unapproachable light, whom no man has seen or can see. To Him *be* honor and eternal dominion! Amen.

17 Instruct those who are rich in this present world not to be conceited or to fix their hope on the uncertainty of riches, but on God, who richly supplies us with all things to enjoy.

18 *Instruct them* to do good, to be rich in good works, to be generous and ready to share,

19 storing up for themselves the treasure of a good foundation for the future, so that they may take hold of that which is life indeed.

20 O Timothy, guard what has been entrusted to you, avoiding worldly *and* empty chatter *and* the opposing arguments of what is falsely called "knowledge"—

21 which some have professed and thus gone astray from the faith.

Grace be with you.

THE SECOND LETTER OF PAUL TO TIMOTHY

Timothy Charged to Guard His Trust

1 Paul, an apostle of Christ Jesus by the will of God, according to the promise of life in Christ Jesus,

2 To Timothy, my beloved son: Grace, mercy *and* peace from God the Father and Christ Jesus our Lord.

3 I thank God, whom I serve with a clear conscience the way my forefathers did, as I constantly remember you in my prayers night and day,

4 longing to see you, even as I recall your tears, so that I may be filled with joy.

5 For I am mindful of the sincere faith within you, which first dwelt in your grandmother Lois and your mother Eunice, and I am sure that *it is* in you as well.

6 For this reason I remind you to kindle afresh the gift of God which is in you through the laying on of my hands.

7 For God has not given us a spirit of timidity, but of power and love and discipline.

8 Therefore do not be ashamed of the testimony of our Lord or of me His prisoner, but join with *me* in suffering for the gospel according to the power of God,

9 who has saved us and called us with a holy calling, not according to our works, but according to His own purpose and grace which was granted us in Christ Jesus from all eternity,

10 but now has been revealed by the appearing of our Savior Christ Jesus, who abolished death and brought life and immortality to light through the gospel,

11 for which I was appointed a preacher and an apostle and a teacher.

12 For this reason I also suffer these things, but I am not ashamed; for I know whom I have believed and I am convinced that He is able to guard what I have entrusted to Him until that day.

13 Retain the standard of sound words which you have heard from me, in the faith and love which are in Christ Jesus.

14 Guard, through the Holy Spirit who dwells in us, the treasure which has been entrusted to *you.*

15 You are aware of the fact that all who are in Asia turned away from me, among whom are Phygelus and Hermogenes.

16 The Lord grant mercy to the house of Onesiphorus, for he often refreshed me and was not ashamed of my chains;

17 but when he was in Rome, he eagerly searched for me and found me—

18 the Lord grant to him to find mercy from the Lord on that day—and you know very well what services he rendered at Ephesus.

Be Strong

2 You therefore, my son, be strong in the grace that is in Christ Jesus.

2 The things which you have heard from me in the presence of many witnesses, entrust these to faithful men who will be able to teach others also.

3 Suffer hardship with *me,* as a good soldier of Christ Jesus.

4 No soldier in active service entangles himself in the affairs of everyday life, so that he may please the one who enlisted him as a soldier.

5 Also if anyone competes as an athlete, he does not win the prize unless he competes according to the rules.

6 The hard-working farmer ought to be the first to receive his share of the crops.

7 Consider what I say, for the Lord will give you understanding in everything.

8 Remember Jesus Christ, risen from the dead, descendant of David, according to my gospel,

9 for which I suffer hardship even to imprisonment as a criminal; but the word of God is not imprisoned.

10 For this reason I endure all things for the sake of those who are chosen, so that they also may obtain the salvation which is in Christ Jesus *and* with *it* eternal glory.

11 It is a trustworthy statement:
For if we died with Him, we will also live with Him;

12 If we endure, we will also reign with Him;
If we deny Him, He also will deny us;

13 If we are faithless, He remains faithful, for He cannot deny Himself.

14 Remind *them* of these things, and solemnly charge *them* in the presence of God not to wrangle about words, which is useless *and leads* to the ruin of the hearers.

15 Be diligent to present yourself approved to God as a workman who does not need to be ashamed, accurately handling the word of truth.

16 But avoid worldly *and* empty chatter, for it will lead to further ungodliness,

17 and their talk will spread like [1]gangrene. Among them are Hymenaeus and Philetus,

18 *men* who have gone astray from the truth saying that the resurrection has already taken place, and they upset the faith of some.

19 Nevertheless, the firm foundation of God stands, having this seal, "The Lord knows those who are His," and, "Everyone who names the name of the Lord is to abstain from wickedness."

20 Now in a large house there are not only gold and silver vessels, but also vessels of wood and of earthenware, and some to honor and some to dishonor.

21 Therefore, if anyone cleanses himself from these *things*, he will be a vessel for honor, sanctified, useful to the Master, prepared for every good work.

22 Now flee from youthful lusts and pursue righteousness, faith, love *and* peace, with those who call on the Lord from a pure heart.

23 But refuse foolish and ignorant speculations, knowing that they produce quarrels.

24 The Lord's bond-servant must not be quarrelsome, but be kind to all, able to teach, patient when wronged,

25 with gentleness correcting those who are in opposition, if perhaps God may grant them repentance leading to the knowledge of the truth,

26 and they may come to their senses *and escape* from the snare of the devil, having been held captive by him to do his will.

"Difficult Times Will Come"

3 But realize this, that in the last days difficult times will come.

2 For men will be lovers of self, lovers of money, boastful, arrogant, revilers, disobedient to parents, ungrateful, unholy,

3 unloving, irreconcilable, malicious gossips, without self-control, brutal, haters of good,

4 treacherous, reckless, conceited, lovers of pleasure rather than lovers of God,

5 holding to a form of godliness, although they have denied its power; Avoid such men as these.

6 For among them are those who enter into households and captivate weak women weighed down with sins, led on by various impulses,

7 always learning and never able to come to the knowledge of the truth.

8 Just as Jannes and Jambres opposed

Moses, so these *men* also oppose the truth, men of depraved mind, rejected in regard to the faith.

9 But they will not make further progress; for their folly will be obvious to all, just as Jannes' and Jambres' folly was also.

10 Now you followed my teaching, conduct, purpose, faith, patience, love, perseverance,

11 persecutions, *and* sufferings, such as happened to me at Antioch, at Iconium *and* at Lystra; what persecutions I endured, and out of them all the Lord rescued me!

12 Indeed, all who desire to live godly in Christ Jesus will be persecuted.

13 But evil men and impostors will proceed *from bad* to worse, deceiving and being deceived.

14 You, however, continue in the things you have learned and become convinced of, knowing from whom you have learned *them*,

15 and that from childhood you have known the sacred writings which are able to give you the wisdom that leads to salvation through faith which is in Christ Jesus.

16 All Scripture is inspired by God and profitable for teaching, for reproof, for correction, for training in righteousness;

17 so that the man of God may be adequate, equipped for every good work.

"Preach the Word"

4 I solemnly charge *you* in the presence of God and of Christ Jesus, who is to judge the living and the dead, and by His appearing and His kingdom:

2 preach the word; be ready in season *and* out of season; reprove, rebuke, exhort, with great patience and instruction.

3 For the time will come when they will not endure sound doctrine; but *wanting* to have their ears tickled, they will accumulate for themselves teachers in accordance to their own desires,

4 and will turn away their ears from the truth and will turn aside to myths.

5 But you, be sober in all things, endure hardship, do the work of an evangelist, fulfill your ministry.

6 For I am already being poured out as a drink offering, and the time of my departure has come.

7 I have fought the good fight, I have finished the course, I have kept the faith;

8 in the future there is laid up for me the crown of righteousness, which the Lord, the righteous Judge, will award to me on that day; and not only to me, but also to all who have loved His appearing.

9 Make every effort to come to me soon;

10 for Demas, having loved this present world, has deserted me and gone to Thessalonica; Crescens *has gone* to Galatia, Titus to Dalmatia.

11 Only Luke is with me. Pick up Mark and bring him with you, for he is useful to me for service.

---

1. Or *cancer*

12 But Tychicus I have sent to Ephesus.

13 When you come bring the cloak which I left at Troas with Carpus, and the books, especially the parchments.

14 Alexander the coppersmith did me much harm; the Lord will repay him according to his deeds.

15 Be on guard against him yourself, for he vigorously opposed our teaching.

16 At my first defense no one supported me, but all deserted me; may it not be counted against them.

17 But the Lord stood with me and strengthened me, so that through me the proclamation might be fully accomplished, and that all the Gentiles might hear; and I was rescued out of the lion's mouth.

18 The Lord will rescue me from every evil deed, and will bring me safely to His heavenly kingdom; to Him *be* the glory forever and ever. Amen.

19 Greet Prisca and Aquila, and the household of Onesiphorus.

20 Erastus remained at Corinth, but Trophimus I left sick at Miletus.

21 Make every effort to come before winter. Eubulus greets you, also Pudens and Linus and Claudia and all the brethren.

22 The Lord be with your spirit. Grace be with you.

THE LETTER OF PAUL TO TITUS

Salutation

1 Paul, a bond-servant of God and an apostle of Jesus Christ, for the faith of those chosen of God and the knowledge of the truth which is according to godliness,

2 in the hope of eternal life, which God, who cannot lie, promised long ages ago,

3 but at the proper time manifested, *even* His word, in the proclamation with which I was entrusted according to the commandment of God our Savior,

4 To Titus, my true child in a common faith: Grace and peace from God the Father and Christ Jesus our Savior.

5 For this reason I left you in Crete, that you would set in order what remains and appoint elders in every city as I directed you,

6 *namely,* if any man is above reproach, the husband of one wife, having children who believe, not accused of dissipation or rebellion.

7 For the overseer must be above reproach as God's steward, not self-willed, not quick-tempered, not addicted to wine, not pugnacious, not fond of sordid gain,

8 but hospitable, loving what is good, sensible, just, devout, self-controlled,

9 holding fast the faithful word which is in accordance with the teaching, so that he will be able both to exhort in sound doctrine and to refute those who contradict.

10 For there are many rebellious men, empty talkers and deceivers, especially those of the circumcision,

11 who must be silenced because they are upsetting whole families, teaching things they should not *teach* for the sake of sordid gain.

12 One of themselves, a prophet of their own, said, "Cretans are always liars, evil beasts, lazy gluttons."

13 This testimony is true. For this reason reprove them severely so that they may be sound in the faith,

14 not paying attention to Jewish myths and commandments of men who turn away from the truth.

15 To the pure, all things are pure; but to those who are defiled and unbelieving, nothing is pure, but both their mind and their conscience are defiled.

16 They profess to know God, but by *their* deeds they deny *Him*, being detestable and disobedient and worthless for any good deed.

Duties of the Older and Younger

2 But as for you, speak the things which are fitting for sound doctrine.

2 Older men are to be temperate, dignified, sensible, sound in faith, in love, in perseverance.

3 Older women likewise are to be reverent in their behavior, not malicious gossips nor enslaved to much wine, teaching what is good,

4 so that they may encourage the young women to love their husbands, to love their children,

5 *to be* sensible, pure, workers at home, kind, being subject to their own husbands, so that the word of God will not be dishonored.

6 Likewise urge the young men to be sensible;

7 in all things show yourself to be an example of good deeds, *with* purity in doctrine, dignified,

8 sound *in* speech which is beyond reproach, so that the opponent will be put to shame, having nothing bad to say about us.

9 *Urge* bondslaves to be subject to their own masters in everything, to be well-pleasing, not argumentative,

10 not pilfering, but showing all good faith so that they will adorn the doctrine of God our Savior in every respect.

11 For the grace of God has appeared, bringing salvation to all men,

12 instructing us to deny ungodliness and worldly desires and to live sensibly, righteously and godly in the present age,

13 looking for the blessed hope and the appearing of the glory of our great God and Savior, Christ Jesus,

14 who gave Himself for us to redeem us from every lawless deed, and to purify for Himself a people for His own possession, zealous for good deeds.

15 These things speak and exhort and reprove with all authority. Let no one disregard you.

Godly Living

3 Remind them to be subject to rulers, to authorities, to be obedient, to be ready for every good deed,

2 to malign no one, to be peaceable, gentle, showing every consideration for all men.

3 For we also once were foolish ourselves, disobedient, deceived, enslaved to various lusts and pleasures, spending our life in malice and envy, hateful, hating one another.

4 But when the kindness of God our Savior and *His* love for mankind appeared,

5 He saved us, not on the basis of deeds which we have done in righteousness, but according to His mercy, by the washing of regeneration and renewing by the Holy Spirit,

6 whom He poured out upon us richly through Jesus Christ our Savior,

7 so that being justified by His grace we would be made heirs according to *the* hope of eternal life.

8 This is a trustworthy statement; and concerning these things I want you to speak confidently, so that those who have believed God will be careful to engage in good deeds. These things are good and profitable for men.

9 But avoid foolish controversies and genealogies and strife and disputes about the Law, for they are unprofitable and worthless.

10 Reject a factious man after a first and second warning,

11 knowing that such a man is perverted and is sinning, being self-condemned.

12 When I send Artemas or Tychicus to you, make every effort to come to me at Nicopolis, for I have decided to spend the winter there.

13 Diligently help Zenas the lawyer and Apollos on their way so that nothing is lacking for them.

14 Our people must also learn to engage in good deeds to meet pressing needs, so that they will not be unfruitful.

15 All who are with me greet you. Greet those who love us in *the* faith.

Grace be with you all.

THE LETTER OF PAUL TO PHILEMON

Salutation

1 Paul, a prisoner of Christ Jesus, and Timothy our brother,

To Philemon our beloved *brother* and fellow worker,

2 and to Apphia our sister, and to Archippus our fellow soldier, and to the church in your house:

3 Grace to you and peace from God our Father and the Lord Jesus Christ.

4 I thank my God always, making mention of you in my prayers,

5 because I hear of your love and of the faith which you have toward the Lord Jesus and toward all the saints;

6 *and I pray* that the fellowship of your faith may become effective [1]through the knowledge of every good thing which is in you for Christ's sake.

7 For I have come to have much joy and comfort in your love, because the hearts of the saints have been refreshed through you, brother.

8 Therefore, though I have enough confidence in Christ to order you *to do* what is proper,

9 yet for love's sake I rather appeal *to you*—since I am such a person as Paul, the aged, and now also a prisoner of Christ Jesus—

10 I appeal to you for my child [2]Onesimus, whom I have begotten in my imprisonment,

11 who formerly was useless to you, but now is useful both to you and to me.

12 I have sent him back to you in person, that is, *sending* my very heart,

13 whom I wished to keep with me, so that on your behalf he might minister to me in my imprisonment for the gospel;

14 but without your consent I did not want to do anything, so that your goodness would not be, in effect, by compulsion but of your own free will.

15 For perhaps he was for this reason separated *from you* for a while, that you would have him back forever,

16 no longer as a slave, but more than a slave, a beloved brother, especially to me, but how much more to you, both in the flesh and in the Lord.

17 If then you regard me a partner, accept him as *you would* me.

18 But if he has wronged you in any way or owes you anything, charge that to my account;

19 I, Paul, am writing this with my own hand, I will repay it (not to mention to you that you owe to me even your own self as well).

20 Yes, brother, let me benefit from you in the Lord; refresh my heart in Christ.

21 Having confidence in your obedience, I write to you, since I know that you will do even more than what I say.

22 At the same time also prepare me a lodging, for I hope that through your prayers I will be given to you.

23 Epaphras, my fellow prisoner in Christ Jesus, greets you,

24 *as do* Mark, Aristarchus, Demas, Luke, my fellow workers.

25 The grace of the Lord Jesus Christ be with your spirit.[3]

---

1. Or *in*   2. I.e. useful   3. One early ms adds *Amen*

THE LETTER TO THE HEBREWS

God's Final Word in His Son

1 God, after He spoke long ago to the fathers in the prophets in many portions and in many ways,

2 in these last days has spoken to us in His Son, whom He appointed heir of all things, through whom also He made the world.

3 And He is the radiance of His glory and the exact representation of His nature, and upholds all things by the word of His power. When He had made purification of sins, He sat down at the right hand of the Majesty on high,

4 having become as much better than the angels, as He has inherited a more excellent name than they.

5 For to which of the angels did He ever say,
"YOU ARE MY SON,
TODAY I HAVE BEGOTTEN YOU"?
And again,
"I WILL BE A FATHER TO HIM
AND HE SHALL BE A SON TO ME"?

6 And when He again brings the firstborn into the world, He says,
"AND LET ALL THE ANGELS OF GOD WORSHIP HIM."

7 And of the angels He says,
"WHO MAKES HIS ANGELS WINDS,
AND HIS MINISTERS A FLAME OF FIRE."

8 But of the Son *He says,*
"YOUR THRONE, O GOD, IS FOREVER AND EVER,
AND THE RIGHTEOUS SCEPTER IS THE SCEPTER OF ¹HIS KINGDOM.

9 "YOU HAVE LOVED RIGHTEOUSNESS AND HATED LAWLESSNESS;
THEREFORE GOD, YOUR GOD, HAS ANOINTED YOU
WITH THE OIL OF GLADNESS ABOVE YOUR COMPANIONS."

10 And,
"YOU, LORD, IN THE BEGINNING LAID THE FOUNDATION OF THE EARTH,
AND THE HEAVENS ARE THE WORKS OF YOUR HANDS;

11 THEY WILL PERISH, BUT YOU REMAIN;
AND THEY ALL WILL BECOME OLD LIKE A GARMENT,

12 AND LIKE A MANTLE YOU WILL ROLL THEM UP;
LIKE A GARMENT THEY WILL ALSO BE CHANGED.
BUT YOU ARE THE SAME,
AND YOUR YEARS WILL NOT COME TO AN END."

13 But to which of the angels has He ever said,
"SIT AT MY RIGHT HAND,
UNTIL I MAKE YOUR ENEMIES
A FOOTSTOOL FOR YOUR FEET"?

14 Are they not all ministering spirits, sent out to render service for the sake of those who will inherit salvation?

Give Heed

2 For this reason we must pay much closer attention to what we have heard, so that we do not drift away *from it.*

2 For if the word spoken through angels proved unalterable, and every transgression and disobedience received a just penalty,

3 how will we escape if we neglect so great a salvation? After it was at the first spoken through the Lord, it was confirmed to us by those who heard,

4 God also testifying with them, both by signs and wonders and by various miracles and by gifts of the Holy Spirit according to His own will.

5 For He did not subject to angels the world to come, concerning which we are speaking.

6 But one has testified somewhere, saying,
"WHAT IS MAN, THAT YOU REMEMBER HIM?
OR THE SON OF MAN, THAT YOU ARE CONCERNED ABOUT HIM?

7 "YOU HAVE MADE HIM FOR A LITTLE WHILE LOWER THAN THE ANGELS;
YOU HAVE CROWNED HIM WITH GLORY AND HONOR,

²AND HAVE APPOINTED HIM OVER THE WORKS OF YOUR HANDS;

8 YOU HAVE PUT ALL THINGS IN SUBJECTION UNDER HIS FEET."
For in subjecting all things to him, He left nothing that is not subject to him. But now we do not yet see all things subjected to him.

9 But we do see Him who was made for a little while lower than the angels, *namely,* Jesus, because of the suffering of death crowned with glory and honor, so that by the grace of God He might taste death for everyone.

10 For it was fitting for Him, for whom are all things, and through whom are all things, in bringing many sons to glory, to perfect the author of their salvation through sufferings.

11 For both He who sanctifies and those who are sanctified are all from one *Father;* for which reason He is not ashamed to call them brethren,

12 saying,
"I WILL PROCLAIM YOUR NAME TO MY BRETHREN,
IN THE MIDST OF THE CONGREGATION I WILL SING YOUR PRAISE."

13 And again,
"I WILL PUT MY TRUST IN HIM."
And again,
"BEHOLD, I AND THE CHILDREN WHOM GOD HAS GIVEN ME."

14 Therefore, since the children share in flesh and blood, He Himself likewise also partook of the same, that through death He might render powerless him who had the power of death, that is, the devil,

15 and might free those who through fear of death were subject to slavery all their lives.

16 For assuredly He does not give help to

---

1. **Late mss read** Your 2. **Two early mss do not contain** And...hands

angels, but He gives help to the descendant of Abraham.

17 Therefore, He had to be made like His brethren in all things, so that He might become a merciful and faithful high priest in things pertaining to God, to make propitiation for the sins of the people.

18 For since He Himself was tempted in that which He has suffered, He is able to come to the aid of those who are tempted.

Jesus Our High Priest

3 Therefore, holy brethren, partakers of a heavenly calling, consider Jesus, the Apostle and High Priest of our confession;

2 He was faithful to Him who appointed Him, as Moses also was in all His house.

3 For He has been counted worthy of more glory than Moses, by just so much as the builder of the house has more honor than the house.

4 For every house is built by someone, but the builder of all things is God.

5 Now Moses was faithful in all His house as a servant, for a testimony of those things which were to be spoken later;

6 but Christ *was faithful* as a Son over His house—whose house we are, if we hold fast our confidence and the boast of our hope firm until the end.

7 Therefore, just as the Holy Spirit says,
"TODAY IF YOU HEAR HIS VOICE,

8 DO NOT HARDEN YOUR HEARTS AS WHEN THEY PROVOKED ME,

AS IN THE DAY OF TRIAL IN THE WILDERNESS,

9 WHERE YOUR FATHERS TRIED *Me* BY TESTING *Me*,

AND SAW MY WORKS FOR FORTY YEARS.

10 "THEREFORE I WAS ANGRY WITH THIS GENERATION,

AND SAID, 'THEY ALWAYS GO ASTRAY IN THEIR HEART,

AND THEY DID NOT KNOW MY WAYS';

11 AS I SWORE IN MY WRATH,

'THEY SHALL NOT ENTER MY REST.' "

12 Take care, brethren, that there not be in any one of you an evil, unbelieving heart that falls away from the living God.

13 But encourage one another day after day, as long as it is *still* called "Today," so that none of you will be hardened by the deceitfulness of sin.

14 For we have become partakers of Christ, if we hold fast the beginning of our assurance firm until the end,

15 while it is said,
"TODAY IF YOU HEAR HIS VOICE,

DO NOT HARDEN YOUR HEARTS, AS WHEN THEY PROVOKED ME."

16 For who provoked *Him* when they had heard? Indeed, did not all those who came out of Egypt *led* by Moses?

17 And with whom was He angry for forty years? Was it not with those who sinned, whose bodies fell in the wilderness?

18 And to whom did He swear that they would not enter His rest, but to those who were disobedient?

19 *So* we see that they were not able to enter because of unbelief.

The Believer's Rest

4 Therefore, let us fear if, while a promise remains of entering His rest, any one of you may seem to have come short of it.

2 For indeed we have had good news preached to us, just as they also; but the word they heard did not profit them, because it was not united by faith in those who heard.

3 For we who have believed enter that rest, just as He has said,
"AS I SWORE IN MY WRATH,

THEY SHALL NOT ENTER MY REST,"

although His works were finished from the foundation of the world.

4 For He has said somewhere concerning the seventh *day:* "AND GOD RESTED ON THE SEVENTH DAY FROM ALL HIS WORKS";

5 and again in this *passage,* "THEY SHALL NOT ENTER MY REST."

6 Therefore, since it remains for some to enter it, and those who formerly had good news preached to them failed to enter because of disobedience,

7 He again fixes a certain day, "Today," saying through David after so long a time just as has been said before,
"TODAY IF YOU HEAR HIS VOICE,

DO NOT HARDEN YOUR HEARTS."

8 For if Joshua had given them rest, He would not have spoken of another day after that.

9 So there remains a Sabbath rest for the people of God.

10 For the one who has entered His rest has himself also rested from his works, as God did from His.

11 Therefore let us be diligent to enter that rest, so that no one will fall, through *following* the same example of disobedience.

12 For the word of God is living and active and sharper than any two-edged sword, and piercing as far as the division of soul and spirit, of both joints and marrow, and able to judge the thoughts and intentions of the heart.

13 And there is no creature hidden from His sight, but all things are open and laid bare to the eyes of Him with whom we have to do.

14 Therefore, since we have a great high priest who has passed through the heavens, Jesus the Son of God, let us hold fast our confession.

15 For we do not have a high priest who cannot sympathize with our weaknesses, but One who has been tempted in all things as *we are,* yet without sin.

16 Therefore let us draw near with confidence to the throne of grace, so that we may receive mercy and find grace to help in time of need.

The Perfect High Priest

5 For every high priest taken from among men is appointed on behalf of men in things pertaining to God, in order to offer both gifts and sacrifices for sins;

2 he can deal gently with the ignorant and misguided, since he himself also is beset with weakness;

3 and because of it he is obligated to offer *sacrifices* for sins, as for the people, so also for himself.

4 And no one takes the honor to himself, but *receives it* when he is called by God, even as Aaron was.

5 So also Christ did not glorify Himself so as to become a high priest, but He who said to Him,

"YOU ARE MY SON,

TODAY I HAVE BEGOTTEN YOU";

6 just as He says also in another *passage*,

"YOU ARE A PRIEST FOREVER

ACCORDING TO THE ORDER OF MEL-CHIZEDEK."

7 In the days of His flesh, He offered up both prayers and supplications with loud crying and tears to the One able to save Him from death, and He was heard because of His piety.

8 Although He was a Son, He learned obedience from the things which He suffered.

9 And having been made perfect, He became to all those who obey Him the source of eternal salvation,

10 being designated by God as a high priest according to the order of Melchizedek.

11 Concerning [1]him we have much to say, and *it is* hard to explain, since you have become dull of hearing.

12 For though by this time you ought to be teachers, you have need again for someone to teach you the elementary principles of the oracles of God, and you have come to need milk and not solid food.

13 For everyone who partakes *only* of milk is not accustomed to the word of righteousness, for he is an infant.

14 But solid food is for the mature, who because of practice have their senses trained to discern good and evil.

The Peril of Falling Away

6 Therefore leaving the elementary teaching about the Christ, let us press on to maturity, not laying again a foundation of repentance from dead works and of faith toward God,

2 of instruction about washings and laying on of hands, and the resurrection of the dead and eternal judgment.

3 And this we will do, if God permits.

4 For in the case of those who have once been enlightened and have tasted of the heavenly gift and have been made partakers of the Holy Spirit,

5 and have tasted the good word of God and the powers of the age to come,

6 and *then* have fallen away, it is impossible

1. Lit *whom* or *which*

to renew them again to repentance, since they again crucify to themselves the Son of God and put Him to open shame.

7 For ground that drinks the rain which often falls on it and brings forth vegetation useful to those for whose sake it is also tilled, receives a blessing from God;

8 but if it yields thorns and thistles, it is worthless and close to being cursed, and it ends up being burned.

9 But, beloved, we are convinced of better things concerning you, and things that accompany salvation, though we are speaking in this way.

10 For God is not unjust so as to forget your work and the love which you have shown toward His name, in having ministered and in still ministering to the saints.

11 And we desire that each one of you show the same diligence so as to realize the full assurance of hope until the end,

12 so that you will not be sluggish, but imitators of those who through faith and patience inherit the promises.

13 For when God made the promise to Abraham, since He could swear by no one greater, He swore by Himself,

14 saying, "I WILL SURELY BLESS YOU AND I WILL SURELY MULTIPLY YOU."

15 And so, having patiently waited, he obtained the promise.

16 For men swear by one greater *than themselves*, and with them an oath *given* as confirmation is an end of every dispute.

17 In the same way God, desiring even more to show to the heirs of the promise the unchangeableness of His purpose, interposed with an oath,

18 so that by two unchangeable things in which it is impossible for God to lie, we who have taken refuge would have strong encouragement to take hold of the hope set before us.

19 This hope we have as an anchor of the soul, a *hope* both sure and steadfast and one which enters within the veil,

20 where Jesus has entered as a forerunner for us, having become a high priest forever according to the order of Melchizedek.

Melchizedek's Priesthood Like Christ's

7 For this Melchizedek, king of Salem, priest of the Most High God, who met Abraham as he was returning from the slaughter of the kings and blessed him,

2 to whom also Abraham apportioned a tenth part of all *the spoils*, was first of all, by the translation *of his name*, king of righteousness, and then also king of Salem, which is king of peace.

3 Without father, without mother, without genealogy, having neither beginning of days nor end of life, but made like the Son of God, he remains a priest perpetually.

4 Now observe how great this man was to

whom Abraham, the patriarch, gave a tenth of the choicest spoils.

5 And those indeed of the sons of Levi who receive the priest's office have commandment in the Law to collect a tenth from the people, that is, from their brethren, although these are descended from Abraham.

6 But the one whose genealogy is not traced from them collected a tenth from Abraham and blessed the one who had the promises.

7 But without any dispute the lesser is blessed by the greater.

8 In this case mortal men receive tithes, but in that case one *receives them*, of whom it is witnessed that he lives on.

9 And, so to speak, through Abraham even Levi, who received tithes, paid tithes,

10 for he was still in the loins of his father when Melchizedek met him.

11 Now if perfection was through the Levitical priesthood (for on the basis of it the people received the Law), what further need *was there* for another priest to arise according to the order of Melchizedek, and not be designated according to the order of Aaron?

12 For when the priesthood is changed, of necessity there takes place a change of law also.

13 For the one concerning whom these things are spoken belongs to another tribe, from which no one has officiated at the altar.

14 For it is evident that our Lord was descended from Judah, a tribe with reference to which Moses spoke nothing concerning priests.

15 And this is clearer still, if another priest arises according to the likeness of Melchizedek,

16 who has become *such* not on the basis of a law of physical requirement, but according to the power of an indestructible life.

17 For it is attested *of Him*,

"YOU ARE A PRIEST FOREVER
ACCORDING TO THE ORDER OF MEL-
CHIZEDEK."

18 For, on the one hand, there is a setting aside of a former commandment because of its weakness and uselessness

19 (for the Law made nothing perfect), and on the other hand there is a bringing in of a better hope, through which we draw near to God.

20 And inasmuch as *it was* not without an oath

21 (for they indeed became priests without an oath, but He with an oath through the One who said to Him,

"THE LORD HAS SWORN
AND WILL NOT CHANGE HIS MIND,
'YOU ARE A PRIEST FOREVER' ");

22 so much the more also Jesus has become the guarantee of a better covenant.

23 The *former* priests, on the one hand, existed in greater numbers because they were prevented by death from continuing,

24 but Jesus, on the other hand, because He continues forever, holds His priesthood permanently.

25 Therefore He is able also to save forever those who draw near to God through Him,

since He always lives to make intercession for them.

26 For it was fitting for us to have such a high priest, holy, innocent, undefiled, separated from sinners and exalted above the heavens;

27 who does not need daily, like those high priests, to offer up sacrifices, first for His own sins and then for the *sins* of the people, because this He did once for all when He offered up Himself.

28 For the Law appoints men as high priests who are weak, but the word of the oath, which came after the Law, *appoints* a Son, made perfect forever.

A Better Ministry

8 Now the main point in what has been said *is this:* we have such a high priest, who has taken His seat at the right hand of the throne of the Majesty in the heavens,

2 a minister in the sanctuary and in the true tabernacle, which the Lord pitched, not man.

3 For every high priest is appointed to offer both gifts and sacrifices; so it is necessary that this *high priest* also have something to offer.

4 Now if He were on earth, He would not be a priest at all, since there are those who offer the gifts according to the Law;

5 who serve a copy and shadow of the heavenly things, just as Moses was warned *by God* when he was about to erect the tabernacle; for, "SEE," He says, "THAT YOU MAKE all things ACCORDING TO THE PATTERN WHICH WAS SHOWN YOU ON THE MOUNTAIN."

6 But now He has obtained a more excellent ministry, by as much as He is also the mediator of a better covenant, which has been enacted on better promises.

7 For if that first *covenant* had been faultless, there would have been no occasion sought for a second.

8 For finding fault with them, He says,
"BEHOLD, DAYS ARE COMING, SAYS THE LORD,
WHEN I WILL EFFECT A NEW COVENANT
WITH THE HOUSE OF ISRAEL AND WITH THE
HOUSE OF JUDAH;

9 NOT LIKE THE COVENANT WHICH I MADE
WITH THEIR FATHERS
ON THE DAY WHEN I TOOK THEM BY THE
HAND
TO LEAD THEM OUT OF THE LAND OF EGYPT;
FOR THEY DID NOT CONTINUE IN MY
COVENANT,
AND I DID NOT CARE FOR THEM, SAYS THE
LORD.

10 "FOR THIS IS THE COVENANT THAT I WILL
MAKE WITH THE HOUSE OF ISRAEL
AFTER THOSE DAYS, SAYS THE LORD:
I WILL PUT MY LAWS INTO THEIR MINDS,
AND I WILL WRITE THEM ON THEIR HEARTS.
AND I WILL BE THEIR GOD,
AND THEY SHALL BE MY PEOPLE.

11 "AND THEY SHALL NOT TEACH EVERYONE HIS
FELLOW CITIZEN,
AND EVERYONE HIS BROTHER, SAYING,
'KNOW THE LORD,'
FOR ALL WILL KNOW ME,

From the least to the greatest of them.

12 "For I will be merciful to their iniquities,

And I will remember their sins no more."

13 When He said, "A new *covenant*," He has made the first obsolete. But whatever is becoming obsolete and growing old is ready to disappear.

The Old and the New

9 Now even the first *covenant* had regulations of divine worship and the earthly sanctuary.

2 For there was a tabernacle prepared, the outer one, in which *were* the lampstand and the table and the sacred bread; this is called the holy place.

3 Behind the second veil there was a tabernacle which is called the Holy of Holies,

4 having a golden altar of incense and the ark of the covenant covered on all sides with gold, in which was a golden jar holding the manna, and Aaron's rod which budded, and the tables of the covenant;

5 and above it *were* the cherubim of glory overshadowing the mercy seat; but of these things we cannot now speak in detail.

6 Now when these things have been so prepared, the priests are continually entering the outer tabernacle performing the divine worship,

7 but into the second, only the high priest *enters* once a year, not without *taking* blood, which he offers for himself and for the sins of the people committed in ignorance.

8 The Holy Spirit *is* signifying this, that the way into the holy place has not yet been disclosed while the outer tabernacle is still standing,

9 which *is* a symbol for the present time. Accordingly both gifts and sacrifices are offered which cannot make the worshiper perfect in conscience,

10 since they *relate* only to food and drink and various washings, regulations for the body imposed until a time of reformation.

11 But when Christ appeared *as* a high priest of the good things [1]to come, *He entered* through the greater and more perfect tabernacle, not made with hands, that is to say, not of this creation;

12 and not through the blood of goats and calves, but through His own blood, He entered the holy place once for all, having obtained eternal redemption.

13 For if the blood of goats and bulls and the ashes of a heifer sprinkling those who have been defiled sanctify for the cleansing of the flesh,

14 how much more will the blood of Christ, who through the eternal Spirit offered Himself without blemish to God, cleanse your conscience from dead works to serve the living God?

15 For this reason He is the mediator of a new covenant, so that, since a death has taken place

for the redemption of the transgressions that were *committed* under the first covenant, those who have been called may receive the promise of the eternal inheritance.

16 For where a covenant is, there must of necessity be the death of the one who made it.

17 For a covenant is valid *only* when men are dead, [2]for it is never in force while the one who made it lives.

18 Therefore even the first *covenant* was not inaugurated without blood.

19 For when every commandment had been spoken by Moses to all the people according to the Law, he took the blood of the calves and goats, with water and scarlet wool and hyssop, and sprinkled both the book itself and all the people,

20 saying, "This is the blood of the covenant which God commanded you."

21 And in the same way he sprinkled both the tabernacle and all the vessels of the ministry with the blood.

22 And according to the Law, *one may* almost *say*, all things are cleansed with blood, and without shedding of blood there is no forgiveness.

23 Therefore it was necessary for the copies of the things in the heavens to be cleansed with these, but the heavenly things themselves with better sacrifices than these.

24 For Christ did not enter a holy place made with hands, a *mere* copy of the true one, but into heaven itself, now to appear in the presence of God for us;

25 nor was it that He would offer Himself often, as the high priest enters the holy place year by year with blood that is not his own.

26 Otherwise, He would have needed to suffer often since the foundation of the world; but now once at the consummation of the ages He has been manifested to put away sin by the sacrifice of Himself.

27 And inasmuch as it is appointed for men to die once and after this *comes* judgment,

28 so Christ also, having been offered once to bear the sins of many, will appear a second time for salvation without *reference to* sin, to those who eagerly await Him.

One Sacrifice of Christ Is Sufficient

10 For the Law, since it has *only* a shadow of the good things to come *and* not the very form of things, [3]can never, by the same sacrifices which they offer continually year by year, make perfect those who draw near.

2 Otherwise, would they not have ceased to be offered, because the worshipers, having once been cleansed, would no longer have had consciousness of sins?

3 But in those *sacrifices* there is a reminder of sins year by year.

4 For it is impossible for the blood of bulls and goats to take away sins.

5 Therefore, when He comes into the world, He says,

---

1. Two early mss read *that have come*   2. Two early mss read *for is it then...lives?*   3. Two early mss read *they can*

"SACRIFICE AND OFFERING YOU HAVE NOT DESIRED,
BUT A BODY YOU HAVE PREPARED FOR ME;
6 IN WHOLE BURNT OFFERINGS AND *sacrifices* FOR SIN YOU HAVE TAKEN NO PLEASURE.
7 "THEN I SAID, 'BEHOLD, I HAVE COME
(IN THE SCROLL OF THE BOOK IT IS WRITTEN OF ME)
TO DO YOUR WILL, O GOD.' "
8 After saying above, "SACRIFICES AND OFFERINGS AND WHOLE BURNT OFFERINGS AND *sacrifices* FOR SIN YOU HAVE NOT DESIRED, NOR HAVE YOU TAKEN PLEASURE *in them*" (which are offered according to the Law),
9 then He said, "BEHOLD, I HAVE COME TO DO YOUR WILL." He takes away the first in order to establish the second.
10 By this will we have been sanctified through the offering of the body of Jesus Christ once for all.
11 Every priest stands daily ministering and offering time after time the same sacrifices, which can never take away sins;
12 but He, having offered one sacrifice for sins for all time, SAT DOWN AT THE RIGHT HAND OF GOD,
13 waiting from that time onward UNTIL HIS ENEMIES BE MADE A FOOTSTOOL FOR HIS FEET.
14 For by one offering He has perfected for all time those who are sanctified.
15 And the Holy Spirit also testifies to us; for after saying,
16 "THIS IS THE COVENANT THAT I WILL MAKE WITH THEM
AFTER THOSE DAYS, SAYS THE LORD:
I WILL PUT MY LAWS UPON THEIR HEART,
AND ON THEIR MIND I WILL WRITE THEM,"
He then says,
17 "AND THEIR SINS AND THEIR LAWLESS DEEDS I WILL REMEMBER NO MORE."
18 Now where there is forgiveness of these things, there is no longer *any* offering for sin.
19 Therefore, brethren, since we have confidence to enter the holy place by the blood of Jesus,
20 by a new and living way which He inaugurated for us through the veil, that is, His flesh,
21 and since *we have* a great priest over the house of God,
22 let us draw near with a sincere heart in full assurance of faith, having our hearts sprinkled *clean* from an evil conscience and our bodies washed with pure water.
23 Let us hold fast the confession of our hope without wavering, for He who promised is faithful;
24 and let us consider how to stimulate one another to love and good deeds,
25 not forsaking our own assembling together, as is the habit of some, but encouraging *one another;* and all the more as you see the day drawing near.
26 For if we go on sinning willfully after receiving the knowledge of the truth, there no longer remains a sacrifice for sins,

27 but a terrifying expectation of judgment and THE FURY OF A FIRE WHICH WILL CONSUME THE ADVERSARIES.
28 Anyone who has set aside the Law of Moses dies without mercy on *the testimony of* two or three witnesses.
29 How much severer punishment do you think he will deserve who has trampled under foot the Son of God, and has regarded as unclean the blood of the covenant by which he was sanctified, and has insulted the Spirit of grace?
30 For we know Him who said, "VENGEANCE IS MINE, I WILL REPAY." And again, "THE LORD WILL JUDGE HIS PEOPLE."
31 It is a terrifying thing to fall into the hands of the living God.
32 But remember the former days, when, after being enlightened, you endured a great conflict of sufferings,
33 partly by being made a public spectacle through reproaches and tribulations, and partly by becoming sharers with those who were so treated.
34 For you showed sympathy to the prisoners and accepted joyfully the seizure of your property, knowing that you have for yourselves a better possession and a lasting one.
35 Therefore, do not throw away your confidence, which has a great reward.
36 For you have need of endurance, so that when you have done the will of God, you may receive what was promised.
37 FOR YET IN A VERY LITTLE WHILE,
HE WHO IS COMING WILL COME, AND WILL NOT DELAY.
38 BUT MY RIGHTEOUS ONE SHALL LIVE BY FAITH;
AND IF HE SHRINKS BACK, MY SOUL HAS NO PLEASURE IN HIM.
39 But we are not of those who shrink back to destruction, but of those who have faith to the preserving of the soul.

The Triumphs of Faith

11 Now faith is the assurance of *things* hoped for, the conviction of things not seen.
2 For by it the men of old gained approval.
3 By faith we understand that the worlds were prepared by the word of God, so that what is seen was not made out of things which are visible.
4 By faith Abel offered to God a better sacrifice than Cain, through which he obtained the testimony that he was righteous, God testifying about his gifts, and through faith, though he is dead, he still speaks.
5 By faith Enoch was taken up so that he would not see death; AND HE WAS NOT FOUND BECAUSE GOD TOOK HIM UP; for he obtained the witness that before his being taken up he was pleasing to God.
6 And without faith it is impossible to please *Him,* for he who comes to God must believe that He is and *that* He is a rewarder of those who seek Him.

7 By faith Noah, being warned *by God* about things not yet seen, in reverence prepared an ark for the salvation of his household, by which he condemned the world, and became an heir of the righteousness which is according to faith.

8 By faith Abraham, when he was called, obeyed by going out to a place which he was to receive for an inheritance; and he went out, not knowing where he was going.

9 By faith he lived as an alien in the land of promise, as in a foreign *land*, dwelling in tents with Isaac and Jacob, fellow heirs of the same promise;

10 for he was looking for the city which has foundations, whose architect and builder is God.

11 By faith even Sarah herself received ability to conceive, even beyond the proper time of life, since she considered Him faithful who had promised.

12 Therefore there was born even of one man, and him as good as dead at that, *as many descendants* AS THE STARS OF HEAVEN IN NUMBER, AND INNUMERABLE AS THE SAND WHICH IS BY THE SEASHORE.

13 All these died in faith, without receiving the promises, but having seen them and having welcomed them from a distance, and having confessed that they were strangers and exiles on the earth.

14 For those who say such things make it clear that they are seeking a country of their own.

15 And indeed if they had been thinking of that *country* from which they went out, they would have had opportunity to return.

16 But as it is, they desire a better *country*, that is, a heavenly one. Therefore God is not ashamed to be called their God; for He has prepared a city for them.

17 By faith Abraham, when he was tested, offered up Isaac, and he who had received the promises was offering up his only begotten *son;*

18 *it was he* to whom it was said, "IN ISAAC YOUR DESCENDANTS SHALL BE CALLED."

19 He considered that God is able to raise *people* even from the dead, from which he also received him back as a type.

20 By faith Isaac blessed Jacob and Esau, even regarding things to come.

21 By faith Jacob, as he was dying, blessed each of the sons of Joseph, and worshiped, *leaning* on the top of his staff.

22 By faith Joseph, when he was dying, made mention of the exodus of the sons of Israel, and gave orders concerning his bones.

23 By faith Moses, when he was born, was hidden for three months by his parents, because they saw he was a beautiful child; and they were not afraid of the king's edict.

24 By faith Moses, when he had grown up, refused to be called the son of Pharaoh's daughter,

25 choosing rather to endure ill-treatment with the people of God than to enjoy the passing pleasures of sin,

26 considering the reproach of Christ greater riches than the treasures of Egypt; for he was looking to the reward.

27 By faith he left Egypt, not fearing the wrath of the king; for he endured, as seeing Him who is unseen.

28 By faith he kept the Passover and the sprinkling of the blood, so that he who destroyed the firstborn would not touch them.

29 By faith they passed through the Red Sea as though *they were passing* through dry land; and the Egyptians, when they attempted it, were drowned.

30 By faith the walls of Jericho fell down after they had been encircled for seven days.

31 By faith Rahab the harlot did not perish along with those who were disobedient, after she had welcomed the spies in peace.

32 And what more shall I say? For time will fail me if I tell of Gideon, Barak, Samson, Jephthah, of David and Samuel and the prophets,

33 who by faith conquered kingdoms, performed *acts of* righteousness, obtained promises, shut the mouths of lions,

34 quenched the power of fire, escaped the edge of the sword, from weakness were made strong, became mighty in war, put foreign armies to flight.

35 Women received *back* their dead by resurrection; and others were tortured, not accepting their release, so that they might obtain a better resurrection;

36 and others experienced mockings and scourgings, yes, also chains and imprisonment.

37 They were stoned, they were sawn in two, ¹they were tempted, they were put to death with the sword; they went about in sheepskins, in goatskins, being destitute, afflicted, ill-treated

38 (*men* of whom the world was not worthy), wandering in deserts and mountains and caves and holes in the ground.

39 And all these, having gained approval through their faith, did not receive what was promised,

40 because God had provided something better for us, so that apart from us they would not be made perfect.

Jesus, the Example

12 Therefore, since we have so great a cloud of witnesses surrounding us, let us also lay aside every encumbrance and the sin which so easily entangles us, and let us run with endurance the race that is set before us,

2 fixing our eyes on Jesus, the author and perfecter of faith, who for the joy set before Him endured the cross, despising the shame, and has sat down at the right hand of the throne of God.

3 For consider Him who has endured such hostility by sinners against Himself, so that you will not grow weary and lose heart.

---

1. One early ms does not contain *they were tempted*

4 You have not yet resisted to the point of shedding blood in your striving against sin;

5 and you have forgotten the exhortation which is addressed to you as sons,

"MY SON, DO NOT REGARD LIGHTLY THE DISCIPLINE OF THE LORD,

NOR FAINT WHEN YOU ARE REPROVED BY HIM;

6 FOR THOSE WHOM THE LORD LOVES HE DISCIPLINES,

AND HE SCOURGES EVERY SON WHOM HE RECEIVES."

7 It is for discipline that you endure; God deals with you as with sons; for what son is there whom *his* father does not discipline?

8 But if you are without discipline, of which all have become partakers, then you are illegitimate children and not sons.

9 Furthermore, we had earthly fathers to discipline us, and we respected them; shall we not much rather be subject to the Father of spirits, and live?

10 For they disciplined us for a short time as seemed best to them, but He *disciplines us* for *our* good, so that we may share His holiness.

11 All discipline for the moment seems not to be joyful, but sorrowful; yet to those who have been trained by it, afterwards it yields the peaceful fruit of righteousness.

12 Therefore, strengthen the hands that are weak and the knees that are feeble,

13 and make straight paths for your feet, so that *the limb* which is lame may not be put out of joint, but rather be healed.

14 Pursue peace with all men, and the sanctification without which no one will see the Lord.

15 See to it that no one comes short of the grace of God; that no root of bitterness springing up causes trouble, and by it many be defiled;

16 that *there be* no immoral or godless person like Esau, who sold his own birthright for a *single* meal.

17 For you know that even afterwards, when he desired to inherit the blessing, he was rejected, for he found no place for repentance, though he sought for it with tears.

18 For you have not come to *a mountain* that can be touched and to a blazing fire, and to darkness and gloom and whirlwind,

19 and to the blast of a trumpet and the sound of words which *sound was such that* those who heard begged that no further word be spoken to them.

20 For they could not bear the command, "IF EVEN A BEAST TOUCHES THE MOUNTAIN, IT WILL BE STONED."

21 And so terrible was the sight, *that* Moses said, "I AM FULL OF FEAR and trembling."

22 But you have come to Mount Zion and to the city of the living God, the heavenly Jerusalem, and to myriads of angels,

23 to the general assembly and church of the firstborn who are enrolled in heaven, and to

God, the Judge of all, and to the spirits of *the* righteous made perfect,

24 and to Jesus, the mediator of a new covenant, and to the sprinkled blood, which speaks better than *the blood* of Abel.

25 See to it that you do not refuse Him who is speaking. For if those did not escape when they refused him who warned *them* on earth, much less *will* we *escape* who turn away from Him who *warns* from heaven.

26 And His voice shook the earth then, but now He has promised, saying, "YET ONCE MORE I WILL SHAKE NOT ONLY THE EARTH, BUT ALSO THE HEAVEN."

27 This *expression,* "Yet once more," denotes the removing of those things which can be shaken, as of created things, so that those things which cannot be shaken may remain.

28 Therefore, since we receive a kingdom which cannot be shaken, let us show gratitude, by which we may offer to God an acceptable service with reverence and awe;

29 for our God is a consuming fire.

The Changeless Christ

13 Let love of the brethren continue.

2 Do not neglect to show hospitality to strangers, for by this some have entertained angels without knowing it.

3 Remember the prisoners, as though in prison with them, *and* those who are ill-treated, since you yourselves also are in the body.

4 Marriage *is to be held* in honor among all, and the *marriage* bed *is to be* undefiled; for fornicators and adulterers God will judge.

5 *Make sure that* your character is free from the love of money, being content with what you have; for He Himself has said, "I WILL NEVER DESERT YOU, NOR WILL I EVER FORSAKE YOU,"

6 so that we confidently say,

"THE LORD IS MY HELPER, I WILL NOT BE AFRAID.

WHAT WILL MAN DO TO ME?"

7 Remember those who led you, who spoke the word of God to you; and considering the result of their conduct, imitate their faith.

8 Jesus Christ *is* the same yesterday and today and forever.

9 Do not be carried away by varied and strange teachings; for it is good for the heart to be strengthened by grace, not by foods, through which those who were so occupied were not benefited.

10 We have an altar from which those who serve the tabernacle have no right to eat.

11 For the bodies of those animals whose blood is brought into the holy place by the high priest *as an offering* for sin, are burned outside the camp.

12 Therefore Jesus also, that He might sanctify the people through His own blood, suffered outside the gate.

13 So, let us go out to Him outside the camp, bearing His reproach.

14 For here we do not have a lasting city, but we are seeking *the city* which is to come.

15 Through Him then, let us continually offer

up a sacrifice of praise to God, that is, the fruit of lips that give thanks to His name.

16 And do not neglect doing good and sharing, for with such sacrifices God is pleased.

17 Obey your leaders and submit *to them*, for they keep watch over your souls as those who will give an account. Let them do this with joy and not with grief, for this would be unprofitable for you.

18 Pray for us, for we are sure that we have a good conscience, desiring to conduct ourselves honorably in all things.

19 And I urge *you* all the more to do this, so that I may be restored to you the sooner.

20 Now the God of peace, who brought up from the dead the great Shepherd of the sheep through the blood of the eternal covenant, *even* Jesus our Lord,

21 equip you in every good thing to do His will, working in us that which is pleasing in His sight, through Jesus Christ, to whom *be* the glory forever and ever. Amen.

22 But I urge you, brethren, bear with this word of exhortation, for I have written to you briefly.

23 Take notice that our brother Timothy has been released, with whom, if he comes soon, I will see you.

24 Greet all of your leaders and all the saints. Those from Italy greet you.

25 Grace be with you all.

THE LETTER OF JAMES

Testing Your Faith

1 James, a bond-servant of God and of the Lord Jesus Christ,

To the twelve tribes who are dispersed abroad: Greetings.

2 Consider it all joy, my brethren, when you encounter various trials,

3 knowing that the testing of your faith produces endurance.

4 And let endurance have *its* perfect result, so that you may be perfect and complete, lacking in nothing.

5 But if any of you lacks wisdom, let him ask of God, who gives to all generously and without reproach, and it will be given to him.

6 But he must ask in faith without any doubting, for the one who doubts is like the surf of the sea, driven and tossed by the wind.

7 For that man ought not to expect that he will receive anything from the Lord,

8 *being* a double-minded man, unstable in all his ways.

9 But the brother of humble circumstances is to glory in his high position;

10 and the rich man *is to glory* in his humiliation, because like flowering grass he will pass away.

11 For the sun rises with a scorching wind and withers the grass; and its flower falls off and the beauty of its appearance is destroyed; so too the rich man in the midst of his pursuits will fade away.

12 Blessed is a man who perseveres under trial; for once he has been approved, he will receive the crown of life which *the Lord* has promised to those who love Him.

13 Let no one say when he is tempted, "I am being tempted by God"; for God cannot be tempted by evil, and He Himself does not tempt anyone.

14 But each one is tempted when he is carried away and enticed by his own lust.

15 Then when lust has conceived, it gives birth to sin; and when sin is accomplished, it brings forth death.

16 Do not be deceived, my beloved brethren.

17 Every good thing given and every perfect gift is from above, coming down from the Father of lights, with whom there is no variation or shifting shadow.

18 In the exercise of His will He brought us forth by the word of truth, so that we would be a kind of first fruits among His creatures.

19 [1]This you know, my beloved brethren. But everyone must be quick to hear, slow to speak *and* slow to anger;

20 for the anger of man does not achieve the righteousness of God.

21 Therefore, putting aside all filthiness and *all* that remains of wickedness, in humility receive the word implanted, which is able to save your souls.

22 But prove yourselves doers of the word, and not merely hearers who delude themselves.

23 For if anyone is a hearer of the word and not a doer, he is like a man who looks at his natural face in a mirror;

24 for *once* he has looked at himself and gone away, he has immediately forgotten what kind of person he was.

25 But one who looks intently at the perfect law, the *law* of liberty, and abides by it, not having become a forgetful hearer but an effectual doer, this man will be blessed in what he does.

26 If anyone thinks himself to be religious, and yet does not bridle his tongue but deceives his *own* heart, this man's religion is worthless.

27 Pure and undefiled religion in the sight of *our* God and Father is this: to visit orphans and widows in their distress, *and* to keep oneself unstained by the world.

The Sin of Partiality

2 My brethren, do not hold your faith in our glorious Lord Jesus Christ with *an attitude of* personal favoritism.

2 For if a man comes into your assembly with a gold ring and dressed in fine clothes, and there also comes in a poor man in dirty clothes,

3 and you pay special attention to the one who is wearing the fine clothes, and say, "You sit here in a good place," and you say to the

---

1. Or *Know* this

poor man, "You stand over there, or sit down by my footstool,"

4 have you not made distinctions among yourselves, and become judges with evil motives?

5 Listen, my beloved brethren: did not God choose the poor of this world *to be* rich in faith and heirs of the kingdom which He promised to those who love Him?

6 But you have dishonored the poor man. Is it not the rich who oppress you and personally drag you into court?

7 Do they not blaspheme the fair name by which you have been called?

8 If, however, you are fulfilling the royal law according to the Scripture, "YOU SHALL LOVE YOUR NEIGHBOR AS YOURSELF," you are doing well.

9 But if you show partiality, you are committing sin *and* are convicted by the law as transgressors.

10 For whoever keeps the whole law and yet stumbles in one *point*, he has become guilty of all.

11 For He who said, "DO NOT COMMIT ADULTERY," also said, "DO NOT COMMIT MURDER." Now if you do not commit adultery, but do commit murder, you have become a transgressor of the law.

12 So speak and so act as those who are to be judged by *the* law of liberty.

13 For judgment *will be* merciless to one who has shown no mercy; mercy triumphs over judgment.

14 What use is it, my brethren, if someone says he has faith but he has no works? Can that faith save him?

15 If a brother or sister is without clothing and in need of daily food,

16 and one of you says to them, "Go in peace, be warmed and be filled," and yet you do not give them what is necessary for *their* body, what use is that?

17 Even so faith, if it has no works, is dead, *being* by itself.

18 But someone may *well* say, "You have faith and I have works; show me your faith without the works, and I will show you my faith by my works."

19 You believe that [1]God is one. You do well; the demons also believe, and shudder.

20 But are you willing to recognize, you foolish fellow, that faith without works is useless?

21 Was not Abraham our father justified by works when he offered up Isaac his son on the altar?

22 You see that faith was working with his works, and as a result of the works, faith was perfected;

23 and the Scripture was fulfilled which says, "AND ABRAHAM BELIEVED GOD, AND IT WAS RECKONED TO HIM AS RIGHTEOUSNESS," and he was called the friend of God.

24 You see that a man is justified by works and not by faith alone.

25 In the same way, was not Rahab the harlot also justified by works when she received the messengers and sent them out by another way?

26 For just as the body without *the* spirit is dead, so also faith without works is dead.

The Tongue Is a Fire

3 Let not many *of you* become teachers, my brethren, knowing that as such we will incur a stricter judgment.

2 For we all stumble in many *ways*. If anyone does not stumble in what he says, he is a perfect man, able to bridle the whole body as well.

3 Now if we put the bits into the horses' mouths so that they will obey us, we direct their entire body as well.

4 Look at the ships also, though they are so great and are driven by strong winds, are still directed by a very small rudder wherever the inclination of the pilot desires.

5 So also the tongue is a small part of the body, and *yet* it boasts of great things. See how great a forest is set aflame by such a small fire!

6 And the tongue is a fire, the *very* world of iniquity; the tongue is set among our members as that which defiles the entire body, and sets on fire the course of *our* life, and is set on fire by hell.

7 For every species of beasts and birds, of reptiles and creatures of the sea, is tamed and has been tamed by the human race.

8 But no one can tame the tongue; *it is* a restless evil *and* full of deadly poison.

9 With it we bless *our* Lord and Father, and with it we curse men, who have been made in the likeness of God;

10 from the same mouth come *both* blessing and cursing. My brethren, these things ought not to be this way.

11 Does a fountain send out from the same opening *both* fresh and bitter *water*?

12 Can a fig tree, my brethren, produce olives, or a vine produce figs? Nor *can* salt water produce fresh.

13 Who among you is wise and understanding? Let him show by his good behavior his deeds in the gentleness of wisdom.

14 But if you have bitter jealousy and selfish ambition in your heart, do not be arrogant and *so* lie against the truth.

15 This wisdom is not that which comes down from above, but is earthly, natural, demonic.

16 For where jealousy and selfish ambition exist, there is disorder and every evil thing.

17 But the wisdom from above is first pure, then peaceable, gentle, reasonable, full of mercy and good fruits, unwavering, without hypocrisy.

18 And the seed whose fruit is righteousness is sown in peace by those who make peace.

Things to Avoid

4 What is the source of quarrels and conflicts among you? Is not the source your

---

1. One early ms reads *there is one God*

pleasures that wage war in your members?

2 You lust and do not have; *so you commit* murder. You are envious and cannot obtain; *so* you fight and quarrel. You do not have because you do not ask.

3 You ask and do not receive, because you ask with wrong motives, so that you may spend *it* on your pleasures.

4 You adulteresses, do you not know that friendship with the world is hostility toward God? Therefore whoever wishes to be a friend of the world makes himself an enemy of God.

5 Or do you think that the Scripture speaks to no purpose: "[1]He jealously desires the Spirit which He has made to dwell in us"?

6 But He gives a greater grace. Therefore *it* says, "GOD IS OPPOSED TO THE PROUD, BUT GIVES GRACE TO THE HUMBLE."

7 Submit therefore to God. Resist the devil and he will flee from you.

8 Draw near to God and He will draw near to you. Cleanse your hands, you sinners; and purify your hearts, you double-minded.

9 Be miserable and mourn and weep; let your laughter be turned into mourning and your joy to gloom.

10 Humble yourselves in the presence of the Lord, and He will exalt you.

11 Do not speak against one another, brethren. He who speaks against a brother or judges his brother, speaks against the law and judges the law; but if you judge the law, you are not a doer of the law but a judge *of it.*

12 There is *only* one Lawgiver and Judge, the One who is able to save and to destroy; but who are you who judge your neighbor?

13 Come now, you who say, "Today or tomorrow we will go to such and such a city, and spend a year there and engage in business and make a profit."

14 Yet you do not know what your life will be like tomorrow. You are *just* a vapor that appears for a little while and then vanishes away.

15 Instead, *you ought* to say, "If the Lord wills, we will live and also do this or that."

16 But as it is, you boast in your arrogance; all such boasting is evil.

17 Therefore, to one who knows *the* right thing to do and does not do it, to him it is sin.

Misuse of Riches

5 Come now, you rich, weep and howl for your miseries which are coming upon you.

2 Your riches have rotted and your garments have become moth-eaten.

3 Your gold and your silver have rusted; and their rust will be a witness against you and will consume your flesh like fire. It is in the last days that you have stored up your treasure!

4 Behold, the pay of the laborers who mowed your fields, *and* which has been withheld by you, cries out *against you;* and the outcry of those who did the harvesting has reached the ears of the Lord of Sabaoth.

5 You have lived luxuriously on the earth and led a life of wanton pleasure; you have fattened your hearts in a day of slaughter.

6 You have condemned and put to death the righteous *man;* he does not resist you.

7 Therefore be patient, brethren, until the coming of the Lord. The farmer waits for the precious produce of the soil, being patient about it, until it gets the early and late rains.

8 You too be patient; strengthen your hearts, for the coming of the Lord is near.

9 Do not complain, brethren, against one another, so that you yourselves may not be judged; behold, the Judge is standing right at the door.

10 As an example, brethren, of suffering and patience, take the prophets who spoke in the name of the Lord.

11 We count those blessed who endured. You have heard of the endurance of Job and have seen the outcome of the Lord's dealings, that the Lord is full of compassion and *is* merciful.

12 But above all, my brethren, do not swear, either by heaven or by earth or with any other oath; but your yes is to be yes, and your no, no, so that you may not fall under judgment.

13 Is anyone among you suffering? *Then* he must pray. Is anyone cheerful? He is to sing praises.

14 Is anyone among you sick? *Then* he must call for the elders of the church and they are to pray over him, anointing him with oil in the name of the Lord;

15 and the prayer offered in faith will [2]restore the one who is sick, and the Lord will raise him up, and if he has committed sins, they will be forgiven him.

16 Therefore, confess your sins to one another, and pray for one another so that you may be healed. The effective prayer of a righteous man can accomplish much.

17 Elijah was a man with a nature like ours, and he prayed earnestly that it would not rain, and it did not rain on the earth for three years and six months.

18 Then he prayed again, and the sky poured rain and the earth produced its fruit.

19 My brethren, if any among you strays from the truth and one turns him back,

20 let him know that he who turns a sinner from the error of his way will save his soul from death and will cover a multitude of sins.

---

1. Or *The spirit which He has made to dwell in us lusts with envy* 2. Or *save*

THE FIRST LETTER OF PETER

A Living Hope, and a Sure Salvation

1 Peter, an apostle of Jesus Christ,
To those who reside as aliens, scattered throughout Pontus, Galatia, Cappadocia, Asia, and Bithynia, who are chosen

2 according to the foreknowledge of God the Father, by the sanctifying work of the Spirit, to obey Jesus Christ and be sprinkled with His blood: May grace and peace be yours in the fullest measure.

3 Blessed be the God and Father of our Lord Jesus Christ, who according to His great mercy has caused us to be born again to a living hope through the resurrection of Jesus Christ from the dead,

4 to *obtain* an inheritance *which is* imperishable and undefiled and will not fade away, reserved in heaven for you,

5 who are protected by the power of God through faith for a salvation ready to be revealed in the last time.

6 In this you greatly rejoice, even though now for a little while, if necessary, you have been distressed by various trials,

7 so that the proof of your faith, *being* more precious than gold which is perishable, even though tested by fire, may be found to result in praise and glory and honor at the revelation of Jesus Christ;

8 and though you have not seen Him, you love Him, and though you do not see Him now, but believe in Him, you greatly rejoice with joy inexpressible and full of glory,

9 obtaining as the outcome of your faith the salvation of [1]your souls.

10 As to this salvation, the prophets who prophesied of the grace that *would come* to you made careful searches and inquiries,

11 seeking to know what person or time the Spirit of Christ within them was indicating as He predicted the sufferings of Christ and the glories to follow.

12 It was revealed to them that they were not serving themselves, but you, in these things which now have been announced to you through those who preached the gospel to you by the Holy Spirit sent from heaven—things into which angels long to look.

13 Therefore, prepare your minds for action, keep sober *in spirit*, fix your hope completely on the grace to be brought to you at the revelation of Jesus Christ.

14 As obedient children, do not be conformed to the former lusts *which were yours* in your ignorance,

15 but like the Holy One who called you, be holy yourselves also in all *your* behavior;

16 because it is written, "YOU SHALL BE HOLY, FOR I AM HOLY."

17 If you address as Father the One who impartially judges according to each one's work, conduct yourselves in fear during the time of your stay *on earth;*

18 knowing that you were not redeemed with perishable things like silver or gold from your futile way of life inherited from your forefathers,

19 but with precious blood, as of a lamb unblemished and spotless, *the blood* of Christ.

20 For He was foreknown before the foundation of the world, but has appeared in these last times for the sake of you

21 who through Him are believers in God, who raised Him from the dead and gave Him glory, so that your faith and hope are in God.

22 Since you have in obedience to the truth purified your souls for a sincere love of the brethren, fervently love one another from [2]the heart,

23 for you have been born again not of seed which is perishable but imperishable, *that is,* through the living and enduring word of God.

24 For,
"ALL FLESH IS LIKE GRASS,
AND ALL ITS GLORY LIKE THE FLOWER OF GRASS.
THE GRASS WITHERS,
AND THE FLOWER FALLS OFF,
25 BUT THE WORD OF THE LORD ENDURES FOREVER."
And this is the word which was preached to you.

As Newborn Babes

2 Therefore, putting aside all malice and all deceit and hypocrisy and envy and all slander,

2 like newborn babies, long for the pure milk of the word, so that by it you may grow in respect to salvation,

3 if you have tasted the kindness of the Lord.

4 And coming to Him as to a living stone which has been rejected by men, but is choice and precious in the sight of God,

5 you also, as living stones, are being built up as a spiritual house for a holy priesthood, to offer up spiritual sacrifices acceptable to God through Jesus Christ.

6 For *this* is contained in Scripture:
"BEHOLD, I LAY IN ZION A CHOICE STONE, A PRECIOUS CORNER *stone,*
AND HE WHO BELIEVES IN HIM WILL NOT BE DISAPPOINTED."

7 This precious value, then, is for you who believe; but for those who disbelieve,
"THE STONE WHICH THE BUILDERS REJECTED,
THIS BECAME THE VERY CORNER *stone,*"

8 and,
"A STONE OF STUMBLING AND A ROCK OF OFFENSE";
for they stumble because they are disobedient to the word, and to this *doom* they were also appointed.

9 But you are A CHOSEN RACE, A royal

---

1. One early ms does not contain *your* 2. Two early mss read *a clean heart*

How do you experience the blood of Jesus? By being baptized into His death.
Read Romans 6:1-4 on page 122.

PRIESTHOOD, A HOLY NATION, A PEOPLE FOR *God's* OWN POSSESSION, so that you may proclaim the excellencies of Him who has called you out of darkness into His marvelous light;

10 for you once were NOT A PEOPLE, but now you are THE PEOPLE OF GOD; you had NOT RECEIVED MERCY, but now you have RECEIVED MERCY.

11 Beloved, I urge you as aliens and strangers to abstain from fleshly lusts which wage war against the soul.

12 Keep your behavior excellent among the Gentiles, so that in the thing in which they slander you as evildoers, they may because of your good deeds, as they observe *them*, glorify God in the day of [1]visitation.

13 Submit yourselves for the Lord's sake to every human institution, whether to a king as the one in authority,

14 or to governors as sent by him for the punishment of evildoers and the praise of those who do right.

15 For such is the will of God that by doing right you may silence the ignorance of foolish men.

16 *Act* as free men, and do not use your freedom as a covering for evil, but *use it* as bondslaves of God.

17 Honor all people, love the brotherhood, fear God, honor the king.

18 Servants, be submissive to your masters with all respect, not only to those who are good and gentle, but also to those who are unreasonable.

19 For this *finds* favor, if for the sake of conscience toward God a person bears up under sorrows when suffering unjustly.

20 For what credit is there if, when you sin and are harshly treated, you endure it with patience? But if when you do what is right and suffer *for it* you patiently endure it, this *finds* favor with God.

21 For you have been called for this purpose, since Christ also suffered for you, leaving you an example for you to follow in His steps,

22 WHO COMMITTED NO SIN, NOR WAS ANY DECEIT FOUND IN HIS MOUTH;

23 and while being reviled, He did not revile in return; while suffering, He uttered no threats, but kept entrusting *Himself* to Him who judges righteously;

24 and He Himself bore our sins in His body on the cross, so that we might die to sin and live to righteousness; for by His wounds you were healed.

25 For you were continually straying like sheep, but now you have returned to the Shepherd and Guardian of your souls.

Godly Living

3 In the same way, you wives, be submissive to your own husbands so that even if any *of them* are disobedient to the word, they may be won without a word by

the behavior of their wives,

2 as they observe your chaste and respectful behavior.

3 Your adornment must not be *merely* external—braiding the hair, and wearing gold jewelry, or putting on dresses;

4 but *let it be* the hidden person of the heart, with the imperishable quality of a gentle and quiet spirit, which is precious in the sight of God.

5 For in this way in former times the holy women also, who hoped in God, used to adorn themselves, being submissive to their own husbands;

6 just as Sarah obeyed Abraham, calling him lord, and you have become her children if you do what is right without being frightened by any fear.

7 You husbands in the same way, live with *your wives* in an understanding way, as with someone weaker, since she is a woman; and show her honor as a fellow heir of the grace of life, so that your prayers will not be hindered.

8 To sum up, all of you be harmonious, sympathetic, brotherly, kindhearted, and humble in spirit;

9 not returning evil for evil or insult for insult, but giving a blessing instead; for you were called for the very purpose that you might inherit a blessing.

10 For,

"THE ONE WHO DESIRES LIFE, TO LOVE AND
  SEE GOOD DAYS,
MUST KEEP HIS TONGUE FROM EVIL AND HIS
  LIPS FROM SPEAKING DECEIT.

11 "HE MUST TURN AWAY FROM EVIL AND DO
  GOOD;
HE MUST SEEK PEACE AND PURSUE IT.

12 "FOR THE EYES OF THE LORD ARE TOWARD
  THE RIGHTEOUS,
AND HIS EARS ATTEND TO THEIR PRAYER,
BUT THE FACE OF THE LORD IS AGAINST
  THOSE WHO DO EVIL."

13 Who is there to harm you if you prove zealous for what is good?

14 But even if you should suffer for the sake of righteousness, *you are* blessed. AND DO NOT FEAR THEIR INTIMIDATION, AND DO NOT BE TROUBLED,

15 but [2]sanctify Christ as Lord in your hearts, always *being* ready to make a defense to everyone who asks you to give an account for the hope that is in you, yet with gentleness and reverence;

16 and keep a good conscience so that in the thing in which you are slandered, those who revile your good behavior in Christ will be put to shame.

17 For it is better, if God should will it so, that you suffer for doing what is right rather than for doing what is wrong.

18 For Christ also died for sins once for all, *the* just for *the* unjust, so that He might bring us to God, having been put to death in the flesh, but made alive in the spirit;

He bore our sins.

---

1. I.e. Christ's coming again in judgment   2. I.e. set apart

Those who practice sin will not go to heaven.
Read Galatians 5:18-21 on pages 149 and 150.

19 in which also He went and made proclamation to the spirits *now* in prison,

20 who once were disobedient, when the patience of God kept waiting in the days of Noah, during the construction of the ark, in which a few, that is, eight persons, were brought safely through *the* water.

21 Corresponding to that, baptism now saves you—not the removal of dirt from the flesh, but an appeal to God for a good conscience—through the resurrection of Jesus Christ,

22 who is at the right hand of God, having gone into heaven, after angels and authorities and powers had been subjected to Him.

Keep Fervent in Your Love

4 Therefore, since Christ has [1]suffered in the flesh, arm yourselves also with the same purpose, because he who has suffered in the flesh has ceased from sin,

2 so as to live the rest of the time in the flesh no longer for the lusts of men, but for the will of God.

3 For the time already past is sufficient *for you* to have carried out the desire of the Gentiles, having pursued a course of sensuality, lusts, drunkenness, carousing, drinking parties and abominable idolatries.

4 In *all* this, they are surprised that you do not run with *them* into the same excesses of dissipation, and they malign *you;*

5 but they will give account to Him who is ready to judge the living and the dead.

6 For the gospel has for this purpose been preached even to those who are dead, that though they are judged in the flesh as men, they may live in the spirit according to *the will of* God.

7 The end of all things is near; therefore, be of sound judgment and sober *spirit* for the purpose of prayer.

8 Above all, keep fervent in your love for one another, because love covers a multitude of sins.

9 Be hospitable to one another without complaint.

10 As each one has received a *special* gift, employ it in serving one another as good stewards of the manifold grace of God.

11 Whoever speaks, *is to do so* as one who is speaking the utterances of God; whoever serves *is to do so* as one who is serving by the strength which God supplies; so that in all things God may be glorified through Jesus Christ, to whom belongs the glory and dominion forever and ever. Amen.

12 Beloved, do not be surprised at the fiery ordeal among you, which comes upon you for your testing, as though some strange thing were happening to you;

13 but to the degree that you share the sufferings of Christ, keep on rejoicing, so that also at the revelation of His glory you may rejoice with exultation.

14 If you are reviled for the name of Christ, you are blessed, because the Spirit of glory and of God rests on you.

15 Make sure that none of you suffers as a murderer, or thief, or evildoer, or a troublesome meddler;

16 but if *anyone suffers* as a Christian, he is not to be ashamed, but is to glorify God in this name.

17 For *it is* time for judgment to begin with the household of God; and if *it begins* with us first, what *will be* the outcome for those who do not obey the gospel of God?

18 AND IF IT IS WITH DIFFICULTY THAT THE RIGHTEOUS IS SAVED, WHAT WILL BECOME OF THE GODLESS MAN AND THE SINNER?

19 Therefore, those also who suffer according to the will of God shall entrust their souls to a faithful Creator in doing what is right.

Serve God Willingly

5 Therefore, I exhort the elders among you, as *your* fellow elder and witness of the sufferings of Christ, and a partaker also of the glory that is to be revealed,

2 shepherd the flock of God among you, exercising oversight not under compulsion, but voluntarily, according to *the will of* God; and not for sordid gain, but with eagerness;

3 nor yet as lording it over those allotted to your charge, but proving to be examples to the flock.

4 And when the Chief Shepherd appears, you will receive the unfading crown of glory.

5 You younger men, likewise, be subject to *your* elders; and all of you, clothe yourselves with humility toward one another, for GOD IS OPPOSED TO THE PROUD, BUT GIVES GRACE TO THE HUMBLE.

6 Therefore humble yourselves under the mighty hand of God, that He may exalt you at the proper time,

7 casting all your anxiety on Him, because He cares for you.

8 Be of sober *spirit*, be on the alert. Your adversary, the devil, prowls around like a roaring lion, seeking someone to devour.

9 But resist him, firm in *your* faith, knowing that the same experiences of suffering are being accomplished by your brethren who are in the world.

10 After you have suffered for a little while, the God of all grace, who called you to His eternal glory in Christ, will Himself perfect, confirm, strengthen *and* establish you.

11 To Him *be* dominion forever and ever. Amen.

12 Through Silvanus, our faithful brother (for so I regard *him*), I have written to you briefly, exhorting and testifying that this is the true grace of God. Stand firm in it!

13 She who is in Babylon, chosen together with you, sends you greetings, and *so does* my son, Mark.

14 Greet one another with a kiss of love.
Peace be to you all who are in Christ.

---

1. I.e. suffered death

Have you obeyed the gospel? Read Acts 22:16 on page 112.

THE SECOND LETTER OF PETER

Growth in Christian Virtue

1 Simon Peter, a bond-servant and apostle of Jesus Christ,

To those who have received a faith of the same kind as ours, by the righteousness of our God and Savior, Jesus Christ:

2 Grace and peace be multiplied to you in the knowledge of God and of Jesus our Lord;

3 seeing that His divine power has granted to us everything pertaining to life and godliness, through the true knowledge of Him who called us by His own glory and excellence.

4 For by these He has granted to us His precious and magnificent promises, so that by them you may become partakers of *the* divine nature, having escaped the corruption that is in the world by lust.

5 Now for this very reason also, applying all diligence, in your faith supply moral excellence, and in *your* moral excellence, knowledge,

6 and in *your* knowledge, self-control, and in *your* self-control, perseverance, and in *your* perseverance, godliness,

7 and in *your* godliness, brotherly kindness, and in *your* brotherly kindness, love.

8 For if these *qualities* are yours and are increasing, they render you neither useless nor unfruitful in the true knowledge of our Lord Jesus Christ.

9 For he who lacks these *qualities* is blind *or* short-sighted, having forgotten *his* purification from his former sins.

10 Therefore, brethren, be all the more diligent to make certain about His calling and choosing you; for as long as you practice these things, you will never stumble;

11 for in this way the entrance into the eternal kingdom of our Lord and Savior Jesus Christ will be abundantly supplied to you.

12 Therefore, I will always be ready to remind you of these things, even though you *already* know *them*, and have been established in the truth which is present with *you.*

13 I consider it right, as long as I am in this *earthly* dwelling, to stir you up by way of reminder,

14 knowing that the laying aside of my *earthly* dwelling is imminent, as also our Lord Jesus Christ has made clear to me.

15 And I will also be diligent that at any time after my departure you will be able to call these things to mind.

16 For we did not follow cleverly devised tales when we made known to you the power and coming of our Lord Jesus Christ, but we were eyewitnesses of His majesty.

17 For when He received honor and glory from God the Father, such an utterance as this was made to Him by the Majestic Glory, "This is My beloved Son with whom I am well-pleased"—

18 and we ourselves heard this utterance made from heaven when we were with Him on the holy mountain.

19 *So* we have the prophetic word *made* more sure, to which you do well to pay attention as to a lamp shining in a dark place, until the day dawns and the morning star arises in your hearts.

20 But know this first of all, that no prophecy of Scripture is *a matter* of one's own interpretation,

21 for no prophecy was ever made by an act of human will, but men moved by the Holy Spirit spoke from God.

The Rise of False Prophets

2 But false prophets also arose among the people, just as there will also be false teachers among you, who will secretly introduce destructive heresies, even denying the Master who bought them, bringing swift destruction upon themselves.

2 Many will follow their sensuality, and because of them the way of the truth will be maligned;

3 and in *their* greed they will exploit you with false words; their judgment from long ago is not idle, and their destruction is not asleep.

4 For if God did not spare angels when they sinned, but cast them into hell and committed them to pits of darkness, reserved for judgment;

5 and did not spare the ancient world, but preserved Noah, a preacher of righteousness, with seven others, when He brought a flood upon the world of the ungodly;

6 and if He condemned the cities of Sodom and Gomorrah to destruction by reducing *them* to ashes, having made them an example to those who would live ungodly *lives* thereafter;

7 and *if* He rescued righteous Lot, oppressed by the sensual conduct of unprincipled men

8 (for by what he saw and heard *that* righteous man, while living among them, felt *his* righteous soul tormented day after day by *their* lawless deeds),

9 *then* the Lord knows how to rescue the godly from temptation, and to keep the unrighteous under punishment for the day of judgment,

10 and especially those who indulge the flesh in *its* corrupt desires and despise authority.

Daring, self-willed, they do not tremble when they revile angelic majesties,

11 whereas angels who are greater in might and power do not bring a reviling judgment against them before the Lord.

12 But these, like unreasoning animals, born as creatures of instinct to be captured and killed, reviling where they have no knowledge, will in the destruction of those creatures also be destroyed,

13 suffering wrong as the wages of doing wrong. They count it a pleasure to revel in the daytime. They are stains and blemishes,

reveling in their ¹deceptions, as they carouse with you,

14 having eyes full of adultery that never cease from sin, enticing unstable souls, having a heart trained in greed, accursed children;

15 forsaking the right way, they have gone astray, having followed the way of Balaam, the *son* of Beor, who loved the wages of unrighteousness;

16 but he received a rebuke for his own transgression, *for* a mute donkey, speaking with a voice of a man, restrained the madness of the prophet.

17 These are springs without water and mists driven by a storm, for whom the black darkness has been reserved.

18 For speaking out arrogant *words* of vanity they entice by fleshly desires, by sensuality, those who barely escape from the ones who live in error,

19 promising them freedom while they themselves are slaves of corruption; for by what a man is overcome, by this he is enslaved.

20 For if, after they have escaped the defilements of the world by the knowledge of the Lord and Savior Jesus Christ, they are again entangled in them and are overcome, the last state has become worse for them than the first.

21 For it would be better for them not to have known the way of righteousness, than having known it, to turn away from the holy commandment handed on to them.

22 It has happened to them according to the true proverb, "A DOG RETURNS TO ITS OWN VOMIT," and, "A sow, after washing, *returns* to wallowing in the mire."

Purpose of This Letter

3 This is now, beloved, the second letter I am writing to you in which I am stirring up your sincere mind by way of reminder,

2 that you should remember the words spoken beforehand by the holy prophets and the commandment of the Lord and Savior *spoken* by your apostles.

3 Know this first of all, that in the last days mockers will come with *their* mocking, following after their own lusts,

4 and saying, "Where is the promise of His coming? For *ever* since the fathers fell asleep, all continues just as it was from the beginning of creation."

5 For when they maintain this, it escapes

their notice that by the word of God *the* heavens existed long ago and *the* earth was formed out of water and by water,

6 through which the world at that time was destroyed, being flooded with water.

7 But by His word the present heavens and earth are being reserved for fire, kept for the day of judgment and destruction of ungodly men.

8 But do not let this one *fact* escape your notice, beloved, that with the Lord one day is like a thousand years, and a thousand years like one day.

9 The Lord is not slow about His promise, as some count slowness, but is patient toward you, not wishing for any to perish but for all to come to repentance.

10 But the day of the Lord will come like a thief, in which the heavens will pass away with a roar and the elements will be destroyed with intense heat, and the earth and its works will be ²burned up.

11 Since all these things are to be destroyed in this way, what sort of people ought you to be in holy conduct and godliness,

12 looking for and hastening the coming of the day of God, because of which the heavens will be destroyed by burning, and the elements will melt with intense heat!

13 But according to His promise we are looking for new heavens and a new earth, in which righteousness dwells.

14 Therefore, beloved, since you look for these things, be diligent to be found by Him in peace, spotless and blameless,

15 and regard the patience of our Lord *as* salvation; just as also our beloved brother Paul, according to the wisdom given him, wrote to you,

16 as also in all *his* letters, speaking in them of these things, in which are some things hard to understand, which the untaught and unstable distort, as *they do* also the rest of the Scriptures, to their own destruction.

17 You therefore, beloved, knowing this beforehand, be on your guard so that you are not carried away by the error of unprincipled men and fall from your own steadfastness,

18 but grow in the grace and knowledge of our Lord and Savior Jesus Christ. To Him *be* the glory, both now and to the day of eternity. Amen.

THE FIRST LETTER OF JOHN

Introduction The Incarnate Word

1 What was from the beginning, what we have heard, what we have seen with our eyes, what we have looked at and touched with our hands, concerning the Word of Life—

2 and the life was manifested, and we have seen and testify and proclaim to you the eternal life, which was with the Father and was manifested to us—

3 what we have seen and heard we proclaim to you also, so that you too may have fellowship with us; and indeed our fellowship is with the Father, and with His Son Jesus Christ.

4 These things we write, so that our joy may be made complete.

5 This is the message we have heard from Him and announce to you, that God is Light, and in Him there is no darkness at all.

---

1. **One early ms reads** *love feasts* 2. **Two early mss read** *discovered*

6 If we say that we have fellowship with Him and *yet* walk in the darkness, we lie and do not practice the truth;

7 but if we walk in the Light as He Himself is in the Light, we have fellowship with one another, and the blood of Jesus His Son cleanses us from all sin.

8 If we say that we have no sin, we are deceiving ourselves and the truth is not in us.

9 If we confess our sins, He is faithful and righteous to forgive us our sins and to cleanse us from all unrighteousness.

10 If we say that we have not sinned, we make Him a liar and His word is not in us.

Christ Is Our Advocate

2 My little children, I am writing these things to you so that you may not sin. And if anyone sins, we have an [1]Advocate with the Father, Jesus Christ the righteous;

2 and He Himself is the propitiation for our sins; and not for ours only, but also for *those of* the whole world.

3 By this we know that we have come to know Him, if we keep His commandments.

4 The one who says, "I have come to know Him," and does not keep His commandments, is a liar, and the truth is not in him;

5 but whoever keeps His word, in him the love of God has truly been perfected. By this we know that we are in Him:

6 the one who says he abides in Him ought himself to walk in the same manner as He walked.

7 Beloved, I am not writing a new commandment to you, but an old commandment which you have had from the beginning; the old commandment is the word which you have heard.

8 On the other hand, I am writing a new commandment to you, which is true in Him and in you, because the darkness is passing away and the true Light is already shining.

9 The one who says he is in the Light and *yet* hates his brother is in the darkness until now.

10 The one who loves his brother abides in the Light and there is no cause for stumbling in him.

11 But the one who hates his brother is in the darkness and walks in the darkness, and does not know where he is going because the darkness has blinded his eyes.

12 I am writing to you, little children, because your sins have been forgiven you for His name's sake.

13 I am writing to you, fathers, because you know Him who has been from the beginning. I am writing to you, young men, because you have overcome the evil one. I have written to you, children, because you know the Father.

14 I have written to you, fathers, because you know Him who has been from the beginning. I have written to you, young men, because you are strong, and the word of God abides in you, and you have overcome the evil one.

15 Do not love the world nor the things in the world. If anyone loves the world, the love of the Father is not in him.

16 For all that is in the world, the lust of the flesh and the lust of the eyes and the boastful pride of life, is not from the Father, but is from the world.

17 The world is passing away, and *also* its lusts; but the one who does the will of God lives forever.

18 Children, it is the last hour; and just as you heard that antichrist is coming, even now many antichrists have appeared; from this we know that it is the last hour.

19 They went out from us, but they were not *really* of us; for if they had been of us, they would have remained with us; but *they went out,* so that it would be shown that they all are not of us.

20 But you have an anointing from the Holy One, and you all know.

21 I have not written to you because you do not know the truth, but because you do know it, and because no lie is of the truth.

22 Who is the liar but the one who denies that Jesus is the Christ? This is the antichrist, the one who denies the Father and the Son.

23 Whoever denies the Son does not have the Father; the one who confesses the Son has the Father also.

24 As for you, let that abide in you which you heard from the beginning. If what you heard from the beginning abides in you, you also will abide in the Son and in the Father.

25 This is the promise which He Himself made to us: eternal life.

26 These things I have written to you concerning those who are trying to deceive you.

27 As for you, the anointing which you received from Him abides in you, and you have no need for anyone to teach you; but as His anointing teaches you about all things, and is true and is not a lie, and just as it has taught you, you abide in Him.

28 Now, little children, abide in Him, so that when He appears, we may have confidence and not shrink away from Him in shame at His coming.

29 If you know that He is righteous, you know that everyone also who practices righteousness is born of Him.

Children of God Love One Another

3 See how great a love the Father has bestowed on us, that we would be called children of God; and *such* we are. For this reason the world does not know us, because it did not know Him.

2 Beloved, now we are children of God, and it has not appeared as yet what we will be. We know that when He appears, we will be like Him, because we will see Him just as He is.

3 And everyone who has this hope *fixed* on Him purifies himself, just as He is pure.

4 Everyone who practices sin also practices lawlessness; and sin is lawlessness.

---

1. Gr *Paracletos*, one called alongside to help; or *Intercessor*

5 You know that He appeared in order to take away sins; and in Him there is no sin.

6 No one who abides in Him sins; no one who sins has seen Him or knows Him.

7 Little children, make sure no one deceives you; the one who practices righteousness is righteous, just as He is righteous;

8 the one who practices sin is of the devil; for the devil has sinned from the beginning. The Son of God appeared for this purpose, to destroy the works of the devil.

9 No one who is born of God practices sin, because His seed abides in him; and he cannot sin, because he is born of God.

10 By this the children of God and the children of the devil are obvious: anyone who does not practice righteousness is not of God, nor the one who does not love his brother.

11 For this is the message which you have heard from the beginning, that we should love one another;

12 not as Cain, who was of the evil one and slew his brother. And for what reason did he slay him? Because his deeds were evil, and his brother's were righteous.

13 Do not be surprised, brethren, if the world hates you.

14 We know that we have passed out of death into life, because we love the brethren. He who does not love abides in death.

15 Everyone who hates his brother is a murderer; and you know that no murderer has eternal life abiding in him.

16 We know love by this, that He laid down His life for us; and we ought to lay down our lives for the brethren.

17 But whoever has the world's goods, and sees his brother in need and closes his heart against him, how does the love of God abide in him?

18 Little children, let us not love with word or with tongue, but in deed and truth.

19 We will know by this that we are of the truth, and will assure our heart before Him

20 in whatever our heart condemns us; for God is greater than our heart and knows all things.

21 Beloved, if our heart does not condemn us, we have confidence before God;

22 and whatever we ask we receive from Him, because we keep His commandments and do the things that are pleasing in His sight.

23 This is His commandment, that we believe in the name of His Son Jesus Christ, and love one another, just as He commanded us.

24 The one who keeps His commandments abides in Him, and He in him. We know by this that He abides in us, by the Spirit whom He has given us.

Testing the Spirits

4 Beloved, do not believe every spirit, but test the spirits to see whether they are from God, because many false prophets have gone out into the world.

2 By this you know the Spirit of God: every spirit that confesses that Jesus Christ has come in the flesh is from God;

3 and every spirit that does not confess Jesus is not from God; this is the spirit of the antichrist, of which you have heard that it is coming, and now it is already in the world.

4 You are from God, little children, and have overcome them; because greater is He who is in you than he who is in the world.

5 They are from the world; therefore they speak as from the world, and the world listens to them.

6 We are from God; he who knows God listens to us; he who is not from God does not listen to us. By this we know the spirit of truth and the spirit of error.

7 Beloved, let us love one another, for love is from God; and everyone who loves is born of God and knows God.

8 The one who does not love does not know God, for God is love.

9 By this the love of God was manifested in us, that God has sent His only begotten Son into the world so that we might live through Him.

10 In this is love, not that we loved God, but that He loved us and sent His Son to be the propitiation for our sins.

11 Beloved, if God so loved us, we also ought to love one another.

12 No one has seen God at any time; if we love one another, God abides in us, and His love is perfected in us.

13 By this we know that we abide in Him and He in us, because He has given us of His Spirit.

14 We have seen and testify that the Father has sent the Son to be the Savior of the world.

15 Whoever confesses that Jesus is the Son of God, God abides in him, and he in God.

16 We have come to know and have believed the love which God has for us. God is love, and the one who abides in love abides in God, and God abides in him.

17 By this, love is perfected with us, so that we may have confidence in the day of judgment; because as He is, so also are we in this world.

18 There is no fear in love; but perfect love casts out fear, because fear involves punishment, and the one who fears is not perfected in love.

19 We love, because He first loved us.

20 If someone says, "I love God," and hates his brother, he is a liar; for the one who does not love his brother whom he has seen, cannot love God whom he has not seen.

21 And this commandment we have from Him, that the one who loves God should love his brother also.

Overcoming the World

5 Whoever believes that Jesus is the [1]Christ is born of God, and whoever loves the Father loves the child born of Him.

2 By this we know that we love the children of God, when we love God and observe His commandments.

3 For this is the love of God, that we keep

---

1. I.e. Messiah

His commandments; and His commandments are not burdensome.

4 For whatever is born of God overcomes the world; and this is the victory that has overcome the world—our faith.

5 Who is the one who overcomes the world, but he who believes that Jesus is the Son of God?

6 This is the One who came by water and blood, Jesus Christ; not with the water only, but with the water and with the blood. It is the Spirit who testifies, because the Spirit is the truth.

7 For there are three that testify:

8 [1]the Spirit and the water and the blood; and the three are in agreement.

9 If we receive the testimony of men, the testimony of God is greater; for the testimony of God is this, that He has testified concerning His Son.

10 The one who believes in the Son of God has the testimony in himself; the one who does not believe God has made Him a liar, because he has not believed in the testimony that God has given concerning His Son.

11 And the testimony is this, that God has given us eternal life, and this life is in His Son.

12 He who has the Son has the life; he who does not have the Son of God does not have the life.

13 These things I have written to you who believe in the name of the Son of God, so that you may know that you have eternal life.

14 This is the confidence which we have before Him, that, if we ask anything according to His will, He hears us.

15 And if we know that He hears us *in* whatever we ask, we know that we have the requests which we have asked from Him.

16 If anyone sees his brother committing a sin not *leading* to death, he shall ask and *God* will for him give life to those who commit sin not *leading* to death. There is a sin *leading* to death; I do not say that he should make request for this.

17 All unrighteousness is sin, and there is a sin not *leading* to death.

18 We know that no one who is born of God sins; but He who was born of God keeps him, and the evil one does not touch him.

19 We know that we are of God, and that the whole world lies in *the power of* the evil one.

20 And we know that the Son of God has come, and has given us understanding so that we may know Him who is true; and we are in Him who is true, in His Son Jesus Christ. This is the true God and eternal life.

21 Little children, guard yourselves from idols.

THE SECOND LETTER OF JOHN

Walk According to His Commandments

1 The elder to the chosen lady and her children, whom I love in truth; and not only I, but also all who know the truth,

2 for the sake of the truth which abides in us and will be with us forever:

3 Grace, mercy *and* peace will be with us, from God the Father and from Jesus Christ, the Son of the Father, in truth and love.

4 I was very glad to find *some* of your children walking in truth, just as we have received commandment *to do* from the Father.

5 Now I ask you, lady, not as though I *were* writing to you a new commandment, but the one which we have had from the beginning, that we love one another.

6 And this is love, that we walk according to His commandments. This is the commandment, just as you have heard from the beginning, that you should walk in it.

7 For many deceivers have gone out into the world, those who do not acknowledge Jesus Christ *as* coming in the flesh. This is the deceiver and the antichrist.

8 Watch yourselves, that you do not lose what we have accomplished, but that you may receive a full reward.

9 Anyone who goes too far and does not abide in the teaching of Christ, does not have God; the one who abides in the teaching, he has both the Father and the Son.

10 If anyone comes to you and does not bring this teaching, do not receive him into *your* house, and do not give him a greeting;

11 for the one who gives him a greeting participates in his evil deeds.

12 Though I have many things to write to you, I do not want to *do so* with paper and ink; but I hope to come to you and speak face to face, so that your joy may be made full.

13 The children of your chosen sister greet you.

---

1. A few late mss add ...*in heaven, the Father, the Word, and the Holy Spirit, and these three are one. And there are three that testify on earth, the Spirit*

THE THIRD LETTER OF JOHN

1 The elder to the beloved Gaius, whom I love in truth.

2 Beloved, I pray that in all respects you may prosper and be in good health, just as your soul prospers.

3 For I was very glad when brethren came and testified to your truth, *that is,* how you are walking in truth.

4 I have no greater joy than this, to hear of my children walking in the truth.

5 Beloved, you are acting faithfully in whatever you accomplish for the brethren, and especially *when they are* strangers;

6 and they have testified to your love before the church. You will do well to send them on their way in a manner worthy of God.

7 For they went out for the sake of the Name, accepting nothing from the Gentiles.

8 Therefore we ought to support such men, so that we may be fellow workers with the truth.

9 I wrote something to the church; but Diotrephes, who loves to be first among them, does not accept what we say.

10 For this reason, if I come, I will call attention to his deeds which he does, unjustly accusing us with wicked words; and not satisfied with this, he himself does not receive the brethren, either, and he forbids those who desire *to do so* and puts *them* out of the church.

11 Beloved, do not imitate what is evil, but what is good. The one who does good is of God; the one who does evil has not seen God.

12 Demetrius has received a *good* testimony from everyone, and from the truth itself; and we add our testimony, and you know that our testimony is true.

13 I had many things to write to you, but I am not willing to write *them* to you with pen and ink;

14 but I hope to see you shortly, and we will speak face to face.

15 Peace *be* to you. The friends greet you. Greet the friends by name.

THE LETTER OF JUDE

The Warnings of History to the Ungodly

1 Jude, a bond-servant of Jesus Christ, and brother of James,

To those who are the called, beloved in God the Father, and kept for Jesus Christ:

2 May mercy and peace and love be multiplied to you.

3 Beloved, while I was making every effort to write you about our common salvation, I felt the necessity to write to you appealing that you contend earnestly for the faith which was once for all handed down to the saints.

4 For certain persons have crept in unnoticed, those who were long beforehand marked out for this condemnation, ungodly persons who turn the grace of our God into licentiousness and deny our only Master and Lord, Jesus Christ.

5 Now I desire to remind you, though you know all things once for all, that ¹the Lord, after saving a people out of the land of Egypt, subsequently destroyed those who did not believe.

6 And angels who did not keep their own domain, but abandoned their proper abode, He has kept in eternal bonds under darkness for the judgment of the great day;

7 just as Sodom and Gomorrah and the cities around them, since they in the same way as these indulged in gross immorality and went after strange flesh, are exhibited as an example in undergoing the punishment of eternal fire.

8 Yet in the same way these men, also by dreaming, defile the flesh, and reject authority, and revile angelic majesties.

9 But Michael the archangel, when he disputed with the devil and argued about the body of Moses, did not dare pronounce against him a railing judgment, but said, "The Lord rebuke you!"

10 But these men revile the things which they do not understand; and the things which they know by instinct, like unreasoning animals, by these things they are destroyed.

11 Woe to them! For they have gone the way of Cain, and for pay they have rushed headlong into the error of Balaam, and perished in the rebellion of Korah.

12 These are the men who are hidden reefs in your love feasts when they feast with you without fear, caring for themselves; clouds without water, carried along by winds; autumn trees without fruit, doubly dead, uprooted;

13 wild waves of the sea, casting up their own shame like foam; wandering stars, for whom the black darkness has been reserved forever.

14 *It was* also about these men *that* Enoch, *in* the seventh *generation* from Adam, prophesied, saying, "Behold, the Lord came with many thousands of His holy ones,

15 to execute judgment upon all, and to convict all the ungodly of all their ungodly deeds which they have done in an ungodly way, and of all the harsh things which ungodly sinners have spoken against Him."

16 These are grumblers, finding fault, following after their *own* lusts; they speak arrogantly, flattering people for the sake of *gaining an* advantage.

17 But you, beloved, ought to remember the words that were spoken beforehand by the apostles of our Lord Jesus Christ,

---

1. Two early mss read *Jesus*

18 that they were saying to you, "In the last time there will be mockers, following after their own ungodly lusts."

19 These are the ones who cause divisions, worldly-minded, devoid of the Spirit.

20 But you, beloved, building yourselves up on your most holy faith, praying in the Holy Spirit,

21 keep yourselves in the love of God, waiting anxiously for the mercy of our Lord Jesus Christ to eternal life.

22 And have mercy on some, who are doubting;

23 save others, snatching them out of the fire; and on some have mercy with fear, hating even the garment polluted by the flesh.

24 Now to Him who is able to keep you from stumbling, and to make you stand in the presence of His glory blameless with great joy,

25 to the only God our Savior, through Jesus Christ our Lord, *be* glory, majesty, dominion and authority, before all time and now and forever. Amen.

THE REVELATION TO JOHN

The Revelation of Jesus Christ

1 The Revelation of Jesus Christ, which God gave Him to show to His bond-servants, the things which must soon take place; and He sent and communicated *it* by His angel to His bond-servant John,

2 who testified to the word of God and to the testimony of Jesus Christ, *even* to all that he saw.

3 Blessed is he who reads and those who hear the words of the prophecy, and heed the things which are written in it; for the time is near.

4 John to the seven churches that are in Asia: Grace to you and peace, from Him who is and who was and who is to come, and from the seven Spirits who are before His throne,

5 and from Jesus Christ, the faithful witness, the firstborn of the dead, and the ruler of the kings of the earth. To Him who loves us and released us from our sins by His blood—

6 and He has made us *to be* a kingdom, priests to His God and Father—to Him *be* the glory and the dominion forever and ever. Amen.

7 BEHOLD, HE IS COMING WITH THE CLOUDS, and every eye will see Him, even those who pierced Him; and all the tribes of the earth will mourn over Him. So it is to be. Amen.

8 "I am the Alpha and the Omega," says the Lord God, "who is and who was and who is to come, the Almighty."

9 I, John, your brother and fellow partaker in the tribulation and kingdom and perseverance *which are* in Jesus, was on the island called Patmos because of the word of God and the testimony of Jesus.

10 I was ¹in the Spirit on the Lord's day, and I heard behind me a loud voice like *the sound* of a trumpet,

11 saying, "Write in a book what you see, and send *it* to the seven churches: to Ephesus and to Smyrna and to Pergamum and to Thyatira and to Sardis and to Philadelphia and to Laodicea."

12 Then I turned to see the voice that was speaking with me. And having turned I saw seven golden lampstands;

13 and in the middle of the lampstands *I saw* one like ²a son of man, clothed in a robe reaching to the feet, and girded across His chest with a golden sash.

14 His head and His hair were white like white wool, like snow; and His eyes were like a flame of fire.

15 His feet *were* like burnished bronze, when it has been made to glow in a furnace, and His voice *was* like the sound of many waters.

16 In His right hand He held seven stars, and out of His mouth came a sharp two-edged sword; and His face was like the sun shining in its strength.

17 When I saw Him, I fell at His feet like a dead man. And He placed His right hand on me, saying, "Do not be afraid; I am the first and the last,

18 and the living One; and I was dead, and behold, I am alive forevermore, and I have the keys of death and of Hades.

19 "Therefore write the things which you have seen, and the things which are, and the things which will take place after these things.

20 "As for the mystery of the seven stars which you saw in My right hand, and the seven golden lampstands: the seven stars are the angels of the seven churches, and the seven lampstands are the seven churches.

Message to Ephesus

2 "To the angel of the church in Ephesus write:
The One who holds the seven stars in His right hand, the One who walks among the seven golden lampstands, says this:

2 'I know your deeds and your toil and perseverance, and that you cannot tolerate evil men, and you put to the test those who call themselves apostles, and they are not, and you found them *to be* false;

3 and you have perseverance and have endured for My name's sake, and have not grown weary.

4 'But I have *this* against you, that you have left your first love.

5 'Therefore remember from where you have fallen, and repent and do the deeds you did at first; or else I am coming to you and will remove your lampstand out of its place—unless you repent.

6 'Yet this you do have, that you hate the deeds of the Nicolaitans, which I also hate.

7 'He who has an ear, let him hear what the Spirit says to the churches. To him who

---

1. **Or** *in spirit* 2. **Or** *the Son of Man*

overcomes, I will grant to eat of the tree of life which is in the Paradise of God.'

8 "And to the angel of the church in Smyrna write:

The first and the last, who was dead, and has come to life, says this:

9 'I know your tribulation and your poverty (but you are rich), and the blasphemy by those who say they are Jews and are not, but are a synagogue of Satan.

10 'Do not fear what you are about to suffer. Behold, the devil is about to cast some of you into prison, so that you will be tested, and you will have tribulation for ten days. Be faithful until death, and I will give you the crown of life.

11 'He who has an ear, let him hear what the Spirit says to the churches. He who overcomes will not be hurt by the second death.'

12 "And to the angel of the church in Pergamum write:

The One who has the sharp two-edged sword says this:

13 'I know where you dwell, where Satan's throne is; and you hold fast My name, and did not deny My faith even in the days of Antipas, My witness, My faithful one, who was killed among you, where Satan dwells.

14 'But I have a few things against you, because you have there some who hold the teaching of Balaam, who kept teaching Balak to put a stumbling block before the sons of Israel, to eat things sacrificed to idols and to commit *acts of* immorality.

15 'So you also have some who in the same way hold the teaching of the Nicolaitans.

16 'Therefore repent; or else I am coming to you quickly, and I will make war against them with the sword of My mouth.

17 'He who has an ear, let him hear what the Spirit says to the churches. To him who overcomes, to him I will give *some* of the hidden manna, and I will give him a white stone, and a new name written on the stone which no one knows but he who receives it.'

18 "And to the angel of the church in Thyatira write:

The Son of God, who has eyes like a flame of fire, and His feet are like burnished bronze, says this:

19 'I know your deeds, and your love and faith and service and perseverance, and that your deeds of late are greater than at first.

20 'But I have *this* against you, that you tolerate the woman Jezebel, who calls herself a prophetess, and she teaches and leads My bond-servants astray so that they commit *acts of* immorality and eat things sacrificed to idols.

21 'I gave her time to repent, and she does not want to repent of her immorality.

22 'Behold, I will throw her on a bed *of* sickness, and those who commit adultery with her into great tribulation, unless they repent of ¹her deeds.

23 'And I will kill her children with pestilence, and all the churches will know that I am He

who searches the minds and hearts; and I will give to each one of you according to your deeds.

24 'But I say to you, the rest who are in Thyatira, who do not hold this teaching, who have not known the deep things of Satan, as they call them—I place no other burden on you.

25 'Nevertheless what you have, hold fast until I come.

26 'He who overcomes, and he who keeps My deeds until the end, TO HIM I WILL GIVE AUTHORITY OVER THE NATIONS;

27 AND HE SHALL RULE THEM WITH A ROD OF IRON, AS THE VESSELS OF THE POTTER ARE BROKEN TO PIECES, as I also have received *authority* from My Father;

28 and I will give him the morning star.

29 'He who has an ear, let him hear what the Spirit says to the churches.'

Message to Sardis

3 "To the angel of the church in Sardis write: He who has the seven Spirits of God and the seven stars, says this: 'I know your deeds, that you have a name that you are alive, but you are dead.

2 'Wake up, and strengthen the things that remain, which were about to die; for I have not found your deeds completed in the sight of My God.

3 'So remember what you have received and heard; and keep *it*, and repent. Therefore if you do not wake up, I will come like a thief, and you will not know at what hour I will come to you.

4 'But you have a few people in Sardis who have not soiled their garments; and they will walk with Me in white, for they are worthy.

5 'He who overcomes will thus be clothed in white garments; and I will not erase his name from the book of life, and I will confess his name before My Father and before His angels.

6 'He who has an ear, let him hear what the Spirit says to the churches.'

7 "And to the angel of the church in Philadelphia write:

He who is holy, who is true, who has the key of David, who opens and no one will shut, and who shuts and no one opens, says this:

8 'I know your ²deeds. Behold, I have put before you an open door which no one can shut, because you have a little power, and have kept My word, and have not denied My name.

9 'Behold, I will cause *those* of the synagogue of Satan, who say that they are Jews and are not, but lie—I will make them come and bow down at your feet, and *make them* know that I have loved you.

10 'Because you have kept the word of My perseverance, I also will keep you from the hour of testing, that *hour* which is about to come upon the whole world, to test those who dwell on the earth.

11 'I am coming quickly; hold fast what you have, so that no one will take your crown.

12 'He who overcomes, I will make him a pillar in the temple of My God, and he will not go out from it anymore; and I will write on him

1. One early ms reads *their* 2. Or *deeds (behold...shut), that you have*

the name of My God, and the name of the city of My God, the new Jerusalem, which comes down out of heaven from My God, and My new name.

13 'He who has an ear, let him hear what the Spirit says to the churches.'

14 "To the angel of the church in Laodicea write:

The Amen, the faithful and true Witness, the [1]Beginning of the creation of God, says this:

15 'I know your deeds, that you are neither cold nor hot; I wish that you were cold or hot.

16 'So because you are lukewarm, and neither hot nor cold, I will spit you out of My mouth.

17 'Because you say, "I am rich, and have become wealthy, and have need of nothing," and you do not know that you are wretched and miserable and poor and blind and naked,

18 I advise you to buy from Me gold refined by fire so that you may become rich, and white garments so that you may clothe yourself, and *that* the shame of your nakedness will not be revealed; and eye salve to anoint your eyes so that you may see.

19 'Those whom I love, I reprove and discipline; therefore be zealous and repent.

20 'Behold, I stand at the door and knock; if anyone hears My voice and opens the door, I will come in to him and will dine with him, and he with Me.

21 'He who overcomes, I will grant to him to sit down with Me on My throne, as I also overcame and sat down with My Father on His throne.

22 'He who has an ear, let him hear what the Spirit says to the churches.' "

Scene in Heaven

4 After these things I looked, and behold, a door *standing* open in heaven, and the first voice which I had heard, like *the sound* of a trumpet speaking with me, said, "Come up here, and I will show you what must take place after these things."

2 Immediately I was [2]in the Spirit; and behold, a throne was standing in heaven, and One sitting on the throne.

3 And He who was sitting *was* like a jasper stone and a sardius in appearance; and *there was* a rainbow around the throne, like an emerald in appearance.

4 Around the throne *were* twenty-four thrones; and upon the thrones *I saw* twenty-four elders sitting, clothed in white garments, and golden crowns on their heads.

5 Out from the throne come flashes of lightning and sounds and peals of thunder. And *there were* seven lamps of fire burning before the throne, which are the seven Spirits of God;

6 and before the throne *there was something* like a sea of glass, like crystal; and in the center and around the throne, four living creatures full of eyes in front and behind.

7 The first creature *was* like a lion, and the second creature like a calf, and the third creature had a face like that of a man, and the fourth creature *was* like a flying eagle.

8 And the four living creatures, each one of them having six wings, are full of eyes around and within; and day and night they do not cease to say,

"HOLY, HOLY, HOLY *is* THE LORD GOD, THE ALMIGHTY, WHO WAS AND WHO IS AND WHO IS TO COME."

9 And when the living creatures give glory and honor and thanks to Him who sits on the throne, to Him who lives forever and ever,

10 the twenty-four elders will fall down before Him who sits on the throne, and will worship Him who lives forever and ever, and will cast their crowns before the throne, saying,

11 "Worthy are You, our Lord and our God, to receive glory and honor and power; for You created all things, and because of Your will they existed, and were created."

The Book with Seven Seals

5 I saw in the right hand of Him who sat on the throne a book written inside and on the back, sealed up with seven seals.

2 And I saw a strong angel proclaiming with a loud voice, "Who is worthy to open the book and to break its seals?"

3 And no one in heaven or on the earth or under the earth was able to open the book or to look into it.

4 Then I *began* to weep greatly because no one was found worthy to open the book or to look into it;

5 and one of the elders *said to me, "Stop weeping; behold, the Lion that is from the tribe of Judah, the Root of David, has overcome so as to open the book and its seven seals."

6 And I saw [3]between the throne (with the four living creatures) and the elders a Lamb standing, as if slain, having seven horns and seven eyes, which are the seven Spirits of God, sent out into all the earth.

7 And He came and took the book out of the right hand of Him who sat on the throne.

8 When He had taken the book, the four living creatures and the twenty-four elders fell down before the Lamb, each one holding a harp and golden bowls full of incense, which are the prayers of the saints.

9 And they *sang a new song, saying,

"Worthy are You to take the book and to break its seals; for You were slain, and purchased for God with Your blood *men* from every tribe and tongue and people and nation.

10 "You have made them *to be* a kingdom and priests to our God; and they will reign upon the earth."

11 Then I looked, and I heard the voice of many angels around the throne and the living creatures and the elders; and the number of them was myriads of myriads, and thousands of thousands,

12 saying with a loud voice,

1. I.e. Origin or Source   2. Or *in spirit*   3. Lit *in the middle of the throne and of the four living creatures, and in the middle of the elders*

"Worthy is the Lamb that was slain to receive power and riches and wisdom and might and honor and glory and blessing."

13 And every created thing which is in heaven and on the earth and under the earth and on the sea, and all things in them, I heard saying,

"To Him who sits on the throne, and to the Lamb, *be* blessing and honor and glory and dominion forever and ever."

14 And the four living creatures kept saying, "Amen." And the elders fell down and worshiped.

The First Seal—Rider on White Horse

6 Then I saw when the Lamb broke one of the seven seals, and I heard one of the four living creatures saying as with a voice of thunder, "Come."

2 I looked, and behold, a white horse, and he who sat on it had a bow; and a crown was given to him, and he went out conquering and to conquer.

3 When He broke the second seal, I heard the second living creature saying, "Come."

4 And another, a red horse, went out; and to him who sat on it, it was granted to take peace from the earth, and that *men* would slay one another; and a great sword was given to him.

5 When He broke the third seal, I heard the third living creature saying, "Come." I looked, and behold, a black horse; and he who sat on it had a pair of scales in his hand.

6 And I heard *something* like a voice in the center of the four living creatures saying, "A ¹quart of wheat for a ²denarius, and three quarts of barley for a denarius; and do not damage the oil and the wine."

7 When the Lamb broke the fourth seal, I heard the voice of the fourth living creature saying, "Come."

8 I looked, and behold, an ashen horse; and he who sat on it had the name Death; and Hades was following with him. Authority was given to them over a fourth of the earth, to kill with sword and with famine and with pestilence and by the wild beasts of the earth.

9 When the Lamb broke the fifth seal, I saw underneath the altar the souls of those who had been slain because of the word of God, and because of the testimony which they had maintained;

10 and they cried out with a loud voice, saying, "How long, O Lord, holy and true, will You refrain from judging and avenging our blood on those who dwell on the earth?"

11 And there was given to each of them a white robe; and they were told that they should rest for a little while longer, until *the number of* their fellow servants and their brethren who were to be killed even as they had been, would be completed also.

12 I looked when He broke the sixth seal, and there was a great earthquake; and the sun became black as sackcloth *made* of hair, and the whole moon became like blood;

13 and the stars of the sky fell to the earth, as a fig tree casts its unripe figs when shaken by a great wind.

14 The sky was split apart like a scroll when it is rolled up, and every mountain and island were moved out of their places.

15 Then the kings of the earth and the great men and the ³commanders and the rich and the strong and every slave and free man hid themselves in the caves and among the rocks of the mountains;

16 and they *said to the mountains and to the rocks, "Fall on us and hide us from the presence of Him who sits on the throne, and from the wrath of the Lamb;

17 for the great day of their wrath has come, and who is able to stand?"

An Interlude

7 After this I saw four angels standing at the four corners of the earth, holding back the four winds of the earth, so that no wind would blow on the earth or on the sea or on any tree.

2 And I saw another angel ascending from the rising of the sun, having the seal of the living God; and he cried out with a loud voice to the four angels to whom it was granted to harm the earth and the sea,

3 saying, "Do not harm the earth or the sea or the trees until we have sealed the bond-servants of our God on their foreheads."

4 And I heard the number of those who were sealed, one hundred and forty-four thousand sealed from every tribe of the sons of Israel:

5 From the tribe of Judah, twelve thousand *were* sealed, from the tribe of Reuben twelve thousand, from the tribe of Gad twelve thousand,

6 from the tribe of Asher twelve thousand, from the tribe of Naphtali twelve thousand, from the tribe of Manasseh twelve thousand,

7 from the tribe of Simeon twelve thousand, from the tribe of Levi twelve thousand, from the tribe of Issachar twelve thousand,

8 from the tribe of Zebulun twelve thousand, from the tribe of Joseph twelve thousand, from the tribe of Benjamin, twelve thousand *were* sealed.

9 After these things I looked, and behold, a great multitude which no one could count, from every nation and *all* tribes and peoples and tongues, standing before the throne and before the Lamb, clothed in white robes, and palm branches *were* in their hands;

10 and they cry out with a loud voice, saying, "Salvation to our God who sits on the throne, and to the Lamb."

11 And all the angels were standing around the throne and *around* the elders and the four living creatures; and they fell on their faces before the throne and worshiped God,

12 saying,

"Amen, blessing and glory and wisdom and thanksgiving and honor and power and might, *be* to our God forever and ever. Amen."

---

1. Gr *choenix*; i.e. a dry measure almost equal to a qt 2. The denarius was equivalent to a day's wages 3. I.e. chiliarchs, in command of one thousand troops

13 Then one of the elders answered, saying to me, "These who are clothed in the white robes, who are they, and where have they come from?" 14 I said to him, "My lord, you know." And he said to me, "These are the ones who come out of the great tribulation, and they have washed their robes and made them white in the blood of the Lamb.

15 "For this reason, they are before the throne of God; and they serve Him day and night in His temple; and He who sits on the throne will spread His tabernacle over them.

16 "They will hunger no longer, nor thirst anymore; nor will the sun beat down on them, nor any heat;

17 for the Lamb in the center of the throne will be their shepherd, and will guide them to springs of the water of life; and God will wipe every tear from their eyes."

The Seventh Seal—the Trumpets

8 When the Lamb broke the seventh seal, there was silence in heaven for about half an hour.

2 And I saw the seven angels who stand before God, and seven trumpets were given to them.

3 Another angel came and stood at the altar, holding a golden censer; and much incense was given to him, so that he might add it to the prayers of all the saints on the golden altar which was before the throne.

4 And the smoke of the incense, with the prayers of the saints, went up before God out of the angel's hand.

5 Then the angel took the censer and filled it with the fire of the altar, and threw it to the earth; and there followed peals of thunder and sounds and flashes of lightning and an earthquake.

6 And the seven angels who had the seven trumpets prepared themselves to sound them.

7 The first sounded, and there came hail and fire, mixed with blood, and they were thrown to the earth; and a third of the earth was burned up, and a third of the trees were burned up, and all the green grass was burned up.

8 The second angel sounded, and *something* like a great mountain burning with fire was thrown into the sea; and a third of the sea became blood;

9 and a third of the creatures which were in the sea and had life, died; and a third of the ships were destroyed.

10 The third angel sounded, and a great star fell from heaven, burning like a torch, and it fell on a third of the rivers and on the springs of waters.

11 The name of the star is called Wormwood; and a third of the waters became wormwood, and many men died from the waters, because they were made bitter.

12 The fourth angel sounded, and a third of the sun and a third of the moon and a third of the stars were struck, so that a third of them would be darkened and the day would not shine for a third of it, and the night in the same way.

13 Then I looked, and I heard an eagle flying in midheaven, saying with a loud voice, "Woe, woe, woe to those who dwell on the earth, because of the remaining blasts of the trumpet of the three angels who are about to sound!"

The Fifth Trumpet—the Bottomless Pit

9 Then the fifth angel sounded, and I saw a star from heaven which had fallen to the earth; and the key of the bottomless pit was given to him.

2 He opened the bottomless pit, and smoke went up out of the pit, like the smoke of a great furnace; and the sun and the air were darkened by the smoke of the pit.

3 Then out of the smoke came locusts upon the earth, and power was given them, as the scorpions of the earth have power.

4 They were told not to hurt the grass of the earth, nor any green thing, nor any tree, but only the men who do not have the seal of God on their foreheads.

5 And they were not permitted to kill anyone, but to torment for five months; and their torment was like the torment of a scorpion when it stings a man.

6 And in those days men will seek death and will not find it; they will long to die, and death flees from them.

7 The appearance of the locusts was like horses prepared for battle; and on their heads appeared to be crowns like gold, and their faces were like the faces of men.

8 They had hair like the hair of women, and their teeth were like *the teeth* of lions.

9 They had breastplates like breastplates of iron; and the sound of their wings was like the sound of chariots, of many horses rushing to battle.

10 They have tails like scorpions, and stings; and in their tails is their power to hurt men for five months.

11 They have as king over them, the angel of the abyss; his name in Hebrew is ¹Abaddon, and in the Greek he has the name Apollyon.

12 The first woe is past; behold, two woes are still coming after these things.

13 Then the sixth angel sounded, and I heard a voice from the ²four horns of the golden altar which is before God,

14 one saying to the sixth angel who had the trumpet, "Release the four angels who are bound at the great river Euphrates."

15 And the four angels, who had been prepared for the hour and day and month and year, were released, so that they would kill a third of mankind.

16 The number of the armies of the horsemen was two hundred million; I heard the number of them.

17 And this is how I saw in the vision the horses and those who sat on them: the riders had breastplates *the color* of fire and of hyacinth and of brimstone; and the heads of the

---

1. I.e. destruction 2. Two early mss do not contain *four*

horses are like the heads of lions; and out of their mouths proceed fire and smoke and brimstone.

18 A third of mankind was killed by these three plagues, by the fire and the smoke and the brimstone which proceeded out of their mouths.

19 For the power of the horses is in their mouths and in their tails; for their tails are like serpents and have heads, and with them they do harm.

20 The rest of mankind, who were not killed by these plagues, did not repent of the works of their hands, so as not to worship demons, and the idols of gold and of silver and of brass and of stone and of wood, which can neither see nor hear nor walk;

21 and they did not repent of their murders nor of their sorceries nor of their immorality nor of their thefts.

The Angel and the Little Book

10 I saw another strong angel coming down out of heaven, clothed with a cloud; and the rainbow was upon his head, and his face was like the sun, and his feet like pillars of fire;

2 and he had in his hand a little book which was open. He placed his right foot on the sea and his left on the land;

3 and he cried out with a loud voice, as when a lion roars; and when he had cried out, the seven peals of thunder uttered their voices.

4 When the seven peals of thunder had spoken, I was about to write; and I heard a voice from heaven saying, "Seal up the things which the seven peals of thunder have spoken and do not write them."

5 Then the angel whom I saw standing on the sea and on the land lifted up his right hand to heaven,

6 and swore by Him who lives forever and ever, WHO CREATED HEAVEN AND THE THINGS IN IT, AND THE EARTH AND THE THINGS IN IT, AND THE SEA AND THE THINGS IN IT, that there will be delay no longer,

7 but in the days of the voice of the seventh angel, when he is about to sound, then the mystery of God is finished, as He preached to His servants the prophets.

8 Then the voice which I heard from heaven, *I heard* again speaking with me, and saying, "Go, take the book which is open in the hand of the angel who stands on the sea and on the land."

9 So I went to the angel, telling him to give me the little book. And he *said to me, "Take it and eat it; it will make your stomach bitter, but in your mouth it will be sweet as honey."

10 I took the little book out of the angel's hand and ate it, and in my mouth it was sweet as honey; and when I had eaten it, my stomach was made bitter.

11 And they *said to me, "You must prophesy again concerning many peoples and nations and tongues and kings."

The Two Witnesses

11 Then there was given me a measuring rod like a staff; and someone said, "Get up and measure the temple of God and the altar, and those who worship in it.

2 "Leave out the court which is outside the temple and do not measure it, for it has been given to the nations; and they will tread under foot the holy city for forty-two months.

3 "And I will grant *authority* to my two witnesses, and they will prophesy for twelve hundred and sixty days, clothed in sackcloth."

4 These are the two olive trees and the two lampstands that stand before the Lord of the earth.

5 And if anyone wants to harm them, fire flows out of their mouth and devours their enemies; so if anyone wants to harm them, he must be killed in this way.

6 These have the power to shut up the sky, so that rain will not fall during the days of their prophesying; and they have power over the waters to turn them into blood, and to strike the earth with every plague, as often as they desire.

7 When they have finished their testimony, the beast that comes up out of the abyss will make war with them, and overcome them and kill them.

8 And their dead bodies *will lie* in the street of the great city which [1]mystically is called Sodom and Egypt, where also their Lord was crucified.

9 Those from the peoples and tribes and tongues and nations *will* look at their dead [2]bodies for three and a half days, and will not permit their dead bodies to be laid in a tomb.

10 And those who dwell on the earth *will* rejoice over them and celebrate; and they will send gifts to one another, because these two prophets tormented those who dwell on the earth.

11 But after the three and a half days, the breath of life from God came into them, and they stood on their feet; and great fear fell upon those who were watching them.

12 And they heard a loud voice from heaven saying to them, "Come up here." Then they went up into heaven in the cloud, and their enemies watched them.

13 And in that hour there was a great earthquake, and a tenth of the city fell; seven thousand people were killed in the earthquake, and the rest were terrified and gave glory to the God of heaven.

14 The second woe is past; behold, the third woe is coming quickly.

15 Then the seventh angel sounded; and there were loud voices in heaven, saying,

"The kingdom of the world has become *the kingdom* of our Lord and of His [3]Christ; and He will reign forever and ever."

16 And the twenty-four elders, who sit on their thrones before God, fell on their faces and worshiped God,

17 saying,

---

1. Lit *spiritually*   2. Lit *body*   3. I.e. **Messiah**

"We give You thanks, O Lord God, the Almighty, who are and who were, because You have taken Your great power and have begun to reign.

18 "And the nations were enraged, and Your wrath came, and the time *came* for the dead to be judged, and *the time* to reward Your bond-servants the prophets and the saints and those who fear Your name, the small and the great, and to destroy those who destroy the earth."

19 And the temple of God which is in heaven was opened; and the ark of His covenant appeared in His temple, and there were flashes of lightning and sounds and peals of thunder and an earthquake and a great hailstorm.

The Woman, Israel

12 A great sign appeared in heaven: a woman clothed with the sun, and the moon under her feet, and on her head a crown of twelve stars;

2 and she was with child; and she *cried out, being in labor and in pain to give birth.

3 Then another sign appeared in heaven: and behold, a great red dragon having seven heads and ten horns, and on his heads *were seven diadems.

4 And his tail *swept away a third of the stars of heaven and threw them to the earth. And the dragon stood before the woman who was about to give birth, so that when she gave birth he might devour her child.

5 And she gave birth to a son, a male *child, who is to rule all the nations with a rod of iron; and her child was caught up to God and to His throne.

6 Then the woman fled into the wilderness where she *had a place prepared by God, so that there she would be nourished for one thousand two hundred and sixty days.

7 And there was war in heaven, Michael and his angels waging war with the dragon. The dragon and his angels waged war,

8 and they were not strong enough, and there was no longer a place found for them in heaven.

9 And the great dragon was thrown down, the serpent of old who is called the devil and Satan, who deceives the whole world; he was thrown down to the earth, and his angels were thrown down with him.

10 Then I heard a loud voice in heaven, saying,

"Now the salvation, and the power, and the kingdom of our God and the authority of His Christ have come, for the accuser of our brethren has been thrown down, he who accuses them before our God day and night.

11 "And they overcame him because of the blood of the Lamb and because of the word of their testimony, and they did not love their life even when faced with death.

12 "For this reason, rejoice, O heavens and you who dwell in them. Woe to the earth and the sea, because the devil has come down to you,

having great wrath, knowing that he has *only* a short time."

13 And when the dragon saw that he was thrown down to the earth, he persecuted the woman who gave birth to the male *child.

14 But the two wings of the great eagle were given to the woman, so that she could fly into the wilderness to her place, where she *was nourished for a time and times and half a time, from the presence of the serpent.

15 And the serpent poured water like a river out of his mouth after the woman, so that he might cause her to be swept away with the flood.

16 But the earth helped the woman, and the earth opened its mouth and drank up the river which the dragon poured out of his mouth.

17 So the dragon was enraged with the woman, and went off to make war with the rest of her children, who keep the commandments of God and hold to the testimony of Jesus.

The Beast from the Sea

13 And the dragon stood on the sand of the seashore.

Then I saw a beast coming up out of the sea, having ten horns and seven heads, and on his horns *were ten diadems, and on his heads *were blasphemous names.

2 And the beast which I saw was like a leopard, and his feet were like *those* of a bear, and his mouth like the mouth of a lion. And the dragon gave him his power and his throne and great authority.

3 *I saw one of his heads as if it had been slain, and his fatal wound was healed. And the whole earth was amazed *and followed* after the beast;

4 they worshiped the dragon because he gave his authority to the beast; and they worshiped the beast, saying, "Who is like the beast, and who is able to wage war with him?"

5 There was given to him a mouth speaking arrogant words and blasphemies, and authority to act for forty-two months was given to him.

6 And he opened his mouth in blasphemies against God, to blaspheme His name and His tabernacle, *that is*, those who dwell in heaven.

7 It was also given to him to make war with the saints and to overcome them, and authority over every tribe and people and tongue and nation was given to him.

8 All who dwell on the earth will worship him, *everyone* whose name has not been ¹written from the foundation of the world in the book of life of the Lamb who has been slain.

9 If anyone has an ear, let him hear.

10 If anyone ²is *destined* for captivity, to captivity he goes; if anyone kills with the sword, with the sword he must be killed. Here is the perseverance and the faith of the saints.

11 Then I saw another beast coming up out of the earth; and he had two horns like a lamb and he spoke as a dragon.

12 He exercises all the authority of the first beast in his presence. And he makes the earth

---

1. Or *written in the book...slain from the foundation of the world*   2. Or *leads into captivity*

and those who dwell in it to worship the first beast, whose fatal wound was healed.

13 He performs great signs, so that he even makes fire come down out of heaven to the earth in the presence of men.

14 And he deceives those who dwell on the earth because of the signs which it was given him to perform in the presence of the beast, telling those who dwell on the earth to make an image to the beast who *had the wound of the sword and has come to life.

15 And it was given to him to give breath to the image of the beast, so that the image of the beast would even ¹speak and cause as many as do not worship the image of the beast to be killed.

16 And he causes all, the small and the great, and the rich and the poor, and the free men and the slaves, to be given a mark on their right hand or on their forehead,

17 and he provides that no one will be able to buy or to sell, except the one who has the mark, either the name of the beast or the number of his name.

18 Here is wisdom. Let him who has understanding calculate the number of the beast, for the number is that of a man; and his number is ²six hundred and sixty-six.

The Lamb and the 144,000 on Mount Zion

14 Then I looked, and behold, the Lamb was standing on Mount Zion, and with Him one hundred and forty-four thousand, having His name and the name of His Father written on their foreheads.

2 And I heard a voice from heaven, like the sound of many waters and like the sound of loud thunder, and the voice which I heard was like the sound of harpists playing on their harps.

3 And they *sang a new song before the throne and before the four living creatures and the elders; and no one could learn the song except the one hundred and forty-four thousand who had been purchased from the earth.

4 These are the ones who have not been defiled with women, for they ³have kept themselves chaste. These are the ones who follow the Lamb wherever He goes. These have been purchased from among men as first fruits to God and to the Lamb.

5 And no lie was found in their mouth; they are blameless.

6 And I saw another angel flying in midheaven, having an eternal gospel to preach to those who live on the earth, and to every nation and tribe and tongue and people;

7 and he said with a loud voice, "Fear God, and give Him glory, because the hour of His judgment has come; worship Him who made the heaven and the earth and sea and springs of waters."

8 And another angel, a second one, followed saying, "Fallen, fallen is Babylon the great, she who has made all the nations drink of the wine of the passion of her immorality."

9 Then another angel, a third one, followed them, saying with a loud voice, "If anyone worships the beast and his image, and receives a mark on his forehead or on his hand,

10 he also will drink of the wine of the wrath of God, which is mixed in full strength in the cup of His anger; and he will be tormented with fire and brimstone in the presence of the holy angels and in the presence of the Lamb.

11 "And the smoke of their torment goes up forever and ever; they have no rest day and night, those who worship the beast and his image, and whoever receives the mark of his name."

12 Here is the perseverance of the saints who keep the commandments of God and their faith in Jesus.

13 And I heard a voice from heaven, saying, "Write, 'Blessed are the dead who die in the Lord from now on!' " "Yes," says the Spirit, "so that they may rest from their labors, for their deeds follow with them."

14 Then I looked, and behold, a white cloud, and sitting on the cloud was one like ⁴a son of man, having a golden crown on His head and a sharp sickle in His hand.

15 And another angel came out of the temple, crying out with a loud voice to Him who sat on the cloud, "Put in your sickle and reap, for the hour to reap has come, because the harvest of the earth is ripe."

16 Then He who sat on the cloud swung His sickle over the earth, and the earth was reaped.

17 And another angel came out of the temple which is in heaven, and he also had a sharp sickle.

18 Then another angel, the one who has power over fire, came out from the altar; and he called with a loud voice to him who had the sharp sickle, saying, "Put in your sharp sickle and gather the clusters from the vine of the earth, because her grapes are ripe."

19 So the angel swung his sickle to the earth and gathered the clusters from the vine of the earth, and threw them into the great wine press of the wrath of God.

20 And the wine press was trodden outside the city, and blood came out from the wine press, up to the horses' bridles, for a distance of ⁵two hundred miles.

A Scene of Heaven

15 Then I saw another sign in heaven, great and marvelous, seven angels who had seven plagues, which are the last, because in them the wrath of God is finished.

2 And I saw something like a sea of glass mixed with fire, and those who had been victorious over the beast and his image and the number of his name, standing on the sea of glass, holding harps of God.

3 And they *sang the song of Moses, the

---

1. One early ms reads speak, and he will cause 2. One early ms reads 616 3. Lit are chaste men 4. Or the Son of Man
5. Lit sixteen hundred stadia; a stadion was approx 600 ft

bond-servant of God, and the song of the Lamb, saying,

"Great and marvelous are Your works,
O Lord God, the Almighty;
Righteous and true are Your ways,
King of the ¹nations!

4 "Who will not fear, O Lord, and glorify Your name?
For You alone are holy;
For ALL THE NATIONS WILL COME AND WORSHIP BEFORE YOU,
For YOUR RIGHTEOUS ACTS HAVE BEEN REVEALED."

5 After these things I looked, and the temple of the tabernacle of testimony in heaven was opened,

6 and the seven angels who had the seven plagues came out of the temple, clothed in ²linen, clean *and* bright, and girded around their chests with golden sashes.

7 Then one of the four living creatures gave to the seven angels seven golden bowls full of the wrath of God, who lives forever and ever.

8 And the temple was filled with smoke from the glory of God and from His power; and no one was able to enter the temple until the seven plagues of the seven angels were finished.

Six Bowls of Wrath

16 Then I heard a loud voice from the temple, saying to the seven angels, "Go and pour out on the earth the seven bowls of the wrath of God."

2 So the first *angel* went and poured out his bowl on the earth; and it became a loathsome and malignant sore on the people who had the mark of the beast and who worshiped his image.

3 The second *angel* poured out his bowl into the sea, and it became blood like *that* of a dead man; and every living ³thing in the sea died.

4 Then the third *angel* poured out his bowl into the rivers and the springs of waters; and they became blood.

5 And I heard the angel of the waters saying, "Righteous are You, who are and who were, O Holy One, because You judged these things;

6 for they poured out the blood of saints and prophets, and You have given them blood to drink. They deserve it."

7 And I heard the altar saying, "Yes, O Lord God, the Almighty, true and righteous are Your judgments."

8 The fourth *angel* poured out his bowl upon the sun, and it was given to it to scorch men with fire.

9 Men were scorched with fierce heat; and they blasphemed the name of God who has the power over these plagues, and they did not repent so as to give Him glory.

10 Then the fifth *angel* poured out his bowl on the throne of the beast, and his kingdom became darkened; and they gnawed their tongues because of pain,

11 and they blasphemed the God of heaven because of their pains and their sores; and they did not repent of their deeds.

12 The sixth *angel* poured out his bowl on the great river, the Euphrates; and its water was dried up, so that the way would be prepared for the kings from the east.

13 And I saw *coming* out of the mouth of the dragon and out of the mouth of the beast and out of the mouth of the false prophet, three unclean spirits like frogs;

14 for they are spirits of demons, performing signs, which go out to the kings of the whole world, to gather them together for the war of the great day of God, the Almighty.

15 ("Behold, I am coming like a thief. Blessed is the one who stays awake and keeps his clothes, so that he will not walk about naked and men will not see his shame.")

16 And they gathered them together to the place which in Hebrew is called ⁴Har-Magedon.

17 Then the seventh *angel* poured out his bowl upon the air, and a loud voice came out of the temple from the throne, saying, "It is done."

18 And there were flashes of lightning and sounds and peals of thunder; and there was a great earthquake, such as there had not been since man came to be upon the earth, so great an earthquake *was it, and* so mighty.

19 The great city was split into three parts, and the cities of the nations fell. Babylon the great was remembered before God, to give her the cup of the wine of His fierce wrath.

20 And every island fled away, and the mountains were not found.

21 And huge hailstones, about ⁵one hundred pounds each, *came down from heaven upon men; and men blasphemed God because of the plague of the hail, because its plague *was extremely severe.

The Doom of Babylon

17 Then one of the seven angels who had the seven bowls came and spoke with me, saying, "Come here, I will show you the judgment of the great harlot who sits on many waters,

2 with whom the kings of the earth committed *acts of* immorality, and those who dwell on the earth were made drunk with the wine of her immorality."

3 And he carried me away ⁶in the Spirit into a wilderness; and I saw a woman sitting on a scarlet beast, full of blasphemous names, having seven heads and ten horns.

4 The woman was clothed in purple and scarlet, and adorned with gold and precious stones and pearls, having in her hand a gold cup full of abominations and of the unclean things of her immorality,

5 and on her forehead a name *was* written, a mystery, "BABYLON THE GREAT, THE MOTHER OF HARLOTS AND OF THE ABOMINATIONS OF THE EARTH."

6 And I saw the woman drunk with the blood of the saints, and with the blood of the

---

1. Two early mss read *ages* 2. One early ms reads *stone* 3. Lit *soul* 4. Two early mss read *Armageddon* 5. Lit *the weight of a talent* 6. Or *in spirit*

witnesses of Jesus. When I saw her, I wondered greatly.

7 And the angel said to me, "Why do you wonder? I will tell you the mystery of the woman and of the beast that carries her, which has the seven heads and the ten horns.

8 "The beast that you saw was, and is not, and is about to come up out of the abyss and [1]go to destruction. And those who dwell on the earth, whose name has not been written in the book of life from the foundation of the world, will wonder when they see the beast, that he was and is not and will come.

9 "Here is the mind which has wisdom. The seven heads are seven mountains on which the woman sits,

10 and they are seven kings; five have fallen, one is, the other has not yet come; and when he comes, he must remain a little while.

11 "The beast which was and is not, is himself also an eighth and is *one* of the seven, and he goes to destruction.

12 "The ten horns which you saw are ten kings who have not yet received a kingdom, but they receive authority as kings with the beast for one hour.

13 "These have one purpose, and they give their power and authority to the beast.

14 "These will wage war against the Lamb, and the Lamb will overcome them, because He is Lord of lords and King of kings, and those who are with Him *are the* called and chosen and faithful."

15 And he *said to me, "The waters which you saw where the harlot sits, are peoples and multitudes and nations and tongues.

16 "And the ten horns which you saw, and the beast, these will hate the harlot and will make her desolate and naked, and will eat her flesh and will burn her up with fire.

17 "For God has put it in their hearts to execute His purpose by having a common purpose, and by giving their kingdom to the beast, until the words of God will be fulfilled.

18 "The woman whom you saw is the great city, which reigns over the kings of the earth."

Babylon Is Fallen

18 After these things I saw another angel coming down from heaven, having great authority, and the earth was illumined with his glory.

2 And he cried out with a mighty voice, saying, "Fallen, fallen is Babylon the great! She has become a dwelling place of demons and a prison of every unclean spirit, and a prison of every unclean and hateful bird.

3 "For all the nations [2]have drunk of the wine of the passion of her immorality, and the kings of the earth have committed *acts of* immorality with her, and the merchants of the earth have become rich by the wealth of her sensuality."

4 I heard another voice from heaven, saying, "Come out of her, my people, so that you will not participate in her sins and receive of her plagues;

5 for her sins have piled up as high as heaven, and God has remembered her iniquities.

6 "Pay her back even as she has paid, and give back *to her* double according to her deeds; in the cup which she has mixed, mix twice as much for her.

7 "To the degree that she glorified herself and lived sensuously, to the same degree give her torment and mourning; for she says in her heart, 'I SIT *as* A QUEEN AND I AM NOT A WIDOW, and will never see mourning.'

8 "For this reason in one day her plagues will come, pestilence and mourning and famine, and she will be burned up with fire; for the Lord God who judges her is strong.

9 "And the kings of the earth, who committed *acts of* immorality and lived sensuously with her, will weep and lament over her when they see the smoke of her burning,

10 standing at a distance because of the fear of her torment, saying, 'Woe, woe, the great city, Babylon, the strong city! For in one hour your judgment has come.'

11 "And the merchants of the earth weep and mourn over her, because no one buys their cargoes any more—

12 cargoes of gold and silver and precious stones and pearls and fine linen and purple and silk and scarlet, and every *kind of* citron wood and every article of ivory and every article *made* from very costly wood and bronze and iron and marble,

13 and cinnamon and spice and incense and perfume and frankincense and wine and olive oil and fine flour and wheat and cattle and sheep, and *cargoes* of horses and chariots and slaves and human lives.

14 "The fruit you long for has gone from you, and all things that were luxurious and splendid have passed away from you and *men* will no longer find them.

15 "The merchants of these things, who became rich from her, will stand at a distance because of the fear of her torment, weeping and mourning,

16 saying, 'Woe, woe, the great city, she who was clothed in fine linen and purple and scarlet, and adorned with gold and precious stones and pearls;

17 for in one hour such great wealth has been laid waste!' And every shipmaster and every passenger and sailor, and as many as make their living by the sea, stood at a distance,

18 and were crying out as they saw the smoke of her burning, saying, 'What *city* is like the great city?'

19 "And they threw dust on their heads and were crying out, weeping and mourning, saying, 'Woe, woe, the great city, in which all who had ships at sea became rich by her wealth, for in one hour she has been laid waste!'

20 "Rejoice over her, O heaven, and you saints and apostles and prophets, because God has pronounced judgment for you against her."

---

1. One early ms reads *is going* 2. Two early ancient mss read *have fallen by*

21 Then a strong angel took up a stone like a great millstone and threw it into the sea, saying, "So will Babylon, the great city, be thrown down with violence, and will not be found any longer.

22 "And the sound of harpists and musicians and flute-players and trumpeters will not be heard in you any longer; and no craftsman of any craft will be found in you any longer; and the sound of a mill will not be heard in you any longer;

23 and the light of a lamp will not shine in you any longer; and the voice of the bridegroom and bride will not be heard in you any longer; for your merchants were the great men of the earth, because all the nations were deceived by your sorcery.

24 "And in her was found the blood of prophets and of saints and of all who have been slain on the earth."

The Fourfold Hallelujah

19 After these things I heard something like a loud voice of a great multitude in heaven, saying,

"Hallelujah! Salvation and glory and power belong to our God;

2 BECAUSE HIS JUDGMENTS ARE TRUE AND RIGHTEOUS; for He has judged the great harlot who was corrupting the earth with her immorality, and HE HAS AVENGED THE BLOOD OF HIS BOND-SERVANTS ON HER."

3 And a second time they said, "Hallelujah! HER SMOKE RISES UP FOREVER AND EVER."

4 And the twenty-four elders and the four living creatures fell down and worshiped God who sits on the throne saying, "Amen. Hallelujah!"

5 And a voice came from the throne, saying, "Give praise to our God, all you His bond-servants, you who fear Him, the small and the great."

6 Then I heard *something* like the voice of a great multitude and like the sound of many waters and like the sound of mighty peals of thunder, saying,

"Hallelujah! For the Lord our God, the Almighty, reigns.

7 "Let us rejoice and be glad and give the glory to Him, for the marriage of the Lamb has come and His bride has made herself ready."

8 It was given to her to clothe herself in fine linen, bright *and* clean; for the fine linen is the righteous acts of the saints.

9 Then he *said to me, "Write, 'Blessed are those who are invited to the marriage supper of the Lamb.' " And he *said to me, "These are true words of God."

10 Then I fell at his feet to worship him. But he *said to me, "Do not do that; I am a fellow servant of yours and your brethren who hold the testimony of Jesus; worship God. For the testimony of Jesus is the spirit of prophecy."

11 And I saw heaven opened, and behold, a white horse, and He who sat on it *is* called Faithful and True, and in righteousness He judges and wages war.

12 His eyes *are* a flame of fire, and on His head *are* many diadems; and He has a name written *on Him* which no one knows except Himself.

13 *He is* clothed with a robe dipped in blood, and His name is called The Word of God.

14 And the armies which are in heaven, clothed in fine linen, white *and* clean, were following Him on white horses.

15 From His mouth comes a sharp sword, so that with it He may strike down the nations, and He will rule them with a rod of iron; and He treads the wine press of the fierce wrath of God, the Almighty.

16 And on His robe and on His thigh He has a name written, "KING OF KINGS, AND LORD OF LORDS."

17 Then I saw an angel standing in the sun, and he cried out with a loud voice, saying to all the birds which fly in midheaven, "Come, assemble for the great supper of God,

18 so that you may eat the flesh of kings and the flesh of [1]commanders and the flesh of mighty men and the flesh of horses and of those who sit on them and the flesh of all men, both free men and slaves, and small and great."

19 And I saw the beast and the kings of the earth and their armies assembled to make war against Him who sat on the horse and against His army.

20 And the beast was seized, and with him the false prophet who performed the signs in his presence, by which he deceived those who had received the mark of the beast and those who worshiped his image; these two were thrown alive into the lake of fire which burns with brimstone.

21 And the rest were killed with the sword which came from the mouth of Him who sat on the horse, and all the birds were filled with their flesh.

Satan Bound

20 Then I saw an angel coming down from heaven, holding the key of the abyss and a great chain in his hand.

2 And he laid hold of the dragon, the serpent of old, who is the devil and Satan, and bound him for a thousand years;

3 and he threw him into the abyss, and shut *it* and sealed *it* over him, so that he would not deceive the nations any longer, until the thousand years were completed; after these things he must be released for a short time.

4 Then I saw thrones, and they sat on them, and judgment was given to them. And I *saw* the souls of those who had been beheaded because of their testimony of Jesus and because of the word of God, and those who had not worshiped the beast or his image, and had not received the mark on their forehead and on their hand; and they came to life and reigned with Christ for a thousand years.

5 The rest of the dead did not come to life

---

1. I.e. chiliarchs, in command of one thousand troops

until the thousand years were completed. This is the first resurrection.

6 Blessed and holy is the one who has a part in the first resurrection; over these the second death has no power, but they will be priests of God and of Christ and will reign with Him for a thousand years.

7 When the thousand years are completed, Satan will be released from his prison,

8 and will come out to deceive the nations which are in the four corners of the earth, Gog and Magog, to gather them together for the war; the number of them is like the sand of the seashore.

9 And they came up on the broad plain of the earth and surrounded the camp of the saints and the beloved city, and fire came down from heaven and devoured them.

10 And the devil who deceived them was thrown into the lake of fire and brimstone, where the beast and the false prophet are also; and they will be tormented day and night forever and ever.

11 Then I saw a great white throne and Him who sat upon it, from whose presence earth and heaven fled away, and no place was found for them.

12 And I saw the dead, the great and the small, standing before the throne, and books were opened; and another book was opened, which is *the book* of life; and the dead were judged from the things which were written in the books, according to their deeds.

13 And the sea gave up the dead which were in it, and death and Hades gave up the dead which were in them; and they were judged, every one *of them* according to their deeds.

14 Then death and Hades were thrown into the lake of fire. This is the second death, the lake of fire.

15 And if anyone's name was not found written in the book of life, he was thrown into the lake of fire.

The New Heaven and Earth

21 Then I saw a new heaven and a new earth; for the first heaven and the first earth passed away, and there is no longer *any* sea.

2 And I saw the holy city, new Jerusalem, coming down out of heaven from God, made ready as a bride adorned for her husband.

3 And I heard a loud voice from the throne, saying, "Behold, the tabernacle of God is among men, and He will dwell among them, and they shall be His people, and God Himself will be among them, [1]

4 and He will wipe away every tear from their eyes; and there will no longer be *any* death; there will no longer be *any* mourning, or crying, or pain; the first things have passed away."

5 And He who sits on the throne said, "Behold, I am making all things new." And He

*said, "Write, for these words are faithful and true."

6 Then He said to me, "It is done. I am the Alpha and the Omega, the beginning and the end. I will give to the one who thirsts from the spring of the water of life without cost.

7 "He who overcomes will inherit these things, and I will be his God and he will be My son.

8 "But for the cowardly and unbelieving and abominable and murderers and immoral persons and sorcerers and idolaters and all liars, their part *will be* in the lake that burns with fire and brimstone, which is the second death."

9 Then one of the seven angels who had the seven bowls full of the seven last plagues came and spoke with me, saying, "Come here, I will show you the bride, the wife of the Lamb."

10 And he carried me away [2]in the Spirit to a great and high mountain, and showed me the holy city, Jerusalem, coming down out of heaven from God,

11 having the glory of God. Her brilliance was like a very costly stone, as a stone of crystal-clear jasper.

12 It had a great and high wall, with twelve gates, and at the gates twelve angels; and names *were* written on them, which are *the names* of the twelve tribes of the sons of Israel.

13 *There were* three gates on the east and three gates on the north and three gates on the south and three gates on the west.

14 And the wall of the city had twelve foundation stones, and on them *were* the twelve names of the twelve apostles of the Lamb.

15 The one who spoke with me had a gold measuring rod to measure the city, and its gates and its wall.

16 The city is laid out as a square, and its length is as great as the width; and he measured the city with the rod, [3]fifteen hundred miles; its length and width and height are equal.

17 And he measured its wall, [4]seventy-two yards, *according to* human measurements, which are *also* angelic *measurements*.

18 The material of the wall was jasper; and the city was pure gold, like clear glass.

19 The foundation stones of the city wall were adorned with every kind of precious stone. The first foundation stone was jasper; the second, sapphire; the third, chalcedony; the fourth, emerald;

20 the fifth, sardonyx; the sixth, sardius; the seventh, chrysolite; the eighth, beryl; the ninth, topaz; the tenth, chrysoprase; the eleventh, jacinth; the twelfth, amethyst.

21 And the twelve gates were twelve pearls; each one of the gates was a single pearl. And the street of the city was pure gold, like transparent glass.

22 I saw no temple in it, for the Lord God the Almighty and the Lamb are its temple.

23 And the city has no need of the sun or of

---

1. One early ms reads, and be *their God* 2. Or *in spirit* 3. Lit *twelve thousand stadia*; a stadion was approx 600 ft 4. Lit *one hundred forty-four cubits*

the moon to shine on it, for the glory of God has illumined it, and its lamp *is* the Lamb.

24 The nations will walk by its light, and the kings of the earth will bring their glory into it.

25 In the daytime (for there will be no night there) its gates will never be closed;

26 and they will bring the glory and the honor of the nations into it;

27 and nothing unclean, and no one who practices abomination and lying, shall ever come into it, but only those whose names are written in the Lamb's book of life.

The River and the Tree of Life

22 Then he showed me a river of the water of life, clear as crystal, coming from the throne of God and of ¹the Lamb,

2 in the middle of its street. On either side of the river was the tree of life, bearing twelve ²*kinds of* fruit, yielding its fruit every month; and the leaves of the tree were for the healing of the nations.

3 There will no longer be any curse; and the throne of God and of the Lamb will be in it, and His bond-servants will serve Him;

4 they will see His face, and His name *will be* on their foreheads.

5 And there will no longer be *any* night; and they will not have need of the light of a lamp nor the light of the sun, because the Lord God will illumine them; and they will reign forever and ever.

6 And he said to me, "These words are faithful and true"; and the Lord, the God of the spirits of the prophets, sent His angel to show to His bond-servants the things which must soon take place.

7 "And behold, I am coming quickly. Blessed is he who heeds the words of the prophecy of this book."

8 I, John, am the one who heard and saw these things. And when I heard and saw, I fell down to worship at the feet of the angel who showed me these things.

9 But he *said to me, "Do not do that. I am a fellow servant of yours and of your brethren the prophets and of those who heed the words of this book. Worship God."

10 And he *said to me, "Do not seal up the words of the prophecy of this book, for the time is near.

11 "Let the one who does wrong, still do wrong; and the one who is filthy, still be filthy; and let the one who is righteous, still practice righteousness; and the one who is holy, still keep himself holy."

12 "Behold, I am coming quickly, and My reward *is* with Me, to render to every man according to what he has done.

13 "I am the Alpha and the Omega, the first and the last, the beginning and the end."

14 Blessed are those who wash their robes, so that they may have the right to the tree of life, and may enter by the gates into the city.

15 Outside are the dogs and the sorcerers and the immoral persons and the murderers and the idolaters, and everyone who loves and practices lying.

16 "I, Jesus, have sent My angel to testify to you these things for the churches. I am the root and the descendant of David, the bright morning star."

17 The Spirit and the bride say, "Come." And let the one who hears say, "Come." And let the one who is thirsty come; let the one who wishes take the water of life without cost.

18 I testify to everyone who hears the words of the prophecy of this book: if anyone adds to them, God will add to him the plagues which are written in this book;

19 and if anyone takes away from the words of the book of this prophecy, God will take away his part from the tree of life and from the holy city, which are written in this book.

20 He who testifies to these things says, "Yes, I am coming quickly." Amen. Come, Lord Jesus.

21 The grace of the Lord Jesus be with ³all. Amen.

---

1. Or *the Lamb. In the middle of its street, and on either side of the river, was* 2. Or *crops of fruit* 3. One early ms reads *the saints*

Guide to
Eternal Life

YOUR NAME: _____

PART 1: THE PATH TO ETERNAL LIFE

1. How many ways are there to heaven? Acts 4:12; John 14:6

2. In addition to eternal life in heaven, what kind of life does Jesus promise us on earth? John 10:10 (see also Galatians 5:22, 23)

3. What is our guide to spiritual life? 2 Timothy 3:16, 17 (see also 2 Peter 1:3)

4. Which part of the Bible should we follow today? Hebrews 8:6–13 (see also Ephesians 2:15; Colossians 2:14; Romans 7:6, 7; Galatians 3:10–14; 2 Corinthians 3:3–16)

5. How important is it for you to be on the right spiritual path? Matthew 7:13, 14; 21–23 (see also 1 John 1:6, 7)

6. On what basis is eternal life given through Jesus Christ? Ephesians 2:8; Acts 6:7

7. Have you ever made a commitment to Jesus?
   If so, how?
   Were you baptized?   If so, how?
   At what age?   For what reason?
   Did you believe you were saved before or after your baptism?

PART 2: STEPPING ONTO THE PATH

1. What is the first step of faith in accepting God's gift of eternal life through Jesus? John 3:16; 8:24

2. What did Jesus do to make it possible for you to have everlasting life with God in heaven? Romans 5:8, 9; 2 Corinthians 5:21 *(see also 1 Peter 1:18–21)*

3. What is the second step of faith? Acts 17:30; 26:20
   What is repentance, and why should we repent? Acts 3:19
   How bad is sin? Romans 6:23; 1 Corinthians 15:3
   How bad is your sin? *(see Galatians 5:19–21)*

4. What is the third step of faith in accepting the gift of eternal salvation? Romans 10:9, 10 *(see also Matthew 10:32, 33; Acts 22:16)*

5. What is the fourth and final step of faith at which time we are saved, receive the forgiveness of our sins, and enter through Jesus onto the path that leads to eternal life? Mark 16:16; Acts 2:37–41; Ephesians 4:4, 5 *(see also 1 Peter 3:20, 21; John 3:3–5; Matthew 28:19)*

6. What is the purpose of baptism? Acts 22:16 *(see also Mark 16:16; Acts 2:38)*

7. Is the one valid baptism for today sprinkling, pouring, or immersion? Acts 8:35–39; Romans 6:3–5

8. Who should be baptized? *(see Mark 16:16; Acts 2:38; 22:16)*
   Why does God require baptism as the final step in accepting the gift of salvation? Romans 6:3–6
   How do your answers on Part 1, question 7 compare to what the Bible says?

PART 3: THE CHURCH

1. To what church does the Lord add people when they are baptized? Acts 2:47; Galatians 3:26–28 *(see also 1 Corinthians 12:13)*

2. Who is the head of the church? Colossians 1:18; Romans 16:16 *(see also Ephesians 1:22, 23)*

3. In whose name should all things be done in the church? Colossians 3:17 *(see also Matthew 28:18–20)* What should the followers of Christ be called? 1 Peter 4:16 *(see also Acts 11:26; Romans 16:16)*

4. Does Jesus want His followers to be united or divided? Ephesians 4:4, 5; John 17:21–23 Why is there so much religious division? 1 Corinthians 1:10–13; 3:3, 4 How closely should we abide by the Word of God? Revelation 22:18, 19

PART 4: WORSHIP IN SPIRIT AND IN TRUTH

1. What does Jesus want members of His church to do regularly? John 4:23, 24; Hebrews 10:25

2. How does Jesus want Christians to remember Him when they assemble with His church? 1 Corinthians 11:23–26; Matthew 26:26–29 Would it be all right to have other foods with the Lord's Supper in addition to what Jesus specified?

3. On which day of the week should Christians partake of the Lord's Supper? Acts 20:7 What else should take place in the assembly?

4. What other act of worship and sacrifice should Christians offer in the Lord's Day assembly? 1 Corinthians 16:1, 2 *(see also 2 Corinthians 9:6, 7)*

5. What else should Christians do together when they assemble? 1 Timothy 2:1, 8; Acts 2:42

6. What other expression of praise and mutual encouragement do Christians offer to God in the church? Ephesians 5:19; Colossians 3:16 *(see also Hebrews 2:12; James 5:13)* What kind of music does God specify in these verses?

7. How important is it to worship God from the heart in the way that He desires? Matthew 15:8, 9; John 4:23, 24 *(see also 2 John 9)*

PART 5: CONTINUING FAITHFULLY WITH JESUS

1. What should be your spiritual food as you walk with Jesus on the narrow way that leads to eternal life? 1 Peter 2:2; 2 Timothy 2:15

2. What kind of life does the Lord want you to live as you walk the narrow way? Titus 2:11–14; Matthew 28:19, 20 (see also Romans 12:1, 2)

3. What is the cost of following Jesus? Matthew 10:37–39
   What would you do if your family tried to prevent you from following Jesus?
   If a religious leader's teachings were different from those of Jesus, which would you follow?

4. How long should you follow Jesus? Revelation 2:10

5. When should you begin to follow Jesus and start receiving His blessings? 2 Corinthians 6:2; Acts 22:16

Are you ready now to begin your walk with Jesus on the narrow way to eternal life, by expressing your faith in Him, turning away from your sins, being baptized by immersion for the forgiveness of those sins, and allowing the Lord to save you and add you to His church, of which He is the only head?

Are you then ready to continue to walk in the light, which involves continued obedience to Jesus, meeting with His church, remembering Him in the Lord's Supper, receiving continual spiritual teaching, giving as you have been prospered, and praying and singing from your heart?

Are you also ready to grow spiritually through the study of His Word and to live a life that pleases and glorifies God until that day when you receive eternal life?

If not now, when?
Read James 4:14, 17.   Read John 14:15, 21.